CONSTITUTING EUROPE

At fifty, the European Court of Human Rights finds itself in a new institutional setting. With the EU joining the European Convention on Human Rights in the near future, and the Court increasingly having to address the responsibility of states in UN-led military operations, the Court faces important challenges at the national, European and international levels. In light of recent reform discussions, this volume addresses the multilevel relations of the Court by drawing on existing debates, pointing to current deficits and highlighting the need for further improvements.

ANDREAS FØLLESDAL is Professor of Political Philosophy at the Norwegian Centre for Human Rights, Faculty of Law, University of Oslo.

BIRGIT PETERS is a post-doctoral researcher and lecturer at the Faculty of Law of the University of Münster.

GEIR ULFSTEIN is Professor of International Law at the Department of Public and International Law, University of Oslo.

CONSTITUTING EUROPE

The European Court of Human Rights in a National,
European and Global Context

Edited by
ANDREAS FØLLESDAL, BIRGIT PETERS
and GEIR ULFSTEIN

CAMBRIDGE UNIVERSITY PRESS
Cambridge, New York, Melbourne, Madrid, Cape Town,
Singapore, São Paulo, Delhi, Mexico City

Cambridge University Press
The Edinburgh Building, Cambridge CB2 8RU, UK

Published in the United States of America by Cambridge University Press, New York

www.cambridge.org
Information on this title: www.cambridge.org/9781107024441

© Cambridge University Press 2013

This publication is in copyright. Subject to statutory exception
and to the provisions of relevant collective licensing agreements,
no reproduction of any part may take place without
the written permission of Cambridge University Press.

First published 2013

Printed and bound in the United Kingdom by the MPG Printgroup

A catalogue record for this publication is available from the British Library

Library of Congress Cataloguing in Publication data

Constituting Europe : The European Court of Human Rights in a National, European, and
Global Context / edited by Andreas Føllesdal, Birgit Peters, and Geir Ulfstein.
p. cm.
Includes bibliographical references and index.
ISBN 978-1-107-02444-1 (Hardback)
1. European Court of Human Rights. 2. Court of Justice of the European Communities.
3. Human rights. I. Føllesdal, Andreas. II. Peters, Birgit. III. Ulfstein, Geir, 1951–
KJC5138.C66 2013
342.2408'50269–dc23
2012038090

ISBN 978-1-107-02444-1 Hardback

Cambridge University Press has no responsibility for the persistence or
accuracy of URLs for external or third-party internet websites referred to
in this publication, and does not guarantee that any content on such
websites is, or will remain, accurate or appropriate.

CONTENTS

List of contributors vii
Preface and acknowledgements xi
Table of cases xiii
Table of international instruments xxxvii
List of abbreviations xl

1 Introduction 1
   ANDREAS FØLLESDAL, BIRGIT PETERS AND GEIR ULFSTEIN

2 The Court and the member states: procedural aspects 25
   IAIN CAMERON

3 The margin of appreciation doctrine: a theoretical analysis of Strasbourg's variable geometry 62
   YUTAKA ARAI-TAKAHASHI

4 The ECHR as a living instrument: its meaning and legitimacy 106
   GEORGE LETSAS

5 No longer offering fine mantras to a parched child? The European Court's developing approach to remedies 142
   PHILIP LEACH

6 National implementation of ECHR rights 181
   MADS ANDENAS AND EIRIK BJORGE

7 The Court as a part of the Council of Europe: the Parliamentary Assembly and the Committee of Ministers 263
   ELISABETH LAMBERT-ABDELGAWAD

8 Should the European Union ratify the European Convention on Human Rights? Some remarks on the relations between the European Court of Human Rights and the European Court of Justice   301
   LEONARD F.M. BESSELINK

9 The European Court of Human Rights and the United Nations   334
   CHRISTIAN TOMUSCHAT

10 Conclusions   389
   ANDREAS FØLLESDAL, BIRGIT PETERS AND GEIR ULFSTEIN

Bibliography   403
Index   430

LIST OF CONTRIBUTORS

MADS ANDENAS is Professor of Law at the University of Oslo, the former Director of the Centre of European Law, King's College, University of London and the former Director of the British Institute of International and Comparative Law, London. He is one of the UN Special Human Rights Mandate Holders, and a member of the UN Working Group on Arbitrary Detention.

YUTAKA ARAI-TAKAHASHI is a Reader in International Law and International Human Rights Law at University of Kent at Brussels (UKB), Belgium and University of Kent at Canterbury (UKC), England. He has published widely on international and European human rights law, as well as on international humanitarian and international criminal law, including the law on occupation (*The Law of Occupation: The Continuity and Change of International Humanitarian Law, and its Interaction with International Humanitarian Law* (2009).

LEONARD BESSELINK is Professor of Constitutional Law at the University of Amsterdam. He was a Henry G. Schermers Fellow at the Netherlands Institute for Advance Study in the Humanities and Social Sciences from 1 September 2011 to 30 June 2012. He studied law at the University of Leiden (Netherlands), the Johns Hopkins School of Advanced International Studies (Bologna Center), and holds a doctorate in social and political science of the European University Institute, Florence, Italy.

EIRIK BJORGE, who holds an M. Jur. from Oxford University, is currently a Research Fellow at the University of Oslo. In 2011–12 he was *pensionnaire étranger* at the École normale supérieure and Visiting Researcher at Sciences Po, Paris.

IAIN CAMERON is Professor in Public International Law at the University of Uppsala. He has served as an expert to a number of Swedish government commissions of inquiry proposing legislation, and written major reports for the Swedish government, the Council of Europe and the European Parliament on targeted sanctions. In 2006, the Swedish government appointed him as a member of the Commission on Democracy through Law (Venice Commission, the advisory body of the Council of Europe on constitutional law and international law).

ANDREAS FØLLESDAL is a Professor of Philosophy and Political Theory at the Norwegian Centre for Human Rights, University of Oslo, Norway. He is currently director of a research project funded by the European Research Council on the Legitimacy of the Multi-Level Human Rights Judiciary (Multirights) and co-editor of the book series *Studies on Human Rights Conventions*, Cambridge University Press.

ELISABETH LAMBERT-ABDELGAWAD is CNRS Research Director (SAGE, University of Strasbourg). She was Senior Expert at the Fundamental Rights Agency for France until 2011. She has published widely on victims' remedies and access to the European Court of Human Rights. Previous publications include *Preventing and Sanctioning Hindrances to the Right of Individual Petition before the European Court of Human Rights* (ed., 2011), and *Quel filtrage des requêtes par la Cour européenne des droits de l'homme?* (co-ed., ed. du Conseil de l'Europe, 2011).

PHILIP LEACH is Professor of Human Rights Law at Middlesex University, London, where he is also Director of the European Human Rights Advocacy Centre (EHRAC). In 2012 he co–authored a report on 'Democratic Legitimacy in Human Rights Implementation: the role of parliaments in the execution of judgments of the European Court of Human Rights,' supported by the Nuffield Foundation, which is to be published by Oxford University Press.

GEORGE LETSAS is the Co-Director of the UCL Institute for Human Rights and Reader in Philosophy of Law & Human Rights at University College London (UCL), Faculty of Laws. He is the author of numerous articles and of the monograph, *A Theory of Interpretation of the European Convention on Human Rights* Oxford University Press (2009).

BIRGIT PETERS is a post-doctoral researcher and lecturer at the Faculty of Law, the University of Münster, Germany. She is affiliated with the research project Multirights at the Norwegian Centre for Human Rights. Her latest publications include 'Interpretation of Human Rights by Human Rights

Treaty Bodies' in Keller and Ulfstein, *Human Rights Treaty Bodies* (Cambridge University Press, 2012).

CHRISTIAN TOMUSCHAT is Professor Emeritus of the Law Faculty of Humboldt University Berlin. He was a member of the Human Rights Committee and the UN International Law Commission. He authored *Human Rights: Between Idealism and Realism* (2nd edn., 2008) and is one of the co-editors of the *Commentary on the Statute of the International Court of Justice* (2nd edn., 2012).

GEIR ULFSTEIN is a Professor of International Law at the University of Oslo, Norway. In 2010–11, he was co-director of the research project 'Should states ratify human rights treaties?' at the Centre for Advanced Studies in Oslo. He is co-editor of the book series *Studies on Human Rights Conventions*, Cambridge University Press.

PREFACE AND ACKNOWLEDGEMENTS

The European Court of Human Rights (the ECtHR, or the Court) has in recent years been the subject of heated debate. It is a cornerstone of human rights protection for over 850 million, but the Court is struggling with an overload of more than 150,000 pending cases. In this sense it is a victim of its own success. At the same time, the Court's interference in national democracy and judiciary is increasingly questioned. How it should ensure effective human rights protection while paying due respect to national sovereignty has been the subject of several inter-governmental conferences: Interlaken, Izmir, and most recently, Brighton in 2012.

It has long been discussed whether the ECtHR slowly assumes the role of a constitutional court for Europe in relation to its member states. However, the envisaged ratification of the European Convention for the Protection of Human Rights and Fundamental Freedoms (ECHR) by the European Union raises new issues, particularly concerning the relationship between the ECtHR and the Court of Justice of the European Union (CJEU) (formerly the European Court of Justice, ECJ). The Court must also find its role among the other organs of the Council of Europe, particularly the Committee of Ministers and the Parliamentary Assembly. Finally, the ECtHR must increasingly address actions by other international organisations, such as the United Nations. Hence, the Court finds itself in a new institutional setting. In addition to its relationship to national legal systems, questions of an inter-institutional character at the European and global level become increasingly important. This book examines these new institutional settings.

This is the second book in the Cambridge University Press series *Studies on Human Rights Conventions*. This series is the result of a larger research project, 'Should states ratify human rights conventions?', at the Centre for Advanced Study, Norway. The project was led by Andreas Føllesdal and Geir Ulfstein. We are grateful for the hospitality of the Centre under Scientific Director, Gro Steinsland and Office Manager, Maria M.L. Sætre.

The book was developed over a period of two years, including two author meetings in Oslo. These meetings were important in shaping a common approach to this study. The chapters of the book seek to address the legitimacy challenges of the Court in terms of some common principles, such as the rule of law, the principle of subsidiarity, the principle of effectiveness, as well as the principles of implied powers and proportionality. However, the authors have been left with considerable freedom in their choice of approach to their respective chapters.

We would like to thank Nienke van Schaverbeke and Finola O'Sullivan at Cambridge University Press for professional assistance and guidance. In Oslo, Leiry Cornejo Chavez and Stian Øby Johansen provided effective and unremitting help in making sure that the style guide was respected (not an easy task), and compiling the registers of the book. Svenja Rebenstörp, Arlena Skalecki and Ante Spalink helped with the compilation of the bibliography and the final manuscript. Lastly, we thank our contributing authors for a great learning process!

Andreas Føllesdal, Birgit Peters and Geir Ulfstein

TABLE OF CASES

European Court and Commission of Human Rights

A v. *Norway* (Appl. No. 28070/06), Judgment (First Section), 9 April 2009, not reported   84, n. 104

A and Others v. *United Kingdom* (Appl. No. 3455/05), Judgment (Grand Chamber), 19 February 2009, Reports 2009   92, n. 143; 187, n. 26

A, B and C v. *Ireland* (Appl. No. 25579/05), Judgment (Grand Chamber), 16 December 2010, Reports 2010   13, 92 n. 181; 187 n. 27; 100, 397

Abbasov v. *Azerbaijan* (Appl. No. 24271/05), Judgment (First Section), 17 January 2008, not reported   153 n. 58, 279 n. 64

Abuyeva and Others v. *Russia* (Appl. No. 27065/05), Judgment (First Section), 2 December 2010, not reported   174, n. 139, 141

ADT v. *UK* (Appl. No. 35765/97), Judgment (Third Section), 31 July 2000, Reports 2000-IX   89 n. 129

Advisory opinion on certain legal questions concerning the lists of candidates submitted with a view to the election of judges to the ECtHR (Grand Chamber), 12 February 2008   268 n. 19, 269

Advisory opinion on certain legal questions concerning the lists of candidates submitted with a view to the election of judges to the ECtHR (No. 2) (Grand Chamber), 22 January 2010   268 n. 20, 270, 27 n. 32

Aksoy v. *Turkey* (Appl. No. 21987/93), Judgment (Chamber), 12 December 1995, Reports 1996-6   129 n. 70

AL v. *Italy* (Appl. No. 41387/98), Decision (Second Section), 11 May 2000, not reported   337 n. 11

Al-Adsani v. *United Kingdom* (Appl. No. 35763/97), Judgment (Grand Chamber), 21 November 2001, Reports 2001-XI   M7 n. 38

Aleksandr Zaichenko v. *Russia* (Appl. No. 39660/02), Judgment (First Section), 18 February 2010, not reported   153 n. 58

Aleksanyan v. *Russia* (Appl. No. 46468/06), Judgment (First Section), 22 December 2008, not reported   158, 158 n. 75

Aliev v. *Ukraine* (Appl. No. 41220/98), Judgment (Fourth Section), 29 April 2003, not reported   96 n. 162, 163

Al-Jedda v. *United Kingdom* (Appl. No. 27021/08), Judgment (Grand Chamber), 7 July 2011, not reported   4 n. 14; 10

Al-Khawaja and Tahery v. *United Kingdom* (Appl. Nos. 26766/05 and 22228/06), Judgment (Grand Chamber), 15 December 2011, not reported   211 n. 132; 212; 216; 217 n. 161

Al-Saadoon and Mufdhi v. *UK* (Appl. No. 61498/08), Judgment (Fourth Section), 2 March 2010, Reports 2010   169 n. 121; 367 n. 110; 381 n. 169

Al-Skeini and Others v. *United Kingdom* (Appl. No. 55721/07), Judgment (Grand Chamber), 7 July 2011, not reported   4 n. 13; 10; 176; 257 362 n. 96, 364, 366, 404

Aquilina v. *Malta* (Appl. No. 25642/94), Judgment (Grand Chamber), 29 April 1999, Reports 1999-III   142; 146

Assanidze v. *Georgia* (Appl. No. 71503/01), Judgment (Grand Chamber), 8 April 2004, Reports 2004-II   145 nn. 14–15; 157 n. 72; 153; 171; 173

Asselbourg and 78 others and Greenpeace Association-Luxembourg v. *Luxembourg* (Appl. No. 29121/95), Judgment (Second Section), 29 June 1999, Reports 1999-VI   113 n. 22

Axel Springer AG v. *Germany* (Appl. No. 39954/08), Judgment (Grand Chamber), 7 February 2012, not reported   77 n. 71; 92 n. 142

B and L v. *UK* (Appl. No. 36536/02), Judgment (Fourth Section), 13 September 2005, not reported   101 n. 188

Bankovic and Others v. *(all involved NATO states)* (Appl. No. 52207/99), Judgment (Grand Chamber), 12 December 2001, Reports 2001-XII   361 n. 94; 362

Bayatyan v. *Armenia* (Appl. No. 23459/03), Judgment (Grand Chamber), 7 July 2011, not reported   176 n. 143

Beer and Regan v. *Germany* (Appl. No. 28934/95), Judgment (Grand Chamber), 18 February 1999, not reported   337 n. 11

Behrami and Behrami v. *France*: and *Saramati* v. *France, Germany and Norway* (Appl. Nos. 71412 and 78166/01), Judgment (Grand Chamber), 2 May 2007, not reported   10; 24; 342 n. 21; 347, 351; 352

Bekos and Koutropoulos v. *Greece* (Appl. No. 15250/02), Judgment (Fourth Section), 13 December 2005, not reported   117

Berić and Others v. *Bosnia and Herzegovina* (Appl. No. 36357/04), Decision (Fourth Section), 16 October 2007, not reported   342 n. 23; 352 n. 66

Biret v. *France* (Appl. No. 13762/04), Decision (Fifth Section), 9 December 2008, not reported   9 n. 35; 381 n. 170

Boivin v. *34 State Members of the Council of Europe* (Appl. No. 73250/01), Decision (Fifth Section), 9 September 2008, Reports 2008   337 n. 10

Boso v. *Italy* (Appl. No. 50490/99), Decision (First Section), 5 September 2002, Reports 2002-VII   72 n. 45; 88 n. 119

Bosphorus Hava Yollari Turızm ve Ticaret Anonim Şirketi v. *Ireland* (Appl. No. 45036/98), Judgment (Grand Chamber), 30 June 2005, Reports 2005-VI   9, 10, 308–12

Bottazzi v. *Italy* (Appl. No. 34884/97), Judgment (Grand Chamber), 28 July 1999, Reports 1999-V   167

TABLE OF CASES

Bozcaada Kimisis Teodoku Rum Ortodoks Kilisesi Vakfi v. *Turkey (No. 2)* (Appl. Nos. 37639 and 37655/03; 26736 and 42670/04), Judgment (Second Section), 3 March 2009, not reported   151

Brannigan and McBride v. *UK* (Appl. Nos. 14553 and 14554/89), Judgment (Plenary), 26 May 1993, Series A, Vol. 258-B   129 n. 70

Broniowski v. *Poland* (Appl. No. 31443/96), Judgment (Grand Chamber), 22 June 2004, Reports 2004-V   77 n. 60; 162 n. 83; 165, 170

Brumarescu v. *Romania* (Appl. No. 28342/95), Judgment (Grand Chamber), 23 January 2001, Reports 2001-I   150

Brusco v. *France* (Appl. No. 1466/07), Judgment (Fifth Section), 14 October 2010, not reported   246 n. 310

Buckley v. *United Kingdom* (Appl. No. 28323/95), CommHR (First Chamber), 26 February 1997, Reports 1997   130 n. 70

Burden v. *UK* (Appl. No. 13378/05), Judgment (Grand Chamber), 29 April 2008, Reports 2008   95 n. 160

Burdov v. *Russia (No. 2)* (Appl. No. 33509/04), Judgment (First Section), 15 January 2009, Reports 2009   163, 281

Buscarini and Others v. *San Marino* (Appl. No. 24645/94), Judgment (Grand Chamber), 18 February 1999, Reports 1999-I   102 n. 191

C v. *Finland* (Appl. No. 18249/02), Judgment (Fourth Section), 9 May 2006, not reported   148 n. 33

Cahit Demirel v. *Turkey* (Appl. No. 18623/03), Judgment (Second Section), 7 July 2009, not reported   167 n. 107

Campbell and Cosans v. *United Kingdom (Article 50)* (Appl. Nos. 7511 and 7743/76), Judgment (Chamber), 23 March 1983, Series A, Vol. 60   146 n. 19

Campbell and Fell v. *United Kingdom* (Appl. Nos. 7819 and 7878/77), Judgment (Chamber), 28 June 1984, Series A, Vol. 80   113 n. 18

Case relating to certain aspects of the laws on the use of languages in education in Belgium (*Belgian Linguistic* case) (Appl. Nos. 1474, 1677 and 1691/62), Report (Commission), 24 June 1965, Series B, Vol. 3; Judgment of 23 July 1968, Series A, Vol. 6   16, 17, 67, 87 n. 116

Ceylan v. *Turkey (No. 2)* (Appl. No. 46454/99), Judgment (Second Section), 11 October 2005, not reported   289 n. 107

Cha'are Shalom Ve Tsedek v. *France* (Appl. No. 27417/95), Judgment (Grand Chamber), 27 June 2000, Reports 2000-VII   101 n. 186

Chahal v. *UK* (Appl. No. 22414/93), Judgment (Grand Chamber), 15 November 1996, Reports 1996-V   76 n. 63

Chappell v. *UK* (Appl. No. 10461/83), Judgment (Chamber), 30 March 1989, Series A, Vol. 159   307 n. 14

Chassagnou and Others v. *France* (Appl. Nos. 25088/94; 28331 and 28443/95), Judgment (Grand Chamber), 29 April 1999, Reports 1999-III   113 n. 17

Chauvy v. *France* (Appl. No. 64915/01), Judgment (Second Section), 29 June 2004, Reports 2004-VI   78

Christine Goodwin v. *United Kingdom* (Appl. No. 28957/95), Judgment (Grand Chamber), 11 July 2002, Reports 2002-VI   87 n. 118; 89 n. 130; 116–23; 188–9

Claes and Others v. *Belgium* (Appl. Nos. 46825, 47132, 47502, 49010, 49104, 49195 and 49716/99), Judgment (First Section), 2 June 2005, not reported   155, 153, 180

Connolly v. *15 EU Member States* (Appl. No. 73274/01), Judgment (Fifth Section), 9 December 2008, not reported   9, 304

Cooper v. *United Kingdom* (Appl. No. 48843/99), Judgment (Grand Chamber), 16 December 2003, Reports 2003-XII   213

Cooperatieve Producentenorganisatie Van De Nederlandse Kokkelvisserij U.A. v. *The Netherlands* 05), Judgment /05), Judgment (Third Section), 29 January 2009   9, 308

Cossey v. *UK* (Appl. No. 10843/84), Judgment (Plenary), 27 September 1990, Series A, Vol. 184, Reports 2009   35 n. 30; 114, 186 n. 19; 189

Cudak v. *Lithuania* (Appl. No. 15869/02), Judgment (Grand Chamber), 23 March 2010, Reports 2010   156, 176 n. 148

Cyprus v. *Turkey* (Appl. No. 25781/94), Judgment (Grand Chamber), 10 May 2001, Reports 2011-IV   16, 335

Dacia S.R.L. v. *Moldova* (Appl. No. 3052/04), Judgment (Fourth Section), 19 February 2009, not reported   150

Dahlab v. *Switzerland* (Appl. No. 42393/98), Decision (Second Section), 15 February 2001, Reports 2001-V   103

De Wilde, Ooms and Versyp v. *Belgium* (*Vagrancy* case) (Appl. Nos. 2832, 2835 and 2899/66), Judgment (Plenary), 18 June 1971, Series A, Vol. 12   67 n. 24

Demir and Baykara v. *Turkey* (Appl. No. 34503/97), Judgment (Grand Chamber), 12 November 2008, Reports 2008   117

Demir and Others v. *Turkey* (Appl. Nos. 21380, 21381 and 21383/93), Judgment (Chamber), 23 September 1998, Reports 1998-VI   129 n. 70

Dickson v. *United Kingdom* (Appl. No. 44362/04), Judgment (Grand Chamber), 4 December 2007, Reports 2007-V   96 n. 163; 146

Dimitrov and Hamanov v. *Bulgaria* (Appl. Nos. 48059/06 and 2708/09), Judgment (Fourth Section), 10 May 2011, not reported   85, 163

Djavit An v. *Turkey* (Appl. No. 20652/92), Judgment (Third Section), 20 February 2003, Reports 2003-III   148 n. 37

Doğan and Others v. *Turkey* (Appl. Nos. 8803–8811, 8813 and 8815–8819/02), Judgment (Third Section), 29 June 2004, Reports 2004-VI   167 n. 106

Driza v. *Albania* (Appl. No. 33771/02), Judgment (Fourth Section), 13 November 2007, Reports 2007-V   168 n. 110

Drozd and Janousek v. *France and Spain* (Appl. No. 12747/87), Judgment (Plenary), 26 June 1992, Series A, Vol. 240   351

Dubenko v. *Ukraine* (Appl. No. 74221/01), Judgment (Second Section), 11 January 2005, Reports 2006-9   278 n. 61

Dubus S.A. v. *France* (Appl. No. 5242/04), Judgment (Fifth Section), 11 July 2009, not reported   32, 218

Dudgeon v. *UK* (Appl. No. 7525/76), Judgment (Plenary), 22 October 1981, Series A, Vol. 45   89 n. 129; 111; 114; 123

Dybeku v. *Albania* (Appl. No. 41153/06), Judgment (Fourth Section), 18 December 2007, not reported   170

EB v. *France* (Appl. No. 43546/02), Judgment (Grand Chamber), 22 January 2008, not reported   89 n. 129; 119 n. 48; 247 n. 317

Egeland and Hanseid v. *Norway* (Appl. No. 34438/04), Judgment (First Section), 16 April 2009, not reported   121 n. 52

Elsholz v. *Germany* (Appl. No. 25735/94), Judgment (Grand Chamber), 13 July 2000, Reports 2000-VIII   78 n. 78

Emre v. *Switzerland (No. 2)* (Appl. No. 5056/10), Judgment (Second Section), 11 October 2011, not reported   282; 291 n. 112

Engel and Others v. *The Netherlands (Article 50)* (Appl. Nos. 5100, 5101 and 5102/71; 5354 and 5370/72), Judgment (Plenary), 23 November 1976, Series A, No. 22   67 n. 23; 113 n. 18; 123; 146 n. 23; 189 n. 37

Eriksen v. *Norway* (Appl. No. 17391/90), Judgment (Chamber), 27 May 1997, Reports 1997-III   113 n. 24

Eriksson v. *Sweden* (Appl. No. 11373/85), Judgment (Plenary), 22 June 1989, Series A, Vol. 156   78 n. 72

Evans v. *UK* (Appl. No. 6339/05), Judgment (Grand Chamber), 10 April 2007, Reports 2007-I   88 n. 121; 99 n. 181; 149 n. 44

Faimblat v. *Romania* (Appl. No. 23066/02), Judgment (Third Section), 13 January 2009, not reported   163 n. 96

Fakiridou and Schina v. *Greece* (Appl. No. 6789/06), Judgment (First Section), 14 November 2008, not reported   156

Fatullayev v. *Azerbaijan* (Appl. No. 40984/07), Judgment (First Section), 22 April 2010, not reported   159

Filiz Uyan v. *Turkey* (Appl. No. 7496/03), Judgment (Second Section), 3 January 2009, not reported   207–9

Findlay v. *United Kingdom* (Appl. No. 22107/93), Judgment (Chamber), 25 February 1997, Reports 1997-I   213 n. 140

Folgerø and Others v. *Norway* (Appl. No. 15472/02), Judgment (Grand Chamber), 29 June 2007, Reports 2007-III   99

Former King of Greece and Others v. *Greece* (Appl. No. 25701/94), Judgment (Grand Chamber), 23 November 2000, Reports 2000-XII   71 n. 38; 113 n. 20; 129 n. 70; 151

Fretté v. *France* (Appl. No. 36515/97), Judgment (Third Section), 26 February 2002, Reports 2002-I   99 n. 181; 119; 120; 124

Frydlender v. *France* (Appl. No. 30979/96), Judgment (Grand Chamber), 27 June 2000, Reports 2000-VII   113

Gäfgen v. *Germany* (Appl. No. 22978/05), Judgment (Grand Chamber), 1 June 2010, Reports 2010   176, 246

Gaglione and Others v. *Italy* (Appl. Nos. 45867/07 and 474 others), Judgment (Second Section), 21 December 2010, not reported   38 n. 38; 290 n. 111

Gajic v. *Germany* (Appl. No. 31446/02), Decision (Fifth Section), 28 August 2007, not reported   342 n. 23; 352 n. 66

Galić and Blagojević v. *The Netherlands* (Appl. Nos. 22617 and 49032/07), Decision (Third Section), 9 June 2009, not reported   337 n. 8; 339 n. 14; 352 n. 66

Garaudy v. *France* (Appl. No. 65831/01), Decision (Fourth Section), 24 June 2003, Reports of Judgments and Decisions 2003-IX   78 n. 74

Gasparini v. *Italy and Belgium* (Appl. No. 10750/03), Judgment (Second Section), 12 May 2009, not reported   383

Gasus Dosier- und Fördertechnik GmbH v. *The Netherlands* (Appl. No. 15375/89), Judgment (Chamber), 23 February 1995, Series A, Vol. 306-B   113 n. 20; 129 n. 70

Gay News Ltd. and Lemon v. *UK* (Appl. No. 8710/79), Decision of 7 May 1982, 5 EHRR 123   98

Geerks v. *Switzerland* (Appl. No. 7640/76), Decision of 7 March 1978, 12 Decisions and Reports 103   98 n. 174

Gençel v. *Turkey* (Appl. No. 53431/99), Judgment (Third Section), 23 October 2003, not reported   152 n. 58; 289 n. 107

Gillow v. *United Kingdom* (Appl. No. 9063/80), Judgment (Chamber), 24 November 1986, Series A, Vol. 109   130; n. 70

Glass v. *United Kingdom* (Appl. No. 61827/00), Judgment (Fourth Section), 9 March 2004, Reports 2004-II   170 n. 39

Golder v. *UK* (Appl. No. 4451/70), Judgment (Plenary), 21 February 1975, Series A, Vol. 18   67 n. 24; 122 n. 54; 123

Goodwin v. *United Kingdom* (Appl. No. 17488/90), Judgment (Grand Chamber), 27 March 1996, Reports 1996-II   87, 116, 117 n. 37; 119; 121; 122; 123; 188, 189

Görgülü v. *Germany* (Appl. No. 74969/01), Judgment (Third Section), 26 February 2004, not reported   7; 220, 234

Grant v. *UK* (Appl. No. 32570/03), Judgment (Fourth Section), 23 May 2006, Reports 2006-VII   90 n. 130

Greece v. *UK (Cyprus* case*)* (Appl. No. 176/56), YB 2 (1958–9), 174   66 n. 16

Greens and MT v. *UK* (Appl. Nos. 60041 and 60054/08), Judgment (Fourth Section), 23 November 2010, Reports 2010   38 n. 39; 163 n. 92; 165; 166; 281

Grori v. *Albania* (Appl. No. 25336/04), Judgment (Fourth Section), 7 July 2009, not reported   149 n. 44

Guiso-Gallisay v. *Italy* (Appl. No. 58858/00), Judgment (Second Section), 21 October 2008, not reported   168 n. 110

Gülmez v. *Turkey* (Appl. No. 16330/02), Judgment (Second Section), 20 May 2008, not reported   168 n. 112

Gurov v. *Moldova* (Appl. No. 36455/02), Judgment (Fourth Section), 11 July 2006, not reported   155

Guzzardi v. *Italy* (Appl. No. 7367/76), Judgment (Plenary), 6 November 1980, Series A, Vol. 39   112 n. 15

TABLE OF CASES xix

H v. Norway (Appl. No. 17004/90), Decision (Commission), 19 May 1992, not reported   88 n. 119

Hachette Filipacchi Associés v. France (Appl. No. 71111/01), Judgment (First Section), 14 June 2007, not reported   98 n. 176

Handyside v. United Kingdom (Appl. No. 5493/72), Judgment (Plenary), 7 December 1976, Series A, Vol. 24   20 n. 78; 68; 97; 102 n. 190; 114; 123, 129 n. 70; 186 n. 23

Hasan and Eylem Zengin v. Turkey (Appl. No. 1448/04), Judgment (Second Section), 9 October 2007, not reported   99, 168

Hatton v. United Kingdom (Appl. No. 36022/97), Judgment (Grand Chamber), 8 July 2003, Reports 2003-VIII   386 n. 182

Hirschhorn v. Romania (Appl. No. 29294/02), Judgment (Third Section), 26 July 2007, not reported   150 n. 48

Hirst v. UK (No. 2) (Appl. No. 74025/01), Judgment (Grand Chamber), 6 October 2005, Reports 2005-IX   88 n. 122; 96 n. 162; 100 n. 184; 119–22; 165–6; 281; 287; 398

Holy Synod of the Bulgarian Orthodox Church (Metropolitan Inokentiy) and Others v. Bulgaria (Merits) (Appl. Nos. 412/03 and 35677/04), Judgment (Fifth Section), 22 January 2009, not reported   84 n. 104; 168 n. 114

Hornsby v. Greece (Appl. No. 18357/91), Judgment, 19 March 1997, at 40, Report 1997-II   278 n. 61

Hutten-Czapska v. Poland (Appl. No. 35014/97), Judgment (Grand Chamber), 19 June 2006, Reports 2006-VIII   84 n. 104; 95 n. 159; 162 n. 83; 170

I v. UK (Appl. No. 25680/94), Judgment (Grand Chamber), 11 July 2002, not reported   89 n. 130

Iatridis v. Greece (Appl. No. 31107/96), Judgment (Grand Chamber), 25 March 1999; Judgment (Grand Chamber), 19 October 2000, Reports 1999-II   113 n. 20; 143 n. 4; 144 n. 7

İçyer v. Turkey (Appl. No. 18888/02), Admissibility Decision (Third Section), 12 January 2006, Reports 2006-I   167 n. 106

Iglesias Gil and AUI v. Spain (Appl. No. 56673/00), Judgment (Fourth Section), 29 April 2003, Reports 2003-V   70 n. 37

Ilascu and Others v. Russia and Moldova (Appl. No. 48787/99), Judgment (Grand Chamber), 8 July 2004, Reports 2004-VII   171; 363

Ilatovskiy v. Russia (Appl. No. 6945/04), Judgment (First Section), 9 July 2009, not reported   153 n. 61

Ionescu v. Romania (Appl. No. 36659/04), Decision (Third Section), 1 June 2010, not reported   36 n. 33

Ireland v. UK (Appl. No. 5310/71), Judgment (Plenary), 18 January 1978, Series A, Vol. 25   66 n. 18; 93 n. 151; 129 n. 70; 145 n. 17

Isayeva v. Russia (Appl. No. 57950/00), Judgment (First Section), 24 February 2005, not reported   174

Issa and Others v. Turkey (Appl. No. 31821/96), Judgment (Second Section), 16 November 2004, not reported   363

Iversen v. *Norway* (Appl. No. 1468/62), Decision (Commission), 17 December 1963, YB 6 (1963)   66 n. 19

Jahn and Others v. *Germany* (Appl. Nos. 46720/99; and 72203 and 72552/01), Judgment (Third Section), 22 January 2004, not reported; Judgment (Grand Chamber), 30 June 2005, Reports 2005-VI   71 nn. 38, 40

James and Others v. *United Kingdom* (Appl. No. 8793/79), Judgment (Plenary), 21 February 1986, Series A, Vol. 98   71 n. 38; 129 n. 70

Jendrowiak v. *Germany* (Appl. No. 30060/04), Judgment (Fifth Section), 14 April 2011, not reported   226, 228

Johansen v. *Norway* (Appl. No. 17383/90), Judgment (Chamber), 7 August 1996, Reports 1996-III   78 n. 72

Johansson v. *Finland* (Appl. No. 10163/02), Judgment (Fourth Section), 6 September 2007, not reported   37 n. 35

Jokela v. *Finland* (Appl. No. 28856/95), Judgment (Fourth Section), 21 May 2002, Reports 2002-IV   129 n. 70

Jussila v. *Finland* (Appl. No. 73053/01), Judgment (Grand Chamber), 23 November 2006, Reports 2006-XIV   54 n. 76

K and T v. *Finland* (Appl. No. 25702/94), Judgment (Grand Chamber), 12 July 2001, Reports 2001-VII   78 n. 72

KA v. *Finland* (Appl. No. 22751/95), Judgment (Fourth Section), 14 January 2003, not reported   147 n. 29

Kallweit v. *Germany* (Appl. No. 17792/07), Judgment (Fifth Section), 13 January 2011, not reported   226 n. 204; 228–9; 231

Karakurt v. *Austria* (Appl. No. 32441/96), Judgment (Third Section), 14 September 1999, not reported   113 n. 17

Karandja v. *Bulgaria* (Appl. No. 69180/01), Judgment (Fifth Section), 7 October 2010, not reported   148 n. 43

Karanović v. *Bosnia and Herzegovina* (Appl. No. 39462/03), Judgment (Fourth Section), 20 November 2007, not reported   152 n. 57

Karatas v. *Turkey* (Appl. No. 23168/94), Judgment (Grand Chamber), 8 July 1999, Reports 1999-IV   94

Kasumaj v. *Greece* (Appl. No. 6974/05), Decision (First Section), 5 July 2007, not reported   342; 352

Katz v. *Romania* (Appl. No. 29739/03), Judgment (Third Section), 20 January 2009, not reported   164 n. 96

Kauczor v. *Poland* (Appl. No. 45219/06), Judgment (Fourth Section), 3 February 2009, not reported   167 n. 107

Kemevuako v. *Netherlands* (Appl. No. 65938/09), Decision (Third Section), 1 June 2010, not reported   29 n. 11

Kingsley v. *United Kingdom* (Appl. No. 35605/97), Judgment (Grand Chamber), 28 May 2002, Reports 2002-IV   142

Klass v. *Germany* (Appl. No. 15473/89), Judgment (Chamber), 22 September 1993, Series A, Vol. 269   70 n. 31

TABLE OF CASES   xxi

Kokkelvisserij v. *Netherlands* (Appl. No. 13645/05), Decision (Third Section), 20 January 2009, Reports 2009   9 n. 35; 308 n. 17; 379 n. 166

Kokkinakis v. *Greece* (Appl. No. 14307/88), Judgment (Chamber), 25 May 1993, Series A, Vol. 260-A   102 n. 191; 123

Konig v. *Germany* (Appl. No. 6232/73), Judgment (Plenary), 28 June 1978, Series A, Vol. 27   113 n. 19

Konstantin Markin v. *Russia* (Appl. No. 30078/06), Judgment (First Section), 7 October 2010, not reported   168 n. 111; 290 n. 111

Korolev (II) v. *Russia* (Appl. No. 25551/05), Decision (First Section), 27 July 2010, Reports 2010   36 n. 33

Kozacıoğlu v. *Turkey* (Appl. No. 2334/03), Judgment (Grand Chamber), 19 February 2009, not reported   75 n. 60

Kozak v. *Poland* (Appl. No. 13102/02), Judgment (Fourth Section), 9 February 2010, not reported   89 n. 129

Kudla v. *Poland* (Appl. No. 30210/96), Judgment (Grand Chamber), 26 October 2000, Reports 2000-XI   256

Kurić and Others v. *Slovenia* (Appl. No. 26828/06), Judgment (Third Section), 13 July 2010, not reported   169

Kutzner v. *Germany* (Appl. No. 46544/99), Judgment (Fourth Section), 26 February 2002, Reports 2002-I   148 n. 40

Kyprianou v. *Cyprus* (Appl. No. 73797/01), Judgment (Grand Chamber), 15 December 2005, Reports 2005-XIII   148 n. 39

L v. *Lithuania* (Appl. No. 27527/03), Judgment (Second Section), 11 September 2007, Reports 2007-IV   170 n. 123

Laska and Lika v. *Albania* (Appl. Nos. 12315 and 17605/04), Judgment (Fourth Section), 20 April 2010, not reported   152 n. 57

Lautsi and Others v. *Italy* (Appl. No. 30814/06), Judgment (Grand Chamber), 18 March 2011, not yet reported   7; 13; 50; 99; 120; 124; 187; 391

Lawless v. *Ireland* (Appl. No. 332/57), Report (Commission, Plenary), 19 December 1959, Series, Vol. 1 (1960–1)   66

Lehideux and Isorni v. *France* (Appl. No. 24662/94), Judgment (Grand Chamber), 23 September 1998, Reports 1998-VII   78 n. 74

Lesjak v. *Croatia* (Appl. No. 25904/06), Judgment (First Section), 18 February 2010, not reported   156 n. 69

Lithgow v. *United Kingdom* (Appl. Nos. 9006/80; and 9262, 9263, 9265, 9266, 9313 and 9405/81), Judgment (Plenary), 8 July 1986, Series A, Vol. 102   129 n. 70

Loizidou v. *Turkey (Merits)* (Appl. No. 15318/89), 23 March 1995, Series A, Vol. 310; *(Preliminary Objections)*, Judgment (Grand Chamber), 18 December 1996, Reports 1996-VI   354

Lucà v. *Italy* (Appl. No. 33354/96), Judgment (First Section), 27 February 2001, Reports 2001-II   211 n. 133

Lukenda v. *Slovenia* (Appl. No. 23032/02), Judgment (Third Section), 6 October 2005, Reports 2005-X   167 n. 106

Lundevall v. *Sweden* (Appl. No. 38629/97), Judgment (Fourth Section), 12 November 2002, not reported   146

Lungoci v. *Romania* (Appl. No. 62710/00), Judgment (Third Section), 26 January 2006, not reported   155

Lustig-Prean and Beckett v. *UK* (Appl. Nos. 31417 and 32377/96), Judgment (Third Section), 27 September 1999, not reported   89 n. 129

Lyons and Others v. *UK* (Appl. No. 15227/03) *(Admissibility Decision)*, 8 July 2003, Reports 2003-IX   146 n. 20

M v. *Germany* (Appl. No. 19359/04), Judgment (Fifth Section), 17 December 2009, Reports 2009   21, 189

M.S.S. v. *Belgium and Greece* (Appl. No. 30696/09), Judgment (Grand Chamber), 21 January 2011, Reports 2011   333 n. 62; 378 n. 160; 381 n. 170

Maksimov v. *Azerbaijan* (Appl. No. 38228/05) *(Operative Provision 3)*, Judgment (First Section), 8 October 2009, not reported   154; 155

Malama v. *Greece* (Appl. No. 43622/98), Judgment (Second Section), 1 March 2001, Reports 2001-II   129 n. 70

Mamatkulov and Askarov v. *Turkey* (Appl. Nos. 46827 and 46951/99), Judgment (Grand Chamber), 4 February 2005, Reports 2005-I   47 n. 62; 149 n. 45

Manole and Others v. *Moldova* (Appl. No. 13936/02), Judgment (Fourth Section), 17 September 2009, Reports 2009   168

Mansur Pad and Others v. *Turkey* (Appl. No. 60167/00), Decision (Third Section), 28 June 2007, not reported   362 n. 95

Marckx v. *Belgium* (Appl. No. 6833/74), Judgment (Plenary), 13 June 1979, Series A, Vol. 31   110–17; 123–4

Margareta and Roger Andersson v. *Sweden* (Appl. No. 12963/87), Judgment (Chamber), 25 February 1992, Series A, Vol. 226-A   78 n. 72

Maria Atanasiu and Others v. *Romania* (Appl. Nos. 30767/05 and 33800/06), Judgment (Third Section), 12 October 2010, not reported   162 n. 84; 163–164

Matthews v. *UK* (Appl. No. 24833/94), Judgment (Grand Chamber), 18 February 1999, Reports 1999-I   122 n. 55; 381 n. 169

Mautes v. *Germany* (Appl. No. 20008/07), Judgment (Fifth Section), 13 January 2011, not reported   226–231

MC v. *Bulgaria* (Appl. No. 39272/98), Judgment (First Section), 4 December 2003, Reports 2003-XII   147 n. 32

Medova v. *Russia* (Appl. No. 25385/04), Judgment (First Section), 15 January 2009, Reports 2009   173

Medvedyev and Others v. *France* (Appl. No. 3394/03), Judgment (Grand Chamber), 29 March 2010, Reports 2010   366 n. 109

Mehemi v. *France* (Appl. No. 25017/94), Judgment (Chamber), 26 September 1997, Reports 1997-VI   145 n. 18

Mehemi v. *France (No. 2)* (Appl. No. 53470/99), Judgment (Third Section), 10 April 2003, Reports 2003-IV   281

Messina v. Italy (No. 2) (Appl. No. 25498/94), Judgment (Second Section), 28 August 2000, Reports 2000-X   167 n. 105

MGN Limited v. The United Kingdom (Appl. No. 39401/04), Judgment (Fourth Section), 18 January 2011, not reported   77 n. 71

Modinos v. Cyprus (Appl. No. 15070/89), Judgment (Chamber), 22 April 1993, Series A, Vol. 259   89 n. 129

Monnat v. Switzerland (Appl. No. 73604/01), Judgment (Third Section), 21 September 2006, Reports 2006-X   78 n. 74

Morel v. France (Appl. No. 54559/00), Decision (Second Section), 3 June 2003, Reports 2003-IX   54 n. 76

Morris v. United Kingdom (Appl. No. 38784/97), Judgment (Third Section), 26 February 2002, Reports 2002-I   147 n. 31, 213

Muller and Others v. Switzerland (Appl. No. 10737/84), Judgment (Chamber), 24 May 1988, Series A, Vol. 133   114 n. 27

Niemietz v. Germany (Appl. No. 13710/88), Judgment (Chamber), 16 December 1992, Series A, Vol. 251-B   401

Nikolova v. Bulgaria (Appl. No. 31195/96), Judgment (Grand Chamber), 25 March 1999, Reports 1999-II   147 n. 26

Norbert Sikorski v. Poland (Appl. No. 17599/05), Judgment (Fourth Section), 22 October 2009, not reported   167 n. 108

Norris v. Ireland (Appl. No. 10581/83), Judgment (Plenary), 26 October 1988, Series A, Vol. 142   89 n. 129

OAO Neftyanaya Kompaniya Yukos v. Russia (Appl. No. 14902/04), Judgment (First Section), 20 September 2011, not reported   184 n. 13; 261 n. 355

Öcalan v. Turkey (Appl. No. 46221/99), Judgment (First Section), 12 March 2003, not reported; Judgment (Grand Chamber), 12 May 2005, Reports 2005-IV   149 n. 44; 363

Öcalan v. Turkey (Appl. No. 5980/07), Decision (Second Section), 6 July 2010, not reported   281 n. 76

Odièvre v. France (Appl. No. 42326/98), Judgment (Grand Chamber), 13 February 2003, Reports 2003-III   72 n. 45; 87 n. 118; 121 n. 52

Olaru and Others v. Moldova (Appl. Nos. 476/07; 22539/05; 17911/08; and 13136/07), Judgment (Fourth Section), 28 July 2009, not reported   163

Olsson v. Sweden (No. 1) (Appl. No. 10465/83), Judgment (Plenary), 24 March 1988, Series A, Vol. 130   78 n. 72

Oneryildiz v. Turkey (Appl. No. 48939/99), Judgment (Grand Chamber), 30 November 2004, Reports 2004-XII   116 n. 33

Opuz v. Turkey (Appl. No. 33401/02), Judgment (Third Section), 9 June 2009, Reports 2009   53 n. 75; 176 n. 149

Orchowski v. Poland (Appl. No. 17885/04), Judgment (Fourth Section), 22 October 2009, not reported   167 n. 108

Osman v. United Kingdom (Appl. 23452/94), Judgment (Grand Chamber), 28 October 1998, Reports 1998-VIII   60 n. 91; 258; 260; 261

Otto-Preminger-Institut v. *Austria* (Appl. No. 13470/87), Judgment (Chamber), 20 September 1994, Series A, Vol. 295-A   87 n. 118; 98 n. 175; 114

Palomo Sánchez and Others v. *Spain* (Appl. Nos. 28955, 28957, 28959 and 28964/06), Judgment (Grand Chamber), 12 September 2011, Reports 2011   77 n. 71; 92 n. 142, 176 n. 149

Papamichalopoulos and Others v. *Greece* (Appl. No. 14556/89), Judgment (Chamber), 31 October 1995, Series A, Vol. 330-B   149 n. 47

Paradysz v. *France* (Appl. No. 17020/05), Judgment (Fifth Section), 29 October 2009, not reported   209 n. 125; 210

Peck v. *United Kingdom* (Appl. No. 44647/98), Judgment (Fourth Section), 28 January 2003, Reports 2003-I   148 n. 34

Pellegrin v. *France* (Appl. No. 28541/95), Judgment (Grand Chamber), 8 December 1999, Reports 1999-VIII   113 n. 23

Piersack v. *Belgium* (Appl. No. 9186/80), Judgment (Court, Plenary), 26 October 1984, Series A, Vol. 85   289 n. 104

Pincova and Pinc v. *Czech Republic* (Appl. No. 36548/97), Judgment (Second Section), 5 November 2002, Reports 2002-VIII   129 n. 70

Pine Valley Developments Ltd and Others v. *Ireland* (Appl. No. 12742/87), Judgment (Chamber), 29 November 1991, Series A, Vol. 222   99 n. 159

Pishchalnikov v. *Russia* (Appl. No. 7025/04), Judgment (First Section), 24 September 2009, not reported   153 n. 58

Pittito v. *Italy* (Appl. No. 19321/03), Judgment (Second Section), 12 June 2007, not reported   238–9

Pla and Puncernau v. *Andorra* (Appl. No. 69498/01), Judgment (Fourth Section), 13 July 2004, Reports 2004-VIII   70 n. 34; n. 39

Poghosyan v. *Georgia* (Appl. No. 9870/07), Judgment (Second Section), 24 February 2009, not reported   170 n. 122

Prežec v. *Croatia* (Appl. No. 48185/07), Judgment (First Section), 15 October 2009, not reported   154 n. 63

RL v. *The Netherlands* (Appl. No. 22942/91), EComHR, Decision of 18 March 1995, not reported   113 n. 16

Ramadhi and 5 others v. *Albania* (Appl. No. 38222/02), Judgment (Fourth Section), 13 November 2007, not reported   168 n. 110

Raninen v. *Finland* (Appl. No. 152/1996), Judgment (Chamber), 16 December 1997, Reports 1997-VIII   207 n. 115

Rantsev v. *Cyprus and Russia* (Appl. No. 25965/04), Judgment (First Section), 7 January 2010, Reports 2010   118–24

Ravnsborg v. *Sweden* (Appl. No. 14220/88), Judgment (Chamber), 23 March 1992, Series A, No. 283-B   113 n. 18

RD v. *Poland* (Appl. Nos. 29692/96 and 34612/97), Judgment (Fourth Section), 18 December 2001, not reported   148 n. 35

Rees v. *United Kingdom* (Appl. No. 9532/81), Judgment (Plenary), 17 October 1986, Series A, Vol. 106   188

Refah partisi (The Welfare Party) and Others v. *Turkey* (Appl. Nos. 41340, 41342 and 41343/98), Judgment (Grand Chamber), 13 February 2003, Reports 2003-II   75 n. 58; 102–3
Reynolds v. *The United Kingdom* (Appl. No. 2694/08), Judgment (Chamber), 13 March 2012, (2012) ECHR 437   255, 257
Rohde v. *Denmark* (Appl. No. 69332/01), Judgment (First Section), 21 July 2005, not reported   123
RR v. *Italy* (Appl. No. 42191/02), Judgment (Third Section), 9 June 2005, not reported
Rumpf v. *Germany* (Appl. No. 46344/06), Judgment (Fifth Section), 2 September 2010, Reports 2010   167 n. 109
Russian Conservative Party of Entrepreneurs and Others v. *Russia* (Appl. Nos. 55066 and 55638/00), Judgment (First Section), 11 January 2007, not reported   117 n. 34
Saadi v. *Italy* (Appl. No. 37201/06), Judgment (Grand Chamber), 28 February 2008, Reports 2008   76 n. 63
Saadi v. *United Kingdom* (Appl. No. 13229/03), Judgment (Grand Chamber), 29 January 2008, Reports 2008   123
Sadak and Others v. *Turkey* (Appl. Nos. 29900, 29901, 29902 and 29903/96), Judgment (First Section), 17 July 2001, Reports 2001-VIII   148 n. 38; 289
Saghinadze and Others v. *Georgia* (Appl. No. 18768/05), Judgment (Second Section), 27 May 2010, not reported   150
Sahin v. *Germany* (Appl. No. 30943/96), Judgment (Grand Chamber), 8 July 2003, not reported   78 n. 73
Salduz v. *Turkey* (Appl. No. 36391/02), Judgment (Grand Chamber), 27 November 2008, Reports 2008   153; 244; 245; 246; 250–1
Sampanis and Others v. *Greece* (Appl. No. 32526/05), Judgment (First Section), 5 June 2008, not reported   287
Schalk and Kopf v. *Austria* (Appl. No. 30141/04), Judgment (Chamber), 24 June 2010, not reported   89 n. 129; 101; 120–124; 187 n. 27; 205 n. 108
Schmautzer v. *Austria* (Appl. No. 15523/89), Court (Chamber), 23 October 1995, Series A, Vol. 328-A   146 n. 20
Schmidt and Dahlström v. *Sweden* (Appl. No. 5589/72), Judgment (Chamber), 6 February 1976, Series A, Vol. 21   67 n. 22
Schmitz v. *Germany* (Appl. No. 30493/04), Judgment (Fifth Section), 9 June 2011, not reported   235 n. 256
Schummer v. *Germany* (Appl. Nos. 27360/04 and 42225/07), Judgment (Fifth Section), 13 January 2011, not reported   226; 228; 229 n. 227; 231
Schweighofer and Others v. *Austria* (Appl. Nos. 35673, 35674, 36082 and 37579/97), Judgment (Third Section), 24 August 1999, not reported   234 n. 50
Scoppola v. *Italy (No. 2)* (Appl. No. 10249/03), Judgment (Grand Chamber), 17 September 2009, not reported   148 n. 42; 156; 157; 323 n. 48
Scoppola v. *Italy (No. 3)* (Appl. No. 126/05), Judgment (Second Section), 18 January 2011, not reported   166 n. 103

Scordino v. *Italy (No. 1)* (Appl. No. 36813/97), Judgment (First Section), 29 July 2004; Judgment (Grand Chamber), 29 March 2006, Reports 2006-V 167 n. 110
Scordino v. *Italy (No. 3)* (Appl. No. 43662/98), Judgment (Fourth Section), 17 May 2005, not reported; Judgment (Chamber), 6 March 2007, not reported 168 n. 110
Scozzari and Giunta v. *Italy* (Appl. Nos. 39221 and 41963/98), Judgment (Grand Chamber), 13 July 2000, Reports 2000-VIII 144 n. 6
Sejdić and Finci v. *Bosnia and Herzegovina* (Appl. Nos. 27996 and 34836/06), Judgment (Grand Chamber), 22 December 2009, Reports 2009 289 n. 99; 288 n. 100
Sejdovic v. *Italy* (Appl. No. 56581/00), Judgment (Chamber) 10 November 2004; Judgment (Grand Chamber), 1 March 2006, Reports 2006-II 167 n. 109
Selçuk and Asker v. *Turkey* (Appl. Nos. 23184 and 23185/94), Judgment (Chamber), 24 April 1998, Reports 1998-II 143 n. 5; 145 n. 16
SH and Others v. *Austria* (Appl. No. 57813/00), Judgment (First Section), 1 April 2010; Judgment (Grand Chamber), 3 November 2011, [2011] EHCR 1879 84 n. 104
Sheffield and Horsham v. *United Kingdom* (Appl. Nos. 31-2/1997;15-816/1018-/1998), Judgment (Grand Chamber), 30 July 1998, Reports 1998-V 114-16; 123-4; 189
Siliadin v. *France* (Appl. No. 73316/01), Judgment (Second Section), 26 July 2005, Reports 2005-VII 117 n. 41; 123-4
Sławomir Musiał v. *Poland* (Appl. No. 28300/06), Judgment (Fourth Section), 20 January 2009, not reported 170 n. 122
Slivenko v. *Latvia* (Appl. No. 48321/99), Judgment (Grand Chamber), 9 October 2003, Reports 2003-X 71 n. 37
Smith and Grady v. *UK* (Appl. Nos. 33985 and 33986/96), Judgment (Third Section), 27 September 1999, Reports 1999-VI 20 n. 78; 89 n. 129
Šneersone and Kampanella v. *Italy* (Appl. No. 14737/09), Judgment (Second Section), 12 July 2011, not reported 327; 333 n. 62
Somogyi v. *Italy* (Appl. No. 67972/01), Judgment (Second Section), 18 May 2004, Reports 2004-IV 152 n. 58
Sorensen and Rasmussen v. *Denmark* (Appl. Nos. 52562 and 52620/99), Judgment (Grand Chamber), 11 January 2006, Reports 2006-I 117 n. 36
Sporrong and Lönnroth v. *Sweden* (Appl. Nos. 7151 and 7152/75), Judgment (Plenary), 23 September 1982, Series A, Vol. 52 75 n. 60; 95 n. 159; 113 n. 19
Steel and Morris v. *United Kingdom* (Appl. No. 68416/01), Judgment (Fourth Section), 15 February 2005, Reports 2005-II 147 n. 31
Stephens v. *Cyprus, Turkey and the UN* (Appl. No. 45267/06), Decision (First Section), 11 December 2008, not reported 339 n. 14; 346 n. 35
Stjerna v. *Finland* (Appl. No. 18131/91), Judgment (Chamber), 25 November 1994, Series A, Vol. 299-B 87 n. 118
Stoichkov v. *Bulgaria* (Appl. No. 9808/02), Judgment (First Section), 24 March 2005, not reported 153 n. 58

Strain v. *Romania* (Appl. No. 57001/00), Judgment (Third Section), 21 July 2005, Reports 2005-VII   288 n. 101
Stran GK Refineries and Stratis Andreadis v. *Greece* (Appl. No. 13427/87), Judgment (Chamber), 9 December 1994, Series A, Vol. 301-B   289 n. 102
Stretch v. *United Kingdom* (Appl. No. 44277/98), Judgment (Fourth Section), 24 June 2003, not reported   148 n. 36
Stübing v. *Germany* (Appl. No. 43547/08), Judgment (Third Section), 19 April 2012   391
Suljagić v. *Bosnia and Herzegovina* (Appl. No. 27912/02), Judgment (Fourth Section), 3 November 2009, not reported   163 n. 91; 164
Sürmeli v. *Germany* (Appl. No. 75529/01), Judgment (Grand Chamber), 8 June 2006, Reports 2006-VII   163 n. 93; 281 n. 72
Swedish Engine Drivers' Union v. *Sweden* (Appl. No. 5614/72), Judgment (Chamber), 6 February 1976, Series A, Vol. 20   67 n. 22
T v. *United Kingdom* (Appl. No. 24724/94), Judgment (Grand Chamber), 16 December 1999, not reported   87 n. 118
Taskin and Others v. *Turkey* (Appl. No. 46117/99), Judgment (Third Section), 10 November 2004, Reports 2004-X   117 n. 40
Tătar v. *Romania* (Appl. No. 67021/01), Judgment (Third Section), 27 January 2009, Reports 2009   95 n. 161
Tehrani and Others v. *Turkey* (Appl. Nos. 32940, 41626 and 43616/08), Judgment (Second Section), 13 April 2010, not reported   158
The Sunday Times v. *UK (No. 2)* (*Spycatcher* case) (Appl. No. 13166/87), Judgment (Plenary), 26 November 1991, Series A, Vol. 217   79 n. 78
Times Newspapers Ltd (Nos. 1 and 2) v. *UK* (Appl. Nos. 3002 and 23676/03), Judgment (Fourth Section), 10 March 2009, Reports - 2009   84 n. 104
Tyrer v. *United Kingdom* (Appl. No. 5856/72), Judgment (Chamber), 25 April 1978, Series A, Vol. 26   109–14; 123
Ullens De Schooten and Rezabek v. *Belgium* (Appl. Nos. 3989 and 38353/07), Judgment (Second Section), 20 September 2011, not reported   324, n. 50
Umayeva v. *Russia* (Appl. No. 1200/03), Judgment (First Section), 4 December 2008, not reported   173 n. 137
Union of Belgian Police v. *Belgium* (Appl. No. 4464/70), Judgment (Plenary), 27 October 1975, Series A, Vol. 19   67 n. 22
United Communist Party of Turkey and Others v. *Turkey*, Judgment (Grand Chamber), 30 January 1998, Reports 1998-I   102 n. 190
Urbárska obec Trenčianske Biskupice v. *Slovakia* (Appl. No. 74258/01), Judgment (Fourth Section), 27 November 2007, not reported   168 n. 113
Van der Heijden v. *Netherlands* (Appl. No. 42857/05), Judgment (Grand Chamber), 3 April 2012, not reported   368 n. 182
Van Kück v. *Germany* (Appl. No. 35968/97), Judgment (Third Section), 12 June 2003, Reports 2003-VII   90 n. 130

Varnava and Others v. *Turkey* (Appl. Nos. 16064, 16065, 16066, 16068, 16069, 16070, 16071, 16072 and 16073/90), Judgment (Grand Chamber), 18 September 2009, Reports 2009   173; 174 n. 138; 176 n. 149

Vassilios Athanasiou and Others v. *Greece* (Appl. No. 50973/08), Judgment (First Section), 21 December 2010, not reported   163; 290 n. 111

Verein gegen Tierfabriken Schweiz (VgT) v. *Switzerland* (Appl. No. 32772/02), Judgment, (Fifth Section), 4 October 2007, not reported   289 n. 105

Verein gegen Tierfabriken Schweiz (VgT) v. *Switzerland (No. 2)* (Appl. No. 32772/02), Judgment (Fifth Section), 4 October 2007; Judgment (Grand Chamber), 30 June 2009, Reports 2009   144 n. 10

Vereinigung Bildender Künstler v. *Austria* (Appl. No. 68354/01), Judgment (First Section), 25 January 2007, not reported   70 n. 33

Viaşu v. *Romania* (Appl. No. 75951/01), Judgment (Third Section), 9 December 2008, not reported   163 n. 96

Vladimir Romanov v. *Russia* (Appl. No. 41461/02), Judgment (First Section), 24 July 2008, not reported   153

Vo v. *France* (Appl. No. 53924/00), Judgment (Grand Chamber), 8 July 2004, Reports 2004-VIII   72 n. 45; 88 n. 119

Von Hannover v. *Germany* (Appl. No. 59320/00), Judgment (Third Section), 24 June 2004, Reports 2004-VI, para. 59   60 n. 92; 98 n. 176

Von Hannover v. *Germany (No. 2)* (Appl. Nos. 40660 and 60641/08), Judgment (Grand Chamber), 7 February 2012, Reports 2012   60 n. 92; 77 n. 71; 92 n. 142

Wegera v. *Poland* (Appl. No. 141/07), Judgment (Fourth Section), 19 January 2010, not reported   290 n. 111

Werner v. *Poland* (Appl. No. 26760/95), Judgment (Fourth Section), 15 November 2001, not reported   147 n. 30

White and Kennedy v. *Germany* (Appl. No. 26083/94), Judgment (Grand Chamber), 18 February 1999, Reports 1999-I   337 n. 11

Wingrove v. *UK* (Appl. No. 17419/90), Judgment (Chamber), 25 November 1996, Reports 1996-V   79 n. 78; 87 n. 118; 98 n. 174; 114 no. 29

Winterwerp v. *The Netherlands* (Appl. No. 6301/73), Judgment (Chamber), 24 October 1979, Series A, Vol. 33   70 n. 37

Witold Litwa v. *Poland* (Appl. No. 26629/95), Judgment (Second Section), 4 April 2000, Reports 2000-III   113 n. 24

Witomila Wołk-Jezierska and Others v. *Russia* (Appl. Nos. 55508/07 and 29520/09), Judgment (Fifth Section), 16 April 2012, not reported   184 n. 14

X, Y and Z v. *UK* (Appl. No. 21830/93), Judgment (Grand Chamber), 22 April 1997, Reports 1997-II   87 n. 118

Xenides-Arestis v. *Turkey* (Appl. No. 46347/99), Judgment (Third Section), 22 December 2005, not reported   167 n. 106

TABLE OF CASES   xxix

Yetiş and Others v. *Turkey* (Appl. No. 40349/05), Judgment (Second Section), 6 July 2010, not reported   169 n. 119

Young, James and Webster v. *United Kingdom* (Appl. Nos. 7601/76 and 7806/77), Judgment (Chamber), 13 August 1981, Series A, Vol. 55   123

Yuriy Nikolayevich Ivanov v. *Ukraine* (Appl. No. 40450/04), Judgment (Fifth Section), 15 October 2009, not reported   163 n. 86

Z v. *Finland* (Appl. No. 22009/93), Judgment (Chamber), 25 February 1997, Reports 1997-I   81 n. 90

Z and Others v. *UK* (Appl. No. 29392/95), Judgment (Grand Chamber), 10 May 2001, Reports 2001-V   60 n. 91

Zolotukhin v. *Russia* (Appl. No. 14939/03), Judgment (Grand Chamber), 10 February 2009, Reports 2009   60 n. 93; 176 n. 149

Zvolsky and Zvolska v. *The Czech Republic* (Appl. No. 46129/99), Judgment (Second Section), 12 November 2002, Reports 2002-IX   71 n. 38

Zwierzynski v. *Poland* (Appl. No. 34049/96), Judgment (First Section), 2 July 2002, not reported   150 n. 48

Court of Justice of the European Union (previously European Court of Justice of the European Communities, ECJ)

Case C-273/99 P, *Bernard Connolly* v. *Commission of the European Communities* [2001] ECR I-1575   304 n. 7

Case C-84/95, *Bosphorus Hava Yollari Turizm ve Ticaret AS* v. *Minister of Transport, Energy and Communications and Others* [1996] ECR I-3953   380, n. 168

Case 120/78, *Cassis de Dijon Rewe Zentral, AG* v. *Bundesmonopolverwaltung für Branntwein* [1979] ECR 649   19 n. 77

Case C-411/06, *Commission* v. *Parliament and Council* [2009] ECR I-7585   185 n. 17

Case 29/69, *Erich Stauder* v. *City of Ulm – Sozialamt* [1969] ECR 419   303 n. 4

Case 314/85, *Foto Frost* v. *Hauptzollamt Lübeck-Ost* [1987] ECR 4199   368 n. 111

Case C-27/09 P, *French Republic* v. *People's Mojahedine Organization of Iran* [2011] ECR 0000   379 n. 165

Case 1/58, *Friedrich Stork & Cie* v. *High Authority of the European Coal and Steel Community* [1959]   303 n. 3

Joined Cases 46/87 and 227/88, *Hoechst AG* v. *Commission of the European Communities* [1989] ECR 2859   306 n. 11

Case 11/70, *Internationale Handelsgesellschaft mbH* v. *Einfuhr- und Vorratsstelle für Getreide und Futtermittel* [1970] ECR 1125   19 n. 77; 304 n. 5

Case 4/73, *J. Nold, Kohlen- und Baustoffgroßhandlung* v. *Commission of the European Communities* [1974] ECR 491   304 n. 5

Case C-491/10 PPU, *Joseba Andoni Aguirre Zarraga* v. *Simone Pelz* [2010] ECR 2010   329 n. 59

Case 44/79, *Liselotte Hauer* v. *Land Rheinland-Pfalz* [1979] ECR 03727   304 n. 5
Case C—188 and 189/10, *Melki and Abdeli* [2010] ECR I-5667   368 n. 111
Case C—119/05, *Ministero dell'Industria, del Commercio e dell'Artigianato* v. *Lucchini SpA* [2007] ECR I-6199   368 n. 111
Joined Cases C-411 and 493/10, *N.S.* v. *Secretary of State for the Home Department and others* [2011] ECR I-2011   333 n. 62
Joined Cases 36, 37, 38 and 40/59, *Präsident Ruhrkohlen-Verkaufsgesellschaft mbH, Geitling Ruhrkohlen-Verkaufsgesellschaft mbH, Mausegatt Ruhrkohlen-Verkaufsgesellschaft mbH and I. Nold KG* v. *High Authority of the European Coal and Steel Community* [1960]   303 n. 3
Case 265/87, *Schrader* v. *Hauptzollamt Gronau* [1989] ECR 2237   19 n. 77; 368 n. 111
Case C-402 and 415/05P, *Yassin Abdullah Kadi and Al Barakaat International Foundation* v. *Council of the European Union and Commission of the European Communities* [2008] ECR I-6351   376 n. 149

General Court of the European Union (previously Court of First Instance, CFI)

Case T-253/02, *Ayadi* v. *Council of the European Union* [2006] All ER (D) 155 (Jul)   375 n. 148
Case T-47/03, *Jose Maria Sison* v. *Council of the European Union* [2009] ECR II-1483   379 n. 165
Case T-315/01, *Kadi* v. *Council and Commission* [2005] ECR II-3649   374 n. 145
Case T-228/02, *Organisation des Modjahedines du peuple d'Iran* v. *Council of the European Union* [2006] ECR II-4665   379 n. 165
Case T-256/07, *People's Mojahedin Organization of Iran* v. *Council of the European Union* [2008] ECR II-3019   379 n. 165
Case T-85/09, *Yassin Abdullah Kadi* v. *European Commission* [2010] ECR 0000   377 n. 158
Case T—306/01, *Yusuf and Al Barakaat* v. *Council and Commission* [2005] ECR II-3353   374 n. 145

International Organisations

Arbitral Tribunals

Arbitration regarding the Iron Rhine (*'Ijzeren Rijn'*) Railway (*Belgium* v. *The Netherlands*), Award, 24 May 2005   192
British Claims in the Spanish Zone of Marroco (*Spain* v. *United Kingdom*) 2 RIAA 615 (1923)   192 n. 49
Romak S.A. (*Switzerland* v. *The Republic of Uzbekistan*), Award, 26 November 2009   192 n. 51

TABLE OF CASES   xxxi

Inter-American Court of Human Rights (IACtHR)

Baena Ricardo et al. v. *Panama,* Judgment, 2 February 2001, Ser. C, No. 61   172 n. 128
Bamaca Velasquez v. *Guatemala (Reparations),* Judgment, 22 February 2002, Ser. C, No. 91   172 n. 131; 175 n. 144
Cantoral Benavides v. *Peru (Reparations),* Judgment, 3 December 2001, Ser. C, No. 88   172 n. 127
El Amparo v. *Venezuela,* Judgment, 14 September 1996, Ser. C, No. 28   172 n. 132
Garrido and Baigorria v. *Argentina (Reparations),* Judgment, 27 August 1998, Ser. C, No. 39   173 n. 133
González et al. ('Cotton Field') v. *Mexico,* Judgment, 16 November 2009, Ser. C, No. 205   175
Loayza Tamayo v. *Peru,* Judgment, 27 November 1998, Ser. C, No. 42   172 n. 129
Monsignor Oscar Arnulfo Romero y Galdemez v. *El Salvador,* Report (2000), No. 37/00, Case 11.481   175 n. 143
Myrna Mack Chang v. *Guatemala,* Judgment, 25 November 2003, Ser. C, No. 101   172 n. 130; 173 n. 134
Paniagua Morales et al. v. *Guatemala (Reparations),* Judgment, 25 May 2001, Ser. C, No. 7   173 n. 133

International Centre for Settlement of Investment Disputes (ICSID)

Mondev International Ltd. v. *United States of America,* Award, 11 October 2002, Case No. ARB(AF)/99/2   192 n. 51
Tecnicas Medioambientales Tecmed S.A. v. *The United Mexican States,* Award, 29 May 2003, Case No. ARB(AF)/00/2   192 n. 51

International Court of Justice (ICJ)

Ahmadou Sadio Diallo (Republic of Guinea v. *Democratic Republic of the Congo)* ICJ Reports (2010)   190 n. 40
Application of the Convention on the Prevention and Punishment of the Crime of Genocide (Bosnia and Herzegovina v. *Serbia and Montenegro),* ICJ Reports (2007) 43   353 n. 69
Armed Activities on the Territory of the Congo (Democratic Republic of the Congo v. *Uganda),* Judgment, ICJ Reports (2005) 168   190 n. 40; 362 n. 96
Case Concerning the Application of the International Convention on the Elimination of All Forms of Racial Discrimination (Georgia v. *Russian Federation)* ICJ Reports (2011)   191 n. 44
Jurisdictional Immunities of the State (Germany v. *Italy: Greece Intervening),* 3 February 2012, not yet reported   386 n. 181
Kasikili/Sedudu Island (Botswana v. *Namibia)* ICJ Reports (1999)   191 n. 46
Legal Consequences of the Construction of a Wall in the Occupied Palestinian Territory, Advisory Opinion, ICJ Reports (2004) 136   362 n. 96
Military and Paramilitary Activities in and against Nicaragua (Nicaragua v. *United States of America),* Merits, ICJ Reports (1986) 14   353 n. 69; 356

International Criminal Tribunal for the Former Yugoslavia (ICTY)

Case IT-94-1-A, *Prosecutor* v. *Dusko Tadic*, 15 July 1999, ILM 38 (1999) 1518   352 n. 65

Permanent Court of International Justice (PCIJ)

Nationality Decrees Issued in Tunis and Morocco (French Zone) Advisory Opinion, PCIJ Series B, No. 4 (1923)   190 n. 40

United Nations (UN)

Human Rights Committee

Abdeel Keerem Hassan Aboushanif v. *Norway*, views of 17 July 2008, Communication No. 1542/2007   207

Elgueta v. *Chile*, Decision on admissibility, 28 July 2009, Communication No. 1536/2006   18 n. 72

Robert Faurisson v. *France*, Communication No. 550/1993, Decision on admissibility, 19 July 1995; Decision on the merit, 8 November 1996, UN Doc. CCPR/C/58/D/550/1993 (1996)   78 n. 74

World Trade Organization (WTO)

Appellate Body

China – *Measures Affecting Trading Rights and Distribution Services for Certain Publications and Audiovisual Entertainment Products (China – Publications and Audiovisual Products)*, Report, WT/DS353/AB/R (circulated 21 December 2009, adopted 19 January 2010)   192 n. 51

National Courts

Austria

Superior Court of Appeal, Vienna, Judgment, 26 February 1979, 77 ILR 470 Belgium   347 n. 44

Constitutional Court

Decision 159/2004, 20 October 2004   205
Decision 202/2004, 21 December 2004   206 n. 109
Decision 131/2005, 19 July 2005   206 n. 109
Decision 151/2006, 18 October 2006   206 n. 109

TABLE OF CASES   xxxiii

Canada

Federal Courts

Abdelrazik v. The Minister of Foreign Affairs, Decision, June 2009, 2009 FC 580   371

Czech Republic

Constitutional Court

Decision of 3 November 2009 Judgment 2010/04/13 – I1. ÚS 485/10   193 n. 52

France

Conseil d'État

Benjamin (No. 17413), 19 May 1933   197 n. 75
Hyver CE, 10 October 1990   195 n. 65
Kerouaa [1992] Actualités Juridique Droit Administratif 833
Marie and Hardoun CE Ass. Plén., 17 February [1995] AJDA 420-1   195 n. 65
Assemblée, M. Planchenault (No. 290420) [2007] AJDA 2404   196 n. 69
Assemblée, Boussouar (No. 290730), 14 December 2007   195-6
Dubus (No. 266735), 25 July 2007   218
Association pour la promotion de l'image et autres (No. 317827 et al.), 26 October 2011   197

Conseil constitutionnel

Decision No. 2008-562DC, 21 February 2008   236

Germany

Bundesverfassungsgericht

BVerfG, 1 BvR 400/51, BVerfGE 7, 198 (Lüth), Judgment, 15 January 1958   19 n. 75; 85 n. 111
BVerfG, 2 BvR 197/83, BVerfGE 73, 339 (Solange II), Decision, 22 October 1986   382
BVerfG, 2 BvR 589/79, BVerfGE 74, 358, Decision, 26 March 1987   218 n. 167; 220 nn. 173-4
BVerfG, 2 BvG 1/89, BVerfGE 82, 106, Judgment, 29 May 1990   218 n. 167
BVerfGE 92, 203, Judgment, 22 March 1995   341 n. 20
BVerfG, 2 BvL 1/97, BVerfGE 102, 147, (Banana Market), Decision, 7 June 2000   382 n. 174
BVerfG, 2 BvR 2029/01, BVerfGE 109, 133, Judgment, 5 February 2004   232 n. 242
BVerfG, 2 BvR 1975/07, BVerfGE 111, 289 (Görgülü), Judgment, 12 October 2004   234 n. 251

BVerfG, 2 BvR 2365/09, BVerfGE 111, 307, Decision, 14 October 2004   220 nn. 173–4
BVerfG 1 BvR 2790/04, Decision, 28 December 2004   222 n. 187
BVerfG, 1 BvR 596/56, BVesfG 7, 377 (*Apotheken-Urteil*), Decision, 1 December 2005   19 n. 75
BVerfG 1 BvR 1174/01, Judgment, 9 February 2007   220 n. 177
BVerfG, 2 BvE 2/08; NJW 2009, 2267, BVerfGE 123, 267(*Lisbon Treaty*), Judgment, 30 June 2009   183 n. 9
BVerfG, 2 BvR 2365/09 (*Preventive Detention*), Judgment, 22 December 2009   7 n. 27; 226 n. 189; 231–4
BVerfG, 2 BvR 2307/06, Decision, 4 February 2010   236; 382 n. 174
BVerfG, 2 BvR 2661/06, BVerfGE 126, 286 (*Honeywell*), Decision, 6 July 2010
BverfG, 2 BvR 987/10, Judgment, 7 September 2011   341 n. 20
Bundesgerichtshof (Federal Supreme Court) 5 StR 60/10 (5 StR 21/09) Judgment, 21 July 2010   227 n. 206

Italy

Corte constituzionale

Judgment No. 348 and 349/2007   237

Corte di Cassazione

FAO v. *Colagrossi*, Judgment, 18 May 1992, *Rivista di diritto internazionale* 75 (1992) 407   337

Other courts

Milan Court of Appeal, 286/2008, Judgment 12 April 2010   238 n. 271

Norway

Supreme Court

Judgment *Corrugated Cardboard* (1994) Norsk Retstidende 610   198
Judgment (1999) Norsk Retstidende 961   198
Judgment *Bøhler* (2000) Norsk Retstidende 996   198–202
Judgment *KRL* (2001) Norsk Retstidende 1006   99, 199
Judgment (2003) Norsk Retstidende 359   200
Judgment (2005) Norsk Retstidende 833   200
Judgment (2008) Norsk Retstidende 1409   201; 200
Judgment (2009) Norsk Retstidende 1118   201
Decision HR-2010-01703-S, 12 October 2010   183 n. 8
Decision HR-2011-00182-A, 26 January 2011   206 n. 110

Switzerland

Swiss Federal Court, *Nada* v. *SECO*, Judgment, 14 November 2007, French text (translation from German): *Revue suisse de droit international et de droit européen* (2008) 467–72   378 n. 161; 380

The Netherlands

College van Beroep voor het bedrijfsleven (Industrial Appeals Court), 23 April 2008, LJN BD0646, AB 2008, 233 (*Socopa*)   309 n. 18
President Rechtbank (District Court), Den Haag, 23 June 2009, LJN BJ0893   309 n. 18
Gerechtshof (The Hague Court of Appeals), *Mustafic* v. *Netherlands*, 5 July 2011, case 200-020.173/01   360 n. 91

United Kingdom

Supreme Court (House of Lords until 1 October 2009)

Ambrose v. *Harris* [2011] UKSC 43; [2011] 1 WLR 2435   250–5
Antaios Compania Neviera SA v. *Salen Rederierna AB* [1985] 1 AC 191   194 n. 60
Attorney-General v. *Nissan* [1969] 1 All ER 639   346 n. 36
Berkshire Community Health NHS Trust and others (Respondents) and two other actions (FC) [2005] UKHL 23   204
Cadder v. *Her Majesty's Advocate* [2010] UKSC 43; [2010] WLR 268   182–183; 243–6
Dickson v. *HM Advocate* 2001 JC 203   34; 244
Dresser UK Ltd. v. *Falcongate Ltd* [1992] QB 502   215 n. 153
Fitzpatrick v. *Sterling Housing Association Ltd* [2001] 1 AC 27   194 n. 55
G, In re (Adoption: Unmarried Couple) [2009] 1 AC 173   93 n. 144
Her Majesty's Treasury (Respondent) v. *Mohammed Jabar Ahmed and others (FC) (Appellants) Her Majesty's Treasury (Respondent)* v. *Mohammed al-Ghabra (FC) (Appellant) R (on the application of Hani El Sayed Sabaei Youssef) (Respondent)* v. *Her Majesty's Treasury (Appellant)* [2010] UKSC 2   371 n. 129; 378 n. 162
JD (FC) (Appellant) v. *East Hertfordshire Police (Original Appellant and Cross-respondent)* v. *Van Colle (administrator of the estate of GC (deceased) and another (Original Respondents and Cross-appellants) and Smith (FC) (Respondent)* v. *Chief Constable of Sussex Police (Appellant)* [2008] UKHL 50   209 n. 95
Manchester City Council (Respondent) v. *Pinnock (Appellant)* [2010] UKSC 45   216
Paton v. *Richie* 2000 JC 271   244 n. 295
Pioneer Shipping Ltd v. *BTP Tioxide Ltd (The Nema)* [1982] AC 724   194 n. 60
R (Alconbury Developments Ltd) v. *Secretary of State for the Environment, Transport and the Regions* [2001] UKHL 23; [2003] 2 AC 295   245
R (Al-Skeini) v. *Secretary of State for Defence* [2007] UKHL 26; [2008] AC 153   247 n. 315; 364 n. 103

R (Anderson) v. *Secretary of State for the Home Department* [2002] UKHL 46; [2003] 1 AC 837   245
R (Ullah) v. *Special Adjudicator* [2004] UKHL 26; [2004] 2 AC 323   247; 249–54
R v. *Davis* [2008] UKHL 36; [2008] AC 1128   214 n. 148
R v. *Horncastle and Others* [2009] UKSC 14; [2010] 2 WLR 47   211–18; 243; 245; 246
R v. *Ireland* [1998] AC 147   194 n. 57
R v. *Spear and others* [2002] UKHL 31; [2003] 1 AC   213–14; 245
Rabone and another v. *Pennine Care NHS Foundation Trust* [2012] UKSC 2   255–9
Secretary of State for the Home Department v. *JJ and others* [2007] UKHL 45; [2008] AC 385   254
Secretary of State for the Home Department v. *AF (No. 3)* [2009] UKHL 28; [2009] 3 WLR 74   212 n. 136
Yemshaw (Appellant) v. *London Borough of Hounslow (Respondent)* [2011] UKSC 3   194

Other UK Courts

A and Others v. *HM Treasury* [2008] EWCA Civ 1187; [2009] 3 WLR 25   371 n. 129
Associated Provincial Picture Houses Ltd v. *Wednesbury Corporation* [1948] 1 KB 223   79 n. 77
Barrett v. *Enfield LBC* [2001] 2 AC 550   260 n. 351
Duke of Dorset v. *Girdler* (1720) Prec. Ch. 531–32, 24 E.R. 238   214
Her Majesty's Advocate v. *McLean* [2009] HCJAC 97; 2010 SLT 73   244
R (Faizovas) v. *Secretary of State for Justice* [2009] EWCA Civ 373   206–10; 218

TABLE OF INTERNATIONAL INSTRUMENTS

International treaties

Charter of the United Nations (26 June 1945) 59 Stat 1031; TS 993; 3 Bevans 1153, entered into force 24 October 1945   10; 335

Consolidated Version of the Treaty on the Functioning of the European Union (30 March 2010) Official Journal 2010 C 83/1   9; 23; 301; 312

Convention for the Protection of Human Rights and Fundamental Freedoms (4 November 1950) 213 UNTS 222; 312 ETS 5, entered into force 3 September 1953   xi

Convention on the Privileges and Immunities of the Specialized Agencies, 33 UNTS 261, 21 November 1947, entered into force 2 December 1948   337

Convention on the Privileges and Immunities of the UN, 1 UNTS 15, 13 February 1946, entered into force 17 September 1946   336

Convention on the Rights of Persons with Disabilities (13 December 2006) 2515 UNTS 3, entered into force 3 May 2008   302

International Convention on the Elimination of All Forms of Racial Discrimination (21 December 1965), 660 UNTS 195, entered into force 4 January 1969   107

International Covenant on Civil and Political Rights (16 December 1966) 999 UNTS 171, entered into force 23 March 1976   103

International Covenant on Economic, Social and Cultural Rights (16 December 1966) 993 UNTS 3, entered into force 3 January 1976   107

Model Agreement Between the United Nations and Member States Contributing Personnel and Equipment to United Nations Peace-Keeping Operations, UN Doc. A/46/185, 23 May 1991   345

Treaty on European Union (7 February 1992) Official Journal C 325 (24 December 2002), entered into force 1 November 1993 (as amended)   9; 23; 301; 312

EU legislation

Commission Regulation (EC) No. 1190/2008 of 28 November 2008, amending for the 101st time Council Regulation (EC) No. 881/2002 imposing certain specific restrictive measures directed against certain persons and entities associated with Usama bin Laden, the Al-Qaida network and the Taliban, OJ 2008 L 322/25   377

Council Directive 89/552/EEC, 3 October 1989 on the coordination of certain provisions laid down by law, regulation or administrative action in Member States concerning the pursuit of television broadcasting activities, OJ L 298/23, 17 October 1989   341

Council Regulation (EC) No. 2201/2003 of 27 November 2003 concerning jurisdiction and the recognition and enforcement of judgments in matrimonial matters and matters of parental responsibility   327, 328

Council Regulation (EC, Euratom) No. 723/2004 of 22 March 2004, OJ L 124/1   304

EEC Council Regulation No. 17: First Regulation implementing articles 85 and 86 of the Treaty (as amended)   307

Regulation (EEC, Euratom, ECSC) No. 259/68 of the Council of 29 February 1968 (Staff Regulations) OJ 56, 4.3.1968   304

Regulation (EC) No. 881/2002 of 27 May 2002 imposing certain restrictive measures directed against certain persons and entities associated with, inter alia, Al-Qaida and the Taliban, OJ L 139, 25.5.2002   377

United Nations General Assembly (GA) resolutions

Establishment of a United Nations Administrative Tribunal, Resolution 351A (IV), 24 November 1949   336

Declaration on Principles of International Law Concerning Friendly Relations and Co-operation Among States in Accordance with the Charter of the United Nations, GA Resolution 2625, 24 October 1970   356

Responsibility of States for Internationally Wrongful Acts, Resolution 56/83, 12 December 2001   350

World Summit Outcome, Resolution 60/1, 16 September 2005   338, 374, 381

Administration of Justice at the United Nations, Resolutions 61/261, 4 April 2007; 62/228, 22 December 2007; 63/253, 24 December 2008   336

Resolution 66/98, Report of the International Law Commission on the work of its sixty-third session, 9 December 2011   346

Security Council (SC) resolutions

Resolution 83 (1950) concerning Korea, 27 June 1950   358
Resolution 84 (1950) concerning Korea, 7 July 1950   358
Resolution 253 (1968) concerning Southern Rhodesia (Zimbabwe), 29 May 1968   369
Resolution 665 (1990) concerning Iraq, 25 August 1990   348
Resolution 678 (1990) concerning Iraq and Kuwait, 29 November 1990   348
Resolution 748 (1992) concerning Libya, 31 March 1992   370
Resolution 827(1993), Establishment of an international tribunal for the prosecution of persons responsible for serious violations of international humanitarian law committed in the territory of the former Yugoslavia, 25 May 1993   336

TABLE OF INTERNATIONAL INSTRUMENTS   xxxix

Resolution 1127 (1997) concerning Angola, 28 August 1997   369
Resolution 1137 (1997) concerning Iraq, 12 November 1997   369
Resolution 1244 (1999) concerning Kosovo, 10 June 1999   354; 358–9
Resolution 1267 (1999) concerning Al-Qaida and the Taliban and associated individuals and entities, 15 October 1999   373; 377
Resolution 1333 (2000) concerning Afghanistan, 19 December 2000   370; 373
Resolution 1373 (2001) concerning terrorism, 28 September 2001   370; 373
Resolution 1390 (2002) concerning Afghanistan, 28 January 2002   373
Resolution 1452 (2002) concerning terrorism, 20 December 2002
Resolution 1483 (2003) concerning Iraq, 22 May 2003   365
Resolution 1500 (2003) concerning Iraq and establishing the United Nations Assistance Mission for Iraq (UNAMI), 14 August 2003   365
Resolution 1511 (2003) concerning Iraq, 16 October 2003   359
Resolution 1526 (2004) concerning state communication with listed persons, 30 January 2004   365
Resolution 1546 (2004) concerning Iraq, 8 June 2004   366
Resolution 1572 (2004) concerning Côte d'Ivoire, 15 November 2004   370
Resolution 1591 (2005) concerning the Sudan, 29 March 2005   370
Resolution 1718 (2006) concerning the Democratic People's Republic of Korea, 14 October 2006   370
Resolution 1737 (2006) concerning Iran, 25 December 2005   370
Resolution 1747 (2007) concerning Iran, 24 March 2007   370
Resolution 1803 (2008) concerning Iran, 3 March 2008   370
Resolution 1904 (2009) concerning terrorism, 17 December 2009   373, 371
Resolution 1970 (2011) concerning Libya, 26 February 2011   370
Resolution 1973 (2011) concerning Libya, 17 March 2011   370
Resolution 1988 (2011) concerning Palestine, 17 June 2011   370
Resolution 1989 (2011) concerning threats to international peace and security caused by terrorist acts, 17 June 2011   374

International Law Commission (ILC)

Draft Articles on Responsibility of States for Internationally Wrongful Acts, adopted by the International Law Commission at its fifty-third session (2001), Official Records of the General Assembly, Fifty-sixth session, Supplement No. 10 (A/56/10), chp.IV. E.1, November 2011   144; 350
Draft Articles on the Responsibility of International Organizations 2011, adopted by the International Law Commission at its sixty-third session, in 2011, submitted to the General Assembly as a part of the Commission's report covering the work of that session (A/66/10, para. 87)   11; 346

LIST OF ABBREVIATIONS

ACHPR	African Charter on Human and Peoples' Rights
ACtHPR	African Court on Human and Peoples' Rights
ACHR	American Convention on Human Rights
ASR	(Draft) Articles on State Responsibility
BVerfG	Bundesverfassungsgericht
BVerfGE	Entscheidungen des Bundesverfassungsgerichts
CAT	Convention against Torture and Other Cruel, Inhuman or Degrading Treatment or Punishment
CAT	Committee against Torture
CDDH	Steering Committee for Human Rights (Council of Europe)
CEDAW	Convention on the Elimination of All Forms of Discrimination against Women
CEDAW	Committee on the Elimination of Discrimination against Women
CERD	Convention on the Elimination of All Forms of Racial Discrimination
CERD	Committee on the Elimination of Racial Discrimination
CFI	Court of First Instance (now General Court) of the European Union
CMW	International Convention on the Protection of the Rights of All Migrant Workers and Members of Their Families
CMW	Committee on Migrant Workers
CoE	Council of Europe
CoM	Committee of Ministers of the Council of Europe
CRC	Convention on the Rights of the Child
CRC	Committee on the Rights of the Child
CPED	Convention on the Protection of All Persons from Enforced Disappearance
CRPD	Convention on the Rights of Persons with Disabilities
CRPD	Committee on the Rights of Persons with Disabilities
CPT	European Committee for the Prevention of Torture and Inhuman or Degrading Treatment or Punishment
DARIO	Draft Articles on the Responsibility of International Organizations
EC	European Commission

LIST OF ABBREVIATIONS

ECHR	Convention for the Protection of Human Rights and Fundamental Freedoms, as amended (European Convention on Human Rights)
ECtHR	European Court of Human Rights
ECommHR	European Commission of Human Rights
ECJ	European Court of Justice
ECOSOC	Economic and Social Council (European Union)
ECSC	European Coal and Steel Community
ECSR	European Committee of Social Rights
ETS	European Treaty Series
EU	European Union
HRC	Human Rights Committee
HRCouncil	Human Rights Council
IACtHR	Inter-American Court of Human Rights
IACommHR	Inter-American Commission on Human Rights
ICC	International Criminal Court
ICCPR	International Covenant on Civil and Political Rights
ICESCR	International Covenant on Economic, Social and Cultural Rights
ICESCR	Committee on Economic, Social and Cultural Rights
ICJ	International Court of Justice
ICSID	International Centre for Settlement of Investment Disputes
ICTY	International Criminal Tribunal for the Former Yugoslavia
ILA	International Law Association
ILC	International Law Commission
ILM	International Legal Materials
ILO	International Labour Organization
ILOAT	International Labour Organization Administrative Tribunal
IMF	International Monetary Fund
NGO	Non-governmental organisation
OHCHR	Office of the High Commissioner for Human Rights
OSCE	Organization for Security and Co-operation in Europe
PACE	Parliamentary Assembly of the Council of Europe
PCIJ	Permanent Court of International Justice
UDHR	Universal Declaration of Human Rights
UN	United Nations
UN Charter	Charter of the United Nations
UN GA	United Nations General Assembly
UN GAOR	United Nations General Assembly Official Records
UN SC	United Nations Security Council
UNAT	United Nations Administrative Tribunal
UNTS	United Nations Treaty Series
UPR	Universal Periodic Review
VCLT	Vienna Convention on the Law of Treaties
WTO	World Trade Organization

1

Introduction

ANDREAS FØLLESDAL, BIRGIT PETERS AND
GEIR ULFSTEIN

1. The European Court of Human Rights in a new institutional setting

At 50, the European Court of Human Rights (ECtHR, or the Court) is without doubt one of the most successful international human rights treaty bodies. The Court has been praised as the driving force of fundamental rights jurisprudence in Europe, contributing to a common European standard in a Europe of 47 member states and over 850 million inhabitants, from the Arctic Ocean to the Caspian Sea. With a case law which outnumbers that of any other regional and international human rights instrument, the Court accounts for changes in many national policies, laws and living conditions in the wider Europe.

The Court today reaches out to a far larger group of states, institutions and potential petitioners than envisaged in 1949 by the ten founding states of the Treaty of London. This growth has implications both for the Court's institutional architecture and the relationship of the Court to the Council of Europe, its member states, as well as to other international organisations. The ECtHR needs to adapt to new floods of petitioners, to changing social and living conditions in the member states, to new governments and to forms of governance at the national and international levels. Consider that in 1994 (former) President of the ECtHR Bernhardt noted that the 'character of the Convention as a "Human Rights Constitution" has become more important than the treaty character; … in the great majority of cases decided by the European Court, violations of the most fundamental human rights are no longer at stake…'.[1] Whilst in 2002, Paul Mahoney, then registrar at the Court, remarked that it had acquired a new mission after the fall of the Berlin

---

[1] R. Bernhardt, 'Human Rights and Judicial Review: The European Court of Human Rights', in D.M. Beatty, *Human Rights and Judicial Review: A Comparative Perspective* (The Hague: Martinus Nijhoff, 1994) 297–319, at 304.

Wall: 'Until 1989, the Convention could be described as an international control mechanism for fine-tuning sophisticated national democratic engines that were, on the whole, working well. Now, and in the foreseeable future, this is not a blanket assumption that can be made for many of the participating States that are starting out on the democratic path.'[2] The year 1989 marked but one of the major turning points in the Court's institutional framework. Mikael Rask Madsen and Jonas Christoffersen recently argued that the ECtHR has undergone at least four major structural changes since its inauguration in 1950. During the first phase, the Court developed institutional autonomy and jurisprudence; the second demarcated the Court's will to develop a progressive jurisprudence, with the doctrines of the margin of appreciation and dynamic interpretation. During the third phase, the ECtHR contributed to the transitions to democracy in Eastern Europe; the last phase consists of the Court's increased focus on the effectiveness of the European Convention on Human Rights (ECHR, or the Convention) in domestic law, which culminated in the recent reform discussions at Interlaken, Izmir and Brighton.[3]

The Court has continuously sought to define and redefine its proper role in the changing institutional landscape of the wider Europe. The recent emphasis on the effectuation of the ECHR at the national levels, and an increased focus on the responsibility of the state members to the ECHR, is not the end. Protocol 14 to the ECHR and the modifications agreed at the Brighton Conference of April 2012 introduced important procedural changes.[4] They emphasised the main responsibility of member states to implement the Court's judgments, as well as the duty of member states to abide with the final decisions of the Court. At the same time, they highlighted the principle of subsidiarity, as well as the margin of appreciation doctrine as main elements of the Court's jurisprudence.[5]

---

[2] P. Mahoney, 'New Challenges for the European Court of Human, Rights Resulting from the Expanding Case Load and Membership', *Penn State International Law Review* 21:1 (2002) 101–14, at 104.

[3] J. Christoffersen and M.R. Madsen (eds.), *The European Court of Human Rights between Law and Politics* (Oxford University Press, 2011) (hereinafter Christoffersen and Madsen, *The ECtHR between Law and Politics*), at 3.

[4] For example, the recent declaration commended a deletion of the words 'and provided that no case may be rejected on this ground which has not been duly considered by a domestic tribunal' which had been introduced into a modified art. 35(3)(b) with Protocol 14.

[5] See Council of Europe (CoE), *High Level Conference on the Future of the European Court of Human Rights*, Brighton, 20 April 2012, paras. 2 and 3.

But the enlargement of membership to the Council of Europe and ever-more petitioners hoping that the Court may provide effective remedies may require even further adaptations. The number of applications pending before the Court is increasing and has just passed the vertiginous count of 153,850.[6] Just to respond to the pending applications without accepting new cases would keep the Court busy for the next six years, a period of justice delayed which it considers unacceptable at the national level.[7] The final shape and impact of the reform proposals still remain unclear.

The recent Brighton Declaration was preceded by several grand debates in academia, by politicians and other stakeholders. They argued about the comparative benefits and disadvantages of a strong ECtHR with 'constitutional' powers to strike out applications lacking constitutional import, and a precedential effect of its judgments.[8] It could be supported by national states which take ownership over the Convention and strong courts at the member state level,[9] or the ECtHR could be devoted to individual justice, with the right of individual petition and individual remedy.[10] It is not yet clear whether the compromissory lines of the Declaration are able to put an end to those controversies. In one sense, the Court will always be an unpopular institution from the perspective of the member states. After all, it decides on the claims of individual persons against their (democratically elected) governments.[11]

---

[6] See the statistics for 2011: www.echr.coe.int/NR/rdonlyres/7B68F865-2B15-4DFC-85E5-DEDD8C160AC1/0/Statistics_2011.pdf.

[7] Based on the figures provided in *ibid.*, the Court can adjudge around 1,700 cases per year on the merits. In 2010, it decided a total of 29,102 communications, of which a total of 27,345 were inadmissibility decisions, or cases struck out of the list.

[8] M. O'Boyle and A. Lester have argued that judgments of the ECtHR should have an 'erga omnes' effect in cases of 'constitutional import' at the member state level. M. O'Boyle, 'The Future', in E. Myjer *et al.* (eds.), *The Conscience of Europe: 50 Years of the European Court of Human Rights* (London: Council of Europe, Third Millennium Publishing Limited, 2010) 197–201, at 201; European Commission of Human Rights (ECoHR) Council of Europe, *High Level Conference on the Future of the European Court of Human Rights*, Interlaken, 2010, B.4.c; A. Lester, 'The European Court of Human Rights after 50 Years', in Christoffersen and Madsen, *The ECtHR between Law and Politics*, 98–115, at 115.

[9] J. Christoffersen, 'Individual and Constitutional Justice', in *ibid.*, 181–203 (hereinafter Christoffersen, 'Individual and Constitutional Justice'), at 202–3.

[10] Compare H. Keller, A. Fischer and D. Kühne, 'Debating the Future of the European Court of Human Rights after the Interlaken Conference: Two Innovative Proposals', *European Journal of International Law* 21:4 (2010) 1025–48 (hereinafter Keller, Fischer and Kühne, 'Debating the Future').

[11] S. Greenberg, 'New Horizons for Human Rights: the European Convention, Court and Commission', *Columbia Law Review* 63 (1963) 1384–412, at 1409.

The envisaged ratification of the ECHR by the European Union (EU, or the Union) raises further issues. A draft Agreement on the Accession of the EU to the ECHR has been agreed upon,[12] but the details of the relationship between the ECtHR and the Court of Justice of the European Union (CJEU, formerly the European Court of Justice, ECJ) are yet to be defined. Finally, the ECtHR must increasingly address actions by international organisations such as the United Nations (UN). The *Al-Skeini*[13] and *Al-Jedda*[14] judgments of the Court touch upon its relation to the UN Security Council. They give a hint of questions which need further discussion. To conclude, the Court finds itself in a new institutional setting toward national courts, and toward institutions at the European and global level.

This book examines these new institutional settings of the Court. Few contributions have hitherto concentrated on these multiple relationships of the ECtHR.[15] The most recent contribution to deal explicitly with the Court's institutional role is Christoffersen and Madsen's *The European Court of Human Rights between Law and Politics*.[16] It concentrates on extrapolating the Court's institutional role, largely leaving aside the proper relationship between the member states, the EU or the organs of the Council of Europe. Some articles have assessed the alleged

---

[12] CoE, Steering Committee for Human Rights, 'Report to the Committee of Ministers on the Elaboration of Legal Instruments for the Accession of the European Union to the European Convention on Human Rights', No. CDDH(2011)009, 14 October 2011.

[13] ECtHR, *Al-Skeini and Others v. United Kingdom* (Appl. No. 55721/07), Judgment (Grand Chamber), 7 July 2011, not reported.

[14] ECtHR, *Al-Jedda v. United Kingdom* (Appl. No. 27021/08), Judgment (Grand Chamber), 7 July 2011, not reported. See comments by C. Chinkin, 'International Humanitarian Law, Human Rights and the UK Courts', in L. Boisson de Chazournes and M.G. Kohen (eds.), *International Law and the Quest for its Implementation: Liber Amicorum Vera Gowlland-Debbas* (Leiden and Boston: Brill, 2010) 243–64, at 252–64; C. Tomuschat, 'Human Rights in a Multi-Level System of Governance and the Internment of Suspected Terrorists', *Melbourne Journal of International Law* 9 (2008) 391–404 (predicting that the judgment would not stand scrutiny by the ECtHR).

[15] Compare P. Popelier, C. v.d. Heyning and P.V. Nuffel (eds.), *Human Rights Protection in the European Legal Order: The Interaction between the European and the National Courts (Law and Cosmopolitan Values)* (Portland, OR: Intersentia, 2011); E. Bates (ed.), *The Evolution of the European Convention on Human Rights: From its Inception to the Creation of a Permanent Court of Human Rights* (Oxford University Press, 2010); H. Keller and A. Stone Sweet, *A Europe of Rights: The Impact of the ECHR on National Legal Systems* (Oxford University Press, 2008); R. Blackburn and J. Polakiewicz, *Fundamental Rights in Europe: The European Convention on Human Rights and its Member States, 1950–2000* (Oxford and New York: Oxford University Press, 2001).

[16] Christoffersen and Madsen, *The ECtHR between Law and Politics*.

constitutional role which the Court assumes within the European context.¹⁷ Although suggestions about the future relationship of the Court and the EU are in circulation,¹⁸ not many have sought to assess this relationship in a more principled manner.

[17] Compare A. Stone Sweet, 'A Cosmopolitan Legal Order: Constitutional Pluralism and Rights Adjudication in Europe', *Journal of Global Constitutionalism* 1:1 (2012) 53–9. S. Greer, 'Constitutionalizing Adjudication under the European Convention on Human Rights', *Oxford Journal of Legal Studies* 23:3 (2003) 405–33; J.R.Z. Pérez, 'The Dynamic Effect of the Case-Law of the European Court of Human Rights and the Role of the Constitutional Courts', in ECtHR, *Dialogue between Judges* (Strasbourg; Council of Europe, 2007) 36–52; E.A. Alkema, 'The European Convention as a Constitution and its Court as a Constitutional Court', in P. Mahoney *et al.* (eds.), *Protecting Human Rights: The European Perspective: Studies in Memory of Rolv Ryssdal* (Cologne, Bonn: Karl Heymanns Verlag, 2000) 41; F. Tulkens, 'The European Convention on Human Rights Between International Law and Constitutional Law', in ECtHR, *Dialogue between Judges*, 8–15; R. Harmsen, 'The European Court of Human Rights as a "Constitutional Court"', *Judges, Transition and Human Rights* (2007) 33–53; X. Groussot, '"European Rights" and Dialogues in the Context of Constitutional Pluralism', *Scandinavian Studies in Law* 55 (2010) 45–75.

[18] T. Lock, 'Accession of the EU to the ECHR: Who Would Be Responsible in Strasbourg?', *SSRN eLibrary* (2010); T. Lock, 'The ECJ and the ECtHR: The Future Relationship between the Two European Courts', *The Law and Practice of International Courts and Tribunals* 8:3 (2009) 375–98; J. Puente Egido, 'Adhesión de la Unión Europea al Convenio Europeo para la Protección de los Derechos Humanos?', *Soberanía del estado y derecho internacional* 2 (2005) 1119–44; T. Jaag, 'Beitritt der EG zur EMRK?: zum Gutachten 2/94 des Europäischen Gerichtshofs', *Aktuelle juristische Praxis* 5:8 (1996) 980–4; J. Boulouis, 'De La Compétence de la Communauté Européenne Pour Adhérer à la Convention de Sauvegarde des Droits de l'Homme et des Libertés Fondamentales: Avis de la Cour de Justice des Communautés', *Libertés* 2 (1994) 315–22; G. Minichmayr, *Der Beitritt der Europäischen Gemeinschaft zur Konvention zum Schutze der Menschenrechte und Grundfreiheiten* (*Euro-Jus, Schriftenreihe der Abteilung für Europäische Integration*) (Krems: Donau Universität, 1999); S. Winkler, *Der Beitritt der Europäischen Gemeinschaften zur Europäischen Menschenrechtskonvention* (*Schriftenreihe Europäisches Recht, Politik und Wirtschaft*) (Baden-Baden: Nomos, 2000); A. Bleckmann, *Die Bindung der Europäischen Gemeinschaft an die Europäische Menschenrechtskonvention* (Cologne: C. Heymann, 1986); M. Ruffert, 'Die künftige Rolle des EuGH im europäischen Grundrechtsschutzsystem: Bemerkungen zum EuGH-Urteil v. 20.5.2003', *Europäische Grundrechte-Zeitschrift* 31:16/18 (2004) 466–71; A. Haratsch, 'Die Solange-Rechtsprechung des Europäischen Gerichtshofs für Menschenrechte: das Kooperationsverhältnis zwischen EGMR und EuGH', *Zeitschrift für Ausländisches Öffentliches Recht und Völkerrecht* 66:4 (2006) 927–47; J.M. Bergmann, 'Diener dreier Herren?: Der Instanzrichter zwischen BVerfG, EuGH und EGMR', *Europarecht* 41:1 (2006) 101–17; N. Philippi, 'Divergenzen im Grundrechtsschutz zwischen EuGH und EGMR', *Zeitschrift für europarechtliche Studien* 3:1 (2000) 97–126; M. Hilf, 'Europäische Union und Europäische Menschenrechtskonvention', MPI für ausländisches öffentliches Recht und Völkerrecht (ed.), *Recht zwischen Umbruch und Bewahrung: Festschrift für Rudolf Bernhardt* (Berlin, Heidelberg: Springer, 1995) 1193–210; U. Everling, 'Europäische Union, Europäische Menschenrechtskonvention und Verfassungsstaat: Schlusswort auf dem

The book aims to assess the relationship between the Court and the member states, the EU, the UN and the other organs of the Council of Europe, partly by referring to a specific set of normative criteria, and taking into consideration their respective needs and their own institutional functions. It seeks to provide a coherent overview and some more principled answers to the current reform debate and future design of the Court and of its relationship to the national, European and global level. The book's main areas of consideration and main objectives are outlined in the following sections.

1.1 The Court and the member states

The Court's relationship with the member states is crucial. Its relationship to national courts has long been debated, in particular, whether the Court slowly assumes the role of a constitutional court for Europe. While judgments of the ECtHR have no direct effect at the national level, the increasing *de facto* importance of the Strasbourg case law challenges national legal orders, questions the role of the national constitutional legislature and judiciary, and ultimately, the sovereignty of member states.[19] States, as well as the Court, therefore seek institutional solutions to deal with Strasbourg's case law in the domestic orders whilst preserving national particularities, institutionally as well as legally. The Interlaken process, including the recent Interlaken, Izmir and Brighton Declarations of February 2010, April 2011 and April 2012,[20] respectively, have set a focal point on the principle of subsidiarity for the Court's

---

Symposion am 11. Juni 2005 in Bonn', *Europarecht* 40:4 (2005) 411–18; L. Wildhaber, 'Europäischer Grundrechtsschutz aus der Sicht des Europäischen Gerichtshofs für Menschenrechte', *Europäische Grundrechtezeitschrift* (2005) 689-92; E. Pache and F. Rösch, 'Europäischer Grundrechtsschutz nach Lissabon: die Rolle der EMRK und der Grundrechtecharta in der EU', *Europäische Zeitschrift für Wirtschaftsrecht* 19:17 (2008) 519–22; T. Ahmed, 'The European Union and Human Rights: An International Law Perspective', *European Journal of International Law* 17:4 (2006) 771–801; G. Quinn, 'The European Union and the Council of Europe on the Issue of Human Rights: Twins Separated at Birth?', *McGill Law Journal* 46:4 (2001) 849–74; J. Polakiewicz, 'The European Union's Charter of Fundamental Rights and the European Convention on Human Rights: Competition or Coherence in Fundamental Rights Protection in Europe', *Revue Européenne de Droit Public* 14:1 (2002) 853–78.

[19] G. Canivet, *Cours Suprêmes Nationales et Convention Européenne des Droits de l'Homme Nouveau Rôle Ou Bouleversement de L'ordre Juridique Interne?* (Paris: Cour de Cassation, 2005) 9, 3–5 (hereinafter Canivet, *Cours suprêmes*).

[20] CoE, *High Level Conference on the Future of the European Court of Human Rights*, Izmir, 2011.

relationship with the member states. Both the Izmir and Interlaken conferences emphasised the 'fundamental role which national authorities, i.e. governments, courts and parliaments, must play in guaranteeing and protecting human rights at the national level'.[21] This led state representatives at Brighton to conclude that 'for reasons of transparency and accessibility' the principle of subsidiarity and the margin of appreciation be included in the Preamble to the Convention.[22] The Declaration further encourages 'open dialogues between the Court and the States Parties as a means of developing an enhanced understanding of their respective roles in carrying out their shared responsibility for applying the Convention'.[23] Yet, whether the codification of subsidiarity will indeed lead to less friction and an increased dialogue between the Court and the member states remains to be seen. States presently eye the ECtHR with mixed feelings. On the one hand, comparative studies of Europe's higher court judges and Members of Parliament suggest that the ECtHR actually enjoys a legitimacy credit rather than a legitimacy deficit.[24] On the other hand, scholars, as well as politicians, question the authority of the Court and criticise the widening grip of Strasbourg.[25] They have questioned the legitimacy of the Court and several particular judgments. Some, such as the *Lautsi* case concerning whether crucifixes may hang in public classrooms in Italy, tackle sensitive and highly political issues.[26] Such judgments are taken to go to the very core of national decision-making. Some judgments have thus provoked strong reactions among the states parties to the ECHR. Ten states intervened as 'third parties' in the *Lautsi* proceedings before the Court's Grand Chamber. Similarly, the proper relationship between the Court and German courts was discussed in Germany in the aftermath of the Federal Constitutional Court's *Görgülü* decision (2004) concerning custody and contact with children born out of wedlock.[27] In Norway, the Court has been

---

[21] ECoHR Council of Europe, *High Level Conference on the Future of the European Court of Human Rights*, Interlaken, 2010, para. 6.
[22] Brighton Declaration, para. 12(b). [23] *Ibid.*, para. 12(c).
[24] B. Çali, 'The Legitimacy of the European Court of Human Rights: The View from the Ground' (Department of Political Science, University College London, 2011) (hereinafter Çali, 'The Legitimacy of the ECtHR') 35.
[25] Canivet, *Cours suprêmes*.
[26] ECtHR, *Lautsi and Others v. Italy* (Appl. No. 30814/06), Judgment (Grand Chamber), 18 March 2011, not reported. Compare B. Schlütter, 'Crucifixes in Italian Classrooms: *Lautsi v Italy*', *European Human Rights Law Review* 6 (2011) 86–92 for a discussion.
[27] Bundesverfassungsgericht, *Preventive Detention*, No. 2 BvR 2365/09, Judgment, 4 May 2011.

criticised for its approach to evolutive treaty interpretation, of being too concerned with details, and for extending its scope of jurisdiction with regard to substantive law as well as to subjects.[28] In the United Kingdom (UK) a repeal of the Human Rights Act, which implements the ECHR, has been openly debated since May 2010,[29] though the results of the Brighton Conference may have soothed some of the harshest critics.[30]

1.2 The Court and the Council of Europe institutions

The current reform process to overcome the overload of cases culminated in the amendment and introduction of new admissibility procedures as contained in the Brighton Declaration, as well as in the earlier Protocol 14 to the ECHR. So far, this process has mostly dealt with internal reform of the Court and its procedures. The Brighton process also addressed the Court's relationship to other Council of Europe institutions: toward the Committee of Ministers, and its relationship toward the Parliamentary Assembly. In particular, the Brighton meeting discussed the election of judges to the Court.[31] In the longer term, the Court needs to reflect on the implementation of its judgments and the role of the Committee of Ministers in the supervision of this task, as well as its possible budgetary independence from the other Council of Europe institutions.

1.3 The Court and the EU

The relationship of the Court with the EU also needs reconsideration. During the past four years, the Court has had to clarify its relationship with the CJEU. A main reason is the 2009 Lisbon Treaty, which stated the

---

[28] Compare: Norges Offentlige Utredninger, *Makt og demokrati, Sluttrapport fra Makt- og demokratiutredningen* (Oslo: Statens forvaltningstjeneste Informasjonsforvaltning, 2003) 32.

[29] I. Dunt, 'Clarke: "No Question" of Human Rights Withdrawal', available at www.politics.co.uk/news/legal-and-constitutional/clarke-no-question-of-human-rights-withdrawal-$21387359.htm; N. Barber, 'The Commission on the Human Rights Act and the European Court of Human Rights', 10 September 2011, at http://ukconstitutionallaw.org/2011/09/10/nick-barber-the-commission-on-the-human-rights-act-and-the-european-court-of-human-rights/; G. Bindman, 'Britain Should be Proud of the Human Rights Act – And Protect It', *The Guardian*, 29 August 2011, at www.guardian.co.uk/commentisfree/2011/aug/29/human-rights-act-protect.

[30] Compare J. Rozenberg, 'Draft Brighton Declaration is a Breath of Fresh Air', *The Guardian*, 9 April 2012.

[31] Compare Brighton Declaration, paras. 21 and 22.

EU's obligation to ratify the ECHR.[32] The current draft accession agreement brought the formal preparations for the EU's accession a considerable step further.[33] Once ratification takes place by the 47 member states, new questions require attention. According to the draft Agreement, the EU may act as both a respondent and a co-respondent to the ECtHR proceedings. Procedurally, this means that complaints can be aimed directly against the Union, and that it can join the proceedings as a party in cases which involve the compatibility of EU legislation with the ECHR.[34] From a substantive point of view, the *Bosphorus* jurisprudence of the ECtHR may need to be modified. This jurisprudence established the rebuttable presumption that the standard of human rights protection at EU level is equivalent to that provided by the ECHR. Accordingly, the ECtHR will only exceptionally assess the compatibility of EU legislation implemented by member states with the ECHR.[35] The Court may also need to discuss whether the acts complained against can be attributed to the EU, a particular member state, or both. The CJEU, or the ECtHR, or both, must tackle the relationship between the ECHR and the Charter of Fundamental Rights which has become an essential part of the Treaty on European Union (TEU)[36] and stands on the same footing as primary EU law.

1.4 The Court and other international organisations, in particular, the UN

The Court must also address its relationship with the Security Council and international territorial administrations established by the UN. The Court is a regional body. Even if a case before it concerns states which are part of the wider Europe, the Court cannot directly control the UN. Nonetheless, issues of attribution may arise for UN-authorised peace

---

[32] See art. 6(2) of the TEU.
[33] See CoE Steering Committee for Human Rights, *supra* note 12.   [34] *Ibid.*, art. 3.
[35] ECtHR, *Bosphorus Hava Yolları Turizm ve Ticaret Anonim Şirketi v. Ireland* (Appl. No. 45036/98), Judgment (Grand Chamber), 30 June 2005, Reports 2005-VI. The *Bosphorus* doctrine was later refined, for example, in ECtHR, *Biret v. 15 EU Member States* (Appl. No. 73250/01), Decision (Fifth Section), 9 September 2008, Reports 2008; ECtHR, *Connolly v. 15 EU Member States* (Appl. No. 73274/01), Decision (Fifth Section), 9 December 2008, not reported; ECtHR, *Cooperatieve Producentenorganisatie van de Nederlandse Kokkelvisserij U.A. v. The Netherlands* (Appl. No. 13645/05), Decision (Third Section), 29 January 2009, Reports 2009.
[36] Article 6(1) of the TEU.

operations. Consider if human rights violations occur that involve member states who have ratified the ECHR. The Court's jurisprudence, such as the *Behrami* and *Saramati* cases, addressed the complex issues of authorship and attribution, as well as further questions involving the supremacy of member states' obligations under the UN Charter. The cases have often been criticised for deviating from the general law of international responsibility. On the other hand, recent cases like *Al-Skeini* and *Al-Jedda* illustrate that member states may not always hide behind international organisations who authorise an operation. Further questions may arise, if UN-mandated action with impact on individual rights is first implemented by a regional organisation like the EU and then executed by the individual member states, a situation which was before the Court in the *Kadi* and *Bosphorus* proceedings. Finally, future cases may not be confined to questions concerning the authorisation of acts by the UN, but may concern regional security organisations like the North Atlantic Treaty Organisation (NATO).

2. Principles and concepts guiding the analyses in this book

The need to rethink the Court's role toward member states and international organisations is imminent. Several maxims and principles may guide such reflections on the future role of the Court.[37] Among the most frequently named are principles of the rule of law,[38] the principle of subsidiarity, the principle of effectiveness,[39] as well as the principles of implied powers and proportionality.[40] These are not novel notions: they stem from discussions

---

[37] For the character of the principle of proportionality as a maxim, rather than a principle of legal rule, compare F. Wieacker, 'Geschichtliche Wurzeln des Prinzips der verhältnismäßigen Anwendung', M. Lutter, W. Simpel and H. Wiedemann (eds.), *Festschrift für Robert Fischer* (Berlin, New York: Walter de Gruyter, 1997) 867–81 (hereinafter Wieacker, 'Geschichtliche'), at 867.

[38] *Ibid.*; J.A. Brauch, 'The Margin of Appreciation and the Jurisprudence of the European Court of Human Rights: Threat to the Rule of Law', *Columbia Journal of European Law* 11:1 (2004–5) 113–50, at 113.

[39] M.D.S. Lasser, *Judicial Deliberations: A Comparative Analysis of Judicial Transparency and Legitimacy* (Oxford University Press, 2004). For the effectiveness criterion, in particular, compare Y. Shany, 'Assessing the Effectiveness of International Courts: Can the Unquantifiable Be Quantified?', SSRN eLibrary (2010).

[40] Compare J.E. Alvarez, *International Organizations as Law-Makers* (Oxford University Press, 2005) at 123, referring to intent instead of consensus. See also, K.A. Young, *The Law and Process of the U.N. Human Rights Committee (The Procedural Aspects of International Law Monograph Series)* (Ardsley, New York: Transnational Publishers, 2002) at 67–9.

within the Council of Europe, or from the Court itself, and have been used frequently in the course of its reform process. These are also either firmly established or arguably increasingly recognised in general international law.[41] Subsidiarity and the criterion of effectiveness were essential in the reform discussions at the Izmir, Interlaken and Brighton conferences.[42] These principles are used by the ECtHR on a regular basis. The principle of proportionality is also exercised by the Court, and has found entry into many national and international review procedures.

Many of the stated principles have gained prominence in discussions on more general overarching theoretical concepts, such as the legitimacy of international institutions and notions of constitutionalism.[43] The Court's present and future performance is often discussed in light of these two paradigms. The constitutionalist notion is often seen as a counterweight to the idea of individual justice.[44] Yet some of the criteria that arguably form part of legitimacy and constitutionalism, such as effectiveness, proportionality and subsidiarity, can, do and should also favour delivering individual justice. Their ultimate impact is not predetermined by either of the two approaches. In short, the set of principles leaves room for further theoretical deliberations.[45]

---

[41] On the importance of practice for rules binding on international institutions, see UN, Office of Legal Affairs, 'Comments and Observations of the Office of Legal Affairs on the Draft Articles on Responsibility of International Organizations, Adopted by the International Law Commission on First Reading in 2009' (2011) 2, 5. On the relevance of practice for the attributability of a certain conduct of an international organisation under international law, see art. 8 of the DARIO.

[42] Compare Brighton Declaration, paras. 12 and 32.

[43] A. Stone Sweet, *Governing with Judges: Constitutional Politics in Europe* (Oxford University Press, 2000); R. Hirschl, *Towards Juristocracy: The Origins and Consequences of the New Constitutionalism* (Cambridge, MA: Harvard University Press, 2004). For the constitutionalist approach to international law, compare J. Klabbers, G. Ulfstein and A. Peters, *The Constitutionalization of International Law* (Oxford Scholarship Online, Oxford University Press, 2009); A. Peters, 'Rechtsordnungen und Konstitutionalisierung: Zur Neubestimmung der Verhältnisse', *Zeitschrift für Öffentliches Recht* 65 (2010) 3–63; A. Stone Sweet and J. Mathews, 'Proportionality, Judicial Review, and Global Constitutionalism', in G. Bongiovanni, G. Sartor and C. Valentini (eds.), *Reasonableness and Law* (Law and Philosophy Library) (Dordrecht, Heidelberg: Springer Netherlands, 2009) 171–214.

[44] S. Hennette-Vauchez, 'Constitutional v. International? When Unified Reformatory Rational Mismatch the Plural Paths of Legitimacy of ECHR Law', in Christoffersen and Madsen, *The ECtHR between Law and Politics*, 144–63; Christoffersen, 'Individual and Constitutional Justice', 181–203, at 183.

[45] R.A. Schapiro, *Polyphonic Federalism: Toward the Protection of Fundamental Rights* (University of Chicago Press, 2009) for an innovative approach to the subsidiarity principle.

The editors' argumentative framework adheres to these principles and concepts to identify areas of potential improvement of the European human rights system in dire need of further reform. It seems possible and sensible to analyse the ECtHR's relationship to member states and its inter-institutional performance according to these principles, and to base recommendations for qualitative improvements on some of those yardsticks. For the purposes of this book, the editors allow differing approaches by the contributing authors with regard to these principles. The individual contributions develop their own theoretical frameworks as necessary, and decide whether, and which, principles should be included in their analysis. Indeed, the best interplay of those principles might only be answered on a case-by-case basis, considering all relevant circumstances. The following section illustrates the relevance of some of these principles.

2.1 The legitimacy of the ECtHR

The current institutional crisis of the ECtHR is increasingly interpreted and addressed as a threat to the Court's legitimacy.[46] This may partly be fuelled by, and fuel, broader concerns about the legitimacy of international institutions which have gained prominence in law, political science and political philosophy. Thus, some authors invoking concerns about legitimacy are concerned with the growing authority of international institutions and claim that it should be accompanied by an increase in accountability.[47]

With regard to the ECtHR, legitimacy concerns revolve around the difficulties in its present and future functioning, its distance from the European polity, as well as fears that it encroaches upon the sovereignty of its member states.[48] As an institution, the Court has undergone

---

[46] Christoffersen and Madsen, *The ECtHR between Law and Politics*, (who address problems related to the legitimacy of the ECtHR in part 2 on the legitimation of the Court); K. Dzehtsiarou and A. Greene, 'Legitimacy and the Future of the European Court of Human Rights: Critical Perspectives from Academia and Practitioners', *German Law Journal* 12:10 (2011) 1707–15 (hereinafter Dzehtsiarou and Greene, 'Legitimacy and the Future of the ECtHR'); Cali, 'The Legitimacy of the ECtHR'; A. Føllesdal, 'The Legitimacy of International Human Rights Review: The Case of the European Court of Human Rights', *Journal of Social Philosophy* 40:4 (2009) 595–607.

[47] C. Janik, 'Die EMRK und internationale Organisationen – Ausdehnung und Restriktion der equivalent protection Formel in der neuen Rechtsprechung des EGMR', *Zeitschrift für Ausländisches Öffentliches Recht und Völkerrecht* 70 (2010) 127–79, at 130.

[48] Dzehtsiarou and Greene, 'Legitimacy and the Future of the ECtHR', at 1707.

significant changes since its establishment in the 1970s. The Strasbourg system has developed from a Commission and Court division into a full quasi-constitutional review structure, with the Grand Chamber exercising the right to appeal first instance decisions of either the complainant or the state. The move to a two-chamber structure by Protocol 11 to the ECHR has sometimes been mentioned as one major cause of the increased number of complaints to the Court. Prior to the new chamber structure, relatively few individual complainants reached the Court; now, it is overrun with cases and has accumulated a huge backlog.[49] It is often held to have become a victim of its success.

The Court adjudicates cases of Europe-wide significance on a frequent basis. It has developed certain standards, such as the margin of appreciation doctrine, which some perceive as unique to the ECHR system. This doctrine serves to avoid undue interference in national democracy and traditions. But the Court is often conceived of as an island disconnected from the polity or the general public in the member states. For example, many regard the nominating and appointment process for the judges of the Court as opaque, even though the Parliamentary Assembly has sought to improve the procedure over the last seven years.[50] Moreover, the ECtHR's interpretative techniques, as well as controversial cases like *A, B and C* v. *Ireland* or *Lautsi* v. *Italy* have caused scepticism among the member states. States without a national constitutional court, but with a long and strong national tradition of parliamentary autonomy, like the Nordic countries and the UK, feel that the Court's decisions in difficult cases encroach upon their parliamentary sovereignty and autonomy.[51] Such concerns are only partly alleviated by the Court's margin of appreciation doctrine.

---

[49] *Supra* note 6.
[50] Compare CoE Parliamentary Assembly, Resolutions 1200 (1999), 1646 (2009).
[51] E. Hale, 'Beanstalk or Living Instrument?', in ECtHR, *Dialogue between Judges* (Strasbourg: Council of Europe, 2011) 11–18, at 18; J.E. Helgesen, 'What are the Limits to the Evolutive Interpretation of the Convention?', in *ibid.*, 19–28, at 22, 23; R. English, 'Human Rights – Strasbourg or Luxembourg?', *UK Human Rights Blog*, 9 September 2011; P. Association, 'Cameron Warned over Human Rights', *The Independent*, 22 August 2011; G. Bindman, 'Britain should be Proud of the Human Rights Act – and Protect it', *The Guardian*, 29 August 2011; 'Deputy PM Nick Clegg Defends UK Human Rights Laws', *BBC News UK Politics*, 26 August 2011; 'UK "should cut links to European Court of Human Rights"', *BBC News UK*, 7 February 2011; A. Wagner, 'Bill of Rights Commission publishes Advice (and Squabbles) on European Court of Human Rights Reform', *UK Human Rights Blog*, 9 September 2011.

The concept of legitimacy can be understood and defined in various ways. Many see democratic legitimacy as the core. But a special challenge is the balance between democratic control and ensuring the independence of the Court. Furthermore, democratic institutions are primarily anchored at the national level.[52] Franck's much-invoked framework of legitimacy concentrates on process legitimacy, i.e. the way decisions are made. It emphasises the accountability of international institutions, the coherence and consistency of the decisions made by them, and the adherence of the institution itself to some underlying normative framework.[53] Other frameworks assess legitimacy from a social perspective, focusing on the compliance and lack thereof by various actors participating in and affected by the exercise of authority by international institutions.[54] Lastly, claims concerned with substantive legitimacy revolve around the substantive output of international institutions and make recommendations on how this output should best be generated.[55] Thus, the content of the concept of legitimacy varies, not least across disciplines: political science scholars sometimes use concepts which deviate from those invoked by international lawyers or political philosophers. For example, legitimacy concepts advanced by political scientists often include criteria like the observance of international human rights standards or legality.[56] However, many international lawyers emphasise that in international law an action may be legal, but illegitimate.[57] We perceive legitimacy as a standard related to, but usually exceeding, legality. It is comprised of criteria which international law is still not fully conversant with, including such notions as fairness and effectiveness.

---

[52] Compare A. von Staden, 'The Democratic Legitimacy of Judicial Review Beyond the State: Normative Subsidiarity and Judicial Standards of Review', *Jean-Monnet Working Paper* 10/11, at 9.

[53] T. Franck, 'Legitimacy in the International System', *American Journal of International Law* 82:4 (1988) 705–59; T. Franck, *The Power of Legitimacy Among Nations* (Oxford University Press, 1990).

[54] A. Føllesdal, 'Legitimacy Deficits beyond the State: Diagnoses and Cures', in A. Hurrelmann, S. Schneider and J. Steffek Houndmills (eds.), *Legitimacy in an Age of Global Politics* (Basingstoke: Palgrave, 2007) 211–28; I. Hurd, 'Legitimacy and Authority in International Politics', *International Organization* 53:2 (1999) 379–408, at 387–9; J. Dowling and J. Pfeffer, 'Organizational Legitimacy: Social Values and Organizational Behavior', *The Pacific Sociological Review* 18:1 (1975) 122–36.

[55] For the distinction between output and input legitimacy, see F. Scharpf, 'Problem-Solving Effectiveness and Democratic Accountability in the EU', *MPIfG Working Paper* 3:1(2003).

[56] Compare Cali, 'The Legitimacy of the ECtHR'.

[57] Independent International Commission on Kosovo, *The Kosovo Report: Conflict, International Response, Lessons Learned* (Oxford University Press, 2000), at 186.

The ultimate aim of the book is to assess and indicate prospects for the ECtHR's functioning within the inter-institutional framework of the Council of Europe, the EU, the UN and other international organisations, as well as with the member states. Factors that focus on the processes of interaction and decision-making may contribute to the further improvement and strengthening of the Court's role. Factors like effectiveness and subsidiarity, and criteria such as adherence, coherence and the concurrence with a wider European consensus, may be among the elements of a standard of legitimacy applicable at the ECHR level. The subsequent section will explain those principles, which we regard as crucial for an assessment of the ECtHR's institutional interaction and legitimacy.

2.2 Principles governing judicial cooperation and interaction: comity and subsidiarity

Some principles are concerned with the *modus operandi* of (international) judicial institutions and their relation to member states, national courts of the member states and other courts at the international level. At the level of jurisdiction, the principle of *res judicata* includes the acknowledgement of decisions made by another court on the same matter at the factual level, and the exhaustion of local remedies. More generally, such principles affect the judicial interaction and dialogue between the Court and the national courts of the member states and other European and international courts.

One of the more general commands applying to the general forms of international judicial dialogue and cooperation is comity. Based on the implied powers doctrine,[58] it calls upon courts 'to defer, when appropriate, to other courts and to treat their procedures and decisions with courtesy and respect'.[59] This may sometimes follow from the broader notion of subsidiarity in the form of deference to the decision-making body closest to the case at hand. Thus, each court or tribunal must exercise the competences assigned to it with due regard to the competences of others. Nonetheless, comity is a rather vague concept; it can mean anything from rules of jurisdiction to the discretion to decline a

---

[58] Y. Shany, *Regulating Jurisdictional Relations between National and International Courts* (*International Courts and Tribunals*) (Oxford University Press, 2007), at 172.
[59] *Ibid.*, at 166.

case, or mere courtesy.⁶⁰ It applies at the level of competences of an international institution, as well as at the level of substantive law. Different notions of comity stem from common or civil law, and they have varying underlying perceptions of the international judicial system as a coherent, hierarchical or fragmented legal order.⁶¹ A number of measures emphasised in the Interlaken, Izmir and Brighton processes fall within the wider range of this principle, such as the fourth instance doctrine, the secondment of national judges to the ECtHR, or the cooperation with other relevant national bodies and the national level's taking into account the Court's case law.

The principle of subsidiarity has dominated reform considerations on the future of the ECtHR all around. Its most general form builds upon respect for smaller entities by larger ones. Its legal adaptation concentrates on the exercise of deference or deferral in the form of preference to the exercise of authority by the entity closer to the individuals affected, as opposed to the larger or hierarchically higher authority.⁶² It applies at the substantive rights level and/or at the procedural level, regulating the general relationship of the ECtHR with the member states.⁶³ Various rules at the procedural level express the legal conception of subsidiarity, amongst others the local remedies rule, the fourth instance doctrine and the implementation of remedies at the national level. The ECtHR has underlined the subsidiary character of its own jurisprudence, i.e. the fourth instance doctrine. Thus, in the *Belgian Linguistic* case, it held that 'the Court ... cannot assume the role of the competent national authorities, for it would thereby lose sight of the subsidiary nature of the international machinery of the collective enforcement established by the Convention. The national authorities remain free to choose the measures which they consider appropriate in those matters which are governed by the Convention. Review by the Court concerns only the

---

⁶⁰ W.T. Worster, 'Competition and Comity in the Fragmentation of International Law', *Brooklyn Journal of International Law* 34, 2008 (2009), at 121; J.R. Paul, 'Comity in International Law', *Harvard International Law Journal* 32:1 (1991) 1–80, at 4.
⁶¹ Worster, 'Competition and Comity', at 122, 123, 148 and 149.
⁶² Compare A. Føllesdal, 'Subsidiarity', *Journal of Political Philosophy* 6 (1998) 190–218, at 190; J. Isensee, 'Subsidiarität, das Prinzip und seine Prämissen', P. Blickle, T.O. Hüglin and D. Wyduckel (eds.), *Subsidiarität als rechtliches und politisches Ordnungsprinzip in Kirche, Staat und Gesellschaft, Rechtstheorie, Beiheft 20* (Berlin: Duncker and Humboldt, 2001) 129–77, at 145 *et seq*.
⁶³ Føllesdal, 'Subsidiarity'.

conformity of these measures with the requirements of the convention.'[64] The margin of appreciation doctrine represents subsidiarity considerations at the substantive rights level.

Yet, the shape and prerequisites of subsidiarity beyond this more descriptive character of deference to the national level are more unclear. Some authors hold that the proportionality test could be added as a second test to the principle of subsidiarity. Kumm argues that proportionality could function as 'a "cost-benefit analysis" which focused on the advantages and disadvantages for ratcheting up the level of decision-making'.[65] Such responses may solve collective action problems that involve both the national and the international level.[66] There are diverse opinions on where the primary authority to review human rights violations should be located, i.e. at the supranational, or the ECHR level.[67] Some scholars point to the dysfunctional judiciary of some of the member states of the Council of Europe and conclude that subsidiarity cannot provide a solution for the relationship of the ECtHR with those states.[68] Others hold that the ECtHR should only be involved if there are good reasons to depart from the interpretation at the national level.[69]

2.3 Effectiveness

The principle of effectiveness is part and parcel of all human rights conventions. It is enshrined in several provisions of the ECHR, and is part of the international treaty and customary law concerning the application, interpretation and implementation of international treaties. Together with the principle of subsidiarity, it has been crucial in the

---

[64] ECtHR, *Case relating to certain aspects of the laws on the use of languages in education in Belgium (Belgian Linguistic* case) (Appl. Nos. 1474, 1677 and 1691/62; 1769 and 1994/63; and 2163/64), Judgment (Plenary), 23 July 1968, Series A, Vol. 6, para. 10.

[65] M. Kumm, 'The Legitimacy of International Law: A Constitutionalist Framework of Analysis', *European Journal of International Law* 15 (2004) 907–31, at 921 (hereinafter Kumm, 'The Legitimacy of International Law').

[66] *Ibid.*

[67] G. Ulfstein, 'International Constitutionalization: A Research Agenda', Guest Editorial, *ESIL Newsletter* (2010) 2; G. Ulfstein, 'The International Judiciary', in J. Klabbers, G. Ulfstein and A. Peters (eds.), *The Constitutionalization of International Law* (Oxford University Press, 2009) 126–52 (hereinafter Ulfstein, 'The International Judiciary'), at 144; Keller, Fischer and Kühne, 'Debating the Future'.

[68] *Ibid.*, at 1032.

[69] Ulfstein, 'The International Judiciary', at 144; Kumm, 'The Legitimacy of International Law', at 921.

debate on institutional reform of the Court. Several provisions of the ECHR provide for an effective implementation of the rights of the Convention. Above all, the preamble calls for an 'effective recognition and observance of the rights therein declared' and establishes that the Convention rights are best preserved by 'an effective political democracy'. It must be read together with the general provision of article 1 ECHR, which commends: 'The High Contracting Parties shall secure to everyone within their jurisdiction the rights and freedoms defined in Section I of this Convention.'[70] Also, article 13 demands the provision of an 'effective remedy' to those whose rights have been violated, and article 34 calls for an effective implementation of the right of individual complainants to launch complaints before the Court.

Several other provisions of the general international law on treaties also encompass the general provision of effective treaty implementation. One crucial international treaty provision with the status of customary international law, the Vienna Convention on the Law of Treaties (VCLT), in its article 31, provides for an interpretation in good faith of international treaty provisions. Effectiveness is both inherent in this notion as well as in the notion to interpret treaties following their object and purpose, according to article 31(1).[71] In their recent discussion of a case concerning reservations under the Optional Protocol, members of the Human Rights Committee held that the provisions of the International Covenant on Civil and Political Rights (ICCPR), as well as of the Optional Protocol, must be interpreted to render utmost effect of the individual rights concerned.[72]

Concerning the current reform of the ECtHR, considerations of effectiveness apply both to the proper functioning of the Court and its Registry, and to the realisation of the rights of the Convention for the individuals affected. However, whether the general effectiveness of the system or individual protection should take precedence may have to be decided case-by-case and often requires careful balancing of all interests

---

[70] Convention as amended by its Protocol No. 14 (CETS No. 194) as from the date of its entry into force on 1 June 2010.
[71] R. Gardiner, *Treaty Interpretation* (Oxford University Press, 2008), at 160.
[72] Human Rights Commission, *Elgueta* v. *Chile*, Communication No. 1536/2006, 7 September 2009, UN Doc. CCPR/C/96/D/1593/2006, Individual Opinion of Ms. Helen Keller and Mr. Fabián Salvioli, para. 11; compare F. Salvioli, 'Un Analisis desde el Principio pro Persona Sobre el Valor Juridico de las Decisiones de la Comision Interamericana de Derechos Humanos', *En Defensa de la Constitución: Libro Homenaje a Germán Bidart Campos* (Buenos Aires: Ediar, 2003) 143–55, 143.

involved. Particular reforms may be at the expense of the individual seeking remedies for serious human rights violations. In particular, minor claims may seriously block the workability of the Court.[73]

2.4. Proportionality

Closely connected to the principle of effectiveness is the principle of proportionality. One of the first provisions which contained a rough notion of proportionality is article 74 of the Prussian General Law (Preussisches Allgemeines Landrecht) of 1794, which allowed the police to take the 'necessary measures', thereby focusing on necessity of the measures involved.[74] Considerations of proportionality measure the intensity of limitations to individual human rights, and assess the trade-off between the interests of the state involved and the individual. Concerning the judicial review of constitutional rights, the German Constitutional Court cultivated and promoted proportionality analysis in an analytical direction, to achieve a reasoned balance between conflicting interests involved.[75] Other national courts also base their analysis of lawful limitations of constitutional rights on a proportionality analysis.[76] The CJEU employs the principle in its assessment of restrictions to the EU Fundamental Freedoms.[77] As of today, proportionality analysis has found its way into many national legal systems, including hybrid and common law based, as well as into the case law of the ECtHR. The Court applies the principle regularly, in particular when assessing the

---

[73] Keller, Fischer and Kühne, 'Debating the Future'.
[74] 'The office of the police is to take the necessary measures for the maintenance of public peace, security and order' (translation in A. Stone Sweet, 'Proportionality Balancing and Global Constitutionalism', *Columbia Journal of Transnational Law* 47 (2008) 68–149, at 100) (hereinafter Stone Sweet, 'Proportionality Balancing'). Compare Wieacker, 'Geschichtliche', 867–81.
[75] BVerfG *Apothekenurteil*, BVerfGE 7, 377 at 405; BVerfG *Lüth*, BVerfGE 7, 198, at 212; Stone Sweet, 'Proportionality Balancing', 104 *et seq.*
[76] Stone Sweet pointed, amongst others, to the Canadian, Israeli and New Zealand use of proportionality analysis. Stone Sweet, 'Proportionality Balancing', at 113–38.
[77] According to Stone Sweet, *ibid.*, at 139, starting with ECJ Case 11/70, *Internationale Handesgesellschaft mbH* v. *Einfuhr und Vorratstelle für Getreide und Futtermittel*, Judgment, 17 December 1970, [1970] ECR 1125, 1146. Others argue that ECJ Case 265/87, *Schrader* v. *Hauptzollamt Gronau*, Judgment, 11 July 1989, [1989] ECR 2237, 2269, was the first judgment where the Court referred to proportionality. For the employment of the principle with regard to the fundamental freedoms, see ECJ Case 120/78, *Cassis de Dijon Rewe Zentral AG* v. *Bundesmonopolverwaltung für Branntwein*, Judgment, 20 February 1979, [1979] ECR 649, 662.

limitations to human rights provisions, e.g. in its analyses of articles 8–11 and article 14 of the Convention.[78] Except for the deference to the interests concerned[79] and a call to carefully balance all the rights affected, the principle does not contain a strong normative claim. Rather, it provides an analytical framework,[80] which can mitigate certain legitimacy concerns,[81] mostly in that it provides a coherent procedure to assess the decision-making process. This is particularly valuable in situations where the law evolves primarily through judicial interpretation and application; where provisions are relatively open-ended; and where courts monitor both the constitution and the decision-making by the political branches of government.[82]

3. The plan of this book

Following the institutional structure and environment of the Court, the book consists of three parts. The states parties to the ECHR are still the primary guarantors of the rights enshrined in the Convention, and Part I (chapters 2–6) concentrates on the relationship of the states parties to the ECHR and the Court. Part II (chapters 7–8) concentrates on the Court and Europe. It explores the Court's relationship with the Council of Europe and the EU. Part III (chapter 9) of the book deals with the relationship between the Court and the UN. A final chapter draws conclusions.

3.1 The Court and the member states

3.1.1 Procedural aspects

The Court has to ensure effective protection of human rights in the face of an overload of cases produced by a handful of states. There is also a need to ensure consistency, that the parties are heard, and that states and the general public have confidence in the Court – including the need for transparency. Iain Cameron's chapter examines the various proposals, which have been made addressing those issues, by Protocol 14, the two

---

[78] Compare Stone Sweet, 'Proportionality Balancing', at 147. ECtHR, *Handyside v. United Kingdom* (Appl. No. 5493/72), Judgment (Plenary), 7 December 1976, Series A, Vol. 24; ECtHR, *Smith and Grady v. United Kingdom* (Appl. Nos. 33985 and 33986/96), Judgment (Third Section), 27 September 1999, Reports 1999-VI.
[79] In the form of the least restrictive means analysis.
[80] Stone Sweet, 'Proportionality Balancing', at 76.   [81] *Ibid.*, at 77.
[82] *Ibid.*, at 80 and 89.

expert reports – i.e. the Woolf Report and the 2007 Wise Persons Report, which were adopted before Protocol 14 came into force – as well as the changes suggested at the state party meetings at Interlaken, Izmir and Brighton, touching upon, amongst others, the admissibility criteria, admissibility decisions taken by the single judge procedure, possible filtering mechanisms, the need for more reasoned non-admissibility decisions, and the Court's priority policy and increased use of oral hearings. Amongst further procedural aspects, like the introduction of court fees, the newly suggested advisory opinion system, as well as the newly introduced and already modified article 35(3)(b), are also addressed. Iain Cameron discusses those proposals in light of the ongoing debate about the Court as a court of individual justice or constitutional court.

3.1.2 The margin of appreciation

Yutaka Arai-Takahashi's chapter addresses the margin of appreciation doctrine as a central element whereby the Court allows discretion to member states. The chapter explores central issues concerning this doctrine, namely (1) the balance between ensuring effective implementation of international obligations and the need to protect national autonomy, (2) whether the Court should differentiate between different areas of substantive human rights law when applying the margin of appreciation and (3) the need to ensure a consistent application of the ECHR, and of the margin of appreciation doctrine itself.

3.1.3 Dynamic interpretation

The Court applies an evolutive (dynamic) interpretation: the Convention is regarded as a 'living instrument'. George Letsas' chapter addresses how the Court balances the need for developing the standards of the Convention, e.g. by comparative analysis of member states' law and practice, while respecting the limits of the Convention's human rights protection, as well as the interests of member states. The chapter also addresses the role of consent in the dynamic interpretation of the ECHR. The Court has often based dynamic interpretations of the Convention on the change of social, factual or legal circumstances within the member states. Accordingly, the ECtHR frequently referred to the consensus of the member states, which supported the respective change in interpretation of the provisions of the Convention. George Letsas frames his considerations about the dynamic interpretation doctrine of the Court along the lines of the debates which have unfolded around the Court's legitimacy.

3.1.4 Remedies

Philip Leach's chapter focuses on the remedy system of the Court, which must accommodate two important considerations: subsidiarity and the coherence of the Court's judgments. Leach points to the changes in the findings on remedies of the Court, which have become much more specific over time. He compares the Court's former and current approaches to non-pecuniary remedies to the approach of the Inter-American Court of Human Rights, which has a known practice for proposing specific remedies. He also discusses the Court's approach to remedy systemic violations of the Convention, in particular the pilot judgment procedure, as well as to gross and systemic human rights violations. Also with regard to this category of cases, the case law of the Court is contrasted with the approach of the Inter-American Court of Human Rights which, to date, takes a much more 'prescriptive and disaggregated approach' toward measures of redress than the ECtHR.

3.1.5 The reception and implementation of the ECHR by national courts

Mads Andenas and Eirik Bjorge assess the reception and implementation of the ECHR in the courts of Belgium, the Czech Republic, France, Germany, Norway, Russia and the UK. They address and assess the effectiveness of judgments by the ECtHR and the subsidiary role of the ECHR, with a particular focus on the dynamic interpretation of ECHR rights, the national margin of appreciation of states, as well as the doctrine of proportionality, which is often linked to the margin of appreciation. In doing so, they touch upon certain further vital questions, namely, whether national courts succeed in resisting the interpretive force of the ECtHR concerning the rights enshrined in the ECHR and what (possibly guiding or interpretive) role the ECHR and the ECtHR's judgments assume in national jurisdictions.

3.2 The Court and Europe

3.2.1 The Court as part of the Council of Europe: the Parliamentary Assembly and the Committee of Ministers

Elisabeth Lambert-Abdelgawad's chapter assesses and evaluates the following three issues: (1) the election of judges; (2) the implementation of judgments; and (3) budgetary aspects. The assessment concentrates in particular on the interplay of the three organs of the Council of Europe when dealing with those issues, i.e. the Committee of Ministers, the Parliamentary Assembly and the Court. The quality of the judges is fundamental to the credibility and legitimacy of the Court. The Parliamentary Assembly plays a pivotal role in their election. The Committee of Ministers is the organ of the Council of Europe in charge of supervision of the execution of the Court's judgments. Building on considerations of adequacy and effectiveness of the relations of the three organs, the Court, the Parliamentary Assembly and the Committee of Ministers, Elisabeth Lambert-Abdelgawad assesses whether the current distribution of tasks among them needs further adjustment, against the backdrop of the reform suggestions made at Interlaken, Brighton and further institutional reform proposals. The chapter also discusses the pros and cons of greater financial autonomy of the Court, and contemplates to what extent the Court should be influenced by policy guidelines adopted by the Council of Europe.

3.2.2   The Court and the EU

Leonard Besselink's chapter on the relationship between the EU and the ECtHR recapitulates this relationship in light of the commitment of the EU to accede to the ECHR, as provided for in the new Protocol 14 to the ECHR, and envisaged in TEU article 6(2). It focuses on the benefits and disadvantages of such an accession by looking at the current process, which is still underway. The ECtHR has accommodated the relationship between member states implementing EU law and the Court in its *Bosphorus* approach. It has been argued that the EU's ratification of the ECHR will not ease problems between the CJEU and the ECtHR. Leonard Besselink discusses aspects, such as which court can and will be the final arbiter of human rights in Europe, and delineates how the present relationship of the ECtHR and the CJEU is regulated. He ponders whether principles like subsidiarity or the ECtHR's characterisation as a constitutional court can guide a sensible development of the ECtHR, the EU institutions and the CJEU. In the light of the foregoing, Leonard Besselink assesses the possible future role of the *Bosphorus* doctrine, the procedural aspects of the EU becoming a direct respondent to proceedings before the Court, as well as possible scenarios of what could be the outcome of the recent accession negotiations. He concludes with a perspective on whether the accession of the EU to the ECHR is ultimately beneficial for the system of European human rights protection.

3.3 The Court and the UN

3.3.1 Attribution of responsibility/the substantive law aspects

Christian Tomuschat's chapter on the attribution and substantive law aspects of the relationship of the Court with the UN touches upon questions which, at the time of the negotiation of the Treaty of London, were neither acute nor obvious to the negotiating states. It was the common perception that international organisations would be immune from jurisdiction of national and international courts. The responsibility of such organisations for individual human rights violations is, however, becoming more urgent. With the end of the Cold War, the UN has taken on new responsibilities: the Security Council has mandated regional organisations and member states to use military force under Chapter VII of the Charter, and the UN has taken on territorial administration of post-conflict states, or 'failed' states. Drawing upon pronouncements of the ECtHR on this controversial issue, like the *Behrami and Saramati* case, the chapter discusses the responsibility of the UN for human rights violations, and questions of attribution of responsibilities between the UN and Council of Europe member states, both in regard to military operations and territorial administration.

3.4 Conclusion

In the final chapter of the book, the editors reflect on the different contributions and on the implications of the suggestions made for the future of the Court in Europe and in the world at large. The chapter focuses on some key elements which various chapters have brought to bear on the multilevel human rights protection system: effectiveness, consistency, transparency and subsidiarity. The chapter explores whether these elements are able and suitable to bring forward further discussions on the reform of the Court. It also contemplates whether there are further elements which should govern the multi-level human rights protection systems in Europe, in particular.

2

The Court and the member states: procedural aspects

IAIN CAMERON*

1. Introduction

This chapter will examine procedural issues relating to the reform of the European Court of Human Rights (hereinafter the ECtHR, or the Court). As noted in the Introduction to the present volume, the background to this chapter is the huge backlog of cases the Court is facing and the fact that a large part of the Court's time has been spent dealing with applications which do not disclose a violation of the Convention. Of the remaining time, much has been taken up with so-called 'repetitive cases'. Since 2001 with the report of the Evaluation Group,[1] there has been an almost continual discussion about procedure.

Protocol 14, adopted in 2004, was designed to solve the Court's immediate, not long-term, problems in this respect. In the period between the adoption of Protocol 14 and the present time, two expert groups reported on reforms: the Woolf Report in 2005[2] and the Report of Wise Persons in 2007.[3] A number of the reforms proposed in these two expert reports could be (and have been) implemented by the Court itself. However, some proposed reforms require further

---

* I am grateful to Elisabeth Fura and the participants in the project meeting in October 2011 for helpful comments.
[1] Report of the Evaluation Group to the Committee of Ministers on the European Court of Human Rights, EG Court (2001)1, 27 September 2001.
[2] Review of the Working Methods of the European Court of Human Rights December 2005 (Woolf Report) at www.echr.coe.int/ECHR/Resources/Home/-LORDWOOLFREVIEW-ONWORKINGMETHODS.pdf.
[3] Report of the Group of Wise Persons to the Committee of Ministers, CM(2006)203, 15 November 2006, https://wcd.coe.int/wcd/ViewDoc.jsp?id=1063779&Site=CM.

amendment of the Convention. The latest series of discussions of the states parties on reform were at conferences in Interlaken,[4] Izmir[5] and Brighton.[6]

The procedural reforms which have been made are, not surprisingly, reactions to crises, or anticipated crises. Thus, a chronological approach is useful, and the chapter will broadly follow this. I will begin with sketching out in the introduction the system envisaged by Protocol 14. I will then turn to the relevant proposals made by the Woolf Report and the report of the Group of Wise Persons. Following this, I will analyse the changes which have been made with the entry into force of Protocol 14, in particular, the working of the single judge procedure and the new admissibility criterion. Thereafter, I will look at the effect of the Court's 'priority policy' and the ongoing reform discussions. I take up different proposals to introduce various new types of 'filtering' mechanism. I also touch upon a number of other procedural innovations which have been proposed and which would involve amendments to the Convention, *inter alia*, creating a statute and delegating to the Court the power to make more substantive amendments to its own procedure, expanding the possibility of giving advisory opinions, the introduction of fees and a requirement to be represented by a lawyer.

I should note that while the focus in this chapter is procedure, the discussion inevitably comes around to the issue of substance, which is at the heart of the idea of a multilevel European architecture for rights protection, namely, what is the ECtHR *for*? Underlying the discussion of procedural issues is not simply the desire to increase efficiency, but also the imperative to maintain (or improve) the Court's legitimacy. One of these threats is the problem of ensuring the quality and internal consistency of the case law, if the Court is delivering in excess of 2,000 judgments per year, and I look at this in the final section.[7]

---

[4] Council of Europe (CoE), *High Level Conference on the Future of the European Court of Human Rights* (Interlaken: 2010).
[5] CoE, *High Level Conference on the Future of the European Court of Human Rights* (Izmir: 2011).
[6] CoE, *High Level Conference on the Future of the European Court of Human Rights* (Brighton: 2012).
[7] Another significant problem, which I will not deal with, is ensuring the quality of the judges themselves. See Lambert-Abdelgawad, Chapter 7 this volume.

THE COURT AND THE MEMBER STATES: PROCEDURAL ASPECTS 27

Turning now to Protocol 14, this was designed primarily to increase the amount of time the judges have available for important cases, first by making it easier to dismiss applications and second, by simplifying treatment of repetitive cases. Many people wanted to go further with Protocol 14, and create a proper 'constitutional court' for Europe, with the power to choose freely which cases it wished to take up. Others stressed the continued need for a court to which anyone whose rights had been violated could apply for justice, especially bearing in mind the continued poor state of national rights protection in many of the new member states. Protocol 14 is thus a compromise between these two competing goals. It was evident even when it was adopted that it could not solve the problem of the continually increasing caseload. As is well known, due to obstruction tactics from the Russian Parliament,[8] it was 1 June 2010 before this protocol entered into force. This delay added to the Court's pending cases: on 31 October 2011, it had 153,850 applications allocated to a judicial formation.

The basic idea behind the protocol was that the Court was to be organised so that clearly inadmissible applications should be dealt with by single judges, routine 'repetitive' cases by three-judge committees, ordinary cases by chambers of seven, or five, judges and very important cases by the Grand Chamber of 17 judges. One major time saving would be that a single judge would deal with clearly inadmissible issues, instead of the existing system of committees of three judges. Another would be that time would be saved by combining of the admissibility and merits phases. As regards the first of these, a practice developed that the committees did not meet physically, but instead the lists of inadmissible cases were circulated, and the judges individually appended their signatures approving the list. As regards the second of these, by the time Protocol 14 had entered into force, the Court itself had already introduced this reform by creatively interpreting article 29 which, at the time, allowed this 'in exceptional cases'.[9] Part of the improved efficiency from Protocol 14 has thus been in evidence for a while.

---

[8] Eventually, the other states parties adopted a special treaty in 2009, Protocol 14bis, ETS 204, providing that a state could consent to certain of the procedural innovations in Protocol 14 applying in applications against that state. Faced with this, Russia finally ratified Protocol 14.

[9] Article 29(1) of the ECHR now provides that the decision on admissibility *may* be taken separately, and this is only supposed to be the norm for inter-state cases (art. 29(2)).

2. The main proposals of the Woolf Report

The Woolf Report contained recommendations relating to the working methods of the Court. I will not deal with all of them here. Many of them dealt with technical, training and practical changes, such as proper introduction procedures for, and monitoring of the work of, new judges, and management innovations in the Registry. In retrospect, it is strange why most of these proposals had not been introduced many years ago. The explanation lies partly in the fact that the Court historically was under-utilised. It did not receive a case until 1961. For most of the 1960s and the 1970s it received very few cases from the Commission. There were only 14 states which recognised the right of individual petition in 1980. Another important aspect to remember is that it is an entity mixing 47 legal cultures, and consisting not only of people with many years of experience of full-time judging (who should know something about the practicalities of running a court),[10] but also of professors and advocates. The law is a conservative force, and courts are, not surprisingly, conservative institutions. Changes in the rules of procedure were, and are, a matter for the plenary Court. In these circumstances, where one strives to achieve consensus before making significant changes, reform can be a long time in coming. It is in the light of these factors that one should see the Court's initial tardiness in getting its house in order. But if the Court was slow to react to begin with, as sections 4–6 make clear, the last few years have seen it taking many different steps, including radical steps, to improve efficiency.

The Woolf Report recommended changes to the rules of procedure to clarify what constitutes an application and to make clear that there is no application until the receipt by the Court of a completed application form. Both these changes have been made. There are tighter time limits, which are held to strictly. If the applicant does not reply to the Registry's request for more information on the substance of the complaint and exhaustion of domestic remedies, the file is destroyed.[11]

---

[10] Although it depends upon the legal culture: the ordinary and administrative courts in many European states show considerable inefficiencies. See generally the data on the website of the Commission on the Efficiency of Justice, www.coe.int/T/dghl/cooperation/cepej/default_en.asp.

[11] ECtHR, 'Practice Direction: Institution of Proceedings', 1 November 2003, amended 22 September 2008 and 24 June 2009, www.echr.coe.int/NR/rdonlyres/9F0B9646-3806-4814-A7CF-345304DCCDB2/0/PracticeDirectionsInstitutionOfProceedingsOctober2010.pdf, provides that: '8. (a) An applicant should be diligent in conducting correspondence with the Court's Registry. (b) A delay in replying or failure to reply may be regarded as a

Part of the problem of the flood of cases was perceived to be informational: people did not know that their complaint was without any prospect of success. Woolf recommended the compilation of a handbook on admissibility. A practical guide for lawyers was published in December 2010 in (so far) six languages.[12] It was more recently complemented with an online admissibility checklist.[13]

Another proposal was for the creation of an 'Article 41 Unit' in the Registry, to assist judges and ensure greater consistency in compensation. Woolf considered that the Court should also publish guidelines as to rates of compensation in order to assist and encourage parties to resolve cases domestically. The issue of consistency in compensation is now under the general supervision of the Jurisconsult in the Registry. The role of the Court in just satisfaction is considered elsewhere in this volume.[14] It will suffice to say here that assessing just satisfaction can involve complex issues of national law, necessitating contacts with national authorities, conducted by or together with the Committee of Ministers, and so may result in considerable delay.[15]

Woolf proposed greater use of friendly settlements and the establishment of a specialist unit in the Registry. The latter proposal has not been followed, as there appears to be unanimity that the case-handling officer is best placed to organise a friendly settlement. In 2010, 1,223 applications were struck out by a decision or judgment following a friendly settlement or unilateral declaration, a steep rise

---

sign that the applicant is no longer interested in pursuing his or her application. 9. Failure to provide further information or documents at the Registry's request ... may result in the application not being examined by the Court or being declared inadmissible or struck out of the Court's list of cases.' Applications must be completed within 8 weeks, and this time limit is strictly adhered to, see ECtHR, *Kemevuako* v. *Netherlands* (Appl. No. 65938/09), Decision (Third Section), 1 June 2010, not reported.

[12] ECtHR, 'Practical Guide on Admissibility Criteria', www.echr.coe.int/ECHR/EN/Header/Case-Law/Case-law+analysis/Admissibility+guide/.

[13] ECtHR, 'Applicant Check List', published (in French) 6 December 2011, http://appform.echr.coe.int/echrappchecklist/default.aspx?lang=eng&cookieCheck=true.

[14] See Leach, Chapter 5 this volume.

[15] See further, the recommendation of the Group of Wise Persons, below, section 3. O'Boyle considers that by awarding damages in large numbers of cases applying well-established case law, the Court 'took a wrong turning': M. O'Boyle, 'The Future', in E. Myjer *et al.* (eds.), *The Conscience of Europe: 50 Years of the European Court of Human Rights* (London: Council of Europe, Third Millennium Publishing Limited, 2010) (hereinafter O'Boyle, 'The Future'), at 198.

from 625 in 2009.[16] The working, and potential for increased use of, friendly settlements have been analysed by others.[17] Suffice to say here that they are not a cure for the backlog.

Two more radical proposals made by Woolf can be mentioned here. The first was that satellite offices of the Registry should be established in certain high case count states. In making this proposal, Woolf was inspired by the – relative – success of a pilot project in Warsaw providing potential applicants with information on the likely admissibility of their complaints.[18] However, Woolf considered that satellite offices could also carry out the initial processing of applications so that those that proceed to Strasbourg are ready for allocation. In other words, Woolf envisaged not only improved information, but in addition, a filtering mechanism at the national level.

He also argued for this solution on the basis that a specialist branch of the Registry, consisting of local lawyers, conversant with the language and the legal culture, would be better placed to work together with existing national institutions, such as the ombudsmen. Applications which disclosed no violation of the Convention, but which did indicate that there might have been maladministration, could thus obtain a remedy. This proposal has not been acted upon. One reason for this is budgetary. Another is the practical difficulty involved in establishing and maintaining an independent subsidiary organ of the Registry, consisting of local employees, in more 'hostile' cultural environments.

The second, more radical proposal, was the introduction of a priority policy, considered below in section 5.

3. The main proposals of the Report of the Group of Wise Persons

The Group of Wise Persons was established in 2005 to look at the long-term effectiveness of the ECHR control mechanism, going beyond the Protocol 14 changes, while 'preserving the basic philosophy underlying

---

[16] ECtHR, *Annual Report 2010* (Strasbourg: Registry of the European Court of Human Rights, 2011), www.echr.coe.int/NR/rdonlyres/F2735259-F638-4E83-82DF-AAC7E934A1D6/0/2010_Rapport_Annuel_EN.pdf, at 160.

[17] H. Keller, M. Forowicz and L. Engi, *Friendly Settlements before the European Court of Human Rights: Theory and Practice* (Oxford University Press, 2010).

[18] H. Machinska, 'Pilot Lawyer Project Developed by the Council of Europe to Make Direct Access to the ECtHR Easier and More Effective for Individuals', in E. Lambert-Abdelgawad (ed.), *Preventing and Sanctioning Hindrances to the Right of Individual Petition before the ECtHR* (Antwerp: Intersentia, 2011).

the Convention'. It made a number of proposals. To begin with, it dismissed summarily the idea that the Court be given a power to select cases to decide on the merits, on the basis that 'a power of this kind would be alien to the philosophy of the European human rights protection system' (para. 42). A greater margin of appreciation would also 'entail a risk of politicising the system as the Court would have to select cases for examination. The choices made might lead to inconsistencies and might even be considered arbitrary.'

Instead, the Group proposed dealing with the case overload, and repetitive cases, by establishing a 'Judicial Committee' which would be separate from, but attached to the Court. It would have jurisdiction to hear all applications raising admissibility issues and all cases which could be declared manifestly well-founded or manifestly ill-founded on the basis of well-established case law of the Court. In other words, it would do the work to be done (when Protocol 14 entered into force) of single judge formations and committees. It would exercise the same powers as the Court in respect of just satisfaction. Its members would be judges 'enjoying full guarantees of independence' (para. 52). In this respect, it attempted to meet the criticism directed against the earlier proposal by the Evaluation Group in 2001, that this work could be handled by non-judicial rapporteurs in the Registry. The Judicial Committee would be a smaller body than the Court, but it would 'reflect a geographical balance as well as a harmonious gender balance and should be based on a system of rotation between states' (para. 53). It would be assisted by the Registry. Its decisions could not be appealed to the Court, but the Court could decide, *proprio motu*, to review a case with which it disagreed.

As the new body would take over a large part of the work of the present Court, the implication was that the number of judges of the Court should be reduced, 'bringing it into line with the Court's functional requirements and the need to ensure consistency of case law' (para. 120). Judges would be elected on the basis of a system of rotation among states. The national perspective in individual cases would be maintained by allowing *ad hoc* judges.

The Group also proposed to transfer to the national legal system the function of assessing the level of compensation required to afford just satisfaction to an applicant, on the basis that this might be more effectively performed by a national organ.

It proposed that, in order to reinforce the subsidiary nature of the system, and foster dialogue with the highest national courts, advisory opinions be introduced. This was the first official endorsement of this idea, analysed below in section 6.

The Group proposed that certain of the rules now to be found in the Convention be moved to a statute, which could be more easily amended – by the Committee of Ministers, with the approval of the Court. Finally, it wanted practical measures to strengthen the authority of the Court's case law in the states parties, mainly by a duty to translate and spread these among courts, and that domestic remedies for Convention remedies be enhanced. These proposals are expressions of the principle of subsidiarity.

This last group of proposals was easily accepted, even though the Court signalled, as regards the statute, its need for full control: it wanted both the power of initiative and the power of approval.[19] The present state of this proposal is discussed in section 6. Certain of the other proposals – advisory opinions, the separate Judicial Committee – received a cautious welcome from the Court, although it stressed that more investigation was needed. The Court was not persuaded, however, that the task of determining the level of just satisfaction would be more efficiently handled by a judicial body at national level.

Other commentators were much less sure that the Judicial Committee would be an improvement.[20] It was pointed out, *inter alia*, that it was shifting the overload from a new, more 'constitutional'-oriented Court, to a subsidiary body, but that anyway the Registry would continue to bear the brunt of the work. It was most unlikely to be cheaper. States would not accept the reduction of judges on the Court proper. And, a not insignificant factor, it would be difficult to recruit good candidates to the Judicial Committee, because the work would be, to put it mildly, very boring.[21]

---

[19] Opinion of the Court on the Wise Persons' Report, 2 April 2007, www.echr.coe.int/NR/rdonlyres/26457EAB-2840-4D71-9ED7-85F0F8AE0026/0/OpinionoftheCourtontheWisePersonsReport.pdf.

[20] M. Eaton, 'The New Judicial Filtering Mechanism: Introductory Comments', in Directorate General of Human Rights (ed.), *Future Developments of the European Court of Human Rights in the Light of the Wise Persons' Report: Colloquy Organized by the San Marino Chairmanship of the Committee of Ministers of the Council of Europe*, San Marino, 22–3 March 2007 (France: Council of Europe, 2007).

[21] In this respect, one can note the comment of the chairperson of the committee which interviews candidates for judges, Mrs. Herta Däubler-Gmelin, that 'often candidates are good, but not outstanding'. PACE Committee on Legal Affairs and Human Rights, 'The Future of the Strasbourg Court and Enforcement of ECHR Standards: Reflections on the Interlaken Process', 21 January 2010, AS/Jur(2010)06.

4. Protocol 14 enters into force

4.1 *Filtering*

When the protocol entered into force, the president decided that there should be 20 single judges, serving for one year at a time. Each single judge works approximately 25 per cent of the time on this task, and otherwise continues to carry out his/her other duties within the section to which s/he is assigned.[22] For most states, a single judge is sufficient. The exceptions are Russia (5 judges), Turkey (4), Romania (3), Ukraine (3) and Poland (2). The same person can be a single judge for three states (two low-count and one high-count state). As regards Registry support, instead of deputy section heads handling these cases, it is now a non-judicial rapporteur[23] who decides initially whether the case should be assigned to a single judge, a committee, or a chamber (art. 24(2)), or just tabled while new information is requested.[24] A specialist 'filtering' section has been created in Registry. This has apparently worked well. It has, *inter alia*, attempted proactively to identify patterns, or 'problem areas', for each state.

As the single judge will seldom be familiar with the language, legal system and legal culture of the states s/he has been assigned, the non-judicial rapporteur has a key role in the process. In fact, the lists the single judge receives usually consist of extremely summary information on each case, a sentence or two on what the case is about and the relevant Convention right. The single judge normally has a two-week period to consider the drafts presented. Should s/he disagree with a proposal, s/he indicates whether the case should be sent to a committee or a chamber.

The single judge procedure thus preserves the form of a judicial determination of each application, but in practice, in almost all cases, it is the non-judicial rapporteur who decides. The system thus requires that judges have a high level of trust in the professionalism and competence of the Registry, particularly their non-judicial rapporteurs. Bearing this in mind, it is surprising how little discussion there has

---

[22] ECtHR, 'Rule 27A1', Rules of Court, www.echr.coe.int/NR/rdonlyres/6AC1A02E-9A3C-4E06-94EF-E0BD377731DA/0/RulesOfCourt_April2011.pdf (1 April 2011). The Court is currently discussing whether five single judges should instead be tasked with working almost full-time on single judge cases.

[23] This is a senior lawyer in the Registry. The term is used to distinguish them from members of the Court (judges) who act as rapporteurs in judgments.

[24] Spot checks are made by the single judges to monitor the work of their non-judicial rapporteurs.

been of the procedures (selection, training etc.) applied by the Court to ensure that Registry personnel attain and maintain a very high standard of objectivity in dealing with cases which will often come from their home state.[25] Moreover, there has been little discussion of the existing practice (encouraged by the Court) of certain states in providing and paying for temporary qualified legal staff (usually junior judges) to strengthen the Registry and speed up handling of cases concerning their own state. Several states, among them Sweden, have done this for a number of years. Russia has recently sent some 20 junior judges to assist with the backlog of Russian cases. These seconded junior judges are not non-judicial rapporteurs, but nonetheless they must be assumed to have considerable influence over whether or not a case is declared admissible.[26]

The single judge figures indicate relatively high levels of 'efficiency'. As already noted, single judge chambers have only been functioning since June 2010. All of the new cases coming in from Ukraine and Poland identified for treatment by single judge are being dealt with immediately. For Romania, the figure being dealt with immediately is more than 90 per cent. For Russia and Turkey, the Filtering Section is able to deal immediately with roughly 75 per cent of the single judge cases.[27] The figures for 2011 (to 31 October 2011) reveal that 39,882 cases were declared inadmissible, the great majority by single judge formations. This was a 46 per cent increase on the same period in 2010.[28]

The Registry calculated in 2010 that, with 80 assistant lawyers preparing decisions in approximately 400 single judge cases each per year, and with 20 single judges who devote approximately 25 per cent of their time to work on these cases, the Court would be able

---

[25] The same can be said of the use of interns – *stageurs* – in preparing cases, including using the manifestly ill-founded admissibility criterion. Cf. B. Jones, 'European Court of Human Rights: is the admissions system transparent enough?' http://ukhumanrightsblog.com/2012/01/27/european-court-of-human-rights-is-the-admissions-system-transparent-enough-ben-jones/.

[26] There is a degree of control. The Court specifies criteria the candidates must satisfy. The sending state submits a list of applicants which it considers satisfies these criteria, and the Court makes the final selection. When in place, the work of the seconded staff is subject to supervision by the heads of division, and their work is quality controlled.

[27] ECtHR, 'Filtering Section Speeds up Processing of Cases from Highest Case-Count Countries', undated, www.echr.coe.int/NR/rdonlyres/F484672E-0C6A-4815-9449-44157ED9C89C/0/Bilan_filtrage_EN.pdf.

[28] ECtHR, 'Statistics 2011 (compared to 2010)', www.echr.coe.int/NR/rdonlyres/7B68F865-2B15-4DFC-85E5-DEDD8C160AC1/0/Stats_EN_31102011.pdf.

to produce some 32,000 decisions. Thus, the formations have been even more effective than expected. Still, at the end of 2010, over 90,000 cases were pending before the single judge formation. Thus, even without the constant influx of new cases, it would take over two years for the Court to clear this backlog. And, if present trends hold, it seems clear that there will be more than 39,000 incoming clearly inadmissible cases per year in the future.[29]

4.2 New chambers

One possibility provided for by Protocol 14, the creation of five judge chambers, also seemed to hold out the potential for increasing efficiency. However, this option has not yet been implemented. The Interlaken Declaration urged the Court to introduce this. There are two main reasons why it has not yet done so.

The first is that deciding the composition of the sections is not easy. It is important that there are not too many judges from one geographical region, as this could make a judgment susceptible to attack by a state which loses the case and considers that too many judges from 'alien' legal cultures have dominated the Court.[30] Moreover, there should not be too many new judges who are, or at least might be, inexperienced in interpreting and applying human rights provisions. And the caseload should not vary too much between the sections.[31] It has thus not proved to be easy to move without loss of efficiency from the present system of sections consisting of 9–10 judges (7 for a chamber, and two reserves) to a new system of 7 judge sections (5 plus two reserves).

The second reason relates to the fact that more chambers will mean increased difficulties in maintaining the internal consistency in the case law.

---

[29] Steering Committee for Human Rights, CDDH (2011) R72 Add. I (1 April 2011), appendix IV, para. 18.
[30] Important differences in approach in, e.g. family matters, have occasionally arisen between judges from the 'progressive' 'North' and the 'traditional' 'South'. See, e.g., the Dissenting Opinions of Judges Palm, Foighel and Pekkanen in ECtHR, *Cossey* v. *UK* (Appl. No. 10843/84), Judgment (Plenary), 27 September 1990, Series A, No. 184.
[31] For discussions of the problems involved in composing sections, see A. Drzemczewski, 'The Internal Organisation of the European Court of Human Rights: The Composition of Chambers and the Grand Chamber', *European Human Rights Law Review* 3 (2000) 233–48.

4.3 The new admissibility ground

One of the reforms introduced by Protocol 14 was the subject of much discussion, connected to the above-mentioned division of opinion between those who argued for and against a more explicit 'constitutional' role for the Court. This was the introduction of a new ground of admissibility. The proposal that the Court should be able to rule inadmissible applications raising 'no substantial issue' was not adopted. Instead, the new ground, article 35(3)(b), provides that an application can be declared inadmissible if the applicant 'has not suffered a significant disadvantage, unless respect for human rights ... requires an examination of the application on the merits and provided that no case may be rejected on this ground which has not been duly considered by a domestic tribunal'. This provision moves focus from the (objective) insignificance of the *issue* to the (subjective) disadvantage of the applicant – something which, at least in monetary terms, will obviously vary from applicant to applicant. For a transitional period of two years it is not to be applied by the single judge formations deciding upon admissibility, but only committees, chambers and the Grand Chamber.[32]

How significant can, and should, this ground of inadmissibility be? This depends upon how one views its purpose. There have already been a number of cases in which the chambers have invoked it.[33] However, it is not likely to be invoked in very many cases – unless it is creatively interpreted. The overload problem is partially caused by the large number of *clearly* inadmissible cases, not *otherwise admissible* cases which do not raise 'important' issues. Moreover, the link that is made between admissibility and effective local remedies will mean that this admissibility ground, as it is worded at present, cannot be used to deal with many applications from states with structural deficiencies in their judicial systems, either generally, or in dealing with certain types of complaints.[34]

---

[32] The drafters took the view that time should elapse to allow interpretative case law to develop, 'Explanatory Report to Protocol 14', para. 106.

[33] There were some 30 cases up to the end of February 2012. ECtHR, 'Preliminary Opinion of the Court in Preparation for the Brighton Conference', 20 February 2012 (hereinafter, ECtHR, 'Preliminary Opinion'), para. 10. See, e.g., ECtHR, *Korolev (II)* v. *Russia* (Appl. No. 25551/05), Decision (First Section), 27 July 2010, Reports 2010 (damages claim for less than €1); ECtHR, *Ionescu* v. *Romania* (Appl. No. 36659/04), Decision (Third Section), 1 June 2010 (damages claim amounting to €90), not reported.

[34] See further below, section 6.6.

The Court already decides that a very high proportion of all applications are inadmissible. Thus, making it *even easier* to declare cases inadmissible is not necessarily a step forward. Would the Court not suffer a legitimacy problem if it raised its overall inadmissibility ratio from around 90 per cent (where it is today – even if the ratio varies considerably from state to state) to 99 per cent? The other part of the Court's problems simply put, is that some states produce relatively high numbers of *admissible* cases.

The number of applications received per year varies enormously from state to state, as does the inadmissibility ratio. This depends to a large extent on the size of the population, but it also varies according to the knowledge the general public (and the legal profession) have of the Convention system in the different states, and how positively these groups look upon the Convention system compared to their own national systems for protection of rights. If a state has a well-functioning national rights system, there may seldom be a need to take a matter to the Court. As pointed out in the Introduction to this volume, there is a group of high case producing states. This group is responsible *both* for large numbers of clearly inadmissible applications *and* large numbers of admissible applications.

Having said that, this new inadmissibility ground may contribute, albeit in a small way, to maintaining or strengthening the Court's legitimacy as amongst the member states which are *not* producing large numbers of admissible cases. A complaint which is heard, at least in certain member states, is that the ECtHR should not be taking up issues which are better dealt with by national courts, at least in states which are well-functioning democracies, with efficient courts.[35] I have heard this complaint, openly or privately, from judges in states with a strong or relatively strong national system for the protection of human rights. Of course, the argument has often been made by state representatives that the Convention regime is a necessary and important safeguard *for other states*, but that the ECtHR can and should leave one's own state alone.

---

[35] See Føllesdal, Peters and Ulfstein, 'Introduction', this volume, nn. 19–21. As regards the Swedish discussion, see the article critical, *inter alia*, of the judgment in ECtHR, *Johansson v. Finland* (Appl. No. 10163/02), Judgment (Fourth Section), 6 September 2007, not reported, by former President of the Supreme Administrative Court, Sten Heckscher, 'Finns det någon europeisk rätt?', C. Wong (ed.), *Festskrift till Per Ole Träskman* (Stockholm: Norstedts, 2011).

This criticism, paradoxically perhaps, can be seen as evidence of the fact that national courts are trying loyally to implement ECtHR case law in their own systems.[36] If the ECtHR was routinely ignored, judges would not bother criticising 'erroneous' or 'inappropriate' ECtHR case law (or even be aware of it). Still, the criticism of friends is often more important to listen to than the criticism of enemies. Article 35(3)(b) – if it is used – allows the Court to claim with greater force that the issues it takes up genuinely need to be taken up.

4.4 Other changes, particularly regarding repetitive cases

Protocol 14 made other important changes. However, these are dealt with elsewhere in this volume.[37] As regards the impact of the pilot procedure on numbers of applications, or repetitive cases, it will suffice to state the following. The procedure can be a way of bundling together groups, even large groups, of applications and/or repetitive cases.[38] However, it is not a panacea either for the number of applications or for the repetitive cases problem, because the procedure requires favourable political conditions for its effective application.[39] Several of the states which suffer most from structural deficiencies in human rights protection are also those states which are least inclined to make, or least capable of making, structural reforms. As already mentioned, the high case-producing states are also responsible for most of the repetitive cases.

---

[36] What evidence there is indicates that the ECtHR has, generally speaking, relatively high status among European judges. B. Çalı, A. Koch and N. Bruch, *The Legitimacy of the European Court of Human Rights: The View from the Ground* (University College London, Department of Political Science, 2011).

[37] As already noted, I will not go into the issue of selection of judges. I will content myself with noting that while the non-renewable term of office of nine years (art. 23 ECHR) strengthens the Court's independence, and so adds to legitimacy, it causes a problem in that it takes time to learn the work of any court. 'Settling-in' in an international court with 47 legal cultures takes time. The Court has previously chosen its leaders from amongst the most experienced judges on the bench, and these will have to 'learn quicker'.

[38] See, e.g., ECtHR, *Gaglione and Others* v. *Italy* (Appl. No. 45867/07 and 474 others), Judgment (Second Section), 21 December 2010, not reported (475 applications).

[39] See Rule 61 of the Rules of Procedure, 21 February 2011; ECtHR, *Greens and M.T.* v. *UK* (Appl. Nos. 60041 and 60054/08), Judgment (Fourth Section), 23 November 2010, Reports 2010; and Leach, Chapter 5 this volume. See also, W. Sadurski, 'Partnering with Strasbourg: Constitutionalisation of the European Court of Human Rights, the Accession of Central and East European States to the Council of Europe, and the Idea of Pilot Judgments', *Human Rights Law Review* 9 (2009) 397–453.

The more than 30,000 repetitive cases at present pending before the Court can be seen as the its problem. One solution, which the Court has advocated, would be to develop a practice whereby the Registry refers a list of cases directly to the relevant government to be settled in an appropriate way. In the absence of any justified objections from the government, failure to provide redress within a fixed period of time would lead to a 'default judgment' awarding compensation to the applicant.[40] However, one can instead see the problem as belonging to the Committee of Ministers, to whom the main function of supervising the execution of the Court's judgment falls under article 46(2). The issue of supervision, and the different options open for the Court (infringement proceedings etc.), are discussed elsewhere in this volume.[41]

Three points should, however, be made here, as they have a direct bearing on procedure. First, any search for a solution to the overload of cases must focus on the real cause(s) of the problem. Both much of the backlog problem, and much of the repetitive case problem, could be solved at a stroke by the expulsion from the Council of Europe of the three 'worst offenders'. One can argue that the scale of the problems revealed in these states indicates that they do not fulfil the requirements of membership. But no one seriously contemplates expulsion. The identity and destiny of Europe is bound up with that of Russia and Turkey. Self-serving reasons for European states – strategic in the case of Turkey, a bridge between Europe and the Islamic world, strategic/energy in the case of Russia – mean that they must be a part of Europe. Above all, the progressive forces in the Russian, Turkish and Ukrainian administrations and civil societies would have their work terribly damaged if Europe (not simply the European Union (EU)) 'turned its back' on these countries.

Second, the repetitive cases are largely because of the absence of effective local remedies. Courts might exist, but lack jurisdiction (e.g. over military personnel), or there may be practical obstacles in either getting the case to the court, or implementing its judgment in the face of opposition from central or local power structures.

These factors vary in strength according to the state in question. It is not possible to go into detail in such complicated issues of legal and political

---

[40] ECtHR, 'Preliminary Opinion', para. 21.
[41] See Lambert-Abdelgawad, Chapter 7 this volume. See also generally, E. Lambert-Abdelgawad, *The Execution of Judgments of the European Court of Human Rights*, 2nd edn (Strasbourg: Council of Europe Publishing, 2008).

culture, but something brief must be said to give an idea of the depth of the problems which the ECtHR has – indirectly – been landed with.

As regards Russia, the local courts may well be corrupt, but even where they are not, they may have little power to check senior officials who ignore the law and/or are corrupt. So they may be of little use for an individual complainant. This is a problem for the whole country, not only for the big cities.[42] Moreover, a constitutional court, such as the Russian Constitutional Court, which is limited to controlling the constitutionality of the laws themselves and which cannot rectify human rights violations caused by the wrong application of a law, is of little practical use either. Thus, it does not function as a filter on applications to the ECtHR. Similar points apply to the Ukraine.[43]

As regards Turkey, it has provided re-opening remedies for administrative, criminal and civil cases. It has also recently reformed its laws and the procedure of the Constitutional Court, providing that individuals can complain to it of violations of their constitutional rights where these fall within the scope of the ECHR.[44] It remains to be seen whether this – residual – remedy[45] will be regarded as sufficiently attractive to cut down significantly on applications to the Court, but it is clearly a step forward. The main problems are the ongoing low-intensity conflict in the country, something which is never conducive to respect for human rights, combined with a more general resistance to the Convention on the part of the military, sections of the bureaucracy and sections of the legal establishment.[46]

---

[42] A. Nußberger, 'The Reception Process in Russia and Ukraine', in H. Keller and A. Stone Sweet (eds.), *A Europe of Rights: The Impact of the ECHR on National Legal Systems* (Oxford University Press, 2008) 604–77, at 631–2 (hereinafter Keller and Stone Sweet (eds.), *A Europe of Rights*).

[43] *Ibid.*, at 650. She adds, 'the population does not trust the judges in general. The large number of individual applications before the Court is, therefore, a sign of deeply rooted problems in Russia's and Ukraine's post-Soviet societies.'

[44] See Law on the Establishment and Rules of Procedure of the Constitutional Court of Turkey (Law No. 6216, adopted 30 March 2011, arts. 45–51), available at www.venice.coe. int.

[45] Article 47(5) of Law No. 6216 provides that it is only applicable 'in case no legal remedy is provided for'. If this, and other, Turkish remedies come to qualify as 'effective', then the ECtHR will require exhaustion of these, meaning that the number of admissible applications from Turkey will decline, probably considerably.

[46] İ.O. Kaboğlu and S.-I.G. Koutnatzis, 'The Reception Process in Greece and Turkey', in Keller and Stone Sweet, *A Europe of Rights* 452–531, at 522. The authors conclude that 'the climate in Turkey is not conducive to independent human rights bodies, while judicial review of State action also faces significant limitations'.

As regards the other high-count states, the following can be said. Poland is a high-count country for primarily two reasons: length of proceedings and detention on remand.[47] To these can be added property problems, many connected to the 'Bug river' claims, now largely resolved. As regards Italy, here, too, it is length of proceedings together with property issues, fair trial and family law issues which are responsible for the largest groups of cases.[48] More or less the same applies to Romania, where property and fair trial make up the largest groups of cases, together with smaller numbers of cases concerning length of proceedings, liberty/security and family life.[49] The intensity of the rights violations in Poland, Romania and Italy are thus nowhere near as serious as in the other three states, even if their persistence is, putting it mildly, very embarrassing for EU members which are supposed to be *Rechtsstaaten*.[50]

Third, the amount of the case law shows the difficulties which courts, acting alone, have in *changing* societies. Courts are gatekeepers of social change.[51] They can facilitate it, but when powerful social forces resist change, they need the support of the executive branch. There is nothing new here. In the 1960s and 1970s, the US Supreme Court found itself unable to ensure the implementation of its progressive judgments regarding racial equality in several states. It took a long period of time for this to happen, and when it did it was mainly a result of changes in

---

[47] ECtHR, '50 Years of Activity: The European Court of Human Rights Some Facts and Figures', www.echr.coe.int/NR/rdonlyres/ACD46A0F-615A-48B9-89D6-8480AFCC 29FD/0/FactsAndFigures_EN.pdf. For discussion, see M. Krzyżanowska-Mierzewska, 'The Reception Process in Poland and Slovakia', in Keller and Stone Sweet (eds.), *A Europe of Rights* (hereinafter Krzyżanowska-Mierzewska, 'The Reception Process in Poland and Slovakia'), at 567–8.
[48] ECtHR, '50 Years of Activity'. Number of judgments finding at least one violation were (to 2009), respectively: 1,095 (length of proceedings), 229 (property issues), 291 (fair trial), 128 (family life).
[49] '50 Years of Activity', *ibid.* Numbers of judgments finding at least one violation were (to 2009), respectively: 373 (property), 304 (fair trial), 62 (length), 45 (liberty/security), 35 (family life).
[50] Krzyżanowska-Mierzewska, 'The Reception Process in Poland and Slovakia', at 567 points out for Poland that the introduction of a right of individual constitutional complaint, which happened as far back as 1996, did little to stem the flow of applications to Strasbourg, even if the ECtHR since 2003 regards this as a local remedy to be exhausted.
[51] Cf. Lord Devlin's remark: 'There is always a host of new ideas galloping around the outskirts of a society's thought. All of them seek admission but each must first win its spurs ... In a changing society ... the law acts as a valve.' P. Devlin, *The Judge* (Oxford University Press, 1981), at 1.

local government and public opinion brought about by the voting public, together with a combination of carrots and sticks at the federal level. The 'least dangerous branch' of government steers by legitimacy, not force or money. It is clear that, for powerful factions in the executive branch of several of the high producing states, it is still force or money which are the really strong arguments.[52]

5. The priority policy

The Court has always been able to give priority to a particular case, and has done so on occasion. However, a quite different issue is general criteria for priority applying to classes of case. In June 2009, the Court amended Rule 41 of its Rules of Court to provide that 'the Court shall have regard to the importance and urgency of the issues raised on the basis of criteria fixed by it. The Chamber, or its President, may, however, derogate from these criteria so as to give priority to a particular application.' These fixed criteria, dividing cases into seven categories, were later published in November 2010.[53]

The first three categories, in order of significance, are urgent applications (in particular, risk to life or health of the applicant, other circumstances linked to the personal or family situation of the applicant), applications raising questions capable of having an impact on the effectiveness of the Convention system, or applications raising an important question of general interest and applications which on their face raise main complaints issues under articles 2, 3, 4 or 5(1) of the Convention. Thereafter come potentially well-founded applications based on other articles, applications raising issues already dealt with in a pilot/leading

---

[52] The following point made by US Supreme Court Justice Breyer on political maturity is instructive. Justice Breyer noted President Eisenhower's decision in the 1950s to enforce the Supreme Court's desegregation decisions with the US Army, in the face of resistance by the state national guard, and stated that: 'Many people were upset with the Supreme Court's decision in *Bush* v. *Gore*. But while that decision has inspired a wide range of different responses and emotions, I have yet to read about the need for deploying paratroopers. Tracing the trajectory of the rule of law in this country reveals that we have arrived at the point where people will accept the fundamental legitimacy of judicial decisions even if they disagree with the outcomes of those decisions. This acceptance of the rule of law has come to exist only over time in this country. And it is an ideal that is not yet universal.' S. Breyer, 'Introduction of President Luzius Wildhaber', *American University International Law Review* 22:4 (2007) 517–20.

[53] ECtHR, 'The Court's Priority Policy', 2010, www.echr.coe.int/NR/rdonlyres/DB6EDF5E-6661-4EF6-992E-F8C4ACC62F31/0/Priority_policyPublic_communication_EN.pdf.

judgment (i.e. 'repetitive cases'), applications identified as giving rise to a problem of admissibility, and applications which are manifestly inadmissible.

What are the effects of this? The priority policy is a radical step, but it does not mean that the Court can choose which individual cases it selects. Instead, it has identified certain categories of case for fast(er) treatment. The main problem it involves is for the category of well-founded non-repetitive cases concerning 'less-important' articles. These will only come up for decision many years after filing of the case.[54] Most applicants can be assumed to have lost interest by then, and this will undoubtedly damage the legitimacy of the Court. The priority policy is a consequence of the insistence of the state parties, and much of the non-governmental organisation (NGO) community, that the right of individual petition be preserved. It has been preserved, but at the price that large numbers of applications will not, in practice, be examined. At present, two rights are at the centre of a considerable proportion of the applications, namely, the right to a fair trial and the right to property. These can still be the subject of a pilot judgment, but judgments on 'follow-on' cases will not be forthcoming for many years.[55] It also goes in the opposite direction from two of the ideas behind Protocol 14, i.e. that inadmissible cases be dealt with rapidly and that 'repetitive cases' would be dealt with by a Committee. If the priority policy remains unchanged, and the Court receives no additional funding, the likelihood is that the number of committee judgments will decline sharply.

6. Interlaken, Izmir, Brighton and ongoing reform discussions

6.1 Introduction

The initiative for a conference of states parties came in 2009 from the President of the Court, who wanted them to recognise the enormity of

---

[54] The majority of the category I 'urgent' applications (79%) have been pending for less than two years; 65% of the category II applications (pilot or leading cases) have at least been communicated to the government; 64% of the category III applications (complaints about articles 2, 3, 4 or 5(1) of the Convention) are still waiting for a first examination by the Court; and 50% of all the applications in this category have been pending for more than two years. See ECtHR, 'Analysis of Statistics 2010', January 2011, www.echr.coe.int/NR/rdonlyres/0A35997B-B907-4A38-85F4-A93113A78F10/0/Analysis_of_statistics_2010.pdf. See also below, section 7.

[55] Compare the comment by A. Buyse, 'The Court's New Priority Policy', 17 November 2010, http://echrblog.blogspot.com/2010/11/courts-new-priority-policy.html.

the problems facing the Court and to make a political commitment to support it.[56] The Swiss government in response organised a conference in Interlaken. The Izmir Conference came soon after, too soon to be particularly meaningful, and adds little new to Interlaken. The declaration commits the parties in an 'Action Plan' to a timetable of discussion and evaluation. The main forum for the continued discussions is the Steering Committee for Human Rights (CDDH). The Committee of Ministers is to evaluate, during 2012 to 2015, to what extent the implementation of Protocol 14 and of the Action Plan has improved the situation of the Court. On the basis of this evaluation, it should decide, before the end of 2015, on whether there is a need for further action. Before the end of 2019, it should decide on whether the measures adopted have proven to be sufficient to assure sustainable functioning of the control mechanism of the Convention, or whether more profound changes are necessary. The Brighton Conference makes some important additions to the Interlaken undertakings.

In this section, I will discuss briefly a number of procedural proposals noted in either or both of the Interlaken and Brighton declarations, namely, a statute, the possible introduction of fees, a mandatory requirement of legal representation, advisory opinions, an additional, or amended, filtering mechanism, an increased emphasis on subsidiarity and changes to the admissibility criteria and, finally, improvements to the mechanisms for ensuring consistency of case law.

6.2 A statute

The procedure for amending the Convention is very time-consuming and, as the Russian obstruction tactics concerning Protocol 14 showed, uncertain. When a relatively minor change in how the Court deals with a procedural issue requires a new protocol, a crisis which has been building up for a long time can be exacerbated even further. The solution is to give the Court more control over its working methods by moving parts of Section II of the Convention to a statute that could be subject to a simplified amendment procedure. The provisions the CDDH has provisionally identified are: article 24(2), concerning (non-judicial) rapporteurs assisting single judges; article 26(1), insofar as it concerns the size of non-singular judicial formations, but excluding their type; article 26(2),

---

[56] ECtHR, 'Memorandum of the President of the European Court of Human Rights to the States with a View to Preparing the Interlaken Conference', 3 July 2009, www.coe.int.

concerning reduction in the size of chambers; article 26(5), concerning the composition of the Grand Chamber; article 27, insofar as it concerns the competence of single judges, but excluding the principle of judicial decision-making; article 28, insofar as it concerns the competence of committees, but excluding the principle of judicial decision-making; article 29, insofar as it concerns decisions by chambers on admissibility and merits, but excluding the principle of judicial decision-making; article 30 concerning relinquishment of jurisdiction to the Grand Chamber; article 31 concerning powers of the Grand Chamber; article 39(2)–(4) concerning friendly settlements, but excluding the 'essential' principle; article 42 concerning finality of chamber judgments; article 43 (2) and (3) concerning referral to the Grand Chamber, but excluding the grounds on which the panel of five judges shall accept requests for referral; article 44(2) concerning finality of chamber judgments; article 47(3) concerning Committee of Ministers' procedure for requesting advisory opinions; and article 48 concerning the Court's advisory jurisdiction.[57] The CCDH was not unanimous on all of these, and it noted that the final choice of provisions that could be subject to a simplified amendment procedure will also depend on the modality eventually retained for introducing such a procedure.

The CDDH also concluded that the following issues currently found outside the Convention (i.e. in the Rules of Court or the Court's case law) may be suitable for 'upgrading', namely, Rule 39 of the Rules of Court on interim measures; the pilot judgment procedure; and unilateral declarations. There are various ways in which this can be accomplished.[58] One problem is that national constitutional laws might prohibit a state from ratifying a protocol that introduced a simplified amendment procedure, or from accepting proposed amendments without first submitting them to parliamentary approval.[59]

---

[57] CoE, 'Interim Activity Report', CDDH(2011)R72 Addendum I, 72nd meeting, Strasbourg, 29 March–1 April 2011.

[58] The most comprehensive approach is to amend the Convention and the Rules of Court, and create a separate statute all at the same time. See H. Keller, A. Fischer and D. Kühne, 'Draft Statute for the European Court of Human Rights – A Contribution to Reforming the European System', *Human Rights Law Journal* 30 (2011) 1–12.

[59] For example, under Chapter 10, para. 7 of the Swedish Constitution, (1974:152, as amended) delegation of competence to an international judicial organ is only permitted 'to a limited extent'. This should not, however, constitute an insuperable obstacle, bearing in mind the fact that Sweden has accepted both the right of the ICJ and the CJEU to amend their own statutes.

As regards the procedure itself, the CDDH considered that amendments could be proposed by states parties or the Court; and the Committee of Ministers would adopt these by consensus (i.e. unanimity within the meaning of article 20(a) of the Statute of the Council of Europe). The CCDH, interestingly, considered that the Court should be consulted (in the case that the proposal does not come from it), but does not appear to give it a veto. If this is so, then it shows desire on the part of the states parties to retain strong control over the Convention and a rather worrying lack of willingness to trust the Court. Worse, if the Court does not have full control over the content of the changes, there is a risk that the states parties, by making, or threatening to make, a procedural change, can influence the Court's case law.

The states parties in the Brighton Declaration contented themselves with noting with appreciation the continuing discussions on the issue and calling for a swift conclusion to these discussions (para. 37). A statute covering the powers set out above would undoubtedly strengthen the Court, even if it would not decisively change its character as a half-international, half-constitutional court. It is difficult for states openly to deny the advantages for flexibility a statute on these lines would entail. Still, it seems clear that some, or even many, of the states parties are reluctant to strengthen the Court in this way.

6.3 Fees

The idea of Court fees has been floating about for a while. The purpose is to deter wholly *unmeritorious* applications.[60] In this respect, a comparative perspective might be useful. A Venice Commission comparative study[61] reveals that fees before a constitutional court are exceptional. In the United States there is a fee of $300 for lodging a petition to grant a writ of *certiorari* before the Supreme Court; in Russia, the fee amounts to one minimum wage, in Armenia to five minimum wages, in Switzerland a minimum of 200 and a maximum of 5,000 CHF, and in Austria the fee is €220. In Israel, there is a fee of approximately $400 to file a petition with the Supreme Court, sitting as the High Court of Justice, but the

---

[60] As is all too clear from the experience of all the international mechanisms for rights protection, a tried and tested method some states apply for discouraging both meritorious and unmeritorious applications is to send men around to a complainant's house.

[61] Venice Commission, 'Study on Individual Access to Constitutional Justice', adopted at 85th Plenary Session, Venice, 17–18 December 2010, CDL-AD(2010)039, paras. 116–17.

petitioner is entitled to file a request, supported by special circumstances, to receive a waiver or reduction of fees.

The Venice Commission recommended that in view of increasingly more comprehensive human rights protection, court fees for individuals ought to be relatively low and that it should be possible to reduce them in accordance with the financial situation of the applicant. Their primary aim should be to deter obvious abuse.

The CCDH has not yet taken a stand on fees. It did consider that if they were introduced, then whatever form they take, they will have the effect of deterring at least *some* meritorious applications.[62] Fees would have to be differential, to take into account the very different salary levels and costs of living in different states. Moreover, some form of waiver system would seem to be necessary, as otherwise it would remove Convention protection from the very people who need it most: the poor. All of this will be time-consuming, and probably costly, to administer.

In any event, bearing in mind the Venice Commission study, fees would have to be set at a low level. The problem will be that, in this case, a fee is unlikely to deter the present flood of applications from Russia and the Ukraine (and possibly, Turkey), because, simply put, many applicants will reason that paying the fee to the ECtHR is worth it; at least one has a *chance* of justice, and compensation, in Strasbourg. Thus, fees are unlikely to have a sufficiently significant reducing effect on unmeritorious applications. The Court has expressed its opposition to fees. After Izmir, the idea appears to be dead.[63]

6.4 Legal representation

As regards the proposal that legal representation be mandatory, this, too, is meant to cut down on unmeritorious applications. The idea is that the lawyer, by referring to the admissibility guides produced (above, section 2) should act as a filter. The position as regards applications to constitutional courts in Council of Europe states varies. It is

---

[62] Compare ECtHR, *Mamatkulov and Askarov* v. *Turkey* (Appl. Nos. 46827 and 46951/99), Judgment (Grand Chamber), 4 February 2005, Reports 2005-I, para. 102: '...applicants should be able to communicate freely with the Court without being subjected to any form of pressure from the authorities to withdraw or modify their complaints'.

[63] ECtHR, 'Preliminary Opinion', para. 30. The same can probably be said for the idea that a sanction be introduced for 'obviously futile' applications. See Council of Europe, 'Report', CDDH (2011) R73 73rd meeting, 6–9 December 2011, www.coe.int/t/dghl/standardsetting/cddh/Meeting%20reports%20committee/73_en.pdf, appendix IV.

obligatory in Andorra, Austria, Azerbaijan, Czech Republic, France, Italy, Luxembourg, Monaco, Portugal, Slovakia, Spain and Switzerland (if the individual is 'clearly unable' to represent him- or herself). No such obligation exists in Albania, Armenia, Belgium, Croatia, Estonia, Georgia, Hungary, Latvia, Liechtenstein, Poland, Romania, Russia, Slovenia, Sweden, Switzerland, The former Yugoslav Republic of Macedonia and Ukraine.[64]

In practice, many applicants to the ECtHR are already represented by lawyers.[65] If and when an application reaches the stage of being reported to the respondent government, this is almost invariably the case. A mandatory requirement to employ a lawyer is likely in practice to cost applicants more, or much more, than a fee system. Thus, the same objections of principle apply to it. Moreover, it is no guarantee of the quality of the application. There is no indication that the admissibility rate of applications introduced through a lawyer is significantly higher. Even where a lawyer does counsel against making an application, the complainant does not have to listen. Again, the Court is opposed to this idea, which now appears to be dead.[66]

6.5 *Advisory opinions*

The idea behind advisory opinions here is that national supreme or constitutional courts could be given the possibility to refer a case to the ECtHR, which in turn would have discretion to take up the request. There are several potential advantages to such a system.[67] It would be in keeping with the principle of subsidiarity and the idea of multilevel protection of rights,[68] as it would institutionalise dialogue between the ECtHR and national courts and emphasise the cooperative nature of the ECHR enterprise. The national court would feel more 'ownership' of the issue, and, hopefully, a high degree of willingness to implement the (non-binding) advisory opinion, as it had chosen to refer the question in the first place.

---

[64] *Ibid.*
[65] Although some high-count countries, such as Poland, have a relatively low proportion of cases submitted through a lawyer.
[66] ECtHR, 'Preliminary Opinion', para. 30.   [67] O'Boyle, 'The Future', at 199.
[68] A. Voßkuhle, 'Multilevel Cooperation of the European Constitutional Courts: Der Europäische Verfassungsgerichtsverbund', *European Constitutional Law Review* 6 (2010) 175–98.

Advisory opinions are in a sense a natural consequence of the ECtHR's assertion (accepted by the states parties in the Interlaken Declaration) that states must take into account judgments affecting other states, not simply judgments against their own state. However, this can be easier said than done, because it involves 'translating' a 'foreign' judgment to one's own national context. The ECtHR might have found law W or practice X in State Y in violation of the Convention because of factors Z1–Z6. But what are the exact implications of this for a national supreme court in State A, which has a similar, but not identical, law or practice? An advisory opinion can help clarify this situation.

Historically, the ECtHR tended to approach the issues raised by cases in a narrow fashion, unlike the European Court of Justice (ECJ) (now Court of Justice of the European Union, CJEU) which, through relatively abstract preliminary rulings, deliberately tries to lay down general interpretative guidelines for national courts. Nowadays, there are much clearer indications that the Court is attempting to lay down clearer, uniform standards of interpretation of the Convention for domestic courts. This is seen, *inter alia*, in how the Court now tends to begin its assessment of the legal issues in a case: by sketching out the applicable principles which apply generally to the area, these having been distilled from its earlier judgments.

On the other hand, there are a number of question marks. The first of these is whether advisory opinions would strengthen or weaken the 'constitutional' nature of the ECtHR. If the issuing of a non-binding opinion would *exclude* later concrete applications concerning the 'same' issue, then this would undoubtedly weaken the Court. But even if this is not the case, and the intention is to strengthen the Court, the next question is: do we want to do this? What the Court does just now is to decide in a concrete case whether a state has got the balance 'right'. Giving it the power to rule more *in abstracto* will involve it doing something different. There is also, for EU members, the question of whether we need, or can have, two courts – the ECtHR and the CJEU – both issuing more *in abstracto* rulings.[69]

The second question mark is the more practical issue of the work this would involve for an already overworked ECtHR. The third is that there is already a mechanism for informing the ECtHR that a pending case has

---

[69] I look at the different approaches of national constitutional courts, the CJEU and the ECtHR in more detail in 'Competing Rights?', in S. de Vries, S. Weatherill and U. Bernitz, *The Protection of Fundamental Rights in the EU after Lisbon* (Oxford: Hart Publishing, 2013).

implications for other states with similar laws and practices, namely, *amicus curiae* briefs. Admittedly, this comes in at the stage of a pending case, although it can also be by way of an appeal to the Grand Chamber. As already noted in the Introduction, ten states handed in *amicus curiae* briefs in the *Lautsi* case. One can also say that this mechanism would duplicate a mechanism which already exists within the Council of Europe, in that the Venice Commission today receives, and replies to, requests for *amicus curiae* briefs from national constitutional courts.

An advisory opinion is obviously designed to influence a state, even if it is, formally speaking, non-binding. A prerequisite for making a system work is that the national constitutional or supreme court genuinely is interested in hearing the opinion of the ECtHR. This should not be taken for granted, even (or especially?) in states with well-functioning national systems for the protection of human rights. Unless advisory opinions are given first priority, there will be considerable delays, and no court wants to wait on another. Even if advisory opinions are introduced, it is likely that a period of 'confidence-building' will have to elapse before national supreme and constitutional courts start asking for them. This period will vary according to the judicial culture of the state in question. The EU preliminary reference procedure is now so well established that it is easy to forget that it took considerable time for the courts in several EU states to overcome their natural reluctance to involve another 'foreign' court in 'their' business.

It is also important to understand that advisory opinions, whatever other advantages they might have, are not a solution to the case overload problem. For advisory opinions to have a genuine impact on the national legal culture, an implicit prerequisite is that the national supreme or constitutional court is powerful enough to impose its will on the executive or legislature. In my opinion this is not, at present, the case in at least two (possibly three) of the highest-count states.

Despite the unanswered questions, the Brighton Declaration paragraph 12(d) commits the states to produce, by the end of 2013, a draft additional protocol providing for an option for states to request advisory opinions.

6.6 *Filtering again*

Very briefly, as regards a new filtering mechanism, little need be added to the discussions in sections 3 and 4. The CCDH is currently discussing three options: national judges *ad litem*, creating a new specialist type of judge for filtering, and strengthening the Registry in different ways. The first two options are close to each other, and both possess the benefit of flexibility (the number of such judges could be adjusted as needed). Both would mean a judge with judicial qualifications, but not necessarily 'qualified for high judicial office', a much shorter period of office, and chosen after a quick selection process. Bearing in mind the boring nature of the work, the short period of office may make it more attractive, although in terms of efficiency, as it will take time to learn the work, the period must not be too short.

I do not see the value of either of these options. The option of strengthening the Registry requires no amendment of the Convention and – to my mind – seems the most cost-effective, the quickest and the most flexible option. But formally recognising that the Registry can decide on clearly inadmissible cases would require amendment of the Convention, even if this is the reality of the present situation.[70] There is agreement in the CCDH, even among those that are in favour of the Registry option, that the Registry's competence should be limited to clearly inadmissible cases and that it should not deal finally with repetitive cases.

The Brighton Declaration (para. 20(e)) provides that a decision on whether to amend the Convention to provide for some such system should be taken by the end of 2013.

6.7 Subsidiarity and proposed changes to processing and admissibility

In the earlier drafts produced by the UK government prior to the Brighton Conference, the powers of the Court were to be cut significantly by an amendment to the Convention providing that applications should be classed inadmissible unless a national court 'erred' in interpreting the Convention.[71] However, the final text of the declaration was much watered down. Subsidiarity and the margin of appreciation are to be written into the preamble to the Convention (para. 12(b)), something which is likely to have only symbolic importance. Instead of putting all the blame on the Court, the Brighton Declaration follows the Interlaken Declaration by stressing that responsibility for cutting down on

---

[70] Arguably, one could say that the 'judicial scrutiny' requirement could be fulfilled by employing people qualified for judicial office to the Registry and giving them security of tenure and the other necessary guarantees of independence etc.
[71] www.guardian.co.uk/law/interactive/2012/feb/28/echr-reform-uk-draft.

inadmissible applications and dealing effectively with repetitive applications is placed primarily on the states parties.

As already pointed out (above, section 4.4), as the main problems are caused by a small number of states, the need for further changes in the institutions and procedure of the Court will depend very much on whether they do what they are supposed to.[72]

A particular concern expressed in the context of the Izmir Conference was the increased inflow of requests for interim measures under Rule 39 of the Rules of Court. The Court had, during 2009 and 2010, accepted applications for issuing interim measures in urgent deportation cases where the documentation was not complete. It did so out of concern for applicants faced with – possibly – irrevocable damage to their interests. However, the number of such applications exploded, and so the Court, in effect, created a lot of extra work for itself, as well as irritation in several states parties which were ordered not to carry out (well-founded) deportations. Thus, in 2011, the Court reorganised its internal set-up for dealing with these urgent requests and changed its procedures at both the judicial and administrative level, requiring complete documentation. It also revised its practice direction, and, through its president, made a public statement on the situation.[73]

The Brighton Declaration goes beyond both Interlaken and Izmir in making undertakings to amend two of the admissibility grounds. These are designed to cut down on the number of applications. The first of these is to introduce a tighter time limit during which the applicant can complain to the Court, reducing it from the present 6 months from the date of final decision, to 4 months (para. 15(a)). This proposed amendment to article 35(1) might seem radical, but the Court itself suggested it.[74]

The second proposed amendment is to remove the words 'and provided that no case may be rejected on this ground which has not been duly considered by a domestic tribunal' from article 35(3)(b). As already indicated (above, section 4.3), the present wording of the article means that 'minor' violations which have nonetheless not been duly considered by domestic courts, cannot be dismissed on this ground. This

---

[72] Compare A. Mowbray, 'The Interlaken Declaration: The Beginning of a New Era for the European Court of Human Rights?', *Human Rights Law Review* 10:3 (2010) 519–28, at 528.

[73] www.echr.coe.int/NR/rdonlyres/B76DC4F5-5A09-472B-802C-07B4150BF36D/0/20110211_ART_39_Statement_EN.pdf.

[74] ECtHR, 'Preliminary Opinion', para. 37.

amendment means, in effect, that the Court can choose not to take up cases concerning 'minor' violations, even from states parties where there are structural deficiencies in local remedies.

The Court is also 'invited to develop its case law' in a number of ways. One of these is to interpret the exhaustion of domestic remedies so as to *require* an applicant, where a domestic remedy was available to them, to have argued the alleged violation of the Convention rights or an equivalent provision of domestic law before the national courts or tribunals, thereby allowing the national courts an opportunity to apply the Convention in light of the case law of the Court (para. 15(g)). The Court is also encouraged to use the manifestly ill-founded ground to dismiss applications which have been duly considered by a domestic court (para. 15(d)). These are both things the Court already does (see further below, section 7).

Finally, as regards processing, one possibility of speeding up consideration of cases is to allow the Court to decide more cases in committee form. This means a more expansive interpretation of 'well-established case law', the meaning of article 28(1). Here there is a delicate issue of state sovereignty. An issue may be well established in case law dealing with *other* states. But is it exactly the same issue? The 'translation' problem (above, section 6.5) again raises its head. The Court itself may consider that its case law has *some* form of *erga omnes* effect.[75] But some (or many?) of the states parties still have concerns in this respect. At any rate, the Court is requested to consult with the states parties in how it applies article 28(1), and to 'bear in mind the non-binding character of judgments against another State Party' (para. 20(f)).

In my view, none of these proposed Convention changes or 'developments' in the case law are particularly problematic for the Court. There is, however, unlikely to be unanimity among academics on the desirability of the proposed change to article 35(3)(b), reflecting the continuing debate on the role of the Court (constitutional/international) for the protection of even 'minor' human rights in Europe.

6.8 Consistency of case law

One of the criticisms directed against the Court prior to the Brighton Declaration concerned the consistency of its case law. A Court divided

---

[75] See, e.g., ECtHR, *Opuz* v. *Turkey* (Appl. No. 33401/02), Judgment (Third Section), 9 June 2009, Reports 2009, para. 163.

into five chambers (perhaps seven in the future) delivering over 2,000 judgments a year, is bound to experience consistency problems.[76] As noted above (section 6.5) the 'translation' problem can make it difficult for a national court to understand what is required of it. This is exacerbated when the Court has decided cases from various states involving *similar* fact situations in (slightly or considerably) different ways, without sufficiently explaining the reasons for the differences in treatment. One can argue that a more open presentation of why cases are being 'distinguished' would be advisable. At the same time, the Court might naturally want to leave itself room for manoeuvre in future cases. And it might not want to be too specific about why it treats state A differently from state B (A's safeguards are working in practice, B's are not). Moreover, it is not, ultimately, the Court's job to lay down one 'uniform' interpretation of the Convention, and the states parties certainly do not want it to do so. It is thus no easy matter to square the circle of clarity and consistency in the case law (demanded by the states parties) with the square of the margin of appreciation (also demanded by the states parties).

The Brighton Declaration notes that the Court is considering amending its Rules of Procedure to *require* chambers to relinquish jurisdiction to the Grand Chamber. This, in turn, means that parties to the case should not be able to object to this (as at present they have the possibility to do). Accordingly, the Declaration (para. 25(d)) proposes that an amendment to article 30 be adopted by 2013, removing the words 'unless one of the parties to the case objects'. In the meantime, states parties are encouraged to refrain from objecting to any proposal for relinquishment by a Chamber. The Court is also invited to consider whether the composition of the Grand Chamber would be enhanced by the *ex officio* inclusion of the vice presidents of each section (para. 25(e)).

7. Legitimacy problems and concluding remarks

In this concluding section, I return to the legitimacy issue I took up in the Introduction, and make a number of concluding remarks.

---

[76] Compare the number of judgments (approx. 100) given every year by the US Supreme Court. For an example from the ECtHR, see *Morel* v. *France* (Appl. No. 54559/00), Decision (Second Section), 3 June 2003, Reports 2003-IX, where a chamber found that a 10% tax surcharge did not fall under the criminal head of art. 6. This was not in accordance with other case law, and caused confusion until clarified by the Grand Chamber in ECtHR, *Jussila* v. *Finland* (Appl. No. 73053/01), Judgment (Grand Chamber), 23 November 2006, Reports 2006-XIV.

Barkenhysen and van Emmerik argue that the legitimacy of the ECtHR can be challenged on the basis that it rarely holds hearings with the applicant, it only gives very brief reasoning in admissibility decisions, there is no right of appeal against these, that the conclusions of pilot judgments are sometimes applied in cases which are not legally identical and the proceedings before it are very lengthy.[77] They add that, after Protocol 14 has entered into force, these problems are exacerbated on the basis that admissibility decisions are in practice being taken by the Registry, the new admissibility ground is unclear, and that the applicant (unlike the respondent state) cannot object to the pilot judgment procedure being applied to him/her. I will not deal with their points on the pilot judgment procedure, but I will take up the other points below.

It is difficult to disagree with Barkenhysen and van Emmerik that admissibility decisions are subject to huge delays and are often not reasoned well, or at all; nor that the Registry, in practice, is determining inadmissibility. What an applicant can receive after three or more years is a short decision, of which perhaps only two sentences are 'operative', and which may well be a simple assertion 'no violation of the Convention is disclosed'. In the circumstances, one can indeed ask: what is the added value in Strasbourg? If legitimacy is to be measured on the basis of whether the aggrieved individuals who applied to the Court are any less aggrieved after having done so, then I guess that the Court's legitimacy is near zero. Would this near-zero legitimacy be improved if the Court offered every applicant an oral hearing, and the possibility of an appeal against an inadmissibility decision? Perhaps, but I doubt it. Most applicants want a result, not 'no' after a fair and – perhaps extremely – lengthy procedure.[78]

One can argue that the 'reasoning deficit' in admissibility decisions has now been corrected, at least partly, by the publication of the detailed guide to admissibility (above, section 3). But more importantly, I think there are other ways of viewing the legitimacy of the Strasbourg system, its (alleged) loss of legitimacy and, if so, how it can go about recovering this.[79]

---

[77] T. Barkhuysen and M. van Emmerik, 'Legitimacy of European Court of Human Rights Judgments: Procedural Aspects', in N. Huls, M. Adams and J. Bornhoff (eds.), *The Legitimacy of Highest Courts' Rulings* (The Hague: T.M.C. Asser Press, 2009), (hereinafter Barkhuysen and van Emmerik, 'Legitimacy'), at 442–3.
[78] Both are utterly impracticable proposals as far as admissibility is concerned, although they are more feasible for decisions on the merits.
[79] If, indeed, we can accurately measure legitimacy at all. Compare R. de Lange, 'Judicial Deliberations and Human Rights Adjudication', in Huls, Adams and Bornhoff (eds.), *The Legitimacy of Highest Courts' Rulings* at 465.

Much of the debate concerning the Court's legitimacy is framed in terms of a choice between a 'constitutional' court or a court which dispenses individual justice.[80] One's approach to this issue is strongly affected by the judicial system one is most familiar with. A supreme court which accepts all appeals on 'points of law', such as the French Cour de Cassation, can be said to possess a high level of legitimacy in the sense, first, that it has fuller control over lower courts (and so can enforce its views on them) and, second, that it provides answers to a wide spectrum of legal queries. The fact of mass production means that its 'argumentive' or 'discursive' legitimacy (i.e. the persuasiveness of its reasoning) will inevitably be less, but this might be seen as of less importance.[81]

Another point made here, often associated with NGOs, relates to the level and seriousness of human rights violations in the three highest-count states, Russia, Turkey and Ukraine. The 'constitutional court' option can be viewed as an abandonment of the victims of human rights violations in these three states in particular, and so a denial of the *raison d'être* of a human rights court, established for the very purpose of addressing human rights violations.[82] Faced with the argument that the flood of cases will never stop, the response is that improvements are being made, shown, *inter alia*, by the recent improvement in remedies in Turkey, and that the creation of a *Rechtsstaat* is a slow process.

An argument can be made that giving the Court the option to pick and choose between cases would, according to some, involve it in moving

---

[80] Amongst many authorities, see I. Cameron, 'Protocol 11 to the ECHR: The European Court of Human Rights as a Constitutional Court?', *Yearbook of European Law* 15 (1995) 219–62; S. Greer, *The European Convention on Human Rights: Achievements, Problems and Prospects* (Cambridge University Press, 2006) at xv and *passim*; E. Bates, *The Evolution of the European Convention on Human Rights: From its Inception to the Creation of a Permanent Court of Human Rights* (Oxford University Press, 2010) 436–72; and J. Christoffersen, 'Individual and Constitutional Justice: Can the Power Balance of Adjudication be Reversed?', in J. Christoffersen and M.R. Madsen (eds.), *The European Court of Human Rights between Law and Politics* (Oxford University Press, 2011) 181–203, at 187–90.

[81] A. Pinna, 'Filtering Applications, the Number of Judgments Delivered and Judicial Decisions by Supreme Courts: Some Thoughts Based on the French Example', in Huls, Adams and Bornhoff (eds.), *The Legitimacy of Highest Courts' Rulings* at 181–2. She adds an argument that, from a common law perspective one can only describe as bizarre, namely, that it is the solution which counts, much less its external motivation. As controversial decisions will always be controversial, it does not really matter how well they are motivated (at 185).

[82] See, e.g., P. Leach, 'Access to the ECtHR – From a Legal Entitlement to a Lottery?', *Human Rights Law Journal* 27 (2006) 11–25.

away from 'objective' admissibility criteria into the realm of 'politics', and in 'negotiating' with states parties. Moreover, this is said to risk giving states parties the idea that certain human rights violations are less important (and therefore, more acceptable) than others.[83]

Writers coming from countries which accept a larger degree of judicial law-making, and who may also come from countries with relatively well-functioning systems of protection of human rights, have perhaps less difficulty in giving the Court the power to pick and choose amongst applications.

I agree with Michael O'Boyle when he states that 'the debate about possible restrictions on the right of individual petition is a false one, in which the passionate confront the pragmatic in a never ending discussion'.[84] He adds that the Evaluation Group, the Woolf and Wise Persons reports, never proposed such a step because the Court's existing differentiated system for dealing with applications has in fact found the 'right balance between maintaining the right of petition and weeding out unfounded applications'.[85]

The presentation of the existing filtering in section 4 above shows that there is already something resembling a *certiorari* system. Even before the introduction of the 'no significant disadvantage' rule, the manifestly ill-founded admissibility ground provides, *inter alia*, for the possibility of picking and choosing. It involves a discretionary decision by the Court that something is not a violation of the Convention.[86] It has existed from the beginning of the Convention system and is thus hardly 'alien' to it.

Moreover, the priority policy[87] means that, instead of picking and choosing individual cases, whole classes of complaint will not be addressed. In other words, the message has already gone out that some human rights violations *are* less important than others. But the priority policy affects the high-count states most. And to be cynical, the Court can put up with a degree of loss of legitimacy amongst complainants from these states. It does not want lots of inadmissible applications. And

---

[83] See above, section 3; and Barkhuysen and van Emmerik, 'Legitimacy', at 441, 448.
[84] O'Boyle, 'The Future', at 197.   [85] Ibid.
[86] Compare Harris *et al.*, who note that it covers 'a spectrum of standards', 'ranging from totally unmeritorious to no prima facie breach' and regard it as something of a misnomer '[how can] a case be rejected as *manifestly* ill-founded after extensive legal argument, often involving an oral hearing and a lengthy reasoned decision of the Court on which not all judges agree?': D.J. Harris *et al.*, *Law of the ECHR*, 2nd edn (Oxford University Press, 2009) at 785.
[87] Section 5.

even if it loses status, it will probably still have a higher status than the national supreme/constitutional courts in these states.

Wildhaber argues that the issue is really deciding what cases the Court should handle and what cases it should not. He proposes nine categories of cases, which, having been declared admissible, should be taken up for decisions on the merits, namely: (a) right to life, prohibition of torture, prohibition of slavery; (b) long periods of illegal detention; (c) wholly arbitrary and unfair procedures; (d) overruling of well-established ECtHR precedents; (e) issues gravely affecting national constitutions; (f) issues vital to the survival of a democracy and a democracy's right to defend itself against its enemies; (g) guidelines for structural and systemic problems; (h) pilot judgments; and (i) interstate applications.[88] To those who might argue that this is radical, he responds that, on the contrary, the end result would be similar to the system presently in force and that he is only being honest.

Of course, it is not a good argument to say that the Court should *become* more 'constitutional' because it is no longer capable of doing the job of dispensing individual justice. But I do not see Wildhaber's and others' similar arguments in this light. They are, rather, about finding a legitimate role for the Court where most states in the system have well-functioning national mechanisms and institutions for protecting human rights, but some states have very poor such remedies or mechanisms (and are not very democratic either).

What sort of Court should exist for such a situation? This is not easy to answer. It is tied up with the future accession of the EU to the ECHR. Speculation is beyond the scope of the present chapter. Suffice it to say that I do not think that the states parties, in the foreseeable future, will accept a Court where they do not have 'their own' judge. And once you have a Court of 47 judges, it naturally has to find something to do. Human rights, ultimately, are about controversial moral and political (resource distribution) issues. There will always be, and should be, room for disagreements between different political communities about these questions. Amongst – relatively – like-minded states there should thus be room for a body which can give an objective second opinion – in the form of a binding judgment – on the need for a particular restriction in a right in a concrete case.[89]

---

[88] L. Wildhaber, 'Rethinking the European Court of Human Rights', in Christoffersen and Madsen (eds.), *The European Court of Human Rights between Law and Politics*, 204–29 at 225.
[89] I look at some of these issues in more detail in 'Competing Rights?', *supra* note 69.

It is easier to answer the question: what sort of Court do the states parties want? They probably want a Court which gives them a clean bill of health while exposing all the other parties to searching scrutiny. This is obviously not possible. One can probably, albeit with a degree of arbitrariness, divide the 47 states parties into A, B and C groups with sliding scales of well-functioning rights protection systems. However, applying the 'Convention lite' to the 'A' group, the 'Convention normal' to the 'B' group and the 'Convention extreme' to the 'C' group is not possible either. On the contrary, even-handedness on the part of the Court is a vital part of its legitimacy. This will mean that there will be cases concerning states with otherwise well-functioning systems for rights protection where the Court will 'err' on the side of interference. These states will just have to put up with this.

Can one say that the Court continues to serve a function for states in the first category? I would echo the words of Lady Justice Arden, that the ECtHR does have an added value.[90] It subjects the institutions of the state to outside scrutiny, particularly important in states where there is a strong doctrine of parliamentary sovereignty, and there is (perceived) public pressure to take action against unpopular groups (e.g. suspected terrorists). Where an administrative decision involves a limitation on a Convention right, the ECHR can heighten the applicable administrative standards and/or lower the threshold for review by a domestic court. The existence of a supranational court, establishing human rights principles, empowers the domestic judiciary and strengthens their independence as against other institutions of their own state. The Convention system gives Europeans a legitimate interest in how other countries in Europe treat their citizens. Finally, the influence of the ECtHR stretches far beyond the shores of Europe.

But what does it have to do, procedurally, to maintain this role? Above all, the Court must remember that the people it most has to persuade are the national legislature, put in the irritating position of possibly having to amend its laws, and the national courts, trying to understand ECtHR case law to interpret national laws, or even more awkwardly, having to refuse to apply national law.

Here it is not admissibility which is at the centre of the Court's legitimacy, instead it is the quality and comprehensibility of the Court's

---

[90] ECtHR, *Dialogue between Judges 2010* (Strasbourg: Council of Europe, 2011), at 23.

reasoning in its judgments. This quality relates to the interpretation of the Convention, including how well it builds upon its own case law. It also means consistency in case law. The legitimacy of the Court is naturally also damaged if it misunderstands national law,[91] or goes against a national supreme or constitutional court and does not motivate its reasoning sufficiently.[92] Irritation can also be caused at national level where it explicitly reverses its own case law where a state has relied upon the earlier interpretation to frame its law.[93]

How the Court applies the principle of subsidiarity is also vital. This is a large issue, discussed by many. Suffice it to say here that the challenge to the Court, in every important case, is finding the right balance between 'guidance' and 'interference'. In drawing this balance, the Court has to remember that its case law operates not just *vis-à-vis* the respondent state, but states generally, and moreover, can affect the domestic power balance within states. I would say that, as long as it does this, the Court will perform a useful function. The radical changes that have been made in procedure mean that it can continue to 'muddle through'. The big changes necessary to reduce its caseload lie not in its hands, but in the hands of the high-count states. I do not see this changing in the next few years. If, as a direct or indirect result of the economic crisis, we see more authoritarian governments emerging and/or more violations of the rights of the disadvantaged, then we can expect new high-count states to join the present group. The huge caseload means that there are losers who

---

[91] See, e.g., the problems caused to the UK by the ruling in ECtHR, *Osman v. UK* (Appl. No. 23452/94), Judgment (Grand Chamber), 28 October 1998, Reports 1998-VIII, that it was violation of art. 6 for a court summarily to dismiss a case where it had been concluded that it was not fair, just or reasonable to impose a duty of care, later corrected in ECtHR, *Z and others v. UK* (Appl. No. 29392/95), Judgment (Grand Chamber), 10 May 2001, Reports 2001-V, paras. 87, 98 and 101.

[92] See ECtHR, *Von Hannover v. Germany* (Appl. No. 59320/00), Judgment (Third Section), 24 June 2004, Reports 2004-VI, which later caused the German Constitutional Court to amend its case law. However, the thinly motivated balance drawn in the case between integrity and freedom of expression has also proved problematic to states such as Sweden, which has a constitutional protection which favours the second over the first value. The Court later 'clarified' its judgment in ECtHR, *Von Hannover (No. 2) v. Germany* (Appl. Nos. 40660 and 60641/08), Judgment (Grand Chamber), 7 February 2012, Reports 2012.

[93] See, e.g., the problems caused for the Swedish system of administrative tax penalties by the explicit change in case law in ECtHR, *Zolotukhin v. Russia* (Appl. No. 14939/03), Judgment (Grand Chamber), 10 February 2009, Reports 2009.

will, with good reason, be disenchanted with the Court. The losers in the present system are those applicants who have a good case on the merits, but concerning an issue which is not a matter of priority. Adopting proposals such as Wildhaber's would not change this, but it would have the virtue of being honest with these applicants.

3

The margin of appreciation doctrine: a theoretical analysis of Strasbourg's variable geometry

YUTAKA ARAI-TAKAHASHI

1. Introduction

The concept of a margin of appreciation,[1] which has been developed in the jurisprudence of the European Convention on Human Rights (ECHR, or the Convention), suggests an ambit of discretion, 'latitude of deference or error',[2] or 'room for manoeuvre',[3] given to national authorities in assessing appropriate standards of the Convention rights, taking into account particular values and other distinct factors woven into the fabric of local laws and practice.

From the outset, the rationale for the margin of appreciation has been closely intertwined with the original conception that the Convention would be supplementary to national constitutional systems in their role

---

[1] For assessment of this doctrine, apart from the sources cited, see A. Ejima, 'Yoroppa Jinken-Saibansho-niokeru "Hyoka-no-yochi" Riron-no Aratana Hatten' ('New Development of the "Margin of Appreciation" Doctrine in the European Court of Human Rights'), *Meiji University Graduate School (Law) Review* 29 (1992) 55–73; E. Kastanas, *Unité et diversité: Notions Autonomes et Marge d'Appréciation des États dans la Jurisprudence de la Cour Européenne des droits de l'Homme* (Brussels: Bruylant, 1996); P. Lambert, 'Marge nationale d'appréciation et contrôle de proportionnalité', F. Sudre (ed.), *L'interprétation de la Convention Européenne des droits de l'Homme* (Brussels: Bruylant, 1998) 63–89; *Human Rights Law Journal* (1998) special issue, *The Doctrine of the Margin of Appreciation under the European Convention on Human Rights: Its Legitimacy in Theory and Application in Practice* (with contributions by P. Mahoney, J. Callewaert, C. Ovey, S. Prebensen, V. Winisdoerffer, J. Schokkenbroek and M. O'Boyle); T. Nishikata, 'Oushu-Jinken-Joyaku derogation-joko-to "Hyoka-no-Yochi": Jinken-Saibansho-no Tosei-wo Chushin-ni' ('The Derogation Clause of the ECHR – Judicial Control by the European Court of Human Rights'), *Kobe Hogaku-Zasshi (Kobe Law Journal)* 50:2 (2000) 149–86; S. van Drooghenbroeck, *La Proportionnalité dans le Droit de la Convention Européenne des Droits de l'Homme – Prendre l'idée Simple au Sérieux* (Brussels: Bruylant, 2001) 483–548.
[2] H.C. Yourow, *The Margin of Appreciation Doctrine in the Dynamics of European Human Rights Jurisprudence* (The Hague: Martinus Nijhoff Publishers, 1996), at 13.
[3] S. Greer, *The Margin of Appreciation: Interpretation and Discretion under the European Convention on Human Rights*, Human Rights Files No. 17, (Strasbourg: Council of Europe, 2000) (hereinafter Greer, *The Margin of Appreciation*), at 5.

in safeguarding fundamental rights. With the concept of sovereignty embedded in the consciousness of drafters, it was contemplated that the ECHR as an international treaty would serve as the lowest common denominator among diverse member states. The judges in Strasbourg have been aware that the enforcement of their judgment and decisions has to rely ultimately on the good faith and cooperation of the contracting states.[4] Since the inception, this consideration has impacted upon the judicial policy of the Strasbourg organs (the European Court of Human Rights (ECtHR, or the Court) and the erstwhile European Commission of Human Rights) in mitigating 'damaging confrontations' between them and the member states by allocating 'spheres of authority'.[5]

This chapter begins by outlining a genealogical development of this doctrine. Its analysis then turns to the nature of the doctrine and the main strands of criticisms levelled at its *modus operandi*. Next, it provides analytical accounts of the circumstances in which this doctrine operates. Numerous commentators have already examined a margin of appreciation doctrine, at times exploring its rational structure[6] or its relevance in a global context.[7] The doctrine has invited by far more

---

[4] Waldock noted that '[t]he doctrine of the "margin of appreciation" ... is one of the more important safeguards developed by the Commission and the Court to reconcile the effective operation of the Convention with the sovereign powers and responsibilities of governments in a democracy': H. Waldock, 'The Effectiveness of the System set up by the European Convention on Human Rights', *Human Rights Law Journal* 1 (1980) 1–12, at 9.

[5] Macdonald emphasises that the process of realising a Europe-wide system of human rights protection and the 'uniform standard' of human rights must be 'gradual' because: 'the entire legal framework rests on the fragile foundations of the consent of the Contracting Parties. The margin of appreciation gives the flexibility needed to avoid damaging confrontations between the Court and Contracting States over their respective spheres of authority and enables the Court to balance the sovereignty of Contracting Parties with their obligations under the Convention.' R.St.J. Macdonald, 'The Margin of Appreciation', in R.St.J. Macdonald, F. Matscher and H. Petzold (eds.), *The European System for the Protection of Human Rights* (Dordrecht, London: Martinus Nijhoff, 1993) (hereinafter Macdonald, 'The Margin of Appreciation') 83–124, at 123.

[6] G. Letsas, 'Two Concepts of the Margin of Appreciation', *Oxford Journal of Legal Studies* 26:4 (2006) (hereinafter Letsas, 'Two Concepts of the Margin of Appreciation') 705–32; G. Letsas, *A Theory of Interpretation of the European Convention on Human Rights* (Oxford University Press, 2007) (hereinafter Letsas, *A Theory of Interpretation*) 80–98; F. Tulkens and L. Donnay, 'L'Usage de la Marge d'Appréciation par la Cour Européenne des Droits de l'Homme. Paravent Juridique Superflu ou Mécanisme Indispensable par Nature?', *Revue de Science Criminelle et de Droit Pénal Comparé* 1 (2006), at 3–23.

[7] E. Brems, 'The Margin of Appreciation Doctrine in the Case-Law of the European Court of Human Rights', *Zeitschrift für Ausländisches Öffentliches Recht und Völkerrecht* 56:1–2 (1996) (hereinafter Brems, 'The Margin of Appreciation') 240–314; and Y. Shany, 'Toward a General Margin of Appreciation Doctrine in International Law?',

criticism than praise.[8] For this reason, we need to examine at length the main strands of criticisms before shifting our analysis to some positive features that this chapter defends in later sections. By undertaking theoretical inquiries into the nature and the function of the margin of appreciation doctrine, this chapter aims to ascertain sustainable rationales for the application of this doctrine in the ECHR context.

2. The origin and development of a margin of appreciation

2.1 The doctrinal mimesis from theories of administrative discretion

It is possible to argue that the margin of appreciation, conceived as the doctrine of discretion given to national authorities, has developed as a doctrinal mimesis of comparable theories on administrative discretion under national administrative laws. The pervasiveness of discourses on the variable scope of a margin of appreciation is a clear indication of the impact that the doctrines on national public law have had on the discourse on international human rights law.[9] However, it is clear that while they represent the cases of isomorphism, structurally there is an important difference between the margin of appreciation and the doctrine of administrative discretion. On one hand, the former deals with the 'downward' deference given to the national authorities in the vertical relationship between international and national organs. On the other hand, the doctrines on administrative discretion serve on a horizontal level in the domestic context, and they explain the inter-governmental distribution of power in terms of discretion given by the judiciary to administrative agents.

The doctrine on administrative discretion can be found in the jurisprudence of all the systems of administrative law within civil law jurisdictions.[10] Among them, the highly systematised and refined doctrinal

---

European Journal of International Law 16:5 (2005) (hereinafter Shany, 'Toward a General Margin of Appreciation Doctrine') 907-40.

[8] See P. Mahoney, 'Marvellous Richness of Diversity or Invidious Cultural Relativism?', *Human Rights Law Journal* 19:1 (1998) (hereinafter Mahoney, 'Marvellous Richness of Diversity') 1-6.

[9] P.G. Carozza, 'Subsidiarity as a Structural Principle of International Human Rights Law', *American Journal of International Law* 97 (2003) 38-79 (hereinafter Carozza, 'Subsidiarity'), at 62.

[10] F. Matscher, 'Methods of Interpretation of the Convention', in Macdonald *et al.* (eds.), *The European System for the Protection of Human Rights*, 63-81, at 76.

discourses on administrative discretion in Germany stand out.[11] Nevertheless, the German administrative courts are distinctly much more intent on narrowing the parameters of administrative discretion (*Ermessensspielraum*) than the French counterparts, or the ECtHR when invoking the notion of a margin of appreciation.[12] The conceptual dimension of a margin of appreciation is covalent with the doctrines on variable intensity/standard of review,[13] deference, and judicial self-restraint[14] that have been fleshed out in the US Supreme Court's jurisprudence.[15]

2.2 The genesis and evolution of a margin of appreciation in the jurisprudence of the ECHR

The first seed of the margin of appreciation doctrine was sown in the context of a derogation clause under the ECHR. The Commission probably never foresaw that its casual reference to the term 'a certain measure of discretion', which the UK authorities were allowed to exercise in evaluating the proportionality of a derogating measure in relation to the exigency in the then British colony of Cyprus, heralded the inception

---

[11] See A. Bleckmann, 'Der Beurteilungsspielraum in Europa – und im Völkerrecht', *Europäische Grundrechte Zeitschrift* (1979) 485–95, at 490–2, and the literature cited in *infra*. n. 38; G. Nolte, 'General Principles of German and European Administrative Law – A Comparison in Historical Perspective', *Modern Law Review* 57 (1994) 191–212; and S. Oeter, 'Die Kontrolldichte hinsichtlich unbestimmter Begriffe und des Ermessens', J.A. Frowein (ed.), *Die Kontrolldichte bei der gerichtlichen Überprüfung von Handlungen der Verwaltung* (Berlin: Springer, 1993), at 266–77. For a comparative examination of German administrative law and common law, see M.P. Singh, *German Administrative Law – In Common Law Perspective*, 2nd edn (Berlin: Springer, 2001).

[12] See Y. Arai-Takahashi, 'Administrative Discretion in German Law: Doctrinal Discourse Revisited', *European Public Law* 6:1 (2000) 69–80 (hereinafter Arai-Takahashi, 'Administrative Discretion in German Law'); and Y. Arai-Takahashi, *The Margin of Appreciation Doctrine and the Principle of Proportionality in the Jurisprudence of the ECHR* (Antwerp: Intersentia, 2002) (hereinafter Arai-Takahashi, *The Margin of Appreciation*), at 3.

[13] Macdonald, 'The Margin of Appreciation', at 84; and T. O'Donnell, 'The Margin of Appreciation Doctrine: Standards in the Jurisprudence of the European Court of Human Rights', *Human Rights Quarterly* 4 (1982) 474–96, at 478.

[14] *Ibid.*, at 477.

[15] Judicial deference is understood as a form of judicial restraint that debars international judges from examining *de novo* and second-guessing the decisions reached by the national authorities: Letsas, 'Two Concepts of the Margin of Appreciation', at 722. Indeed, in Victorian England, Jeremy Bentham had already intimated the constitutional constraint on the right of judges to annul laws enacted by the Parliament: J. Bentham, 'A Fragment on Government', in F.C. Montague (ed.), *A Fragment of Government* (Oxford: Clarendon Press, 1891), at 221, para. XXXII.

of a long 'saga' of one of the most controversial doctrines of the ECHR.[16] Shortly afterwards, this rudimentary concept was replicated by the Court in the *Lawless* case, where the Irish government was accorded 'a certain discretion – a certain margin of appreciation' in assessing the existence of public emergency.[17] Any denominational doubt over this crude formula was soon to be settled in favour of the term 'margin of appreciation' in the subsequent case of *Ireland* v. *UK*, where the Court recognised the sliding scale on which the ambit of margin would vary. There, the national authorities confronted with emergency circumstances were given a 'wide margin of appreciation' in assessing: first, the 'fact-intensive' and more epistemic question of the existence or otherwise of an emergency; and second, a more technical question of the nature and scope of derogating measures chosen to stave it off.[18]

Retrospectively, the first invocation of this concept *outside the context of derogation* was almost accidental. This was in the Norwegian case relating to forced labour under article 4, in which the Commission drew an analogy of a state of emergency under article 15 in relation to the dire shortage of dentists in a sparsely populated region.[19] Thereafter, until the late 1970s, the Strasbourg organs' application of the concept of margin of appreciation was experimental. The concept remained far from being a 'doctrine'. Their underlying thought on the margin of appreciation was closely tied to the concept of subsidiarity. This can be gleaned from the

---

[16] ECommHR, *Greece* v. *UK (Cyprus* Case) (Appl. No. 176/56), YB 2 (1958–9), 174, at 176.
[17] ECommHR, *Lawless* v. *Ireland* (Appl. No. 332/57), Report (Commission), 19 December 1959, Series. Vol. 1 (1960–1), at 82.
[18] ECtHR, *Ireland* v. *UK* (Appl. No. 5310/71), Judgment (Plenary), 18 January 1978, Series A, Vol. 25, para. 207.
[19] The relevant paragraph reads as follows:

> the Commission has frequently held that, although a certain margin of appreciation should be given to a government in determining the existence of a public emergency within the meaning of Article 15 in its own country, the Commission has the competence and the duty to examine and pronounce upon the consistency with the Convention of a government's determination of this question ... in the analogous circumstances of the present case, the Commission cannot question the judgment of the Norwegian Government and Parliament as to the existence of an emergency as there is evidence before the Commission showing reasonable grounds for such judgment.

ECommHR, *Iversen* v. *Norway* (Appl. No. 1468/62), Decision (Commission), 17 December 1963, YB 6 (1963), 278, at 330.

Belgian Linguistic case, concerning the right to education under article 2 of the First Protocol, as well as the principle of non-discrimination under article 14.[20] The Court recognised the intrinsically subsidiary nature of its European supervision with respect to regulations of the system of education.[21] Thereafter, the experimental spheres of the margin of appreciation were expanded to cover issues of the freedom of peaceful assembly and association under article 11, with specific regard to trade union activities.[22]

Subsequently, the concept of a margin of appreciation has been spread in a spectacular manner in relation to substantive rights provisions, in particular due process guarantees under articles 5–6[23] and the 'personal freedom' rights under articles 8–11,[24] and two supplementary provisions of articles 13 and 14.[25] The rationales for the dynamic evolution of this concept were most saliently spelt out in cases addressing the limitation clauses under articles 8–11 and article 1 of the First Protocol.

---

[20] The Commission emphasised that the first sentence of art. 2 of the Protocol allows states 'a certain discretion' with regard to the measures to be taken to secure the enjoyment of the right guaranteed: ECommHR, *Case relating to Certain Aspects of the Laws on the Use of Languages in Education in Belgium* (*Belgian Linguistic* case) (Appl. Nos. 1474, 1677 and 1691/62), Report (Commission), 24 June 1965, Series B, Vol. 3, at 307, para. 401.

[21] The Court noted as follows:

> The right to education guaranteed by the first sentence of Article 2 of the Protocol by its very nature calls for regulation by the State, regulation which may vary in time and place according to the needs and resources of the community and of individuals. It goes without saying that such regulation must never injure the substance of the right to education nor conflict with other rights enshrined in the Convention.

ECtHR, *Belgian Linguistic* case, para. 5. See also *ibid.*, para. 10.

[22] The Strasbourg organs allowed the national authorities 'a free choice of means' to realise the interests of trade unions: ECtHR, *Union of Belgian Police* v. *Belgium* (Appl. No. 4464/70), Judgment (Plenary), 27 October 1975, Series A, Vol. 19, para. 39; ECtHR, *Swedish Engine Drivers' Union* v. *Sweden* (Appl. No. 5614/72), Judgment (Chamber), 6 February 1976, Series A, Vol. 20, para. 40; and ECtHR, *Schmidt and Dahlström* v. *Sweden* (Appl. No. 5589/72), Judgment (Chamber), 6 February 1976, Series A, Vol. 21, para. 36.

[23] ECtHR, *Engel and Others* v. *The Netherlands (Article 50)* (Appl. Nos. 5100, 5101 and 5102/71; 5354 and 5370/72), Judgment (Plenary), 8 June 1976, Series A, Vol. 22, para. 72.

[24] The first recourse to this concept was seen in ECtHR, *De Wilde, Ooms and Versyp* v. *Belgium* (*Vagrancy* case) (Appl. Nos. 2832, 2835 and 2899/66), Judgment (Plenary), 18 June 1971, Series A, Vol. 12, para. 93. See also ECtHR, *Golder* v. *UK* (Appl. No. 4451/70), Judgment (Plenary), 21 February 1975, Series A, Vol. 18, para. 45 (restrictions on the right to correspondence).

[25] As is well known, Protocol No. 12 has made art. 14 a stand-alone, substantive right for the states parties to this protocol.

Among them, the Court's famous dictum in the *Handyside* case has spelt out the deferential approach that endorsed the latitudes of national discretion in assessing the concept 'necessary in a democratic society' under the limitation clause of article 10. More precisely, a national margin of appreciation was recognised in assessing whether there existed 'pressing social need' that would warrant interference for the alleged purpose of protecting 'public morals':

> it is not possible to find in the domestic law of the various Contracting States a uniform European conception of morals. The view taken by their respective laws of the requirements of morals varies from time to time and from place to place, especially in our era which is characterised by a rapid and far-reaching evolution of opinions on the subject. By reason of their direct and continuous contact with the vital forces of their countries, State authorities are in principle in a better position than the international judge to give an opinion on the exact content of these requirements as well as on the 'necessity' of a 'restriction' or 'penalty' intended to meet them. The Court notes at this juncture that whilst the adjective 'necessary', within the meaning of Article 10 § 2, is not synonymous with 'indispensable' [cf. in Articles 2 § 2 and 6 § 1, the words 'absolutely necessary' and 'strictly necessary' and, in Article 15 § 1, the phrase 'to the extent strictly required by the exigencies of the situation'], neither has it the flexibility of such expressions as 'admissible', 'ordinary' [cf. Article 4 § 3], 'useful' [cf. the French text of the first paragraph of Article 1 of Protocol No. 1], 'reasonable' [cf. Articles 5 § 3 and 6 § 1] or 'desirable'. Nevertheless, it is for the national authorities to make the initial assessment of the reality of the pressing social need implied by the notion of 'necessity' in this context. Consequently, Article 10 § 2 leaves to the Contracting States a margin of appreciation. This margin is given both to the domestic legislator ['prescribed by law'] and to the bodies, judicial amongst others, that are called upon to interpret and apply the laws in force ...[26]

With hindsight, the *Handyside* judgment has provided the prototype of 'margin' analysis not only in the context of the limitation clauses,[27] but also in any other context. For that reason, it is only since that *cause célèbre* that it has become fairly justifiable to consider a margin of appreciation as a 'doctrine'.

---

[26] ECtHR, *Handyside v. UK* (Appl. No. 5493/72), Judgment (Plenary), 7 December 1976, Series A, Vol. 24, para. 48.

[27] These include not only the second paragraphs of arts. 8–11, but also the third paragraph of art. 2 of Protocol No. 4. A similar formula can be seen in respect of the right to property guaranteed in art. 1 of the First Protocol and art. 1 of Protocol No. 7.

3. Analysing the circumstances in which the margin of appreciation may be invoked

3.1 Overview

Analytically, the main contours of debates on the margin of appreciation take shape in five processes: (i) the process of fact-finding and ascertainment of fact; (ii) the process of interpreting and applying national laws; (iii) the process of evaluating the conceptual parameters of a specific ECHR right and applying them in relation to a specific issue arising from a member state's concrete (measure to implement) laws; (iv) the process of balancing between an individual person's right and a public interest ground, including the evaluation of the means to achieve the social ends sought after;[28] and (v) weighing in balance two competing rights and freedoms. The second process is related to the question of interpretive disagreements over a specific human rights norm, the profound question that in turn gives rise to judicial discretion. The third process links the first phase of empirical questions with the second phase of delineating the ambit of Convention rights. This process necessitates examining specific (measures of) national laws in the light of the 'autonomous' standards of the ECHR rights. The fourth and fifth processes of balancing appear most frequently in the assessment of the limitation clauses appertaining to articles 8–11 ECHR and article 1 of the First Protocol.

3.2 The process of fact-finding and ascertainment of fact

The first pattern of the operation of the margin of appreciation is seen in relation to the discretion given to national or local authorities in ascertaining relevant facts because of their greater access to information and social forces at hand.[29] Deference to national decisions is corroborated by the comparative advantage of local administrative authorities in fact-finding.[30]

---

[28] Shany, 'Toward a General Margin of Appreciation Doctrine', at 917, 935.
[29] Carozza, 'Subsidiarity', at 73; and Judge Dean Spielmann, 'Allowing the Right Margin the European Court of Human Rights and the National Margin of Appreciation Doctrine: Waiver or Subsidiarity of European Review?', CELS Working Paper Series, February 2012 (hereinafter Spielmann, 'Allowing the Right Margin'), available at www.cels.law.cam.ac.uk, at 8–9. In essence, this is what Greer calls the 'implementation discretion': S. Greer, 'Constitutionalising Adjudication under the European Convention on Human Rights', Oxford Journal of Legal Studies 23 (2003) 405–33 (hereinafter Greer, 'Constitutionalising Adjudication'), at 423.
[30] Shany, 'Toward a General Margin of Appreciation Doctrine', at 927.

In this respect, the Court has consistently held that 'it is not normally within the province of the European Court to substitute its own assessment of the facts for that of the domestic courts and as a general rule, it is for these courts to assess the evidence before them'.[31] The most salient examples would be the assessment of 'fact-intensive' elements. These include a state of emergency that would authorise a member state to invoke the derogation clause under article 15, evidence for criminal convictions, and 'evaluative' concepts susceptible of greater room for subjectivity,[32] such as sexual propriety and obscenity.[33] As a result, arguably the most lax form of review can be exhibited by the Court in those areas.[34]

Nevertheless, several caveats ought to be entered. Clearly, the assertion that this phase is altogether 'value-free' or 'ideologically neutral or free'[35] is contestable. The manner in which empirical data are amassed with the reconstruction of past reality can be susceptible to subjective evaluations. Further, even in respect of such a process of gathering factual information, the Court reserves the right to second-guess the outcomes of national assessment.[36]

3.3 The process of evaluating national laws

Akin to the evaluation of questions of fact, the appraisal of domestic law is in principle considered to fall outside the scope of the Court's review. The consistent jurisprudence amply demonstrates that 'it is in the first place for the national authorities, and in particular the courts of first instance and appeal, to construe and apply the domestic law'.[37] This

---

[31] See, for instance, ECtHR, *Klaas v. Germany* (Appl. No. 15473/89), Judgment (Chamber), 22 September 1993, Series A, Vol. 269, para. 29.

[32] Compare this, however, with E. Voyiakis, 'International Law and the Objectivity of Value', *Leiden Journal of International Law* 22:1 (2009) 51–78 (hereinafter Voyiakis, 'International Law').

[33] Compare, for instance, ECtHR, *Müller and Others v. Switzerland* (Appl. No. 10737/84), Judgment (Chamber), 24 May 1988, Series A, Vol. 133; and ECtHR, *Vereinigung Bildender Künstler v. Austria* (Appl. No. 68354/01), Judgment (First Section), 25 January 2007, not reported.

[34] See, for instance, ECtHR, *Pla and Puncernau v. Andorra* (Appl. No. 69498/01), Judgment (Fourth Section), 13 July 2004, Reports 2004-VIII, para. 46 (holding that the Court's review can intervene only when 'the national courts' assessment of the facts ... were manifestly unreasonable or arbitrary or blatantly inconsistent with the fundamental principles of the Convention').

[35] Shany, 'Toward a General Margin of Appreciation Doctrine', at 937.

[36] See Spielmann, 'Allowing the Right Margin', at 8.

[37] See, *inter alia*, ECtHR, *Winterwerp v. The Netherlands* (Appl. No. 6301/73), Judgment (Chamber), 24 October 1979, Series A, Vol. 33, at 20, para. 46; ECtHR, *Iglesias Gil and*

process necessitates the evaluation of national policy choices in relation to socio-economic issues under article 1 of the First Protocol.[38] The second phase can be integrated into the first process of evaluating empirical data. As such, this phase is also amenable to a deferential approach. The Strasbourg Court's intervention tends to be confined to cases where national assessment is regarded as 'manifestly unreasonable or arbitrary',[39] or 'manifestly without reasonable foundation'.[40]

3.4 The process of evaluating the human rights norms in the ECHR

This phase essentially concerns the interpretation of the terms of ECHR rights and the determination of their meaning and scope. Human rights law, while providing 'deontological constraints' and pulling judicial decisions in the direction of optimising rights, does not prescribe their content and ambit exhaustively.[41] Indeed, despite inexorable increase in normative instruments and monitoring mechanisms of international human rights law both at universal and regional levels, it remains the case that one of the most conspicuous weaknesses of the current human rights system is the 'lack of a thick normative content', that is, the question of indeterminacy of human rights concepts.[42] Hence, there remains ineluctably a measure of interpretive latitudes for determining their scope and meaning, and for reconciling conflicting liberties in case of clashes between them. In the ECHR context, where the normative ambit and meaning of a human rights norm is indefinite, the Court is receptive to the deferential policy, on the ground that national authorities

---

AUI v. Spain (Appl. No. 56673/00), Judgment (Fourth Section), 29 April 2003, Reports 2003-V, para. 61; ECtHR, *Slivenko v. Latvia* (Appl. No. 48321/99), Judgment (Grand Chamber), 9 October 2003, Reports 2003-X, para. 105; and *Pla and Puncernau v. Andorra*, para. 46.

[38] See, inter alia, ECtHR, *James and Others v. United Kingdom* (Appl. No. 8793/79), Judgment (Plenary), 21 February 1986, Series A, Vol. 98, at 32, para. 46; ECtHR, *Former King of Greece and Others v. Greece* (Appl. No. 25701/94), Judgment (Grand Chamber), 23 November 2000, Reports 2000-XII, para. 87; ECtHR, *Zvolsky and Zvolska v. The Czech Republic* (Appl. No. 46129/99), Judgment (Second Section), 12 November 2002, Reports 2002-IX, para. 67 *in fine*; and ECtHR, *Jahn and Others v. Germany* (Appl. Nos. 46720/99, 72203 and 72552/01), Judgment (Grand Chamber), 30 June 2005, Reports 2005-VI, para. 91.

[39] *Pla and Puncernau v. Andorra*, para. 46.   [40] *Jahn and Others v. Germany*, para. 91.

[41] G. Pavlakos, 'Constitutional Rights, Balancing and the Structure of Autonomy', *Canadian Journal of Law and Jurisprudence* 24:1 (2011) 129–54 (hereinafter Pavlakos, 'Constitutional Rights'), at 132.

[42] Carozza, 'Subsidiarity', at 58–9, 62.

are better placed to ascertain concrete measures implementing the abstract Convention right in specific circumstances.[43] The problem of ambiguity of some human rights norms remains unresolved, not least because of the absence of 'common social or moral order' in Europe that would serve as a metric for normative guidance.[44]

Human rights norms are often deliberately drafted in a general and ambiguous manner to accommodate multiple eventualities in the future.[45] Such an open-ended norm encompasses: (i) an ill-defined or inherently ambiguous norm;[46] and (ii) an intrinsically discretion-conferring norm.[47] Legal norms inherently entail what Waismann and Hart describe as an 'open texture'.[48] Hart explains that '[w]hichever

---

[43] In the context of minority rights protection, see P. Keller, 'Re-thinking Ethnic and Cultural Rights in Europe', *Oxford Journal of Legal Studies* 18 (1998) 29–59, at 52–3.

[44] S. Wheatley, 'Minorities under the ECHR and the Construction of a "Democratic Society"', *Public Law* (2007) 770–92 (hereinafter Wheatley, 'Minorities'), at 789. The line of argument is redolent of the hermeneutic postulation that the pre-understanding of judges, which is shaped by 'the shared topoi of an ethical tradition' serves to forge 'the flexible connections between norms and states of affairs' on the basis of 'received, and historically corroborated principles': J. Habermas, *Between Facts and Norms* (Cambridge, MA: MIT Press, 1996) (hereinafter Habermas, *Between Facts*), at 200.

[45] Shany, 'Toward a General Margin of Appreciation Doctrine', at 910. See ECtHR, *Odièvre v. France* (Appl. No. 42326/98), Judgment (Grand Chamber), 13 February 2003, Reports 2003-III, para. 40; ECtHR, *Boso v. Italy* (Appl. No. 50490/99), Decision (First Section), 5 September 2002, Reports 2002-VII; and ECtHR, *Vo v. France* (Appl. No. 53924/00), Judgment (Grand Chamber), 8 July 2004, Reports 2004-VIII, para. 82 (recognising that 'the issue of when the right to life begins comes within the margin of appreciation which the Court generally considers that states should enjoy in this sphere, notwithstanding an evolutive interpretation of the Convention').

[46] For instance, see the notion of 'protection of ... morals' under art. 8(2) ECHR. For the discussions on the German public law doctrine on indefinite norms (*unbestimmte Begriffe*), see Arai-Takahashi, 'Administrative Discretion in German Law'.

[47] Shany calls this a 'result-oriented norm': Shany, 'Toward a General Margin of Appreciation Doctrine', at 917. When analysing the theory of the margin of appreciation in the *general* context of international law, Shany argues that special features of the result-oriented norms are that: (i) these norms are indifferent to the manner in which a desired legal end is attained, insofar as its attainment is guaranteed; (ii) state authorities are given discretion over choice of means and manner of implementing such norms; and (iii) the path to the desired social/public end is uncertain: *ibid*.

[48] H.L.A. Hart, *The Concept of Law*, 2nd edn (Oxford University Press, 1994) (hereinafter Hart, *The Concept of Law*), at 127–8. Brian Bix explains that the term 'open texture' derives from the idea of the same name proposed by Waismann, a colleague of Hart's at Oxford: B. Bix, 'Questions in Legal Interpretation', in A. Marmor (ed.), *Law and Interpretation: Essays in Legal Philosophy* (Oxford: Clarendon Press, 1995) 137–54, at 138. See also B. Bix, *Law, Language, and Legal Determinacy* (Oxford: Clarendon Press, 1993), at 7–17.

device ... is chosen for the communication of standards of behaviour, these, however smoothly they work over the great mass of ordinary cases, will, at some point where their application is in question, prove indeterminate; they will have what has been termed an *open texture*.[49] In a different work, he refers to 'problems of the penumbra' or 'a penumbra of uncertainty' that surround all legal rules, which make it hard to assert that the application of legal rules to specific cases is merely a matter of logical deduction or automation.[50] Hart accepts that uncertainty and indeterminacy concerning the requirement of the law is inevitably susceptible to adjudicative discretion.[51] In his view, if a legal norm lacks 'objective' content (namely, an objectively correct answer to what the norm requires), then judges are given a scope of discretion to determine the content of the norm on the basis of extralegal considerations, including moral and political values.[52] Where moral norms lack 'objective'

---

[49] Hart, *The Concept of Law*, at 127–8, emphasis in the original.

[50] H.L.A. Hart, 'Positivism and the Separation of Law and Morals', *Harvard Law Review* 71 (1957) 593–629 (hereinafter Hart, 'Positivism'), at 607–8. In cases where legal disputes raise a question of law concerning a rule's open texture, 'uncertainties as to the form of behaviour required by them may break out in particular concrete cases': Hart, *The Concept of Law*, at 126.

[51] Hart observes that 'In every legal system a large and important field is left open for the exercise of discretion by courts and other officials in rendering initially vague standards determinate, in resolving the uncertainties of statutes, or in developing and qualifying rules only broadly communicated by authoritative precedents': *ibid.*, at 136.

In another work, he aptly observes that:

> The point must be not merely that a judicial decision to be rational must be made in the light of some conception of what ought to be, but that the aims, the social policies and purposes to which judges should appeal if their decisions are to be rational, are themselves to be considered as part of the law in some suitably wide sense of 'law' which is held to be more illuminating than that used by the Utilitarians.
>
> [...]
>
> ...instead of saying that the recurrence of penumbral questions shows us that legal rules are essentially incomplete, and that, when they fail to determine decisions, judges must legislate and so exercise a creative choice between alternatives, we shall say that the social policies which guide the judges' choice are in a sense there for them to discover; the judges are only 'drawing out' of the rule what ... is 'latent' within it.

Hart, 'Positivism', at 612. However, he is careful in stating that to describe such judicial role of 'drawing out' as judicial legislation 'is to obscure some essential continuity between the clear cases of the rule's application and the penumbral decisions': *ibid.*

[52] He argues that 'if it is an open question whether moral principles and values have objective standing, it must also be an open question whether 'soft positivist' provisions

standing, as they often do, then the only way, according to Hart, to give effect to a legal norm entailing moral language, is to construe it as guiding judges to exercise their 'law-making discretion' in harmony with their 'best understanding of morality'.[53] In essence, receptiveness of such indefinite or discretion-giving norms to a margin of appreciation can be explained by the difficulty in evaluating the moral, political and other value-laden considerations underlying such norms.

3.5 The process of balancing individual persons' rights and public interest grounds

Arguably, the application of a margin of appreciation is most discernible and tenacious in this phase of balancing. The national authorities may be given latitudes of discretion in ascertaining the means (types, suitability, proportionality, etc.) to attain social objectives in a particular factual circumstance.[54] This corresponds to the process of what Greer[55] terms 'structured balancing' between a right and a public good, or of reconciling clashes between rights. Similarly, Letsas' 'substantive concept of the margin of appreciation' doctrine is set in motion to rationalise the relationship between rights of individual persons and the collective interests.[56] It ought to be noted that the term 'margin of appreciation' in this context might be redundant if the

---

purporting to include conformity with them among the tests for existing law can have that effect or instead, can only constitute directions to courts to make law in accordance with morality': Hart, *The Concept of Law*, at 253–4. See also K.E. Himma, 'Inclusive Legal Positivism', in J. Coleman and S. Shapiro (eds.), *The Oxford Handbook of Jurisprudence and Philosophy of Law* (Oxford University Press, 2002) 125–65, at 145–6.

[53] Hart, *The Concept of Law*, at 253.

[54] Shany, 'Toward a General Margin of Appreciation Doctrine', at 917 and 935. In this phase, for instance, the proportionality of incriminating measure (penalty) may be assessed.

[55] S. Greer, '"Balancing" and the European Court of Human Rights: A Contribution to the Habermas-Alexy Debate', *Cambridge Law Journal* 63 (2004) 412–34, at 434.

[56] Letsas, 'Two Concepts of the Margin of Appreciation', at 709. Letsas distinguishes between the 'structural' and 'substantive' concepts of the margin of appreciation. The structural concept refers to the limit of the review conducted by the Court and the scope of discretion given to the national authorities on the basis of the vertical relationship between the Court and the national authorities. On the other hand, Letsas contemplates that the 'substantive concept of the margin of appreciation' adverts to interpretive discretion in the area of substantive moral issues, such as the appropriate balance to be struck between an individual person's right and the public interest as a whole: *ibid.*, at 705–32; and Letsas, 'A Theory of Interpretation', at 80–1, 84–92.

notion of a 'fair balance' that the Court has frequently invoked were more systematic and coherent.[57]

When weighing the rights of individual persons against public goods essential to the Convention's 'constitutional' order, the Court ought to provide a considered judgment based on substantive moral arguments.[58] As noted by some commentators,[59] the variable margin as a means to adjust the intensity of its review has much to do with the Court's struggle to make a hard choice of political morality when it is grappling with a complex balance of values between community goals and individual persons' rights.[60] The propensity for a deferential approach is enhanced, where decisions entail complex policy or political issues that are closely bound up not merely with the demand of sovereignty, but with that of legitimacy of the national or local community.[61] Alexy recognises that decision-makers enjoy 'structural discretion' when assessing competing interests that are crudely of equal weight and where a single answer is unlikely to be inferred from a balancing appraisal.[62]

---

[57] Compare A. Mowbray, 'A Study of the Principle of Fair Balance in the Jurisprudence of the European Court of Human Rights', *Human Rights Law Review* 10 (2010) 289–317 (hereinafter Mowbray, 'A Study of the Principle of Fair Balance'), at 289 (describing this notion as a 'principle').

[58] Letsas, 'Two Concepts of the Margin of Appreciation', at 709. In the *Refah partisi* case, the Court affirmed that '[p]luralism and democracy are based on a compromise that requires various concessions by individuals or groups of individuals, who must sometimes agree to limit some of the freedoms they enjoy in order to guarantee greater stability of the country as a whole': ECtHR, *Refah partisi (The Welfare Party) and Others* v. *Turkey* (Appl. Nos. 41340, 41342 and 41343/98), Judgment (Grand Chamber), 13 February 2003, Reports 2003-II, para. 99.

[59] Mowbray, 'A Study of the Principle of Fair Balance', at 316. See also Carozza, 'Subsidiarity', at 73.

[60] The restrained review standard has been discerned in cases regarding town planning, social and economic policy issues (including the transition from a community system to a free-market economy), the manner of taking cultural property into public ownership: *Sporrong and Lönnroth* v. *Sweden* (Appl. Nos. 7151 and 7152/75), Judgment (Plenary), 23 September 1982, Series A, Vol. 52; *Broniowski* v. *Poland* (Appl. No. 31443/96), Judgment (Grand Chamber), 22 June 2004, Reports 2004-V. Compare these with *Kozacıoğlu* v. *Turkey* (Appl. No. 2334/03), Judgment (Grand Chamber), 19 February 2009, para. 53 (confirming the general principle that 'Finding it natural that the margin of appreciation available to the legislature in implementing social and economic policies should be a wide one, the Court will respect the legislature's judgment as to what is "in the public interest" unless that judgment is manifestly without reasonable foundation'; yet the Court finding a proportionate balance to be upset).

[61] Mowbray, 'A Study of the Principle of Fair Balance', at 316.

[62] R. Alexy, *A Theory of Constitutional Rights* (Oxford University Press, 2002) (hereinafter Alexy, *A Theory of Constitutional Rights*), at 414–25. See also M. Kumm, 'Constitutional

With respect to non-derogable rights, there is no scope of balancing, with the width of a margin of appreciation shrinking to zero.[63] Judge Spielmann of the ECtHR affirms that 'the margin of appreciation is virtually inexistent when it comes to the non-derogable rights' (right to life, prohibition of torture, prohibition of slavery and forced labour, prohibition of retroactive legislation, the *ne bis in idem* rule).[64] What is more, deontological critics, including Ronald Dworkin, who proposes individual persons' rights as 'trumps',[65] are averse to the idea of balancing with respect to all human rights, be they non-derogable or not. These critics may consider that all human rights are unsusceptible of balancing.[66] After all, the central tenet of Dworkin's thesis is to place emphasis on the singular nature of human rights.[67] Along this line, other

---

Rights as Principles: On the Structure and Domain of Constitutional Justice' – A Review Essay on *A Theory of Constitutional Rights*', *International Journal of Constitutional Law* 2:3 (2004) 574–96 (hereinafter Kumm, 'Constitutional Rights as Principles'), at 581 and 588. Finnis argues that in a 'hard case', the requirements of moral soundness and *fit* in Ronald Dworkin's theory of interpretation leave more than one answer that is morally and legally '*not wrong*', allowing leeway of discretion to those that interpret laws: J. Finnis, 'Natural Law: The Classical Tradition', in Coleman and Shapiro (eds.), *The Oxford Handbook of Jurisprudence and Philosophy of Law*, 1–60, at 36. According to Dworkin, 'hard cases' are discernible in instances where 'reasonable lawyers' disagree and 'where no settled rule dictates a decision either way': R. Dworkin, *Taking Rights Seriously* (London: Duckworth, 1977) (hereinafter Dworkin, *Taking Rights Seriously*), at xiv and 83.

[63] For instance, in cases involving anticipatory form of torture, the Court has consistently treated as irrelevant the conduct of applicants at issue, including the claim that they are allegedly posing a threat to national security: see ECtHR, *Chahal* v. *UK* (Appl. No. 22414/93), Judgment (Grand Chamber), 15 November 1996, Reports 1996-V, para. 80; and ECtHR, *Saadi* v. *Italy* (Appl. No. 37201/06), Judgment (Grand Chamber), 28 February 2008, Reports 2008, para. 138.

[64] Spielmann, 'Allowing the Right Margin', at 11.

[65] R. Dworkin, 'Rights as Trumps', in J. Waldron (ed.), *Theories of Rights* (Oxford University Press, 1984) 153–67. See also, M. Cohen-Eliya and I. Porat, 'The Hidden Foreign Law Debate in Heller: The Proportionality Approach in American Constitutional Law', *San Diego Law Review* 46:2 (2009) 367–413, at 395 (arguing that 'American constitutional culture holds a more traditional view of rights as strong trumps or side constraints vis-à-vis government action', and that this 'is the result of the great suspicion with which both government and the judiciary are regarded').

[66] See also Rawls' theory based on 'priority of the right over the good': J. Rawls, *Political Liberalism* (New York: Columbia University Press, 1993), at 173; and Kumm, 'Constitutional Rights as Principles', at 590 (considering that this strand of thought can ultimately trace its origin to Immanuel Kant's theory premised on the ideas of dignity and autonomy as opposed to the collective interference of 'the good').

[67] See, for instance, R. Dworkin, 'Even Bigots and Holocaust Deniers Must Have Their Say', *The Guardian*, 14 February 2006 (concerning the highly controversial Danish cartoons lampooning the Prophet Mohamed).

authors criticise the process of balancing for dispensing with, or worse, even impairing, substantive rationalisation based on political morality.[68] In the present author's view, when invoking a margin of appreciation in assessing the balance between a human right and a social end, the Court should provide moral rationales that can help delineate the boundaries of individual persons' autonomy within the emerging 'constitutional' framework of the ECHR.[69]

3.6 The balance between competing rights and freedoms

The margin of appreciation can also serve to demarcate the conceptual parameters of two rival rights and liberties claimed by individual persons. This operational sphere is not dissimilar to the cases in which the margin of appreciation is invoked to assess a reasonable or fair balance between an individual person's right and the common good. Mowbray observes that weighing in balance the rights at stake, as well as the gains and losses of different individuals involved in the national legal system, is 'an exceptionally difficult exercise' that calls for, 'in the nature of things, a wide margin of appreciation'.[70]

A clash of rights can be exemplified in a number of cases, including the case of conflict between the privacy right grounded under article 8 and the freedom of expression of the media enunciated under article 10.[71] The discordance between two countervailing rights can also be contemplated in the case of limitations on the right of access of biological parents to their

---

[68] See, for instance, S. Tsakyrakis, 'Proportionality: An Assault on Human Rights?: A Rejoinder to Madhav Khosla', *International Journal of Constitutional Law* 8:2 (2010) 307–10, at 309.
[69] Compare Pavlakos, 'Constitutional Rights'. One can postulate that the Court's balancing is a species of 'constitutional rights reasoning', and that it is in the process of 'constitutionalising' the ECHR, that is, transforming the normative significance of this regional human rights treaty into a systematic, uniform and vertical normative order grounded on effective guarantees of human rights in Europe.
[70] Mowbray, 'A Study of the Principle of Fair Balance', at 313.
[71] See, for instance, ECtHR, *Axel Springer AG v. Germany* (Appl. No. 39954/08), Judgment (Grand Chamber), 7 February 2012, not reported, para. 88; and ECtHR, *Von Hannover v. Germany (No. 2)* (Appl. Nos. 40660 and 60641/08), Judgment (Grand Chamber), 7 February 2012, not reported, para. 107. See also ECtHR, *Palomo Sánchez and Others v. Spain* (Appl. Nos. 28955, 28957, 28959 and 28964/06), Judgment (Grand Chamber), 12 September 2011, Reports 2011, para. 57 (the clash between the right to honour and reputation and free speech); and ECtHR, *MGN Limited v. The United Kingdom* (Appl. No. 39401/04), Judgment (Fourth Section), 18 January 2011 (breach of confidentiality and the free speech right of the press), not reported, paras. 150 and 155.

children placed in foster parents' custody,[72] and in the case of a welfare authority's intervention to remove a child from his/her natural parents on the basis of emergency (or normal) care orders. In those cases disputed under article 8, the social-democratic ethos of national societies that prioritise the well-being of children may contravene the idea of privacy and family life (including natural parents' access to their children).[73] Further, a similarly intractable friction of two rights is discernible in case of the national measures to constrain Holocaust denials, and other genres of odious hate speeches.[74] Given the special historical experience, it is legitimate to be vigilant of the virulent and rampant dissemination of neo-Nazi or other extremist publications in many continental European countries.

4. Main strands of criticism against the margin of appreciation doctrine

4.1 Overview

The margin of appreciation is a judge-made doctrine that lacks explicit legal basis in the Convention text.[75] As an interpretive technique of

---

[72] See, *inter alia*, ECtHR, *Olsson v. Sweden (No. 1)* (Appl. No. 10465/83), Judgment (Plenary), 24 March 1988, Series A, Vol. 130; ECtHR, *Eriksson v. Sweden* (Appl. No. 11373/85), Judgment (Plenary), 22 June 1989, Series A, Vol. 156; ECtHR, *Margareta and Roger Andersson v. Sweden* (Appl. No. 12963/87), Judgment (Chamber), 25 February 1992, Series A, Vol. 226-A; ECtHR, *Johansen v. Norway* (Appl. No. 17383/90), Judgment (Chamber), 7 August 1996, Reports 1996-III; and ECtHR, *K and T v. Finland* (Appl. No. 25702/94), Judgment (Grand Chamber), 12 July 2001, Reports 2001-VII.

[73] See, *inter alia*, ECtHR, *Elsholz v. Germany* (Appl. No. 25735/94), Judgment (Grand Chamber), 13 July 2000, Reports 2000-VIII, para. 49 (examination under art. 8 of the question of father's right to access to a child born out of wedlock, after his relationship with child's mother broke up); and ECtHR, *Sahin v. Germany* (Appl. No. 30943/96), Judgment (Grand Chamber), 8 July 2003 (a father's right of access to a child born out of wedlock, examined under art. 14 taken in tandem with art. 8), not reported. See also ECtHR, *K and T v. Finland* (Appl. No. 25702/94), Judgment (Grand Chamber), 12 July 2001, Reports 2001-VII (an emergency care order and a normal care order in relation to a psychiatrically ill mother).

[74] ECtHR, *Lehideux and Isorni v. France* (Appl. No. 24662/94), Judgment (Grand Chamber), 23 September 1998, Reports 1998-VII; ECtHR, *Garaudy v. France* (Appl. No. 65831/01), Decision (Fourth Section), 24 June 2003, Reports 2003-IX; ECtHR, *Chauvy v. France* (Appl. No. 64915/01), Judgment (Second Section), 29 June 2004, Reports 2004-VI. Compare ECtHR, *Monnat v. Switzerland* (Appl. No. 73604/01), Judgment (Third Section), 21 September 2006, Reports 2006-X. See also Human Rights Committee (HRC), *Robert Faurisson v. France*, Communication No. 550/1993, Decision on Admissibility, 19 July 1995; Decision on the Merits, 8 November 1996, UN Doc. CCPR/C/58/D/550/1993 (1996).

[75] Spielmann, 'Allowing the Right Margin', at 2.

adjudicative justification in a specific case, the margin of appreciation doctrine is criticised for furnishing only 'a very thin analytical basis' for a systematic politico-legal or 'constitutional' thinking of the ECHR rights.[76] The Strasbourg Court's judicial self-restraint based on a broad margin of appreciation may go so far as to be approximated to such a lax test as 'the test for reasonableness [that] signifies little more than a lack of arbitrariness'.[77] Without succumbing to legal scepticism, one might even contend that lurking beneath the application of the margin of appreciation doctrine is the presumptive *Conventionnalité* of national measures. Such a presumption may weigh heavily on the onus of proof required of individual applicants. As noted in the Introduction, in view of the prevalence of criticisms levelled at the use of this doctrine in the existing literature, it is of special importance to summarise several strands of criticisms.

4.2 Diluting normative expectation and inconsistent human rights standards

First, the margin of appreciation doctrine is condemned for its inconsistent and opaque modality of operation.[78] Vagueness and indeterminacy of normative meaning might stultify the rationality expectation.[79] The proponents of the certainty of legal rules charge the doctrine for vitiating

---

[76] Carozza, 'Subsidiarity', at 69–70; Greer, 'The Margin of Appreciation', at 32; Lord Lester of Herne Hill, 'Universal versus Subsidiarity: A Reply', *European Human Rights Law Review* (1998) 73–81, at 75; O. de Schutter, 'L'Interprétation de la Convention Européenne des Droits de l'Homme: un Essai en Démolition', *Revue de Droit International de Sciences Diplomatiques, Politiques, et Sociales* 70 (1992) 83–127.

[77] P. Keller, 'Re-thinking Ethnic and Cultural Rights in Europe', *Oxford Journal of Legal Studies* 18 (1998) 29–59, at 52–3. See also the *Wednesbury* unreasonableness principle established in English law: G. de Búrca, 'The Influence of European Legal Concepts on UK Law: Proportionality and Wednesbury Unreasonableness', *European Public Law* 3 (1993) 561–87; *Associated Provincial Picture Houses Ltd v. Wednesbury Corporation* [1948] 1 KB 223. This principle was largely criticised as giving too much deference to unreasonable agents without articulating principled criteria: A. Lester, 'Beyond *Wednesbury*: Substantive Principles of Administrative Law', *Public Law* (1987) 368.

[78] The inconsistent element is most salient seen in the case law on art. 10 ECHR. For the *causes célèbres* featuring incoherency, contrast, for instance, the case law on national security grounds: ECtHR, *The Sunday Times v. UK (No. 2) (Spycatcher* case*)* (Appl. No. 13166/87), Judgment (Plenary), 26 November 1991, Series A, Vol. 217, and the case law relating to public morality grounds: ECtHR, *Wingrove v. UK* (Appl. No. 17419/90), Judgment (Chamber), 25 November 1996, Reports 1996-V.

[79] J.A. Brauch, 'The Margin of Appreciation and the Jurisprudence of the European Court of Human Rights: Threat to the Rule of Law', *Columbia Journal of European Law* 11

the normative guidance of substantive rights provisions of the ECHR[80] and fostering normative ambiguity. Lord Lester forcefully argues that in the context of article 10 ECHR, 'its [the Court's] reasoning has always suffered from a use of ad hoc balancing under the margin of appreciation doctrine which lacks legal certainty and adherence to clear principles'.[81] The ambiguity in human rights standards that are cumulatively brought about by the case law might negatively impact upon the dignity of individual persons in concrete cases by failing to respect their autonomy.[82] As a corollary of such normative erosion, there is a risk that the overall effectiveness in safeguarding the Convention rights might be undermined. Further, the standards of the Convention rights might be differently applied in the seemingly similar cases,[83] leading to inconsistent standards of human rights.[84]

4.3 Non-accountability and corrosive effect on the rule of law

Second, such a proneness to diluting normative expectation might in turn handicap the development of judge-made law and have a potentially damaging implication for the very legitimacy of the Court.[85] Excessive reliance on the judicial self-restraint rationale risks fostering a habit of non-accountability[86] and abdicating the supervisory role of the

---

(2004–5) 113–50 (hereinafter Brauch, 'The Margin of Appreciation'), at 148. Compare K. Kress, 'Legal Indeterminacy', *California Law Review* 77 (1989) 283–337, at 285–95.

[80] Shany, 'Toward a General Margin of Appreciation Doctrine', at 937.

[81] Lord Lester of Herne Hill, 'The European Court of Human Rights after 50 Years', *European Human Rights Law Review* 4 (2009) 461–78, at 474.

[82] See J. Raz, *The Authority of Law* (Oxford: Clarendon Press, 1979), at 222.

[83] E. Benvenisti, 'Margin of Appreciation, Consensus, and Universal Standards', *New York University Journal of International Law and Politics* 31 (1998–9) 843–54 (hereinafter Benvenisti, 'Margin of Appreciation'), at 844. See also F. Ní Aoláin, 'The Emergence of Diversity: Differences in Human Rights Jurisprudence', *Fordham International Law Journal* 19 (1995–6) 101–42 (hereinafter Ní Aoláin, 'The Emergence of Diversity'), at 114, 119.

[84] Benvenisti, 'Margin of Appreciation'; and D. McGoldrick, 'Multiculturalism and its Discontents', *Human Rights Law Review* 5 (2005) 27–56 (hereinafter McGoldrick, 'Multiculturalism').

[85] Shany, 'Toward a General Margin of Appreciation Doctrine', at 922–3. See also Spielmann, 'Allowing the Right Margin', at 28.

[86] Compare the discussions on the Framework Convention for the Protection of National Minorities: C.F. Furtado, Jr. 'Guess Who's Coming to Dinner? Protection for National Minorities in Eastern and Central Europe under the Council of Europe', *Columbia Human Rights Law Review* 34 (2003) 333–412, at 364–5.

Court.[87] In essence, the weakening normative guidance might yield a corrosive effect on the overarching principle of the rule of law.[88]

4.4 Subjective and relativist standards and risk of fragmentation

Third, as threadbare as it may be, the application of the doctrine might be seen as furtively introducing subjective and relativist standards into treaty provisions of human rights treaties, formal sources of international law. In other words, a margin of appreciation might be deployed as a conceptual 'Trojan horse' for the purpose of fragmenting the unity and harmony of the established Convention standards. Such a potential risk would run counter to the universal claim, 'universalising project', of human rights.[89] Precisely for this reason, in *Z v. Finland*, Judge De Meyer, in his Partly Dissenting Opinion, noted that 'I believe that it is high time for the court to banish that concept [of margin of appreciation] from its reasoning. It has already delayed too long in abandoning this hackneyed phrase and recanting the relativism it implies.'[90] Such a tendency would risk generating judicial double standard,[91] unfairness[92] or bias.[93] The Court might err on the side of becoming altogether obtuse over such serious consequences.

4.5 Strategies to address the criticisms

These strands of criticisms are levelled mainly at the doctrine's modality of application. In the present writer's view, the bulk of such criticisms can be addressed by a tripartite strategy: (i) clarifying the normative nature of

---

[87] Brauch argues that 'The empty phrases concerning the states' margin of appreciation – repeated in the court's judgments for too long already – are unnecessary circumlocutions, serving only to indicate abstrusely that the States may do anything the Court does not consider incompatible with human rights': Brauch, 'The Margin of Appreciation', at 148.

[88] For such a strand of criticism, see, for instance, *ibid.*, at 125. See also P. Macklem, 'Militant Democracy, Legal Pluralism, and the Paradox of Self-Determination', *International Journal of Constitutional Law* 4 (2006) 488–516.

[89] Benvenisti, 'Margin of Appreciation', at 843–4; and McGoldrick, 'Multiculturalism', at 55.

[90] ECtHR, *Z v. Finland* (Appl. No. 22009/93), Judgment (Chamber), 25 February 1997, Reports 1997-I, Partly Dissenting Opinion of Judge De Meyer, Section III.

[91] Benvenisti, 'Margin of Appreciation', at 844. See also Ní Aoláin, 'The Emergence of Diversity', at 114, 119 (suggesting that states that adhere to democratic principles can be subject to less exacting scrutiny).

[92] Shany, 'Toward a General Margin of Appreciation Doctrine', at 912.

[93] Benvenisti, 'Margin of Appreciation', at 850; and Shany, 'Toward a General Margin of Appreciation Doctrine', at 923–4.

a margin of appreciation doctrine; (ii) structurally locating the doctrine's place in the ECHR's 'constitutional' normative order, which can address the question of institutional competence (who should assume the final responsibility for this question: national v. European, and judicial or non-judicial organs, etc.);[94] and (iii) identifying robust substantive rationales that underlie the application of a margin of appreciation.

5. Determining the nature of the margin of appreciation

5.1 The margin of appreciation as a principle?

Many commentators agree that a margin of appreciation, as an evaluative concept, should not be treated sophomorically as a rhetorical device for window-dressing. Instead, this concept, as a fruit of the conscientious judicial policy of the ECtHR, is worthy of serious theoretical explanations in respect of its nature and underlying rationales.[95] Our examinations will turn first to the question whether a margin of appreciation can be described as a general *principle* governing the entire corpus of the ECHR. For that purpose, we will make a brief inquiry into what features characterise *principles* in the normative order.

Dworkin stresses that many standards other than 'rules' are operative within the legal order, including 'principles, policies and other sorts of standards'. Principles or policies are not part of the law, but are treated more as 'extra-legal standards'.[96] He describes a principle as 'a standard that is to be observed, not because it will advance or secure an economic, political, or social situation deemed desirable, but because it is a requirement of justice or fairness or some other dimension of morality'.[97]

The first and foremost special trait of principles is the malleable nature of its normative force. This can be illustrated by Robert Alexy's idea of

---

[94] S. Greer, 'What's Wrong with the European Convention on Human Rights?', *Human Rights Quarterly* 30 (2008) 680–702 (hereinafter Greer, 'What's Wrong with the ECHR?'), at 696. See also J. Rivers, 'Proportionality and Variable Intensity of Review', *Cambridge Law Journal* 65:1 (2006) 174–207 (hereinafter Rivers, 'Proportionality'), at 207 (arguing that '[j]udicial deference and restraint are both practically required and constitutionally appropriate as expression of the different institutional competences and legitimacy of governmental powers in the joint project of rendering rights definitive').

[95] Cohen-Eliya and Porat contend that the margin of appreciation, together with proportionality, constitutes a 'standard-based doctrine': M. Cohen-Eliya and I. Porat, 'Proportionality and the Culture of Justification', *American Journal of Comparative Law* 59:2 (2010) 463–90 (hereinafter Cohen-Eliya and Porat, 'Proportionality'), at 468.

[96] Dworkin, *Taking Rights Seriously*, at 35.   [97] *Ibid.*, at 22.

principles as 'optimization requirements' that 'can be satisfied to varying degrees'. The amenable nature of a principle suggests its capacity of greater resilience. Hence, it can survive intact, even in circumstances where it cannot prevailingly provide a basis for a precise normative outcome.[98]

The malleable nature of principles is all the more ascertainable when they are compared to rules. Building his theoretical framework on the assumption that constitutional rights are hybrids of rules and principles,[99] Alexy argues that in contrast to rules that are considered to entail 'definitive commands', principles are 'reasons for concrete ought-judgment'[100] that represent 'norms requiring that something be realized to the greatest extent possible, given the factual and legal possibilities at hand'.[101] Similarly, for Ronald Dworkin, in contrast to a 'rule' that is inclined to stipulate a discrete resolution because of its specificity and concrete character, a principle 'states a reason that argues in one direction, but does not necessitate a particular decision'. According to Dworkin, a principle is susceptible to evaluations in terms of its relative importance. This marks a contrast to a rule that operates in an all-or-nothing manner, so that the conflict of rules is resolved by allowing one to supersede the other.[102] Further, a principle is deemed more receptive than a rule to moral reasoning in the inclusive positivist sense.[103] Put differently, it is generally considered that the proclivity to be backed up by some substantive rationales is more potent for principles than with respect to rules.

While susceptible of flexible interpretation, principles are capable of foreseeing normative outcomes with relative consistency, the capacity

---

[98] This can be contrasted to rules, which may be changed, or fall into desuetude, when drastically failing to dictate their normative direction and outcomes, such as in the case where a contrary result continues to be yielded: Dworkin, *ibid.*, at 35-6.

[99] See K. Möller, 'Balancing and the Structure of Constitutional Rights', *International Journal of Constitutional Law* 5:3 (2007) 453-68, at 456.

[100] Alexy, 'A Theory of Constitutional Rights', at 60. Kumm usefully summarises Alexy's characterisation of principles as an 'ideal-ought': Kumm, 'Constitutional Rights as Principles', at 577.

[101] R. Alexy, 'The Construction of Constitutional Rights', *Law and Ethics of Human Rights* 4 (2010) 20-32, at 21. See also Alexy, 'A Theory of Constitutional Rights', at 47-8 and 57.

[102] Dworkin, *Taking Rights Seriously*, at 24, and 26-7.

[103] J. Waldron, 'Judges as Moral Reasoners', *International Journal of Constitutional Law* 7 (2009) 2-24 (hereinafter Waldron, 'Judges as Moral Reasoners'), at 10. See also E. Sherwin, 'Rule-Oriented Realism', *Michigan Law Review* 103 (2005) 1578-94, at 1591 (contending that 'the rule-sensitive particularism [which highlights evaluating an ideal outcome according to available reasons] does not treat rules as *constraints* in judicial reasoning; rather, it calls on judges to give appropriate weight to the value of rules in the process of unconstrained moral reasoning'; emphasis in original).

that tends to be lacking in respect of the margin of appreciation. For instance, in some instances, the Court has invoked the notion 'margin of appreciation' only as a rhetorical tool. In other words, the Court's express reference to this notion has had little bearing on the actual course of its review.[104] In those cases, the allusion to this notion gives a façade or pretence of 'assurance' to national authorities against a possible criticism of what they may perceive as unfounded judicial activism, while in reality the Court does not hesitate to engage itself in stringent scrutiny. The notion of a margin of appreciation used as a rhetorical tool is diametrically opposite to the idea of illocutionary function that the language of legal terms is expected to undertake.[105] These considerations cast a certain doubt on this notion's eligibility for a fully-fledged 'principle'.

5.2 The margin of appreciation as a 'principle of secondary order'

Greer furnishes a distinct theoretical framework within which he classifies the margin of appreciation, together with proportionality and

---

[104] See, *inter alia*, ECtHR, *A v. Norway* (Appl. No. 28070/06), Judgment (First Section), 9 April 2009, not reported, paras. 66 and 74 (the right to reputation in respect of defamation under art. 8); ECtHR, *Holy Synod of the Bulgarian Orthodox Church (Metropolitan Inokentiy) and Others v. Bulgaria* (Appl. Nos. 412/03 and 35677/04), Judgment (Fifth Section), 22 January 2009, not reported, paras. 119, 131 and 159 (finding a disproportionate interference with the leadership disputes in the Bulgarian Orthodox Church, notwithstanding 'a wide margin of appreciation' left to the national authorities states in regulating its relations with religious communities); ECtHR, *SH and Others v. Austria* (Appl. No. 57813/00), Judgment (First Section), 1 April 2010, paras. 69, 89–90, 92–4 (dispute over the ban on heterologous artificial procreation techniques for *in vitro* fertilisation under the Austrian Artificial Procreation Act, examined under art. 14 taken together with art. 8; overturned by the Grand Chamber's judgment of 3 November 2011); and ECtHR, *Hutten-Czapska v. Poland* (Appl. No. 35014/97), Judgment (Grand Chamber), 19 June 2006, Reports 2006-VIII, paras. 165, 166, 223 and 224 (rebuking the laws imposing tenancy agreements and setting an inadequate amount of rent as a violation of art. 1 of Protocol No. 1, despite a broad margin of appreciation that the domestic authorities enjoyed in implementing social and economic policies in the post-community era). Compare *Times Newspapers Ltd (Nos. 1 and 2) v. UK* (Appl. Nos. 3002 and 23676/03), Judgment (Fourth Section), 10 March 2009, Reports 2009, paras. 43, 45, 46–9 (the Court undertaking a relatively meticulous examination of the case in question, albeit finding no violation of art. 10 and recognising the national margin of appreciation in setting limitation periods for libel actions).

[105] Wittgenstein considers uses of words as moves in language games. According to him, words are not labels that can be pinned down to concrete objects, and their meaning can be determined by rules for their use: T.A.O. Endicott, 'Law and Language', in Coleman and Shapiro (eds.), *The Oxford Handbook of Jurisprudence and Philosophy of Law* 935–68, at 946–7 and 949.

non-discrimination, as forming the body of 'secondary principles' of the ECHR. According to him, such second-order principles supplement the three 'primary constitutional principles': the 'rights' principle; the 'democracy' principle; and 'the priority-to-rights' principle.[106] In Greer's view, the 'rights principle' requires that in democracy, the Convention rights ought to be safeguarded by national courts and the ECtHR through the medium of law. The 'democracy principle' then demands that collective ends be sought after by democratically accountable national non-judicial organs. The 'priority-to-rights principle' (or 'priority principle') in turn functions as the mediator between these two principles. It requires that the Convention rights 'take procedural and evidential, but not conclusive, priority over the democratic pursuit of the public interest, according to the terms of given Convention provisions'.[107] This principle will impose an onerous burden of proof on respondent states to rationalise their meddling with individual persons' rights.[108] In a more nuanced manner, Kumm argues that 'The priority of rights can only mean that individual rights should not be treated lightly but should be given the weight they deserve within a general conception of political justice grounded in the basic ideas of dignity and autonomy.'[109] According to Greer, the 'legality' principle (or the 'rule of law' principle), while worthy of being categorised as the fourth primary constitutional principle, is fully integral to each of the three principles.[110] Greer's panoply of those 'primary principles' in his theoretical framework is instrumental in systematically accounting for the emerging, 'constitutional' pillars of the ECHR. In his structure, when classified as a 'secondary principle', a margin of appreciation is an 'inferred' principle of interpretation[111] that is ancillary to the 'primary principles' that govern the entire edifice of the ECHR. For the purpose of shedding more light on normative features of a margin of appreciation as a 'secondary principle', this chapter will turn to another strand of explanations.

---

[106] Greer, 'What's Wrong with the ECHR?', at 697.   [107] Ibid.
[108] Ibid., at 700.   [109] Kumm, 'Constitutional Rights as Principles', at 591.
[110] Greer, 'What's Wrong with the ECHR?', at 697.
[111] It can be contended that though there is no explicit basis for this doctrine, its genesis owes much to the way in which the Convention rights are structured, in particular, in respect of the limitation and derogation clauses: Brauch, 'The Margin of Appreciation', at 116. Note that in the Lüth case, the German Federal Constitutional Court (Bundesverfassungsgericht, or BVerfG) found that the principle of proportionality can be deduced from the very nature of the constitutional rights themselves: Lüth, Bundesverfassungsgericht (BVerfG), 15 January 1958, 7 Entscheidung des Bundesverfassungsgerichts (BVerfGE) 198 (concerning the freedom of opinion).

5.3 The margin of appreciation as a policy standard

This author agrees with Greer's view that a margin of appreciation is a 'secondary' or 'auxiliary' principle that is short of a 'fully-fledged' principle. Still, it will be argued that a margin of appreciation can most fittingly be characterised as a 'policy standard' that emanates from the conscious decisional choice of the Court. Distinguishing it from a 'principle' in a narrow sense,[112] Dworkin defines a 'policy' or a 'policy standard' as a 'kind of standard that sets out a goal to be reached, generally an improvement in some economic, political, or social feature of the community'.[113] A margin of appreciation can be deemed as an inevitable spin-off of the notion of balancing inherent in the Convention (between two clashing Convention rights, or between a Convention right and a public purpose). An adjunct nature of the margin of appreciation can also be corroborated by the view that this is an expression of the principle of good faith within the meaning of article 31 of the Vienna Convention on the Law of Treaties, whereby a member state is entrusted with addressing 'hard cases' in a municipal context.[114]

As compared with a principle, a policy standard is equipped with two salient traits that can fit the description of a margin of appreciation in respect of its operational modality and normative feature. First, a 'policy standard' (or simply, a 'policy') entails normative advantages of a principle such as flexibility and resilience. Still, a policy standard is even more malleable than a principle.[115] Second, as compared with a principle, a policy standard does not require itself to be an outcome of the Court's deliberations on overarching moral rationales. Instead, it is not excluded that a policy standard may be predicated solely on the Court's utilitarian calculation of judicial economy or other considerations of expediency.[116]

---

[112] Admittedly, Dworkin occasionally employs the term 'principles' generically to refer to all those normative standards other than rules. Yet, in the main, he segregates a 'policy' from a principle: Dworkin, *Taking Rights Seriously*, at 22.

[113] *Ibid.*

[114] Crema describes the concept of margin of appreciation as an expression of the principle of good faith within the meaning of art. 31 of the Vienna Convention on the Law of Treaties, granting to a state the room to address hard cases: L. Crema, 'Disappearance and New Sightings of Restrictive Interpretation(s)', *European Journal of International Law* 21 (2010) 681–700, at 699.

[115] Dworkin at times employs the terms 'principles' to refer to any other extra-legal standards that operate in adjudication: Dworkin, *Taking Rights Seriously*, at 22.

[116] Indeed, it can be submitted that this ought to be the interpretive ethic of all monitoring bodies of human rights treaties: see G. Letsas, 'Strasbourg's Interpretive Ethic: Lessons for the International Lawyer', *European Journal of International Law* 21 (2010) 509–41,

In other words, a policy standard is not bound as strictly as a principle ought to be, by the idea that the judicial reasoning marshalled in human rights decision-making should articulate a coherent set of arguments on underlying political morality.[117]

6. The normative relationship between a margin of appreciation, European consensus and evolutive interpretation

As is well known, one of the rational premises that the Court has consistently invoked to vindicate the application of a margin of appreciation is the absence of 'European consensus'.[118] The complexity in ascertaining a particular matter closely related to a social policy of each national society may be compounded by the evolution of scientific progress and of corresponding social opinions. The lack of European consensus in regulatory approaches, due to different cultural interpretation

---

at 520 (arguing that 'The Court's interpretive ethic became one of looking at the substance of the human right at issue and the moral value it serves in a democratic society, rather than engaging in linguistic exercises about the meaning of words or in empirical searches about the intentions of drafters').

[117] Ronald Dworkin characterises the judicial review undertaken by the US Supreme Court as being of the kind that ensures that 'the most fundamental issues of political morality' will be examined as 'issues of principles and not political power alone': R. Dworkin, *A Matter of Principle* (Cambridge, MA: Harvard University Press, 1985), at 70.

[118] See, *inter alia*, ECtHR, *X, Y and Z* v. *UK* (Appl. No. 21830/93), Judgment (Grand Chamber), 22 April 1997, Reports 1997-II (the right of a post-operational transsexual to be registered as the parent of a child conceived by artificial insemination); ECtHR, *Stjerna* v. *Finland* (Appl. No. 18131/91), Judgment (Chamber), 25 November 1994, Series A, Vol. 299-B (condition on change of surname); ECtHR, *Otto-Preminger-Institut* v. *Austria* (Appl. No. 13470/87), Judgment (Chamber), 20 September 1994, Series A, Vol. 295-A; ECtHR, *Wingrove* v. *UK* (Appl. No. 17419/90), Judgment (Chamber), 25 November 1996, Reports 1996-V (relative significance of freedom of religion as compared with freedom of expression); ECtHR, *Odièvre* v. *France* (Appl. No. 42326/98), Judgment (Grand Chamber), 13 February 2003, Reports 2003-III, see, in particular, the French government's pleading at para. 37, and para. 15 of the Joint Dissenting Opinion of Judges Wildhaber, Sir Nicolas Bratza, Bonello, Loucaides, Cabral Barreto, Tulkens and Pellonpää. Still, see the ground-breaking decision in *Christine Goodwin* v. *UK*, where the Court found sufficient European consensus to depart from its earlier conservative stance to recognise the rights of transsexuals under art. 8: ECtHR, *Christine Goodwin* v. *UK* (Appl. No. 28957/95), Judgment (Grand Chamber), 11 July 2002, Reports 2002-VI. Though in principle not entailing a margin of appreciation because the case involved alleged violation of art. 3 (in relation to the minimum age of criminal responsibility), the absence of such a consensus was used as a rationale for rejecting the claim: ECtHR, *T* v. *United Kingdom* (Appl. No. 24724/94), Judgment (Grand Chamber), 16 December 1999, not reported, paras. 71–2.

and understanding of the matter, rationalises the Court's deference and the non-substitution principle (namely, the Court's decision not to substitute its view for a national understanding). There is no European consensus on such issues as the impact of human embryo research on the beginning of human life,[119] and IVF treatment, including ova donation for IVF[120] and rights of a mother to bear an offspring once her eggs are fertilised through IVF treatment.[121] Even so, one ought to add a caveat that in the case of ostensibly excessive measures affecting the Convention right of fundamental importance, the Court may feel uninhibited to jettison the deferential approach based on the lack of European 'consensus' and to embark on an assertive policy of review.[122]

It ought to be highlighted that the Court identifies such European consensus in its own 'objectivised' manner. The concept 'European consensus' is different from mere numerical majority of the member states. Indeed, this is related to a more substantive idea.[123] For instance, in some cases the Court's identification of the evolving European consensus, on closer inspection, is altogether independent of the empirical data. Such consensus may remain flimsy,[124] or it may have yet to be rigorously tested.[125]

---

[119] ECtHR, *Vo v. France* (Appl. No. 53924/00), Judgment (Grand Chamber), 8 July 2004, Reports 2004-VIII, paras. 78, 82 and 85. Compare ECommHR, *H v. Norway* (Appl. No. 17004/90), Decision (Commission), 19 May 1992; and ECtHR, *Boso v. Italy* (Appl. No. 50490/99), Decision (First Section), 5 September 2002, Reports 2002-VII.

[120] ECtHR, *SH and Others v. Austria*, paras. 97 and 106.

[121] ECtHR, *Evans v. UK* (Appl. No. 6339/05), Judgment (Grand Chamber) 10 April 2007, Reports 2007-I, paras. 77–8, 80–2, 85, 90 and 92.

[122] In this light, see, for instance, ECtHR, *Hirst v. UK (No. 2)* (Appl. No. 74025/01), Judgment (Grand Chamber), 6 October 2005, Reports 2005-IX, para. 81 (the Court holding that 'even if no common European approach to the problem [of the exclusion of convicted prisoners from voting in national and local elections] can be discerned, this cannot in itself be determinative of the issue').

[123] See G. Letsas, 'The Truth in Autonomous Concepts: How to Interpret the ECHR', *European Journal of International Law* 15 (2004) 279–305; and Letsas, Chapter 4, this volume.

[124] Such a pattern may risk crossing the borderline between interpretation and invention of a rule and becoming arbitrary: R. Dworkin, *Law's Empire* (Oxford: Hart Publishing, 1986) (hereinafter Dworkin, *Law's Empire*), at 66.

[125] This has been seen in cases of discrimination against illegitimate children. See, for instance, *Marckx v. Belgium*, in which the Court noted that the existence of the European treaties aimed at removing discrimination against 'illegitimate' children was 'a clear measure of common ground', despite the small number of states parties to those treaties: ECtHR, *Marckx v. Belgium* (Appl. No. 6833/74), Judgment (Plenary), 13 June 1979, Series A, Vol. 31, para. 41.

THE MARGIN OF APPRECIATION DOCTRINE   89

In contrast to the propensity for judicial self-restraint that appears in the absence of such European consensus, once such 'consensus' is ascertained, this can warrant a teleological step to deploy evolutive interpretation assertively in favour of uniform (namely, harmonised) and autonomous European standards. This line of reasoning is consonant with Mahoney's suggestion that the margin of appreciation and evolutive interpretation operate on the flip sides of the same coin.[126] When applying the margin of appreciation, the Court may be signalling a message that it is awaiting the formation of a 'European consensus'.[127] This may be aptly described as a 'deferral approach'. Invoking the presence (or lack) of such European consensus as a benchmark for adjusting the standard of review is a singular hallmark of the Court.

So far, such a teleological construction has been applied to the benefit of rights of individual persons, including those who are members of vulnerable, and historically and socially discriminated-against (minority) groups. As is well known, this judicial strategy, which is predicated on the interplay between a narrow margin and stringent scrutiny, has been instrumental in challenging residual prejudice in relation to issues of children born out of wedlock,[128] homosexuals[129] and transsexuals.[130]

---

[126] P. Mahoney, 'Judicial Activism and Judicial Self-Restraint in the European Court of Human Rights: Two Sides of the Same Coin', *Human Rights Law Journal* 11 (1990) 57–80 (hereinafter Mahoney, 'Judicial Activism').

[127] The author expresses special gratitude to George Letsas for this suggestion.

[128] See, for instance, ECtHR, *Marckx v. Belgium*, para. 41.

[129] See, *inter alia*, ECtHR, *Dudgeon v. UK* (Appl. No. 7525/76), Judgment (Plenary), 22 October 1981, Series A, Vol. 45, para. 60; ECtHR, *Norris v. Ireland* (Appl. No. 10581/83), Judgment (Plenary), 26 October 1988, Series A, Vol. 142; ECtHR, *Modinos v. Cyprus* (Appl. No. 15070/89), Judgment (Chamber), 22 April 1993, Series A, Vol. 259; ECtHR, *Lustig-Prean and Beckett v. UK* (Appl. Nos. 31417 and 32377/96), Judgment (Third Section), 27 September 1999, not reported, para. 90; ECtHR, *Smith and Grady v. UK* (Appl. Nos. 33985 and 33986/96), Judgment (Third Section), 27 September 1999, Reports 1999-VI, para. 97; ECtHR, *ADT v. UK* (Appl. No. 35765/97), Judgment (Third Section), 31 July 2000, Reports 2000-IX, para. 38 (conviction of gross indecency with respect to private video-recording of non-violent homosexual activities); ECtHR, *Kozak v. Poland* (Appl. No. 13102/02), Judgment (Fourth Section), 9 February 2010, not reported, paras. 92 and 98 (denial of the right to succeed to the tenancy of a flat in which the applicant lived with his late homosexual partner); and ECtHR, *EB v. France* (Appl. No. 43546/02), Judgment (Grand Chamber), 22 January 2008, not reported paras. 91–2 (refusal to grant a single homosexual woman an authorisation to adopt a child, which was held to be discriminatory based on her sexual orientation); *contra*: ECtHR, *Schalk and Kopf v. Austria* (Appl. No. 30141/04), Judgment (First Section), 24 June 2010, Reports 2010 (denial of the right of same-sex marriage under art. 12).

[130] *Christine Goodwin v. UK*, paras. 74–5, 85; ECtHR, *I v. UK* (Appl. No. 25680/94), Judgment (Grand Chamber), 11 July 2002, not reported paras. 54–5 and 65; ECtHR,

7. The conceptual linkage between a margin of appreciation and the principle of subsidiarity

7.1 Overview

In the light of the foregoing criticisms, this section proposes that one main locus of analysing the notion of margin of appreciation should be situated in a 'constitutional' dimension manifested by the principle of subsidiarity.[131] At the root of the substantive discourse on international human rights law, the principle of subsidiarity embodies disparate and axiomatic ideas of a constitutional nature. This principle also functions as a crucial analytical vehicle for ascertaining divergent features of international human rights law. For the purpose of our analysis, the institutional dimension of this principle (allocation of competences between national and international organs) can elucidate: (i) the nature and extent of 'devolution of interpretive authority' that can be given to the national authorities (the question of interpretive discretion, or a margin of appreciation); and (ii) the question of the scope of judicial review along a sliding scale.[132] The special relevance of the principle of subsidiarity in the discourse on a margin of appreciation lies in its mediating role in finding an appropriate equilibrium between national constitutional

---

Van Kück v. Germany (Appl. No. 35968/97), Judgment (Third Section), 12 June 2003, Reports 2003-VII, paras. 52, 55–6, 81–2 (examining, under arts. 65 and 8, the onus of proving the need of gender reassignment operation in national court proceedings as regards claims for reimbursement of medical expenses against a private health insurance company); ECtHR, *Grant* v. *UK* (Appl. No. 32570/03), Judgment (Fourth Section), 23 May 2006, Reports 2006-VII, paras. 41–4;

[131] For the same view, see E. Brems, *Human Rights: Universality and Diversity* (The Hague: Kluwer, 2001), at 422; and Carozza, 'Subsidiarity', at 69. For the assessment of the principle of subsidiarity in general, see *ibid.*; K. Endo, 'The Principle of Subsidiarity: From Johannes Althusius to Jacques Delors', *Hokkaido Law Review* 44:6 (1994) 553–652. For its analysis in EU law, see G.A. Bermann, 'Taking Subsidiarity Seriously: Federalism in the European Community and the United States', *Columbia Law Review* 94 (1994) 332; L.F.M. Besselink, 'Entrapped by the Maximum Standard: On Fundamental Rights, Pluralism and Subsidiarity in the European Union', *Common Market Law Review* 35 (1998) 629; and R. Schütze, 'Subsidiarity after Lisbon: Reinforcing the Safeguards of Federalism?', *Cambridge Law Journal* 68 (2009) 525. Assessment of this principle in the ECHR context is limited, but see: P. Mahoney, 'Universality versus Subsidiarity in the Strasbourg Case Law on Free Speech: Explaining Some Recent Judgments', *European Human Rights Law Review* 4 (1997) 364; H. Petzold, 'The Convention and the Principle of Subsidiarity', in Macdonald *et al.* (eds.), *The European System for the Protection of Human Rights*, 41–62 (hereinafter Petzold, 'The Convention').

[132] Carozza, 'Subsidiarity', at 55–6, and 62.

protection systems on one hand, and regional or universal systems on the other. National constitutions, which are intrinsic national symbols of member states, synthesise three main fundamental 'values' of sovereignty, local culture and political legitimacy. They are structurally polarised against a pan-European and cosmopolitan clamour for unitary standard-setting.[133] Determining the right balance in a specific circumstance depends on evaluating what is seen as the necessary degree of international cooperation and intervention in matters that occur within national sovereign jurisdictions.[134]

The notion of subsidiarity can be considered inherent in any decision-making process of international human rights law,[135] or international law in general. Akin to the margin of appreciation, the principle of subsidiarity should be considered to encompass a more substantive function connected to the interwoven ideas about individuals, society, state and international organisation.[136] The bounds of our discourse ought not to be reduced by approximating this principle to attributes of national sovereignty.[137] The notion of sovereignty, albeit pertinent, is unable to resolve what Carozza terms an 'anxious dialectic between universal and particular', that is, the tension between the demand for pan-European (or universal) standards of human rights law that transcend particular values of member states on one hand, and the yearning for autonomy and self-governance on the other.[138] In contrast, the principle of subsidiarity can embrace both the universalising aspirations of human rights and the relative autonomy of national and local communities.[139] Carozza argues that by assuming such a paradoxical function, 'subsidiarity seeks to overcome the bind of modernism that Koskenniemi has laid out – the problem of basing international order on some substantive conception of the good without succumbing to the temptation of authoritarianism'.[140]

---

[133] *Ibid.*, at 64.   [134] *Ibid.*, at 40.   [135] *Ibid.*, at 69.
[136] *Ibid.*, at 42. Contending that the rationales of the notion of subsidiarity that are rooted only in technical and institutional functions may impoverish our debates. Compare the discussion under EU law: *ibid.*, at 52.
[137] K. Endo, 'Subsidiarity and its Enemies: To What Extent is Sovereignty Contested in the Mixed Commonwealth of Europe?', EUI Working Papers, RSC No. 2001/24 at 36, available at www.eui.eu/RSCAS/WP-Texts/01_24.pdf (last accessed 30 January 2012).
[138] Carozza, 'Subsidiarity', at 64 and 67.   [139] *Ibid.*, at 68.
[140] *Ibid.* See also his other assertion that: 'Its [subsidiarity's] paradoxical quality helps keep alive the unceasing tension between the competing ideals of belonging to a particular and affirming a universal unity and helps avoid the collapse of international law into either the romanticism of the nation-state or the ideological abstraction of "pure" internationalism': *ibid.*

7.2 Institutional/structural dimension of subsidiarity

Article 12 of Protocol No. 14, which has amended article 35(3)(b) ECHR, can be considered to incorporate the structural sense of subsidiarity in the Court's admissibility scrutiny.[141] Article 12 reads:

> Paragraph 3 of Article 35 of the Convention shall be amended to read as follows:
> '3. The Court shall declare inadmissible any individual application submitted under Article 34 if it considers that:
>
> a. the application is incompatible with the provisions of the Convention or the Protocols thereto, manifestly ill-founded, or an abuse of the right of individual application; or
> b. the applicant has not suffered a significant disadvantage, unless respect for human rights as defined in the Convention and the Protocols thereto requires an examination of the application on the merits and provided that no case may be rejected on this ground which has not been duly considered by a domestic tribunal.'

The more the ECHR is domestically implemented, the greater the number of cases dealing with the clash of two competing Convention rights, where the highest instance of the national courts has had to engage itself in reasoned judgment with due application of the criteria developed by the Court. In such circumstances, apart from the reflection of judicial economy, the Court may see it as advisable to refrain from heavily criticising decisions reached by the highest instance of national courts.[142]

In *A and Others v. UK*, the ECtHR held that: 'The doctrine of the margin of appreciation has always been meant as a tool to define relations between the domestic authorities and the Court.'[143] The Court added that this doctrine 'cannot have the same application to the relations between the organs of State at the domestic level'. That the margin of appreciation doctrine is designed to apply to the vertical relationship

---

[141] Spielmann, 'Allowing the Right Margin', at 26–7.

[142] This pattern of giving a margin of appreciation to national courts is recognised by Judge Dean Spielmann: *ibid.*, at 23. Indeed, the recent case law of the Court seems to endorse this approach: *Axel Springer AG v. Germany*, para. 88; and *Von Hannover v. Germany (No. 2)*, para. 107. See also *Palomo Sánchez and Others v. Spain*, para. 57; and *MGN Limited v. The United Kingdom*, paras. 150 and 155. See also Baroness Hale, 'Argentoratum Locutum: Is the Strasbourg or the Supreme Court Supreme?', *Human Rights Law Review* 12:1 (2012) 65–78, at 77.

[143] *A and Others v. UK* (Appl. No. 3455/05), Judgment (Grand Chamber), 19 February 2009, Reports 2009, para. 184.

between the ECtHR and national authorities, and not to the horizontal relationship between two or more national organs, has been recognised explicitly by the UK courts.[144] What Letsas calls the 'structural concept of the margin of appreciation'[145] is closely intertwined with the institutional/structural dimension of subsidiarity,[146] which underpins the rationale of distributive justice. This structural dimension of a margin of appreciation is predicated on the vertical distribution of powers between the supranational judiciary and national constitutional mechanisms.[147]

The institutional dimension of the principle of subsidiarity can also be corroborated by the technical considerations of judicial economy.[148] Against the backdrop of an exponential number of applications and a chronic backlog of cases,[149] the Court is bound, based as it is on the consideration of judicial economy, to allocate its limited judicial resources equitably. In the light of a 'resource gap'[150] in collecting and analysing evidence or other empirical data, such a utilitarian rationale bolsters the Strasbourg judges' decision to endorse the national authorities' fact-finding and to ascertain a state of emergency.[151]

---

[144] See, for instance, *In re G (Adoption: Unmarried Couple)* [2009] 1 AC 173, at 187–8, per Lord Hoffmann. See also D. Pannick, 'Principles of Interpretation of Convention Rights under the Human Rights Act and the Discretionary Area of Judgment', *Public Law* (1998) 545, 548; R. Singh, 'Is There a Role for the "Margin of Appreciation" in National Law after the Human Rights Act?', *European Human Rights Law Review* (1999) 15; and Rivers, 'Proportionality', at 175.

[145] The gist of this concept is that 'the Court's power to review decisions taken by domestic authorities should be more limited than the powers of a national constitutional court or other national bodies that monitor or review compliance with an entrenched bill of rights': Letsas, 'Two Concepts of the Margin of Appreciation', at 721.

[146] J.A. Sweeney, 'Margins of Appreciation: Cultural Relativity and the European Court of Human Rights in the Post-Cold War Era', *International and Comparative Law Quarterly* 54 (2005) 459–74 (hereinafter Sweeney, 'Margins of Appreciation'), at 474.

[147] Petzold, 'The Convention', at 49. See also *A and Others* v. *UK*, para. 184 (holding that: 'The doctrine of the margin of appreciation has always been meant as a tool to define relations between the domestic authorities and the Court. It cannot have the same application to the relations between the organs of State at the domestic level').

[148] Arai-Takahashi, 'The Margin of Appreciation', at 239–41.

[149] Greer, 'What is Wrong with the ECHR?', at 687–91; and H. Keller, A. Fischer and D. Kühne, 'Debating the Future of the European Court of Human Rights after the Interlaken Conference: Two Innovative Proposals', *European Journal of International Law* 21 (2010) 1025–48.

[150] Shany, 'Toward a General Margin of Appreciation Doctrine', at 918.

[151] ECtHR, *Ireland* v. *UK* (Appl. No. 5310/71), Judgment (Plenary), 28 January 1978, Series A, Vol. 25, para. 214 (asserting that the Court's evaluation must be made not with the advantage of hindsight, but from the standpoint of the conditions prevailing at the time of emergency). Shany argues that the *ex post facto* nature of attributing state

8. The substantive dimension of a margin of appreciation

8.1 Overview

Having explained the structural dimension of a margin of appreciation within the framework of the principle of subsidiarity, the analysis now turns to the substantive dimension of a margin of appreciation doctrine. The present section argues that such a substantive dimension of this doctrine can be considered to highlight two interconnected ideas: (i) deference to, and, recognition of, national legitimacy, when the Court itself is patently aware of the lack of its democratic accountability;[152] and (ii) respect for an expression of diverse cultural values in Europe. Some authors consider that these two ideas are also encompassed within the notion of subsidiarity by introducing the 'substantive' dimension of subsidiarity.[153]

8.2 Deference to national legitimacy

The rationale underpinning the margin of appreciation based on legitimacy has been recognised by judges of the ECtHR themselves. In their Dissenting Opinion in *Karatas v. Turkey*, Judges Wildhaber, Pastor Ridruejo, Costa and Baka observed that 'the democratic legitimacy of measures taken by democratically elected governments commands a degree of judicial self-restraint'.[154] Along this line, Cohen-Eliya and Porat portray the function of the margin of appreciation positively, at least in its formative years, as reinforcing the legitimacy of the Court.[155]

By applying the margin of appreciation, the Court is endorsing 'an open and fair process of public deliberation' at a national level.[156]

---

responsibility for violations of vague, primary norms might be perceived as a manifestation of 'dubious legitimacy': Shany, 'Toward a General Margin of Appreciation Doctrine', at 918.

[152] For a consistent critique of the thesis that judges are better suited than the democratically elected legislature to grapple with disputes on fundamental rights through the mechanism of their judicial review, see Waldron, 'Judges as Moral Reasoners', at 24; and J. Waldron, 'The Core of the Case against Judicial Review'. *Yale Law Journal* 115 (2006) 1346.

[153] Carozza refers to the demarcation of a 'conceptual territory in which unity and plurality interact, pull at one another, and seek reconciliation': Carozza, 'Subsidiarity', at 52.

[154] ECtHR, *Karatas v. Turkey* (Appl. No. 23168/94), Judgment (Grand Chamber), 8 July 1999, Reports 1999-IV, Joint Partly Dissenting Opinion of Judges Wildhaber, Pastor Ridruejo, Costa and Baka.

[155] Cohen-Eliya and Porat, 'Proportionality', at 468.

[156] Wheatley, 'Minorities', at 790.

Here, the notion of a margin of appreciation serves as a solvent against 'unfounded' judicial activism of international adjudications. It signifies the Court's willingness to hold joint 'ownership' of the juridical tasks with the national authorities,[157] incrementally facilitating 'normative internalisation' of the ECHR standards by domestic courts.[158]

The legitimacy-based rationales are of special pertinence in assessing policy-affecting questions, and the extent to which positive obligations that can be inferred from a specific right ought to be implemented in a particular national society. The principle of subsidiarity underscores the Court's deference to general policy choices of national governments in areas of socio-economic matters[159] and fiscal policy[160] under article 1 of the First Protocol, and of environmental policies under article 8.[161] Further, the notion of subsidiarity can be considered to impact on the Court's decision in more *specific* policy-related questions, such as restrictions on a prisoner's rights under the Convention, including their right

---

[157] Shany, 'Toward a General Margin of Appreciation Doctrine', at 922.

[158] H.H. Koh, 'Bringing International Law Home', *Houston Law Review* 35 (1998) 623-81, at 648-50. Incorporating a national adjudicative technique of interpretive discretion in turn helps bolster the Court's own legitimacy among the member states as well: Carozza, 'Subsidiarity', at 74.

[159] See, inter alia, ECtHR, *Pine Valley Developments Ltd and Others v. Ireland* (Appl. No. 12742/87), Judgment (Chamber), 29 November 1991, Series A, Vol. 222, para. 59; ECtHR, *Sporrong and Lönnroth v. Sweden* (Appl. Nos. 7151 and 7152/75), Judgment (Plenary), 23 September 1982, Series A, Vol. 52, para. 69. Compare ECtHR, *Hutten-Czapska v. Poland* (Appl. No. 35014/97), Judgment (Grand Chamber), 19 June 2006, Reports 2006-VIII, paras. 165, 166, 223 and 224 (a stringent scrutiny, despite recognising that as a general rule, a broad margin of appreciation is accorded to the national authorities in implementing social and economic policies).

[160] See, for example, ECtHR, *Burden v. UK* (Appl. No. 13378/05), Judgment (Grand Chamber), 29 April 2008, Reports 2008, paras. 59-60 (inheritance tax relating to unmarried and cohabiting, elderly sisters).

[161] In *Tătar v. Romania*, the Court held that:

> La Cour esitime n'avoir pas qualité pour substituer son propre point de vue à celui des autorités locales quant à la meilleure politique à adopter en matière environnementale et industrielle: il y va de l'ample marge d'appréciation que sa jurisprudence reconnaît aux Etats dans des domaines sociaux et techniques difficiles ... En l'espèce, les mesures preventives requises étaient celles qui rentraient dans le cadre des pouvoirs conférés aux autorité et qui pouvaient raisonnablement passer pour aptes à pallier les risques portés à leur connaissance.

ECtHR, *Tătar v. Romania* (Appl. No. 67021/01), Judgment (Third Section), 27 January 2009, Reports 2009, para. 108.

to vote under article 3 of the First Protocol,[162] and their rights to private and family life under article 8.[163]

8.3 Cases of 'tyranny of the majority' and denial of the margin of appreciation

However, an appeal to deference to local legitimacy loses persuasive force when the constitutional edifice for national legitimacy is disturbingly shaky and morally questionable. Not merely the authoritarian regimes, but also states with democratically elected governments, may flout rights of a member of a minority (the case of a tyranny of the majority).[164]

As Europe's historical experience of having democratically elected extreme right-wing leaders demonstrates, there is no assurance that the majority's prevailing view is always morally defensible, and/or 'progressive' in the sense of enhanced effectiveness in guaranteeing individual persons' rights.[165] Indeed, the assumption that the doctrine's rational basis is rooted principally in deference to the legitimacy of democratic governments may be usurped in a diametrically opposite direction, namely, to the detriment of minority rights protection. There is a grave danger that the democratic majority may opt to deprive members belonging to any minority of their fundamental rights. Clearly, such an outcome 'would be illegitimate because [it is] contrary to the foundational values of democracy itself'.[166] Political or social minority members would be divested of means to redress injustice through democratic political procedures. In such circumstances, the application of a margin of appreciation would give the wrong impression that the Court is

---

[162] See, for instance, *Hirst* v. *UK (No. 2)*, (finding a violation of art. 3 of the First Protocol in view of the blanket nature of prisoners' disenfranchisement, without any regard to gravity of their offences and to nature of their sentences). See also, ECtHR, *Aliev* v. *Ukraine* (Appl. No. 41220/98), Judgment (Fourth Section), 29 April 2003, not reported (a prisoner's right to receive an intimate conjugal visit by his partner).

[163] See, for instance, ECtHR, *Dickson* v. *UK* (Appl. No. 44362/04), Judgment (Grand Chamber), 4 December 2007, selected for publication in Reports of Judgments and Decisions (the right to receive an intimate conjugal visit by their partner and the right to be given artificial insemination facilities to conceive a baby). See also, *Aliev* v. *Ukraine*, paras. 187–9.

[164] Greer, 'Constitutionalising Adjudication', at 420; and Shany, 'Toward a General Margin of Appreciation Doctrine', at 921.

[165] See, for instance, T. Meron, 'Martens Clause, Principles of Humanity, and Dictates of Public Conscience', *American Journal of International Law* 94 (2000) 78–89, at 85.

[166] Ibid.

abandoning its institutional and 'constitutional' role as the external guarantor of human rights against the 'tyranny of the majority'.[167] Indeed, it may even be argued that the operation of the margin of appreciation doctrine and the very 'balance' metaphor that this doctrine implies are preventing the Court from playing a meaningful role in resolving majority/minority dissensions.[168] Here, it is pertinent to take heed of Sadurski's concept of 'democracy-plus'. This concept suggests that in order to be 'fully legitimate', democracy should be predicated not only on correct procedures, but also on substantive values, such as human dignity, liberty and equal concern for all.[169]

8.4 Recognition of cultural diversity

The substantive dimension of a margin of appreciation doctrine can also be robustly explained as an expression of the due recognition of cultural diversity among the member states. The Court's rationale for the application of the margin of appreciation, which was marshalled in the *Handyside* case, has become a 'mantra' that, even after the lapse of several decades, provides crucial guidelines. First and foremost, the Court has recognised that certain standards of morality are neither uniform nor capable of being harmonised, and that they are not static either.[170] Second, because of direct access to dynamic social forces at hand, national and local authorities are better placed to evaluate an act/omission reflecting sensitive moral and religious values. This second prong of reasoning is clearly derived from the structural/institutional dimension of subsidiarity.

When justifying the application of a margin of appreciation by invoking the deference to a cultural value in a specific society, the Court is

---

[167] Wheatley, 'Minorities', at 791. Note that Bruce Ackerman suggests that those who place philosophical emphasis on fundamental rights ('rights foundationalists', in his term), assume that democracy ought to be constrained by such commitment to protection of rights: B. Ackerman, 'Constitutional Politics/Constitutional Law', *Yale Law Journal* 99 (1989) 453–547, at 465–71.
[168] Wheatley, 'Minorities'.
[169] W. Sadurski, 'Law's Legitimacy and "Democracy-Plus"', *Oxford Journal of Legal Studies* 26 (2006) 377, at 377. Compare Ronald Dworkin's argument that democracy is an 'interpretive' concept and must, however, be guided and constrained by the 'non-negotiable' principle of treating all subjects with 'equal concern': R. Dworkin, 'Do Values Conflict? A Hedgehog's Approach', *Arizona Law Review* 43 (2001) 251, at 254–5 and 259.
[170] Arai-Takahashi, 'The Margin of Appreciation', at 206–8.

considered to endorse an overarching, 'ethical decentralizing'[171] rationale against the conformist trend.[172] In such judicial thinking, the idea of cultural diversity is recognised as among essential social goods in human rights decision-making. This helps assure the national authorities that a normative objective contemplated in each of the Convention rights can be attained without entailing strict uniform standards.[173]

The consistent jurisprudence suggests that the Court has shown a greater inclination to a restrained approach when ascertaining issues of morality understood in a broad sense, including the questions of obscenity and sexual propriety.[174] The deferential stance has also been upheld in cases where the Court has been asked to demarcate the conceptual parameters of free speech against the competing interest in safeguarding the freedom of religion.[175] Similarly, the national authorities may be given latitudes of discretion in delineating what they perceive as appropriate conceptual boundaries of such intrinsic notions as privacy and family life that are set against the freedom of the press.[176]

Deference to national cultural policies as a rationale for the margin of appreciation can be corroborated not least in educational matters, the area that epitomises how to make a coherent explication of abundant forces of distinct local values. The fact that national education curricula devote a large proportion of time to knowledge of locally dominant

---

[171] Sweeney, 'Margins of Appreciation', at 472–4.
[172] See, for instance, Mahoney, 'Marvellous Richness of Diversity'; and Sweeney, 'Margins of Appreciation'. Compare C. Nowlin, 'The Protection of Morals under the European Convention for the Protection of Human Rights and Fundamental Freedoms', *Human Rights Quarterly* 24 (2002) 264–86.
[173] Greer, 'Constitutionalising Adjudication', at 409; and Shany, 'Toward a General Margin of Appreciation Doctrine'.
[174] See, for instance, ECtHR, *Wingrove v. United Kingdom* (Appl. No. 17419/90), Judgment (Chamber), 25 November 1996, Reports 1996-V; ECommHR, *Geerks v. Switzerland* (Appl. No. 7640/76), Decision (Commission), 7 March 1978, 12 Decisions and Reports 103 (friendly settlement, Commission's Report of 4 May 1979, 16 DR 56); and ECommHR, *Gay News Ltd. and Lemon v. UK* (Appl. No. 8710/79), Decision (Commission), 7 May 1982, 5 EHRR 123.
[175] ECtHR, *Otto-Preminger-Institut v. Austria* (Appl. No. 13470/87), Judgment (Chamber), 20 September 1994, Series A, No. 295-A.
[176] Publishing photographs and images containing intimate private aspects of individuals or their family is a serious affront to their right to good reputation, honour and privacy: ECtHR, *Von Hannover v. Germany* (Appl. No. 59320/00), Judgment (Third Section), 24 June 2004, Reports 2004-VI, para. 59; ECtHR, *Von Hannover v. Germany (No. 2)* (Appl. Nos. 40660 and 60641/08), Judgment (Grand Chamber), 7 February 2012, Reports 2012, paras. 82, 104–7, 126; and ECtHR, *Hachette Filipacchi Associés v. France* (Appl. No. 71111/01), Judgment (First Section), 14 June 2007, (2009) 49 EHRR 515, para. 42.

religion is not in itself considered to constitute indoctrination and to infringe the principles of pluralism and objectivity in breach of article 2 of Protocol No. 1. The conceptual device of a margin of appreciation is deployed to rationalise national discretion in planning and setting up educational curricula.[177] However, as found in *Folgerø and Others v. Norway*[178] and *Hasan and Eylem Zengin v. Turkey*,[179] in cases where the system of partial exemption from a mandatory religious class entails the risk of compelling the parents unduly to disclose intimate aspects of their own religious and philosophical convictions,[180] this would upset a fair balance. It would contravene the principle that the information contained in the curriculum be conveyed in an 'objective, critical and pluralistic' manner as required under article 2 of Protocol No. 1.

As discussed above, the absence of European consensus over the relative importance of a particular cultural issue is a factor that may prompt the Court to widen the ambit of a national margin.[181] In *Lautsi*

---

[177] In *Folgerø and Others v. Norway*, the Grand Chamber of the Court found that the fact that the syllabus of the 'Christianity, religion and philosophy' (KRL) module provided a larger proportion to knowledge of Christianity than to that of other religions could not in itself be viewed as a departure from the principles of pluralism and objectivity amounting to indoctrination. On this matter, the Court recognised the Norwegian margin of appreciation in regulating its educational curriculum while acknowledging its history and tradition dominated by Christianity: ECtHR, *Folgerø and Others v. Norway* (Appl. No. 15472/02), Judgment (Grand Chamber), 29 June 2007, Reports 2007-III, para. 89. Similarly, in *Hasan and Eylem Zengin v. Turkey*, where Alevist applicants complained that the Turkish syllabus for 'religious culture and ethics' classes gave greater prominence to knowledge of Islam, the Court recognised the Turkish authorities' margin of appreciation in examining its educational curriculum on the ground that Islam is the majority religion practised in Turkey: ECtHR, *Hasan and Eylem Zengin v. Turkey* (Appl. No. 1448/04), Judgment (Second Section), 9 October 2007, not reported, para. 63.

[178] *Folgerø and Others v. Norway*. para. 102.

[179] *Hasan and Eylem Zengin v. Turkey*, para. 75. Decisive for the Court in this case to find a violation of art. 2 of Protocol No.1 was the fact that even after request for partial exemption was made, whether or not to grant such a request for exemption was subject to discretion of the relevant educational authorities.

[180] *Folgerø and Others v. Norway*, paras. 98 and 100.

[181] Such a *general* understanding is summarised by the dictum that 'Where ... there is no consensus within the member States of the Council of Europe, either as to the relative importance of the interest at stake or as to the best means of protecting it, particularly where the case raises sensitive and ethical issues, the margin will be wider...': *S.H. and Others v. Austria*, para. 94. See also *ibid.*, para. 97; *Evans v. UK*, para. 77; ECtHR, *Fretté v. France* (Appl. No. 36515/97), Judgment (Third Section), 26 February 2002, Reports 2002-I, para. 41; *A, B. and C. v. Ireland* (Appl. No. 25579/05), Judgment (Grand Chamber), 16 December 2010, Reports 2010, para. 232.

and Others v. *Italy*, the presence of such a powerfully religious symbol as a crucifix at a state-run primary school was contested as being at odds with both the requirement of secularism, and rights of pupils and their parents to entertain different religious and philosophical beliefs and convictions.[182] In that case, the Grand Chamber was adamant that the absence of European consensus would justify its judicial self-restraint and its deference to what the Italian government pleaded as a manifestation of a community's deeply-rooted Catholic values.[183]

In some cases, the Court has gone to the length of considering cultural justifications as sufficiently potent to dilute the solidly established methodology based on European consensus and to rebuff the need for evolutive interpretation. In *A, B and C* v. *Ireland*, where highly sensitive issues of abortion were at stake, the Court held:

> ...even if it appears from the national laws ... that most Contracting Parties may in their legislation have resolved those conflicting rights and interests [conflicting rights of the mother and of foetuses] in favour of greater legal access to abortion, *this consensus cannot be a decisive factor* in the Court's examination of whether the impugned prohibition on abortion in Ireland for health and well-being reasons struck a fair balance between the conflicting rights and interests, *notwithstanding an evolutive interpretation of the Convention.*[184]

When invoked, the notion of a margin of appreciation can be viewed as a metaphor that funnels into the 'constitutional' discourse a more profound, *cultural dialogue* about the implications of international human rights on different national societies, and on their identities and cultural values. In other words, the variable parameters of the margin are the reserved domain of *Kulturkampf* in which quest for culturally specific

---

[182] *Lautsi and Others* v. *Italy* (Appl. No. 30814/06), Judgment (Grand Chamber), 18 March 2011, Reports 2011, paras. 68–70 and 76.

[183] The Italian government submitted as follows: 'That presence [the presence of crucifixes] was the expression of a "national particularity", characterised notably by close relations between the State, the people and Catholicism attributable to the historical, cultural and territorial development of Italy and to a deeply rooted and long-standing attachment to the values of Catholicism. Keeping crucifixes in schools was therefore a matter of preserving a centuries-old tradition.' *Lautsi and Others* v. *Italy*, para. 36.

[184] *A, B and C.* v. *Ireland*, para. 237, emphasis added. For the same line of argument deployed not in cultural matters, but in social and economic policy areas, see the case disputing disenfranchisement of a prisoner under art. 3 of the First Protocol: *Hirst* v. *UK (No. 2)*, para. 81 (albeit the Court finding a violation of this provision due to a blanket nature of restrictions on all convicted prisoners, irrespective of the length of their sentence and gravity of their offences).

and socially contextualised understanding of ECHR standards is still cognisable.[185] It is in this line of reasoning that the most cogent and sustainable application of the margin of appreciation can be defended. As a caveat, one might argue that the Court's deference to the cultural (and religious) tradition prevalent among the majority of the local society can be contrasted to its relatively curt treatment of issues that are reflective of a minority group's distinct cultural values.[186]

It may be argued that the very idea of human rights as such already entails and articulates a degree of cultural pluralism and diversity in society.[187] In *Schalk and Kopf* v. *Austria*, which involved denial of the right of marriage to a same-sex couple, the Court held that:

> marriage has deep-rooted social and cultural connotations which may differ largely from one society to another. The Court reiterates that it must not rush to substitute its own judgment in place of that of the national authorities, who are best placed to assess and respond to the needs of society...[188]

In that specific case, admittedly, the Court seems to retreat evasively into the thinly disguised veneer of cultural relativism.[189] Even so, the least that

---

[185] For this discussion in respect of the principle of subsidiarity, see Carozza, 'Subsidiarity', at 79.

[186] See, for instance, *Cha'are Shalom Ve Tsedek* v. *France* (Appl. No. 27417/95), Judgment (Grand Chamber), 27 June 2000, Reports 2000-VII (refusal to grant the applicant association an approval to authorise its ritual slaughterers to perform ritual slaughter to get '*glatt*' meat, in contrast to another Jewish association that received such an approval and to which the vast majority of the observing Jewish population in France were affiliated).

[187] Carozza, 'Subsidiarity', at 47.

[188] *Schalk and Kopf* v. *Austria*, para. 62. See also *ibid.*, paras. 108–9 (complaint under arts. 14 and 8); but *contra*, the Joint Dissenting Opinions of Judges Rozakis, Spielmann and Jebens (finding a violation under arts. 14 and 8). Compare *B and L* v. *UK* (Appl. No. 36536/02), Judgment (Fourth Section), 13 September 2005 (ban on parents-in-law marrying children-in-law, unless both outlive their former spouses), paras. 31–3 (the government's reliance on moral arguments) and paras. 36–40 (the Court recognising the subsidiary principle in view of the 'divided' nature of the question of a marriage of a close degree of affinity, but finding inconsistency of the stated aims of the ban in question and the waiver applicable in some cases).

[189] The above-quoted argument seems less persuasive than the frank admission that judicial interpretation, even by way of teleological strategy, finds it hard to surmount the clear textual meaning (unlike art. 9 of the Charter of the Fundamental Rights of the European Union, which avoids any reference to men and women, art. 12 ECHR expressly mentions a union of opposite sex). This was the first line of reasoning provided by the Court in *Schalk and Kopf* v. *Austria*, 129, para. 60.

this dictum demonstrates is the potency of the culture-based arguments in human rights decision-making.

Embedded consciousness of cultural diversity is borne out by the Court's repeated emphasis on the principle of 'pluralism, tolerance and broadmindedness',[190] and on its affiliated notion of religious pluralism and democracy.[191] In this sphere, one may contend that the margin of appreciation, as interpretive leeway given to local decision-making agents, serves as a more nuanced but sensible conceptual device than a politically charged rhetoric of cultural relativism in ascertaining legitimacy of applying human rights constructs in culturally enriched Europe.[192] If invoked, the idea of cultural relativism might 'ensnare' the Court into the most deferential standard of review. At least on a level of perception among citizens, the Court's failure to tap into the capacity to make a non-reviewable judgment would detract from its role as the final and authoritative arbiter of all human rights decisions in Europe.[193]

8.5 The rejection of cultural values: a harmonisation approach reinstated

In contrast, it ought to be noted that even if demands of specific cultural values are in issue, the Court does not compromise what it conceives as

---

[190] It is crucial to recall the 'classic' *Handyside* case, in which this principle was explained as follows:

> Subject to paragraph 2 of article 10, it [freedom of expression] is applicable not only to information or ideas that are favourably received or regarded as inoffensive or as a matter of indifference, but also to those that offend, shock or disturb the State or any sector of the population. Such are the demands of that pluralism, tolerance and broadmindedness without which there is no democratic society.

[191] ECtHR, *Handyside* v. *UK*, para. 49. See also *Refah partisi (The Welfare Party) and Others* v. *Turkey*, para. 89; and *United Communist Party of Turkey and Others* v. *Turkey* (Appl. No. 19392/92), Judgment (Grand Chamber), 30 January 1998, Reports 1998-I, paras. 42–3. ECtHR, *Refah partisi (The Welfare Party) and Others* v. *Turkey*, para. 90. See also *Kokkinakis* v. *Greece* (Appl. No. 14307/88), Judgment (Chamber), 25 May 1993, Series A, Vol. 260-A, para. 31; and *Buscarini and Others* v. *San Marino* (Appl. No. 24645/94), Judgment (Grand Chamber), 18 February 1999, Reports 1999-I, para. 34. See also the Framework Convention on the Protection of National Minorities, preamble and art. 6(1).

[192] Carozza, 'Subsidiarity', at 62.

[193] See Dworkin's second 'weak sense' of discretion: Dworkin, *Taking Rights Seriously*, at 31–4, 68–71 and 327–30. See also, W. Lucy, 'Adjudication', in Coleman and Shapiro (eds.), *The Oxford Handbook of Jurisprudence and Philosophy of Law*, 206–67, at 215.

foundational principles underpinning the normative backbone of the ECHR. Indeed, in such cases, the Court does not hesitate to reject outright deference to cultural diversity.

For instance, in the *Refah Partisi* case, the Court rebuked the introduction of the *sharia* law as being irreconcilable with the primordial principles of gender equality and secularism.[194] Similarly, in *Dahlab v. Switzerland*, the Court did not baulk at endorsing the Swiss Federal Court's reasoning that wearing of an Islamic headscarf by a primary school teacher was problematic on two grounds: it was imposed only on women as a precept derived from the Koran; and that this was incompatible with gender equality and demands of tolerance and respect for others. Admittedly, in this specific case, these two rationales were given greater weight than the consideration, according to which the wearing of 'a powerful external symbol', such as a headscarf, might have some proselytising effect on tender minds of young pupils.[195] Be that as it may, what matters most here is that the Court's approach is clearly geared toward autonomous (and 'objective') pan-European standards. This is also in tune with the Human Rights Committee's universalist premise that 'traditional, historical, religious or cultural attitudes' should not legitimate violations of intrinsic rights, such as women's rights under the International Covenant on Civil and Political Rights.[196]

9. Conclusion

Any discourses on international human rights law necessitates intensively locating an appropriate intersection between 'a communicable common good' of normative standards desired to be uniformly implemented on

---

[194] The ECtHR held that: '... such a system [based on a plurality of legal systems including the sharia law] would undeniably infringe the principle of non-discrimination between individuals as regards their enjoyment of public freedoms, which is one of the fundamental principles of democracy. A difference in treatment between individuals in all fields of public and private law according to their religion or beliefs manifestly cannot be justified under the Convention, and more particularly article 14 thereof': *Refah partisi (The Welfare Party) and Others v. Turkey*, para. 119 (confirming chamber's Judgment of 31 July 2002, para. 70).

[195] *Dahlab v. Switzerland* (Appl. No. 42393/98), Decision (Second Section), 15 February 2001, Reports 2001-V. In the present writer's view, it is the second and third ground that should have been considered preponderant in this case.

[196] HRC, *General Comment No. 28: Equality of Rights between Men and Women (Article 3)*: 29/03/2000, CCPR/C/21/Rev.1/Add.10, para. 5. See also HRC, *General Comment No. 31 [80]: Nature of the General Legal Obligation Imposed on States Parties to the Covenant*: 26/05/2004, CCPR/C/21/Rev.1/Add.13, para. 14 (observing that a failure to abide by the obligations to comply with the ICCPR rights cannot be justified by reference to cultural considerations).

one hand, and national and local particularities fully reflected in domestic constitutional projects on the other.[197] Lurking behind such an endeavour is the search for 'an equilibrium between unity and diversity' that would allow the formation of a common normative framework on international human rights while accommodating respect for fundamental values manifested in national constitutional decision-making.[198]

The margin of appreciation, as an interpretive doctrine that is an outcome of the Strasbourg judges' practical reasoning, cannot function as a fixed benchmark in moral space. It can be considered a fruit of the Strasbourg judges' process of deliberation, which is purported to optimise the protection of rights among a plethora of competing values. As such, the doctrine's operative sphere is set against the backdrop of the need to balance between the relevant reasons for action.[199]

As is well known, Habermas's model of deliberative democracy (democracy as 'a legally mediated form of political integration')[200] is receptive of a diverse European cultural landscape. This model demands that any individual be able to flourish meaningfully in his/her private and public autonomy.[201] Cohen-Eliya and Porat argue that 'under the theory of deliberative democracy, laws and democratically reached decisions gain legitimacy only if they are the outcomes of a deliberative process, the result of a public discourse in which a public attempt is made to justify arguments and claims in terms of reason'.[202] The deliberative process suggests that a construction of a common European edifice of human rights is an incremental step, while account needs to be taken of the plurality of cultural particularities. Such a gradational approach is precisely what the Court envisages when applying the doctrine of a margin of appreciation. The legal space and flexibility proffered by this doctrine allows the national authorities to engage themselves in such legitimacy-enhancing, deliberative processes in the quest for agreements over divisive issues. Set against the background of European deliberative

---

[197] I owe the term 'communicable common good' to Carozza, 'Subsidiarity', at 58, n. 118.
[198] For a discussion in the EU law context, see *ibid.*, at 53.
[199] Pavlakos, 'Constitutional Rights', at 150–2.
[200] J. Habermas, 'Toward a Cosmopolitan Europe', *Journal of Democracy* 14 (2003) 86–100, at 97–8.
[201] Habermas, 'Between Facts', at 419.
[202] M. Cohen-Eliya and I. Porat, 'Proportionality and the Culture of Justification', *American Journal of Comparative Law* 59 (2011) 463–90, at 481.

democracy,[203] or democracy as an 'interpretive' or 'integrated' concept of value,[204] the margin of appreciation doctrine, once comprehended more than as an expedient product of practical reasoning, can help shape Habermas's notion of a 'normative consensus'. Its sustainable rationale resides in its capacity to facilitate the reconciliation of competing political and moral values espoused by divergent and plural national and ethnic groups, and to inculcate the moral sense for tolerating 'others'.[205]

---

[203] The concept of deliberative democracy involves 'an attempt to institutionalize discourse as far as possible as a means of public decision making': R. Alexy, 'Balancing, Constitutional Review, and Representation', *International Journal of Constitutional Law* 3 (2005) 572, at 579. Likewise, Voyiakis highlights the importance of '[d]ebates genuinely focused on discovering truth'. He notes that such debates 'resemble less a group of perspectives battling out until one of them dominates than a process of constant reformulation of each perspective in the light of the other until a mutually satisfactory equilibrium is reached....': Voyiakis, 'International Law', at 76.

[204] R. Dworkin, 'Hart's Postscript and the Character of Political Philosophy', *Oxford Journal of Legal Studies* 24(1) (2004) 1–37, at 9, 14–18 and 23. He postulates that the concept of legitimacy operates in a community that takes 'integrity' as central to politics. He asserts that 'a general commitment to integrity expresses a concern by each for all that is sufficiently special, personal, pervasive, and egalitarian to ground communal obligations': Dworkin, *Law's Empire*, at 216.

[205] J. Habermas, 'Intolerance and Discrimination', *International Journal of Constitutional Law* 1 (2003) 2–12, at 3–4.

4

The ECHR as a living instrument: its meaning and legitimacy

GEORGE LETSAS*

1. Introduction

The idea that constitutions are living organisms that evolve over time is a familiar metaphor in many constitutional traditions.[1] It figures prominently in debates about how constitutional courts should interpret entrenched rights and how far they may or should depart from the constitution's original understanding. These debates are generated by a normative tension that bedevils modern constitutionalism: on one hand constitutions are meant to signal a pre-commitment to a set of fundamental principles that should be immune from ephemeral political changes; but on the other hand the circumstances of human life change constantly and sometimes drastically, calling for a novel interpretation of the constitution which few, if any, of the original actors (drafters, judges, the people) could have foreseen. Advocates of the 'living constitution' oppose the idea that present-day conditions should be fully governed by a document whose drafters died decades or even centuries ago. But they are burdened with the difficulty of explaining what kind of pre-commitment the original constitution is meant to express, if its meaning is not treated as frozen. They also have to justify why courts and not

---

* I am deeply grateful to Andreas Føllesdal, Birgit Peters and Geir Ulfstein for their in-depth comments, editorial suggestions and substantive criticisms. I am also grateful to all the participants in the two workshops held at the University of Oslo in preparation for this volume for their very valuable comments on an earlier draft. I have also benefited from discussions with Colm O'Cinneide, Nicos Stavropoulos and John Tasioulas.

[1] See, e.g., W. Rehnquist, 'The Notion of a Living Constitution', *Texas Law Review* 54 (1976) 693–706; L. Sager, 'The Incorrigible Constitution', *New York University Law Review* 65 (1990) 893–961; A. Scalia, 'Common Law Courts in a Civil Law System: The Role of United States Federal Courts in Interpreting the Constitution and Laws', in A. Gutmann (ed.), *A Matter of Interpretation: Federal Courts and the Law* (Princeton University Press, 1998) 3–48; R. Sharpe, 'The Impact of a Bill of Rights on the Role of the Judiciary: A Canadian Perspective', in P. Alston (ed.), *Promoting Human Rights through Bills of Rights: Comparative Perspectives* (Oxford University Press, 1999) 431–53.

legislatures or constitutional assemblies should have the power to evolve the meaning of the constitution and how far they may go before they start abusing this power.

Similar debates arise in the context of the interpretation of international human rights treaties. To be sure, international human rights treaties are not constitutions. They are multilateral agreements between sovereign states. Contracting states may at any point opt-in or pull out of a human rights treaty.[2] If a state chooses not to join, or chooses to pull out, then the international court or supervisory body has no jurisdiction to hear complaints from individuals within that state. This is so even when a treaty, like the European Convention on Human Rights (ECHR, or the Convention), provides for direct access to a court and makes its jurisdiction compulsory and binding on contracting states. Moreover, human rights treaties, unlike a constitution, are not meant to contain all the fundamental principles of a political community; they are not meant to *constitute* a system of political organisation for a particular people. So the link between international human rights and national institutions is contingent and ultimately conditional on state consent.

Still, a lot remains common between international human rights treaties and constitutional bills of rights. They both contain lists of abstract fundamental rights that individuals have against government. They both face the need to accommodate constant and drastic societal changes in relation to these abstract rights, changes that were not anticipated at the drafting stage – or in the case of treaties, at the stage of state accession. And, in the case of the ECHR and most constitutions, they both create judicial institutions with the power to review whether individuals' *legal* rights have been violated. So just like many constitutional courts, international human rights courts have to take a stand on how far, if at all, the meaning of the abstract legal rights individuals are entitled to

---

[2] It is sometimes argued that two main United Nations Covenants, the International Covenant on Civil and Political Rights (ICCPR) and the International Covenant on Social, Economic and Cultural Rights (ICESCR), do not allow a state that has ratified them to denounce them or withdraw. This is the position of the UN Human Rights Committee, as expressed in General Comment 26 (1996). The Committee bases its argument partly on the fact that the Covenants do not expressly provide for denunciation. Most human rights treaties, however, expressly provide for state denunciation. See, e.g., art. 58 of the European Convention on Human Rights (ECHR), art. 21 of the International Covenant on the Elimination of all Forms of Racial Discrimination (CERD), and art. 78 of the American Convention on Human Rights (ACHR). Note also that the Optional Protocol to the ICCPR, which recognises the competence of the Human Rights Committee to receive and consider individual communications, expressly permits states to denounce it (art. 12).

claim before them, evolves over time. No doubt, no area of law is immune from radical changes in social circumstances. But what is distinctive about human rights law is that it engages abstract values that are meant to serve as general normative standards against which to judge the soundness of a legal system as a whole. Radical changes in societal beliefs about these abstract values poses a distinctive challenge for any court, be it domestic or international, that adjudicates on issues of fundamental human rights.[3]

The idea that the ECHR is a living instrument that must be interpreted according to present-day conditions has been a central feature of Strasbourg's case law from its very early days. This chapter first provides a general account of the way in which the European Court of Human Rights (ECtHR, or the Court) has understood and used evolutive interpretation, by looking at relevant case law and how it has developed over time (sections 2 and 3).[4] I aim to show that there has been an important shift in the Court's use of the doctrine of evolutive interpretation over the years, particularly in relation to the relevance and normative weight of state consensus. I then move on to discuss the rationale and justifiability of the doctrine, particularly in relation to the moral foundations of human rights (section 4). The final section (section 5) is devoted to the relation between evolutive interpretation and the Court's legitimacy over contracting states. It argues that evolutive interpretation, understood as the moral reading of the Convention, is essential to the Court's legitimacy.

2. The ECHR as a living instrument: early cases

In the hands of the ECtHR, the idea of a living instrument has three main features. First, the Court will take into consideration 'present-day standards' as an important factor in interpreting the Convention; it will very rarely inquire into what was thought to be acceptable state conduct when the Convention was drafted, or what specific rights the drafters of the Convention intended to protect. Second, the present-day standards that the Court takes into consideration must somehow be *common* or *shared* amongst contracting states. The Court has never clarified what it means

---

[3] This is also true of courts such as the European Court of Justice (ECJ) or the International Criminal Court (ICC) which, though not designated as human rights courts, routinely face and decide issues of fundamental human rights.

[4] I shall use the terms 'evolutive interpretation' and 'living-instrument approach' interchangeably. Another synonym in the relevant literature is the term 'dynamic interpretation'.

for a standard to be common or shared. As we shall see, the Court does not make it a condition that all contracting states have expressly accepted the standard by way of legislative enactment. Third, the Court will not assign decisive importance to what the respondent state (be it its authorities or public opinion) considers to be an acceptable standard in the case at hand. This is so particularly if the respondent state's practice is out of line with the commonly accepted standards in the Council of Europe. Over time, however, the Court has shifted the emphasis it places on the various aspects of the living instrument approach. This section looks at the early cases decided by the old Court, i.e. before the reform of Protocol 11 to the ECHR (1998).

The idea that the ECHR is a living instrument has figured in Strasbourg's case law since its very early days. The Court first acknowledged it in the judgment of *Tyrer* v. *United Kingdom*, delivered in 1978.[5] The Court had to decide whether judicial corporal punishment of juveniles amounts to degrading punishment within the meaning of article 3 of the Convention. The punishment, having the form of bare-skin birching carried out by a policeman at a police station, was prescribed by law and practised in the Isle of Man, a dependent territory of the United Kingdom, with a significant degree of legislative autonomy. At the time, judicial corporal punishment had been abolished in the rest of the United Kingdom and neither was to be found in the vast majority of the other contracting states. In his submissions, the Attorney-General for the Isle of Man put forward the following argument: judicial corporal punishment could not be considered degrading because it 'did not outrage public opinion in the Isle of Man'.[6] The Court, however, rejected this argument. It noted that public acceptance of judicial corporal punishment could not constitute a criterion as to whether it is degrading or not, because the reason why people favour this type of punishment may well be the fact that corporal punishment is so degrading that it operates as a deterrent. It then went on to add:

> The Court must also recall that the Convention is a living instrument which, as the Commission rightly stressed, must be interpreted in the light of present-day conditions. In the case now before it the Court cannot but be influenced by the developments and commonly accepted standards in the penal policy of the member States of the Council of Europe in this field.[7]

---

[5] ECtHR, *Tyrer* v. *United Kingdom* (Appl. No. 5856/72), Judgment (Chamber), 25 April 1978, Series A, No. 26.
[6] *Ibid.*, at para. 31.   [7] *Ibid.*

The Court moved on to decide the case on purely substantive considerations. It said that 'the very *nature* of judicial corporal punishment is that it involves one human being inflicting physical violence on another human'[8] and that it is an institutionalised assault on a person's dignity and physical integrity, which is precisely what article 3 of the Convention aims to protect. It further added that the institutionalised character of the punishment, the fact that it is inflicted by total strangers on the offender, and the fact that it is administered over the bare posterior, all add up to the punishment being degrading. It concluded that article 3 of the Convention had been breached.

In *Marckx* v. *Belgium*,[9] decided just a few months after *Tyrer*, the applicants, a child born out of wedlock and his unmarried mother, complained that Belgian legislation violated their right to family life under article 8 of the Convention, and discriminated against them, contrary to article 14 of the Convention. Belgian law at the time did not follow the maxim 'mater semper certa est', denying maternal affiliation upon birth to children born out of wedlock ('illegitimate children'). Maternal affiliation between a child born out of wedlock and its biological mother could only be established after birth, either by voluntary recognition or by a court declaration. The Court noted straightforwardly that article 8 ECHR makes no distinction between 'legitimate' and 'illegitimate' family and that such distinction would anyway contradict article 14 of the Convention, which prohibits any discrimination grounded on birth.[10] It then noted that 'respect for family life' may well impose positive obligations on the part of the state and further argued that Belgian law puts illegitimate family under unfavourable and discriminatory conditions.[11] At that point the Court was faced with an objection raised by the Belgian government. The respondent government conceded that the law favoured the traditional family, but maintained that this was for the purpose of ensuring the family's full development as a matter of 'objective and reasonable grounds relating to morals and public order'.[12] The Court took issue at the Belgian government's objection. While admitting that at the time when the Convention was drafted it was regarded as permissible to distinguish between 'legitimate' and 'illegitimate' families, it noted that:

> The domestic law of the great majority of the member States of the Council of Europe has evolved and is continuing to evolve, in company

---

[8] *Ibid.*, at para. 33 (emphasis added).
[9] *Marckx* v. *Belgium* (Appl. No. 6833/74), Judgment (Plenary), 13 June 1979, Series A, No. 31.
[10] *Ibid.*, at para. 31.   [11] *Ibid.*, at paras. 36–9.   [12] *Ibid.*, at para. 40.

with the relevant international instruments, towards full juridical recognition of the maxim 'mater semper certa est'.[13]

The Court concluded that article 8 of the Convention had been breached. There is a noticeable difference between *Tyrer* and *Marckx*. In the latter, the Court went on to refer explicitly to two international conventions (the Brussels Convention on the Establishment of Maternal Affiliation of Natural Children and the European Convention on the Legal Status of Children born out of wedlock) as a way to demonstrate the existence of 'commonly accepted standards'. Yet these two international conventions were far from being signed by the majority of the contracting states at the time. The way the Court justified this was by saying that, 'the existence of these two treaties denotes that there is a clear measure of common ground in this area amongst modern societies'. It added, further, that Belgian law itself showed signs of this 'evolution of rules and attitudes'.

In the case of *Dudgeon v. United Kingdom*, decided in 1981, the main issue was whether penalisation of homosexuality in Northern Ireland violated the right to respect for private life guaranteed by article 8(1). The respondent state drew the Court's attention to the particularities of Northern Ireland: it is a conservative society that places emphasis on religious matters, and in which there was a genuine conviction, shared by a large number of people and institutional actors, that decriminalising homosexuality would be seriously damaging to the moral fabric of the society. The Court took the view that these particularities, and in particular the 'moral climate' of Northern Ireland, are a relevant factor for the purposes of article 8 ECHR. But then it went on to say:

> As compared with the era when that legislation was enacted, there is now a better understanding, and in consequence an increased tolerance, of homosexual behaviour to the extent that in the great majority of the member States of the Council of Europe it is no longer considered to be necessary or appropriate to treat homosexual practices of the kind now in question as in themselves a matter to which the sanctions of the criminal law should be applied.[14]

The Court further added that there had been little enforcement of the criminal prohibition in recent years, and that the respondent state had

---

[13] *Ibid.*, at para. 41.
[14] ECtHR, *Dudgeon v. United Kingdom* (Appl. No. 7525/76), Judgment (Chamber), 24 February 1983, Series A, No. 59, para. 60.

provided no evidence to show that decriminalisation would be injurious to moral standards in Northern Ireland. It concluded that, though a legitimate concern, the moral climate in Northern Ireland did not amount to a pressing social need, capable of outweighing the negative effect that the prohibition had on the life of homosexuals. It found a violation of article 8 of the Convention.

The early cases in which the Court characterised the Convention as a living instrument display a certain pattern. First, the Court is invited to rule on an issue that is morally sensitive in the respondent state: corporal punishment, children born out of wedlock, homosexuality. Second, the Court acknowledges the relevance of the prevailing moral climate within the respondent state to the interpretation of the Convention. Third, the Court appeals to broader developments in the Council of Europe as a counterweight to the prevailing moral climate in the respondent state. And fourth, the Court also examines a number of substantive considerations that do not relate to the prevailing moral climate or to common standards in the Council of Europe. Rather, they relate directly to the purpose of the protected right and to why governmental acts fall short of serving this purpose in the case at hand.[15] In most cases, the pattern results in the finding of a violation.

The use of present-day developments and standards in the Council of Europe as a counterweight to the moral climate prevailing in the respondent state is the central feature of evolutive interpretation as applied by the old Court. It has a negative and a positive side. The negative side is that what the national authorities and the people of the respondent state believe about the applicant's human right claim is *not* decisive for whether she has that right under the Convention. The positive side is that commonly held standards in the Council of Europe are very weighty considerations for whether the applicant has the right she claims. Evolutive

---

[15] In ECtHR, *Guzzardi v Italy* (Appl. No. 7367/76), Judgment (Plenary), 6 November 1980, Series A, No. 39, for example, the Court had to decide whether compulsory residence in an island constitutes deprivation of liberty. The Italian government argued that all that the applicant had suffered was not a deprivation, but a restriction of liberty, which is outside the scope of art. 5. In response, the Court held that 'the difference between deprivation and restriction is one of degree or intensity and not one of nature or substance', that deprivation may take several forms and that 'account must be taken of a whole range of criteria such as the type, duration, effects and manner of implementation of the measure in question'. It concluded that the applicant's condition amounted to deprivation of liberty even though there was no physical barrier to the applicant's movement. Towards the end of its judgment, the Court made reference to 'the notions currently prevailing in democratic states'.

interpretation is therefore linked to two other doctrines of the Court, which complement it: autonomous concepts and the margin of appreciation.

The Court's doctrine of autonomous concepts is linked to the negative aspect of the evolutive interpretation. The Court and the former Commission have held that a number of Convention concepts have autonomous meaning, i.e. they 'must be interpreted as having an autonomous meaning in the context of the Convention and not on the basis of their meaning in domestic law'.[16] On the Court's view, 'definition in national law has only relative value and constitutes no more than a starting point'.[17] The Court has characterised as autonomous a significant number of concepts that figure in the Convention, such as criminal charge,[18] civil rights and obligations,[19] possessions,[20] association,[21] victim,[22] civil servants[23] and lawful detention.[24]

The positive aspect of evolutive interpretation is linked to the role that consensus within the Council of Europe plays in the Court's doctrine of the margin of appreciation.[25] Throughout the 1980s and 1990s, the old

---

[16] ECommHR, *RL v. The Netherlands*, Decision (Commission), 18 March 1995, not reported.

[17] ECtHR, *Chassagnou and Others v. France* (Appl. Nos. 25088/94, 28331 and 28443/95), Judgment (Grand Chamber), 29 April 1999, Reports 1999-III, para. 100; ECtHR, *Karakurt v. Austria* (Appl. No. 32441/96), Judgment (Third Section) not reported, at 4.

[18] ECtHR, *Engel and Others v. The Netherlands (Article 50)* (Appl. Nos. 5100, 5101 and 5102/71; 5354 and 5370/72), Judgment (Plenary), 8 June 1976, Series A, No. 22; ECtHR, *Campbell and Fell v. United Kingdom* (Appl. Nos. 7819 and 7878/77), Judgment (Chamber), 28 June 1984, Series A, No. 80; ECtHR, *Ravnsborg v. Sweden* (Appl. No. 14220/88), Judgment (Chamber), 23 March 1992, Series A, No. 283-B.

[19] ECtHR, *Konig v. Germany* (Appl. No. 6232/73), Judgment (Plenary), 28 June 1978, Series A, No. 27; ECtHR, *Sporrong and Lönnroth v. Sweden* (Appl. Nos. 7151 and 7152/75), Judgment (Plenary), 23 September 1982, Series A, No. 52.

[20] ECtHR, *Gasus Dosier- und Fordertechnik GmbH v. The Netherlands* (Appl. No. 15375/89), Judgment (Chamber), 23 February 1995, Series A, No. 306-B; ECtHR, *Iatridis v. Greece* (Appl. No. 31107/96), Judgment (Grand Chamber), 25 March 1999, Reports 1999-II; ECtHR, *Former King of Greece v. Greece* (Appl. No. 25701/94), Judgment (Grand Chamber), 23 November 2000, Reports 2000-XII.

[21] *Chassagnou and Others v. France*.

[22] ECtHR, *Asselbourg and 78 others and Greenpeace Association-Luxembourg v. Luxembourg* (Appl. No. 29121/95), Judgment (Second Section), 29 June 1999, Reports 1999-VI.

[23] ECtHR, *Pellegrin v. France* (Appl. No. 28541/95), Judgment (Grand Chamber), 8 December 1999, Reports 1999-VIII; ECtHR, *Frydlender v. France* (Appl. No. 30979/96), Judgment (Grand Chamber), 27 June 2000, Reports 2000-VII.

[24] ECtHR, *Eriksen v. Norway* (Appl. No. 17391/90), Judgment (Chamber), 27 May 1997, Reports 1997-III; ECtHR, *Witold Litwa v. Poland* (Appl. No. 26629/95), Judgment (Second Section), 4 April 2000, Reports 2000-III.

[25] See Arai-Takahashi, Chapter 3, this volume.

Court granted a wide margin of appreciation to the respondent state in cases where there was no consensus amongst contracting states on the moral issue raised by the applicant's case, particularly in relation to restrictions based on public morals. These cases concerned a number of controversial issues regarding freedom of expression and private life: the publication of a book containing sexual advice for adolescents,[26] the exhibition of obscene paintings,[27] the screening[28] or licensing[29] of a blasphemous film and the legal reassignment of sex for post-operation transsexuals.[30] In these cases, the old Court found the lack of consensus or of a 'uniform conception of morals' a weighty factor, and in the end did not find a violation. Of particular note are the cases relating to post-operation transsexuals and their unsuccessful claim to have their new gender recognised by law. The old Court decided three such cases (*Rees, Cossey, Sheffield and Horsham*) in a period of twelve years, indicating that the issue amounts to a human rights violation, but finding no consensus amongst contracting states in favour of the applicants.

In sum, until the late 1990s, the Court would cite present-day standards in the Council of Europe as a counterweight factor to the moral climate prevailing in the respondent state, a climate prejudiced against the applicant's claim (*Tyrer, Marckx, Dudgeon*). Once it had done so, it would examine the substance of the right in question and often conclude that there has been a violation. In other cases, however, the Court would be reluctant to recognise that a common standard exists, given that there was no consensus amongst contracting states (*Handyside, Sheffield and Horsham, Otto-Preminger*). In these cases, the Court would perform a less strict scrutiny of the substantive issue in question, granting the respondent state a wide margin of appreciation and ultimately finding no violation. This resulted in a normative tension between the Court's

---

[26] ECtHR, *Handyside* v. *United Kingdom* (Appl. No. 5493/72), Judgment (Plenary), 7 December 1976, Series A, No. 24.

[27] ECtHR, *Muller and Others* v. *Switzerland* (Appl. No. 10737/84), Judgment (Chamber), 24 May 1988, Series A, No. 133.

[28] ECtHR, *Otto-Preminger-Institut* v. *Austria* (Appl. No. 13470/87), Judgment (Chamber), 20 September 1994, Series A, No. 295-A.

[29] ECtHR, *Wingrove* v. *United Kingdom* (Appl. No. 17419/90), Judgment (Chamber), 25 November 1996, Reports 1996-V.

[30] ECtHR, *Rees* v. *United Kingdom* (Appl. No. 9532/81), Judgment (Plenary), 17 October 1986, Series A, No. 106; ECtHR, *Cossey* v. *United Kingdom* (Appl. No. 10843/84), Judgment (Plenary), 27 September 1990, Series A, No. 184; ECtHR, *Sheffield and Horsham* v. *UK* (Appl. Nos. 22985/93 and 23390/94), Judgment (Grand Chamber), 30 July 1998, Reports 1998-V.

reasoning in cases like *Marckx* and in cases like *Rees* and *Sheffield and Horsham*. In *Marckx*, the Court would be satisfied to invoke some abstract common standard, evidenced by the existence of a couple of international conventions which had not been ratified by the majority, let alone all, of the contracting states. And it would do so by citing the idea that the ECHR should be seen as a living instrument. In cases like *Sheffield and Horsham*, however, the Court would raise the bar as to what a common standard is. It would require a 'generally shared approach among the Contracting States' and would grant states a wide margin of appreciation in the absence of it. In the eyes of academic commentators, the doctrine of the margin of appreciation was naturally seen as a constraint to the doctrine of evolutive interpretation: the Court would bring the meaning of the Convention rights up to date, but it would use common ground, or consensus amongst contracting states, as the ultimate limit of how far it can go.[31]

3. The new Court: from consensus to common values

The previous section highlighted a tension between cases in which the old Court found a violation, citing the living instrument approach and cases in which it found no violation, citing the respondent state's margin of appreciation. In the early 2000s, after the coming into force of Protocol 11, this tension started to retreat in favour of the living instrument approach. The new Court started favouring the *Marckx* test over the *Sheffield and Horsham* test. Recall that the Court in *Marckx* relied on some abstract sense of common standards, evidenced by the existence of some international conventions (not ratified by the majority of member states) and by trends of evolution in societal beliefs. By contrast, in cases like *Sheffield and Horsham*, the Court granted the respondent state a wide margin of appreciation in the absence of a 'common ground' or 'shared approach' by the contracting states. Let us look at some examples.

In 2002, the Court revisited the issue of whether the state has a positive duty, under article 8 ECHR, officially to recognise the new gender

---

[31] See, e.g., Y. Arai-Takahashi, *The Margin of Appreciation Doctrine and the Principle of Proportionality in the Jurisprudence of the ECHR* (Antwerp: Intersentia, 2001): 'On the other hand the existence of a common European standard tends to strengthen the Strasbourg organs in the assertive application of evolutive interpretation, shrinking the breadth of margin', at 200.

identity of post-operative transsexuals and to alter public records accordingly. In the cases of *Goodwin* v. *United Kingdom* and *I* v. *United Kingdom*, the Court reversed its previous case law, ruling unanimously in favour of the applicants. In its reasoning, the Court noted that it must have regard to 'the changing conditions within the respondent State and within Contracting States generally' and respond to any 'evolving convergence as to the standards to be achieved'.[32] In other words, it tried to justify reversing its previous case law on the ground that there were significant developments in Europe since *Sheffield and Horsham*. But, in effect, the Court simply loosened its test for the existence of a common, present-day standard. It noted that although the emphasis in *Sheffield and Horsham* was on the lack of a common European approach, this lack is 'hardly surprising' in countries with such diverse legal systems and traditions. And it went on to say:

> The Court accordingly attaches less importance to the lack of evidence of a common European approach to the resolution of the legal and practical problems posed, than to the clear and uncontested evidence of a continuing international trend in favour not only of increased social acceptance of transsexuals but of legal recognition of the new sexual identity of post-operative transsexuals.

Just like *Marckx* and unlike *Sheffield and Horsham*, the Court in *Goodwin* was willing to rely on what it took to be a *trend* of evolution, as a present-day common standard, in order to outweigh the respondent state's appeal for a margin of appreciation. Just like in *Marckx*, the test for the existence of present-day common standards was so loose as to make one wonder whether the Court is paying lip-service to the idea of common ground.

In subsequent cases, the new Court generalised and expanded this approach. It started appealing to evidence of common ground and trends of evolution in international law materials, regardless of whether such materials are binding and whether most contracting states have ratified them. So, for example, the Court has taken into consideration the following materials: recommendations and resolutions of the Committee of Ministers and the Parliamentary Assembly,[33] reports of the 'Venice

---

[32] ECtHR, *Goodwin* v. *United Kingdom* (Appl. No. 17488/90), Judgment (Grand Chamber) 27 March 1996, Reports 1996-II, para. 74.

[33] ECtHR, *Oneryildiz* v. *Turkey* (Appl. No. 48939/99), Judgment (Grand Chamber), 30 November 2004, Reports 2004-XII.

Commission',[34] reports of the European Commission Against Racism,[35] the European Social Charter,[36] the European Union (EU) Charter of Fundamental Rights,[37] the European Convention on State Immunity,[38] the Oviedo Convention on Human Rights and Biomedicine,[39] the Aarhus Convention on Access to Information,[40] and Conventions of the International Labour Organization (ILO).[41] Some of these materials are not legally binding and some of the legally binding materials were not ratified by many contracting states, sometimes including the respondent state in question. Let us look more closely at some of these cases.

In the Grand Chamber judgment of *Demir and Baykara v. Turkey*, the Court found a violation of article 11 ECHR (freedom of association). The authorities of the respondent state refused to recognise the legal personality of a trade union formed by municipal civil servants, and annulled the collective agreement into which the trade union had entered. The Grand Chamber found a violation of article 11 ECHR on both these points. In its reasoning, the Court noted that it 'has never considered the provisions of the Convention as the sole framework of reference for the interpretation of the rights and freedoms therein' and that 'in defining the meaning of terms and notions in the text of the Convention, it can and must take into account elements of international law other than the Convention, the interpretation of such elements by competent organs, and the practice of European States reflecting their *common values*' (emphasis added).[42] Citing *Marckx* in support, the Court said that:

---

[34] ECtHR, *Russian Conservative Party of Entrepreneurs and Others v. Russia* (Appl. Nos. 55066 and 55638/00), Judgment (First Section), 11 January 2007, not reported.
[35] ECtHR, *Bekos and Koutropoulos v. Greece* (Appl. No. 15250/02), Judgment (Fourth Section), 13 December 2005, not reported.
[36] ECtHR, *Sorensen and Rasmussen v. Denmark* (Appl. Nos. 52562 and 52620/99), Judgment (Grand Chamber), 11 January 2006, Reports 2006-I.
[37] ECtHR, *Christine Goodwin v. United Kingdom* (Appl. No. 28957/95), Judgment (Grand Chamber), 11 July 2002, Reports 2002-VI.
[38] ECtHR, *Al-Adsani v. United Kingdom* (Appl. No. 35763/97), Judgment (Grand Chamber), 21 November 2001, Reports 2001-XI.
[39] ECtHR, *Glass v. United Kingdom* (Appl. No. 61827/00), Judgment (Fourth Section), 9 March 2004, Reports 2004-II.
[40] ECtHR, *Taskin and Others v. Turkey* (Appl. No. 46117/99), Judgment (Third Section), 10 November 2004, Reports 2004-X.
[41] ECtHR, *Siliadin v. France* (Appl. No. 73316/01), Judgment (Second Section), 26 July 2005, Reports 2005-VII; ECtHR, *Demir and Baykara v. Turkey* (Appl. No. 34503/97), Judgment (Grand Chamber), 12 November 2008, Reports 2008.
[42] See the extensive analysis by the Court in ECtHR, *Demir and Baykara v. Turkey*, ibid., paras. 69–86.

> [I]t is not necessary for the respondent State to have ratified the entire collection of instruments that are applicable in respect of the precise subject matter of the case concerned. It will be sufficient for the Court that the relevant international instruments denote a continuous evolution in the norms and principles applied in international law or in the domestic law of the majority of member States of the Council of Europe and show, in a precise area, that there is common ground in modern societies.

This was followed by a reference to the living instrument approach, whose purpose the new Court now qualifies as follows: it is to 'reflect the increasingly high standard being required in the area of the protection of human rights, thus necessitating greater firmness in assessing breaches of the fundamental values of democratic societies'.[43]

In another landmark judgment, *Rantsev* v. *Cyprus and Russia*,[44] the Court had to decide whether human trafficking falls within the scope of article 4 ECHR, which prohibits 'slavery', 'servitude' and 'forced or compulsory labour'. After looking at a number of international materials on human trafficking, the Court reasoned as follows in a passage worth quoting in its entirety:

> [T]he absence of an express reference to trafficking in the Convention is unsurprising. The Convention was inspired by the Universal Declaration of Human Rights, proclaimed by the General Assembly of the United Nations in 1948, which itself made no express mention of trafficking. In its Article 4, the Declaration prohibited 'slavery and the slave trade in all their forms'. However, in assessing the scope of Article 4 of the Convention, sight should not be lost of the Convention's special features or of the fact that it is a living instrument which must be interpreted in the light of present-day conditions. The increasingly high standards required in the area of the protection of human rights and fundamental liberties correspondingly and inevitably require greater firmness in assessing breaches of the fundamental values of democratic societies. There can be no doubt that trafficking threatens the human dignity and fundamental freedoms of its victims and cannot be considered compatible with a democratic society and the values expounded in the Convention. In view of its obligation to interpret the Convention in light of present-day conditions, the Court considers it unnecessary to identify whether the treatment about which the applicant complains constitutes 'slavery', 'servitude' or 'forced and compulsory labour'. Instead, the Court concludes that trafficking itself,

---

[43] *Ibid.*, para. 146.
[44] ECtHR, *Rantsev* v. *Cyprus and Russia* (Appl. No. 25965/04), Judgment (First Section), 7 January 2010, Reports 2010.

within the meaning of Article 3(a) of the Palermo Protocol and Article 4(a) of the Anti-Trafficking Convention, falls within the scope of Article 4 of the Convention.[45]

Goodwin, Demir and Bakara and *Rantsev* exemplify the new Court's reliance on *evolving* trends and *emerging* consensus in international law ('present-day conditions') as a justificatory basis for finding a practice (or policy) to be in breach of the Convention. Since the Court does not consider in these cases whether the emerging practice is followed by all or most contracting states, we may infer that, on the new Court's approach, this consideration is irrelevant. Meanwhile, the Court shows clear willingness to restrict the margin of appreciation that states enjoy because of lack of consensus, alongside citing the idea that the Convention is a living instrument. The cases of *EB v. France* and *Hirst v. United Kingdom* are important to mention here.

In *EB*, the applicant was a lesbian who had been refused authorisation to adopt by the French authorities, partly on the ground that there was no paternal referent in her household. The Court held that in the circumstances of the case, this ground was used as a pretext, and that it was the applicant's homosexuality that served, implicitly, as a decisive factor for refusing her authorisation to adopt. It concluded she had suffered a difference in treatment on the basis of her sexual orientation and moved on to examine whether the difference in treatment had an objective and reasonable justification. In the earlier case of *Fretté*,[46] the Court had allowed France a wide margin of appreciation on the basis that there was no common ground in Europe.[47] But in *EB* the Court held that 'where sexual orientation is in issue, there is a need for particularly convincing and weighty reasons to justify a difference in treatment regarding rights falling within Article 8'.[48] In its reasoning, the Grand Chamber made no reference to the margin of appreciation and to

---

[45] *Ibid.*, paras. 272–82.
[46] ECtHR, *Fretté v. France* (Appl. No. 36515/97), Judgment (Third Section), 26 February 2002, Reports 2002-I.
[47] 'Since the delicate issues raised in the case, therefore, touch on areas where there is little common ground amongst the member States of the Council of Europe and, generally speaking, the law appears to be in a transitional stage, a wide margin of appreciation must be left to the authorities of each State', *Fretté v. France, ibid.*, para. 41.
[48] ECtHR, *EB v. France* (Appl. No. 43546/02), Judgment (Grand Chamber), 22 January 2008, not reported, para. 91. For a more extensive discussion of the differences between *EB* and *Fretté*, see G. Letsas, 'No Human Right to Adopt?', *UCL Human Rights Review* 1:1 (2008) 134–53.

whether there is consensus within contracting states in making adoption available to single homosexuals. It paid no attention to the argument put forward by the French government that the division of the scientific community, the contracting states and public opinion over homosexual adoption should weigh against the ruling of a violation. Instead, the Court based its judgment on the principle that the burden should be on the respondent state to provide particularly *weighty* reasons that call for differential treatment when sexual orientation is in issue. Given that no such reasons were put forward, the Court found a violation of article 14 ECHR (non-discrimination) in conjunction with article 8 ECHR, reiterating that the Convention is a living instrument.

In *Hirst v. United Kingdom*,[49] the Court, sitting as a Grand Chamber, held that the UK's blanket restriction on the right of convicted prisoners to vote is disproportionate and in breach of the Convention. Noting that the UK is not alone among Convention countries in depriving all convicted prisoners of the right to vote, it nevertheless remarked: 'Even if no common European approach to the problem can be discerned, this cannot in itself be determinative of the issue.'[50]

This is not to say, however, that there are no cases in which the new Court would assign significant weight to the absence of common ground amongst contracting states. Apart from the earlier cases of *Fretté* (2002) and *Murphy v. Ireland* (2004), the Court has also done so in more recent cases, usually where the applicant is challenging the public morals prevailing within the respondent state. So, for example, in the case of *Schalk and Kopf v. Austria*, the Court had to decide whether the prohibition of same-sex marriage and the absence of an alternative means of legal recognition of same-sex relationships violated article 8 ECHR in conjunction with article 14 ECHR. It concluded that there was no violation, citing in support the fact that there was at the time no consensus amongst contracting states providing legal recognition of same-sex partnerships. And in the case of *Lautsi v. Italy*, the Grand Chamber found that the obligatory display of crucifixes in public classrooms is not in breach of the Convention, holding that the absence of a European consensus counts in favour of granting the respondent state a margin of appreciation.[51]

---

[49] ECtHR, *Hirst v. United Kingdom* (Appl. No. 74025/01), Judgment (Grand Chamber), 6 October 2005, Reports 2005-IX.
[50] *Ibid.*, para. 81.
[51] 'The Court concludes in the present case that the decision whether crucifixes should be present in State-school classrooms is, in principle, a matter falling within the margin of

Still, these cases must be seen as outliers for at least two reasons; first, because they are still outnumbered by cases such as *Goodwin, Demir and Bakara, EB, Rantsev, Hirst* and many others. And second, because reliance on the absence of consensus as the basis for granting a margin of appreciation is now treated by the Court itself as an exception, not the norm. This is evidenced by the fact that it is met with vocal opposition by many of the Court's judges. So, for example, in the case of *Schalk and Kopf v. Austria*, three judges (Spielmann, Jebens and Rozakis) dissented not only on the weight that the Grand Chamber had assigned to the absence of common ground amongst contracting states, but also on its very *relevance*. Here is what they argued:

> Having identified a 'relevantly similar situation', and emphasized that 'differences based on sexual orientation require particularly serious reasons by way of justification', the Court should have found a violation of Article 14 taken in conjunction with Article 8 of the Convention because the respondent Government did not advance any argument to justify the difference of treatment, relying in this connection mainly on their margin of appreciation. However, in the absence of any cogent reasons offered by the respondent Government to justify the difference of treatment, there should be no room to apply the margin of appreciation. Consequently, the 'existence or nonexistence of common ground between the laws of the Contracting States' is irrelevant as such considerations are only a subordinate basis for the application of the concept of the margin of appreciation.

Moreover, the Court's former Vice-President, Christos Rozakis, would often complain about its reference to the margin of appreciation, even though it had found a violation.[52]

In sum, the new Court has moved away from placing decisive weight on the absence of consensus amongst contracting states and from

---

appreciation of the respondent State. Moreover, the fact that there is no European consensus on the question of the presence of religious symbols in State schools speaks in favor of that approach,' ECtHR, *Lautsi and Others v. Italy* (Appl. No. 30814/06), Judgment (Grand Chamber), 18 March 2011, not reported, para. 70.

[52] See the Concurring Opinions of Judge Rozakis in ECtHR, *Odièvre v. France* (Appl. No. 42326/98), Judgment (Grand Chamber), 13 February 2003, Reports 2003-III, and ECtHR, *Egeland and Hanseid v. Norway* (Appl. No. 34438/04), Judgment (First Section), 16 April 2009, not reported. I analyse the contribution of Rozakis's Separate Opinions to the Court's jurisprudence in G. Letsas, 'Judge Rozakis's Separate Opinions and the Strasbourg Dilemma', in Dean Spielmann, Marialena Tsirli and Panayotis Voyatzis (eds.), *The European Convention on Human Rights: A Living Instrument, Essays in Honour of Christos L. Rozakis* (Brussels: Bruylant, 2011) 305–27.

treating it as the ultimate limit on how far it can evolve the meaning and scope of Convention rights. The new Court treats the ECHR as a living instrument by looking for *common values* and *emerging* consensus in international law. In doing so, it often raises the human rights standard *above* what most contracting states currently offer. It reasons mainly by focusing on the substance of the case and by placing the burden on the respondent states to provide *weighty* reasons for interfering with core aspects of Convention rights. If no weighty reasons are provided, the new Court will not normally grant the respondent state a margin of appreciation, even in the absence of consensus amongst contracting states on the question. As the Court said in several cases (*Goodwin*, *Rantsev*), the lack of consensus in the Council of Europe is hardly surprising, and it is not determinative of the issue before the Court (*Hirst*). Whether it will maintain this approach in the face of vocal criticism by several contracting states remains to be seen.

4. The moral reading of the Convention and the problem of legitimacy

What are we to make of the new Court's use of the living instrument approach? Can this use be justified?

The first thing to note is that it coheres with the Court's general approach to legal interpretation, which in a previous work I have called Strasbourg's interpretive *ethic*.[53] This ethic is based on rejecting textualism and intentionalism as methods of interpretation of the Convention. I have already mentioned the Court's doctrine of autonomous concepts, which detaches the meaning of several Convention concepts from the way they are construed within the respondent state. In addition, the Court has read into the Convention rights that are not explicitly mentioned in the text, such as the right of access to court.[54] Finally, the Court has recognised not only rights the drafters could not have intended to protect, such as the right to vote in EU elections,[55] but also rights that they had intended *not* to protect, such as the right not to join a trade

---

[53] See G. Letsas, 'Strasbourg's Interpretive Ethic: Lessons for the International Lawyer', *European Journal of International Law* 21 (2010) 1–33.

[54] ECtHR, *Golder v. United Kingdom* (Appl. No. 4451/70), Judgment (Plenary), 21 February 1975, Series A, No. 18.

[55] ECtHR, *Matthews v. United Kingdom* (Appl. No. 24833/94), Judgment (Grand Chamber), 18 February 1999, Reports 1999-I.

union.[56] In other words, the Court's interpretive ethic has been both anti-textualist and anti-originalist. In fact, one can trace the various stages in the Court's reasoning as the gradual severing of interpretive links with the beliefs of the following groups: the drafters (*Golder, Young, James and Webster*), the respondent state's legal authorities and their classifications (*Engel*), the respondent state's public opinion (*Marckx, Dudgeon*) and finally, the authorities and public opinion of the majority of contracting states (*Hirst, Goodwin*).

Is the severing of these interpretive links justified? In a book first published in 2007,[57] I argued that this severing is fully justified because it is required by the moral foundations of human rights: if human rights are distinctively counter-majoritarian, then it makes no sense conditioning their scope and meaning on what the majority itself believes. For example, if the interpretation of the rights of groups such as children born out of wedlock (*Marckx*), homosexuals (*Dudgeon, Frette, EB, Schalk and Kopf*), juveniles (*Tyrer, Handyside*), prisoners (*Hirst, Rohde v. Denmark*[58]), transsexuals (*Rees, Sheffield and Horsham, Goodwin*), foreigners (*Saadi v. United Kingdom*,[59] *Siliadin v. France*[60]), religious minorities (*Kokkinakis v. Greece*[61]) and many others were made dependent on majoritarian preferences, then these groups would be denied equal protection under the Convention. This is because majoritarian preferences are typically biased against these groups, who are fewer in numbers and cannot bring about a change in domestic law through legislative process. Hence, if the role of the Court is to shield the interests of these groups from majoritarian preferences, then it should not distinguish between the majoritarian preferences prevailing in the respondent state and the majoritarian preferences of the entire Council of Europe. For example, lack of consensus amongst contracting states on whether same-sex

---

[56] ECtHR, *Young, James and Webster* v. *United Kingdom* (Appl. Nos. 7601/76 and 7806/77), Judgment (Chamber), 13 August 1981, Series A, No. 55.
[57] G. Letsas, *A Theory of Interpretation of the European Convention on Human Rights*, 1st edn. (Oxford University Press, 2007), 2nd edn with new Preface and Foreword by Judge Spielmann in 2009 (hereinafter Letsas, *A Theory of Interpretation*).
[58] ECtHR, *Rohde* v. *Denmark* (Appl. No. 69332/01), Judgment (First Section), 21 July 2005, not reported.
[59] ECtHR, *Saadi* v. *United Kingdom* (Appl. No. 13229/03), Judgment (Grand Chamber), 29 January 2008, Reports 2008.
[60] *Siliadin* v. *France*.
[61] ECtHR, *Kokkinakis* v. *Greece* (Appl. No. 14307/88), Judgment (Chamber), 25 May 1993, Series A, No. 260-A.

partnerships should be recognised by law should be as irrelevant as a prejudiced moral climate towards homosexuals in the respondent state.

So borrowing Dworkin's label about the US Constitution,[62] I argued that the Court should engage in the 'moral reading' of the ECHR rights, ignoring consensus and blocking majoritarian preferences from having an effect on fundamental interests of individuals. And I defended the moral reading of the ECHR against the charge of judicial activism, on the ground that it remains within the remit of the Court's legal function: contracting states have given the Court jurisdiction to protect whatever human rights people *in fact* have, and not what human rights domestic authorities or public opinion *think* people have.[63] Contracting states cannot have their cake and eat it: set up a supranational institution to protect people's *real* human rights, but expect the institution to condone violations when it is convenient for them. Not only is the moral reading within the legal limits of the Court's jurisdiction; it is *essential* if the Court is to perform its legal function of protecting individual human rights in the Council of Europe.

At the time when I was writing *A Theory of Interpretation*, the Court's case law was still equivocating between the *Marckx* test, which paid lip-service to the idea of consensus, and the *Sheffield and Horsham* test, which required uniform or shared practice amongst contracting states. My concern at the time was to highlight the normative inconsistency between the Court's doctrines on autonomous concepts and living instrument on one hand and its heavy reliance on consensus in cases like *Murphy* and *Fretté* on the other. After the book was published, the Court moved further away from consensus and towards the abstract idea of 'common values' in international law. It is now less deferential, showing willingness (and confidence) to scrutinise state interference with fundamental individual rights. It shifts the onus on the respondent state to show that weighty reasons necessitated the interference and downplays the significance, or even relevance, of the lack of shared practice amongst contracting states. It recognises rights under the ECHR that would have been unimaginable thirty or forty years ago, such as in relation to trafficking (*Rantsev*), domestic workers (*Siliadin*), prisoners' voting (*Hirst*), gay adoption (*EB*) and many others. Despite the occasional outliers (*Lautsi, Schalk and Kopf* v. *Austria*) the new Court has embraced

---

[62] R. Dworkin, *Freedom's Law: The Moral Reading of the American Constitution* (Oxford University Press, 1996).
[63] Letsas, *A Theory of Interpretation*, chapters 2 and 3.

the moral reading of the Convention rights.[64] And understood as the moral reading of the Convention, evolutive interpretation simply denotes a process of moral discovery: the Court is not expanding or inflating the scope of the ECHR rights by treating the Convention as a living instrument; rather, it *discovers* what these human rights always meant to protect.

Yet the Court's interpretive ethic is not uncontroversial. In recent years, a number of old contracting states have reacted vocally against the Court's adverse rulings[65] and against the retreat of the use of the margin of appreciation. Meanwhile, the issue of the legitimacy of the Court and the role of consensus in its case law has become a lively topic.[66] Even if the morality of human rights requires a counter-majoritarian reading of the Convention, as I argue, does the Court possess the legitimacy to impose its own view about what human rights require upon most or all contracting states? Does the moral reading of the Convention exceed the boundaries of the Court's legitimacy? After all, the Court is an international, not a constitutional court, and its effect is ultimately dependent on state consent. If evolutive interpretation is controversial at domestic level, then it is even more controversial at international level. The next section looks into the question of the Court's legitimacy, both in general and in relation to evolutive interpretation.

5. The legitimacy of the moral reading of the Convention: a defence

The idea that the role of judges is to interpret bills of rights in the light of changing circumstances raises concerns about the legitimacy of them doing so. This is particularly the case if evolutive interpretation is to be understood as the moral reading of rights. For even if we grant that the best moral understanding of rights evolves over time, we still have to

---

[64] I do not, of course, mean to imply that the self-perception of individual judges of the Court is that of the moral philosopher who seeks to discover the moral foundations of human rights. When I say that the Court has embraced the moral reading of the Convention, I mean that its decisions do not, as a matter of outcome, condition the existence of the applicant's human right on a majoritarian understanding of what that right is.

[65] For instance, the UK with respect to *Hirst*, and Italy with respect to the Chamber Judgment in *Lautsi*.

[66] See, e.g., K. Dzehtsiarou, 'Does Consensus Matter? Legitimacy of European Consensus in the Case Law of the European Court of Human Rights', *Public Law* (2011) 534–53.

explain why it is the judicial branch, as opposed to other institutions or branches of government, that gets to decide on what that better understanding is. The question of legitimacy raises an additional concern at the international level, because international courts are not part of a single constitutional order and they exercise supervision over a large number of states, with diverse legal and political structures. How can we justify the legitimacy of international courts, like the ECtHR, to evolve the meaning of legally binding obligations of sovereign states according to what a few judges think is morally best? Concerns about Strasbourg's legitimacy have risen sharply in the last few years, particularly amongst the old contracting states, following the handing down of a number of controversial judgments. This is understandable, because the more prominent the role of an institution, the more it is called to justify it. Yet it is not always clear what it means to question whether an international human rights court has legitimacy.

In the remainder of this chapter, I shall argue that evolutive interpretation, understood as the moral reading of the Convention, does not threaten the legitimacy of the Court. In fact, I will advance a stronger thesis, namely, that the moral reading of the Convention is *essential* to the Court's overall legitimacy, and its only possible ground. In order to do so, I shall have to look at the broader issue of the Court's legitimacy and to show why alternative ways of grounding its legitimacy fail.

I shall begin by distinguishing two different ways in which Strasbourg can be said to possess legitimate authority over contracting states. The first one relates to whether following Strasbourg's judgments can help contracting states better to comply with their human rights obligations than if they were to rely on their own judgment. Call this *authority-based legitimacy*. The second one relates to whether contracting states have an obligation to follow Strasbourg's judgments based on the treaty-based commitment they have undertaken by joining the ECHR. Call this *commitment-based legitimacy*. I shall argue that Strasbourg is unlikely to have authority-based legitimacy for all contracting states and that interpreting the Convention according to the morally best reading is unlikely to be an effective way of acquiring authority-based legitimacy. Commitment-based arguments, by contrast, are more likely to succeed in showing that Strasbourg's judgments are authoritative on all contracting states. And evolutive interpretation, understood as the moral reading of the Convention rights, is essential to commitment-based legitimacy. Or so I will argue.

5.1 Authority-based legitimacy

The traditional understanding of legitimacy, owed largely to the work of Joseph Raz,[67] is to contrast it with the idea of justice or correctness. To ask whether someone has legitimate authority over you is to ask whether his decisions bind you irrespective of merit, regardless, that is, of whether they are just; correct; right.[68] The reason for this understanding draws on the role that authorities are meant to play in our lives: if we were to be bound by authorities *only* when they make just decisions, then they would make no practical difference in our lives. Each one of us would have to figure out what reasons apply to him independently of the authority's decision, and follow the decision only when it matches what one ought to do anyway, according to the balance of reasons. Doing so, however, would make authorities redundant. And authorities are meant to play a practical role in our lives by guiding our action and by imposing obligations. But how can they play that role if we are to follow them only when they are right? And how can they impose obligations when, from a moral point of view, their decisions may not be correct?

Raz's answer to this is that authorities are meant to provide us with a service, namely, to help us comply with reasons we already have. As he puts it, authorities 'mediate between people and the right reasons that apply to them'.[69] According to what he calls the 'normal justification thesis', an authority is legitimate when the alleged subject is likely better to comply with reasons which apply to him if he accepts the directives and tries to follow them than by trying to follow the reasons that apply to him directly. One has a duty to follow someone's directives, even if some of them are incorrect or unjustified, if, on the whole, one increases conformity with right reason by doing so. Raz's normal justification thesis is typically met in two cases. First, when the authority has greater expertise than its subjects in the domain to which its decisions pertain. Second, when the authority can solve coordination problems, for instance, by making one course of action – amongst many alternatives – salient.

---

[67] J. Raz, *The Morality of Freedom* (Oxford University Press, 1986); see also Raz's more recent restatement, in J. Raz, 'The Problem of Authority: Revisiting the Service Conception', *Minnesota Law Review* 90 (2006) 1003–44.
[68] It should be stressed that the question here is not that of *perceived* or *de facto* legitimacy, i.e. whether one *believes* that some authority is legitimate. The question is a normative one, namely, what would make that belief true, i.e. what reasons *in fact* one has to obey an authority.
[69] J. Raz, *Ethics in the Public Domain* (Oxford: Clarendon Press, 1995), at 214.

Raz attaches several conditions and qualifications to the normal justification thesis. The first is what we might call the 'autonomy constraint'. Authorities are not legitimate in relation to matters that individuals should decide themselves. For example, personal aspects of one's life, such as what friends or sexual partners to have, are things that each one of us should reflect on and act autonomously due to the nature of the value that they promote. Even if one would choose better friends by following someone else's directives than by relying on one's own judgment, doing so would defeat the whole point of the value of friendship, because part of that value consists in making one's own choices. The scope of legitimate authority is limited by the autonomy interests of the subjects. Likewise, in the case of international institutions, their authority could plausibly be limited by certain sovereignty interests of state parties.

The second condition relates to manifestly unjust decisions. An outrageously unjust decision, issued by an otherwise legitimate authority, would not obligate its subjects. This is a second way in which legitimate authority is limited. Obeying authorities is meant to be a rational way to improve compliance with one's reasons and duties. When it is manifestly obvious that the authority's directive is unjust or evil, then the subject should ignore it, even if the rest of its directives help him on the whole to do what is right.

Third, not everyone whose directives, if followed, would help me comply with my reasons, is a legitimate authority for me. There are many people out there who know more about finances than I do, but this does not make them legitimate authorities over my financial decisions. Such people are merely theoretical authorities. The legitimacy of an authority may depend on whether it is also a practical authority, i.e. on whether its decisions are *in fact* followed by its subjects, or on whether it has the ability to enforce them. This is particularly the case in coordination issues: arguably, there are institutions or persons (e.g. the International Monetary Fund or the World Bank) who can coordinate the economic activities of EU member states better than the EU institutions. The reason why they do not possess legitimate authority is that the directives of such institutions, unlike those of the EU institutions, are not treated as authoritative by the EU member states. The idea here is that only *de facto* authorities, i.e. authorities that are generally obeyed, are candidates for possessing legitimate authority to solve coordination issues.

Finally, legitimate authority can be *piecemeal*: someone can be a legitimate authority for you, but not for me. When one's legitimate authority is based on expertise, then it can only be possessed over people who know less than the authority on the subject-matter in question. For example, if you know less than the government on medicinal matters, then you have reason to follow the government's health directive mandating a flu vaccine. But if you are a medical expert on flu and know more about it than the Ministry of Health, then the government possess no legitimate authority over you in relation to vaccines.

Now, if this is what we mean by legitimacy, then it is doubtful whether Strasbourg possesses it. The relevant test would be whether each and every contracting state is more likely to comply with their human rights obligations by following Strasbourg's directives than by trying to comply with these obligations directly. The next section raises doubts about whether Strasbourg can meet this test.

5.1.1 Expertise-based legitimacy

Take first the argument from expertise, which is one of the grounds of legitimacy according to the Razian conception. It is doubtful whether Strasbourg judges possess greater expertise about human rights than all or most national institutions, including national constitutional courts with powers of judicial review. Strasbourg surely does not have greater expertise in empirical matters within the contracting states. As Strasbourg itself acknowledges, national authorities are often 'better placed' to establish a number of facts pertaining either to the applicant's situation or to general conditions existing in the respondent states (e.g. what its 'public morals' are).[70] Moreover, it is doubtful whether

---

[70] See ECtHR, *Handyside v. United Kingdom* (Appl. No. 5493/72), Judgment (Plenary), 7 December 1976, Series A, Vol. 24, para. 59; ECtHR, *Ireland v. United Kingdom* (Appl. No. 5310/71), Judgment (Plenary), 18 January 1978, Series A, Vol. 25, para. 207; ECtHR, *Aksoy v. Turkey* (Appl. No. 21987/93) Judgment (Chamber), 18 December 1996, Reports 1996-VI, para. 68; ECtHR, *Demir and Others v. Turkey* (Appl. Nos. 21380, 21381 and 21383/93) Judgment (Chamber), 23 September 1998, Reports 1998-VI, para. 43; ECtHR, *James and Others v. United Kingdom* (Appl. No. 8793/79) Judgment (Plenary), 21 February 1986, Series A, Vol. 98, para. 46; ECtHR, *Lithgow v. United Kingdom* (Appl. Nos. 9006/80; 9262, 9263, 9265, 9266, 9313 and 9405/81), Judgment (Plenary), 8 July 1986, Series A, Vol. 102, para. 122; ECtHR, *Former King of Greece v. Greece*, supra note 20, para. 87; ECtHR, *Pincova and Pinc v. Czech Republic* (Appl. No. 36548/97) Judgment (Second Section), 5 November 2002, Reports 2002-VIII, at para. 47; ECtHR, *Brannigan and McBride v. United Kingdom* (Appl. Nos. 14553 and 14554/89) Judgment (Plenary), 26 May 1993, Series A, Vol. 258-B, para. 43; *Gasus Dosier- und Fordertechnik GmbH v. The Netherlands*, supra note 20, para. 60; ECtHR, *Malama v. Greece* (Appl. No. 43622/98) Judgment (Second Section), 1 March 2001, Reports 2001-II, para. 46; ECtHR, *Jokela v. Finland* (Appl. No. 28856/95) Judgment (Fourth Section), 21 May 2002, Reports 2002-IV, para. 52; ECtHR, *Jahn v. Germany* (Appl. Nos. 46720/99; 72203 and 72552/01) Judgment

Strasbourg judges have greater *moral* expertise than domestic institutions on what human rights we have. Though the quality of Strasbourg's judgments is by no means poor and has improved significantly, there are many reasons to be sceptical that its expertise on human rights is greater than that of many national constitutional courts. First, the Court is relatively new, established as a direct, full-time Court in 1998 with the reform of Protocol 11. Some contracting states have constitutional courts and constitutional rights jurisprudence that are many decades older than Strasbourg's, serving as the repository of accumulated wisdom about rights.

Second, the Court's jurisdiction is based on 'individual justice', having a duty to examine the merits of each and every complaint that meets the requirements of admissibility. As a result, it is overburdened with applications, having less time to consider important matters of human rights principle than domestic courts operating under a more selective, *certiorari* jurisdiction. There are domestic courts, like the UK Supreme Court or the German Constitutional Court, whose judicial reasoning is on average less formulaic and legalistic than Strasbourg's, making for a more substantive engagement with human rights issues.

Third, the procedure for appointing Strasbourg judges, though more transparent and democratic than in other international institutions, is still not as rigorous as it could be. The Parliamentary Assembly of the Council of Europe elects out of a list of three candidates nominated by the government of each contracting state, in ranked order. The Assembly has the right to elect the government's second or third candidate and to refuse to accept the candidate list for want of gender balance or proper qualifications, and it has done so on occasion. In practice, the government's first choice is elected in the majority of appointments.[71] Governments, however, are not really scrutinised domestically for their choice of candidates, and there is in general little publicity surrounding the nomination and appointment process. Hence, there is greater risk that considerations other than merit and expertise might influence who gets appointed to Strasbourg, compared

---

(Third Section), 22 January 2004, not reported, para. 80; ECtHR, *Gillow* v. *United Kingdom* (Appl. No. 9063/80) Judgment (Chamber), 24 November 1986, Series A, Vol. 109, para. 56; ECtHR, *Buckley* v. *United Kingdom* (Appl. No. 20348/92) Judgment (Chamber), 25 September 1996, Reports 1996-IV, para. 75.

[71] For further discussion and analysis of the selection process, see Lambert-Abdelgawad, Chapter 7, this volume.

to procedures for appointing national judges that involve more checks and balances and attract greater publicity.[72]

Fourth, many of the new member states that joined following the collapse of Communism emerge from legal structures that have paid lip-service to the values of human rights, democracy and the rule of law.[73] It is more likely that the judges coming from these states will have little expertise in what these values practically entail, compared to judges trained within states whose legal systems have internalised and realised these values for a longer period. That is not to say that judges from these new member states will more often than not reach the wrong result.[74] The point is that, given that there is a wide spectrum of rights expertise within the Council of Europe, it will always be questionable why states with greater expertise should obey a court composed of judges the majority of whom come from states with lesser expertise.

The above four reasons suffice to show that it is doubtful that Strasbourg judges have better moral expertise on human rights than all national authorities.[75] And if such expertise is essential for engaging in the method I called the moral reading of the Convention, then it would count against this method that it is unlikely to confer legitimacy on the Court's judgments. The Court would have no reason to employ a method that could not confer on it legitimacy over states with higher expertise on rights issues. And it would be open to criticism by states with greater

---

[72] See the extensive criticism of the European Court by Lord Hoffman in his 'The Universality of Human Rights', Judicial Studies Board Annual Lecture (2009), available at: www.judiciary.gov.uk/Resources/JCO/Documents/Speeches/Hoffmann_2009_JSB_Annual_Lecture_Universality_of_Human_Rights.pdf (hereinafter Hoffman, 'The Universality of Human Rights').

[73] See the discussion in Cameron, Chapter 2, this volume.

[74] An assessment of how competent the ECtHR judges from the new member states are is not a purely empirical exercise, because it would require a normative view about what the correct outcome is in each and every case that they have decided. It is a mistake to think that whether a human rights judge is impartial or an activist depends on whether he decides against or in favour of the government, because either decision may, from a normative point of view, be correct. So purely quantitative analyses of how individual judges vote cannot make out a case of greater or lesser expertise on human rights issues. For an example of such an analysis, see E. Voeten, 'The Impartiality of International Judges: Evidence from the European Court of Human Rights', *American Political Science Review* 102:4 (2008) 417–33.

[75] The comparison I have made so far has been between Strasbourg and national courts. It is equally, if not more doubtful, that Strasbourg possesses greater expertise on human rights than non-judicial national institutions, such as legislatures.

expertise on human rights for doing so.[76] At best, the claim that Strasbourg possesses expertise-based legitimate authority would apply mainly to states with worse than average human rights records. Expertise-based arguments would have great difficulty establishing that states with the best human rights records in Europe and a long history of rights-based constitutionalism will respect human rights better by following Strasbourg than by relying on their own judgment.

The likely result of expertise-based argument is a *piecemeal* picture of Strasbourg's legitimate authority: states with poor human rights records are bound by Strasbourg because they will do a better job at complying with their obligations by following the Court than by relying on their own judgment. States with a strong human rights culture, on the other hand, are free to ignore the Court, much like the medical expert who is free to ignore the government's directives on flu vaccines. And the piecemeal picture of Strasbourg's legitimacy would justify the stance of some national authorities, like that of the UK Parliament,[77] to refuse to comply with a Strasbourg judgment that they think is a mistake.

Note, finally, that in striving to maintain expertise-based legitimacy over contracting states with less than average human rights records, the moral reading of the Convention might be a sub-optimal interpretive method. Recall that the moral reading asks the judge to interpret the Convention according to what he takes to be the best understanding of the moral values that underlie human rights. In doing so, he should not be constrained by what is most states' understanding of those values. But if Strasbourg's main authoritative role is to help states with the weakest human rights record in Europe, then it would be better to interpret the Convention according to what states with a strong human rights record do than to try to develop its own vision of human rights. For by taking the protection offered by states with strong human rights records as a yardstick, the Court would be guaranteed to provide weak states with good guidance on human rights issues and to help them reduce violations. By contrast, the moral reading of the Convention will often result

---

[76] Indeed, that is exactly the spirit of Lord Hoffman's critique: 'It is therefore hardly surprising that to the people of the United Kingdom, this judicial body does not enjoy the constitutional legitimacy which the people of the United States accord to their Supreme Court', Hoffman, 'The Universality of Human Rights', at 23. Hoffman is also, of course, very critical of the Court's use of evolutive interpretation.

[77] In February 2011, Members of Parliament backed a backbench cross-party motion supporting the blanket ban by a vote of 234 to 22. See www.guardian.co.uk/politics/2011/feb/10/mps-blanket-ban-prisoners-vote.

in challenging policies taken by strong states and, hence, risks settling on a scheme of rights that offers weaker protection.

5.1.2 Coordination-based legitimate authority

Alternatively, it could be suggested that the Court is in a position to solve some coordination problems that contracting states face, and that its legitimacy stems from this position. Consider the analogy with driving: we want to be able to drive safely and enjoy the goods of transportation, but this is possible only if we all drive on the same side of the road. As far as safety is concerned, it does not matter at all which side we drive on (left or right), what matters is that we all take the same side. However, if either option were open to each one of us, then safe driving would become impossible: we would know that we have to drive on the same side of the road as everybody else, but we would not know what side others will choose to drive on. The government solves this problem by directing us, through traffic codes and legislation, to drive on one of the two sides of the road (left in the UK, right in Continental Europe). The government has the ability to make one of the two alternatives salient in virtue of the fact that it is a *de facto* authority: drivers follow its directives and drive on the side that the government directed. Hence, the legitimate authority of government to direct our driving, the reason why we have a duty to follow traffic rules, need not have anything to do with its expertise on traffic matters. For there is no expert knowledge on whether it is better to drive on the left or on the right – either is permissible, before any practice of driving gets off the ground. The government's legitimate authority here depends partly on its ability to make a course of action salient and partly on the fact that an important good is promoted when everybody follows the same (permissible) course of action.

It is difficult to see what coordination problem the Court is there to solve. It is true that it possesses *de facto* authority, in that its judgments are generally complied with by the contracting states. However, unlike cases of coordination, human rights norms are meant to identify courses of governmental action that are *impermissible*. The Court is meant to identify what states ought not to do to people within their jurisdiction. And unlike cases of coordination, the ability of each contracting state to comply with their human rights obligations does not depend on whether other states comply with theirs. It is not that by ruling something to be a violation of human rights (say, a blanket ban on prisoners' voting) the Court makes salient one amongst many possible alternative ways in which states can promote some common good. The ruling of a human rights violation is meant to identify a *wrong* done to an individual, a wrong whose existence does not depend on what other states do.

Now, it could be argued that there is a mutual benefit whose promotion *does* depend on all contracting states following the Court's directives. Consider the claim that states with a poor human rights record will have no incentive to reduce human rights violations unless they are parties to the same binding mechanisms as states with a strong human rights record. It could then be argued that it is only if *all* states obey the Court that the protection of human rights in Europe will improve. If strong states ignore the Court's judgments, then they will not be in a position to criticise weak states that do the same and to put pressure on them to comply with their human rights obligations. This argument links up with the idea of *piecemeal* authority discussed above. We saw that the Court's expertise can provide a unique service to contracting states with poor human rights records, helping them to comply with their human rights obligations, but little or no service to other states. This would entail that the Court has legitimate authority over some states, but not others. If, however, states with a strong human rights record also have reasons to ensure that the not-so-good states improve their human rights record, *and* the way to do this is by obeying some supranational institution (albeit of lesser expertise), then the Court can come to possess legitimate authority over *all* contracting states. It would have legitimate authority over weak states because it can directly help them comply with their human rights obligation, and it would have legitimate authority over strong states because, by doing what it says, they comply with the reason they have to prevent human rights violations in weaker states.

This argument is familiar from debates about European politics. It is often argued, for instance, that it better serves the interests of Western European states (like the UK or France) if emerging European democracies (like Russia and Turkey) are parties to the ECHR rather than outside it. Empirical evidence suggests that states' human rights records improve by joining an international human rights treaty[78] and that stable democracies do not go to war with each other.[79] By giving up a little bit of sovereignty to supranational human rights institutions, Western states

---

[78] See B. Simmons, *Mobilizing for Human Rights: International Law in Domestic Politics* (Cambridge University Press, 2009) chapters 5–8.

[79] On the so-called 'democratic peace theory', see M. Doyle, 'Kant, Liberal Legacies and Foreign Affairs', *Philosophy and Public Affairs* 12 (1983) 205–23.

gain long-term benefits in peace and stability. Indeed, the entire post-World War II process of European integration started as a means to prevent another costly and catastrophic war.

But there are reasons to doubt the soundness of the above argument. We could first question the claim that emerging democracies will not be motivated to improve their human rights record unless they are parties to the same binding mechanisms as states with a strong human rights record. This is, of course, an empirical question of political science, and I do not claim to have an answer. The more important objection relates to whether states have a responsibility to do something to reduce the human rights violations occurring in *other* states. Suppose we grant that obeying the Court is the only way for European states to help improve, in the long run, the human rights record of Russia or Ukraine. Why is the UK or Germany responsible for improving the human rights record of Russia or Ukraine? Why is it part of their responsibility, given that doing so involves the significant cost of giving up part of their sovereignty and obeying an institution of lesser expertise on human rights issues?

A moral reason, let alone a duty, to ensure that other states improve their human rights records would be unduly burdensome on states. The analogy with interpersonal morality is, I think, apt here: individuals do not normally have a duty to ensure that others comply with the moral reasons that apply to them. For example, I do not normally have a reason to make sure that people with whom I have no connection do not abuse their children. Likewise, states are not normally morally responsible for the human rights violations occurring in other states, nor do they have a moral reason to prevent them, save in exceptional circumstances like genocide.

At best, states would have a *prudential* reason to do so, stemming from their own self-interest: by helping improve the human rights record of weaker states, strong states can protect their own security and economic interests, by reducing the risk that weak states will become aggressive or economically unstable. Prudential reasons, however, will be insufficient to confer legitimacy on the Court over all 47 contracting states. The current risk to security or economic interest posed to several old democracies of Europe is not substantial enough to justify such a strong limit on their sovereignty, particularly when some of the ECHR states are so remote geographically (e.g. Georgia and Azerbaijan). The result would again most likely be one of piecemeal legitimacy: several states would have a weighty reason to obey the Court's judgments because they have prudential reasons to prevent neighbouring states with a poor human rights record from escalating into rogue states. But not all contracting states would have such reasons.

5.2 Commitment-based legitimacy

For *authority-based* arguments, as I have described them, it makes no difference whether we are asking why states should obey the Court's judgments, or whether we are asking why have the ECHR or the Council of Europe in the first place. This is because the authority-based legitimacy of the Court does not depend on whether states have a legal obligation to abide by the Court's judgments. Authority-based views treat the existence of the Court's judgments as a mere *claim* that the Court be obeyed and then they ask what moral reason there could be for obeying it. According to such views, the idea that states are legally bound by the ECHR, which includes the legal duty under article 46 ECHR to abide by the decisions of the Court, is not meant to play any role in grounding the legitimacy of the Court. If it has no greater expertise in human rights issues than contracting states and is not solving some coordination issue, then it has no legitimate authority over them.

By contrast, *commitment-based* arguments for legitimacy treat the fact that states made a voluntary undertaking to be bound by the ECHR, as well as the subsequent practice of honouring that undertaking, as morally relevant. The morality of promises or agreement, encapsulated in the principle *pacta sunt servanda*, here plays a crucial role: just like individuals, states are agents whose will and practice matters in relation to the obligations they have. For example, the promise to my neighbours that I will abide by a joint scheme of recycling, as well as the subsequent compliance with that scheme by everyone, generate reciprocal moral obligations to respect it. It does so, even if the scheme established is sub-optimal in serving the relevant goal and even if some parties to the joint scheme would be in a position to act optimally (e.g. recycle more) were they to violate the scheme.[80] It is important to highlight here that the duty to keep one's promise is by and large independent from whether one had, absent the promise, a duty to do what one promised. For example, my duty to meet you for lunch tomorrow, as I promised, does not depend on whether I had a reason to meet you for lunch or to promise to do so. Likewise, states' duty to respect the judgments of a treaty-based, collective mechanism for enforcing human

---

[80] A number of moral principles to do with fairness, legitimate expectations and reliance account for the obligations that arise out of collective institutional action. I cannot here elaborate on the precise shape of the moral principles that make past institutional practice relevant.

rights obligations does not depend on whether they had, prior to the treaty, a duty to join such a treaty.[81]

To be sure, it is not the case that states have a duty to respect human rights only if they have agreed by treaty to do so. Arguably, a core list of fundamental rights, including – but not limited to – *jus cogens* norms, are binding on all states, whether or not they have signed up to a human rights treaty. Yet it does not follow from the fact that states have non-consent-based obligations that they also have duties to abide by the judgment of particular institutions on what these obligations are. For example, the fact that China has human rights obligations, whether or not it has ratified human rights treaties, does not mean that it is bound by the views of the International Convention on Civil and Political Rights (ICCPR) Human Rights Committee or the judgment of the ECtHR on what these obligations are. This is one part where the commitment and subsequent practice of states makes a difference: in virtue of setting up or joining a treaty with a binding enforcement mechanism, like the ECHR, and of using this mechanism in their institutional practices, states acquire an obligation to respect the joint scheme and judgment of supranational institutions like the Court. This obligation is partly based on the morality of agreements and partly on the fact that past institutional practice, including the practice of international institutions, changes what reasons states have.[82] The force of this obligation is not instrumental, that is, it does not depend on whether following the Court's judgments is beneficial for states or makes it more likely to comply with the reasons that applied to states prior to joining. In other words, treaty-based obligations are not morally neutral or 'formal': they are *deontic*, grounded on principles of political morality that pertain to agreements and collective action; they

---

[81] Admittedly, this account says very little about what reasons states have in the first place for agreeing to create supranational human rights organisations and to be bound by them. For what matters on this account is the existence of state agreement and subsequent international practice, not any prior reasons for agreeing and engaging in that practice. And states can be motivated to set up or join international human rights organisations by a variety of considerations, without there being an actual reason (let alone a duty) for them to do so. On the view defended here, the Court's legitimacy does not depend on there being a reason for states to set up international human rights institutions.

[82] For the idea that past political practice changes what constitutes rightful and wrongful ways for government to act, see N. Stavropoulos, 'Why Principles?', available at http://papers.ssrn.com/sol3/papers.cfm?abstract_id=1023758); and M. Greenberg, 'The Standard Picture and its Discontents', available at http://papers.ssrn.com/sol3/papers.cfm?abstract_id=1103569.

bind states not because of the consequential *effects* of the agreement, but in virtue of the fact that states have made a mutual commitment to respect the judgments of the institution that the treaty established, and followed through on that commitment in their institutional practices, generating requirements of fairness and respecting mutual expectations. The mutual commitment to set up a joint mechanism for the protection of human rights in Europe is clear in the text of the Convention, particularly article 46 paragraph 1 ECHR:

> The High Contracting Parties undertake to abide by the final judgment of the Court in any case to which they are parties.

Moreover, there is no doubt that the ECHR has had a profound effect on the institutional practice of states at both international and domestic level: not only do states comply with the judgments of the Court by awarding compensation to the victims, but they also routinely alter their national policies to make them consistent with the Court's case law.

Of course, treaty-based duties, just like promissory duties, are not absolute; they provide states with a *defeasible* reason to abide by the Court's judgment. But this reason is enough to ground the *pro tanto* legitimacy of the Court. Other things being equal, states have a duty to comply with the Court's judgments, regardless of whether they are good or bad. A state must adduce some pretty weighty considerations for not complying with the Court's judgment. Mere disagreement with the judgment would be insufficient to defeat the treaty-based obligation.

Now, it could be objected that there must be limits to how much of the Court's interpretive authority is justified by states' treaty-based agreement. Did states really agree to give the Court *carte-blanche* on how to interpret the ECHR? Did they consent to the Court using the evolutive interpretation to inflate the scope of ECHR rights and increase the number of ECHR obligations that states have? If the Court's jurisprudence, inspired by evolutive interpretation, has exceeded the bounds of the treaty-based authority, then perhaps it makes sense to challenge its legitimacy and look for alternative bases for its authority, such as expertise or coordination solving.

The above objection raises an important question about how we are to understand states' agreement to create the ECHR, set up the ECtHR, and make its judgments binding. There is no doubt that most old contracting states would not have anticipated the expansive interpretation of the Convention rights by the Court and the burden that the Court's jurisprudence would impose on state sovereignty. On the other hand, however, there is equally no doubt that the ECHR contracting states wanted to create not only legally binding obligations, but also legally binding *determinations* of when these obligations have been breached. Unlike the ICCPR Human Rights Committee or other international 'soft-law' mechanism, the reform of Protocol 11 ECHR clearly established Strasbourg as a court whose judgments are legally binding. They did so, moreover, with a view to promoting specific aims listed stated in the ECHR preamble: first, to 'achieve greater unity' between them and second, 'to take the first steps for the *collective enforcement* of certain of the rights stated in the Universal Declaration' (my emphasis). Greater political unity and collective enforcement of fundamental rights were the abstract background aims of the initial drafting of the ECHR and they continue to be so, until states reform or withdraw from it.

So herein lies the Court's legitimacy to use evolutive interpretation and to develop the meaning of the Convention rights, often against states' expectations or preferences: first, states gave the Court the legal mandate to provide institutional remedies for the violation of people's human rights, whatever these moral rights happen to be. The Convention is meant to protect whatever human rights people *in fact* have, and not what human rights domestic authorities or public opinion *think* people have. As a result, a better understanding of the nature of human rights and the principles that justify them will require an evolving interpretation of the Convention. Second, states also promised to abide by the Court's *determinations* of whether a human right has been violated. They did not, as they could have done, take the Court's judgments to be mere recommendations or soft law. And third, there has been a long institutional practice of contracting states respecting and implementing the scheme of rights that the Court, through its case law, has produced. The existence of such practice generates obligations of fairness amongst contracting states to respect this scheme, even if it is imperfect from the point of view of ideal morality. As we saw in previous sections, the scheme of rights that the Court has produced does not condition the existence of the right that the applicant claims to have under the ECHR on whether there is state consensus to that effect.

However, are there limits to how far the Court can go in seeking to discover the true nature and content of people's human rights? Of course there are. But these limits have nothing to do with the Court's expertise or with the quality of this or that judgment. Nor do they have anything to do with states' consensus on what is and what is not a human rights violation.

The most important limit relates to the character of the Court's reasoning. The Court has two fundamental obligations in this respect. First, to reason in *good faith*, seeking to discover the principles that underlie and justify human rights and to apply them to the case at hand. And second, it has a duty, as any court, to strive to justify its decisions according to a scheme of principles that represents an intelligible and coherent vision of justice.[83] As Ronald Dworkin argues, courts cannot rely on one principle to decide a case and then offend that very same principle to decide the next case.[84] And it is here that the use of evolutive interpretation becomes essential to the Court's legitimacy: the Court should seek to construct a coherent body of principles in its case law by constantly adjusting, modifying and reshaping the scope and meaning of the Convention rights in the light of the body of principles that it uses. It is this need for coherence that the method of evolutive interpretation serves: other things being equal, the Court cannot deny protection in a newly developed problem (say, domestic workers, or trafficking), if its existing principles are applicable. By 'expanding' the scope of the Convention rights, the Court simply applies existing law. Any so-called 'expansive' interpretation of a Convention right is legitimate so long as it is a good-faith application of a principle that the Court has consistently applied and recognised in its case law.

But of course, the duty to reason in good faith and to strive for consistency of principle over time is not the only consideration bearing on the Court. Like any moral duty, it may be outweighed by exceptional cases in which there is a threat of devastating consequences, justifying the Court granting a margin of appreciation, in violation of its principles. But these cases are few and far between, relating to a clear and present danger of drastic repercussions within the respondent state, following an adverse ruling.[85] The mere fact that the respondent state (or a large number of contracting states) will be frustrated by an adverse ruling and that its politicians will make noises, usually for party-political gains, about the legitimacy of the Court, is not a good reason for the Court to compromise its principles.

[83] This is what Dworkin calls 'integrity' in R. Dworkin, *Law's Empire* (Oxford: Hart Publishing, 1986) chapter 6. See also S. Hershovitz, 'Integrity and Stare Decisis', in S. Hershovitz (ed.), *Exploring Law's Empire* (Oxford University Press, 2006) 103–18.
[84] R. Dworkin, *Justice in Robes* (Cambridge, MA: Harvard University Press, 2006), at 53.
[85] Such a case arises, in my view, when there is a clear and present danger that a contracting state with a poor human rights record will withdraw from the ECHR because of the ruling of a violation. See the discussion in Letsas, 'A Theory of Interpretation', chapter 6.

In sum, the advantage of the commitment-based argument for the Court's legitimacy is that, unlike the authority-based argument, it explains why the Court has legitimacy over *all* 47 contracting states. All 47 states undertook a commitment to respect a joint scheme of determining and enforcing human rights obligations and all 47 states have adjusted their institutional practice to make it consistent with the scheme that the Court, through its case law, has developed. The commitment-based argument also explains why its legitimacy is not under threat each time it makes a poor decision or each time a respondent state thinks that the Court went too far. Commitment-based legitimacy *can* be lost if the Court's reasoning lacks certain features: first, if it becomes a bad faith attempt to exceed the Court's legal mandate and to restrict the sovereignty of contracting states. And second, if its reasoning lacks principled consistency, deciding cases arbitrarily. The method of evolutive interpretation, understood as the moral reading of the Convention, is essential if the Court's case law is to be principled and, consequently, if the Court is to preserve its legitimacy. As we have seen in sections 2 and 3, the Court's case law over time has acquired greater depth and consistency, through relying on evolutive interpretation and on the search for common values in international law.

6. Conclusion

It is too early to tell whether the Court's interpretive ethic, crystallised after the reform of Protocol 11, will survive the recent attacks on its legitimacy. The current political climate and the continuing economic crisis put additional pressure on supranational institutions, including the Court, to show greater deference to national authorities. The Court treated the ECHR as a living instrument, nourishing it to become a large and fairly consistent body of rights-based principles for the whole of Europe. The Court's interpretive ethic is a unique asset for Europe and the best example of a successful international system for protecting human rights. If the Court continues to treat the Convention as a living instrument, it will not lose its legitimacy; it will lose it if it does not.

5

No longer offering fine mantras to a parched child? The European Court's developing approach to remedies

PHILIP LEACH

1. Introduction

Any assessment of the nature or extent of redress to be provided by a court needs to grapple with the question of the purpose of its remedial measures. Are they intended to restore, to rectify, to rehabilitate, to compensate, to provide restitution, to deter, to reconcile (but perhaps not to provide retribution)? For a court that adjudicates on violations of broadly-phrased human rights standards, on an international basis, these are especially difficult questions to answer. It is inevitably an imprecise science – how can it be possible to measure the equivalence of a particular remedy to the past violation of a fundamental right? Some violations are, of course, simply irreparable.

The European Court of Human Rights (the Court, or the ECtHR) has had surprisingly little to say about such notions. Apparently constrained by perceptions of state sovereignty, and overly deferential to the principle of subsidiarity, it has traditionally proved to be decidedly unadventurous on the question of redress, favouring a limited, declaratory approach. Consequently, it has often been criticised for its conservatism, as, for example, when one of its own judges suggested that the Court's approach was like trying to quench the thirst of a parched child with fine mantras.[1] However, in recent years the Court's stance has changed markedly, in the light of the manifest inadequacy of declaratory relief and under the weight of increasing numbers of systemic and egregious human rights violations, such that it is now not uncommon for the Court to direct a state to amend or introduce legislation within a matter of months. These developments have not, however, been

---

[1] ECtHR, *Aquilina* v. *Malta* (Appl. No. 25642/94), Judgment (Grand Chamber), 29 April 1999, Reports 1999-III, Partly Dissenting Opinion of Judge Bonello.

met with universal approval, as evidenced for example, by the furore in the UK over prisoner voting rights.

This chapter traces and analyses these developments, and seeks to ask how and why the Court has altered its position so profoundly in relation to non-monetary remedies. It discusses the Court's increasingly prescriptive approach to redress as regards property cases, unfair trials, unlawful detention and in situations where there have been large-scale systemic Convention breaches. It also analyses the suitability of redress awarded in cases concerning egregious violations of the Convention. The chapter considers whether such changes are in compliance, or in conflict, with the principle of subsidiarity, and it also makes some suggestions as to how the Court should develop its position on redress, post-Interlaken.

2. The legal basis for redress

The sources of the Court's remedial powers are both the binding nature of its judgments (under article 46(1) of the European Convention on Human Rights (the Convention, or the ECHR))[2] and its capability (exercised as a discretion) to award 'just satisfaction' to the victims of human rights violations (under article 41).[3] In view of its legally binding nature, it is trite Strasbourg law that the effect of a judgment in which the Court finds a violation of the ECHR is to impose a legal obligation on the respondent state both to put an end to the breach and to make reparation for its consequences in such a way as to restore as far as possible the situation existing before the breach ('*restitutio in integrum*'). Therefore, if *restitutio in integrum* is possible, it is for the state to carry it out (not the Court).[4] If, however, *restitutio in integrum* is in practice impossible, the respondent state is free to choose the means for complying with a judgment,[5] provided that those means are compatible with the conclusions

---

[2] Article 46(1) of the ECHR provides: 'The High Contracting Parties undertake to abide by the final judgment of the Court in any case to which they are parties.'

[3] Article 41 of the ECHR provides: 'If the Court finds that there has been a violation of the Convention or the protocols thereto, and if the internal law of the High Contracting Party concerned allows only partial reparation to be made, the Court shall, if necessary, afford just satisfaction to the injured party.'

[4] See, e.g., ECtHR, *Iatridis* v. *Greece* (Appl. No. 31107/96), Judgment (Grand Chamber), 19 October 2000, Reports 1999-II, paras. 32–3.

[5] See, e.g., ECtHR, *Selçuk and Asker* v. *Turkey* (Appl. Nos. 23184 and 23185/94), Judgment (Chamber), 24 April 1998, Reports 1998-II, para. 125.

set out in the Court's judgment.[6] This 'room to manoeuvre' has been said to reflect the discretion given to states as to how they honour their fundamental obligation under article 1 of the Convention to secure to everyone the rights and freedoms guaranteed by the Convention.[7]

The obligation on the state to do more than simply pay damages to an applicant has been explicitly and repeatedly reiterated by the Court. For example:

> A judgment in which the Court finds a breach imposes on the respondent state a legal obligation not just to pay those concerned the sums awarded by way of just satisfaction, but also to choose, subject to supervision by the Committee of Ministers, the general and/or, if appropriate, individual measures to be adopted in their domestic legal order to put an end to the violation found by the Court and to redress so far as possible the effects.[8]

The Court has also frequently emphasised that the purpose of awarding just satisfaction is 'to provide reparation solely for damage suffered by those concerned to the extent that such events constitute a consequence of the violation that cannot otherwise be remedied'.[9] The jurisprudence of the Court has established that even a partial failure to execute a judgment will engage the state's international responsibility.[10] Furthermore, placing reliance on the law of state responsibility, the Court has held that restitution will be required unless there is material impossibility,[11] or it would involve a disproportionate burden:

> ... a State responsible for a wrongful act is under an obligation to make restitution, consisting in restoring the situation which existed before the wrongful act was committed, provided that restitution is not 'materially impossible' and 'does not involve a burden out of all proportion to the benefit deriving from restitution instead of compensation' (article 35 of the Draft Articles of the International Law Commission on Responsibility of States for Internationally Wrongful Acts...).[12]

---

[6] See, e.g., ECtHR, *Scozzari and Giunta v. Italy* (Appl. Nos. 39221 and 41963/98), Judgment (Grand Chamber), 13 July 2000, Reports 2000-VIII.

[7] See, e.g., *Iatridis v. Greece*, para. 33.

[8] See, e.g., *Scozzari and Giunta v. Italy*, para. 249.   [9] *Ibid.*, para. 250.

[10] ECtHR, *Verein gegen Tierfabriken Schweiz (VgT) v. Switzerland (No. 2)* (Appl. No. 32772/02), Judgment (Grand Chamber), 30 June 2009, Reports 2009, para. 85.

[11] Loucaides has been critical of the Court's past failure adequately to assess the question of whether restitution was impossible, when this point has been argued by respondent states. See L. Loucaides, 'Reparation for Violations of Human Rights under the European Convention and *Restitutio in Integrum*', (2008) *European Human Rights Law Review*, 182–92, at 185–6 (hereinafter Loucaides, 'Reparations').

[12] *Verein gegen Tierfabriken*, para. 86.

THE EUROPEAN COURT'S DEVELOPING APPROACH TO REMEDIES 145

In spite of these explicit Convention obligations to provide reparations, and indeed, to ensure *restitutio in integrum*, the Court's traditional approach to the issue of redress has been cautious and conservative – and certainly mindful of the pitfalls of being perceived to tread on state sovereignty. Such a stance is not unique within international human rights systems, reflecting, it has been suggested, the innovative and developing nature of international human rights procedures, a lack of confidence both about the scope of powers to provide remedies and about states' willingness to comply, an emphasis on cessation and non-repetition of the violation in question, and a lack of national judicial experience amongst international tribunal members.[13] The Court's judgments have therefore been 'essentially declaratory'.[14] Thus, in a case in which the applicant has successfully established that the Convention has been violated, the Court's usual approach has been to issue a declaration to the effect that the Convention has been violated (with detailed reasoning) and to exercise its discretion whether to award compensation (in the form of pecuniary and/or non-pecuniary damages) and legal costs. This predominant approach is also, as Judge Costa has noted, a reflection of the subsidiarity principle:

> The distinction between the choice of means and the obligation to achieve a specific result thus seeks to reconcile the principle of subsidiarity with the collective guarantee of the rights and freedoms protected by the Convention.[15]

Accordingly, as regards the state's wider duty to provide reparation, the Court has been very reluctant to issue 'consequential orders or declaratory statements',[16] such as directing a state to instigate criminal or disciplinary proceedings,[17] ordering a state to allow an excluded applicant to return to the state's territory,[18] or to give undertakings as to future

---

[13] D. Shelton, *Remedies in International Human Rights Law*, 2nd edn (Oxford University Press, 2005) 1–2 (hereinafter Shelton, *Remedies*).
[14] See, e.g., ECtHR, *Marckx v. Belgium* (Appl. No. 6833/74), Judgment (Plenary), 13 June 1979, Series A, No. 31, para. 58; ECtHR, *Assanidze v. Georgia* (Appl. No. 71503/01), Judgment (Grand Chamber), 8 April 2004, Reports 2004-II, para. 202.
[15] *Assanidze v. Georgia*, ibid., Partly Concurring Opinion of Judge Costa, para. 4.
[16] See, e.g., *Selçuk and Asker v. Turkey*, para. 125.
[17] See, e.g., ECtHR, *Ireland v. United Kingdom* (Appl. No. 5310/71), Judgment 18 January 1978, Series A, No. 25, para. 187.
[18] See, e.g., ECtHR, *Mehemi v. France* (Appl. No. 25017/94), Judgment (Chamber), 26 September 1997, Reports 1997-VI, paras. 42–3.

conduct.[19] It has not quashed the decisions of the domestic authorities or courts, reasoning that it could not speculate what the outcome of the domestic proceedings would have been had there been no Convention violation.[20] Nor has the Court's traditional approach been to strike down (or require a state to alter) its legislation. For example, in its 2002 judgment in *Lundevall v. Sweden*,[21] the Court explicitly noted that 'the Convention does not empower it to order a State to alter its legislation'. In 2007, the Grand Chamber found in *Dickson v. United Kingdom*[22] that a refusal to allow the applicant prisoner access to artificial insemination facilities breached article 8 of the Convention, but a request that the government be directed to allow such access was denied, with the Court emphasising the primacy of its function to rule on questions of compatibility with the Convention.

As a consequence of the Court's highly respectful attitude towards state sovereignty, and also because the award of damages and legal costs is in the Court's discretion, it has frequently been the practice of the Court to conclude that the finding of a violation of the Convention constitutes sufficient 'just satisfaction', and therefore even to decline to award any damages at all. This practice has not infrequently been the subject of judicial dissent.[23] When Joseph Aquilina, a teenager in Malta, was arrested and was first taken before a magistrate and charged with defiling his girlfriend in a public place, the Grand Chamber of the Court found that the fact that the magistrate had had no power to order his release violated his rights under article 5(3) of the Convention. However, the majority of the Court declined to award him any non-pecuniary damages, adopting its formula of a finding of a violation constituting sufficient just satisfaction.[24] This was met with stinging criticism by

---

[19] See, e.g., ECtHR, *Campbell and Cosans v. United Kingdom (Article 50)* (Appl. Nos. 7511 and 7743/76), Judgment (Chamber), 23 March 1983, Series A, No. 60, para. 16.

[20] See, e.g., ECtHR, *Schmautzer v. Austria* (Appl. No. 15523/89), Court (Chamber), 23 October 1995, Series A, No. 328-A, paras. 42–4; ECtHR, *Lyons and Others v. UK* (Appl. No. 15227/03), Admissibility Decision, 8 July 2003, Reports 2003-IX.

[21] See, e.g., ECtHR, *Lundevall v. Sweden* (Appl. No. 38629/97), Judgment (Fourth Section), 12 November 2002, not reported, para. 44.

[22] ECtHR, *Dickson v. United Kingdom* (Appl. No. 44362/04), Judgment (Grand Chamber), 4 December 2007, Reports 2007-V.

[23] See, e.g., the Separate Opinions of Judges Ganshof van der Meersch and Evrigenis, and of Judge Bindschedler-Robert in ECtHR, *Engel and Others v. Netherlands (Article 50)* (Appl. Nos. 5100, 5101 and 5102/71; 5354 and 5370/72), Judgment (Plenary), 23 November 1976, Series A, No. 22.

[24] *Aquilina v. Malta*, para. 59.

Judge Bonello in his Partly Dissenting Opinion,[25] who considered it to be 'wholly inadequate and unacceptable that a court of justice should "satisfy" the victim of a breach of fundamental rights with a mere handout of legal idiom'.[26] Putting it another way, he suggested that 'hoping to satisfy a victim of injustice with cunning forms of words is like trying to quench the thirst of a parched child with fine mantras'.[27] Dissenting on the same issue in the subsequent *Kingsley* judgment, Judge Casadevall (joined by Judges Bonello and Kovler) articulated a similar complaint, that 'applicants are entitled to something more than a mere moral victory or the satisfaction of having contributed to enriching the Court's case-law'.[28] Although the particular concern in the *Aquilina* case was the denial of damages, Judge Bonello was clearly also concerned about the Court's limited approach to remedies more generally:

> It is regrettable enough as it is, albeit understandable, that, in the sphere of granting redress, the Court, in its early days, imposed on itself the restriction of never ordering performance of specific remedial measures in favour of the victim. That exercise in judicial restraint has already considerably narrowed the spectrum of the Court's effectiveness. Doubling that restraint, to the point of denying any compensation at all to those found to have been the victims of violations of the Convention, has further diminished the Court's purview and dominion.

The Court is empowered to award both pecuniary and non-pecuniary damages, as well as legal costs and expenses. Awards for non-pecuniary damage have reflected a very wide range of consequences suffered by the victims, including pain and suffering;[29] anguish and distress;[30] disruption to life;[31] trauma;[32] uncertainty, anxiety, stress and feelings of

---

[25] Six judges dissented on this point (with four others publishing Dissenting Opinions: Judges Tulkens, Casadevall, Fischbach and Greve).
[26] See his similar comments in his Dissenting Opinion in ECtHR, *Nikolova* v. *Bulgaria* (Appl. No. 31195/96), Judgment (Grand Chamber), 25 March 1999, Reports 1999-II.
[27] *Aquilina* v. *Malta*, Partly Dissenting Opinion of Judge Bonello.
[28] ECtHR, *Kingsley* v. *United Kingdom* (Appl. No. 35605/97), Judgment (Grand Chamber), 28 May 2002, Reports 2002-IV.
[29] See, e.g., ECtHR, *KA* v. *Finland* (Appl. No. 22751/95), Judgment (Fourth Section), 14 January 2003, not reported.
[30] See, e.g., ECtHR, *Werner* v. *Poland* (Appl. No. 26760/95), Judgment (Fourth Section), 15 November 2001, not reported.
[31] See, e.g., ECtHR, *Steel and Morris* v. *United Kingdom* (Appl. No. 68416/01), Judgment (Fourth Section), 15 February 2005, Reports 2005-II.
[32] See, e.g., ECtHR, *MC* v. *Bulgaria* (Appl. No. 39272/98), Judgment (First Section), 4 December 2003, Reports 2003-XII.

injustice;[33] embarrassment;[34] frustration;[35] inconvenience;[36] feelings of isolation and helplessness;[37] loss of opportunity;[38] loss of reputation;[39] and loss of relationship.[40] There have been frequent criticisms that the principles on which damages awards are made are not clear or have lacked coherency,[41] with an over-reliance on making assessments 'on an equitable basis',[42] or indeed (as discussed above) to make no award at all on the basis that the finding of a violation itself is sufficient. This situation is, in part at least, a reflection of the inherent difficulties in quantifying damages:

> ... a precise calculation of the sums necessary to make complete reparation (*restitutio in integrum*) in respect of the pecuniary losses suffered by the applicant may be prevented by the inherently uncertain character of the damage flowing from the violation. The question to be decided in such cases is the level of just satisfaction, which is a matter to be determined by the Court at its discretion, having regard to what is equitable.[43]

Although damages awards have traditionally represented the mainstay of the Court's approach to redress, they are not the primary concern of this chapter, which will focus instead on the developing picture as regards non-monetary remedies.

---

[33] See, e.g., ECtHR, *C v. Finland* (Appl. No. 18249/02), Judgment (Fourth Section), 9 May 2006, not reported.

[34] See, e.g., ECtHR, *Peck v. United Kingdom* (Appl. No. 44647/98), Judgment (Fourth Section), 28 January 2003, Reports 2003-I.

[35] See, e.g., ECtHR, *RD v. Poland* (Appl. Nos. 29692/96 and 34612/97), Judgment (Fourth Section), 18 December 2001, not reported.

[36] See, e.g., ECtHR, *Stretch v. United Kingdom* (Appl. No. 44277/98), Judgment (Fourth Section), 24 June 2003, not reported.

[37] See, e.g., ECtHR, *Djavit An v. Turkey* (Appl. No. 20652/92), Judgment (Third Section), 20 February 2003, Reports 2003-III.

[38] See, e.g., ECtHR, *Sadak and Others v. Turkey* (Appl. Nos. 29900, 29901, 29902 and 29903/96), Judgment (First Section), 17 July 2001, Reports 2001-VIII.

[39] See, e.g., ECtHR, *Kyprianou v. Cyprus* (Appl. No. 73797/01), Judgment (Grand Chamber), 15 December 2005, Reports 2005-XIII.

[40] See, e.g., ECtHR, *Kutzner v. Germany* (Appl. No. 46544/99), Judgment (Fourth Section), 26 February 2002, Reports 2002-I.

[41] Shelton, *Remedies*, at 197; F. Hampson, 'The Future of the European Court of Human Rights', in G. Gilbert, F. Hampson and C. Sandoval (eds.), *Strategic Visions for Human Rights: Essays in Honour of Professor Kevin Boyle* (London and New York: Routledge, 2011), at 163; P. Leach, *Taking a Case to the European Court of Human Rights*, 3rd edn (Oxford University Press, 2011) 466–8.

[42] See, e.g., ECtHR, *Scoppola v. Italy (No. 2)* (Appl. No. 10249/03), Judgment (Grand Chamber), 17 September 2009, not reported.

[43] ECtHR, *Karandja v. Bulgaria* (Appl. No. 69180/01), Judgment (Fifth Section), 7 October 2010, para. 76, not reported.

3. A more expansive approach?

Latterly, however, the Court has exhibited a far greater degree of flexibility and creativity in its approach to redress, in going beyond its standard, declaratory approach in responding to various types of Convention violations, including the failure to compensate people who had lost property when it was nationalised, unfair trials, and, most starkly, individuals unlawfully detained by the state. As we will see below, this certainly represents a more incisive approach and one therefore that could be characterised as pushing against the boundaries of notions of state sovereignty. These developments are also mirrored in the expanding coverage of interim measures rulings,[44] and indeed in the Court's insistence, since 2005, on the binding nature of such measures,[45] which have become a form of injunctive relief.[46] It is important, therefore, to ask how the Court has done this, and, indeed, why.

3.1 Restitution of property

Requiring a state to take specific, directed steps in order to achieve *restitutio in integrum* has been most prevalent in property-related cases, notably those concerning the nationalisation of property, where applicants have successfully complained of violations of their right to 'peaceful enjoyment' of their possessions under article 1 of Protocol No. 1 to the Convention. In such cases, the Court may require the state to return land and buildings which had been unlawfully and unjustifiably expropriated. In its 1995 judgment in *Papamichalopoulos and Others* v. *Greece*,[47] the Court held that the unlawfulness of an expropriation would affect the criteria for determining the reparation owed, taking inspiration from the judgment of the Permanent Court of International Justice in the *Chorzów Factory* case (of 13 September 1928) and referring to the

---

[44] See, e.g., ECtHR, Öcalan v. Turkey (Appl. No. 46221/99), Judgment (Grand Chamber), 12 May 2005, Reports 2005-IV; ECtHR, Evans v. United Kingdom (Appl. No. 6339/05), Judgment (Grand Chamber), 10 April 2007, Reports 2007-I; ECtHR, Grori v. Albania (Appl. No. 25336/04), Judgment (Fourth Section), 7 July 2009, not reported.

[45] ECtHR, Mamatkulov and Askarov v. Turkey (Appl. Nos. 46827 and 46951/99), Judgment (Grand Chamber), 4 February 2005, Reports 2005-I, para. 128.

[46] Interim measures are not further considered in this chapter, as they are discussed in Lambert-Abdelgawad, Chapter 7, this volume.

[47] ECtHR, Papamichalopoulos and Others v. Greece (Appl. No. 14556/89), Judgment (Chamber), 31 October 1995, Series A, No. 330-B.

principle of restitution in kind. A similar decision was made in *Brumarescu v. Romania*,[48] thereby reinforcing a final domestic court order requiring restitution, but which had not been enforced. Failing such restitution, the Court in the *Brumarescu* judgment required the Romanian state to pay damages equivalent to the current value of the property. A further example is the case of *Dacia S.R.L. v. Moldova*,[49] which concerned the unlawful deprivation of the applicant company's hotel, in violation of article 1 of Protocol No. 1 and article 6. Under article 41, the Court held that the most appropriate form of *restitutio in integrum* would be for the hotel and underlying land to be returned to the applicant company, and for compensation to be paid for any additional losses sustained. In case that were to prove impossible, the Court went on to determine the monetary value of the hotel to be paid in lieu of restitution of it (about €7.6 million, at the current market value), less sums already paid back to the applicant company, so as to avoid any unjust enrichment.[50] A decision to similar effect was made in *Saghinadze and Others v. Georgia*,[51] which concerned the unlawful eviction of an Abkhazian internally displaced person (IDP) from a cottage belonging to the Georgian Ministry of Interior, after ten years' right of occupation. However, in *Saghinadze* the Court also proposed that the provision of an alternative property (presumably of equivalence) would satisfy the obligation to redress. Under article 41, the Court found that:[52]

> ... the most appropriate form of redress would be *restitutio in integrum* under the IDPs Act, that is, to have the cottage restored to the first applicant's possession pending the establishment of conditions which would allow his return, in safety and with dignity, to his place of habitual residence in Abkhazia, Georgia. Alternatively, should the return of the cottage prove impossible, the Court is of the view that the first applicant's claim could also be satisfied by providing him, as an internally displaced person, with other proper accommodation or paying him reasonable compensation for the loss of the right to use the cottage ...

---

[48] ECtHR, *Brumarescu v. Romania* (Appl. No. 28342/95), Judgment (Grand Chamber), 23 January 2001, Reports 2001-I. See also ECtHR, *Zwierzynski v. Poland* (Appl. No. 34049/96), Judgment (First Section), 2 July 2002, not reported; ECtHR, *Hirschhorn v. Romania* (Appl. No. 29294/02), Judgment (Third Section), 26 July 2007, not reported.
[49] ECtHR, *Dacia SRL v. Moldova* (Appl. No. 3052/04), Judgment (Fourth Section), 19 February 2009, not reported.
[50] *Ibid.*, paras. 55–6.
[51] ECtHR, *Saghinadze and Others v. Georgia* (Appl. No. 18768/05), Judgment (Second Section), 27 May 2010, not reported.
[52] *Ibid.*, para. 160.

In cases concerning the violation of property rights, the Court has also obliged states to ensure that landowners are correctly registered. In *Bozcaada Kimisis Teodoku Rum Ortodoks Kilisesi Vakfı* v. *Turkey (No. 2)*,[53] the Court found a violation of article 1 of Protocol No. 1 because the Turkish authorities had refused to enter the applicant, a Greek Orthodox Church foundation, in the land register as the owner of property it had in fact held for more than 20 years. Consequently, the Court required the property to be registered in the applicant foundation's name (within a period of three months), or failing that, the foundation was to be paid €100,000 by way of pecuniary damages.

There are two influences of which the Court has appeared to take particular cognisance in these cases. The first is that the Court may be acting, in effect, to reinforce the domestic law or in support of the approach taken by the national courts. In that sense, it could therefore be said that the principle of subsidiarity is being applied. However, the picture may be a complex one where there are divergences between (and indeed, within) national bodies as to what is the correct approach. In that situation, you may have an international court acting in concert with a national court, against what, in effect, may be the domestic forces of opposition to the implementation of the rule of law by the courts. Such resistance may well have a political basis, but could also result from more mundane problems such as endemic bureaucratic obstacles or lack of funds. The second influence is the nature or extent of the illegality in question. It may therefore be important to consider whether the expropriation of the land was itself unlawful, or whether the Convention violation had a different basis. For example, in *Former King of Greece and Others* v. *Greece*,[54] the Court found a violation of article 1 of Protocol No. 1, not as a result of the state's expropriation, as such, of the applicants' property, but as a result of the failure to pay compensation. Accordingly, in view of the distinction which the Court made between lawful and unlawful expropriations, it was held that it was not appropriate to order *restitutio in integrum*, although the state was said to be free to decide to return some or all of the property to the applicants. Does this indicate that the 'more unlawful' the violation in question, the more

---

[53] ECtHR, *Bozcaada Kimisis Teodoku Rum Ortodoks Kilisesi Vakfı* v. *Turkey (No. 2)* (Appl. Nos. 37639 and 37655/03; 26736 and 42670/04), Judgment (Second Section), 3 March 2009, not reported.
[54] ECtHR, *Former King of Greece and Others* v. *Greece* (Appl. No. 25701/94), Judgment (Grand Chamber), 28 November 2002, not reported.

willing the Court is to 'step in' and direct the national authorities? We will return to this question below when considering unlawful detention.

3.2 Unfair domestic legal proceedings

For several decades, the consequences of the Court finding that an applicant had been convicted in the course of domestic criminal proceedings which were unfair, or had been party to inequitable civil proceedings, were often negligible. There was certainly no right to have the domestic proceedings reopened, nor was there any real expectation of that happening. This illogical state of affairs had, however, changed by the early 2000s.

The Court's evolving stance on this question has enjoyed political support from the Committee of Ministers, which has explicitly recognised that in certain situations the re-examination of a case by the domestic authorities, or the reopening of proceedings, will be the most efficient means of achieving *restitutio in integrum*. A Committee of Ministers Recommendation in 2000[55] urged Convention states to ensure that it is possible to re-examine or reopen cases where the Court has found a violation of the Convention. As a result, many Convention states have now established means by which domestic proceedings can be reopened following a Court finding of a violation of the Convention.[56] Where the domestic legal system does not yet allow for the reopening of proceedings in such circumstances, the Court will urge the state to take steps to ensure that the applicants can be adequately redressed, as it has done, for example, in relation to Bosnia and Herzegovina, and Albania.[57] Since 2003, it has accordingly become common practice for the Court to urge states to reopen criminal proceedings, where it has found those proceedings to have violated the Convention.[58] These are recommendations by the Court which are not strictly legally binding.

---

[55] Committee of Ministers, 'Recommendation No. R(2000)2', 19 January 2000.
[56] See *ibid.*, Explanatory Memorandum, para. 3.
[57] See, e.g., ECtHR, *Karanović* v. *Bosnia and Herzegovina* (Appl. No. 39462/03), Judgment (Fourth Section), 20 November 2007, not reported; ECtHR, *Laska and Lika* v. *Albania* (Appl. Nos. 12315 and 17605/04), Judgment (Fourth Section), 20 April 2010, not reported.
[58] See, e.g., ECtHR, *Gençel* v. *Turkey* (Appl. No. 53431/99), Judgment (Third Section), 23 October 2003, not reported (and a series of other judgments against Turkey of the same date); ECtHR, *Somogyi* v. *Italy* (Appl. No. 67972/01), Judgment (Second Section), 18 May

However, a judicial fault-line began to emerge in 2008, reflecting a view that such recommendations should, indeed, be made obligatory. Thus the Court *may*, but only rarely in practice *does*, require a state to hold a rehearing of the domestic proceedings. This fault line remains volatile, as the Court has not yet established a consistent position. In June 2009, the Grand Chamber explicitly reiterated in *Verein gegen Tierfabriken Schweiz (VgT) v. Switzerland (No. 2)* that the Court does not have jurisdiction to order (as opposed to recommend) the reopening of domestic proceedings.[59] A different view, however, had emerged the previous year. In *Vladimir Romanov v. Russia*,[60] having found a violation of article 6(1) together with article 6(3)(d), because the applicant had been denied an adequate opportunity as a criminal defendant to question witnesses against him, the chamber simply urged the respondent state either to hold a *de novo* trial, or reopen the domestic proceedings. Judges Spielmann and Malinverni argued in their joint concurring opinion that a specific direction to that effect should be included in the operative provisions of judgments where states have made provision for proceedings to be reopened. They reasoned that the reopening of proceedings represented the 'best means' of achieving *restitutio in integrum*. This therefore signalled a significant shift in judicial approach: rather than leaving states with the discretion to decide how to achieve restitution, Judges Spielmann and Malinverni wanted to impose a binding obligation to use the best means of doing so, as interpreted and specified by the Court.[61] This position was then supported by four judges in the Grand Chamber judgment in *Salduz v. Turkey*,[62] which highlighted flaws in criminal proceedings brought against the applicant, arising from an

---

2004, Reports 2004-IV; ECtHR, *Stoichkov v. Bulgaria* (Appl. No. 9808/02), Judgment (First Section), 24 March 2005, not reported; ECtHR, *Claes and Others v. Belgium* (Appl. Nos. 46825, 47132, 47502, 49010, 49104, 49195 and 49716/99), Judgment (First Section), 2 June 2005, not reported; ECtHR, *Abbasov v. Azerbaijan* (Appl. No. 24271/05), Judgment (First Section), 17 January 2008, not reported; ECtHR, *Pishchalnikov v. Russia* (Appl. No. 7025/04), Judgment (First Section), 24 September 2009, not reported; ECtHR, *Aleksandr Zaichenko v. Russia* (Appl. No. 39660/02), Judgment (First Section), 18 February 2010, not reported.

[59] *Verein gegen Tierfabriken Schweiz (VgT) v. Switzerland (No. 2)*, para. 89.
[60] ECtHR, *Vladimir Romanov v. Russia* (Appl. No. 41461/02), Judgment (First Section), 24 July 2008, not reported.
[61] Judges Spielmann and Malinverni issued a similar opinion in ECtHR, *Ilatovskiy v. Russia* (Appl. No. 6945/04), Judgment (First Section), 9 July 2009, not reported.
[62] ECtHR, *Salduz v. Turkey* (Appl. No. 36391/02), Judgment (Grand Chamber), 27 November 2008, Reports 2008.

absence of legal assistance while he was in police custody, as well as deficient disclosure. In their Joint Concurring Opinion, Judges Rozakis, Spielmann, Ziemele and Lazarova Trajkovska were critical of the majority's timidity and cited the position of the Permanent Court of International Justice as regards the essence of reparations in the *Factory at Chorzów* case:

> ... that reparation must, as far as possible, wipe out all the consequences of the illegal act and re-establish the situation which would, in all probability, have existed if that act had not been committed.

They also prayed in aid article 35 of the Draft Articles of State Responsibility, which provides that states must make restitution for an internationally wrongful act unless it is materially impossible or it would involve a burden out of all proportion to the benefit. For Judges Rozakis *et al.*, the award of damages as compensation was accordingly a subsidiary issue.

The following year, in *Prežec v. Croatia*,[63] the First Section of the Court found a violation of article 6 in the course of criminal proceedings against the applicant, due to the failure to provide him with adequate legal aid representation. Judges Spielmann and Malinverni dissented against the majority verdict that the finding of a violation constituted sufficient just satisfaction (see the discussion above on this 'formula'). Noting the anxiety, distress, confusion and frustration that would have been caused to the applicant by being sentenced to five months' imprisonment, the dissenters broadened their attack on the Court's reliance on declarations and its conservative approach to reparations:

> ... one wonders whether the mere finding of a violation of a right – no matter which – protected by the Convention is capable of repairing the harm done to the victim.[64]

In the same month as the *Prežec* judgment was delivered, Judges Spielmann and Malinverni found themselves in the majority on this point in the case of *Maksimov v. Azerbaijan*.[65] Having found that criminal appeal proceedings had been unfair, a chamber majority (reflecting the view of Judges Vajić, Spielmann, Jebens and Malinverni)

---

[63] ECtHR, *Prežec v. Croatia* (Appl. No. 48185/07), Judgment (First Section), 15 October 2009, not reported.

[64] They also cited Judge Bonello's Partly Dissenting Opinion in *Aquilina v. Malta*.

[65] ECtHR, *Maksimov v. Azerbaijan* (Appl. No. 38228/05), Judgment (First Section), 8 October 2009 (operative provision 3), not reported.

held that the state must take all measures to reopen the proceedings. It did so by stipulating this obligation in the operative provisions. Judges Kovler, Steiner and Hajiyev dissented, although apparently more out of pragmatism than principle. They identified three categories of cases in which the Court had previously utilised the operative provisions in such a way: pilot judgments; unlawful detention cases; and cases concerning the non-enforcement of domestic judgments. *Maksimov* fell into none of these categories, and, according to the dissenters, the chamber had overstepped existing practice. In their view, to broaden these categories was a matter for the Grand Chamber. The Court now needs to take steps – by way of a Grand Chamber judgment – to resolve the inconsistency in its case law. The imposition of binding obligations on states to reopen proceedings is to be preferred, as being a logical consequence of the Court's finding of a violation of the right to a fair trial.

The Court has proved less willing to make recommendations advocating re-hearings in respect of civil cases, apparently because of the difficulties this may cause to the other (non-state) parties to the proceedings. Having found that the applicant's civil cases had not been heard by a 'tribunal established by law' in *Gurov v. Moldova*,[66] the Court simply noted that the Moldovan Code of Civil Procedure did allow for proceedings to be reopened following the finding of a Convention violation by the Court. On that basis, the Court then declined to make any monetary award – possibly indicating a more reflective approach as to the relevance and sufficiency of the requisite remedial steps in such cases. By contrast, in the same year (2006), the Third Section of the Court, in the case of *Lungoci v. Romania*,[67] included in its operative provisions a direction to the state to ensure that, if the applicant so desired, the proceedings (civil proceedings to recover possession of property) were reopened within six months of the judgment becoming final. *Lungoci* seems something of an anomaly, as the Court's usual practice subsequently has been to recommend that states should reopen proceedings, rather than imposing a binding legal obligation to do so. For example, this was the outcome in the 2010 judgment in the Grand Chamber case

---

[66] ECtHR, *Gurov v. Moldova* (Appl. No. 36455/02), Judgment (Fourth Section), 11 July 2006, not reported.
[67] ECtHR, *Lungoci v. Romania* (Appl. No. 62710/00), Judgment (Third Section), 26 January 2006, not reported. See also the earlier decision in *Claes and Others v. Belgium*, in which the Court reached a 'half-way house' by stipulating in the operative provisions the payment of damages if the state had not granted a request by the applicants for a retrial or for the proceedings to be reopened.

of *Cudak v. Lithuania*,[68] which concerned the dismissal of a Lithuanian switchboard operator who had been employed at the Polish Embassy in Vilnius – this followed her claim of sexual harassment against another embassy employee. In view of the way in which the principle of state immunity had been used to block her claim, the Court found that the applicant's article 6 rights had been breached, which led the majority of the Grand Chamber to note that a retrial or the reopening of proceedings would be an appropriate response by the Lithuanian authorities. However, in his Concurring Opinion in that case, Judge Malinverni, supported by Judges Casadevall, Cabral Barreto, Zagrebelsky and Popović, argued that this point should have been included in the operative provisions of the judgment. Judge Malinverni's arguments included several points about the Court's approach to redress. First, that the Court should aim, wherever possible, to restore the *status quo ante* – the award of damages under article 41 being a subsidiary matter. Second, he emphasised the importance of the binding effect of the operative provisions of a Court's judgment. Third, he argued that by including specific stipulations in the operative provisions, this would assist the Committee of Ministers in their role of supervising the execution of judgments. Finally, in the particular circumstances of the case, he considered that an award of damages was not sufficient to redress the damage caused to the applicant. She had first and foremost sought a decision to the effect that her dismissal had been unlawful – accordingly, only the reopening of the proceedings would provide 'full satisfaction'.[69]

As regards unfair domestic legal proceedings, the Grand Chamber adopted a more interventionist stance in the *Scoppola (No. 2)* judgment in 2009, in relation to the imposition of a sentence by the Italian courts. Having found a violation of articles 6 and 7 as a result of the exaction of life imprisonment on the applicant (which was heavier than the maximum sentence for which he was liable at the time), the Grand Chamber was unanimous in ordering the state (using its operative provisions) to ensure that the applicant's sentence was replaced with a penalty that was

---

[68] ECtHR, *Cudak v. Lithuania* (Appl. No. 15869/02), Judgment (Grand Chamber), 23 March 2010, Reports 2010.

[69] In the context of civil proceedings, Judges Spielmann and Malinverni have expressed similar views, for example, in ECtHR, *Fakiridou and Schina v. Greece* (Appl. No. 6789/06), Judgment (First Section), 14 November 2008, not reported (violation of art. 1 of Protocol No. 1 arising from expropriation proceedings concerning the applicants' land, which had lasted for several decades), and ECtHR, *Lesjak v. Croatia* (Appl. No. 25904/06), Judgment (First Section), 18 February 2010, not reported.

consistent with the principles enunciated in the judgment.[70] To direct a state to ensure that a specific sentence in a particular case is changed (from life imprisonment to a period of less than thirty years, in accordance with the domestic law) goes significantly further than merely urging – or indeed, requiring – that domestic proceedings be reopened. The rationale for this was simply expressed, and was therefore not illuminating: 'having regard to the particular circumstances of the case and the urgent need to put an end to the breach of articles 6 and 7 of the Convention'.[71] It could be argued that this goes too far – in prescribing not just how the state should respond, but also how the judicial authorities should do so. The equivalent result could have been achieved by ordering a retrial: the conclusions of the Court mean that had the applicant been retried and found guilty, he could not have been sentenced to more than 30 years' imprisonment.

3.3 The release of detainees

The urgency of cases relating to individuals unlawfully detained has led the Court, since 2004, to issue states (primarily, to date, from the former Soviet bloc) with binding directives to secure their release. The first two such instances arose in exceptional situations where a separatist entity had seized *de facto* control from the host country. The applicant in *Assanidze v. Georgia*[72] remained in detention in the Ajarian autonomous province of Georgia three years after the Georgian Supreme Court had acquitted him and ordered his release. The Georgian government had taken both legal and political steps to ensure his release, but without success. The Grand Chamber held that the applicant's continuing detention was arbitrary and in violation of both articles 5(1) and 6(1). In view of its urgency, the Court ordered the respondent state to 'secure the applicant's release at the earliest possible date'. As in the *Scoppola* judgment, the Court's reasoning for taking such an unprecedented step was not especially informative: 'by its very nature, the violation found in the instant case does not leave any real choice as to the measures required to remedy it'. A similar decision was made by the Grand Chamber in *Ilaşcu and Others v. Russia and Moldova*,[73] in which the Court held, *inter*

---

[70] *Scoppola v. Italy (No. 2)*, (operative provision 6(a)).
[71] *Ibid.*, para. 154 and operative provisions, para. 6(a).   [72] *Assanidze v. Georgia*.
[73] ECtHR, *Ilaşcu and Others v. Russia and Moldova* (Appl. No. 48787/99), Judgment (Grand Chamber), 8 July 2004, Reports 2004-VII.

alia, that three applicants had been, and continued to be, unlawfully detained in the 'Moldavian Republic of Transdniestria', a region of Moldova which declared its independence in 1991, but which has not been recognised by the international community. They had been convicted by the 'Supreme Court of the Moldavian Republic of Transdniestria', which had been set up by an entity which was illegal under international law. The Court ordered the two respondent states to secure their immediate release, reasoning that:

> ... any continuation of the unlawful and arbitrary detention of the three applicants would necessarily entail a serious prolongation of the violation of Article 5 found by the Court and a breach of the respondent states' obligation under Article 46(1) of the Convention to abide by the Court's judgment. Regard being had to the grounds on which they have been found by the Court to be in violation of the Convention ... the respondent states must take every measure to put an end to the arbitrary detention of the applicants still detained...[74]

There was a similar conclusion in *Aleksanyan* v. *Russia*,[75] in which the Court found several violations of the Convention relating to the detention on remand of the applicant, Vasiliy Aleksanyan, Mikhail Khodorkovskiy's former lawyer. The Court found that his serious, life-threatening illnesses (he was HIV-positive) could not be adequately treated in his remand prison, and also that his detention did not serve any meaningful purpose under article 5, as the proceedings against him had been suspended and were unlikely to be reopened in the foreseeable future. The Court concluded that his continuing detention was unacceptable, and accordingly ordered the government to introduce other, less stringent measures of restraint, in accordance with Russian law. It was the gravity of the applicant's ill-health which stands out in this case, and which may therefore have been determinative of the Court's stance on ordering his release, but his poor state of health cannot be said to be unique amongst Court applicants. The Court further developed its approach in the case of *Tehrani and Others* v. *Turkey*,[76] which concerned the detention of four Iranian applicants in Turkey because of their involvement with the People's Mojahedin Organisation of Iran (PMOI).

---

[74] *Ibid.*, para. 490.
[75] ECtHR, *Aleksanyan* v. *Russia* (Appl. No. 46468/06), Judgment (First Section), 22 December 2008, not reported.
[76] ECtHR, *Tehrani and Others* v. *Turkey* (Appl. Nos. 32940, 41626 and 43616/08), Judgment (Second Section), 13 April 2010, not reported.

Having found a violation of article 5(1) and (4), because of the absence of clear legal provisions governing their deprivation of liberty, or a mechanism by which they could have the lawfulness of their detention swiftly judicially reviewed, and in view of the 'urgent need' to put an end to it, the Court ordered the Turkish state to secure the release of the two applicants still being held at an accommodation centre. The Court also stipulated that it should not re-detain the other two applicants who had previously been released (an interesting example of a form of 'injunctive relief', with the Court acting in anticipation of a potential future violation of the Convention).

In its 2010 judgment in *Fatullayev v. Azerbaijan*,[77] the First Section of the Court went further than stipulating the release of a detainee because of a procedural breach of the Convention (under article 5), by adopting a similar position in a case highlighting the repression of the media. Criminal proceedings for defamation, threatening terrorism, inciting ethnic hostility and tax evasion, had been brought against the newspaper editor Eynulla Fatullayev, following the publication of his articles on the Nagorno-Karabakh war and concerning Azerbaijan's position as regards US–Iranian relations. As a consequence, he had been sentenced to periods of imprisonment of 2-and-a-half years and 8-and-a-half years. The Court found that the interferences with Mr. Fatullayev's freedom of expression were not justified under article 10(2), and in assessing the severity of the penalties imposed on him, it explicitly found that there was no justification for imprisoning him. Furthermore, the Court was also concerned that the treatment meted out to him was 'capable of producing a chilling effect on the exercise of journalistic freedom of expression in Azerbaijan and dissuading the press from openly discussing matters of public concern'.[78] Invoking article 46, the Court ordered the respondent government to secure his immediate release (even though there had been no such order by a domestic body, as there had been, for example, in *Assanidze*), referring to the urgency of the need to end a continuing violation of the Convention. Such a stipulation was said to be the only way of providing redress: 'by its very nature, the situation found to exist in the instant case does not leave any real choice as to the measures required to remedy the violations of the applicant's Convention rights'. There had been no violation of article 5, and so the decision

---

[77] ECtHR, *Fatullayev v. Azerbaijan* (Appl. No. 40984/07), Judgment (First Section), 22 April 2010, not reported.
[78] *Ibid.*, para. 128.

marks an extension of the Court's practice – to cases where detention resulted from an unjustifiable breach of another of the Convention's substantive provisions, such as the right to freedom of expression.

In each of the three areas considered above (restitution of property, unfair trials and unlawful detention), the application of the maxim *restitutio in integrum* was perceived to be of particular relevance, arguably especially as regards the release of detainees and the return of property. The Court's justification for its more incisive approach as regards redress in these situations is lacking in particularity. The nature and gravity of the Convention violation are certainly relevant and important factors, as, of course, is the efficacy of the particular direction stipulated. In any event, the Court's increasingly directive approach, as exemplified by the cases discussed above, is to be welcomed as providing greater clarity. For the respondent government (and its constituent elements which may be involved in the implementation process) it means that there is a much greater degree of certainty as to what exactly is required of it. In addition, it should aid applicants' understanding of what should follow from Strasbourg judgments. This added clarity and certainty ought to mean swifter implementation, and if that is not the case in practice, it will be easier for the Committee of Ministers to assess whether or not compliance has been achieved. Whether the Court's developing approach to redress complies or conflicts with the principle of subsidiarity needs to be considered 'in the round'. In other words, in order to make such an assessment, the totality of the Court's functions and practice have to be taken into account, as does the wider context in which the Court is now operating. Subsidiarity is reflected and acknowledged by the Court both procedurally (take, for example, the obligation on all applicants to exhaust domestic remedies before going to the Court) and in its substantive case law (to give one important example, by applying the doctrine of the margin of appreciation). The context for the Court has been, increasingly in recent years, one of a heavy burden of applications, caused to a significant extent by the failure to implement the Convention at the national level. Therefore, whilst the Court's position on redress has undoubtedly become more prescriptive, it would not be correct to portray such developments as being in contravention of the subsidiarity principle – as the national authorities will always have had the opportunity to resolve the violations at issue, and only where they have failed to do so will the Court take decisive action. In the face, in particular, of high levels of non-compliance, the Court is justified in its more interventionist stance.

The next section moves on from deserving individual cases, to consider remedies in situations revealing broader, systemic problems.

3.4 Systemic Convention violations

Arguably more significant than the Court's increasing interventionism in the scenarios already discussed has been its development of new measures aimed at resolving structural Convention violations more efficiently. Introduced through judicial innovation in 2004, the pilot judgment procedure was formally codified in the Court's Rules in 2011, and in that period has become one of the central pillars of reform.[79] Allied to this procedure has been the relatively frequent utilisation of article 46 of the Convention, together with article 41, in other cases highlighting systemic Convention breaches. Both developments signal a more incisive activism vis-à-vis the slothfulness, or even recalcitrance, of states which have been the sources of hundreds or thousands of clone cases which have been plaguing the Court. To describe them as 'clone' cases is perhaps to downplay their importance. It is true to say that they relate to issues which have already repeatedly come before the Court, and therefore, perhaps it is justifiable to argue that the Court should not have to bother with them. However, it is their source that is especially important – very large-scale systemic or structural issues often caused by defective legislation. If states can be induced to resolve such issues in a much more efficient way, then this should have a significant impact both within the states and on the Court's overwhelming backlog.

3.4.1 Pilot judgments

Although primarily a result of 'judicial engineering',[80] the development of the pilot judgment procedure appears to have firm support from states, as the Court was explicitly encouraged in the early 2000s by the Committee of Ministers to identify both the prevalent structural problems and their source.[81] It is these aspects which have formed the heart

---

[79] See further, P. Leach et al., *Responding to Systemic Human Rights Violations – An Analysis of Pilot Judgments of the European Court of Human Rights and their Impact at National Level* (Antwerp, Oxford, Portland: Intersentia, 2010) (hereinafter Leach et al., *Responding to Systemic Violations*).

[80] A term used by Judge Spielmann in his presentation to the 'Expert Seminar: The Future of the European Court of Human Rights', Institute for Human Rights, Katholieke Universiteit Leuven, Leuven, 2 September 2011.

[81] Council of Europe, 'Resolution Res(2004)3 of the Committee of Ministers on Judgments Revealing an Underlying Systemic Problem', 12 May 2004.

of the pilot judgment procedure: the identification by the Court of a systemic violation of the Convention and its stipulation of 'general measures' in the operative part of the judgment in order that the respondent state should resolve the systemic issue. It was not until April 2011 that the procedure was confirmed by way of a new Court Rule, marking its 'coming of age'.[82] Rule 61 formalises a flexible judicial tool aimed at resolving large-scale, endemic dysfunctions, and empowers the Court to identify 'the type of remedial measures which the Contracting State concerned is required to take at the domestic level by virtue of the operative provisions of the judgment'. All pilot cases are to be granted priority treatment (in accordance with Rule 41). The rule also codifies another important innovation which had already been a key feature of pilot judgments – that the Court may impose binding time limits (again using its operative provisions) within which the specified remedial measures must be adopted by states. There is a recognition that such time limits may vary, as Rule 61 provides that they are to be set 'bearing in mind the nature of the measures required and the speed with which the problem which it has identified can be remedied at the domestic level'. The Court may also reserve the question of just satisfaction in individual cases, pending the adoption by the state of the stipulated individual and general measures. Furthermore, the Court may adjourn the examination of all similar applications pending the adoption of the remedial measures.

Since the instigation of the procedure in 2004, the majority of pilot judgments to date have been property-related cases (concerning article 1 of Protocol No. 1) and have notably featured the non-enforcement of domestic court judgments and the excessive length of legal proceedings. The respondents have predominantly been states from Eastern Europe (Poland,[83] Romania[84] and Bulgaria[85]) and the former Soviet bloc

---

[82] ECtHR, 'Rule 61 of the Rules of Court', 1 April 2011. It was preceded by the Court's Information Note on the pilot judgment procedure, see: www.echr.coe.int/NR/rdonlyres/DF4E8456-77B3-4E67-8944-B908143A7E2C/0/Information_Note_on_the_PJP_for_Website.pdf. The Court had previously issued an Information Note on the procedure – available at www.echr.coe.int/ECHR/EN/Header/Basic+Texts/The+Convention+and+additional+protocols/The+European+Convention+on+Human+Rights/.

[83] ECtHR, *Broniowski v. Poland* (Appl. No. 31443/96), Judgment (Grand Chamber), 22 June 2004, Reports 2004-V; ECtHR, *Hutten-Czapska v. Poland* (Appl. No. 35014/97), Judgment (Grand Chamber), 19 June 2006, Reports 2006-VIII.

[84] ECtHR, *Atanasiu and Others v. Romania* (Appl. Nos. 30767/05 and 33800/06), Judgment (Third Section), 12 October 2010, not reported.

[85] ECtHR, *Dimitrov and Hamanov v. Bulgaria* (Appl. Nos. 48059/06 and 2708/09), Judgment (Fourth Section), 10 May 2011, not reported.

THE EUROPEAN COURT'S DEVELOPING APPROACH TO REMEDIES 163

(Ukraine,[86] Russia[87] and Moldova[88]). However, more recently, states from Western and Central Europe have also been targeted by pilot judgments: Germany[89] and Greece[90] have been the subject of length of proceedings pilot judgments; Bosnia and Herzegovina has featured in a case concerning lost foreign currency savings;[91] and the UK was the subject of a pilot judgment relating to the disenfranchisement of convicted prisoners.[92]

The Court's stance on remedial measures in these cases has varied in terms of both its specificity and the time periods imposed. As regards endemic problems relating to the length of proceedings, the Court has required states to introduce an effective domestic remedy (or combination of remedies) within one year, as it did in *Rumpf v. Germany*,[93] *Vassilios Athanasiou and Others v. Greece*[94] and *Dimitrov and Hamanov v. Bulgaria*.[95] A similar form of general measures has been stipulated in cases concerning the non-implementation of domestic court judgments, either within six months (*Olaru* and *Burdov*) or twelve months (*Ivanov*). In each of those cases, the respondent states were also required to provide redress to the applicants within a year. The systemic problem identified in the pilot judgment of *Maria Atanasiu and Others v. Romania*[96] was the applicants' inability to obtain restitution of their nationalised properties or

---

[86] ECtHR, *Yuriy Nikolayevich Ivanov v. Ukraine* (Appl. No. 40450/04), Judgment (Fifth Section), 15 October 2009, not reported.
[87] ECtHR, *Burdov v. Russia (No. 2)* (Appl. No. 33509/04), Judgment (First Section), 15 January 2009, Reports 2009 (extracts).
[88] ECtHR, *Olaru and Others v. Moldova* (Appl. Nos. 476/07, 22539/05, 17911/08 and 13136/07), Judgment (Fourth Section), 28 July 2009, not reported.
[89] ECtHR, *Rumpf v. Germany* (Appl. No. 46344/06), Judgment (Fifth Section), 2 September 2010, not reported.
[90] ECtHR, *Vassilios Athanasiou and Others v. Greece* (Appl. No. 50973/08), Judgment (First Section), 21 December 2010, not reported.
[91] ECtHR, *Suljagić v. Bosnia and Herzegovina* (Appl. No. 27912/02), Judgment (Fourth Section), 3 November 2009, not reported.
[92] ECtHR, *Greens and MT v. United Kingdom* (Appl. Nos. 60041 and 60054/08), Judgment (Fourth Section), 23 November 2010, Reports 2010 (extracts).
[93] ECtHR, *Rumpf v. Germany*. See also ECtHR, *Sürmeli v. Germany* (Appl. No. 75529/01), Judgment (Grand Chamber), 8 June 2006, Reports 2006-VII.
[94] ECtHR, *Vassilios Athanasiou and Others v. Greece*.
[95] ECtHR, *Dimitrov and Hamanov v. Bulgaria* (Appl. Nos. 48059/06 and 2708/09), Judgment (Fourth Section), 10 May 2011, not reported.
[96] ECtHR, *Maria Atanasiu and Others v. Romania* (Appl. Nos. 30767/05 and 33800/06), Judgment (Third Section), 12 October 2010, not reported. See also ECtHR, *Viaşu v. Romania* (Appl. No. 75951/01), Judgment (Third Section), 9 December 2008, not reported; ECtHR, *Faimblat v. Romania* (Appl. No. 23066/02), Judgment (Third Section),

to secure compensation. In those circumstances, the Court allowed the state a longer period – 18 months – within which to take the measures needed to resolve the issue. This extended period was not explicitly justified by the Court, but it is likely to have reflected the sheer scale of the problem of property restitution in Romania, the complexity of the relevant legislation and the considerable burden on the state budget, each of which was referred to by the Court in its judgment. In view of such complexity, interestingly the Court was also willing to afford the Romanian authorities a larger degree of discretion as regards the very nature of the general measures to be introduced:

> Balancing the rights at stake, as well as the gains and losses of the different persons affected by the process of transforming the State's economy and legal system, is an exceptionally difficult exercise involving a number of different domestic authorities. The Court therefore considers that the respondent State must have a considerable margin of appreciation in selecting the measures to secure respect for property rights or to regulate ownership relations within the country, and in their implementation.[97]

The granting of such relative leeway in *Maria Atanasiu* can be contrasted with the Court's rather more prescriptive approach in *Suljagić v. Bosnia and Herzegovina*. There, the Court found a systemic violation of article 1 of Protocol No. 1 as a result of the government's failure adequately to reimburse applicants for foreign currency savings deposited in national banks in the former Yugoslavia before 1991. In the operative provisions of the judgment, the Court stipulated that government bonds and outstanding instalments should be issued within six months of the judgment becoming final. This would seem to be an approach that is more invasive of state sovereignty than the more generalised requirements adopted in previous pilot judgments, but it can be explained, as such provisions mirror the obligations already established in domestic legislation, but which had not been effectively implemented. For the Court, 'having undertaken to repay "old" foreign-currency savings in locally based banks and having set up a repayment scheme in this regard, the respondent State must stand by its promises.'[98]

---

13 January 2009, not reported; ECtHR, *Katz v. Romania* (Appl. No. 29739/03), Judgment (Third Section), 20 January 2009, not reported.

[97] Ibid.; *Maria Atanasiu and Others v. Romania*, para. 233.

[98] ECtHR, *Suljagić v. Bosnia and Herzegovina* (Appl. No. 27912/02), Judgment (Fourth Section), 3 November 2009, not reported, para. 56.

One case which stands out in terms of its subject matter and the reactions it has engendered, is the Court's pilot judgment in *Greens and MT v. UK*.[99] In tackling the question of votes for prisoners, this seems far removed from the property-related, endemic problems which have been the usual targets of the pilot judgment procedure. Does the decision, therefore, signal an expansion of the Court's purview? This was only the second judgment on this issue as regards the UK, but it is not unknown for the procedure to be adopted in respect of one of the first cases pending at the Court raising a particular systemic problem, as was the position in *Broniowski v. Poland*, the Court's first pilot judgment. *Greens* followed the Grand Chamber judgment in *Hirst* five years earlier,[100] but the response to that judgment had been procrastination and outright political opposition to the notion of altering the legislative ban on any convicted prisoner from voting whilst they remain in prison.[101] The *Greens* judgment imposed a binding obligation on the UK government to bring forward proposals to amend the legislation within a mere six months of the judgment becoming final. This relatively prescriptive time limit is likely to reflect the relative clarity and ease (legally, if not politically) of resolving the issue – by amending the Representation of the People Act 1983. As the Court had decided in both cases not to award any damages (pecuniary or non-pecuniary) to the prisoner complainants, there would be no need for the UK authorities to establish a system for providing redress to individual applicants (unlike the position in other pilot judgments). This, then, is apparently a development moving closer to what President Costa advocated, when he suggested that consideration be given to introducing 'class actions' and 'collective applications' into the Strasbourg armoury.[102] It represents a step change from the Court's traditional focus on individualised cases, and one which seeks to emphasise the importance of tackling wider systemic issues (which may be common to a number of Council of Europe states). To that extent, the increasing 'constitutionalisation' of the Court is a welcome, and indeed necessary, development.

---

[99] ECtHR, *Greens and MT v. UK*.
[100] ECtHR, *Hirst v. UK (No. 2)* (Appl. No. 74025/01), Judgment (Grand Chamber), 6 October 2005, Reports 2005-IX.
[101] A House of Commons backbench motion in February 2011 to the effect that 'legislative decisions of this nature should be a matter for democratically-elected lawmakers', and supporting the existing ban on sentenced prisoners from voting, was carried by 234 votes to 22.
[102] *Memorandum of the President of the European Court of Human Rights to the States with a View to Preparing the Interlaken Conference* (3 July 2009), 8.

The domestic furore which has followed the *Hirst* and *Greens* judgments results primarily from the contentiousness of the issue at the heart of the cases. The controversy arose because of the unwillingness to implement *Hirst* (which was not a pilot judgment), however, tensions have undoubtedly been heightened by the application of the pilot judgment procedure in the *Greens* case, because of the explicit directive to amend the legislation, and to do so within just six months.[103] As the issue remains unresolved at the time of writing, it is too early to assess whether the use of the pilot judgment procedure will have had a positive or negative impact on implementation in this particular context. The situation has caused a mini-constitutional crisis in the UK, reflecting real concern, in some quarters, that the sovereign will of Parliament is being threatened by judges – and worse, judges from an international court. This position was exemplified by Kenneth Clarke, the then Secretary of State for Justice, when he declared at the Izmir Conference in April 2011:

> If the Strasbourg Court is too ready to substitute its own judgment for that of national parliaments and courts that have through their own processes complied with the Convention, it risks turning the tide of public opinion against the concept of international standards of human rights, and risks turning public opinion against the Convention itself. In Britain, it is going to be really quite difficult to persuade Parliament to pass legislation to comply with the Court's judgment on votes for prisoners. This is regarded by our Parliament as a domestic political issue, on which there are valid arguments on both sides.[104]

3.4.2 Article 46 judgments

Over the same period in which the Court has developed the pilot judgment procedure, it has also been evolving a practice of issuing 'Article 46 judgments'. These are decisions which similarly highlight systemic or structural problems which have been the source of repeated Convention violations. In these decisions, the Court refers to the legal

---

[103] The UK government subsequently intervened as a third party in ECtHR, *Scoppola v. Italy (No. 3)* (Appl. No. 126/05), Judgment (Second Section), 18 January 2011, not reported (Grand Chamber hearing held on 2 November 2011), and was granted an extension of 6 months after the *Scoppola* judgment within which to comply with the *Greens* decision.

[104] Speech by Rt. Hon. Kenneth Clarke QC MP, Secretary of State for Justice, Lord Chancellor, 26 April 2011, High Level Conference on the Future of the European Court of Human Rights, Izmir, 26–7 April 2011. Available at: www.coe.int/t/dghl/standardsetting/conferenceizmir/Speeches/Speech%20UK.pdf.

THE EUROPEAN COURT'S DEVELOPING APPROACH TO REMEDIES 167

obligation on the state under article 46 to introduce general and/or individual measures in the domestic legal system in order to end the violations and provide redress.[105] However, they do not go so far as issuing binding obligations in the operative provisions, and so for that reason, they do not have the same importance or priority status as pilot judgments (as is illustrated by the discussion above about the Court's treatment of cases revealing unfair domestic proceedings).[106]

There is already an abundance of such judgments, encompassing a very broad range of systemic Convention issues, some of which are certainly endemic across a number of Convention states, such as the excessive length of pre-trial detention,[107] prison conditions,[108] the practice of holding trials *in absentia*,[109] and the inadequacy of compensation for expropriated property.[110] Article 46 judgments have also been issued

---

[105] It has not, of course, been unknown for the Court to highlight systemic issues arising from legislative deficiencies and to identify practices considered to be incompatible with the Convention (see, e.g., ECtHR, *Messina v. Italy (No. 2)* (Appl. No. 25498/94), Judgment (Second Section), 28 August 2000, Reports 2000-X (monitoring of prisoners' correspondence) and ECtHR, *Bottazzi v. Italy* (Appl. No. 34884/97), Judgment (Grand Chamber), 28 July 1999, Reports 1999-V (length of proceedings cases)). However, it is the sheer scale of 'article 46 judgments' and the breadth of the range of their subject matter that is unprecedented.

[106] Very exceptionally, an article 46 judgment will also prescribe general measures in the operative part of the judgment (e.g. ECtHR, *Lukenda v. Slovenia* (Appl. No. 23032/02), Judgment (Third Section), 6 October 2005, Reports 2005-X; and ECtHR, *Xenides-Arestis v. Turkey* (Appl. No. 46347/99), Judgment (Third Section), 22 December 2005, not reported). Some commentators have described these decisions as 'pilot judgments', although the Court did not state expressly that it was applying the pilot judgment procedure. The Court's practice in that respect has not always been clear or consistent. For example, the judgment in ECtHR, *Doğan and Others v. Turkey* (Appl. Nos. 8803–8811, 8813 and 8815–8819/02), Judgment (Third Section), 29 June 2004, Reports 2004-VI (concerning the applicants' forced evictions from their homes) was not defined by the Court as a pilot judgment, but in the later admissibility decision in ECtHR, *İçyer v. Turkey* (Appl. No. 18888/02), Admissibility Decision (Third Section), 12 January 2006, Reports 2006-I, the Court referred to *Doğan* as a 'pilot judgment' (paras. 73 and 94).

[107] See, e.g., ECtHR, *Kauczor v. Poland* (Appl. No. 45219/06), Judgment (Fourth Section), 3 February 2009, not reported; ECtHR, *Cahit Demirel v. Turkey* (Appl. No. 18623/03), Judgment (Second Section), 7 July 2009, not reported.

[108] See, e.g., ECtHR, *Orchowski v. Poland* (Appl. No. 17885/04), Judgment (Fourth Section), 22 October 2009, not reported; and ECtHR, *Norbert Sikorski v. Poland* (Appl. No. 17599/05), Judgment (Fourth Section), 22 October 2009, not reported.

[109] ECtHR, *Sejdovic v. Italy* (Appl. No. 56581/00), Judgment (Chamber), 10 November 2004 and Judgment (Grand Chamber), 1 March 2006, Reports 2006-II; ECtHR, *RR v. Italy* (Appl. No. 42191/02), Judgment (Third Section), 9 June 2005, not reported.

[110] ECtHR, *Scordino v. Italy (No. 1)* (Appl. No. 36813/97), Judgment (First Section), 29 July 2004 and Judgment (Grand Chamber), 29 March 2006, Reports 2006-V; ECtHR,

in respect of problems which certainly seem to be less widespread, but which nevertheless have systemic origins, such as the right to parental leave for male military personnel,[111] the right to a hearing for prisoners charged with disciplinary measures,[112] restrictions on the rights of allotment-holders,[113] and laws regulating leadership conflicts in religious communities.[114]

Typically, article 46 judgments identify a flaw in domestic legislation and recommend that the domestic law should be brought into compliance with the Convention. One of the earliest such cases was *Hasan and Eylem Zengin* v. *Turkey*, which exposed the fact that religious teaching within the Turkish educational system failed to respect the parental convictions of adherents to Alevism, in violation of article 2 of Protocol No. 1.[115] As a result, the Court noted that 'bringing the Turkish educational system and domestic legislation into conformity with the ... Convention would represent an appropriate form of compensation which would make it possible to end the violation found',[116] although in its operative provisions it held simply that the finding of a Convention breach constituted sufficient just satisfaction (the applicants not having claimed any pecuniary or non-pecuniary damages). Another example is the important judgment in *Manole and Others* v. *Moldova*,[117] which concerned governmental interference in the domestic law regulating broadcasting, in violation of article 10. Although nothing was said about

---

Scordino v. *Italy (No. 3)* (Appl. No. 43662/98), Judgments (Fourth Section), 17 May 2005 and 6 March 2007, not reported; ECtHR, *Guiso-Gallisay* v. *Italy* (Appl. No. 58858/00), Judgment (Second Section), 21 October 2008, not reported; ECtHR, *Driza* v. *Albania* (Appl. No. 33771/02), Judgment (Fourth Section), 13 November 2007, Reports 2007-V (extracts); ECtHR, *Ramadhi and 5 Others* v. *Albania* (Appl. No. 38222/02), Judgment (Fourth Section), 13 November 2007, not reported.

[111] ECtHR, *Konstantin Markin* v. *Russia* (Appl. No. 30078/06), Judgment (First Section), 7 October 2010, not reported. Note, however that this decision was superseded by a Grand Chamber Judgment of 22 March 2012, Reports 2012.

[112] ECtHR, *Gülmez* v. *Turkey* (Appl. No. 16330/02), Judgment (Second Section), 20 May 2008, not reported.

[113] ECtHR, *Urbárska obec Trenčianske Biskupice* v. *Slovakia* (Appl. No. 74258/01), Judgment (Fourth Section), 27 November 2007, not reported.

[114] ECtHR, *Holy Synod of the Bulgarian Orthodox Church (Metropolitan Inokentiy) and Others* v. *Bulgaria* (Appl. Nos. 412/03 and 35677/04), Judgment (Fifth Section), 22 January 2009, not reported.

[115] ECtHR, *Hasan and Eylem Zengin* v. *Turkey* (Appl. No. 1448/04), Judgment (Second Section), 9 October 2007, not reported.

[116] *Ibid.*, para. 84.

[117] ECtHR, *Manole and Others* v. *Moldova* (Appl. No. 13936/02), Judgment (Fourth Section), 17 September 2009, Reports 2009 (extracts).

reforms in the operative provisions of that judgment, this passage clearly indicates the Court's view of the mandatory nature of the obligation which thereby arose:

> ... the respondent State is under a legal obligation under Article 46 to take general measures at the earliest opportunity to remedy the situation which gave rise to the violation of Article 10. In the light of the deficiencies found by the Court, these general measures should include legislative reform, to ensure that the legal framework complies with the requirements of Article 10...[118]

In addition to such cases where the state is required, in general terms, to amend its laws, the Court may issue more specific directions, as to the nature of the general or individual measures required. Some of these cases have related to 'staple' Convention subjects such as the unfairness of land-expropriation procedures. Thus, in *Yetiş and Others* v. *Turkey*,[119] for example, the Court specifically called for the creation of a mechanism which would take account of depreciation in the value of compensation for expropriation resulting from the length of proceedings or inflation. Other article 46 decisions demonstrate a definite tendency to broaden and deepen the Court's reach. One example is the case of *Kurić and Others* v. *Slovenia*,[120] which concerned the situation of the 'erased' – former Yugoslav citizens whose names had been taken off the register of permanent residents and who became *de facto* stateless after Slovenian independence. As well as urging legislative reform, the Court also called on the Slovenian authorities to issue the applicants retroactively with permanent residence permits. This stipulation mirrored earlier rulings of the Slovenian Constitutional Court which had not been respected. *Al-Saadoon and Mufdhi* v. *UK*[121] concerned the applicants' detention by the British armed forces in Southern Iraq in 2003, and their subsequent transfer to the Iraqi authorities. The Court found that article 3 had been breached because the applicants had been subjected to inhuman mental suffering caused by a fear of execution. This meant a requirement for the UK to take all possible steps to obtain an assurance from the Iraqi

---

[118] *Ibid.*, para. 117.
[119] ECtHR, *Yetiş and Others* v. *Turkey* (Appl. No. 40349/05), Judgment (Second Section), 6 July 2010, not reported.
[120] ECtHR, *Kurić and Others* v. *Slovenia* (Appl. No. 26828/06), Judgment (Third Section), 13 July 2010, not reported.
[121] ECtHR, *Al-Saadoon and Mufdhi* v. *UK* (Appl. No. 61498/08), Judgment (Fourth Section), 2 March 2010, Reports 2010 (extracts).

authorities that the applicants would not be subjected to the death penalty. In cases highlighting the very poor state of health of detainees, the Court has invoked article 46 in order to ensure that the applicants received adequate medical and psychiatric treatment.[122]

Another case resulting in a direction to make legislative changes is *L v. Lithuania*,[123] although the case is something of an anomaly, as no reference was made to article 46. The applicant was a pre-operative transsexual who successfully complained to the Court about the absence of any domestic law regulating full gender reassignment surgery. The applicant's just satisfaction claim included a request for the future costs of surgery. However, the Court's response was to direct the state (using its operative provisions) to enact subsidiary legislation to plug the gap, but if that were to prove impossible, then a sum of €40,000 would have to be paid to the applicant (in order to pay for surgery abroad). Judge Fura-Sandström was concerned that in doing so, the Second Section had acted *ultra vires*. He sought to distinguish the case from pilot judgments like *Broniowski* and *Hutten-Czapska* by suggesting that the Court in *L v. Lithuania* had prescribed general measure to redress an individual complaint. The point he seemed to be making was one of scale – that there were not thousands of similarly-situated individuals. Nevertheless, in identifying a legislative gap, the problem was a systemic one, and around 50 people in Lithuania were believed to have been affected by it.

The explicit identification by the Court of violations of the Convention arising from systemic causes, together with the additional focus and priority that the Court is placing on such cases, are welcome, and indeed necessary, measures. As the further reform of the Court continues to be debated, it is important that the experiences gleaned from pilot judgments and article 46 cases should be built upon, in particular, by closely monitoring the extent to which there is effective compliance with, and implementation of, such cases. Again, the subsidiarity principle is not being ignored – as Sitaropoulos has argued:

> All these jurisprudential techniques [pilot judgments and article 46 judgments] are actually based on the fundamental principle of subsidiarity ...

---

[122] See, e.g., ECtHR, *Dybeku* v. *Albania* (Appl. No. 41153/06), Judgment (Fourth Section), 18 December 2007, not reported; ECtHR, *Sławomir Musiał* v. *Poland* (Appl. No. 28300/06), Judgment (Fourth Section), 20 January 2009, not reported; ECtHR, *Poghosyan* v. *Georgia* (Appl. No. 9870/07), Judgment (Second Section), 24 February 2009, not reported.

[123] ECtHR, *L* v. *Lithuania* (Appl. No. 27527/03), Judgment (Second Section), 11 September 2007, Reports 2007-IV.

By these methods the Court provides guidance to states in order to overcome long-standing dysfunctions in their law and practice affecting Convention rights and freedoms.[124]

4. Gross and systematic human rights violations

A significant influence on the Court in recent years has undoubtedly been the increasing rate of occurrence of extremely serious, systematic breaches of the Convention. Cases such as *Assanidze* and *Ilascu* (discussed above) are representative of situations of manifestly unlawful detention in parts of Europe under the *de facto* control of separatist power blocs. The Kurdish cases (brought against Turkey) first introduced the phenomenon of the 'enforced disappearance' into European human rights jurisprudence in the 1990s, and also led to a series of findings of violations by the Turkish security forces, constituting the large-scale destruction of homes, torture and extra-judicial executions. The security forces in Russia, operating in Chechnya and other republics in the North Caucasus since 1999, have been responsible for a comparable catalogue of egregious breaches of the Convention since 2005. Such cases are undoubtedly significant, but their influence on the Court's approach to redress has not been as marked as might have been expected. Situations entailing gross and systematic human rights violations arguably justify a significant step-up in terms of the remedial response by an international court. The very nature and scale of the violations are likely to require a radical re-think about the suitability of reparations. For example, what constitutes appropriate redress where an applicant's relative has 'been disappeared', no body has been found, and where similar cases are common? There is an extra dimension to be taken into account here – the moral adequacy of redress. As Shelton has argued, remedies also serve moral goals.[125] Moreover, these cases are not just about individual justice; much broader questions arise about wider societal healing and the relevance of principles of restorative justice, such as reintegration and rehabilitation.

The only other international court which has had to adjudicate on a comparable body of egregious, systematic human rights violations is the

---

[124] N. Sitaropoulos, 'Implementation of the European Court of Human Rights' Judgments concerning National Minorities or Why Declaratory Adjudication Does Not Help', *European Society of International Law Conference Paper Series* 4 (2011), at 28.
[125] Shelton, *Remedies*, 1–2.

Inter-American Court of Human Rights, which has often had to deal with such situations since it published its first judgments (relating to enforced disappearances) in the late 1980s. In the ensuing 20 or so years, it has developed a rich and progressive jurisprudence on reparations in cases of egregious violations.[126] For example, the Inter-American Court may order the state to make a public apology to victims, acknowledging its responsibility,[127] or require that a person be reinstated to their former employment.[128] It has acted innovatively by introducing the concept of damages to the victim's 'life plan' ('*proyecto de vida*'), which reflects their circumstances, ambitions and potential.[129] In adjudicating on disappearances and extra-judicial executions, the Inter-American Court has upheld the right of relatives (and of wider society) to be informed about what happened,[130] and has ordered respondent states to locate the remains of victims and provide them to the next-of-kin.[131] The Inter-American Court of Human Rights has explicitly held that the nature and gravity of cases of gross violations of human rights may require rather more than a declaratory response:

> ... while a condemnatory judgment may in itself constitute a form of reparation and moral satisfaction, whether or not there has been recognition on the part of the State, it would not suffice in the instant case, given the extreme gravity of the violation of the right to life and of the moral suffering inflicted on the victims and their next of kin, who should be compensated on an equitable basis.[132]

---

[126] See further, D. Cassel, 'The Expanding Scope and Impact of Reparations Awarded by the Inter-American Court of Human Rights', in K. De Feyter *et al.* (eds.), *Out of the Ashes: Reparation for Victims of Gross and Systematic Human Rights Violations* (Antwerp: Intersentia, 2005); C. Sandoval and M. Duttwiler, 'Redressing Non-pecuniary Damages of Torture Survivors – The Practice of the Inter-American Court of Human Rights', in G. Gilbert, F. Hampson and C. Sandoval, *The Delivery of Human Rights: Essays in Honour of Professor Sir Nigel Rodley* (London and New York: Routledge, 2011) 114–36.

[127] See, e.g., IACtHR, *Cantoral Benavides v. Peru (Reparations)*, Judgment, 3 December 2001, Ser. C, No. 88, operative para. 7.

[128] IACtHR, *Baena Ricardo et al. v. Panama*, Judgment, 2 February 2001, Ser. C, No. 61, operative para. 7. The ECtHR made a reinstatement order for the first time in ECtHR *Oleksandr Volkov v. Ukraine* (Appl. No. 21722/11), judgment (former Fifth Section), 9 January 2013, not reported.

[129] See, e.g., IACtHR, *Loayza Tamayo v. Peru*, Judgment, 27 November 1998, Ser. C, No. 42, paras. 144–54.

[130] See, e.g., IACtHR, *Myrna Mack Chang v. Guatemala*, Judgment, 25 November 2003, Ser. C, No. 101, para. 274.

[131] See, e.g., IACtHR, *Bamaca Velasquez v. Guatemala (Reparations)*, Judgment, 22 February 2002, Ser. C, No. 91, para. 79.

[132] IACtHR, *El Amparo v. Venezuela*, Judgment, 14 September 1996, Ser. C, No. 28, para. 35.

As yet, the ECtHR has not generally been willing to follow the example set by the Inter-American Court as regards its more progressive, nuanced approach toward reparations. There are recent signs, however, of movement by the ECtHR on the question of the need for an investigation into human rights abuses. It has been the common practice of the Inter-American Court to order the respondent state to investigate, prosecute and punish the perpetrators of human rights violations.[133] In doing so, the Inter-American Court has also explicitly recognised that the failure to investigate will lead to situations of 'grave impunity' and thereby foster chronic recidivism.[134]

Similar orders have been sought by applicants to the ECtHR, which have not been successful, although they have found support from judges in the minority.[135] In his Partly Dissenting Opinion in the case *Medova v. Russia*,[136] a case of enforced disappearance from Ingushetia for which the authorities were held to be directly responsible, Judge Spielmann argued that the respondent state should have been ordered to carry out an investigation. It was clearly important to him that in spite of the shortcomings in the investigation identified by the Court, he considered that they could be overcome, even though several years had passed.[137] Explicitly relying on the principle of *restitutio in integrum*, Judge Spielmann expressed similar views about the obligation to investigate in his Concurring Opinion (joined by Judges Ziemele and Kalaydjieva) in *Varnava*

---

[133] See, e.g., *ibid.*, operative para. 4; IACtHR, *Garrido and Baigorria v. Argentina (Reparations)*, Judgment, 27 August 1998, Ser. C, No. 39, operative para. 4; IACtHR, *Paniagua Morales et al. v. Guatemala (Reparations)*, Judgment, 25 May 2001, Ser. C, No. 7, operative para. 2. There is, of course, a quite separate question about the implementation of such measures. In practice, compliance with these orders is rare. Aside from political will, the conduct of investigations is hampered, for example, by amnesty laws, statutes of limitation and the double jeopardy principle.

[134] See, e.g., *Myrna Mack Chang v. Guatemala*, para. 272.

[135] As to the range of international law standards concerning the duty to investigate, see, e.g., P. Leach, 'Quelles sont les réparations adéquates dans les affaires de 'disparitions'? Leçons issues des affaires sur la Tchétchénie', E. Lambert-Abdelgawad and K Martin-Chenut (eds.), *Réparer les violations graves et massives des droits de l'homme: La Cour InterAméricaine, pionnière et modèle?*, Collection de L'UMR De Droit Comparé de Paris (Université de Paris1/CNRS UMR 8103), Vol. XX (Paris: Société de Législation Comparée, 2010).

[136] ECtHR, *Medova v. Russia* (Appl. No. 25385/04), Judgment (First Section), 15 January 2009.

[137] See also his similar Dissenting Opinion in ECtHR, *Umayeva v. Russia* (Appl. No. 1200/03), Judgment (First Section), 4 December 2008, not reported, concerning the wounding of the applicant in an artillery attack by Russian armed forces on Grozny in January 2000.

and Others v. *Turkey*,[138] which concerned the disappearance of nine men in northern Cyprus, following the Turkish occupation of Cyprus in 1974. The 2010 judgment in *Abuyeva and Others* v. *Russia*[139] laid down another important marker. That case concerned a series of fatalities caused by the shelling of the village of Katr-Yurt in Chechnya in 2000 by the Russian armed forces. The decision followed the *Isayeva* judgment in 2005 relating to the same incident.[140] The Court in *Abuyeva* noted 'with great dismay' that an effective investigation had still not been carried out into the attack. It found that the government had 'manifestly disregarded the specific findings of a binding judgment concerning the ineffectiveness of the investigation' and the Court also concluded that an effective investigation into the case was still possible. Therefore, although the state's compliance with the judgment was to be assessed by the Committee of Ministers, the Court considered it 'inevitable that a new, independent, investigation should take place'.[141]

One issue that has been a significant feature of the gross violation cases from both Turkey and Chechnya has been the significant non-disclosure of the investigation files by the respondent governments.[142] This is not just a technical, legal issue; nor are its consequences insignificant. While the Court may, in a disappearance case, find a substantive violation of article 2, because it concludes that state agents were directly responsible for an abduction (and presumed death), many of the vital facts are often left unresolved. Thus, it may not be established how or when the victim was killed, nor who was responsible (nor even which state entity was involved, let alone identifiable individuals). This is an unacceptable lacuna and is one that needs to be tackled. One way to do so would be to acknowledge, in this particular context, the right to know the truth as an integral part of reparations. This is an area where the ECtHR could justifiably draw on the Inter-American jurisprudence. The

---

[138] ECtHR, *Varnava and Others* v. *Turkey* (Appl. Nos. 16064, 16065, 16066, 16068, 16069, 16070, 16071, 16072 and 16073/90), Judgment (Grand Chamber), 18 September 2009, Reports 2009.

[139] ECtHR, *Abuyeva and Others* v. *Russia* (Appl. No. 27065/05), Judgment (First Section), 2 December 2010, not reported.

[140] ECtHR, *Isayeva* v. *Russia* (Appl. No. 57950/00), Judgment (First Section), 24 February 2005, not reported.

[141] *Abuyeva and Others* v. *Russia*, para. 243.

[142] See as regards the Chechen cases, P. Leach, 'The Chechen Conflict: Analysing the Oversight of the European Court of Human Rights', *European Human Rights Law Review* 6 (2008) 732–61.

Inter-American Commission of Human Rights has affirmed the right 'to know the full, complete and public truth as to the events that transpired, their specific circumstances, and who participated in them'.[143] In cases such as disappearances, the Inter-American Court of Human Rights has reiterated both the specific right to know what happened, and the right to know which state agents were responsible.[144] The extent of the right to know the truth was formulated in this way in the '*Cotton Fields*' case:

> The absence of a complete and effective investigation into the facts constitutes a source of additional suffering and anguish for the victims, who have the right to know the truth about what happened. This right to the truth requires the determination of the most complete historical truth possible, which includes determination of the collective patterns of action, and of all those who, in different ways, took part in said violations.[145]

The ECtHR's more conservative approach to redress, in comparison with the position of the Inter-American Court, may reflect differences in the nature of the remedial provisions in their respective conventions. Article 63 of the American Convention on Human Rights expressly provides the power to order remedial measures other than compensation.[146] The ECtHR's tendency has been to interpret its power under article 41 of the ECHR to award 'just satisfaction' in a very limited way, although as Shelton has argued, that term in international practice has not been restricted to monetary compensation.[147] The Inter-American Court may have deemed it necessary to develop a more prescriptive approach, not only because of the prevailing political context of egregious human rights violations being committed with apparent impunity, but also because of the absence of any separate body in the Inter-American

---

[143] See, e.g., IACHR, *Monsignor Oscar Arnulfo Romero y Galdemez* v. *El Salvador*, Report (2000), No. 37/00, Case 11.481, paras. 147–8.

[144] IACtHR, *Bamaca-Velasquez* v. *Guatemala*, para. 74.

[145] IACtHR, *González et al.* (*Cotton Fields*) v. *Mexico*, Judgment, 16 November 2009, Ser. C, No. 205, para. 454.

[146] Article 63(1) of the ACHR provides: 'If the Court finds that there has been a violation of a right or freedom protected by this Convention, the Court shall rule that the injured party be ensured the enjoyment of his right or freedom that was violated. It shall also rule, if appropriate, that the consequence of the measure or situation that constituted the breach of such right or freedom be remedied and that fair compensation be paid to the injured party.'

[147] Shelton, *Remedies*, at 280–1. See also Loucaides, 'Reparations', at 190 ('…the language of Art. 41 is sufficiently wide to allow the possibility of a judgment indicating the specific measures for the execution of the obligation of *restitutio in integrum* resulting from the judgment itself').

system with the role of supervising the enforcement of judgments (comparable to the Committee of Ministers in the European system). Conversely, it has clearly been the case that the ECtHR has been concerned about over-stepping the mark as regards redress, and has been anxious not to tread on the toes of the Committee of Ministers, in the light of its duty of supervision, as stipulated in article 46 of the Convention. However, there need be no confusion in their respective roles, and there is no need for the Court to consider itself fettered by this on the question of redress (as opposed to the question of implementation). As Judge Malinverni has cogently argued:

> ... supervision of the execution of the Court's judgments is the responsibility of the Committee of Ministers. That does not mean, however, that the Court should not play any part in the matter and should not take measures designed to facilitate the Committee of Ministers' task in discharging these functions. To that end, it is essential that in its judgments the Court should not merely give as precise a description as possible of the nature of the Convention violation found but should also, in the operative provisions, indicate to the State concerned the measures it considers the most appropriate to redress the violation.[148]

The ECtHR has certainly become ever-more willing to refer to the Inter-American jurisprudence as regards substantive questions of law,[149] but not, as yet, to draw on its case law relating to redress. However, as has been discussed in this chapter, the Court has recently significantly changed its approach to redress, in making the kind of orders for non-monetary relief which the Inter-American Court has consistently been making for years. Consequently, it makes every sense for the Court to place much greater reliance on the Inter-American case law in this area,

---

[148] *Cudak* v. *Lithuania*. Concurring Opinion of Judge Malinverni, joined by Judges Casadevall, Cabral Barreto, Zagrebelsky and Popović, para. 5.

[149] See, e.g., *Varnava and Others* v. *Turkey* (*ratione temporis* jurisdiction in disappearance cases); ECtHR, *Al-Skeini* v. *UK* (Appl. No. 55721/07), Judgment (Grand Chamber), 7 July 2011, not reported (the duty to investigate); ECtHR, *Opuz* v. *Turkey* (Appl. No. 33401/02), Judgment (Third Section), 9 June 2009, Reports 2009 (the imputability to the state of acts of private persons and discrimination in the context of domestic violence); ECtHR, *Bayatyan* v. *Armenia* (Appl. No. 23459/03), Judgment (Grand Chamber), 7 July 2011, not reported (conscientious objection); ECtHR, *Palomo Sanchez and Others* v. *Spain* (Appl. Nos. 28955, 28957, 28959 and 28964/06), Judgment (Grand Chamber), 12 September 2011, not reported (trade union rights); ECtHR, *Gäfgen* v. *Germany* (Appl. No. 22978/05), Judgment (Grand Chamber), 1 June 2010, Reports 2010 (the scope of the prohibition of torture); ECtHR, *Zolotukhin* v. *Russia* (Appl. No. 14939/03), Judgment (Grand Chamber), 10 February 2009 (the 'double jeopardy' principle).

in view of the Inter-American Court's highly specialised experience in considering cases of gross and systematic human rights violations. Given the problems experienced by the Committee of Ministers in ensuring the effective implementation of such cases in the European context,[150] it is high time that the ECtHR followed the Inter-American Court's lead in taking a more prescriptive and disaggregated approach as regards measures of redress.

5. Interlaken, Brighton and further interpretations of subsidiarity

How might the current pressures on the Court, and the reform debates, impact upon the issue of remedies? The concept of subsidiarity would certainly be interpreted by some as meaning that the Court should not interfere unduly with issues that are properly the domain of national authorities.[151] Interestingly, the criticisms of the Court to the effect that its evolutive interpretation of the Convention has gone too far, have focused on the substantive provisions of the Convention, rather than on the issue of redress.[152] In respect of the particular question of remedies, this line of argument might translate into a call for a reduced role for the Court – fewer perceived illegitimate intrusions into the arena of state sovereignty. In the UK, for example, the Commission on a Bill of Rights has expressed its doubts 'as to whether it is properly the function of an international court of last resort to be entrusted with the task of calculating and awarding just satisfaction'.[153]

---

[150] See, e.g., Committee of Ministers, 'Execution of the Judgments of the European Court of Human Rights in 154 cases against the Russian Federation Concerning Actions of the Security Forces in the Chechen Republic of the Russian Federation', Interim Resolution CM/ResDH(2011)292, 2 December 2011.

[151] See, e.g., D. Raab, *Strasbourg in the Dock: Prisoner Voting, Human Rights and the Case for Democracy* (London: Civitas, 2011), referring, *inter alia*, to 'the scale of judicial legislation and the willingness of the Strasbourg Court to override both the UK courts and Parliament', at 21.

[152] See, e.g., M. Bossuyt, 'It is by ever widening its jurisdiction that the Court of Strasbourg is going too far', seminar paper given at the 'Expert Seminar: The Future of the European Court of Human Rights', Institute for Human Rights, Katholieke Universiteit Leuven, 2 September 2011 (on file with the author). This paper also discusses the increase in interim measures applications.

[153] Letter from the Commission on a Bill of Rights to Rt. Hon. Nick Clegg MP and Rt. Hon. Kenneth Clarke MP QC, 28 July 2011 – available at: www.justice.gov.uk/downloads/about/cbr/cbr-court-reform-chairs-letter.pdf. However, the focus of the Commission's letter was on financial awards, and made no reference to non-monetary relief, as such. Nevertheless, the recommendation is broadly phrased: 'the Government should ensure

At Interlaken, the Convention states parties exhorted the Court 'to take fully into account its subsidiary role in the interpretation and application of the Convention'. There is no sign, however, that this was code for 'you have gone too far on redress'. The Interlaken Declaration was clear that subsidiarity means an obligation on states to 'fully secure' Convention rights at the national level – and the importance of effective national implementation was reiterated by the Brighton Declaration.[154] There is also no suggestion that where states fail to do so, the Court should not be more prescriptive in defining remedial measures. Indeed, the Interlaken Declaration's call for clarity of the Court's case law, its invitation to the Court to make 'maximum use' of the procedural tools at its disposal and its emphasis on the indispensability of the 'full, effective and rapid' execution of Court judgments, would seem to suggest assent to the Court's developing practice. Furthermore, there was explicit support at Interlaken and at Brighton for the Court's response to systemic violations through the pilot judgment procedure – the Declarations encouraged the Court in its policy of the prioritisation of cases and identifying structural and systemic problems, and urged states to cooperate with the Committee of Ministers in relation to pilot judgments, by adopting and implementing general measures aimed at remedying the structural problems.[155]

6. Conclusion

This chapter has sought to analyse the significant developments in the Court's provision of non-monetary remedies in recent years. Although past declaratory judgments have often been implemented, in the sense that they have led to changes in domestic law or practice, the increasing number of systemic problems across the continent which have not been resolved, combined with the backlog of cases, has spurred the Court on to take a more creative and incisive approach (in the realm of both individual and general measures).

---

that a programme of fundamental reform addresses the need to revisit the meaning and effect of Article 41 of the Convention and the role of the Court in awarding "just satisfaction"'. See also *Report of the Group of Wise Persons to the Committee of Ministers*, CM(2006)203, 15 November 2006, paras. 94–9.

[154] CoE, High Level Conference on the Future of the European Court of Human Rights – Brighton Declaration, 20 April 2012, paras. 7–9. Available at www.coe.int/en/20120419-brighton-declaration/.

[155] See also *Report of the Group of Wise Persons to the Committee of Ministers*, paras. 100–5.

The principle of *restitutio in integrum* seems to have been re-visited by the Court, and reinvigorated. There are more situations where restitution is deemed by the Court to be possible in practice, and it is witnessing an increasing number of egregious human rights violations. This has led the Court, in some areas at least, to be more prescriptive, both in terms of the nature of the remedial measures required, and in laying down time periods. The Court's directions have been made in the judicial arena (requiring the release of detainees, ordering the reopening of legal proceedings or a change in a sentence handed down by a national court), but more far-reaching still have been its directions in the legislative field (requiring the state to introduce or amend particular laws).

One (no doubt, intended) consequence of the Court's new strategy is that greater clarity in its judgments should assist the Committee of Ministers in its task of supervising the enforcement of judgments, by reducing the opportunity for debate (or indeed, obfuscation) about what steps are in fact required to be implemented by the state. However, as President Costa commented in *Assanidze* in 2004, it does not necessarily mean simplification politically:

> ... if it has no choice as to the measures to be implemented, the respondent State will be left with only one alternative: either to comply with the Court's order (in which case all will be well), or to run the risk of blocking the situation.[156]

A more incisive approach may have considerably damaging political consequences in particular contexts, as we have seen in relation to the issue of prisoners' right to vote in the UK. Nevertheless, the Court has had no choice, given the prevalence of large-scale structural problems which Council of Europe states have failed to resolve, over long periods. It would be quite wrong to characterise such developments as violating the subsidiarity principle, which is still respected by the practice of the Court, both procedurally and in its substantive case law. This is not unjustified 'judicial activism', but a logical development which imposes an obligation on states to make appropriate reparation for the damage which has been caused. Those who are especially concerned about the Court's expansive tendencies may be able to take some comfort from the suggestion that the pilot judgment procedure represents (in some

---

[156] *Assanidze v. Georgia*, para. 7.

situations, at least) a means of improving the dialogue between the Court and national authorities, especially the national courts.[157]

When we contemplate the adequacy of the Court's position on redress, it should not be forgotten that the role of an international court is to rule on human rights violations which have been committed by the state (as opposed to a private individual). We should also remember that human rights violations are not just committed against individuals, but also represent breaches of the wider social order. In this broader context, the provision of redress accordingly serves the additional, and vital, functions of upholding the public interest and the rule of law.

---

[157] See, e.g., Leach *et al.*, *Responding to Systemic Violations*', 73–4; J. Gerards, 'The Pilot Judgment Procedure before the European Court of Human Rights as an Instrument for Dialogue', in M. Claes and P. Popelier (eds.), *Constitutional Conversations in Europe: Actors, Topics and Procedures* (Antwerp, Oxford, Portland: Intersentia, forthcoming) available at http://papers.ssrn.com/sol3/papers.cfm?abstract_id=1924806.

6

National implementation of ECHR rights

MADS ANDENAS AND EIRIK BJORGE

1. What are the issues?

The effectiveness of the Convention rights and of the judgments of the Strasbourg Court depend in no small measure on national implementation. National legal systems have opened up as an expression of the constitutional *Grundentscheidung für die offene Staatlichkeit*. Christian Tomuschat has stated in the case of Germany that the country could not 'ihre Existenz nicht in selbstherrlicher Isolierung, sondern nur in einem kooperativen Verbund mit den Völkern Europas und der Welt führen kann'.[1] James Crawford's essay, 'International Law as an Open System', regards parallel issues primarily from the vantage point of public international law.[2]

Alec Stone Sweet analyses the rapid development of the European Convention on Human Rights (ECHR, or the Convention) into a cosmopolitan legal order: a transnational legal system in which all public officials bear the obligation to fulfil the fundamental rights of every person within their jurisdiction. The emergence of the system depended on certain deep, structural transformations of law and politics in Europe, where courts are mediating constitutional pluralism at the national level, and of rights cosmopolitanism at the transnational level.[3] As Alec

---

[1] C. Tomuschat, 'Die Staatsrechtliche Entscheidung für die Internationale Offenheit', J. Isensee and P. Kirchhoff (eds.), *Handbuch des Staatsrechts der Bundesrepublik Deutschland*, Vol. VII (Heidelberg: C. F. Müller, 1992) para. 172. See the analysis in A. Proelss, 'Der Grundsatz der Völkerrechtsfreundlichen Auslegung im Lichte der Rechtsprechung des BVerfG', H. Rensen and S. Brink (eds.), *Linien der Rechtsprechung des Bundesverfassungsgerichts – Erörtert Von Den Wissenschatlichen Mitarbeitern* (Berlin: De Gruyter Recht, 2009) 553–84, 552.
[2] See J. Crawford, 'International Law as an Open System', in J. Crawford, *International Law as an Open System* (London: Cameron May Press, 2002) 17–38.
[3] A. Stone Sweet, 'A Cosmopolitan Legal Order: Constitutional Pluralism and Rights Adjudication in Europe', *Journal of Global Constitutionalism* 1:1 (2012) 53–90.

Stone Sweet and Helen Keller have said, 'courts have taken the lead in incorporating the Convention'.[4]

In this chapter we look at the implementation of the Convention in national law in Belgium, the Czech Republic, France, Germany, Norway, Russia and the United Kingdom (UK). In all of these jurisdictions there has been considerable change over the last 10–15 years. Two examples, one from UK law and one from Norwegian law, go a long way in bearing this out.

In *Cadder* v. *Her Majesty's Advocate*, the UK Supreme Court in October 2010 overturned Scottish case law on whether a person detained by the police on suspicion of having committed an offence has, prior to being interviewed, the right of access to a solicitor. The stakes of the case were not trifling were the Supreme Court to find that there was a breach of Convention rights. More than 76,000 cases would potentially be affected, and the rule in breach of the Convention was a long-standing rule of Scots law. The Court, adopting the opinion of Lord Hope, said that the issue 'must be faced up to, whatever the consequences'.[5] The Supreme Court was not convinced by the legal argument of the government; it would be untenable if the solution in the UK should be different from that of the other member states. Such a solution, said Lord Hope on behalf of a unanimous Supreme Court, would be entirely out of keeping with the Strasbourg court's approach to problems posed by the Convention, which is to provide principled solutions that are *universally applicable* in all the contracting states. It aims to achieve a harmonious application of standards of protection throughout the Council of Europe area, not one dictated by national choices and preferences. There is no room in its jurisprudence for, as it were, one rule for the countries in Eastern Europe, such as Turkey, on the one hand, and those on its Western fringes, such as Scotland, on the other.[6]

Later Lord Hope summarised the Supreme Court's approach in *Cadder* in the following way: 'Pride in our own system is one thing; isolationism is quite another.'[7] A ruling in a similar case was handed

---

[4] A. Stone Sweet, 'Assessing the Impact of the ECHR on National Legal Systems', in A. Stone Sweet (ed.), *A Europe of Rights: The Impact of the ECHR on National Legal Systems* (Oxford University Press, 2007) 677–712, at 687 (hereinafter Stone Sweet, 'Assessing the Impact').

[5] *Cadder* v. *Her Majesty's Advocate* [2010] UKSC 43; [2010] WLR 268 at 4.

[6] *Ibid.*, at 40.

[7] Lord Hope, 'Scots Law seen from South of the Border', www.supremecourt.gov.uk/docs/speech_110401.pdf.

down by the Norwegian Supreme Court in the same month as the UK Supreme Court handed down its ruling in *Cadder*. The Norwegian case bore on the reopening of old criminal cases in which the process had been in breach of international human rights.[8] The Norwegian Supreme Court, unanimously adopting the closely argued opinion of Justice Gjølstad, held that the international human rights obligations required reopening, with potentially several thousand more cases to be reopened. It is clear that the Norwegian Supreme Court does not see itself in a bilateral relationship with the international human rights organs. The arguments of the government attorneys, that one ought instead to opt for Norwegian exceptionalism, were thus roundly rejected. In the face of high stakes, the Norwegian Supreme Court's exemplary ruling chose instead to take seriously the universal exigencies which apply to national judges when they are adjudicating on human rights issues.

Lord Hope and Justice Gjølstad focus in their opinions on the universality of solutions adopted by national courts. Armin von Bogdandy, in his criticism of the *Lissabon-Urteil* of the German Federal Constitutional Court,[9] makes the point that the formation of European law is not only the task of politics, but equally that of lawyers, who, in their work, not only have recourse to law, but develop it.[10] It is no surprise that the *Lissabon-Urteil* by the Federal Constitutional Court was read with no small interest in courts all over Europe. German arguments in favour of 'selbstherrlicher Isolierung' over a 'kooperativen Verbund mit den Völkern Europas' would be in demand from those wishing to close the national political and legal systems.

The relationship between Russian law and the Convention has raised questions similar to those addressed by the German Federal Constitutional Court.[11] In the wake of the *Lissabon-Urteil*, the President of the Russian Constitutional Court, Valery Zorkin, criticised several of the

---

[8] Decision HR-2010-01703-S, 12 October 2010.
[9] BVerfG, NJW 2009, 2267 – *Lissabon-Urteil*.
[10] A. von Bogdandy, 'Prinzipien der Rechtsfortbildung im Europäischen Rechtsraum: Überlegungen zum Lissabon-Urteil des BVerfGE', *Neue Juristische Wochenzeitung* 63:1 (2010) 1–5, at 1–2. G. de Búrca and J.H.H. Weiler, 'Introduction' in G. de Búrca and J.H.H. Weiler (eds.), *The Worlds of European Constitutionalism* (Cambridge University Press, 2012) 1–8, point to the role of EU law in mediating between different legal orders in their critical assessment of the discourse on 'constitutional pluralism'.
[11] M. Andenas *et al.*, 'The Federal Russian Law on Foreign Treaties', in R. Mullerson *et al.* (eds.), *Constitutional Reform and International Law in Central and Eastern Europe* (The Hague: Kluwer Law International, 1998) 259–65.

judgments against Russia by the European Court of Human Rights in public speeches.[12] He singled out the complaint made by the Russian opposition about the course of the parliamentary elections held in 2003 (criticised by OSCE observers) and the Strasbourg Court's decision in favour of the Russian military, who were striving for three years' paid child care leave for single parents (in Russia only women are granted this right). The Strasbourg Court had been subject to political and press criticism, and the president may also be seen as warning it about consequences of further adverse findings against Russia in the then ongoing cases concerning Mikhail Khodorkovsky's detention and despoilment (*Yukos* v. *Russia*,[13] and the case regarding the Katyn massacre (*Wołk-Jezierska* v. *Russia*).[14]

The Czech Constitutional Court provides another aspect of the issue. While looking at German law, the Czech court did not follow the German approach but, rather, criticised it. Challenges to the parliamentary ratification of the EU Treaty of Lisbon made the Czech Republic one of the final member states to ratify this Treaty. The Czech Constitutional Court refused to establish the clear limitations on transfers of powers that the German court had done. '[T]he Constitutional Court does not consider it possible, in view of the position that it holds in the constitutional system of the Czech Republic, to create such a catalogue of non-transferrable powers and authoritatively determine "substantive limits to the transfer of powers", as the petitioners request'. It points out that it already stated, in judgment Pl. ÚS 19/08, that 'These limits should be left primarily to the legislature to specify, because this is a priori a political question, which provides the legislature wide discretion'. Responsibility for these political decisions cannot be transferred to the Constitutional Court; it can review them only at the point when they have actually been made on the political level.

For the same reasons, the Constitutional Court does not feel authorised to formulate in advance, in an abstract context, what is the precise content of Article 1(1) of the Constitution, as requested by the petitioners, supported by the president, who welcomes the attempt 'in a final list

---

[12] Notably in a widely reported intervention in St. Petersburg, 18 November 2010, at the International Forum of Constitutional Justice.
[13] ECtHR, *OAO Neftyanaya Kompaniya Yukos* v. *Russia* (Appl. No. 14902/04), Judgment (First Section), 20 September 2011, not reported.
[14] ECtHR, *Witomila Wołk-Jezierska and Others* v. *Russia* (Appl. Nos. 55508/07 and 29520/09), Judgment (Fifth Section), 16 April 2012, not reported.

to define the elements of the "material core" of the constitutional order, or more precisely, of a sovereign democratic state governed by the rule of law', and states (in agreement with the petitioners) that this could 'limit future self-serving definition of these elements based on cases being adjudicated at the time'.[15]

The next subsection of the judgment (IV.C.) has the heading: 'Limiting the Possibility of Unconstitutional Abuse of the Proceeding pursuant to article 87(2) of the Constitution and Permissibility of Supplementing the Petition' and contains a robust reply to the president and senators, who used the constitutional review procedure to delay the ratification. Under the heading 'Democracy in the European Union', the Czech court expressly addressed the German *Lissabon-Urteil*.[16] It is a mistake to claim that 'representative democracy can exist only within states, within sovereign subjects'. To further refute the German court's decision, the Czech court cited Advocate-General Maduro of the European Court of Justice:

> European democracy also involves a delicate balance between national and European dimensions of democracy, without one necessarily outweighing the other.[17]

How best to make sense of these developments in the implementation of European exigencies and more specifically, the ECHR, in national law? It is clear that the implementation by national courts of the ECHR may be measured in different ways. One way is to look at the defining features of the ECHR regime and then see how the national systems relate to these defining features. What, then, are the defining precepts of the ECHR? The defining features of the regime set up by the Convention have been summarised as 'an evolutive approach based upon [the Court's] understanding of the object and purpose of the Convention, but also reflective of its own role as an international human rights court conscious of its subsidiary role in the protection of human rights'.[18]

---

[15] Decision, 3 November 2009, at paras. 111–12. See M. Hofmann, 'Zum Zweiten "Lissabon-Urteil" des Tschechischen Verfassungsgerichts', *Europäische Grundrechtzeitschrift* 37:5–6 (2010) 153–6, 153.
[16] Decision of 3 November 2009, at subsection V.C. of the judgment, see in particular at para. 280.
[17] *Ibid.*, at para. 138. The court cites a longer passage from the Opinion of Advocate General Maduro in C-411/06 *Commission* v. *Parliament and Council* [2009] ECR I-7585, note 5.
[18] R. White, *Jacobs, White & Ovey: The European Convention on Human Rights*, 5th edn (Oxford University Press, 2010), at 81.

On the one hand, reflecting the object and purpose of the Convention, there is the doctrine of evolutive interpretation, according to which the Court will 'ensure that the interpretation of the Convention reflects societal change and remains in line with present-day conditions'.[19] Lucius Wildhaber has described this as 'one of the best known principles of Strasbourg case-law'.[20] This feature of the Convention schema pulls graphically in the direction of unity and coherence; the evolution of the Convention rights leads to heightened rights protection applicable in *all* the member states.[21]

On the other hand, reflecting the subsidiary and supranational role of the Court is the doctrine of the margin of appreciation,[22] according to which the state authorities will in some cases be accorded a measure of deference in determining particularly, but not only, whether interference with a protected right was 'necessary in a democratic society'.[23] Margins of appreciation are closely connected with standards of review, and the determination of the reach of, and the justified restrictions on, substantive rights at the other end of the filters of margins and standards. In the following, we focus on the national margin of appreciation. This doctrine of the national margin of appreciation has been developed by the Court itself, as a tool in the relationship between the domestic authorities and the Court. The margin of appreciation is only one aspect of this relationship.[24]

Jean-Paul Costa has pointed out the importance of the margin of appreciation in ECHR adjudication, but also warned against taking this further at the national level in a way that could lead to municipal authorities following double or triple standards:

---

[19] ECtHR, *Cossey* v. *United Kingdom* (Appl. No. 10843/84), Judgment (Plenary), 27 September 1990, Series A, Vol. 184. A recent example of this doctrine is ECtHR, *Rantsev* v. *Cyprus and Russia* (Appl. No. 25965/04), Judgment (First Section), 7 January 2010, Reports 2010, para. 282.

[20] L. Wildhaber, 'The European Court of Human Rights in Action', *Ritsumeikan Law Review* 83 (2004) 83–92, at 84.

[21] See Letsas, Chapter 4, this volume. [22] See Arai-Takahashi, Chapter 3, this volume.

[23] ECtHR, *Handyside* v. *United Kingdom* (Appl. No. 5493/72), Judgment (Plenary), 7 December 1976, Series A, Vol. 24, para. 49.

[24] See, for instance, the helpful analysis on subsidiarity in the Convention system by S. Besson, 'European Human Rights, Supranational Judicial Review and Democracy – Thinking Outside the Judicial Box', in P. Popelier, C. Van den Heyning and P. Van Nuffel (eds.), *Human Rights Protection in the European Legal Order: Interaction between European Courts and National Courts* (Cambridge: Intersentia, 2011) 97–143, at 102–20.

il faut probablement dans certaines matières laisser une certaine marge d'appréciation aux États, mais ... en même temps il faut éviter à tout prix les doubles ou triples standards selon les pays et en ce qui concerne les mêmes problèmes.[25]

This highlights the issue of municipal courts adopting municipal concepts of the margin of appreciation, and this was also highlighted by the Grand Chamber in A v. United Kingdom:

> The doctrine of the margin of appreciation has always been meant as a tool to define relations between the domestic authorities and the Court. It cannot have the same application to the relations between the organs of State at the domestic level.[26]

The UK courts had rejected adopting a municipal margin of appreciation, with similar reasons. The government lawyers got short shrift when they challenged this rejection before the Grand Chamber. The Grand Chamber did not need to address this question, but used the opportunity given here to clarify this issue.

Questions relating to the margin of appreciation are very much a live issue, not least because the remit of this doctrine seems to be expanding.[27] This issue was front and centre in the *Lautsi* case, in which the Grand Chamber of the Strasbourg Court afforded a generous margin of appreciation to the state in the vexed question of whether public schools may display religious symbols in classrooms.[28] J.H.H. Weiler, who favoured that solution which the Grand Chamber reached in *Lautsi*, has

---

[25] J.-P. Costa, 'Interview Exclusive de Jean-Paul Costa, Président de la Cour Européenne des Droits de l'Homme', *Droits de l'homme – jurisprudence de la cour européenne des droits de l'homme* 5 (2007) 77–80, at 77–8.

[26] ECtHR, *A v. United Kingdom* (Appl. No. 3455/05), Judgment (Grand Chamber), 19 February 2009, Reports 2009, para. 184. We have discussed this in M. Andenas and E. Bjorge, *Menneskerettene Og Oss* (Oslo: Universitetsforlaget, 2012) 83–9, and see also J. Christoffersen, 'Primaritetsprinsippet – Nye Tanker Om EMRKs Stilling i Dansk Ret', J. Christoffersen and M. Rask Madsen (eds.), *Menneskerettighedsdomstolen – 50 års samspil med dansk ret og politik* (Copenhagen: Thomson, 2009), at 173, concluding that 'the doctrine of national margin of appreciation does not have the same application at the national level' ['doktrinen om statenes skønsmargin ikke finder samme anvendelse på national plan'].

[27] See the judgments in ECtHR, *Schalk and Kopf v. Austria* (Appl. No. 30141/04), Judgment (Chamber), 24 June 2010, Reports 2010; ECtHR, *A, B and C v. Ireland* (Appl. No. 25579/05), Judgment (Grand Chamber), 16 December 2010, Reports 2010; ECtHR, *Lautsi and Others v. Italy* (Appl. No. 30814/06), Judgment (Grand Chamber), 18 March 2011, Reports 2011.

[28] *Lautsi and Others*, ibid.

argued that this must be so, as the 'European Court of Human Rights is not an oracle'.[29] In his view, the Strasbourg Court is a dialogical partner with the member states, the legitimacy and persuasiveness of its decisions residing both in their quality and communicative power. The Court, Weiler argues, is simultaneously reflective and constitutive of the European constitutional practices and norms. When there is a diverse constitutional practice among the Convention States – and there certainly is in this area – the Court needs to listen, not only preach, and to be seen to be listening.[30]

Graphically, the doctrine of margin of appreciation pulls in the direction of value pluralism; the effect of the granting by the Court of a margin to the state authorities will in practice lead to differing levels of rights protection in the member states.

We mention briefly another feature, often linked to the margin of appreciation – the doctrine of proportionality. The centrality in ECHR law of proportionality and balancing has long been recognised.[31] Rolv Ryssdal pointed out that '[t]he theme that runs through the Convention and its case law is the need to strike a balance between the general interest of the community and the protection of the individual's fundamental rights'.[32]

The cases before the Court on the rights of transsexuals, which culminated in *Goodwin*[33] – perhaps the leading Strasbourg exemplar of evolutive interpretation – show the relationship between the doctrine of evolution of rights on the one hand and the doctrine of the margin of appreciation on the other: at various stages of the development of this line of cases, both of these defining concepts of the Convention scheme were on display. For years – most notably in *Rees*,[34]

---

[29] J.H.H. Weiler, 'Editorial', *European Journal of International Law* 21:1 (2010) 1–6, at 1.

[30] Ibid. The argument builds on J.H.H. Weiler, *Un' Europa Cristiana: Un saggio esplorativo* (Saggi: BUR, 2003).

[31] See among the many of his works on this, A. Stone Sweet, 'Sur la constitutionnalisation de la Convention Européenne des Droits de l'Homme: Cinquante ans après son installation, la Cour Européenne des droit de l'Homme conçue comme une Cour constitutionnelle', *Revue Trimestrielle des Droits de l'Homme* 80 (2009) 923–44, at 923.

[32] R. Ryssdal, 'Opinion: The Coming of Age of the European Convention on Human Rights', *European Human Rights Law Review* 1:1 (1996) 18–29, at 18, 26; see S. Tsakyrakis, 'Proportionality: An Assault on Human Rights?', *International Journal of Constitutional Law* 7:3 (2009) 468–93, at 475–8.

[33] ECtHR, *Goodwin v. United Kingdom* (Appl. No. 28957/95), Judgment (Grand Chamber), 11 July 2002, Reports 2002-VI.

[34] ECtHR, *Rees v. United Kingdom* (Appl. No. 9532/81), Judgment (Plenary), 17 October 1986, Series A, Vol. 106.

Cossey[35] and *Sheffield and Horsham*[36] – the Court held back from recognising the right of British citizens to receive a birth certificate in accordance with their new sex after sex change. In issue in these cases were article 8 and whether the interference by the UK with the prima facie privacy right to have one's own perceived gender recognised was proportionate. As is clear from this line of cases – especially in light of its culmination, *Goodwin*, in which the Grand Chamber concluded in 2002 that the interference was disproportionate – the acceptability of an evolutive interpretation of the right in issue was a question of whether the interference could be deemed proportionate, which in turn was dependent upon the margin of appreciation to be accorded to the state authorities, itself a function of consensus among the member states.

Other comparators could conceivably have been chosen, too. Another example could have been the notion of 'autonomous concepts', according to which member states cannot define their way out of Convention obligations by, for example, classifying an offence as disciplinary instead of criminal, thus falling outside the remit of articles 6–7.[37] There have been many cases in which the Strasbourg Court has handed down adverse judgments faulting the member state based on the doctrine of autonomous concepts.[38] One recent example of this is the 2009 decision by the Strasbourg Court in *M v. Germany*,[39] which bore on whether preventive detention could be ordered retrospectively against persons convicted of offences committed prior to the publication of the statute setting up the preventive detention scheme. The German scheme of preventive detention – *Sicherungsverwahrung* – in terms of German law was not punishment, whereas the Strasbourg Court held that, no matter what the definition in national law, in terms of ECHR law it was clear that the scheme in issue was punishment according to article 5, and as a consequence, also fell foul of article 7(1).

---

[35] *Cossey v. United Kingdom*.
[36] ECtHR, *Sheffield and Horsham v. United Kingdom* (Appl. Nos. 31-2/1997/15–816/1018–19/1998), Judgment (Grand Chamber), 30 July 1998, Reports 1998-V.
[37] ECtHR, *Engel and Others v. The Netherlands* (Appl. Nos. 5100, 5101, and 5102/71; 5354 and 5370/72), Judgment (Plenary), 8 June 1976, Series A, Vol. 22; see G. Letsas, 'Strasbourg's Interpretive Ethic: Lessons for the International Lawyer', *European Journal of International Law* 21:3 (2010) 509–41, at 523.
[38] G. Letsas, 'The Truth in Autonomous Concepts: How to Interpret the ECHR', *European Journal of International Law* 15:2 (2004) 279–305, 279.
[39] ECtHR, *M v. Germany* (Appl. No. 19359/04), Judgment (Fifth Section), 17 December 2009, Reports 2009.

However, the doctrine of autonomous concepts is really part and parcel of any kind of treaty interpretation.[40] Any treaty whose member states may define themselves away from their treaty obligations will be positively emasculated, as would the notion of the treaty having a final international arbiter. Autonomous concepts have not been given the pride of place which has been accorded to the doctrines of the evolution of Convention rights, the margin of appreciation, and proportionality – nor have they been as important in defining the relationship between the Strasbourg Court and national judges.

Evolution of rights, proportionality and the margin of appreciation, therefore, seem to be apposite points of reference by which to measure the degree of adaptation of the member states. If it is accepted that the three comparators make up a good yardstick, then looking at how the municipal legal systems have related to them would seem a good way of measuring the will of the judiciaries of the member states at issue to comply with the schema of the ECHR. Some of the issues will bleed into one another, and while in some jurisdictions the margin of appreciation has been front and centre in legal debates on implementation, it may have received no attention in others. It has, for example, been the subject of much debate in UK law, while many other jurisdictions have conceptualised implementation in ways which have brought other aspects of the Convention system into the foreground. The opening up of national and international legal systems, as discussed by Tomuschat and Crawford, is a complex process.

2. Development of Convention rights

In spite of, or rather, precisely because of, the fact that in international law 'no matter is more daunting and complicated' than getting one's hands around evolutive interpretation,[41] a large literature over the last few decades has been accorded to this aspect of the ECHR system and interpretation – both in international and national law – in general.[42]

---

[40] See, for a classic example, the 1923 ruling by the Permanent Court of International Justice in *Nationality Decrees Issued in Tunis and Morocco (French Zone)*, Advisory Opinion, PCIJ (1923) Series B, No. 4; a more recent example is found in the 2010 judgment by the International Court of Justice, *Ahmadou Sadio Diallo (Republic of Guinea v. Democratic Republic of the Congo)* ICJ Reports (2010), para. 77.

[41] M. Fitzmaurice, 'Dynamic (Evolutive) Interpretation of Treaties I', *Hague Yearbook of International Law* 21 (2008) 101–57, at 102.

[42] Some examples among many are P.M. Dupuy, 'Evolutionary Interpretation of Treaties: Between Memory and Prophecy', in E. Cannizzaro (ed.), *The Law of Treaties Beyond the*

This technique of interpretation has been particularly associated with human rights treaty regimes, such as that of the Convention.[43] In fact, one is often made to believe that the technique of evolutive interpretation is a concomitant of human rights conventions only, or certainly that it is a more natural ally of human rights conventions than of other conventions.[44] There may be good reason to complicate the picture, as it has a direct bearing on the relationship between national courts and the Strasbourg Court.[45]

Arguably, evolutive – or 'dynamic' – interpretation of human rights treaties is in principle no different from evolutive interpretation of other treaties. What is common between treaty regimes which have been interpreted evolutively is first and foremost the fact that the treaty makers wanted them to be capable of application to new situations, and therefore articulated the treaties' object and purpose in 'generic terms'. A generic term is 'a known legal term, whose content the parties expected would change through time'.[46] When an international tribunal has recourse to evolutive interpretation of generic terms, what it does is to apply, in keeping with the treaty's object and purpose, the generic term on new situations.[47] In the interpretation of all types of treaty, the interpreter will encounter the problem of how the passage of time – and

---

Vienna Convention (Oxford University Press, 2011) 123–37; V. P. Tzevelekos, 'The Use of Article 31(3)(c) of the VCLT in the Case Law of the ECtHR: An Effective Anti-Fragmentation Tool for the Reinforcement of Human Rights Teleology? Between Evolution and Systemic Integration', *Michigan Journal of International Law* 31 (2010) 621–90, at 621; B. Simma, 'Harmonizing Investment Protection and International Human Rights: First Steps towards a Methodology', in C. Binder (ed.), *International Investment Law for the 21st Century* (Oxford University Press, 2009) 685–94; D. French, 'Treaty Interpretation and the Incorporation of Extraneous Legal Rules', *The International and Comparative Law Quarterly* 55:2 (2006) 281–314, 297–300; C. Jennings, *Oppenheim's International Law*, Vol. I (London: Longman, 1992), at 1282.

[43] L. Caflisch, 'Les conventions américaine et européenne des droits de l'homme et le droit international général', *Révue Générale du Droit International* 108:5 (2004) 9–22.

[44] See, for a recent example, Dissenting Opinion of Judge Cançado Trindade in *Case Concerning the Application of the International Convention on the Elimination of All Forms of Racial Discrimination (Georgia v. Russian Federation)* ICJ Reports (2011), para. 169.

[45] See E. Bjorge, 'National Supreme Courts and the Development of ECHR Rights', *International Journal of Constitutional Law* 9:1 (2012) 5–31.

[46] *Kasikili/Sedudu Island (Botswana v. Namibia)*, Declaration of Judge Higgins, ICJ Reports (1999), 1113–14, para. 2.

[47] B. Schlütter, 'Aspects of Human Rights Interpretation by the UN Treaty Bodies', in G. Ulfstein and H. Keller (eds.), *UN Treaty Bodies: Law and Legitimacy* (Cambridge University Press, 2012) 261–319, 278 *et seq.*

attendant changing circumstances – affect the interpretation and application of the treaty. Just as the genius of the Napoleonic codes was their taxonomic elegance and the adaptability of their concepts to apply to new situations,[48] treaties meant to last over long periods of time are often furnished with generic terms, the meaning of which will be capable of new applications. As was pointed out in the *Iron Rhine* case: 'It has long been established that the understanding of conceptual or generic terms in a treaty may be seen as "an essentially relative question; it depends upon the development of international relations".'[49] Another early example is the *Spanish Zone of Morocco Claims*, where the arbitrator, Max Huber, in his 1923 ruling, held that the treaty term in issue, '*maison convenable*', which dated back to 1783, must be interpreted '*au point de vue des exigencies actuelles*' (at the time when the decision was rendered).[50]

Examples of such conventions may be found in many different fields: one finds it, for example, in a field as far removed from human rights law as trade treaties and bilateral investment treaties, where, as a matter of course, generic terms such as 'sound recording', 'distribution', 'investment', 'fair and equitable treatment', 'full protection and security', and 'expropriation' have been the object of evolutive interpretation.[51]

It bears mention at this juncture that interpretative techniques such as evolutive interpretation are in no way foreign to national judges – even independently of the ECHR system. This forms an important part of the background for implementation. A 2010 judgment from the Czech

---

[48] See generally, J.L. Halpérin (ed.), *L'impossible Code Civil* (Paris: Presses Universitaires de France, 1992).

[49] Permanent Court of Arbitration, *Arbitration regarding the Iron Rhine ('Ijzeren Rijn') Railway (Belgium v. The Netherlands)*, Award, 24 May 2005 at 36, para. 79, quoting *Nationality Decrees Issued in Tunis and Morocco*, PCIJ Series B, No. 4 (1923) at 24. See P. Daillier *et al.*, *Droit international public* (Paris: Librairie générale de droit et de jurisprudence, 2009) at 287.

[50] *British Claims in the Spanish Zone of Marroco (Spain v. United Kingdom)* 2 RIAA 615, at 722, 725. See A. McNair, *The Law of Treaties* (Oxford University Press, 1968), at 468.

[51] See WTO Appellate Body, *China – Measures Affecting Trading Rights and Distribution Services for Certain Publications and Audiovisual Entertainment Products (China – Publications and Audiovisual Products)*, Report, WT/DS353/AB/R (circulated 21 December 2009, adopted 19 January 2010) paras. 396-7 ('sound recording' and 'distribution'); *Romak S.A. (Switzerland v. The Republic of Uzbekistan)*, Award, 26 November 2009, paras. 181–95 ('investment'); ICSID, *Mondev International Ltd. v. United States of America*, Award, 11 October 2002, ICSID Case No. ARB(AF)/99/2, para. 116 ('fair and equitable treatment' and 'full protection and security'); ICSID, *Tecnicas Medioambientales Tecmed S.A. v. The United Mexican States*, Award, 29 May 2003, ICSID Case No. ARB(AF)/00/2, para. 116 ('expropriation').

Constitutional Court illustrates the national constitutional perspective. The Czech court applies a 'teleological interpretation' of national constitutional and ECHR provisions. The recently adopted Czech constitutional rights provisions are subjected to the same teleological method. In rejecting a literal approach, the court emphasised how formalism and literalism would open up for 'arbitrariness', which it has developed as its core constitutional concept. The court set out its method and how it has been developed as part of its constant jurisprudence as follows, in a tightly reasoned and referenced passage to which the present translation does not do full justice:

> The Constitutional Court has also referred to the relevance of the teleological method directed at finding the meaning and operation of the law. … The Constitutional Court has accentuated the importance of the teleological method of interpretation as an interpretative approach which is necessary in constitutional law and which … constitutes a significant corrective in identifying the contents of a legal norm.[52]

From the point of view of another legal system, the UK Supreme Court Justice, Lady Hale, said extra-judicially in 2011 that: '[t]he common law is no stranger to the concept of evolutive interpretation, both of precedent case law and of legislation'.[53] When it comes to the interpretation of statutes, except where the Human Rights Act requires otherwise, the UK Supreme Court are in theory looking for the 'intention of Parliament'. This, as Lady Hale explicates, is an illusion, 'because on most points which come before us Parliament did not have any intention at all'. Common law judges then deduce the intention of the legislation from the terms used, read in the light of the statutory purpose. It is, however, rare for an Act of Parliament to have to be construed and applied exactly as it would have been at the time of its promulgation. Statutes, she says, are said to be 'always speaking';[54] the words used must be made to apply to situations which would never even have been contemplated when they were enacted. Thus, a 'member of the family', first used in 1920, could be

---

[52] 2010/04/13 – Ii. ÚS 485/10, para. 21. This and other translations of judgments of the Czech Constitutional Court build on the translations published by the Court and made public on its website.

[53] B. Hale, 'European Court of Human Rights: The Limits to the Evolutive Interpretation of the Convention' at www.echr.coe.int/ECHR/EN/Header/The+Court/Events+at+the+court/Opening+of+the+judicial+year/ (15 April 2011).

[54] 'Always speaking' is the equivalent approach to 'living instrument' in the Common Law tradition.

held in 2001 to include a same-sex partner.[55] As Lord Slynn of Hadley said in *Fitzpatrick v. Sterling Housing Association Ltd*:

> It is not an answer to the problem to assume … that if in 1920 people had been asked whether one person was a member of another same-sex person's family the answer would have been 'No'. That is not the right question. The first question is what the characteristics of a family in the 1920 Act were, and the second whether two same-sex partners can satisfy those characteristics so as today to fall within the word 'family'. An alternative question is whether the word 'family' in the 1920 Act has to be updated so as to be capable of including persons who today would be regarded as being of each other's family, whatever might have been said in 1920.[56]

In the same vein, 'bodily harm', in a statute of 1861, could be held in 1998 to include psychiatric harm.[57] In its recent ruling in *Yemshaw*,[58] the UK Supreme Court gave an illustrative example of just how naturally evolutive interpretation comes to common lawyers. In this case, the generic statutory term in issue was 'violence'. As the Supreme Court in *Yemshaw* said, this kind of generic statutory term 'can change and develop over time'.[59] This, as Lord Brown poignantly underscored, was nothing other than applying a '"living instrument", "always speaking" approach to statutory construction'.[60]

The picture is much the same in French law.[61] French courts, as a matter of course, make use of the Strasbourg Court's method when interpreting the ECHR; the Convention thus becomes a living instrument for effective rights protection through the contribution of French courts.[62] The field in which this interpretative development has been most striking is probably prisoners' rights.[63] On the whole, French administrative courts have lost no time in joining the Strasbourg Court

---

[55] *Fitzpatrick v. Sterling Housing Association Ltd* [2001] 1 AC 27. [56] *Ibid.*, at 35.
[57] *R v. Ireland* [1998] AC 147.
[58] *Yemshaw (Appellant) v. London Borough of Hounslow (Respondent)* [2011] UKSC 3.
[59] *Ibid.*, para. 27.
[60] *Ibid.*, para. 56. See also *Pioneer Shipping Ltd v. BTP Tioxide Ltd (The Nema)* [1982] AC 724 and *Antaios Compania Neviera SA v. Salen Rederierna AB* [1985] 1 AC 191.
[61] See D. Fairgrieve and H. Muir Watt, *Common Law et Tradition Civiliste: Convergence ou Concurrence?* (Paris: Presses Universitaires de France, 2006); B. Stirn *et al.*, *Droits et Libertés en France et au Royaume-Uni* (Paris: Odile Jacob, 2006).
[62] L. Heuschling, 'Comparative Law in French Human Rights Cases', in Esin Örücü (ed.), *Judicial Comparativism in Human Rights Cases* (United Kingdom National Committee of Comparative Law, 2003) 23–47, at 33.
[63] M. Guyomar *et al.*, *Contentieux Administratif* (Paris: Dalloz, 2010), at 235–6.

in evolving rights in this area. Important here are two cases decided on the same day, on the basis of the same *conclusions* by *rapporteur public*, Mattias Guyomar.[64] The first of the cases concerned a decision about a change of the allocation of a detainee, the other, prison employment relegation.

Traditionally, such measures were deemed to be *mesures d'ordre intérieur*, which are not subject to judicial review. In respect of prisons, this practice is very much a vestige of old penitentiary administration traditions. French administrative law has drawn a distinction between them and *actes administratives*. *Mesures d'ordre intérieur administratives* in later years have become eroded by rights-based jurisprudence,[65] so that fewer and fewer are exempt from judicial review. Barring any breach of legal requirement, however, the ordinary operational decisions in the exercise of a discretion which the administration enjoys – the decision, for example, to alter the frequency of services – has been regarded until very recently to lie squarely outside the ambit of judicial review.[66] The authorities on the issue, *Marie* and *Remli*, did not warrant such a move; the *rapporteur public* made clear in his *conclusions* that in his view only a dynamic approach to the Convention rights, going further than Strasbourg, but taking inspiration from the ECHR rights, would allow this.

In *Boussouar*,[67] which was about the right to an effective remedy in article 13, the *Assemblée du contentieux*, the highest body of the Conseil d'État, held that the decision to change the allocation of a detainee from a high-security prison (*maison centrale*) to a detention centre where detainees are being held pending their trial or sentencing (*maison d'arrêt*) was in fact an administrative act, lending itself to judicial review.[68]

---

[64] M. Guyomar, 'Conclusions sur Conseil d'État, Assemblée, 14 December 2007, *M. Planchenault* (1re espèce), et *Garde des sceaux, ministre de la Justice c/ M. Boussouar* (2e espèce)', *Revue Française de Droit Administratif* (2008) 87 (hereinafter Guyomar, 'Conclusions'). Rapporteur public is the new appellation of the *commissaire du gouvernement*: décret no. 2009-14 du 7 janvier 2009 relatif au rapporteur public des juridictions administratives et au déroulement de l'audience devant ces juridictions.

[65] See *Kherouaa* [1992] *Actualités Juridique Droit Administratif* 833; *Hyver* CE 10 Oct. 1990; *Marie and Hardoun* CE Ass. Plén. 17 February [1995] *Actualités Juridique Droit Administratif* 420–21.

[66] See, e.g., J. Bell *et al.*, *Principles of French Law*, 2nd edn (Oxford University Press, 2008), at 181.

[67] Conseil d'État, Assemblée, *Boussouar*, No. 290730, 14 December 2007; Guyomar, 'Conclusions'.

[68] *Ibid.*

The second decision in which the Conseil applied these criteria was *Planchenault*.⁶⁹ At issue was the decision by a penitentiary administration body to deny a prisoner the opportunity to work in the prison kitchen on grounds of his attitude being uncooperative. The effects of this measure on his situation proved to be important to his chances of proving that he was capable of reintegration into society and benefiting from a reduction of his sentence diminished. The Conseil clarified the degree of control afforded in these instances to the judge. Following the extensive conclusions of the *rapporteur public*, which cited ECHR authorities, but also comparative analysis by way of showing the direction in which Belgian, Italian, and UK jurisprudence on the issue was heading, the *Assemblée du contentieux* held that this, too, could no longer be exempt from judicial review by dint of being *mesure d'ordre intérieur*. This effectively meant that the two situations in *Boussouar* and *Planchenault* were held to constitute 'administrative act[s] susceptible of *recours pour excès de pouvoir*'. As the principle of legality in French administrative law prescribes a line of conduct for administration from which the administration cannot depart without committing an *excès de pouvoir*, any violation of the principle can be a ground for review, potentially making the administrative act void. Traditionally, this is based on four grounds, *incompetence*, *vice de forme*, *violation de la loi*, and *détournement de pouvoir*.⁷⁰ The *conclusions*, adopted wholesale by the Conseil in the two judgments, held:

> En premier lieu, l'évolution jurisprudentielle que nous vous proposons qui prolonge les acquis de vos décisions *Marie–Remli* nous paraît de nature à prémunir la France contre toute condamnation de la Cour de Strasbourg. Les deux logiques de contrôle – la vôtre et celle de la Cour européenne – ne coïncident pas exactement. La prise en compte de la jurisprudence européenne vous conduit, dans une certaine mesure, à aller au-delà de ce que la Cour exige dans le cadre de son contrôle *a posteriori* et *in concreto*. ... Refuser de contrôler les décisions aujourd'hui attaquées reviendrait à accepter de fermer les yeux en attendant qu'on les ouvre pour vous à Strasbourg. Telle n'est pas la conception que nous avons de votre office. ... En outre, en élargissant l'accès à votre prétoire, vous conférez sa pleine portée au caractère subsidiaire du contrôle de la cour européenne, prenant en charge dès les instances nationales la vérification du respect des droits conventionnellement garantis.⁷¹

---

⁶⁹ M. *Planchenault*, req. no. 290420 [2007] *AJDA* 2404.
⁷⁰ L. Neville Brown *et al.*, *French Administrative Law*, 5th edn (Oxford: Clarendon Press, 1998), at 239.
⁷¹ Guyomar, 'Conclusions', in the original, of which a translation follows: 'First of all, the jurisprudential evolution which we suggest you take, extending the *acquis* of your

Such an 'attitude décomplexée',[72] according to which the ECHR is subject to overt dynamic interpretation, led the Conseil d'État onto a trajectory of constructive interpretation of the ECHR. Thus, the Conseil not only refuses to have its eyes opened by the Strasbourg Court; it seems plainly to be wide awake, adverting of its own volition to the 'interpretative dynamism' of the European system.[73]

The Conseil d'État has continued in the same vein, opening up its jurisprudence to the principles of the ECHR in a way which is perhaps as enriching to the ECHR as to French law. In the recent ruling in *Association pour la promotion de l'image*, the Conseil d'État, with support in article 8 on the right to privacy and article 2 of Protocol 4 on the freedom of movement, the open approach of the Conseil d'État to the Convention rights was on full display.[74] The Conseil was asked whether a decree regulating the use of and storage of data from biometric passports was lawful. One of the stipulations of the decree was that eight fingerprints were stored by the authorities, while only two were needed for the passport. In a carefully reasoned judgment, the Conseil d'État held that parts of the decree were unlawful, clearly basing itself on Convention principle, as well as legal precepts flowing from national law.[75] There was plainly no judgment from the Court which settled the matter. This, however, did not deter the Conseil d'État from simply applying the principles animating articles 8 and 2 of Protocol 4.

Much the same has been the case in Norwegian law over the last few years. In the 1990s, the Norwegian Supreme Court made an important

---

decisions *Marie* and *Remli*, seems to us to avert that the Strasbourg Court find any breach on the part of France. The two different systems of control – yours and that of the European Court – do not correspond completely. Taking into account the European jurisprudence to a certain measure leads you to go beyond what the Court requires in the scope of its control *a posteriori* and *in concreto*. ... To refuse to overturn the decisions which are attacked today would be tantamount to accept to close one's eyes and wait for Strasbourg to open them for one. This is not the conception we have of your office. ... By enlarging the ambit of judicial review, moreover, you would give full effect to the subsidiary character of the control of the European Court, taking charge of giving full effect before national authorities to Convention rights.'

[72] F. Sudre, 'Du "Dialogue Des Juges" à l'Euro-Compatibilité', *Le Dialogue Des Juges: Mélanges en l'Honneur du Président Bruno Genevois* (Paris: Dalloz 2009) 1015–31, at 1028 (hereinafter Sudre, 'Dialogue des Juges').
[73] *Ibid.*
[74] Conseil d'État, *Association Pour la Promotion de l'Image et Autres*, 26 October 2011, No. 317827 and others.
[75] For example, the decision seems to develop the proportionality test relied on in the classic ruling *Benjamin*: Conseil d'État, 19 May 1933, *Benjamin*, No. 17413.

statement of principle in the *Corrugated Cardboard* case.[76] Concerning illegal price-fixing and ECHR rights, this case allowed the Norwegian Supreme Court to consider in detail the issue of Norwegian and international law. The Court held that when considering relevant human rights provisions, '[f]or a Norwegian court to be justified in setting aside the effects of national rules of procedure, the differing rule which can be based on international law sources must appear sufficiently clear and unequivocal to permit such a decision'.[77]

Imposing a special requirement of 'clarity' on the international law rule to be used, this doctrine underscored that in deciding whether a ruling by an international court should be given precedence in national law, it was of importance whether it was based on a situation factually and legally comparable to the situation in which the Norwegian court was to decide. The doctrine was seen as a signal to lower courts that they need not immerse themselves in what was regarded as vast and sometimes complex international sources when the ECHR was invoked by legal counsel.

At the same time, looming in the background was a question of more far-reaching scope: should the Norwegian Supreme Court play an active role in the development of Convention rights? For it is precisely in the penumbral areas – where the law is *not* clear and unequivocal – that national supreme courts may have a hand in the development of ECHR law.[78] Although criticised in legal doctrine, and by the minority in Rt. 1999 p. 961, as falling short of the wording of the statute incorporating the Convention into Norwegian law, this doctrine survived through the 1990s.[79]

Corrugated Cardboard was overturned by the *Bøhler* case.[80] The Supreme Court in *Bøhler* was at pains to go into considerable detail on the question of the relationship between Norwegian and international law, with the question of the evolution of the ECHR and national courts looming large.

---

[76] Norwegian Supreme Court Judgment (*Corrugated Cardboard*), see (1994) Norsk Retstidende 610 (in Norwegian: *Bølgepappkjennelsen*).
[77] *Ibid.*, at 616–17.
[78] C. Smith, 'The Interaction between the European Convention and the Protection of Human Rights and Fundamental Freedoms within the Norwegian Legal System', in P. Mahoney *et al.* (eds.), *Protecting Human Rights: The European Perspective* (Cologne: Carl Heymanns Verlag, 2000), at 1306–7 (hereinafter Smith, 'Interaction').
[79] Norwegian Supreme Court Judgment, see (1999) Norsk Retstidende 961.
[80] Norwegian Supreme Court Judgment, see (2000) Norsk Retstidende 996 (in Norwegian: *Bøhlerdommen*).

First, in unambiguous terms the judgment set aside the 'clear and unequivocal' reservation. There was no longer any need for the rule following from the ECHR to be 'clear' for it to take precedence over Norwegian law.[81] The Supreme Court held that the question whether there was a conflict between a provision in an incorporated convention and other parts of Norwegian law was not amenable to answer by reference to general principles; it depends on interpretation of the applicable provisions in the circumstances. Having recourse to the newly adopted Human Rights Act 1999 section 3, which seemed to influence the Court considerably, it held that where the solution following from the ECHR appears reasonably clear, it is incumbent on Norwegian courts to give precedence to the ECHR provision, even though this would mean the overturning of well-established Norwegian legislation or practice. The Court later underscored that one ought not to take what it said in *Bøhler* about clarity to mean that some sort of reservation with regard to clarity still obtained; this would be a misconstruction.[82] At times, however, there may be well-founded doubt as to how the ECHR is to be understood. This doubt, the Norwegian Supreme Court said, could stem from the evolutive interpretation of the Convention by the Strasbourg Court.

Although Norwegian courts expressly intend to use the same method of interpretation as the Strasbourg Court, the Supreme Court held that it is primarily for the Strasbourg Court to develop the Convention. The Supreme Court underscored that if doubt obtains as to the impact of the judgments of the Strasbourg Court, it is important whether the decision in question is based on a situation factually and legally comparable to the situation in which the Norwegian court is to decide. To the extent that Norwegian courts have to engage in balancing of various interests, they should also take account of traditional Norwegian priorities, and all the more so if the Norwegian legislature has considered the relationship to the Convention and found no conflict between Norwegian and ECHR law.[83]

In the view of the Supreme Court in *Bøhler*, Norwegian courts do not have the same panoramic view as the Strasbourg Court, not possessing the same knowledge of the ECHR and relevant sources, including case

---

[81] T. Eckhoff, *Rettskildelære* (Oslo: Universitetsforlaget, 2001), at 330–2.
[82] See, for example, Rt. 2001 p. 1006 *KRL* (2001) Norsk Retstidende 1006.
[83] E. Møse, 'Norway', in R. Blackburn *et al.* (eds.), *Fundamental Rights in Europe: The European Convention on Human Rights and its Member States, 1950–2000* (Oxford University Press, 2001), at 636–7 (hereinafter Møse, 'Norway').

law of other member states. Norwegian courts, in going about to balance different interests, may draw especially on priorities and traditions underpinning Norwegian law. In this way, they will be able to engage in reciprocal dialogue with the Strasbourg Court, contributing to the development of the Convention rights. An evolutive approach to the ECHR on the part of Norwegian courts, said the Court in its 2000 ruling, would run the risk of Norwegian courts going too far. They could grant further human rights protection than the ECHR requires, the result of which would be interfering with the balance between the legislature and the judiciary, and engendering unnecessary limitations on legislative powers. Norwegian courts, the Supreme Court concluded, should not interpret the Convention evolutively where there may be doubt as to the interpretation of the ECHR.[84]

The main purport of this doctrine is that the principles of ECHR construction are not the same in Norwegian courts as in other courts, insofar as the former take on a special Norwegian character. This stance was then reiterated in, among others, Rt. 2003 p. 359[85] and Rt. 2005 p. 833.[86] Of the different trajectories a national Supreme Court may follow with respect to the evolution of the Convention, the approach of the Norwegian Supreme Court seems to fit well into the category former Supreme Court President Carsten Smith referred to as the 'enforcement approach', 'passively receiving' as opposed to 'actively contributing' to the evolution of the ECHR.[87]

The Norwegian Supreme Court in Rt. 2002 p. 557,[88] sitting in plenary session, held (8–5) that to bring charges for tax evasion against someone who had already suffered additional taxes over the evasion would run counter to the *non bis in idem* principle as set out in article 4 Protocol 7 ECHR. Although the majority quoted *Bøhler* emphasising that it was not for national courts to develop the Convention, it is plain that the court did just that.[89]

The same seems to hold true for Rt. 2008 p. 1409.[90] The question before the Supreme Court, sitting in plenary session, was whether one

---

[84] *Ibid.*, at 637.
[85] Norwegian Supreme Court Judgment, see (2003) Norsk Retstidende 359.
[86] Norwegian Supreme Court Judgment, see (2005) Norsk Retstidende 833.
[87] Smith, 'Interaction', at 1307.
[88] Norwegian Supreme Court Judgment, see (2002) Norsk Retstidende 557.
[89] J.E.A. Skoghøy, 'Norske domstolers lovkontroll i forhold til inkorporerte menneskerettskonvensjoner', *Lov og Rett* 41:06 (2002) 337–54, at 351–2.
[90] Norwegian Supreme Court Judgment, see (2008) Norsk Retstidende 1409.

can deduce a standard of proof from article 6(2) ECHR. This had not been set out clearly in the jurisprudence of the Strasbourg Court. Both the majority and the minority of the Norwegian Supreme Court pointed out that it is for the Strasbourg Court to develop the Convention, the minority adding that the *Bøhler* reticence would be particularly warranted in a case raising as many difficult questions about the standards of the ECHR as did Rt. 2002 p. 557. The majority, however, held by six votes that article 6(2) ECHR does lay down a standard of proof, and by the same token seemed *not* to shy away from evolutive interpretation of the Convention where there may be doubt as to the correct interpretation of the ECHR.

In judgments Rt. 2002 p. 557 and Rt. 2008 p. 1409, the Norwegian Supreme Court set aside the *Bøhler* doctrine, opening up for changes in its case law. From having been a lock on Norwegian conventional obligations, 'Norwegian values' have been turned into a conduit for a positive contribution by the Norwegian Supreme Court to the development of human rights protection.[91] In Rt. 2008 p. 1764, the Supreme Court was faced with the question whether the Norwegian system of unreasoned decisions to appeal for re-hearing was in conformity with article 14(5) of the International Convention on Civil and Political Rights (ICCPR), which provides that: 'Everyone convicted of a crime shall have the right to his conviction and sentence being reviewed by a higher tribunal according to law.' What prompted this case was that the UN Human Rights Committee had found against Norway on this question in its Communication No. 1542/2007, holding that the failure of the Norwegian rule to guarantee reasoned decisions to appeal for re-hearing was in breach of the ICCPR. In reaching its conclusion, the Supreme Court in Rt. 2008 p. 1764 underscored that the right to reasons in general was a principle with a long pedigree in Norwegian law. By doing this, the Supreme Court effectively held that the guarantees flowing from Norwegian law pulled in the same direction as those of the international human rights system.[92]

This approach was then strengthened in Rt. 2009 p. 1118, where the Supreme Court was faced with the question of how the question in Rt. 2008 p. 1764 would play out with respect to civil as opposed to criminal cases. Was Norwegian law in breach of the due process guarantees in

---

[91] See M. Andenas and A.M. Kravik, 'Norske Verdier og EMK', *Lov og Rett* 49:10 (2010) 579–99 (hereinafter Andenas and Kravik, 'Norske Verdier').
[92] *Ibid.*, at 590.

article 88 of the Norwegian Constitution, article 6 of the ECHR and article 14(1) of the ICCPR? Justice Bårdsen, for the majority, referred at the outset to Rt. 2008 p. 1764; when the Supreme Court had said that there was a right to reasons in criminal cases, it stood to reason that it must have been the will of the legislator that the same should apply in civil cases.[93] Furthermore, said Justice Bårdsen, this would harmonise with the 'purpose and system' of the law at issue. It is plain that Justice Bårdsen's majority opinion must be seen in relation to Rt. 2008 p. 1764, where the Supreme Court had based its decision on international human rights standards. What was new in Rt. 2009 p. 1118, however, was that the Supreme Court established the right by building on national rather than international sources. This shows the interplay between national and international sources in the jurisprudence of the Norwegian Supreme Court. This normative adjustment of the national law paves the way for development of Convention rights on the back of national sources.

Summing up, it is clear what was said in *Bøhler* about Norwegian values as putting a stop on the effect of Convention rights in Norwegian law has not developed into a lock on human rights obligations. This would have been a potentially dangerous approach. The Supreme Court has, rather, turned things around and made out of the *Bøhler* dictum an avenue for positive contributions to the heightening of rights protection, both within the context of ECHR rights and ICCPR rights.

Turning to the Czech and Russian decisions we discuss elsewhere in this chapter, they differ in method and on many other points from one another. But they share a central feature, in that there is no distinction between the domestic sources and the European sources. Both the discussion of the reach of rights and of the legality and proportionality of restrictions combine the sources, merging arguments based on decisions of the Court with arguments from domestic sources. In this respect, the two jurisdictions stand out from the others we have discussed. Most other jurisdictions will operate with spheres of purely domestic rights, and will address the issue of how European rights take effect in the national system in different ways. In particular, the more extensive reasons of the Czech Constitutional Court are accessible to readers from other jurisdictions, and repay study. We will return to this point in different contexts below.

---

[93] I. Lorange Backer, 'Begrunnelse for Avsiling av en Sivil Ankesak', *Lov og Rett* 48:8 (2009) 49–51, at 48, is critical of the judgment.

Another example, closely related to Lady Hale's point and to the Czech and Russian approach, is the development of rights in the common law, particularly the contribution to the development of rights by way of 'common law rights', nationally derived rights which strengthen the development of Convention rights. Examples of this can be found particularly in some of the leading judgments of Lord Bingham, who, on numerous occasions, brought out the relationship between national and international rights, 'melding', to quote the felicitous phrase of Philippe Sands, 'the relationship between long-established principles of common law with the more recent obligations of European and international laws'.[94] In *Van Colle and Smith*,[95] Lord Bingham set out the case for developing the common law action for negligence in the light of the case law of the Strasbourg Court.[96] Considerable argument was devoted to exploration of the relationship between rights arising under the Convention, in particular article 2, and rights and duties arising at common law. The question was: should these two regimes remain entirely separate, or should the common law be developed to absorb Convention rights? Lord Bingham said:

> I do not think that there is a simple, universally applicable answer. It seems to me clear, on the one hand, that the existence of a Convention right cannot call for instant manufacture of a corresponding common law right where none exists.... On the other hand, one would ordinarily be surprised if conduct which violated a fundamental right or freedom of the individual did not find a reflection in a body of law ordinarily as sensitive to human needs as the common law, and it is demonstrable that the common law in some areas has evolved in a direction signalled by the Convention.[97]

Lord Bingham concluded that there was a strong case for developing the common law action for negligence in the light of Convention rights; where a common law duty covers the same ground as a Convention right, it should develop in harmony with it. Parallel issues arose in *JD* v. *East*

---

[94] P. Sands, 'Lord Bingham of Cornhill Obituary', *The Guardian*, 11 September 2010.
[95] *Chief Constable of the Hertfordshire Police (Original Appellant and Cross-respondent)* v. *Van Colle (administrator of the estate of GC (deceased) and another (Original Respondents and Cross-appellants)* and *Smith (FC) (Respondent)* v. *Chief Constable of Sussex Police (Appellant)* (*Van Colle and Smith*) [2008] UKHL 50, para. 58.
[96] See M. Andenas *et al.*,'"There is A World Elsewhere": Lord Bingham and Comparative Law', in M. Andenas *et al.* (eds.), *Tom Bingham and the Transformation of the Law: A Liber Amicorum* (Oxford University Press, 2009) (hereinafter Andenas *et al.*, 'A World Elsewhere').
[97] *Van Colle and Smith*, para. 58.

Berkshire.[98] Should the law of tort evolve, analogically and incrementally, so as to fashion appropriate remedies to contemporary problems, or should it remain essentially static, making only such changes as are forced upon it, leaving difficult and, in human terms, very important problems, to be swept up by the Convention? Lord Bingham's reply was terse: 'I prefer evolution.'[99]

While Lord Chief Justice, before the incorporation into UK law of the Convention, Lord Bingham told the House of Commons that: 'British judges have a significant contribution to make in the development of the law of human rights. It is a contribution which so far we have not been permitted to make.'[100] He went on to quote Milton's *Areopagitica*:

> I hope that incorporation will restore the belief of our people, once an article of faith, that human rights and fundamental freedoms flourish as luxuriantly here as anywhere else in the world. It is after all 350 years since Milton wrote in *Areopagitica*, 'Let not England forget her precedence of teaching nations how to live.'[101]

Addressing the criticism that national courts ought to show restraint in this regard, Lady Hale has said that the criticism that national courts may not interpret the Convention evolutively does not make much sense. 'We cannot commit other Member States or the European Court of Human Rights to our interpretation of the rights – so why should they mind what we do, as long as we do at least keep pace with the rights as they develop over time?'[102]

The Belgian Constitutional Court[103] has developed an interesting jurisprudence on article 53 of the Convention, entitled 'Safeguard for existing human rights', which provides that:

> Nothing in this Convention shall be construed as limiting or derogating from any of the human rights and fundamental freedoms which may be ensured under the laws of any High Contracting Party or under any other agreement to which it is a party.[104]

---

[98] *JD (FC) (Appellant) v. East Berkshire Community Health NHS Trust and others (Respondents) and two other actions (FC)* [2005] UKHL 23.
[99] *Ibid.*, at [50].   [100] Hansard, HL, vol. 582, col. 1245, 3 November 1997.
[101] *Ibid.*, col. 1246.
[102] Lady Hale, *Speech at the Salford Human Rights Conference 2010*, 4 July 2010.
[103] The Cour d'Arbitrage changed its name on 7 May 2007 to Cour constitutionnelle, and we use the English version of the latter title throughout.
[104] The same is expressed in article 5(2) of the United Nations International Covenant on Civil and Political Rights (ICCPR), which provides that: 'There shall be no restriction upon or derogation from any of the fundamental human rights recognized or existing in

In decision 159/2004 the Constitutional Court[105] had been asked to hold unconstitutional the law of 13 February 2003 which had legalised same-sex marriage. The claimants averred that the law was in breach of article 12 of the European Convention, together with article 23 of the ICCPR, read in conjunction with articles 10-11 of the Belgian Constitution. Article 10(3) of the Belgian Constitution says that: '[l]'égalité des femmes et des hommes est garantie'; article 11bis(1) provides that: 'La loi, le décret ou la règle visée à l'article 134 garantissent aux femmes et aux hommes l'égal exercise de leurs droits et libertés, et favorisent notamment leur égal accès aux mandats électifs et publics'. The claimants argued that the effect of these constitutional provisions was that there was in Belgian constitutional law a principle of the 'dualité sexuelle fondamentale du genre humain'.[106]

This the Belgian Constitutional Court rejected. The argument of the court was the following:

> Dans l'interprétation des dispositions conventionnelles citées au moyen, il doit être tenu compte de l'article 53 de la Convention européenne des droits de l'homme et de l'article 5.2 du Pacte international relatif aux droits civils et politiques. ... Il résulte des dispositions citées au B.6.3 [article 53 ECHR and article 5(2) ICCPR] que l'article 12 de la Convention européenne des droits de l'homme et l'article 23.2 du Pacte international relatif aux droits civils et politiques ne peuvent être interprétés en ce sens qu'ils empêcheraient des Etats qui sont parties aux conventions précitées d'accorder le droit garanti par ces dispositions aux personnes qui souhaitent exercer ce droit avec des personnes de même sexe.[107]

It is clear that the Belgian Constitutional Court would not be influenced by the fact that the Strasbourg Court had not held that article 12 of the Convention, in conjunction with article 14, gave the right to same-sex marriage.[108] Instead, it took article 53 seriously, and the notion of domestication of rights protection, holding that it was free to go further than the Strasbourg Court on the question in issue. The Belgian Constitutional Court has done the same in other cases, too. In three cases regarding the principle of legality, the Belgian court went further in its

---

any State Party to the present Covenant pursuant to law, conventions, regulations or custom on the pretext that the present Covenant does not recognize such rights or that it recognizes them to a lesser extent.'

[105] Decision 159/2004, 20 October 2004.   [106] Ibid., para. 5.7.
[107] Ibid., para. 6.1-6.4.
[108] In fact, as at 2011, the Strasbourg Court still has not done this. In its controversial decision, Schalk and Kopf v. Austria (Appl. No. 30141/04), Judgment (Second Section), 24 June 2010, Reports 2010, it held that there was no right to same-sex marriage under the Convention.

rights protection than the Strasbourg Court had done, again explicitly founding its approach on article 53.[109]

The Norwegian Supreme Court has taken the same approach. In a ruling handed down on 26 January 2011,[110] it was faced with questions relating to the right to evidence by child witnesses in court, which is found both in Norwegian due process guarantees and in article 6(3)(d) ECHR. Delivering the judgment of the court, Justice Øie held that:

> When a procedural right follows from the ECHR, and not from internal Norwegian provisions, the question arises whether limitations to the Convention right, as interpreted by the Strasbourg Court, must apply in Norwegian law as well. As is clear from what I have cited from [earlier Norwegian jurisprudence on the issue] on the implementation of the right to the questioning of child witnesses, the Supreme Court adverts only to article 6(3)(d) ECHR, and not to Norwegian provisions. There is, however, a principle granting the right to contradiction in Norwegian law too. In my view it is therefore not reasonable to see the right to the questioning of children as anchored in the Convention, as interpreted by the Strasbourg Court, alone; it has rather been established in interplay between Norwegian law and international human rights.[111]

However, there have also been instances at which UK courts have chosen approaches to the Convention which have been less focused on universal solutions. It is plain, as Alec Stone Sweet and Helen Keller have put it in a more general context, that sometimes it happens that national courts 'decide to ignore the [Strasbourg] Court's interpretation of the Convention even when on point, and even where Convention rights have been domesticated through incorporation'.[112]

The Court of Appeal of England and Wales in *Faizovas*[113] was faced with the question whether it was a violation of article 3 of the Convention

---

[109] See Decisions 202/2004, 21 December 2004, para. 5.4; 131/2005, 19 July 2005, para. 5.2; 151/2006, 18 October 2006, para. 5.6. We thank *Conseiller d'État* Pierre Vandernoot for bringing these cases to our attention.

[110] Decision HR-2011-00182-A, 26 January 2011.

[111] *Ibid.*, para. 30; see M. Andenas and E. Bjorge, 'Norske Domstoler og Utviklingen av Menneskerettene', *Jussens Venner* 46:5 (2011) 251–86.

[112] A. Stone Sweet et al., 'Introduction: The Reception of the ECHR in National Legal Order', in Stone Sweet (ed.), *A Europe of Rights: The Impact of the ECHR on National Legal Systems*, at 14.

[113] *R (Faizovas)* v. *Secretary of State for Justice* [2009] EWCA Civ 373. See the discussion in M. Arden, 'Peaceful or Problematic? The Relationship between National Supreme Courts and Supranational Courts in Europe', in P. Eeckhout et al. (eds.), *Yearbook of European Law 2010* (Oxford University Press, 2010) 3–20, at 8–9 (hereinafter Arden, 'Peaceful or Problematic?').

for prison authorities to handcuff a terminally ill patient while he was receiving chemotherapy treatment at a hospital outside prison. Arden LJ pointed out that according to the jurisprudence of the Strasbourg Court, ill-treatment must meet a minimum level of severity if it is to fall within article 3 of the Convention. It was, however, clear from the jurisprudence of the Strasbourg Court that, for example, a high level of vulnerability experienced by the applicant would impose special obligations on the state.[114] The Strasbourg jurisprudence on the issue had held on the one hand that the wearing of handcuffs by a prisoner when they are outside the prison and there is reason to believe that they will abscond or cause injury does not in general amount to degrading treatment,[115] and on the other hand that the use of restraints such as handcuffs during medical treatment must be justified objectively: there was a violation when the prisoner who was forced to wear handcuffs 'was infirm as a result of his illness'.[116] In a 2009 judgment, however, the Strasbourg Court had held that there was a violation when a female prisoner, who was not infirm, was subject to a gynaecological examination while handcuffed, with male security officers present. It is necessary for present purposes to look at this judgment by the Strasbourg Court in some depth. The Court in *Filiz Uyan* v. *Turkey*,[117] which concerned a woman who had been sentenced to twenty-two years' imprisonment on grounds of membership of a terrorist organisation, had said that the insistence on the use of handcuffs during an examination by a gynaecologist, and the presence of three male security officers in the examination room during consultation, even behind a folding screen, were disproportionate security measures, when there were other practical alternatives. For example, the officers could have secured the room by leaving the female prison guard there and placing one of the gendarmes outside the window of the consultation room.[118]

The Strasbourg Court had cited the standards of the European Committee for the Prevention of Torture and Inhuman or Degrading

---

[114] See generally, E. Bjorge, 'Torture and "Ticking Bomb" Scenarios', *Law Quarterly Review* 127 (2011) 196–9, at 196 (hereinafter Bjorge, 'Ticking Bomb').

[115] ECtHR, *Raninen* v. *Finland* (Appl. No. 152/1996), Judgment (Chamber), 16 December 1997, Reports 1997-VIII, at paras. 55–6.

[116] Arden, 'Peaceful or Problematic?', at 9: this is Mary Arden's summary of ECtHR, *Mouisel* v. *France* (Appl. No. 67263/01), Judgment (First Section), 14 November 2002, Reports 2002-IX, paras. 37 and 47.

[117] ECtHR, *Filiz Uyan* v. *Turkey* (Appl. No. 7496/03), Judgment (Second Section), 8 January 2009, not reported.

[118] *Ibid.*, para. 32.

Treatment or Punishment (CPT), which cautioned against the use of handcuffs in civil hospital examinations:

> If recourse is had to a civil hospital, the question of security arrangements will arise. In this respect, the CPT wishes to stress that prisoners sent to hospital to receive treatment should not be physically attached to their hospital beds or other items of furniture for custodial reasons. Other means of meeting security needs satisfactorily can and should be found; the creation of a custodial unit in such hospitals is one possible solution.[119]

The strict measures at issue failed, in the view of the Strasbourg Court, to allow a flexible and more practical approach to be taken; in particular, the Court found that the government had failed in the case to demonstrate that the applicant presented such an acute security risk that measures of this nature were required for a gynaecological procedure. The Court concluded that there was a violation of article 3, as the security conditions on which the Turkish government had insisted 'must have caused the applicant humiliation and distress, beyond that inevitably associated with the treatment of a prisoner, which was capable of undermining her personal dignity'.[120]

Arden LJ in *Faizovas*[121] noted that: '[t]he Convention is interpreted as a living instrument and it would thus not be surprising if the standards set in earlier cases had been increased in a later decision', bearing testimony to the fact that UK courts are, on a conceptual level, on board with the doctrine of evolutive interpretation of Convention rights.

The claimant in *Faizovas* had suffered from pancreatic cancer which had spread to other organs, for which he was undergoing chemotherapy. During his course of chemotherapy, in the period March 2007–February 2008, he was 'handcuffed by standard handcuffs (one on his arm and one on the arms of a prison officer) and attended by two prison officers'. The standard handcuffs on arrival were replaced by an escort chain of two-and-a-half metres linking him and a prison officer. He received treatment, which took about thirty minutes, while remaining handcuffed, generally on an escort chain. The applicant, on his own admission, had felt shorn of his dignity during treatment. As a result of the infirmities

---

[119] European Committee for the Prevention of Torture and Inhuman or Degrading Treatment or Punishment (CPT), 'The CPT Standards: "Substantive" Sections of the CPT's General Reports' (CPT/Inf/E (2002) 1 – Rev. 2006), at 31 and 34. See *Filiz Uyan*, para. 21.
[120] *Ibid.*, at paras. 34–5.   [121] *R (Faizovas)* v. *Secretary of State for Justice*, 112

caused by his cancer, he died on 21 May 2008.¹²² The risk of harm to the public and of escape had been reduced to low from 11 December 2007 for all but one hospital visit.

As foreshadowed above, much play was made by counsel for the claimant of the Strasbourg Court judgment in *Filiz Uyan*. Counsel had argued that the more stressful the treatment, the greater the need for justification for insisting on handcuffs; there had been no contraindication – the medical term for a circumstance indicating that a particular technique or drug ought not to be used in the case in question – in *Filiz Uyan*, but the effect of handcuffing had been to undermine dignity. Arden LJ was not swayed by this line of argument:

> the Strasbourg court found that [Filiz Uyan] must have suffered humiliation and distress beyond that inevitably associated with being a prisoner. At first sight, it is surprising that the Strasbourg court was willing to assume this without proof. But this was a matter that could be inferred from the fact that the prisoner refused treatment under the conditions under which it was offered. ... In my judgment, the humiliation or distress did not necessarily mean that there had been a violation. Humiliation and distress, however, were an indication that the treatment was degrading. The absence of justification for the security measures in question, having regard to the security risk posed by the prisoner, the particular type of treatment she had to undergo and the possibility of more suitable means of security led to the finding of a violation.¹²³

The Court of Appeal distinguished the case, as *Filiz Uyan* was found to turn on its own particular facts.¹²⁴ Though this particular part of the reasoning of the Court of Appeal in *Faizovas* may be unobjectionable – as what judges do is to adjudicate in cases which turn on their own particular facts – it may also serve as an example of how, in the particular instances of a case, national judges put a stop on characteristic features of the ECHR schema with which they, on a conceptual level, do not have any quarrel. For example, the Strasbourg Court in *Paradysz* v. *France*,¹²⁵ handed down after *Filiz Uyan*, drew other conclusions from its own article 3 line of authority, including *Filiz Uyan*.

The Strasbourg Court in *Paradysz* pointed out that in considering whether article 3 was triggered, one would have to have regard to

---

[122] *Ibid.*, para. 10. [123] *Ibid.*, para. 23.
[124] *Ibid.*, para. 35; Arden, 'Peaceful or Problematic?', at 9.
[125] ECtHR, *Paradysz* v. *France* (Appl. No. 17020/05), Judgment (Fifth Section), 29 October 2009, not reported (available in French only).

'l'ensemble des données de la cause, notamment de la durée du traitement et de ses effets physiques et mentaux, ainsi que, parfois, du sexe, de l'âge et de l'état de santé de la victime'.[126] Only in cases where the wearing of handcuffs was part of lawful detention and did not involve more force or public exposure – 'exposition publique' – than could reasonably be deemed necessary would it be compatible with the exigencies of article 3, said the Court.[127] The Court further pointed out that the applicant complained of the use of shackles only during transport to the hospital and not during medical consultations, and that it was the use of such constraints during medical consultations which remained the main preoccupation of the Court with regard to article 3. The Court did not exclude that the wearing of shackles during transport to the hospital, especially in view of the health of the prisoner, could be in breach of article 3.[128] It did not, however, find that there had been a breach in the present case, and for the following reasons. First, the wearing of the shackles had not affected the applicant physically. Second, his infirmities were not so grave as to gainsay the use of the shackles. Third, considering the penalty he had served, his criminal and violent record, the Court held that the decision to make him wear shackles – limited to three journeys to the hospital – was proportionate with regard to the obtaining exigencies of security.[129]

If one compares the facts and the lines of argument of the two courts in *Paradysz* and *Faizovas*, a picture emerges in which it is not wholly clear that the Court of Appeal in *Faizovas* was right to temper the impact of the ECHR by way of distinguishing the case from the apposite Strasbourg authorities. If one were to take the line of argument of the Strasbourg Court in *Paradysz* as a yardstick for how it might have decided *Faizovas*, the case seems to take on a different complexion. It seems clear, for example, that the level of infirmity of the claimant in *Faizovas* was higher than in *Paradysz* (the fact that the applicant in *Faizovas* died of his cancer shortly after his treatment seems to be a fairly good indication of that); the number of visits in which the applicant was subjected to the measure at issue was eighteen in *Faizovas* as opposed to three in *Paradysz*; and the applicant in *Faizovas* had been deemed to have only a 'low' risk of harm to the public and of escape from 11 December 2007 for all but one hospital visit.

---

[126] *Ibid.*, para. 86 ('all aspects of the case, particularly the duration of the treatment and its mental and physical effects, as well as, at times, gender, age, and the health of the victim').
[127] *Ibid.*, para. 88.   [128] *Ibid.*, para. 94.   [129] *Ibid.*, para. 95.

The question was not so much one of whether the wearing of handcuffs on all eighteen visits, *en bloc*, represented an interference with the claimant's article 3 rights; it would have been enough for there to have been a breach at one of them. In light of this, and the reasons set out above, it is not altogether clear that the Court of Appeal struck the right balance. Though it was not minded to conclude in this way, the better view would be that there had, in fact, been an interference with article 3 during at least some of the last hospital visits.

Some of the same mechanisms, national limitations or locks on ECHR law,[130] are in play in *R. v. Horncastle*.[131] The question with which the Supreme Court was faced in *Horncastle* was whether a conviction based 'solely or to a decisive extent' on the statement of a witness whom the defendant has had no chance of cross-examining necessarily infringes on the defendant's right to a fair trial under article 6(1) and (3)(d) of the Convention. Article 6(1) provides that:

> In the determination of his civil rights and obligations or of any criminal charge against him, everyone is entitled to a fair and public hearing within a reasonable time by an independent and impartial tribunal established by law...

Article 6(3)(d) says that everyone charged with a criminal offence has the right to examine or have examined witnesses against him and to obtain the attendance and examination of witnesses on his behalf under the same conditions as witnesses against him.

The most recent Strasbourg authority on the issue was *Al-Khawaja and Tahery v. United Kingdom*.[132] In the two applications jointly adjudged in this Chamber decision, statements had been admitted in evidence at a criminal trial of a witness who was not called to give evidence. The Strasbourg Court had held that, in both cases, the statement was the 'sole or, at least, the decisive basis' for the applicant's conviction. The Court in *Al-Khawaja* took as one starting point the statement in *Lucà v. Italy*,[133] that:

---

[130] See on the 'lock' terminology, P. Craig, 'The European Union Act 2011: Locks, Limits and Legality', in P. Craig and G. de Búrca (eds.), *The Evolution of EU Law* (Oxford University Press, 2012).

[131] *R. v. Horncastle and Others* [2009] UKSC 14; [2010] 2 WLR 47 (hereinafter *Horncastle*)

[132] ECtHR, *Al-Khawaja and Tahery v. United Kingdom* (Appl. Nos. 26766/05 and 22228/06), Judgment (Grand Chamber), 15 December 2011, Reports 2011.

[133] ECtHR, *Lucà v. Italy* (Appl. No. 33354/96), Judgment (First Section), 27 February 2001, Reports 2001-II.

where a conviction is based solely or to a decisive degree on depositions that have been made by a person whom the accused has had no opportunity to examine or to have examined, whether during the investigation or at the trial, the rights of the defence are restricted to an extent that is incompatible with the guarantees provided by article 6.[134]

Neither the Court of Appeal nor the Supreme Court accepted in *Horncastle* that the Strasbourg Court's decision in *Al-Khawaja* should be determinative of the results of the appeals in the case before them. Both courts held that, in the circumstances of each of the appeals, the claimants had received a fair trial.[135] As, on 16 April 2009, the UK had requested, under article 43(1) of the Convention, that the Chamber decision in *Al-Khawaja* be referred to the Grand Chamber, and the Supreme Court at that time was about to begin to hear *Horncastle*, a Panel of the Grand Chamber on 5 June 2009 adjourned consideration of the request pending the Supreme Court's judgment in *Horncastle*. This gave the Supreme Court a chance to have its say on the issue.

The claimants had submitted that the Supreme Court must treat *Al-Khawaja* as determinative of the success of their appeals. This, they argued, would be the appropriate response to the requirement of section 2(1) of the Human Rights Act 1998 (HRA), which requires a court to 'take into account' any judgment of the Strasbourg Court in determining any question to which such a judgment is relevant. It was submitted in this regard that the decision of the House of Lords in *Secretary of State for the Home Department* v. *AF (No. 3)*[136] exemplified the correct approach to a decision of the Strasbourg Court. In that case their Lordships had held themselves bound to apply a clear statement of principle by the Grand Chamber in respect of the precise issue with which the House was faced.

That submission a unanimous Supreme Court in *Horncastle* could 'not accept':[137]

> The requirement to 'take into account' the Strasbourg jurisprudence will normally result in this Court applying principles that are clearly established by the Strasbourg Court. There will, however, be rare occasions where this court has concerns as to whether a decision of the Strasbourg

---

[134] *Ibid.*, para. 40.   [135] *Horncastle* [2009] EWCA Crim 964; [2009] WLR 173.
[136] *Secretary of State for the Home Department* v. *AF (No. 3)* [2009] UKHL; [2009] 3 WLR 74. See generally, P. Craig, 'Perspectives on Process: Common Law, Statutory and Political', *Public Law* (2010) 275–96.
[137] *Horncastle*, para. 11.

Court sufficiently appreciates or accommodates particular aspects of our domestic process. In such circumstances it is open to this court to decline to follow the Strasbourg decision, giving reasons for adopting this course. This is likely to give the Strasbourg Court the opportunity to reconsider the particular aspect of the decision that is in issue, so that there takes place what may prove to be a valuable dialogue between this court and the Strasbourg Court.[138]

It should perhaps be added that the Strasbourg decision at issue was one against the UK, so the Strasbourg judges – who, as always with cases against the UK, included the British judge, Sir Nicholas Bratza – would perforce have been seised of such salient features of the common law scheme in question as the government presented in court.

Though this non-acceptance was a surprising move by the Supreme Court, it is not the first time one has seen signs of British judges taking issue with Strasbourg jurisprudence.[139] The issue of courts martial in the UK furnishes an apposite example. The Strasbourg Court in *Findlay v. United Kingdom*[140] had held that the UK was in violation of article 6(1) of the Convention, as a soldier successfully challenged the court martial procedure on grounds of lack of independence and impartiality. The UK court martial procedure was reformed by new legislation in 1996. In 2002, in *Morris v. United Kingdom*,[141] the Strasbourg Court held that the new legislation also fell foul of the Convention rights. However, as another case, *R v. Spear and Others*[142] reached the House of Lords in 2002, before new legislation had been introduced in response to the Strasbourg Court's adverse decision in *Morris*, Lord Bingham in *R v. Spear and Others* found that, though it was for UK courts to accept the decisions of the Strasbourg Court, the legislation in issue satisfied the requirements of independence and impartiality. In the wake of *R v. Spear and Others*, a unanimous Grand Chamber of the Strasbourg Court in *Cooper v. United Kingdom*[143] overturned their previous ruling in *Morris*, drawing on Lord Bingham's analysis in *R v. Spear and Others* and giving its imprimatur to his conclusions.[144]

---

[138] *Ibid.*   [139] See Andenas *et al.*, 'A World Elsewhere'.
[140] ECtHR, *Findlay v. United Kingdom* (Appl. No. 22107/93), Judgment (Chamber), 25 February 1997, Reports 1997-I.
[141] ECtHR, *Morris v. United Kingdom* (Appl. No. 38784/97), Judgment (Third Section), 26 February 2002, Reports 2002-I.
[142] *R v. Spear and Others* [2002] UKHL 31; [2003] 1 AC.
[143] ECtHR, *Cooper v. United Kingdom* (Appl. No. 48843/99), Judgment (Grand Chamber), 16 December 2003, Reports 2003-XII.
[144] Andenas *et al.*, 'A World Elsewhere', at 831–66.

As adumbrated above, however, Lord Bingham in *R* v. *Spear and Others* crucially did not say that the House of Lords could choose not to follow the decisions of the Strasbourg Court. Rather, he clarified that they were, in point of fact, following it. *Horncastle* is different, in that it says not only that English law is in reality conforming with the precepts of article 6 of the Convention; it also says that if this is not the case, there is effectively no need for the Supreme Court to follow the Strasbourg jurisprudence. The idea of a 'dialogue' between judges[145] was accepted with alacrity by the Supreme Court in *Horncastle*. To the dialogue the Supreme Court submitted nine conclusions, of which the Supreme Court 'hope[d] that in due course the Strasbourg Court may also take account'.[146]

There are, the Supreme Court put forth as perhaps the most salient of its conclusions, safeguards designed to protect a defendant against unfair prejudice as a result of the admission of hearsay evidence, seen in the context of the more general safeguards which apply to every jury trial. These include the concept that the trial judge acts as a gatekeeper and has a duty to prevent the jury from receiving evidence which will have such an adverse effect on the fairness of the proceedings that it ought not to be received, and hearsay evidence is admissible only in strictly defined circumstances, in which the judge is satisfied beyond reasonable doubt that the prosecution is not able to adduce the evidence by calling the witness.[147]

It bears mention, however, that in *R* v. *Davis*,[148] the House of Lords as recently as 2008 had held unanimously that it was a long-established principle of the English common law that, subject to certain exceptions and statutory qualifications, the defendant in a criminal trial should be confronted by his accusers in order that he may cross-examine them and challenge their evidence.[149] For this Lord Bingham cited common law authorities going back to *Duke of Dorset* v. *Girdler* from 1720, which held that:

> The other side ought not to be deprived of the opportunity of confronting the witnesses, and examining them publicly, which has always been found the most effectual method of discovering of the truth.[150]

---

[145] See, e.g., Sudre, 'Dialogue des Juges', at 1028; A. Torres Pérez, *Conflicts of Rights in the European Union: A Theory of Supranational Adjudication* (Oxford University Press, 2009), particularly 9–26 and 97–140.
[146] *Horncastle*, at 47. [147] *Ibid.*, para. 38.
[148] *R* v. *Davis* [2008] UKHL 36; [2008] AC 1128. [149] *Ibid.*, para. 5.
[150] *Duke of Dorset* v. *Girdler* (1720) Prec. Ch. 531–32, 24 ER 238. Lord Bingham also cited Sir Matthew Hale, *The History of the Common Law of England*, 6th edn (1820), at 345–6; W. Blackstone, *Commentaries on the Law of England Bk. III*, 12th edn (1794), at 373;

Lord Mance in his Concurring Opinion in *R v. Davis* carried out an analysis of the apposite Strasbourg jurisprudence. Lord Bingham adopted Lord Mance's analysis, the effects of which he summarised as follows:

> It is that no conviction should be based solely or to a decisive extent upon the statements or testimony of anonymous witnesses. The reason is that such a conviction results from a trial which cannot be regarded as fair. This is the view traditionally taken by the common law of England.[151]

Lord Bingham's rule seemed to build on age-old precedent, was unanimously agreed to in *R v. Davis*, and would not create any problems vis-à-vis Strasbourg. The Supreme Court in *Horncastle*, however, described the former Senior Law Lord's summary of the law as 'overstated', finding it a more apt summarisation that Parliament has decreed that the question of whether evidence is or is likely to be sole or decisive is relevant as to whether it should be permitted, but that there is 'no mandatory rule prohibiting the admission of such evidence'.[152] Adopting Lord Bingham's reading – and heeding his earlier warning that '[p]rocedural idiosyncracy is not (like national costume or regional cuisine) to be nurtured for its own sake'[153] – would, however, have obviated the need for a stand-off with Strasbourg.

What the Supreme Court said in *Horncastle* was really three things: in the first place, the 'sole or decisive rule' is not a good rule.[154] Second, it does not follow from the Strasbourg jurisprudence anyway.[155] Third, at all events, we are not bound by this rule.[156] This led Lord Phillips, with whose judgment all members of the Court agreed, to conclude with the following:

> In these circumstances I have decided that it would not be right for this court to hold that the sole or decisive test should have been applied rather than the provisions of the 2003 Act, interpreted in accordance with their natural meaning. I believe that those provisions strike the right balance between the imperative that a trial must be fair and the interests of victims in particular and society in general that a criminal should not be immune from conviction where a witness, who has given critical evidence in a statement that can be shown to be reliable, dies or cannot be called to give evidence for some other reason. In so concluding I have taken careful account of the Strasbourg jurisprudence. I hope that in due course the

---

J. Bentham, *Rationale of Judicial Evidence Vol. II, Bk. III* (1827), at 404, 408, 423 (the citations are Lord Bingham's own).
[151] *R v. Davis*, at [25].   [152] *Horncastle*, paras. 54–6.
[153] *Dresser UK Ltd. v. Falcongate Ltd.* [1992] QB 502, 522.
[154] *Horncastle*, paras. 76–94.   [155] *Ibid.*, paras. 63–75.   [156] *Ibid.*, paras. 10–11.

Strasbourg Court may also take account of the reasons that have led me not to apply the sole or decisive test in this case.[157]

One gets the feeling reading *Horncastle* that the Supreme Court views its relationship with the Strasbourg Court as a bilateral one, when, in fact, the Supreme Court represents one of nearly fifty member states. If the other courts of Europe were to take a leaf out of the Supreme Court's book, the result could be a very chaotic situation indeed. It would furthermore hardly be in tune with ideas of 'bringing rights home', as claimants would have to go to Strasbourg to achieve their Convention rights. It bears mention that there is *obiter* support of the *Horncastle* approach in the newly decided *Pinnock*,[158] though in the event, the Supreme Court followed the Strasbourg Court, overturning much of its own case law on the use of the proportionality test in demoted tenancy possession cases.[159]

The President of the European Court in an article published on the eve of the Grand Chamber's decision in *Al-Khawaja*, had the following to say about *Horncastle*:

> I believe that it is right and healthy that national courts should continue to feel free to criticise Strasbourg judgments where those judgments have applied principles which are unclear or inconsistent or where they have misunderstood national law or practices. But I also believe that it is important that the superior national courts should, as Lord Phillips put it in the *Horncastle* judgment, on the rare occasions when they have concerns as to whether a decision of the Strasbourg Court sufficiently appreciates or accommodates particular aspects of the domestic process, 'decline to follow the Strasbourg decision, giving reasons for adopting this course.' If, as has happened in the case of *Al-Khawaja*, Strasbourg is given the opportunity to reconsider the decision in issue, what takes place may indeed as Lord Phillips put it, 'prove to be a valuable dialogue between this court and the Strasbourg Court.' I firmly believe that such dialogue can only serve to cement a relationship between the two courts which, whatever criticisms may be levelled against the Strasbourg Court, is a sound and solid one.[160]

---

[157] *Ibid.*, para. 108.
[158] *Manchester City Council (Respondent)* v. *Pinnock (Appellant)* [2010] UKSC 45.
[159] Lord Bingham had persistently argued for this line, and in *Pinnock* his views finally prevailed. See the background story in Lord Bingham, *Widening Horizons: The Influence of Comparative Law and International Law on Domestic Law* (Cambridge University Press, 2010), at 80–3.
[160] N. Bratza, 'The Relationship Between the UK Courts and Strasbourg', *European Human Rights Law Review* 5 (2011) 505–12, at 512.

The Grand Chamber in its ruling ceded ground to the Supreme Court, admitting that where a hearsay statement is the sole or decisive evidence against a defendant, its admission as evidence will not automatically result in a breach of article 6(1). At the same time, where a conviction is based solely or decisively on the evidence of absent witnesses, the Court must subject the proceedings to the most searching scrutiny. Because of the dangers of the admission of such evidence, it would constitute a very important factor to balance in the scales, to use the words of Lord Mance in *R v. Davis*, and one which would require sufficient counterbalancing factors, including the existence of strong procedural safeguards. The question in each case is whether there are sufficient counterbalancing factors in place, including measures that permit a fair and proper assessment of the reliability of that evidence to take place. This would permit a conviction to be based on such evidence only if it is sufficiently reliable given its importance in the case.[161]

It may be, however, that it was more political exigencies and the immense pressure under which the Court has been finding itself in the last few years, rather than the argumentative force of the *Horncastle* ruling, that made the Court change its mind. At all events, given Lord Bingham's convincing judgment in *R v. Davis*, it is not clear that, while there may be extreme occasions on which a national court should be able to say no, this was a very good case in which to do so. One critical commentator put it in the following way:

> What is genuinely bizarre was the Supreme Court's choice of subject matter. It did not go to bat on behalf of a fundamental common law principle. Instead, it went to bat against it, on behalf of the same dodgy piece of legislation that eroded the right of trial by jury and raised the maximum period of pre-charge detention from seven to 14 days.[162]

We will return below to the relationship between the UK courts and the Strasbourg Court. Mattias Guyomar has said of the French Conseil d'État that: 'it makes every effort to acquire an accurate understanding of the European case-law so as to be able to apply it correctly, to take reasonable steps to anticipate it or even, if it considers it necessary, to depart from it with full knowledge of what it is doing'.[163] The ruling that Guyomar cites as an

---

[161] ECtHR, *Al-Khawaja and Tahery v. United Kingdom*, para. 147 (internal references omitted).
[162] E. Metcalfe, 'Time for the UK Supreme Court to Think Again on Hearsay', *The Guardian*, 15 December 2011.
[163] M. Guyomar, 'Le Dialogue des Jurisprudences Entre le Conseil d'État et la Cour de Strasbourg: Appropriation, Anticipation, Émancipation', *Mélanges en l'Honneur de*

example of the Conseil d'État departing in full knowledge from the jurisprudence of the Court is *Dubus*.[164] In this case, which bore on article 6 rights, the Conseil d'État did not follow the *conclusions* of *commissaire du gouvernement* Mattias Guyomar, in which he had recommended taking a larger view of the jurisprudence of the Court. When the applicant then took the case to Strasbourg, the Court agreed with the approach taken in the *conclusions*.[165] This brings out another facet of dialogue between jurisdictions.

Some of the same mechanisms on display in *Faizovas* and *Horncastle* have also been at play in the saga of the reception in German law of the Strasbourg Court's adverse ruling in *M* v. *Germany*.[166] In this line of cases, however, the end result was other than in the *Horncastle–Al-Khawaja* line of cases; though the principles at stake were perhaps even more important to the identity of German law than had been so in the British case, the German Federal Constitutional Court in the end found another solution, a more universal one, than did the UK Supreme Court.

In order fully to present the situation in German law, and because of the particular importance that so many European courts accord to the role of the German Constitutional Court (*Bundesverfassungsgericht*) and of German law, it is apposite here to say a few words about the way in which the ECHR is implemented in German law. Though article 1(1)–(2) of the German Basic Law provides that '[h]uman dignity is inviolable' and that '[t]he German People therefore acknowledge inviolable and inalienable human rights as the basis of every human community, of peace, and of justice in the world', the rights of the ECHR in German law do not enjoy constitutional authority.[167] The ECHR is incorporated into

---

Jean-Paul Costa (Paris: Dalloz, 2011) 311–20, 313 ['s'attache à connaître précisément la jurisprudence européenne afin de l'appliquer correctement, de raisonnablement l'anticiper ou meme, [s'il] estime cela nécessaire, de s'en écarter en toute connaissance de cause'].

[164] Conseil d'État, *Dubus* (No. 266735), 25 July 2007; Guyomar, 'Conclusions'.
[165] ECtHR, *Dubus S.A.* v. *France* (Appl. No. 5242/04), Judgment (Fifth Section), 11 June 2009, not reported.
[166] *M* v. *Germany*.
[167] See BVerfGE 74, 358 (370); 82, 106 (114); T. Giegerich, 'Wirkung und Rang der EMRK in den Rechtsordnungen der Mitgliedstaaten', R. Grote (ed.), *EMRK/GG: Konkordanzkommentar zum europäischen und deutschen Grundrechtsschutz* (Tübingen: Mohr Siebeck, 2006), at 82 (hereinafter Giegerich, 'Wirkung und Rang'). See generally, W. Heun, *The Constitution of Germany: A Contextual Analysis* (Oxford: Hart Publishing, 2011) 191–229; C. Tomuschat, 'The Effects of the Judgments of the European Court of Human Rights According to the German Constitutional Court', *German Law Journal* 11 (2006) 513–26 (hereinafter Tomuschat, 'Effects'); A. Voßkuhle, 'Multilevel Cooperation of the European Constitutional Courts: *Der Europäische Verfassungsgerichtsverbund*', *European Constitutional Law Review* 6 (2010) 175–98 (hereinafter Voßkuhle, 'Multilevel Cooperation').

German law by way not of constitutional law, but of statute, in the same way as other international treaties which contain provisions capable of being adverted to in national law. As the President of the German *Bundesverfassungsgericht*, Andreas Voßkuhle, has said, 'In the Federal Republic of Germany, the ECHR ... in formal terms has "merely" the rank of an ordinary law, by virtue of the German Act approving it.'[168]

Article 31 of the German Basic Law provides that 'Federal law takes precedence over State [i.e. *Land*] law', and the Act on the Convention for the Protection of Human Rights and Fundamental Freedoms (*Gesetz über die Konvention zum Schutze der Menschenrechte und Grundfreiheiten*) was enacted in 1952:[169] this means that the Convention rights have precedence over any *Land* law. It also means, according to the *lex superior* principle, over any secondary federal legislation and, according to the *lex posterior* principle, that they take precedence over any anterior primary federal legislation. The obverse of this is that the Convention rights, according to the *lex posterior* principle, take second place to later primary federal legislation and, according to the *lex superior* principle, to all constitutional norms.[170]

At all events, the structure of the first chapter of the Basic Law dealing with fundamental rights – articles 1–19 of the Basic Law – have a very close family resemblance to the rights enumerated in the ECHR. It has been pointed out that – obvious differences in the chosen drafting language aside – even the register in which the rights of the Basic Law and the ECHR are couched evinces striking similarities.[171]

The obverse of this strong national protection of fundamental rights is, however, an apparent lack of willingness on the part of the German legal order to go as far in adhering to the ECHR as, for example, have the UK and France. Thomas Giegerich has pointed out that the 'hierarchical infirmity' (*rangmäßige Schwäche*) of the chosen method of incorporation of the Convention rights in German law risks incurring the danger that Germany, through its internal law, should be in breach of its international obligations. In most cases, however, this situation is obviated, as the courts opt for an interpretation which conforms to the Convention rights, of both posterior primary federal legislation, and even

---

[168] Ibid., at 180.
[169] Act on the Convention for the Protection of Human Rights and Fundamental Freedoms (*Gesetz über die Konvention zum Schutze der Menschenrechte und Grundfreiheiten*) 7 August 1952, Federal Law Gazette (Bundesgesetzblatt – BGBl) 1952 II 685.
[170] Giegerich, 'Wirkung und Rang', at 82–3. [171] Tomuschat, 'Effects', at 515.

constitutional norms.[172] The hierarchical infirmity of incorporation is further tempered by the principle of 'openness of the Basic Law towards international law' (*Völkerrechtsfreundlichkeit des Grundgesetzes*), according to which it cannot be assumed that the statutory or constitutional legislator wanted to create a breach of international obligations.[173]

Statute interpretation which is in conformity with the Convention (*konventionskonforme Auslegung*) can go only so far. It is not possible to read down a statute where it is clear that deviation from the Convention rights is the desired result of the legislator.[174] It bears mention, nonetheless, that as at 2010 there had not been a single *Bundesverfassungsgericht* judgment in which the 'rude *lex posterior* principle was resorted [to] to the detriment of the ECHR'.[175]

The leading constitutional case in this regard is the 2004 *Görgülü* judgment.[176] The claimant was a Turkish national living in Germany who was the father of a child born out of wedlock. As the mother was no longer in contact with the father, she did not consult the claimant when, immediately after the child's birth, she gave the child up for adoption. The claimant, when later seised of this development, attempted to obtain custody of the child and to be given access to him. Following a decision which had been favourable to the claimant, the Court of Appeal found against him, holding that it was in the child's best interest to remain in the foster family to which he had been assigned and thus to be separated from the father. The Constitutional Court, in a terse decision giving no grounds, refused to hear the claimant's constitutional complaint.[177] The claimant filed an application with the Strasbourg Court, which unanimously held that there had been a violation of article 8 of the Convention in respect of the refusal of custody and access rights.[178] The Wittenberg Court of First Instance duly gave effect in German law to the Strasbourg ruling, conferring on the claimant custody of his child. The Naumburg Court of Appeal held that the holding in *Görgülü* v. *Germany* was binding only in terms of public international law; the effect of the judgment, therefore, was limited as a matter of law to establishing the

---

[172] Giegerich, 'Wirkung und Rang', at 84.
[173] BVerfG, BVerfGE 74, 358 (370); BVerfGE 111, 307 (317).
[174] BVerfG, BVerfGE 74, 358 (370); BVerfGE 111, 307 (317–28); Giegerich, 'Wirkung und Rang', at 84.
[175] Tomuschat, 'Effects'.   [176] BVerfGE 74, 358.
[177] BVerfG, 1 BvR 1174/01, BVerfGE 11, 307. See Tomuschat, 'Effects', at 520–1.
[178] ECtHR, *Görgülü* v. *Germany* (Appl. No. 74969/01), Judgment (Third Section), 26 February 2004, not reported.

sanction of what in the view of the Strasbourg Court had been a violation of the ECHR and as such was not binding for national courts.[179] The claimant then filed a constitutional complaint with the Constitutional Court, complaining that his right to protection of family life under article 6(1) of the Basic Law had been violated and that the treatment by the Court of Appeal of the adverse Strasbourg judgment was contrary to his right, according to German constitutional principle, to see the rule of law respected. The *Görgülü* decision of the Constitutional Court has been seen as an instance of its taking the occasion to make known, in an amply reasoned manner, its understanding of the relationship between the ECHR and German law. Though, in the event, the holding of the Court of Appeal was criticised by the constitutional judges, it has been suggested that the Constitutional Court in *Görgülü* was showing force vis-à-vis the Strasbourg Court.[180] The Constitutional Court said about the jurisprudence of the Strasbourg Court that it was for 'the authorities and courts of the Federal Republic of Germany ..., under certain conditions, to take account of the European Convention on Human Rights as interpreted by the Strasbourg Court in making their decisions'.[181] It has been pointed out that the chosen wording – 'take account' – is weaker than what had earlier been used – such as 'comply with' and 'abide by'[182] The Constitutional Court went on to say that:

> If ... the Strasbourg Court establishes that there has been a violation of the Convention, and if this is a continuing violation, the decision of the Strasbourg Court must be taken into account in the domestic sphere: that is, the responsible authorities or courts must discernibly consider the decision and, if necessary, justify comprehensibly why they nevertheless do not follow the international interpretation.[183]

Against this backcloth, the Constitutional Court held that the lower courts had not been bound 'regarding the actual outcome' (*im konkreten Ergobnis*).[184] The Constitutional Court shored up its conclusion by pointing out that the application of Convention rights may at times be compounded by the existence of 'multipolar fundamental rights situations',[185] that is to say, situations in which the state action under review is intended to protect the rights of third parties, i.e. rights-holders other than the claimant. In view of this, the Court brought out that there may

---

[179] See the summary given by the Constitutional Court in BVerfGE 111, 307 (312–13).
[180] Tomuschat, 'Effects', at 522.   [181] BVerfG, BVerfGE 111, 307 (315).
[182] Tomuschat, 'Effects', at 523.   [183] BVerfG, BVerfGE 111, 307 (324).
[184] *Ibid.* (332).   [185] *Ibid.* (324).

'be constitutional problems if one of the subjects of fundamental right in conflict with one another obtains a judgment from the Strasbourg Court in his or her favour against the Federal Republic of Germany and German courts schematically apply this decision to the private law relationship'.[186]

This led the lower courts again to find against the claimant, Mr. Görgülü, before the Constitutional Court issued an injunction against the Court of Appeal and then also handed down a judgment setting the matter straight, in favour of the claimant and in keeping with the adverse Strasbourg judgment against Germany.[187]

The balance which *Görgülü* tries to strike is well summarised by the following dictum by the Constitutional Court: 'The Basic Law aims to integrate Germany into the legal community of peaceful and free states, but does not waive the sovereignty encapsulated in the last instance in the German constitution.'[188] This was later cited with approval in the *Lissabon-Urteil* of 2009, where the passage was used to bring out that there would be instances in which the legislator, without breaching the principle of 'openness of the Basic Law towards international law', did not have to take into account international legal obligations, to the extent that they could fall foul of one of the fundamental rights provisions of the Basic Law.[189]

To sum up, this is what *Görgülü* says about the relationship between German law and the Convention rights. The ECHR is incorporated into German law by way not of constitutional law, but of statute, and this is to be taken seriously. If the Strasbourg Court has held against Germany, finding a breach of the Convention rights, and the breach of the Convention is a continuing one, then the German courts must take into account the apposite judgment (*berücksichtigen*). Taking into account, however, means only that comprehensive reasons must be given if the national courts find that they are unable to follow the Strasbourg decision at issue. If the Strasbourg Court has held that a German statute is in breach of the Convention rights, then this may either be interpreted in conformity with the apposite Convention right, or the legislator may change the legislation. The legislation at issue may be interpreted in conformity with Convention rights only to the extent that the interpretation follows the exigencies of rational statute interpretation (*im Rahmen*

---

[186] *Ibid.* (324).   [187] See BVerfGE, 1 BvR 2790/04.
[188] BVerfG, BVerfGE 111, 307 (319).
[189] BVerfG, *Lissabon-Urteil* (*Lisbon Treaty*), BVerfGE 123, 267 (340).

methodisch vertretbarer Gesetzesauslegung); the language may not be strained beyond comprehension. German courts are furthermore obliged to interpret the legislation in conformity with the Convention as far as possible.[190] The position was summed up in a 2010 case from the *Bundesverfassungsgericht*:

> The fact that the ECHR has the status of statute law means that it is incumbent on German courts to apply the Convention as they would other statutes, in accordance with the exigencies of rational statute interpretation. ... The guarantees of the Convention will, however, influence the interpretation of the fundamental rights and the rule of law guarantees of the Basic Law. ... The Convention text and the judgments of the European Court of Human Rights may, on the constitutional level, serve as interpretation tools, in the determination of the content and remit of fundamental rights and rule of law principles of the Basic Law, so long as this does not lead to a restriction – which would be contrary to the Convention, see article 53 ECHR – of the fundamental rights protection afforded by the Basic Law.[191]

We now return to the important *M* case. The European Court of Human Rights in *M* held that the continued preventive detention beyond the ten-year period which had been the maximum for such detention under the legal provisions applicable at the time of the applicant's offence and conviction, was in breach of article 5(1) of the Convention, and that the retrospective extension of the preventive detention to an effectively unlimited period of time was in breach of article 7(1). The Court held that preventive detention as practised in Germany was to be qualified as a 'penalty' and not merely a measure of correction and prevention. As the scheme had not been considered to be a penalty in German law, principles such as the prohibition of retroactive sentences and the *ne bis in idem* rule were not considered to apply by the German judges adjudicating in the case. The German courts, in the application of section 2(6) of the German criminal code, explicitly allowed the retroactive application of a statute intensifying the 'measures of correction and prevention', including preventive detention. After this scheme was introduced in German law in 1998, the courts extended the confinement of inmates in preventive detention beyond the ten-year restriction, even if the

---

[190] BVerfG, BVerfGE 11, 307 (323–4); Grabenwarter, 'Wirkungen eines Urteils des Europäischen Gerichtshofs für Menschenrechte – am Beispiel des Falls M. gegen Deutschland', *JuristenZeitung* 65 (2010) 857–69, at 862 (hereinafter Grabenwarter, 'Wirkungen').
[191] BVerfG, 2 BvR 2307/06.

inmates in issue had been put under the preventive detention scheme before the promulgation of the restriction in 1998.[192]

When M was sentenced in 1986 he could, according to section 67(d)(1) of the criminal code, be kept in preventive detention for no more than ten years. This rule was then amended in 1998, with effect also for the preventive detention orders which had been made prior to the entry into force of the amended provision. Without that change in the law, the courts responsible for the execution of sentences would not have had jurisdiction to extend the duration of the applicant's preventive detention. The Strasbourg Court held that there was not a sufficient causal connection between the applicant's conviction by the sentencing court in 1986 and his continued deprivation of liberty beyond the period of ten years in preventive detention, which was made possible only by the subsequent change in the law in 1998.[193]

The German courts had not examined whether the applicant's preventive detention beyond the ten-year point was justified under any of the sub-paragraphs of article 5(1), as they had not been required to do so under the provisions of the German Basic Law. Under article 5(1)(c), the apposite sub-paragraph, the detention of a person may be justified 'when it is reasonably considered necessary to prevent his committing an offence'. The applicant's continued detention had been justified by the courts responsible for the execution of sentences with reference to the risk that the applicant could commit further serious offences – similar to those of which he had previously been convicted – if released. The Court held, however, that these potential further offences were not sufficiently concrete and specific as regards, in particular, the place and time of their commission and their victims, and did not fall within the ambit of article 5(1)(c). This finding, the Court said, was confirmed by an interpretation of article 5(1)(c) in the light of article 5 as a whole.[194]

The Court also found that there had been a breach of the applicant's right not to have a heavier penalty imposed upon him than the one applicable at the time of his offence. When the applicant committed the attempted murder in 1985, a preventive detention order made by a sentencing court for the first time, read in conjunction with section 67(d)(1) of the criminal code, meant that the applicant could be kept

---

[192] G. Merkel, 'Incompatible Contrasts? Preventive Detention in Germany and the European Convention on Human Rights', *German Law Journal* 11 (2010) 1046–66, at 1051 (hereinafter Merkel, 'Incompatible Contrasts?').
[193] *M v. Germany*, para. 100.   [194] *Ibid.*, para. 102.

in preventive detention for ten years at the most. Based on the subsequent amendment in 1998 of section 67(d) of the Criminal Code, read in conjunction with section 1(a)(3) of the Introductory Act to the Criminal Code, which abolished that maximum duration with immediate effect, in 2001, the courts responsible for the execution of sentences then ordered the applicant's continued preventive detention beyond the ten-year point. Thus, the applicant's preventive detention was prolonged with retrospective effect, under a law enacted after the applicant had committed his offence – and at a time when he had already served more than six years in preventive detention. The Court noted at the outset that, just like a prison sentence, preventive detention entails a deprivation of liberty. The Court did not agree that preventive detention served only a preventive, and not a punitive, purpose. The Court, 'looking behind appearances and making its own assessment', concluded that preventive detention under the German criminal code must be qualified as a 'penalty' for the purposes of article 7(1).[195] The Court therefore found that there had been a breach of article 7. The finding of these two breaches effectively cast a veil of doubt over the whole German system of preventive detention.

The response of the German courts to the adverse judgment in *M* has been a varied one. The responses fall into two categories: on the one hand, decisions holding that the German courts are bound to uphold German law and that the Convention is effectively the handmaiden to national law, and on the other hand, decisions which hold that the apposite German statutes are capable of being interpreted in conformity with the Strasbourg Court's decision in *M*.[196]

After the Strasbourg Court's decision had been handed down, M filed a constitutional complaint with the Constitutional Court, arguing that he should be discharged from detention by way of a temporary injunction, as the Strasbourg Court had said his continued detention was in breach of Convention rights. The *Bundesverfassungsgericht* may exercise its authority to issue a temporary injunction in proceedings through provisional measures (*einstweilige Anordnungen*): section 32 of the Bundesverfassungsgericht Act provides: 'In a dispute the Federal Constitutional Court may deal with a matter provisionally by means of a temporary injunction if this is urgently needed to avert serious detriment, ward off imminent force or for any other important reason for the common

---

[195] *Ibid.*, para. 133.   [196] See Grabenwarter, 'Wirkungen'.

good.'[197] The *Bundesverfassungsgericht*, in the face of the Strasbourg Court decision, ruled that M must remain in detention.[198] The Court's ruling was a terse one. It pointed out the dangers of keeping in detention an individual whom a later constitutional complaint could show ought not to have been kept in detention; the continued deprivation of his liberty, were it to be found unwarranted in a later constitutional judgment, would be a grave injustice, said the Court.[199] In its conclusion, however, the *Bundesverfassungsgericht* found that the detrimental effects of letting loose an individual whom the lower German courts had shown, by way of comprehensible reasoning, to be dangerous, would outweigh the dangers of keeping the claimant in preventive detention.[200]

The tenor of the *Bundesverfassungsgericht*'s decision seems to have served as an exemplar for the German courts in the many cases like M working their way up the German curial hierarchy.[201] The result of this line of authority was four adverse judgments handed down by the Strasbourg Court in January 2011. In *Schummer*,[202] *Mautes*,[203] *Kallweit*,[204] and *Jendrowiak*[205] the Strasbourg Court could do little more than reaffirm its decision in M and point out that German law was still in breach of articles 5 and 7. The German courts by and large responded by digging in, refusing to give effect in German law to the Strasbourg Court's holding in M.

Of late, however, the German courts seem to have shifted tack, proving more amenable to the Strasbourg Court's decision in M. The recent judgment of the German Federal Supreme Court in 5 StR 60/10 furnishes

---

[197] See generally, A. Maurer, 'The Federal Constitutional Court's Emergency Power to Intervene: Provisional Measures Pursuant to Article 32 of the Federal Constitutional Court Act', *German Law Journal* 2 (2001).

[198] BverfG, 2 BvR 2365/09.

[199] *Ibid.*, para. 3.   [200] *Ibid.*, para. 4.

[201] See, for example, Celle Court of Appeal, decision of 25 May 2010, File No. 2 Ws 169-70/10; Stuttgart Court of Appeal, decision of 1 June 2010, File No. 1 Ws 57/10; Koblenz Court of Appeal, decision of 7 June 2010, File No. 1 Ws 108/10; Nuremberg Court of Appeal, decision of 24 June 2010, File No. 1 Ws 315/10; and Cologne Court of Appeal, decision of 14 July 2010, File No. 2 Ws 428/10.

[202] ECtHR, *Schummer* v. *Germany* (Appl. Nos. 27360/04 and 42225/07), Judgment (Fifth Section), 13 January 2011, not reported.

[203] ECtHR, *Mautes* v. *Germany* (Appl. No. 20008/07), Judgment (Fifth Section), 13 January 2011, not reported.

[204] ECtHR, *Kallweit* v. *Germany* (Appl. No. 17792/07), Judgment (Fifth Section), 13 January 2011, not reported.

[205] ECtHR, *Jendrowiak* v. *Germany* (Appl. No. 30060/04), Judgment (Fifth Section), 14 April 2011, not reported.

an apposite example of this development. In its judgment, the German Federal Supreme Court[206] ruled that due to the authority of ECHR law, it was not bound to follow the Strasbourg Court's holding in *M*. In the event, however, the Federal Supreme Court's end result was in line with *M*. The claimant had been sentenced to preventive detention under section 66(b)(a)(2) of the German criminal code. His case was parallel to the one in *M*. In 1997 he had been sentenced to twelve years of imprisonment for several serious sexual offences. He served his sentence to term, and was then, in 2008, sentenced to preventive detention.

The Federal Supreme Court cited the *Bundesverfassungsgericht*'s *Görgülü* rule, that the Convention is incorporated into German law through statute, and therefore, in the hierarchy of norms, has the same status as other statutory legislation, and that the Convention rights 'is to be taken into account and used by national judges in the interpretation of national law, within the bounds of methodically defensible interpretation'.[207] In that regard, the German courts must advert to the decisions of the Strasbourg Court, as they mirror the current development of the Convention rights.[208]

The Federal Supreme Court brought out the holding of the Strasbourg Court in *M*, underscoring that in formal terms the Strasbourg judgment concerned only section 67(d) of the Criminal Code. The Court did, however, make it clear that the same had to apply with respect to section 66(b)(1)(2), the provision in issue, as the Strasbourg Court would indubitably have found that provision to be in breach of the Convention, too.[209] Faced with such a structural breach of the Convention, said the Federal Supreme Court, it was incumbent on the Court to give national law an interpretation which conformed to the Convention. The fact that the Convention enjoys that status of statutory norms only, and not of constitutional norms, means that the Convention rights, as applied in German law, must be applied within the bounds of a 'methodologically defensible interpretation' (*im Rahmen methodisch vertretbarer Auslegung zu beachten und anzuwenden*).[210] This means that the extent to which German law may be interpreted in conformity with Convention rights ends where 'the contrary will of national lawmakers is sufficiently recognisable'; 'Convention friendly' interpretation of national law may not run

---

[206] BGH, 5 StR 60/10 (5 StR 21/09), Judgment, 21 July 2010.
[207] *Ibid.*, para. 10, citing BVerfGE 111, 307 (317).
[208] BGH, 5 StR 60/10, para. 10, citing BVerfGE 111, 307 (319).
[209] BGH, 5 StR 60/10, paras. 11–12.   [210] *Ibid.*, para. 13.

headlong into the meaning intended by the legislator.[211] From these principles it was clear that section 66(1)(2) of the Criminal Code could not be interpreted in light of article 7(1) of the Convention, as this would lead to the complete emasculation of the national law provision.[212] The clear wording, eloquent of an equally clear will of the legislator, could not admit of such an interpretation; there was effectively no room for the use of article 7(1) of the Convention, as section 66(b)(1)(2) of the Criminal Code was explicitly meant to have retroactive effect.[213]

The Court said, however, that the decision must also pass a discretionary test, in which, on the one hand, the interests of the convicted and, on the other hand, the right to protection of the public, would have to be balanced. In this balancing exercise, said the Court, the constitutional principle of proportionality plays a central role:

> The criminal courts must, in the application of s 66(b)(1)(2), bear in mind that the constitutional principle of proportionality may, when in an individual case the right to liberty outweighs the general interest, offer the option of disallowing the effects of the rules of the preventive detention scheme.[214]

In doing so, the Court said, the German judges must take into account the ECHR, as interpreted by the Strasbourg Court; the balancing must be directed by the Convention rights.[215] Thus, the exigencies of the Convention rights, through the constitutional principle of proportionality, are brought to bear on the national law after all.[216] The Court held that the same must apply with respect to article 5(1)(2) of the Convention. Taking a leaf out of the Strasbourg Court's book, the Federal Supreme Court held that the there was not sufficient causal connection between the claimant's continued detention and his conviction.[217] If other German courts, not least the *Bundesverfassungsgericht*, follow suit, the structural problems which have led to the adverse Strasbourg judgments in *M*,[218] *Schummer*,[219] *Mautes*,[220] *Kallweit*[221] and *Jendrowiak*[222] will, by way of an interpretative knight's move on the part of the German courts, be obviated.

---

[211] *Ibid.* For this proposition the Court cited Giegerich, 'Wirkung und Rang', chapter 2.
[212] BGH, 5 StR 60/10, paras. 14–15.   [213] *Ibid.*, para. 15.   [214] *Ibid.*, para. 17.
[215] *Ibid.*, para. 18.
[216] The result reached by the Federal Supreme Court in 5 StR 60/10 – that the Convention is effectively incorporated on an equal footing with constitutional norms – is the same as that suggested by Voßkuhle, 'Multilevel Cooperation', at 175.
[217] BGH, 5 StR 60/10, para. 19.   [218] *M* v. *Germany*.   [219] *Schummer* v. *Germany*.
[220] *Mautes* v. *Germany*.   [221] *Kallweit* v. *Germany*.   [222] *Jendrowiak* v. *Germany*.

In *Preventive Detention*,[223] the response of the top German court in this line of cases, the German Constitutional Court ruled on the compatibility with the ECHR of the German legislation on preventive detention. The case concerned the constitutional complaints lodged by four detainees who challenged the retrospective prolongation of their preventive detention beyond the former ten-year maximum and the retrospective imposition of preventive detention under criminal law relating to adult and juvenile offenders. The Court reviewed the provisions of the Criminal Code and the Juvenile Court Act on the imposition and duration of preventive detention and found them incompatible with the fundamental right to liberty under article 2(2), sentence 2,[224] in conjunction with article 104(1),[225] of the German Constitution (*Grundgesetz*, or Basic Law). The Court ordered that the unconstitutional provisions shall continue to be applicable until the entry into force of new legislation.

As the statutory provisions at issue failed to satisfy the constitutional requirement of establishing a 'distance' (*Abstandsgebot*) between preventive detention and prison sentences, those provisions fell foul of the fundamental right to liberty. The Court also ruled that the legislation failed to comply with the constitutional protection of legitimate expectations guaranteed in a state governed by the rule of law, as read together with the constitutional right to liberty. According to the Court, the protection of legitimate expectations under article 2(2), in conjunction with article 20(3) of the Basic Law,[226] is an expression of the rule-of-law precept.

The *Preventive Detention* judgment, crucially, was the response of the Constitutional Court to a spate of adverse judgments against Germany by the European Court of Human Rights on the highly controversial issue of preventive detention, mainly of sexual offenders.[227] The Strasbourg

---

[223] BVerfG, 4 May, No. 2 BvR 2365/09 (*Preventive Detention*). The basic documents, press releases, and related materials for the judgments of the Constitutional Court are available on the Court's website, www.bundesverfassungsgericht.de. Unless otherwise noted, translations from the German are by the authors.

[224] Grundgesetz (hereinafter GG, Basic Law), May 23 1949, BGBl. 1. GG Article 2(2) provides: 'Everyone has the right to life and to physical integrity. The freedom of the person is inviolable. Intrusion on these rights may be made only pursuant to a statute.'

[225] GG Article 104(1) provides: 'The liberty of the individual may be restricted only by virtue of a formal statute and only in compliance with the forms prescribed therein. Detained persons may not be subjected to mental or to physical ill treatment.'

[226] GG Article 20(3) provides: 'The legislature is bound by the constitutional order; the executive and the judiciary are bound by law and justice.'

[227] *Schummer v. Germany*; *Mautes v. Germany*; *Kallweit v. Germany*.

Court had held in the first of these cases, *M* v. *Germany*,[228] that continued preventive detention beyond ten years, which was the maximum under the applicable law at the time of the applicant's offence and conviction, was in breach of Article 5(1) of the Convention,[229] and that the retrospective extension of the preventive detention to an effectively unlimited period of time was in breach of article 7(1).[230] The Strasbourg Court further found that preventive detention as practised in Germany 'is to be qualified as a "penalty"', and not merely a measure of correction and prevention'.[231] As the scheme had not been considered to be a penalty in German law, the German judges had not believed that such principles as the prohibition of retroactive sentences and the *ne bis in idem* rule were applicable.

When M – the claimant in both *M* in 2009 and *Preventive Detention* in 2011 – was sentenced in 1986, he could be kept in preventive detention for no more than ten years, in accordance with section 67d(1) of the Criminal Code. This rule was amended in 1998 and made applicable in its new form to the preventive detention orders that had been issued prior to the amendment's entry into force. Without that change in the law, the courts responsible for the execution of sentences would not have had the authority to extend the duration of the claimant's preventive detention.

Initially, the German courts did not respond in unison to the adverse judgment in *M*. Some decisions held that the German courts are bound by German law and that the Convention is effectively the handmaiden of national law. Others held that the apposite German statutes were amenable to being interpreted in conformity with the Strasbourg Court's ruling in *M*.[232]

---

[228] *M* v. *Germany*.
[229] Article 5(1)(c) of the Convention, provides: 'Everyone has the right to liberty and security of person. No one shall be deprived of his liberty save in the following cases and in accordance with a procedure prescribed by law: … (c) the lawful arrest or detention of a person effected for the purpose of bringing him before the competent legal authority on reasonable suspicion of having committed an offence or when it is reasonably considered necessary to prevent his committing an offence or fleeing after having done so.'
[230] Article 7(1) of the Convention provides: 'No one shall be held guilty of any criminal offence on account of any act or omission which did not constitute a criminal offence under national or international law at the time when it was committed. Nor shall a heavier penalty be imposed than the one that was applicable at the time the criminal offence was committed.'
[231] *M* v. *Germany*, para. 133.
[232] See Grabenwarter, 'Wirkungen'; Merkel, 'Incompatible Contrasts?'.

After the Strasbourg Court's decision was handed down, M filed a constitutional complaint before the *Bundesverfassungsgericht*, arguing that he ought to be discharged from detention by way of a temporary injunction, since the Strasbourg Court had said his continued detention was in breach of his rights under the Convention. The Constitutional Court, in the face of the Strasbourg Court's decision, by a temporary injunction of 22 December 2009, ordered that M remain in detention.[233]

In the temporary injunction, the Constitutional Court tersely pointed out the dangers of holding an individual in detention who, it might later be shown, ought not to have been so held; the continued deprivation of his liberty, were it to be found unwarranted in a subsequent constitutional judgment, would be a grave injustice.[234] In its conclusion, however, the Court determined that the detrimental effects of freeing an individual whom the German lower courts had demonstrated by plausible reasoning to be dangerous would outweigh the hazards of keeping the claimant in preventive detention.[235]

The tenor of the Constitutional Court's decision seems to have served as an exemplar for the many cases like *M* that were working their way up the German curial hierarchy.[236] This line of authority resulted in January 2011 in the adverse judgments by the Strasbourg Court mentioned above: in *Schummer*, *Mautes* and *Kallweit*, the Court could do little but reaffirm its decision in *M* and point out that German law was still in breach of ECHR articles 5 and 7.[237] The German courts largely responded by digging in and refusing to give effect in national law to the Strasbourg Court's holding in *M*.

Yet, at the same time, some German courts had begun to shift, proving more receptive to accommodating the Strasbourg Court's *M* decision. The Federal Court of Justice (Bundesgerichtshof) – the highest German court in matters of criminal and civil law – for example, ruled in a case also bearing on preventive detention,[238] that it was not bound by ECHR law to follow the holding in *M*. In addition, however, the Court of Justice held that its decision must pass a discretionary test balancing the interests of the convicted and the right of the public to protection. In this

---

[233] BVerfG, 2 BvR 2365/09.   [234] *Ibid.*, para. 3.   [235] *Ibid.*, para. 4.
[236] See, e.g., Oberlandesgericht (OLG, Higher Regional Court) Celle, 25 May 2010, No. 2 Ws 169–70/10; OLG Stuttgart, 1 June 2010, No. 1 Ws 57/10; OLG Koblenz, 7 June 2010, No. 1 Ws 108/10; OLG Nuremberg, 24 June 2010, No. 1 Ws 315/10; OLG Cologne, 14 July 2010, No. 2 Ws 428/10.
[237] *Schummer v. Germany*; *Mautes v. Germany*; *Kallweit v. Germany*.
[238] BGH, 5 StR 60/10.

balancing exercise, the courts must give a central role to the constitutional principle of proportionality.[239] This balancing must furthermore be directed by the ECHR rights; in this way the constitutional principle of proportionality brings the exigencies of the ECHR rights to bear on the national law after all.[240] Though the solution espoused by the Court of Justice was in accordance with the Strasbourg jurisprudence, confusion still prevailed over how best to accommodate *M* in German law, so that the Constitutional Court could definitely no longer stay above the fray – hence the May 2011 decision in *Preventive Detention*.

As adumbrated above, the Constitutional Court held the statutes in issue to be unconstitutional. This result may come as a surprise, and in more than one respect. The main issue was that the preventive detention scheme was in breach of the German Basic Law – even though the Constitutional Court in 2004 had held that the self-same scheme was constitutional, and even though what was really in issue were the exigencies of the Convention. What, then, had changed in seven years? The Constitutional Court explained in *Preventive Detention* that rulings by the Strasbourg Court containing new considerations for the interpretation of the Basic Law are equivalent to legally relevant changes (*rechtserhebliche Änderungen*), which may lead to the supersession of the final and binding effect of a Federal Constitutional Court decision.[241] In a 2004 decision in *M*,[242] the Court had declared constitutional the elimination of the ten-year maximum period for preventive detention that had applied previously, and the application of the new legislation to the so-called old cases. However, the Court had also ruled in that earlier decision that preventive detention did not fall foul of any of the human rights guarantees in the Basic Law but, without going into detail, that there had to be some 'distance' between preventive detention and prison sentences. The final and binding effect of the Constitutional Court's 2004 decision, therefore, did not constitute a procedural bar to the admissibility of the present constitutional complaints.

What *Preventive Detention* says about prisoners' rights and the German legislation on preventive detention is important for several reasons. By departing from its own 2004 decision, the Constitutional Court resolved a fundamental conflict between the German constitutional order and the European system of human rights protection. It gave the reasons for this

---

[239] *Ibid.*, para. 17.   [240] *Ibid.*, para. 18.   [241] BVerfG, 2 BvR 2365/09, para. 82.
[242] BVerfG, 109 BVerfGE 133.

change as follows. The starting point is that the Convention is incorporated into German law by way of statute only; at the national level, the Convention ranks below the Basic Law.[243] The ECHR does, however, serve as an 'aid to interpretation' (*Auslegungshilfe*) of German fundamental rights and the rule-of-law principles of the Basic Law. The provisions of the Basic Law are to be construed in a manner that is open to international law (*völkerrechtsfreundlich*). [244]

Similarly, the Strasbourg jurisprudence will influence the interpretation of the German constitutional precepts. As Constitutional Court President Andreas Voßkuhle had explained on earlier occasions, and the *Preventive Detention* judgment echoes, the Court has effectively raised the ECHR and the Strasbourg jurisprudence 'to the level of constitutional law' as aids to interpretation for determining the content and scope of the fundamental rights and rule-of-law guarantees of the Basic Law.[245] An interpretation that is open to international law does not require the Basic Law's exigencies to be schematically aligned with those of the Convention,[246] but it does require the ECHR values to be taken into consideration to the extent that is methodologically justifiable and compatible with the Basic Law's standards.[247]

The issue before the Court stirred controversy in Germany at the time. Ministers and police, at both the state and the federal levels, warned of the potential consequences of following *M v. Germany*, and in the days before *Preventive Detention* was handed down, those officials made public how in Freiburg – a neighbouring city to Karlsruhe, where the Constitutional Court is based – the allocation of twenty-five police officers to surveil each one of the prisoners released from preventive detention heavily drained police resources.[248]

It is a happy circumstance indeed when, in the words of the German Romantic poet, Friedrich Hölderlin, the danger itself fosters the rescuing power.[249] That is nonetheless precisely what happened in the *Preventive Detention* case. The Court not only followed the Strasbourg jurisprudence;

---

[243] BVerfG, 2 BvR 2365/09, paras. 86–7. [244] *Ibid.*, paras. 86, 89.
[245] *Ibid.*, paras. 82, 88. [246] *Ibid.*, para. 91.
[247] *Ibid.*, para. 93. The Court used the term 'methodologically justifiable interpretation' in the *Görgülü* judgment.
[248] See, e.g., *Ex-Sicherungsverwahrte unter Dauerbewachung*, Rhein-Zeitung, 4 May 2011, at www.rhein-zeitung.de/.
[249] F. Hölderlin, 'Patmos', in E.L. Santner (ed.), *Hyperion and Selected Poems* (New York: Continuum, 1990) 245.

it took the occasion, in this challenging proceeding, to develop its doctrine on the openness of German law to the Convention and the jurisprudence of the Strasbourg Court.

The Court underscored the crucial importance of the role played by human rights in the Basic Law: 'The prominent position that human rights enjoy in the Basic Law is given expression particularly in the attachment of the German people to inviolable and inalienable human rights in articulo 1(2) of the Basic Law'.[250] Notably, the Court had adverted to the position of human rights in the Basic Law before, in the 2004 *Görgülü* case,[251] but had never explicitly referenced article 1(2). The Constitutional Court seems to have given its imprimatur to the approach advocated by Professor Jochen von Bernstorff – that one must take seriously the constitutional fact that the Basic Law itself, in article 1(1) and (2) and 19(2), requires public organs to respect categorical limits on state interference in civil liberties derived not only from national human rights, but also from the international human rights conventions.[252] This significant development goes a long way toward grounding respect for European and international human rights law in the German Constitution.

Another point has to do with the tone of the ruling and its terminology. The Constitutional Court in *Görgülü* had held that: '[t]he authorities and courts of the Federal Republic of Germany are obliged, under certain conditions, to take account of the European Convention on Human Rights as interpreted by the [European Court of Human Rights]' and had been criticised for this weak choice of words by Professors Christian Tomuschat and Armin von Bogdandy.[253] The Court in *Preventive Detention* ruled that the duty to apply the Convention in national law amounted to much more: it was 'not ... a duty only to take into account, for the Basic Law aims ... to avoid conflict between international obligations of the Federal Republic of Germany and national law'.[254] 'The openness of the Basic Law', the Court continued,

---

[250] BVerfG, 2 BvR 2365/09, para. 90.
[251] BVerfG, 111 BVerfGE 289 ('*Görgülü*').
[252] See J. von Bernstorff, *Kerngehalte im Grund- und Menschenrechtsschutz* (Berlin: Duncker und Humbolt, 2012).
[253] Tomuschat, 'Effects', at 522–3 (quoting 111 BVerfGE 289 (315), English translation para. 29, at www.bundesverfassungsgericht.de/); A. von Bogdandy, 'Pluralism, Direct Effect, and the Ultimate Say: On the Relationship between International and Domestic Constitutional Law', *International Journal of Constitutional Law* 6 (2008) 397–413, at 403.
[254] BVerfG, 2 BvR 2365/09, para. 89.

'thus expresses an understanding of sovereignty which not only not opposes international and supranational integration; it presupposes and expects it'.[255]

The overarching question is this: does *Preventive Detention* represent a transformation in German law as compared to *Görgülü*? While it probably does not, one should not underestimate how far the Constitutional Court went to avoid a clash with the Convention and the Strasbourg Court on this highly vexing and politically sensitive matter. As discussed above, the influence of the Convention and the Strasbourg jurisprudence will extend only so far as it may be supported by established German legal methods and principles. German constitutional doctrine had maintained for many decades that preventive detention was not wrong and that it was not 'punishment' (*Strafe*); the German legal method in the field was very clear.

It is therefore difficult to see what kind of restriction, if any, is posed by the words 'methodologically justifiable' (*methodisch vertretbar*), and in that light, too, the decision is remarkable. The question could be asked whether this test of methodological justifiability is really a coherent check on the incorporation of international law in the national legal order. In reality, the test may have no substance, as *Preventive Detention* shows that the extent to which the Basic Law can be interpreted in light of the Convention is very great; no constitutional problem is posed, because the prominent position of human rights in the Basic Law is explicitly expressed in its article 1(2).

The approach of the Constitutional Court in *Preventive Detention* duly received the imprimatur of the Strasbourg Court, which in *Schmitz* v. *Germany* took note of the reversal of the Federal Constitutional Court's case law concerning preventive detention in its leading judgment of 4 May 2011. It welcomed the Federal Constitutional Court's approach of interpreting the provisions of the Basic Law also in the light of the Convention and this Court's case law, which demonstrates that court's continuing commitment to the protection of fundamental rights not only at national, but also at European level.[256]

Since the Constitutional Court ordered that the unconstitutional provisions would continue to apply until they were cured by the entry into force of appropriate new legislation, the affected prisoners would

---

[255] *Ibid.*
[256] ECtHR, *Schmitz* v. *Germany* (Appl. No. 30493/04), Judgment (Fifth Section), 9 June 2011, not reported, para. 41 (citation omitted).

effectively be kept under lock and key pending those legislative changes. Consequently, more cases will surely reach the Strasbourg Court, and the dialogue on preventive detention will just as surely continue.

In any event, the Voßkuhle court went a long way in charting a course that responds to the exigencies of both national constitutional law and European law. In a broader sense, this approach marks a change from the general stance of Voßkuhle's predecessor, Hans-Jürgen Papier, who consistently put a thumb on the scale in favour of national law.[257] What the Constitutional Court did in its sovereignty-based *Lisbon* judgment in 2009,[258] the Voßkuhle court undid in *Honeywell* in 2010.[259] The jurisprudence of the Constitutional Court is now clearly tending toward openness to international and European law, particularly, it seems, in rights cases.

The German Court accordingly follows the example of the French Constitutional Court of many years. In 2008, the French Court even declared unconstitutional a similar statute on preventive detention, on the basis of the exigencies of the Convention as well as those of French constitutional law,[260] and the Strasbourg Court in *M* explicitly cited the French position.[261] The strength of this French view was corroborated by former president of the Constitutional Court, Robert Badinter, who, looking back in 2011 over his legal career, asserted that since the 1980s 'the best defense of our liberties resided in the control by the Strasbourg

---

[257] Hans-Jürgen Papier was President of the Court in the period 10 April 2002 to 16 March 2010, during which the *Görgülü* ruling was handed down. Andreas Voßkuhle took over on 16 March 2010.

[258] BVerfG, 123 BVerfGE 267 (holding that the Constitutional Court is competent to review whether EU legal acts are compatible with the defining characteristics or the constitutional identity of the German Constitution – 'constitutional identity review').

[259] BVerfG, BvR 2661/06 (*Honeywell*) (holding that while the Constitutional Court is competent to carry out *ultra vires* review of EU legal acts, the Court's competence to declare an act of the EU institutions to be *ultra vires* is very restricted, which effectively makes this contingency a remote one); see M. Payandeh, 'Constitutional Review of EU Law After Honeywell: Contextualizing the Relationship Between the German Constitutional Court and the EU Court of Justice', *Common Market Law Review* 48 (2011) 9–38, at 9.

[260] Conseil constitutionnel (hereinafter CC, Constitutional Court), decision No. 2008-562DC, 21 February 2008, Journal Officiel (J.O.), 26 February 2008, at 3272; see B. Stirn, *Les Sources Constitutionnelles du Droit Administratif: Introduction au Droit Public*, 6th edn (Paris: Lextenso Editions, 2008), at 17–18; E. Bjorge, 'National Supreme Courts and the Development of ECHR Rights', *International Journal of Constitutional Law* 9:1 (2011) 5–31.

[261] See B. Stirn, *Les Libertés en Questions*, 7th edn (Paris: Lextenso Éditions, 2010), at 73.

Court of the conformity of our statutes and judgments with the European Convention on Human Rights'.[262] This sentiment now seems to have been endorsed by Andreas Voßkuhle, who has promoted, both extrajudicially and in his capacity as president of the German Constitutional Court, the concept of national constitutional courts as components of the 'multilevel cooperation of European Constitutional Courts'.[263]

The strong rights protection afforded by the Italian Constitution, and the rigorous rights jurisprudence developed in Italian courts, makes the backdrop for national ECHR implementation in Italian law very similar to the German context. The Italian and the German systems evince similarities in their approach, historically and presently, to EU law. The same applies to implementation of Convention rights.

In the twin decisions No. 348 and 349/2007, the Italian Constitutional Court ruled that the ECHR enjoys higher status than statutes.[264] This means that in a case of conflict between Convention rights and a national statute passed after the 1955 law which incorporated the Convention into Italian law, the Convention will take precedence.[265] The Constitutional Court held that a Convention right enjoyed the position between statutory and constitutional norms: a Convention right is 'una norma interposta'.[266] Convention rights no longer have only the status of ordinary laws; 'they are to a degree subordinated to the Constitution, but are intermediate between the Constitution and ordinary status'. The Court in decisions 348 and 349/2007 also held that the exact meaning of the ECHR may be ascertained only by the Strasbourg Court. It followed from this that Italian law must keep pace with the Convention rights as they evolve in the jurisprudence of the Strasbourg Court.

What the Constitutional Court said about how ordinary judges are to deal with the ECHR in national law was interesting. In the analysis of

---

[262] R. Badinter, *Les Épines et les Roses* (Paris: Fayard, 2011), at 240–1 (trans. by authors); see, e.g., CC decision No. 95-360DC, 2 February 1995, J.O., 7 February 1995, at 2097; CC decision No. 2006-540DC, 27 July 2006, J.O., 3 August 2006, at 11541; O. Dutheillet de Lamothe, 'Olivier Dutheillet de Lamothe Member, Conseil Constitutionnel France', *International Journal of Constitutional Law* 3:4 (2005) 550–6; M. Andenas and E. Bjorge, 'Juge National et Interprétation Évolutive de la Convention Européenne des Droits de l'Homme', *Revue du Droit Public* (2011) 997–1014.

[263] See Voßkuhle, 'Multilevel Cooperation'.

[264] *Corte costituzionale*, judgment No. 348 and 349/2007.

[265] See O. Pollicino *et al.*, 'Report on Italy', in O. Pollicino (ed.), *The National Judicial Treatment of the ECHR and EU Laws: A Comparative Perspective* (Groningen: Europa Law Publishing, 2010) 269–95, at 285 (hereinafter Pollicino, 'Italy').

[266] *Corte costituzionale*, judgment No. 348 and 349/2007, para. 4.7.

Oreste Polliciono and Giuseppe Martinico, the Constitutional Court exhorted ordinary judges, before raising a question about the constitutionality of a national law in conflict with the ECHR, to interpret the national law in conformity with the ECHR so far as possible. This was the first time that the ordinary judge was 'assigned a clear constitutional duty to interpret the domestic law in conformity with the international law of human rights'.[267] Were the ordinary courts not to succeed in reading down the statute at issue, they would have to refer the matter to the Constitutional Court. If, however, an ordinary judge is unable to reconcile a statute with the Convention, the judge hearing the case must then preliminarily set the statute aside and seise the Constitutional Court.

Two aspects of the decisions have been criticised by Polliciono and Martinico: 'the exclusion of any power for common judges to set aside national legislation in conflict with ECHR and the consequent risk of losing the effectiveness of ECHR law'.[268] This seems a valid criticism, as the system of seisin of the Constitutional Court is very rigid, and the end result may be that proceedings fall foul of article 6 of the ECHR. The second criticism levelled at the twin decisions homes in on the fact that the ECHR, as opposed to European Union (EU) law, which enjoys constitutional status,[269] has not been given a more prominent place in the Italian legal order. Pollicino and Martinico ask: 'Is it not confusing to put the ECHR and the "Treaty on Principles Governing the Activities of States in the Exploration and Use of Outer Space, Including the Moon and Other Celestial Bodies", on the same level only because they are formally both international Treaties ratified by Italy?'[270] It is not clear any longer, however, that the exclusion of any power for ordinary judges to set aside national legislation in conflict with the ECHR is set in stone. The recent decision in the *Pittito* case handed down by the Court of Appeal of Milan is a case in point where the impact of this potential structural lock is tempered.[271]

Mr. Pittito had been condemned after a trial conducted *in absentia*. He unsuccessfully appealed the judgment in the Italian courts. He then

---

[267] Pollicino, 'Italy', at 287–8.   [268] *Ibid.*, at 290.

[269] Article 117(1) of the Italian Constitution provides that: 'La potestà legislativa è esercitata dallo Stato e dalle Regioni nel rispetto della Costituzione, nonché dei vincoli derivanti dall'ordinamento comunitario e dagli obblighi internazionali.' ('Legislative power belongs to the State and the regions in accordance with the constitution and within the limits set by European Union law and international obligations.' Translation from Polliciono, 'Italy', at 271.)

[270] *Ibid.*   [271] *Corte d'Appello di Milano*, 286/2008, Judgment, 12 April 2010.

filed a claim with the Strasbourg Court, which confirmed its previous decisions on the matter, affirming that the real intention of the accused not to be present in the domestic trial must be ascertained in order to declare him *latitante*, 'on the run', which is a requirement for the trial to be conducted *in absentia*.[272] The Strasbourg Court held that this was not the case, and added that its decision should be a sufficient form of reparation for the wrong done to the applicant. The Italian courts had already gone beyond this approach, as they had decided on many occasions that whenever a trial has been shown to have been conducted in violation of fair trial standards, a form of compensation 'for equivalents' must be granted, such as, for example, partial revision of the trial or the condemnation to a milder penalty.

According to the Strasbourg Court's interpretation of the fair trial standard in article 6, Mr. Pittito would have no right to have his trial started over again, with the procedural guarantees which, going back to the court of first instance, would entail for him. When the Court of Appeal declared void the judgment in which Mr. Pittito had been condemned, and scheduled a retrial, it went further than the Strasbourg Court had said was necessary according to article 6.

As will have become clear, this is an interesting point if one compares the approach of the Milanese Court of Appeal to the exhortation of the Constitutional Court to the lower courts. The Constitutional Court, as was said above, had held in 2007 that Italian law ought to be interpreted in accordance with the ECHR so far as possible, and when this proves to be unfeasible the ordinary judge must seise the *Corte costituzionale*, which will declare void the Italian law contrary to the ECHR. This was not done in the *Pittito* case. The ordinary judge did not ask for the intervention of the *Consulta*, but instead set aside the conflicting law of his own volition. From this it may be concluded that the ECHR in the Italian system has gained the status that Community law has had for some time; it enjoys constitutional status.

The Russian approach, while more sceptical, also evinces certain structural similarities with the German approach. Angelika Nußberger has compared the approach of the Russian Constitutional Court with that of the German. In her view, the Russian Court has a 'much more restrictive' approach than the German, in the sense of further limiting

---

[272] ECtHR, *Pittito* v. *Italy* (Appl. No. 19321/03), Judgment (Second Section), 12 June 2007 (in French only), not reported, paras. 11 and 42.

the effect of the decisions of the Strasbourg Court in national law.[273] In three articles from 2006, the Constitutional Court Justices Vitruk, Zimnenko and Marchenko explain the Russian Court's approach to the case law of the Strasbourg Court. Vitruk is generally critical of the role of case law which, in his view, 'can seriously weaken the Constitution', and also to giving the Strasbourg Court's decisions any binding precedential effect.[274] Zimnenko argues that states are not bound by decisions from the Strasbourg Court.[275] Marchenko explains 'precedent' from the Strasbourg Court as 'a helpful example'.[276]

On President Zorkin's view, judgments 'involving issues of sovereignty' would not be binding for Russia. He further indicated that Russia could denounce the Convention. A declaration was made at the event of Zorkin's intervention about the introduction of 'a mechanism for defending national sovereignty' which would allow the Russian government not to respect judgments issued by the ECHR which are contrary to judgments reached by the Russian Constitutional Court.[277] At the same time, however, President Zorkin in the same speech advocated an increased 'role of the judiciary in the strengthening of interaction between the national and international legal systems, and in more and more active integration of Russia into the international legal space, including the European one'.[278]

---

[273] A. Nußberger, 'The Reception Process in Russia and Ukraine', in H. Keller, *A Europe of Rights: The Impact of the ECHR on National Legal Systems* (Oxford University Press, 2008) 603–76, at 603.

[274] N.V. Vitruk, 'O nekotorykh osobennostyakh ispol'zovaniya resheniy Evropeyskogo Suda po pravam cheloveka v. pratike Konstitutsionnogo Suda Rossiyskoy Fedreratsii i inykh sudov', *Sravnitel'noe konsituttsionnoe obozrenie* 1 (2006) 80–95, at 83.

[275] B.L. Zimnenko, *Mezhdunarodnoe pravo in pravovaya sistema Rossiyskoy Federatsii* (Moskow: Statut, 2006).

[276] M.N. Marchenko, 'Yuridicheskaya priroda i charakter resheny Evropeyskogo Suda po pralam cheloveka', *Gusodarstvo i Pravo* 2 (2006), at 11. However, all three judges relate the binding effect, as precedents, of decisions from the Court to the role of court judgments in general, including those of their own court. So here neither is there any distinction between the domestic sources and the European sources, as also seen in the discussion of the reach of rights and of the legality and proportionality of restrictions, the Russian judges integrate the sources. Applying the same method here can cause particular problems when it allows a court not to follow decisions by the Court.

[277] The International Forum of Constitutional Justice in St. Petersburg on 18 November 2010.

[278] See V. Zorkin, 'Constitutional Justice of the New Democracies in the Conditions of Modern Challenges and Threats' at the Conference on the Occasion of the Twenty Year Anniversary of the Hungarian Constitutional Court in 2009, available at www.mkab.hu/index.php?id=twenty_years_of_the_constitutional_court. We are grateful to Anastasia Maltseva, the Max Planck Institute for Comparative and International Public Law at Heidelberg, for assistance on this point.

In another public statement, President Zorkin underlined that sovereignty under the Russian Constitution 'supposes supremacy and independence of state power, fullness of ... the state's power within its territory, independence in international relations, it is the necessary qualitative feature of the Russian Federation, characterising its constitutional legal status'.[279] In a speech given at the Opening of the Court Year of the European Court of Human Rights in 2005, President Zorkin stated that '[t]he Constitutional Court protects fundamental rights, guaranteed by the Constitution, which are essentially the same as human rights stated in the Convention'.[280]

Article 15(4) of the Russian Constitution of 1993 provides that generally recognised principles and norms of international law and international treaties form 'part of its *legal system*'.[281] In case of conflict between federal law and treaties, the latter apply as *lex superior*, even if the domestic legislation is *lex posterior*. In *Bogdanov*, the Constitutional Court said that the Convention is ratified by the Russian Federation and in force in all its territory, and part of domestic law. The Russian Federation has accepted the jurisdiction of the Strasbourg Court, undertaking to comply fully, also in its judicial functions, 'with the obligations following from the Convention and the Protocols. ... It follows that the [Russian legislative provisions under challenge] should be considered and then consistently applied in normative unity with the Convention provisions.'[282]

This is elaborated on in a 2007 ruling directly addressing the status of judgments from the Strasbourg Court:

> Judgments of the European Court of Human Rights – in that part, in which they, proceeding from the generally recognized principles and

---

[279] Statement of President of the Constitutional Court of the Russian Federation V. Zorkin, 'National Interests, Contemporary World Order and Constitutional Legality' at the scientific conference 'Role of Law in Securing National Interests', available at www.ksrf.ru/news/7.htm.

[280] Speech by V. Zorkin, President of the Constitutional Court of the Russian Federation, available at www.echr.coe.int/NR/rdonlyres/E85D3F3C-67EC-4B3F-B04D-65F1BFE039B9/0/2005__Opening_Jud__Year_WILDHABER_ZORKIN_BIL_.pdf.

[281] See generally, M. Andenas, 'The Federal Russian Law on Foreign Treaties', in R. Mullersohn, *Constitutional Reform and International Law in Central and Eastern Europe* (The Hague: Kluwer Law International, 1998), at 259–65 (emphasis added), explaining the effect of treaties in Russian law.

[282] *I V Bogdanov and Others*, Reasons, at para. 6 (see also the translation by K. Koroteev, 'Judgment of the Russian Constitutional Court on Supervisory Review in Civil Proceedings: Denial of Justice, Denial of Europe', *Human Rights Law Review* 7 (2007) 619–32).

norms of international law, give interpretation of the content of the rights and freedoms provided by of the Convention – form part of the Russian legal system and should be taken into account by the federal legislator during regulation of the social relations and by the law enforcement bodies.[283]

In 1995, the Supreme Court of the Russian Federation passed a resolution (*postanovleniia*) on the application of the constitution in the general courts, instructing lower courts to apply international law.[284] In 2003 it passed another resolution developing the role of international law in Russian courts.[285] The Supreme Court underlined the duty to apply international treaties, and in particular the ECHR. It repeated that international treaties, including the ECHR, take priority over national law. What is of particular interest to us is how the Supreme Court, referring to 'article 31(3)(b) of the Vienna Convention on the Law of Treaties 1996 [*sic.*]' on subsequent treaty practice, made clear that courts must take account of the practice of treaty bodies.[286] This means that the Russian courts must keep pace with the development of ECHR law. Failure to apply international obligations could lead to cassation or revision of judgments. A brief review was also provided of the Strasbourg Court's case law on articles 3, 5, 6 and 13 of the Convention, without referring expressly to any individual decisions. In the parallel commercial court system, there is a circular by the Chief Justice of the Supreme Court of Arbitration on the protection of private property under the ECHR.[287]

---

[283] Judgment of the Constitutional Court of the Russian Federation No. 2, 5 February 2007, *Cabinet of Ministers of the Republic of Tatarstan, applications of Open Stock Companies 'Nizhneftekamskneftekhim' and 'Khakasenergo'*, at para. 2.1. We are grateful to Vera Rusinova, Immanuel Kant Baltic Federal University, for her kind assistance on this point.

[284] 'On Some Questions Concerning the Application of the Constitution of the Russian Federation by Courts', adopted by the Plenum of the Supreme Court, 31 November 1995, *Rossiyaskaya gazeta* 244, 8 December 1995 (in Russian).

[285] 'On the Application by Courts of General Jurisdiction of the Generally-Recognized Principles and Norms of International Law and the International Treaties of the Russian Federation', adopted by the Plenum of the Supreme Court, 10 November 2003, *Rossiyaskaya gazeta* 244, 2 December 2003 (in Russian).

[286] The year here refers to the ratification and publication in the official gazette, *Rossiyaskaya gazeta*.

[287] Circular by Chief Justice of the Supreme Court of Arbitration,'On the Main Provisions Applied by the European Court of Human Rights for the Protection of Property Rights and Right to Justice', 20 December 1995, No. C1-7/CMP1341, *Vestnik Viysschego arbitrazhnogo suda Rossiyskoy Federatsii* (Bulletin of the Supreme Court of Arbitration) No. 2, 2000.

This is not much different from the approach of the UK Supreme Court post-*Horncastle*. We saw above the position that the UK Supreme Court took in that case. After *Horncastle*, the approach has been a very open and forthcoming one. As illustrated, the Supreme Court in *Cadder* v. *Her Majesty's Advocate*,[288] faced with a similar question to the one in *Horncastle*, opted for quite another approach than the one chosen in 2009. The question in *Cadder* was whether a person who has been detained by the police in Scotland on suspicion of having committed an offence has the right of access to a solicitor prior to being interviewed. Sections 14–15 of the Criminal Procedure (Scotland) Act 1995, as amended, allow the police to detain a person whom they have reasonable grounds for suspecting has committed or is committing an offence punishable by imprisonment for up to six hours. During this detention, the police may put questions to the detainee. The detainee is entitled to have a solicitor informed of their detention. In terms of the statute, however, the detainee has no right of access to a solicitor. The question was whether that was a breach of the right to a fair trial guarantee in article 6(1) and (3)(c) of the Convention. The notion that there should be anything wrong with Scots law on this point was quite novel, and could have far-reaching implications, said the Court:

> Countless cases have gone through the courts, and decades have passed, without any challenge having been made [against the Scottish procedure]. Many more are ongoing or awaiting trial – figures were provided to the court which indicate there are about 76,000 such cases – or are being held in the system pending the hearing of an appeal although not all of them may be affected by the decision in this case. There is no doubt that a ruling that the assumption was erroneous will have profound consequences.[289]

As this decision landed in the docquet of the Supreme Court hot on the heels of *Horncastle*, it would ordinarily be a deaf ear that did not detect at this point the direction in which the decision would, by the sound of things, inexorably be headed. The challenge posed by the ECHR to the common law of England in *Horncastle* led the Supreme Court to hand down a ringing defence of English procedural idiosyncracy. The challenge posed by the ECHR to characterising features of Scots law in *Cadder*, however, led a unanimous Supreme Court, in judgments written by the two Scots Justices – Lords Hope and Rodger – to hand down a

---

[288] *Cadder*. See generally, E. Bjorge, 'Exceptionalism and Internationalism in the Supreme Court: *Horncastle* and *Cadder*', *Public Law* 3 (2011) 475–82.
[289] *Cadder*, para. 4.

decision which marries very ill indeed with the criticism which has been levelled against the HRA in the last few years. There was, on the Court's own admission, no room in the situation which faced the Court for a decision which favoured the status quo simply on grounds of expediency. The issue was a difficult one, but '[i]t must be faced up to, whatever the consequences', said the Court in unambiguous terms.[290] In no way did the decision sound in deference[291] or a national species of the margin of appreciation[292] which could blunt the impact of the Convention rights.

The Grand Chamber of the Strasbourg Court in *Salduz* v. *Turkey*[293] had unanimously held that there had been a violation of article 6(1) and (3)(c) of the Convention because the claimant had not had the benefit of legal advice when he was in police custody. Notwithstanding the Strasbourg Court's decision in *Salduz*, a seven-judge panel of the High Court of Justiciary held in *Her Majesty's Advocate* v. *McLean*[294] that it was not a violation of article 6(1) and (3)(c) for the Crown at trial to rely on admissions made by a detainee while being interviewed without having had access to a solicitor. This was because otherwise available guarantees under Scots law, particularly the requirement that there be corroborated evidence for a conviction to be in order, were sufficient to provide for a fair trial.

It was perfectly clear that the High Court of Justiciary's judgment in *McLean* was in line with previous domestic authority.[295] It was equally clear to a unanimous Supreme Court, however, that *Salduz* required a detainee to have had access to a lawyer from the time of the first interview unless there are compelling reasons, in light of particular circumstances of the case, to restrict that right.[296] The exception applies in particular circumstances only; it does not allow a systematic departure

---

[290] *Ibid.*
[291] See A. Kavanagh, 'Defending Deference in Public Law and Constitutional Theory', *Law Quarterly Review* 126 (2010) 222–50.
[292] See P. Sales, 'The General and the Particular: Parliament and the Courts under the Scheme of the European Convention on Human Rights', in Andenas *et al.* (eds.), *Tom Bingham and the Transformation of the Law: A Liber Amicorum*, 163–82; P. Sales *et al.*, 'Rights-Consistent Interpretation and the Human Rights Act 1998', *Law Quarterly Review* 127 (2011) 217–38.
[293] ECtHR, *Salduz* v. *Turkey* (Appl. No. 36391/02), Judgment (Grand Chamber), 27 November 2008, Reports 2008.
[294] *Her Majesty's Advocate* v. *McLean* [2009] HCJAC 97; 2010 SLT 73.
[295] *Paton* v. *Richie* 2000 JC 271; *Dickson* v. *HM Advocate* 2001 JC 203.
[296] *Cadder*, paras. 35–6, 38 and 70.

from the rule such as that set up by the 1995 Act.[297] The majority of those Member States which, prior to *Salduz*, did not afford a right to legal representation at interview – Belgium, France, Ireland and the Netherlands – had initiated reforms to their laws with a view to bringing their law into line with the precepts of the Convention.[298]

Did the Supreme Court have to follow *Salduz* – or could it instead go down the route of *Horncastle*? To answer this question, the Supreme Court took as its starting point section 2(1) of the HRA which, as stated above, provides that a court which is determining a question which has arisen in connection with a Convention right must 'take into account' any decision of the Strasbourg Court. The Supreme Court pointed out that 'the United Kingdom was not a party to the decision in *Salduz* nor did it seek to intervene in the proceedings'.[299] As, crucially, the Lord Justice General had observed in *McLean*,[300] the implications for Scots law could not be said to have been carefully considered. Had the *Cadder* court here been singing from the same hymn sheet as the *Horncastle* court, this would perhaps have settled the issue. But the Court went on instead to cite the words of Lord Slynn in *Alconbury*,[301] that the Court should follow any clear and constant jurisprudence of the Strasbourg Court, and Lord Bingham's exhortation in *R (Anderson)*,[302] that the Court will not without good reason depart from the principles laid down in a carefully considered judgment of the Strasbourg Court sitting as a Grand Chamber.[303] The Supreme Court then referred to *R v. Spear and Others*,[304] before going on to say:

> And in *R v. Horncastle* [2009] UKSC 14, [2010] 2 WLR 47 this court declined to follow a line of cases in the Strasbourg court culminating in a decision of the Fourth Section because, as Lord Phillips explained in para 107, its case law appeared to have been developed largely in cases relating to the civil law without full consideration of the safeguards against an unfair trial that exist under the common law procedure.[305]

As the Supreme Court said, *Salduz* was a unanimous decision of the Grand Chamber, in itself 'a formidable reason for thinking that we should follow it'.[306] Moreover, the judgment has been followed

---

[297] *Ibid.*, para. 41.   [298] *Ibid.*, para. 49.   [299] *Ibid.*, para. 45.
[300] *Her Majesty's Advocate v. McLean*, at [29].
[301] *R (Alconbury Developments Ltd) v. Secretary of State for the Environment, Transport and the Regions* [2001] UKHL 23; [2003] 2 AC 295, para. 26.
[302] *R (Anderson) v. Secretary of State for the Home Department* [2002] UKHL 46; [2003] 1 AC 837, para. 18.
[303] *Cadder*, para. 45.   [304] *R v. Spear*.   [305] *Cadder*, para. 45.   [306] *Ibid.*, para. 46.

repeatedly in subsequent cases.[307] There were, on the other hand, two judgments, one of them by the Grand Chamber, which 'should be noted',[308] presumably as they could handily have been used to make the point, if one were so inclined, that the Strasbourg jurisprudence was not all that 'clear and constant' after all. In *Gäfgen* v. *Germany*[309] Judge Rozakis and five others indicated in a dissent that in their opinion the approach of the Grand Chamber in *Gäfgen* was very difficult to reconcile with *Salduz*. After *Gäfgen*, the *Salduz* judgment was applied in the Chamber judgment, *Brusco* v. *France*.[310] On balance, therefore, it would have been conceivable – as conceivable as it was in *Horncastle* – to say in *Cadder* that the Strasbourg jurisprudence fell somewhat short of being 'clear and constant', and at all events that the Court had – as it had in *Horncastle* – 'concerns as to whether a decision of the Strasbourg Court sufficiently appreciates or accommodates particular aspects of our domestic process'.[311] This Lords Hope and Rodger, both former Presidents, or the most senior judge in Scotland, in their powerful judgments were not minded to do. The way in which they conceived of the question to be solved was markedly different from what the Court did in *Horncastle*. The practice of the Scottish system could not be saved by 'any guarantees otherwise in place there': 'There is no room … for, as it were, one rule for the countries in Eastern Europe such as Turkey on the one hand and those on its Western fringes such as Scotland on the other'.[312]

By approaching the system of the Convention rights not as though the relationship between Strasbourg and the Supreme Court were a bilateral one, but rather, conceiving of the ECHR scheme as an international system providing 'principled solutions that are universally applicable in all the contracting states', the Supreme Court in *Cadder* took an important step towards a universal approach, away from the exceptionalist approach on display in *Horncastle*.

---

[307] See the extensive list of Strasbourg authority marshalled in *ibid.*, para. 48.
[308] *Ibid.*, para. 46.
[309] ECtHR, *Gäfgen* v. *Germany* (Appl. No. 22978/05), Judgment (Grand Chamber), 1 June 2010, Reports 2010. See Bjorge, 'Ticking Bomb', at 196.
[310] ECtHR, *Brusco* v. *France* (Application No. 1466/07), Judgment (Fifth Section), 14 October 2010, not reported.
[311] *Horncastle*, para. 11. This was the approach in *Her Majesty's Advocate* v. *McLean*, para. 29.
[312] *Cadder*, para. 40.

3. Margin of appreciation and possible ways of minimising the effects of ECHR law

In terms of the system of the ECHR, the margin of appreciation is mostly a term encountered on the European as opposed to the national level. There is good reason for this. As discussed in section 1. above, the Strasbourg Court in *A v. United Kingdom* in 2009 held the doctrine of the margin of appreciation has always been intended as a tool to define relations between the domestic authorities and the Court; '[i]t cannot have the same application to the relations between the organs of State at the domestic level'.[313]

Before the Strasbourg Court handed down *A*, there was much debate in UK law about the margin of appreciation. The 2007 judgment, *In re G*, is apposite here. The judgment has been called in scholarly commentary a significant decision.[314] It suggests an exception to the common law *Ullah* rule in cases regarding margin of appreciation. The House of Lords had said in *Ullah*:

> It is of course open to member states to provide for rights more generous than those guaranteed by the Convention, but such provision should not be the product of interpretation of the Convention by national courts, since the meaning of the Convention should be uniform throughout the states party to it. The duty of national courts is to keep pace with the Strasbourg jurisprudence as it evolves over time: no more, but certainly no less.[315]

This was the backdrop to *In re G*. The claimants, an unmarried heterosexual couple, lived in Northern Ireland, whose statutory regulation of adoption, enacted as secondary legislation,[316] prevented courts making an adoption order in favour of an unmarried couple. They argued that this violated their right to be free of discrimination, taken together with their right to respect for family life under articles 8 and 14 of the ECHR. Though the Strasbourg Court had not decided whether denying an unmarried heterosexual couple the opportunity to adopt violated article 14, the Grand Chamber in *EB v. France* had held that preventing adoption by a lesbian, whose partner was loath to take on any responsibility for the child, lay outside the state's margin of appreciation in the case at issue.[317]

---

[313] *A v. United Kingdom*, para. 184.
[314] J. Herring, 'Who Decides on Human Rights?', *Law Quarterly Review* 125 (2009) 1–5, at 1.
[315] *R (Ullah) v. Special Adjudicator* [2004] UKHL 26; [2004] 2 AC 323, at para. 20.
[316] Adoption (Northern Ireland) Order 1987 (SI 1987/2203 (NI 22)), art. 14.
[317] ECtHR, *EB v. France* (Appl. No. 43546/02), Judgment (Grand Chamber), 22 January 2008, not reported.

Lord Walker's dissent represents what one might have been predicted would be the response of the House of Lords to the question raised by the case. His conclusion was that it would be wrong for the House of Lords to amend or invalidate the Order; he wanted instead to defer the issue to the Northern Ireland Assembly, for which he gave three reasons.

First, he noted that the Strasbourg Court had not provided a definitive ruling on the issue. Pointing out that the issue of adoption by unmarried couples was a fraught one, he adverted to the European Convention on the Adoption of Children, which does not require states to allow unmarried couples to adopt. This led him to conclude that it was most likely that the Strasbourg Court would not find a bar on unmarried couples adopting to run counter to the ECHR. Second, he stated that, given the controversial nature of the issue, 'the decision to be made is one that ought to be made by a democratically-elected legislature'.[318] Third, he described the issuing of a declaration that the courts not give effect to the order as a 'blunt instrument', as it would make the law unclear.[319] The majority was not swayed by the weight of these arguments.

Taking as its starting point that section 6 HRA, which provides that a public authority must not act in a way which is incompatible with a Convention right applies for the courts, the majority of the House found that it was required under section 6(1) to apply the secondary legislation in a way which was compatible with Convention rights. If the secondary legislation could not be interpreted in a way compatible with the ECHR, national courts were not to apply it.

The next issue was to determine whether the Order did, in fact, breach Convention rights. The majority all agreed that it did, though for various reasons. Disagreement arose over whether preventing unmarried couples from adopting amounted to unjustifiable discrimination against them for the purposes of article 14. Their Lordships were in agreement that there was no definitive Strasbourg ruling on the issue. Lord Hoffmann, Lord Mance and Lord Hope decided that Strasbourg jurisprudence indicated that the ECHR prohibited such discrimination. On this point Baroness Hale disagreed, believing that it was unclear how the issue would be decided – though thinking it quite possible that the issue would be deemed to be one within the state's margin of appreciation. On Baroness Hale's account, the Strasbourg Court would therefore not find the provision unjustifiably discriminatory. Though she thought the matter would

---

[318] *In re G (Adoption: Unmarried Couple)* [UKHL] 38; [2008] 3 WLR 76, para. 82.
[319] Ibid.

have been found to be within the margin of appreciation, this in her view did not bar a UK court from interpreting the Convention for itself. She therefore, and interestingly, took the view that for the purposes of UK law – though this might pan out differently in Strasbourg – the Order was discriminatory on the grounds of marital status. Lord Hoffmann, Lord Mance and Lord Hope took the view that if Baroness Hale's account of how the Strasbourg Court would deal with the question was correct, they would follow her approach and hold that the UK should find the law in breach of the Convention rights of the applicant.

On the final issue, whether the discrimination was justified or not, the majority were unanimous in finding it was not. It was the bright-line character of the rule, devoid of any recourse to notions of proportionality, which made the rule unjustifiable. Lord Hoffmann said:

> Even if the court considers that an applicant couple pass all these tests – that adoption by them is plainly in the best interests of the child, that the child wishes to be adopted, that their relationship is loving, stable and harmonious – ...the court is bound to refuse the order and take a course which, ex hypothesi, is not in the best interests of the child on the sole ground that the applicants are not married.[320]

Addressing four-square the possibility of their Lordships going further than the Strasbourg Court, Lord Hoffmann said that it was true that Lord Bingham in *Ullah* said that the 'duty of national courts is to keep pace with the Strasbourg jurisprudence as it evolves over time: no more, but certainly no less',[321] but then went on to say that Lord Bingham's remarks were not, however, made in the context of a case in which the Strasbourg Court has declared a question to be within the national margin of appreciation. That means that the question is one for the national authorities to decide for themselves, and it follows that different member states may well give different answers.[322]

> Where the Strasbourg Court has declared something to be within the margin of appreciation, therefore, it would be for the court in the United Kingdom to interpret articles 8 and 14 and to apply the division between the decision-making powers of courts and parliament in the way which appears appropriate for the United Kingdom ... It follows, my Lords, that the House is free to give, in the interpretation of the 1998 Act, what it considers to be a principled and rational interpretation to the concept of discrimination on grounds of marital status.[323]

[320] *Ibid.*, para. 11.   [321] *Ibid.*, para. 30.   [322] *Ibid.*, para. 31.
[323] *Ibid.*, paras. 37–8.

The majority concluded that the Order could not be applied; unmarried couples in Northern Ireland could be considered as potential adopters. What the Supreme Court did was to say that in this type of case, a case in which if the question had reached the Strasbourg Court, that court could conceivably have ended up saying that the national court would have had to be accorded a wide margin of appreciation on the issue, there must be room for the national court to go further in its rights protection than the Strasbourg Court. Perhaps one has to see *In re G* in light of the importance which the *Ullah* principle has enjoyed in UK law since 2004. In its ruling in *In re G*, the House of Lords gave an example of an exception to the *Ullah* doctrine, by saying that national courts in cases such as *In re G* were not bound not to go further than had the Strasbourg Court.

Also, after *In re G*, the question has arisen as to how UK courts should deal with issues under the Convention not explicitly resolved in the jurisprudence of the Strasbourg Court. In *Ambrose v. Harris*[324] there were two opposing views. One was that UK courts should not go where Strasbourg has not yet gone. The other view was that UK courts must seek to give full effect to Convention rights even if not pronounced upon by Strasbourg.

Lord Bingham of Cornhill's approach to the jurisprudence of the European Court in *Ullah* has become the orthodox view of the UK courts:

> It is of course open to member states to provide for rights more generous than those guaranteed by the Convention, but such provision should not be the product of interpretation of the Convention by national courts, since the meaning of the Convention should be uniform throughout the states party to it. The duty of national courts is to keep pace with the Strasbourg jurisprudence as it evolves over time: no more, but certainly no less.[325]

The issues in *Ambrose* were, first, whether the right of access to a lawyer prior to police questioning, which had been established in *Salduz*, applied only to questioning which takes place when the person had been taken into police custody. Second, if the right to a lawyer applies at some earlier stage, what is the moment from which the rule applies? The evidence in *Ambrose* itself (the first of conjoined cases) had been obtained before Mr. Ambrose was taken to the police station for further procedures to be carried out under section 7 of the Road Traffic Act 1988 following his failure of a roadside breath test, and in the two other, anonymised, cases,

---

[324] *Ambrose v. Harris* [2011] UKSC 43; [2011] 1 WLR 2435.   [325] *R (Ullah)*, para. 20.

before the defendants were detained and questioned at a police station under section 14 of the Criminal Procedure (Scotland) Act 1995.

In *Salduz*, the Grand Chamber of the Strasbourg Court had set out the following feature triggering the right to legal advice under article 6:

> The rights of the defence will in principle be irretrievably prejudiced when incriminating statements made during police interrogation without access to a lawyer are used for a conviction.[326]

Lord Hope of Craighead, with whom Lord Brown, Lord Dyson and Lord Matthew Clarke agreed, ruled that there was in the Strasbourg jurisprudence no rule according to which a person had a Convention right of access to a lawyer before answering any questions put to him in the course of a police search. The consequences of such a ruling would be profound, 'as the answers to police questioning in such circumstances would always have to be held – in the absence of compelling reasons for restricting access to a lawyer – to be inadmissible'. For that reason, '[i]f Strasbourg has not yet spoken clearly enough on this issue, the wiser course must surely be to wait until it has done so'.[327] Lord Hope referred here to Lord Bingham's famous dictum in *Ullah*.

On Lord Dyson's view, too, there was no sufficiently clear indication in the Strasbourg jurisprudence of how the Court would resolve the question. The obligation in section 2 of the HRA to take account of rulings of the Court did not compel a decision one way or the other. He went on to say that nor was this the case where, although the Court has not expressly decided the point, it can nevertheless clearly be deduced or inferred from decisions of the Court how it will decide the point if and when it falls to be determined. 'But', said Lord Dyson, 'these statements are not entirely apposite where Strasbourg has spoken on an issue, but there is no clear and constant line of authority.'[328] Lord Dyson accepted that it was arguable that the language of [55] in *Salduz* can and should be interpreted as holding that the *Salduz* principle does apply in such circumstances. In the end, however, he found that the Supreme Court must hold that the *Salduz* principle is confined to statements made by suspects detained or otherwise deprived of their freedom in any significant way. He considered that caution was particularly apposite, and that the Supreme Court should remind itself that 'there exists a supranational court whose purpose is to give authoritative and Europe-wide rulings on the Convention'.[329]

---

[326] *Salduz v. Turkey*, para. 55.   [327] *Ambrose v. Harris*, para. 15.   [328] *Ibid.*, para. 102.
[329] *Ibid.*, para. 105.

Lord Kerr dissented. In his view, article 6 of the ECHR was engaged in each of the respondents' cases at the time that the relevant questions were asked. Whereas the majority would admit the answers to police questioning in such circumstances, on Lord Kerr's view, the answers should be inadmissible. He, too, gave much attention to the *Ullah* principle. In keeping with this principle and its usages, said Lord Kerr, some judges in the UK have evinced what he termed '*Ullah*-type reticence':

> On the basis of this, it is not only considered wrong to attempt to anticipate developments at the supra national level of the Strasbourg court, but there is also the view that we should not go where Strasbourg has not yet gone.[330]

Lord Kerr went on to explain his view of the provenance of Lord Bingham's *Ullah* dictum. Lord Bingham's formulation of the principle which he expressed in *Ullah* had been prompted by consideration of the effect of section 2 of the HRA by which the courts of the UK are enjoined to take into account Strasbourg jurisprudence:

> I greatly doubt that Lord Bingham contemplated – much less intended – that his discussion of this issue should have the effect of acting as an inhibitor on courts of this country giving full effect to Convention rights unless they have been pronounced upon by Strasbourg.[331]

Where there was no clear and direct ruling by the Court, it was not open to the UK courts to adopt an attitude of agnosticism and refrain from giving effect to such a right, simply because the Court had not spoken. Lord Kerr gave three reasons. First, that it is to be expected, and hoped, that not all debates about the ambit of Convention rights would be resolved by the Court. As a practical reality it was inevitable, he said, that many claims to Convention rights should fall to be determined by courts at every level in the United Kingdom without the benefit of unequivocal jurisprudence from the Court.

Lord Kerr's second reason was the Supreme Court's duty to address those issues when they arise, whether or not authoritative guidance from the Court should be available. It was therefore, he said, the duty of this and every court not only to ascertain 'where the jurisprudence of the Strasbourg court clearly shows that it currently stands' but to resolve the question of whether a claim to a Convention right is viable or not, even where the jurisprudence of the Strasbourg Court does not disclose a clear current view.[332]

---

[330] *Ibid.*, para. 126.   [331] *Ibid.*, para. 128.   [332] *Ibid.*, para. 129.

Lord Kerr's third reason was that section 6 of the HRA leaves no alternative to courts called upon to adjudicate on claims made by litigants to a Convention right. This section makes it unlawful for a public authority, including a court, he said, to act in a way which is incompatible with a Convention right. In order to be effective, that statutory obligation must carry with it the requirement that the court in issue determine if the Convention right has the effect claimed for, he continued, whether or not the Court has pronounced upon it. He concluded:

> If the much vaunted dialogue between national courts and Strasbourg is to mean anything, we should surely not feel inhibited from saying what we believe Strasbourg ought to find in relation to those arguments. ... I consider that not only is it open to this court to address and deal with those arguments on their merits, it is our duty to do so.[333]

One way of testing the different approaches in *Ambrose* is to use them on the facts of *Ullah*. The question in *Ullah* was whether a decision to remove two asylum seekers could be challenged on the basis of the right to freedom of religion under article 9 of the Convention. Strasbourg had not yet explicitly spoken on the issue of whether a claim could be based on the threat of religious persecution in the home country. In *Ullah* there was no one Strasbourg case which four-square had settled the issue; the House of Lords had to rely on, and did in fact rely on, the principles developed in the Strasbourg jurisprudence. If one had applied in *Ullah* Lord Hope's approach in *Ambrose*, 'to wait until it has done so', only one outcome would have been possible; no claim could then have been based on article 9.

Lord Bingham, and a unanimous House of Lords, came to the opposite result in *Ullah*; they did not wait until Strasbourg had pronounced on the issue in a way that explicitly resolved it. In the paragraph after the one in which he set out the *Ullah* approach of 'no more, but certainly no less', Lord Bingham said that he found it hard to think that a person could successfully resist expulsion in reliance on article 9 (freedom of religion) without being entitled either to asylum on the ground of a well-founded fear of being persecuted for reasons of religion or personal opinion or to resist expulsion in reliance on article 3 (on torture and degrading and inhuman treatment).[334]

Lord Bingham would nonetheless not rule out such a possibility 'in principle unless the Strasbourg court has clearly done so, and I am not

---
[333] *Ibid.*, para. 130. [334] *R (Ullah)*, para. 21.

sure it has'.³³⁵ So a right to resist expulsion based on article 9 could not be ruled out. Lord Steyn and Lord Carswell in their concurring speeches repeated the point that one could not be sure the Court clearly had ruled out an article 9 right. Certainty and clarity were used here in support of the existence of a right, and not, as in Lord Hope's argument in *Ambrose*, the reverse. In the event, the claimants in *Ullah* did not satisfy the high threshold that would apply under an article 9 right, and their appeals failed.

Lord Hope's 'wiser course' in *Ambrose* would have ruled out the possibility of an article 9 claim, in direct contradiction of Lord Bingham and the House of Lords in *Ullah*. Lord Kerr's approach would not have barred the ruling of the unanimous House in *Ullah*.

Lord Kerr's approach in *Ambrose* conforms with the approach of the House of Lords in *Ullah* and subsequent jurisprudence. In *Secretary of State for the Home Department* v. *JJ and Others*, Lord Bingham, with whom a majority of the House of Lords agreed, held that in cases where there is no ruling from the European court to settle a matter:

> It is inappropriate to seek to align this case with the least dissimilar of the reported cases. The task of the English courts is to seek to give fair effect, on the facts of this case, to the principles which the Strasbourg court has laid down.³³⁶

Lord Bingham developed this principled approach further in the last article he had occasion to write, where he said that the task of the courts in cases such as these is 'to ascertain the true governing principle and apply it'.³³⁷

Lord Hope in *Ambrose* seems to have read down the approach of 'no more, but certainly no less' and, if one looks at what the House of Lords actually did in *Ullah*, also to have read into it terms that limit its purpose. Lord Kerr's opinion represents a more principled approach to the Convention rights; it is also one which is more in line with *Ullah*. The middle ground represented by Lord Dyson's opinion is closer to this approach; Lord Kerr and Lord Dyson agree that waiting for the Court to rule on the

---

³³⁵ *Ibid.*
³³⁶ *Secretary of State for the Home Department* v. *JJ and others* [2007] UKHL 45; [2008] AC 385, para. 19.
³³⁷ T. Bingham, *Lives of the Law: Selected Essays and Speeches 2000–2010* (Oxford University Press, 2011), at 183. See also B. Kerr, 'The UK Supreme Court: The Modest Underworker of Strasbourg?', at www.supremecourt.gov.uk/doc5/speech_120125.pdf (25 January 2012).

specific issue is not a good option. The different positions set out in *Ambrose* reflect different views in the judiciary, and not only the judicial process, but a continuously changing political landscape. It is not surprising that there are still creases to be ironed out.

The ordinary law of tort does not recognise or compensate the anguish suffered by parents who are deprived of the life of their adult child. Does human rights law provide a remedy? Article 2 of the Convention states: 'Everyone's right to life shall be protected by law.' In two judgments, first the UK Supreme Court and then the Strasbourg Court ruled on the breach of the state's duty to protect life under article 2. This issue is illustrated in a recent judgment from the UK Supreme Court, *Rabone*,[338] and a recent judgment from the Strasbourg Court, *Reynolds*.[339] These two cases clearly bring out what is today the nature of the relationship between the UK courts and the Strasbourg Court. Melanie Rabone (24), who suffered from a depressive disorder, had hanged herself from a tree while on home leave from hospital. David Reynolds (35), who had been diagnosed with schizophrenia, broke a window in his hospital room and had fallen from the sixth floor to his death. The hospitals in both instances admitted to negligence, but the ordinary law of tort left the parents of Melanie and David without any cause of action. The hospitals denied liability under the HRA, which offered such a cause of action.

Judgment in *Rabone* was delivered just over a month before *Reynolds*. Both judgments are unanimous. The omissions by the psychiatric hospitals to take appropriate steps to prevent the suicide of a voluntary patient were in breach of article 2. The parents had a right to compensation. Lord Dyson's impressive lead judgment in *Rabone* irons out several creases in tort law and human rights law. The judgments can best be understood in the background of Lady Hale's lament in *Rabone*:

> In this day and age we all expect our children to outlive us. Losing a child prematurely is agony. No-one who reads the hospital's notes of the series of telephone calls made by this patient's father to the hospital on the night in question can be in any doubt of that; or that the agony may be made worse by knowing that the loss both could and should have been prevented.[340]

---

[338] *Rabone and Another v. Pennine Care NHS Foundation Trust* [2012] UKSC 2.
[339] ECtHR, *Reynolds v. The United Kingdom* (Appl. No. 2694/08), Judgment (Fourth Section), 13 March 2012, not reported.
[340] *Rabone*, para. 92.

She adds that it is not surprising that parents are recognised as 'victims' of violations of the right to life of their child under article 2 ECHR, including the failure effectively to protect their child's life. Lord Walker and Lord Brown, who often can be relied on to hold back against the extension of tort liability, expressly supported Lady Hale's Concurring Judgment.

In *Rabone*, a unanimous Supreme Court provided a clearer answer to the question of how UK courts should deal with issues under the Convention not explicitly resolved in the jurisprudence of the Court. Under the Convention, the Court has supervisory functions. Article 1 provides that states 'shall secure to everyone within their jurisdiction the rights and freedoms defined in Section I of this Convention'. Article 13 requires the right to an effective remedy before a national authority. The role of the Court is provided for in article 35(1), it 'may only deal with the matter after all domestic remedies have been exhausted'.

Kudla v. Poland[341] is one of many judgments in which the Court has emphasised how the primary responsibility for implementing and enforcing the guaranteed rights and freedoms rests on the national authorities: 'The machinery of complaint to the Court is thus subsidiary to national systems safeguarding human rights.' The Court further explained that the purpose of Article 35 is to afford the Contracting States the opportunity of preventing or putting right the violations alleged against them before those allegations are submitted to the Court. The object of Article 13, as emerges from the *travaux préparatoires*, is to provide a means whereby individuals can obtain relief at national level for violations of their Convention rights before having to set in motion the international machinery of complaint before the Court.[342]

In the UK, sections 3, 4 and 6 of the HRA 1998 give effect to 'the Convention rights'. It is unlawful for public authorities, including courts, to act in a way which is incompatible with one of the enumerated Convention rights. Legislation shall be applied in a way which is compatible with Convention rights; if this is not possible, courts may make a declaration of incompatibility. Section 2 provides that in interpreting Convention rights, a court 'must take into account any' of four categories of sources, including any 'judgment, decision, declaration or advisory opinion of the European Court of Human Rights', 'whenever made or

---

[341] ECtHR, *Kudla v. Poland* (Appl. No. 30210/96), Judgment (Grand Chamber), 26 October 2000, Reports 2000-XI.
[342] *Ibid.*, para. 152.

given, so far as, in the opinion of the court or tribunal, it is relevant to the proceedings in which that question has arisen'.

Some judges, including Lord Brown in *Al-Skeini*, had reversed the order of words, attempting to invert the approach, by moving the 'certainly' in front of the 'more', and away from the 'no less', emphasising the 'no more'.[343] *Al-Skeini* was, predictably, overturned when it reached the Court.[344] That reversal of words also inverts the subsidiarity principle of the Convention and the HRA. The Court would not remain a supervisory mechanism, subsidiary to national systems safeguarding human rights. The national systems would become subsidiary. National courts and other authorities should wait for the Court to interpret the Convention. In yet other versions, they could wait until there was a judgment from the Court's Grand Chamber, or even for a judgment that the national judge would hold to be sufficiently clear.

In *Rabone*, the Supreme Court took the responsibility of interpreting the Convention. Liability under article 2 would not have been possible if the Supreme Court had relied on the 'certainly no more' approach. The lead judgment of Lord Dyson, and the concurring judgments of Lady Hale and Lord Mance, show how untenable these inverted approaches had become. This is brought into even sharper relief by the Court's judgment in *Reynolds* v. *The United Kingdom*, with similar facts and the same conclusions. The Court in *Reynolds* could build upon and confirm *Rabone*, but had the Supreme Court gone the other way and refused liability, the interpretation of article 2 in such an alternative judgment would have been overturned by *Reynolds*.

Lady Hale's lament is prefaced by her explanation for why 'we are here'. It is 'because the ordinary law of tort does not recognise or compensate the anguish suffered by parents who are deprived of the life of their adult child'. In his judgment, Lord Brown adds to that explanation that if a domestic court is 'content (perhaps even ready and willing) to decide a Convention challenge against a public authority and believes such a conclusion to flow naturally from existing Strasbourg case law (albeit that it could be regarded as carrying the case law a step further), then in my judgment it should take that further step. And that, indeed, is to my mind precisely the position in this very case.'

---

[343] *R (Al-Skeini)* v. *Secretary of State for Defence* [2008] AC 153, para. 106.
[344] ECtHR, *Al-Skeini* v. *United Kingdom* (Appl. No. 55721/07), Judgment (Grand Chamber), 11 July 2011, Reports 2011.

The hospitals in both instances had admitted to negligence, but the ordinary law of tort left the parents of Melanie and David without any cause of action. Mr. Rabone had accepted an amount (for funeral expenses and the balance as general damages for Melanie's pain and suffering during the two-month period before she died) in settlement of the negligence claim, which had been based on the Law Reform (Miscellaneous Provisions) Act 1934. Mr. and Mrs. Rabone had no cause of action, because section 1A of the Fatal Accidents Act 1976 provides that a claim by parents for damages for bereavement for the loss of a child (currently fixed by section 1A(3) at £11,800) shall only be for the benefit of the parents of a minor, and Melanie had been over 18. Having established breach of article 2, the Supreme Court ruled that this did not constitute adequate redress under article 13 or precluded the claim in any other way (at [63]). In establishing breach of article 2, the Supreme Court had to go 'rather further than the evolving jurisprudence of the European Court of Human Rights has yet clearly established to be required', as Lord Brown states in his Concurring Judgment.[345]

A positive duty to protect life in certain circumstances deriving from article 2 was articulated in *Osman*.[346] There is a general duty on the state 'to put in place a legislative and administrative framework designed to provide effective deterrence against threats to the right to life'. There is also an 'operational duty'. The failure of the police to protect the Osman family from threats and harassment from a third party culminated in the murder of Mr. Osman and the wounding of his son. The Court said in *Osman* that in 'well-defined circumstances' the state should take 'appropriate steps' to safeguard the lives of those within its jurisdiction, including a positive obligation to take 'preventative operational measures' to protect an individual whose life is at risk from the criminal acts of another.[347]

The Court had identified other circumstances in which the operational duty may apply. Lord Dyson explained that the Strasbourg jurisprudence showed that there is such a duty to protect persons from a real and immediate risk of suicide, at least, where they are under the control of the state. This duty would include a detained patient, and there was no suggestion that the operational obligation to prevent suicide is limited

---

[345] *Rabone*, para. 111.
[346] ECtHR, *Osman v. United Kingdom* (Appl. No. 23452/94), Judgment (Grand Chamber), 28 October 1998, Reports 1998-VIII.
[347] *Ibid.*, at para. 115.

to prisoners and detainees. But in the generality of cases involving medical negligence, there is no operational duty under article 2.

Lord Dyson concluded that there was no doubt that there was an operational duty in the case to take reasonable steps to protect Melanie Rabone from the real and immediate risk of suicide. Melanie had been admitted to hospital precisely because of the risk that she would take her own life. Voluntary patients at risk from suicide would often take medication which would compromise the ability to make an informed decision, were likely to be detained if they attempted to leave, and may have consented to hospital treatment to avoid detention. It was not meaningful to treat Melanie any differently from detained or involuntary patients. The operational duty had been broken, and the parents were victims of this violation. Lord Dyson, Lady Hale and Lord Mance, in clear and carefully reasoned judgments, contributed to the development of the tort remedies in a way the case required. In doing so, they also clarified the relationship between national courts and the Strasbourg Court in a judgment which will no doubt stand as an authority for a long time.

4. Conclusion

The implementation of the ECHR into national law has been led by the work of national judges; as Alec Stone Sweet and Helen Keller have said, 'courts have taken the lead in incorporating the Convention'.[348] This chapter has brought out not only the relationship between on the one hand a national court, and the Strasbourg Court on the other. Instead, the point has been to look at the relationship between national courts as they relate to the Strasbourg Court. Such an approach is also in keeping with the reflection by the President of the Federal Constitutional Court, Andreas Voßkuhle, that the effects of internationalisation and Europeanisation have given the vocation of comparative constitutional law 'eine neue quantitative und qualitative Dimension'.[349]

With respect to the evolution of rights under the Convention, it is becoming clear that European courts not only accept that they must

---

[348] Stone Sweet, 'Assessing the Impact', at 687.
[349] A. Voßkuhle, 'Europa als Gegenstand wissenschaftlicher Reflexion – eine thematische Annäherung in 12 Thesen', C. Fanzius et al. (eds.), Strukturfragen der Europäischen Union 37–45, at 44–5. See also J.L. Halperin, Les mondialisations du droit (Paris: Dalloz, 2009). These new dimensions are plain from the approach taken in B. Strin, Vers un droit public européenne (Paris: Monchrestion, 2012).

follow the development of the ECHR as interpreted by the Strasbourg Court; they also take a lead in developing the rights. As we have seen, Belgian, French, Italian, Norwegian and UK rights have gone far in this regard. This is very strong testimony to how far many national courts have gone in the implementation. If one is effectively more Strasbourgeois than Strasbourg, interpreting the Convention as having higher standards than the Strasbourg Court has said, then that must be the sign of successful domestication and implementation of Convention rights. This happens in different ways, the Belgian Constitutional Court conceiving of what it is doing as an application of article 53, the Czech Constitutional Court seeing the matter as one of 'teleological interpretation', both of the Czech Charter and of Convention rights. As the Italian jurisprudence shows, Italian judges are moving in the direction of giving the Convention constitutional value and have also gone beyond the interpretations of Strasbourg in the context of article 6. Such locks in Italian law as there have been, structural or interpretative, are being done away with. In Russia, the judges have gone far in implementing the ECHR, though not in any case as far, for example, as the Belgian or French judges. The picture with respect to proportionality gives the same impression. The UK, German, French, Czech and Russian judges have gone very far in implementing the proportionality test into national law. Such differences as persist are largely functions of the respective traits of the rights-protection traditions in the different jurisdictions. The margin of appreciation, though one of the defining features of the scheme of the ECHR, does not have any application nationally. In the UK it has, however, been used in order to develop rights. This leads us to our concluding point.

The Strasbourg Court held in 1998 in its decision in *Osman v. United Kingdom*[350] that English law on tort liability for the police was not in conformity with the Convention rights. The Court considered that English law provided an immunity against liability for police negligence in operational decisions. *Osman* provoked a strongly critical reaction from, among others, two House of Lords justices, Lords Browne-Wilkinson and Hoffmann.[351] A.W. Brian Simpson analysed the British reception of

---

[350] *Osman v. United Kingdom*.
[351] See generally, A.W.B. Simpson, *Human Rights and the End of Empire: Britain and the Genesis of the European Convention* (Oxford University Press, 2001), at 7–8. See for criticism of the decision, *Barrett v. Enfield LBC* [2001] 2 AC 550 (Lord Browne-Wilkinson); Lord Hoffmann, 'Human Rights and the House of Lords', *Modern Law Review* 62 (1999) 159–66.

Osman. He pointed out that the hostility to the adverse Strasbourg ruling arose because of difficulty in adjusting to the existence of a superior European body of law, developed by a court whose members mostly come from alien legal cultures, and which can be driven by concerns which do not seem important from an insular British perspective. He continued:

> None of the English critics of *Osman* adopted a European perspective, or seemed aware of the importance of establishing police accountability in many of the countries now governed by the convention, where the history of policing is not happy.[352]

This very nicely brings out what we believe must be the right perspective on the Convention: a perspective which sees a national court not in a bilateral relationship to the Strasbourg Court, but, rather, in a multilateral relationship with the other national courts as well as the Strasbourg Court.

The *M* saga is a case in point here. On 7–8 February 2011 the *Bundesverfassungsgericht* heard a constitutional complaint by M. During the hearings, President Andreas Voßkuhle criticised the authorities for not having followed sufficiently closely what the *Bundesverfassungsgericht* said in its 2004 ruling on the preventive detention scheme.[353] Yet the German Constitutional Court in *Preventive Detention* found a solution which was satisfactory, both in terms of national constitutional law and in terms of the Strasbourg Court's ruling in *M* – clearly complying with the latter.

This was also the only solution capable of being universalised. It stands to reason that if the German court had decided not to follow Strasbourg, then other European courts, with less happy histories of rights protection than the *Bundesverfassungsgericht*, could interpret this as carte blanche not to follow the decisions of Strasbourg. If the German courts can turn a blind eye to what Strasbourg says about M's detention in *M* v. *Germany*,[354] then surely the Russian courts could have done the same with regard to Mikhail Khodorkovsky's detention in *Yukos* v. *Russia*?[355] For the ECHR system to work, the national courts must interact with Strasbourg only in ways which are capable of being universalised and also applied by other European courts. This was well summarised by Lord Neuberger of Abbotsbury MR, who in 2011 made the point that:

---

[352] Simpson, *Human Rights*, at 7–8.
[353] 2 BvR 2029/01. See, for example, 'Gratwanderung in Karlsruhe', *Zeit Online*, 8 February 2011, http://pdf.zeit.de/politik/deutschland/2011-02/sicherungsverwahrung-verfassungsgericht.pdf.
[354] *M* v. *Germany*.   [355] *OAO Neftyanaya Kompaniya Yukos* v. *Russia*.

The Strasbourg court is in the unenviable position of having to decide human rights law across over 45 countries, ranging from mature free societies to the not so free. It is important that the court ensures that there is consistency across all countries. However, it is sometimes hard for one country, with its different standards and conditions, to accept a decision which is plainly right for another country. We may think that it is inappropriate that Strasbourg pokes its nose into the votes for prisoners issue on the basis that it should be left to our Parliament to decide. However, if Strasbourg said votes for criminals was a matter for national legislatures, it may be that a dictator might see this as a green light to depriving his enemies of the vote by trumping up charges to bring against them. It may be thought to be a small price to pay for a civilised Europe that we sometimes have to adapt our laws a little.[356]

---

[356] Lord Neuberger MR, 'Who are the Masters now? Second Lord Alexander of Weedon Lecture', www.judiciary.gov.uk/Resources/JCO/Documents/Speeches/mr-speech-weedon-lecture-110406.pdf.

7

The Court as a part of the Council of Europe: the Parliamentary Assembly and the Committee of Ministers

ELISABETH LAMBERT-ABDELGAWAD

The aim of this chapter is to consider the relationship between the European Court of Human Rights (ECtHR, the Court), and the Parliamentary Assembly (the PACE, the Assembly) and Committee of Ministers (the CoM), the two main organs of the Council of Europe, and to analyse the impact of these relationships on the functioning and the evolution of the Court. These relationships encompass three main issues: (1) the election of the judges, (2) the implementation of the judgments, and (3) the budget of the Court. This chapter will detail these three issues and focus on the recent evolutions and present and future reforms. The question of the adequacy and effectiveness of these relationships will also be considered, as well as the possible competition between these three actors. Among the guiding principles in this book, the implied powers principle and the principle of effectiveness are of particular relevance. We will demonstrate that both of these principles, and in particular the latter, have been used by the Court to extend its functions beyond its classic judicial role in relation to other European organs. This also means that the constitutional function of the Court in relation to the two other bodies comes into play.

Historically, the general approach was that the judicial function of the Court was restricted to deciding whether or not the European Convention on Human Rights (ECHR) had been breached by a State party. This Montesquieuian understanding of the judicial function has often been referred to as the *jus dicere* role of the Court. Thus, there was a general understanding that the implementation of the judgments was not part of this judicial function and was the sole responsibility of the CoM. This is why the relationships between the Court and the two other organs, the PACE and the CoM, used to be nearly non-existent. This approach was eventually put into question, as it considerably limited the role of the

Court. At the same time, and for more than 20 years, the PACE has had the ambition to play a role in the implementation of some of the judgments of the Court. The PACE is also the main organ responsible for the election of judges and the budget of the Council of Europe. Consequently, as the Court now has the ambition to go beyond its '*jus dicere*' function (*stricto sensu*), the relationship with the PACE and the CoM have to be seen in a different light. What is also noticeable is that the relationships of the Court with the Assembly on the one hand, and with the CoM on the other hand, have always been thought about differently. While there seems to have been a great distrust towards the PACE by the Court, the CoM has benefited from a privileged relationship with the Court.

The topic is therefore fundamentally linked to the role the Court wants to play in Europe. Indeed, there has always been a clash between judges, politicians and scholars, as some want the Court to limit itself to the role it played until the 1990s, while others would like to pave the way for a constitutional Court.

1. The election of judges to the ECtHR

'The election of judges is one of the few powers that the Parliamentary Assembly enjoys and this role is therefore jealously guarded.'[1] Indeed, 'even in the most open and democratic societies, judges are usually chosen by an overtly political process, often involving appointment by an executive, then confirmation by a legislative body.'[2] The judges of the ECtHR, who 'shall be of high moral character and must either possess the qualifications required for appointment to high judicial office or be jurisconsults of recognised competence' (article 21, para. 1), 'shall be elected by the Parliamentary Assembly with respect to each High Contracting Party by a majority of votes cast from a list of three candidates nominated by the High Contracting Party' (article 22).

The CoM has not officially been involved in this process. Even if it was envisaged in 1949 that judges be elected by a single or an absolute

---

[1] J. Limbach *et al.*, *Judicial Independence: Law and Practice of Appointments to the European Court of Human Rights* (Interights, 2003), at 23 (hereinafter Limbach *et al.*, *Judicial Independence*). A. Coomber, 'Judicial Independence: Law and Practice of Appointments to the European Court of Human Rights', *European Human Rights Law Review* 5 (2003) 486–500, at 496 (hereinafter Coomber, 'Judicial Independence').

[2] D. Terris *et al.* (eds.), *The International Judge: An Introduction to the Men and Women who Decide the World's Cases* (Oxford University Press, International Courts and Tribunal Series, 2007), at 148.

majority of votes in the Assembly and in the CoM, each body voting independently,[3] a practice has emerged where the list is first controlled by the Directorate General for Human Rights[4] and is then transmitted to the CoM, which sends it unchanged to the PACE.[5] The role of the CoM would be eventually to reject unacceptable lists, but in practice this has not been the case.[6] An *ad hoc* group of the CoM engages in an 'informal exchange of views on such candidates before the lists are formally transmitted to the CoM for transmission to the Parliamentary Assembly'.[7] According to this mechanism established in 1997, 'it is understood that the results of this exchange of views would neither bind governments, who would retain the right to present candidates of their choosing, nor interfere with the PACE's function of electing judges from the lists provided'.[8]

We will see that the role of the Panel Experts set up in January 2011 is similar to the one formerly exercised by the CoM.

As was stated by the PACE itself: '7. The authority of the Court is contingent on the stature of judges and the quality and coherence of the Court's case law.'[9] The crux of the matter is also linked to the fact

---

[3] Historically, 'the intention was that both the Parliamentary Assembly and the Committee of Ministers would participate in the election', see J. Hedigan, 'The Election of Judges to the European Court of Human Rights', in M. G. Kohen (ed.), *Promoting Justice, Human Rights and Conflict Resolution through International Law: Liber Amicorum Lucius Caflish* (Leiden and Boston: Brill, 2007) 235–53, 235. Limbach *et al.*, *Judicial Independence*, paras. 8–9, at 7–8. Yet, consider Coomber, 'Judicial Independence', at 8: 'With no explanation, that draft that was ultimately adopted omitted reference to the CoM and consolidated the role in the Parliamentary Assembly.'

[4] Limbach *et al.*, *Judicial Independence*, at 20: 'First, the Directorate General for Human Rights (DGHR) reviews the model curriculum vitae of each candidate to ensure that their applications confirm that they fulfill the formal requirements, such as language liability. The assessment is made purely on the basis of material provided in the curriculum vitae: the DGHR does not check any of the information. There are no known cases in which the DGHR has questioned the caliber of candidates submitted by States.'

[5] Limbach *et al.*, *ibid.*, at 8.

[6] *Ibid.*, at 9: 'The CoM, while on paper the body that should be empowered to engage with governments on their nomination procedures and reject unacceptable lists, is concerned more with safeguarding State sovereignty than with ensuring the quality of nominated candidates. Accordingly it fails to engage in meaningful dialogue with States on their internal nomination procedures and to evaluate the quality of candidates submitted.'

[7] Committee of Ministers, 'Informal Procedure for the Examination of Candidatures for the Election of Judges', CM/Del/Dec/Act(96)547/1.3, (CM/Inf(2004)47, 1 December 2004, 593rd meeting, 1997).

[8] *Ibid.*

[9] Parliamentary Assembly, 'Effective Implementation of the ECHR: The Interlaken Process', Res. 1726(2010), 29 April 2010.

that many judges will have to be replaced in the following months.[10] Currently the PACE and the States are the main actors in this matter. What is especially interesting is how the relationships between the Court and the PACE have evolved from a lack of concern to mutual respect.

1.1 The responsibility of the PACE

States are not completely free to select their three candidates. Both the PACE and the Court may interfere in that process. The guidelines very recently issued[11] by the CoM also apply to the national selection stage. They incorporate national good practices and the recommendations made by the PACE. So it appears that the CoM, through this document, intends to bring its formal support to the PACE's practice.

During the last fifteen years, the goal of the PACE has been to harmonise and enhance the quality of the national procedures by imposing a model resume and by inviting States to issue public and open calls for candidatures.[12] In its Resolution adopted on 1 December 2008, The PACE listed the various requirements for States, that is to say: '4.1. Issue public and open calls for candidatures; 4.2. When submitting the names of candidates to the Assembly, describe the manner in which they had been selected; 4.3. Transmit the names of candidates to the Assembly in alphabetical order; 4.4. Candidates should possess an active knowledge of one and a passive knowledge of the other official language of the Council of Europe (see model curriculum vitae appended hereto); and 4.5. That, if possible, no candidate should be submitted whose election might result in the necessity to appoint an ad hoc judge.'[13] A model resume was attached in the appendix.

---

[10] In 2011 the election of the judges took place for Switzerland, Norway, France and Portugal. In 2012, the judges' mandate expired for Belgium, Croatia, the Czech Republic, Poland, the Russian Federation, Sweden and the UK.

[11] Committee of Ministers, 'Guidelines of the Committee of Ministers on the Selection of Candidates for the Post of Judge at the European Court of Human Rights', Explanatory Memorandum, CM(2012)40 addendum final, 29 March 2012.

[12] When submitting the names of candidates to the Assembly, the states are required to describe the manner in which they were selected, see Parliamentary Assembly, 'Nomination of Candidates and Election of Judges to the European Court of Human Rights', Res. 1646(2009), 27 January 2009 (hereinafter Res. 1646(2009)).

[13] Parliamentary Assembly, 'Nomination of Candidates and Election of Judges to the European Court of Human Rights', Doc. 11767 (Rapporteur: C. Chope), 1 December 2008 (hereinafter Doc. 11767).

Nevertheless, the attempts to improve national procedures are not entirely successful; the PACE had to recognise that 'there is still significant variance as concerns fairness, transparency and consistency'.[14] Indeed, it is concerned 'by ad hoc and politicised processes in the nomination of candidates'.[15] An assessment of these national procedures was made in a report dated 1 December 2008.[16] While some national procedures closely follow the Assembly's requirements or are even 'exemplary',[17] very few of them appear to involve an independent organ at the pre-selection stage.

By the books, lists of candidates have to be transmitted directly to the PACE, but in practice lists have been sent first to the Secretary General and to the CoM through ambassadors.[18] The PACE organises personal interviews of candidates by its sub-committee to ensure that candidates selected by States are competent. The sub-committee formulates a recommendation to the Bureau of the Assembly, and the Bureau forwards this recommendation to the Assembly. The candidate, having obtained an absolute majority of votes cast, is declared elected as a member of the Court. If no candidate obtains an absolute majority, a second ballot is held, after which the candidate who has obtained a relative majority of votes is declared elected. In practice, the recommendation formulated by the sub-committee is very often followed by the Assembly.

The above analysis has shown that the processes introduced to facilitate a more transparent election procedure at the national stage have remained relatively ineffective. The following section will demonstrate how the Court has come to take a more active role in the election proceedings.

---

[14] Res. 1646(2009).   [15] *Ibid.*   [16] Doc. 11767.

[17] *Ibid.*, at 14: 'Several states' selection procedures appear exemplary: Belgium makes a public call in the specialised press and transmits the information by other means to all universities and members of the legal profession, conducts interviews (including an assessment of language abilities), and gives an important role to an independent group of experts as well as academics with human rights expertise.' The Netherlands, in addition to making an open call for candidatures in the specialised and general press, holding interviews, and providing for an independent panel of experts, has published a document describing the selection procedure in detail (see document AS/Jur (2008) 52).

[18] A. Drzemczewski, 'The European Human Rights Convention: A New Court of Human Rights in Strasbourg as of 1 November 1998', *Washington and Lee Law Review* 55:3 (1998) 697–736. A. Drzemczewski, 'Election des Juges à la Cour Européenne de Strasbourg: un Aperçu', *L'Europe des libertés* 33 (2010), at 6 (hereinafter Drzemczewski, 'Election des Juges').

1.2 The interference of the Court with the election procedure: bringing the Assembly and the Court into closer connection

The Court may be involved in the election process in two ways. First, it may be consulted by the CoM (and indirectly by the PACE) to deliver consultative opinions on questions related to the election of judges. Second, in its relationships with States, a new panel of experts partly composed of some of the former judges of the ECtHR may advise States before issuing the list of three candidates to the PACE.

1.2.1 The consultative power of the Court

According to article 47(1) of the ECHR, 'the Court may, at the request of the CoM, give advisory opinions on legal questions concerning the interpretation of the Convention and the protocols thereto'. As was stressed by the Explanatory Report, 'the questions on which such opinions may be given must therefore have a legal character'.[19] As the Court mentioned in its first and second advisory opinions, this was stipulated 'in order to rule out any jurisdiction on the Court's part regarding matters of policy'.[20] The Explanatory Report mentions the fact that 'only the CoM shall have the right to request advisory opinions of the Court', but adds that 'the consultative Assembly, the European Commission of Human Rights and the Secretary General may submit proposals for requests for advisory opinions…' At the time, the CoM, 'as a body representing the governments, was [considered to be] the one best qualified to appreciate the advisability of asking the Court for an advisory opinion'.[21] Some of the experts supported the view that the power to request opinions should be extended to the Commission, as it was 'an essential part of the machinery set up by the Convention',[22] but nothing similar was noted in favour of the PACE; however, during the discussions

---

[19] Protocol No. 2 to the Convention for the Protection of Human Rights and Fundamental Freedoms, Conferring upon the European Court of Human Rights Competence to Give Advisory Opinions, ETS No. 44, Explanatory Report, article 1, at 6 (hereinafter Protocol No. 2).

[20] Advisory opinion on certain legal questions concerning the lists of candidates submitted with a view to the election of judges to the ECtHR, Advisory Opinion (Grand Chamber), 12 February 2008, at 36 (hereinafter Certain legal questions, Advisory Opinion). Advisory opinion on certain legal questions concerning the lists of candidates submitted with a view to the election of judges to the ECtHR (No. 2), Advisory Opinion (Grand Chamber), 22 January 2010, at 29 (hereinafter Certain legal questions No. 2, Advisory Opinion).

[21] Protocol No. 2, article 1, paras.1, 5.   [22] *Ibid.*, further commentary, *ibid.*, para. 6.

before the drafting of Protocol 2, 'the examples which were given of issues which might come within this general jurisdiction concerned primarily procedural points such as the election of judges...'[23] The PACE has the competence to submit written comments to the Court when seised by the CoM to give an advisory opinion. Yet it is remarkable that the PACE has never been given the competence to seise the Court, even when the two new forms of requests by the CoM to the Court on execution of judgments were recently discussed and introduced by Protocol 14.[24] There seems to be a long distrust of the PACE.

In its 'Advisory Opinion on certain legal questions concerning the lists of candidates submitted with a view to the election of judges to the European Court of Human Rights', the ECtHR (Grand Chamber, 12 February 2008) confirmed the main responsibility of the PACE with regard to the election process.[25] But the support of the Court to the PACE's activities is not unlimited. This request to the Court to give an advisory opinion related to the gender-based criteria imposed by the PACE to States when submitting a list of candidates.[26] The criteria are not stipulated in article 21, but were added in the Resolutions adopted by the PACE.[27] Indeed, this opinion related to the impasse between one government and the PACE following the refusal of the list sent by the Maltese authorities in July 2006, as it included no candidate belonging to the under-represented sex. The Maltese government invited the PACE to co-sponsor with it a request to the CoM under article 47 for a referral to the Court for an advisory opinion. As the PACE replied that it had no competence on this matter, the Maltese government requested on its own

---

[23] As was recalled by the Court itself in ECtHR, Advisory Opinion, *Decision on the competence of the Court to give an advisory opinion*, 2 June 2004, at 28.

[24] ECHR, article 46, paras. 3, 4 and 5.

[25] Certain legal questions, Advisory Opinion: 'As the body responsible for electing judges, it must also ensure in the final instance that each of the candidates on a given list fulfils all the conditions laid down by Article 21, paragraph 1, in order for it to preserve the freedom of choice conferred on it by Article 22, which it must exercise in the interests of the proper functioning and the authority of the Court.'

[26] A. Mowbray, 'The Consideration of Gender in the Process of Appointing Judges to the European Court of Human Rights', *Human Rights Law Review* 8:3 (2008) 549–59.

[27] Parliamentary Assembly, 'Candidates for the European Court of Human Rights', Resolution 1366(2004), 30 January 2004, at 3: 'The Assembly decides not to consider lists of candidates where ... ii. The list does not include at least one candidate of each sex.' According to Resolution 1426 (2005), Candidates for the ECtHR, PACE, 18 March 2005, at 3, 'the Assembly decides not to consider lists of candidates where: ... ii. The list does not include at least one candidate of each sex, except when the candidates belong to the sex which is under-represented in the Court ...'

that the CoM ask the Court to give an advisory opinion on these matters. The Court started by recalling the attempt to have article 22 of the Convention amended on that point. Nevertheless, the CoM has always replied to the PACE that 'circumstances may exceptionally arise in which,... a Contracting Party may find itself obliged to submit a list containing candidates of only one sex in derogation from that rule, and that it would therefore be undesirable to give such a rule binding force under the Convention'.[28] This question was expressly addressed when discussing Protocol 14, and it was decided not to amend article 22.[29] Consequently, it is clear that this advisory opinion concerns a dispute between a State Party and the PACE. In addition, it deals with conflicting views between the PACE and the CoM on the compulsory or non-compulsory criteria based on gender equality when submitting a list of three candidates. To a certain extent, the Court played the role of an arbitrator, holding that 'there is a need to ensure that the situation which gave rise to the request for an opinion does not cause a blockage in the system'.[30] Even if the Court chose words very carefully and maintained that the question raised before it 'does not lend itself to a straightforward "yes" or "no" answer', it clearly and strongly came down in favour of the State and of the CoM's points of view, affirming that in such circumstances, 'the Assembly may not reject the list in question...'

The second advisory opinion given by the Court followed a dispute between the PACE and the Ukrainian authorities. It raised the issue of the possibility for the State to withdraw a list that had already been submitted to the PACE, where it had already interviewed two of the candidates, the third having withdrawn his candidature for personal reasons. The PACE had asked the authorities to communicate the name of a third candidate in order to complete the list, and opposed the transmission of an entirely new list. Contrary to former practice, this time the PACE took the initiative to recommend the CoM to seek an advisory opinion from the Court.[31] Written comments were sent by sixteen State parties and by the PACE. The Court affirmed that the questions '... also relate to the division of powers between the

---

[28] Committee of Ministers, 'Candidates for the European Court of Human Rights', Parliamentary Assembly Recommendation 1649 (2004), CM/AS(2005)Rec1649final, 20 April 2005, Reply of the CoM to the PACE.
[29] Protocol 14 to the ECHR, 'Amending the Control System of the Convention', Explanatory Report, CETS No. 194, at 49.
[30] Certain legal questions, Advisory Opinion, at 38.
[31] Recommendation 1875 (2009), adopted 23 June 2009.

Contracting States and the Parliamentary Assembly in the context of that procedure'.[32] The Court first recalls one of the three main principles regarding the election of judges, that is to say 'the balance and division of powers between the High Contracting Parties and the Assembly under Article 22 of the Convention' (para. 39), which implies 'that the entities involved – the State concerned and the Assembly – enjoy a certain autonomy, within the limits of their respective powers' (*ibid.*), without going into further details. Unsurprisingly the Court, on the question of the possibility for a State to withdraw a list, held that States parties have such a right, 'but only on condition that they do so before the deadline set for submission of the list to the Parliamentary Assembly. After that date, the High Contracting Parties will no longer be entitled to withdraw their lists' (para. 49). In the same spirit, the Court held that 'candidates on a list withdrawn by the High Contracting Party can no longer be regarded as candidates if the withdrawal occurs before the time-limit' (para. 50). Thus, 'If the withdrawal occurs before the time-limit referred to in paragraph 48 above, the High Contracting Party concerned may either replace any absent candidates or submit a new list of three candidates. If, however, the withdrawal occurs after that date, the High Contracting Party concerned must be restricted to replacing any absent candidates' (para. 57). This advisory opinion is very clear and balanced, drawing a line between the national and the European stages.[33] Moreover, the Court seemed to be sensitive both to the respect of the autonomy of the States and of the PACE.

I do not completely agree that the Court kept a 'low profile' in these advisory opinions.[34] The Court clearly took a stand in favour of one of the options which was at issue, while respecting the requirements set up in the text of the Convention. If the Assembly wished to add some new criteria for the nomination of candidates, these criteria should be added to the text of the ECHR. In this process the Court tried to adopt a balanced approach in respect of the autonomy of the States and of the PACE and clearly assumed its role of an arbitrator by demanding conformity with law. In both opinions, the Court acted on the formal request of the CoM, but the facts related in substance to the relationship between the PACE and member states.

---

[32] Certain legal questions No. 2, Advisory Opinion, at 31.
[33] On the whole procedure, see Drzemczewski, 'Election des Juges', at 6.
[34] J.-F. Flauss and G. Cohen-Jonathan, 'La CourEDH et le droit international', *Annuaire Français de Droit International* 50 (2004), at 781.

1.2.2 The new panel of experts

In the past, the Court has tried to influence the election of new judges; indeed, the President of the ECtHR happened to lobby for the re-election of some judges, and attempted to influence governments (through ambassadors) and the PACE at the election stage.[35] But a new step has recently been taken. The idea came from the former French President of the Court, who suggested[36] that a panel be set up to advise governments before lists of candidates are transmitted to the PACE. This initiative, 'seen from this perspective' (the perspective of the improvement of the quality of lists submitted by the governments) was 'welcomed' by the PACE.[37] The seven-person advisory panel is composed of former judges of the Court and other international courts, members of the highest national courts and lawyers of recognised competence. It has to be geographically and gender balanced. This panel is appointed by the CoM for a three-year term, renewable once upon the proposal of the Court's President.[38] According to former President Costa's letter, it would 'intervene before a list was submitted to the PACE by the contracting party so as not to interfere with the PACE's Convention responsibilities in this area. Moreover, its role would be advisory; in other words, it would make recommendations to the nominating state including, as necessary, proposals to modify the list.'[39]

---

[35] The former President of the ECtHR admitted that he 'lobbied for the re-election of the Moldovan and the Austrian judges' and 'tried to convince the deputies to refuse the lists submitted by the two governments and to inquire why the judge in function was not on the list': F.J. Bruinsma and S. Parmentier, 'Interview with L. Wildhaber, President of the ECHR', *Netherlands Quarterly Review of Human Rights* 21:2 (2003), at 196.

[36] The idea also came from the former President of the Court, L. Wildhaber: Bruinsma and Parmentier, *ibid.*, at 195: 'I think it would be good to have an advisory body at the international level that would look for quality.' This proposal was also mentioned in the Committee of Ministers, 'Report of the Group of Wise Persons to the CoM', CM(2006) 203, 15 November 2006, at 118 (hereinafter 'Report of Wise Persons 2006'), which envisaged the screening of candidatures 'by a committee of prominent personalities possibly chosen from among former members of the Court, current and former members of national supreme or constitutional courts and lawyers with acknowledged competence'.

[37] Parliamentary Assembly, 'National Procedures for the Selection of Candidates for the ECtHR', Resolution 1764 (2010), 8 October 2010; Parliamentary Assembly, 'National Procedures for the Selection of Candidates for the ECtHR', Doc. 12391 (R. Wohlwend), 6 October 2010 (hereinafter Doc. 12391).

[38] *Ibid.*, at 9.

[39] Letter of President Costa. See also, Doc. 12391, at 10: 'My understanding of the manner in which the proposed panel of experts would function is this: the panel would provide advice to governments by examining the *curriculum vitae* of the candidates selected before transmission of the list of the three candidates to the Assembly. This procedure

Nevertheless, some criticisms were expressed by the Reporter of the PACE, stating that:

> This idea, modeled on the independent panel (Article 255 of the Treaty on the Functioning of the EU[40]) set up with the entry into force of the Lisbon Treaty, relates to another type of 'animal'. Under the ECHR it is the PACE which elects judges from a list of three persons (in other words, it has a choice: Article 22), whereas the EU panel looks at the suitability of (single) candidates put forward for appointment by governments to the ECJ. Election of judges by the Assembly, in the Strasbourg system, provides 'democratic legitimacy', something which no other international court possesses. Similarly, states parties to our Convention might consider such a 'hybrid creation' as an inappropriate interference in their own national, hopefully rigorous, transparent and fair, selection procedures (as might also the Assembly, were it ever suggested that such a panel provide the Assembly, rather than states parties, with advice).[41]

This panel was applauded by the former President of the Court, noting that the authority of the Court depends mostly on the quality of the judges.[42] The members of the panel were actually appointed in December 2010. The panel is chaired by the former President of the ECtHR,

---

would be obligatory. If the panel were to find, after an examination of the *curriculum vitae*, that the list to be forwarded to the Assembly is composed of suitable candidates, it would so inform the state concerned without further comment. If, however, the panel were of the view that one or more of the persons on the list (to be) put forward to the Assembly was not suitable, it would provide its views, in a confidential procedure, to the state concerned, indicating to it why the said person or persons should not be on the list. Then, if ever the state concerned were not to heed the "advice" of the panel and transmit, to the Assembly, a list containing one or more persons deemed by the panel not to meet the criteria for office – as provided in Article 21, paragraph 1, of the Convention, – the panel would inform the Assembly of its reasons.'

[40] Consolidated Version of the Treaty on the Functioning of the EU, Official Journal of the EU, C83/47, 30 March 2010, article 255: 'A panel shall be set up in order to give an opinion on candidates' suitability to perform the duties of Judge and Advocate-General of the Court of Justice and the General Court before the governments of the member States make the appointments referred to in Articles 253 and 254. The panel shall comprise seven persons chosen from among former members of the Court of Justice and the General Court, members of national supreme courts and lawyers of recognized competence, one of whom shall be proposed by the European Parliament. The Council shall adopt a decision establishing the panel's operating rules and a decision appointing its members. It shall act on the initiative of the President of the Court of Justice.'

[41] Doc. 12391, at 11.

[42] ECtHR, J.-P. Costa, 'Foreword', *Annual Report 2010*, provisional edition (Council of Europe, Strasbourg), January 2011, at 5.

L. Wildhaber, and is composed of six other experts.[43] If a government refuses to follow the panel's advice that a candidate is unsuitable, 'the panel's reasons would be communicated directly to the latter PACE for its information'.[44] The functioning of the panel, initially settled for a three-year period, will be reviewed.[45] The panel decides on the suitability of each candidate, and not of the whole list. The PACE's approach is to consider the panel's activity as an internal process operating in conjunction with the selection made by governments.

It seems that this initiative is symptomatic of the Court's willingness to be involved in matters which go beyond its *jus dicere* role. It is true that the election of many judges in the coming months and years is of high importance, in order to ensure a certain continuity of the case law of the Court.[46] Taking previous practice into account, it is apparent that this new panel will not have much impact, as it is likely that it will be reluctant to reject candidates submitted by the governments. It is also sensitive to the fact that the PACE has a significant experience in examining lists. The panel held an inaugural meeting at the end of January 2011. In 2011 the panel examined the lists sent by three States: France, Switzerland and Belgium. As the procedure is confidential, it is not possible to know the impact of its examination. The French list was rejected in spring 2011 by the PACE, which had previously rejected eight other lists.[47]

In considering the interim advice sent recently by the British Commission in a bill of rights to the British government, one has the impression that there may be an attempt in the coming months, particularly under the chairmanship of the new British President of the Court, to increase the powers of this panel. In fact, the Commission shares the view that this panel does not go far enough; for example, it cannot interview all nominees

---

[43] Katarzyna Gonera (Poland), Renate Jaeger (Germany), Chief Justice John L. Murray (Ireland), Matti Pellonpää (Finland), Professor Sami Selçuk (Turkey), Valery D. Zorkin (Russian Federation).

[44] Committee of Ministers, Ad Hoc Working Party on the Follow-up Process to the Interlaken Declaration, 'Election of Judges to the European Court of Human Rights', GT-SUIVI.Interlaken(2010)8, 24 June 2010.

[45] Committee of Ministers, 'Report on the Future of the European Court of Human Rights' CM(2011)57 final, follow-up to the Interlaken and Izmir Conferences, 3 May 2011, at 7.

[46] The number of judges to elect in the following years at the ECtHR is: 7 for 2013, 2 for 2014, 11 for 2015, 10 for 2017, 1 for 2018 and 2 for 2019 ('Election of Judges to the European Court of Human Rights', GT-SUIVI.Interlaken(2010)8, 24 June 2010).

[47] Parliamentary Assembly, 'Nomination of Candidates and Election of Judges to the European Court of Human Rights', Doc. 11767, 1 December 2008, para. 8.

before giving its advice to the Assembly.[48] Yet when the panel was set up, the registrar of the Court affirmed that a hearing of the candidates was not necessary, as it was the responsibility of the sub-committee of the PACE.[49] Without putting into question the role of the PACE in that process, the idea may be to put more pressure on it and reduce its influence. The main responsibility should, however, still lie in the hands of the PACE, which has demonstrated its autonomy towards States.

The ECtHR is clearly the only international court where governmental officials do not have full control over elections. There now seems to be four actors: the nominating State, the PACE, the CoM and the Court (indirectly). The role and the authority of the PACE (the only democratic organ of the Council of Europe) should be safeguarded. It is also desirable that the panel acts in accordance with the guidelines set up by the PACE.

The weakest point in securing competent and independent judges is certainly the nomination by States. The fact that the CoM has issued guidelines in this matter and that the Brighton Declaration 'Welcomes the adoption by the Committee of Ministers of the Guidelines on the selection of candidates for the post of judge at the European Court of Human Rights, and encourages the States Parties to implement them (...) and invites the Parliamentary Assembly and the Committee of Ministers to discuss how the procedures for electing judges can be further improved',[50] shows that the competence given to the PACE in this field (by the Statute of the Council of Europe) has been seriously called into question. Labelled as an improvement of the election process, an interference of the executive organ has taken place. This means that the election process will be even more dependent on the governments.

2. The implementation of the Court's judgments

It is well known that 'full execution of judgments helps to enhance the Court's prestige and the effectiveness of its action and has the effect of limiting the number of applications submitted to it'.[51]

---

[48] Commission on a bill of rights, 'Reform of the ECtHR Our Interim Advice to Government', 28 July 2011, http://www.justice.gov.uk/downloads/about/cbr/cbr-court-reform-interim-advice.pdf/ (11 July 2012).

[49] Committee of Ministers, Ad hoc working party on the follow-up process to the Interlaken Declaration, GT-SUIVI.Interlaken(2010)CB5, Synopsis, Meeting of 29 June 2010, 5 July 2010, at 15.

[50] CoE, High Level Conference on the Future of the European Court of Human Rights, Brighton Declaration, 20 April 2012, para. 25(a) and (b).

[51] 'Report of Wise Persons', at 25.

Considering the terminology and distinction used by R. Grant and R. Keohane,[52] I share the view that the European system of human rights protection has evolved towards a 'participatory model of accountability'. This model involves a plurality of actors, and this seems to have enhanced the effectiveness of the monitoring procedure. According to the ECHR, the supervision of the execution of the judgments is a matter for the CoM alone.[53] In reality, the arrangement has become much more complex: the Court has come to play a greater part in the process of supervising this execution. By its own initiative, the PACE has also *de facto* and even *de jure* imposed an increasingly institutionalised right of inspection on the CoM. The following assessment will show that, with regard to the implementation of the judgments, the activities of the CoM and of the Court often overlap, as do the functions of the PACE with the CoM. There is no triangular relationship, but rather, a double bilateral connection; in this regard, the CoM comes under pressure both from the Court and from the PACE. The Court has taken the risk of redefining its relationship with the CoM, raising the argument that its involvement is necessary in order to enhance the effectiveness of the implementation of the judgments.

2.1 The CoM and the Court in a more cooperative interconnection

The workload of the CoM is dramatically increasing (more than 10,000 pending cases) and the last few years have seen a significant increase in the number of cases relating to complex and sensitive issues. For instance, in 2010, the number of new cases was three times the number of cases which had been closed by a final resolution.[54]

To a certain extent, the CoM has to admit its failure to effectively supervise the implementation of the judgments. As the financial and

---

[52] R. Grant and R. Keohane, 'Accountability and Abuses of Power in World Politics', *American Political Science Review* 99:1 (2005) 29–43, 29, who 'distinguish two basic concepts of accountability: delegation and participation', among which they expose a plurality of models. See E. Lambert-Abdelgawad, 'The Execution of the Judgments of the ECtHR: Towards a Non-coercive and Participatory Model of Accountability', *Zeitschrift für ausländisches öffentliches Recht und Völkerrecht* 69:3 (2009) 471–506.

[53] E. Lambert-Abdelgawad, *The Execution of Judgments of the European Court of Human Rights*, Human Rights Files No. 19, 2nd edn (Strasbourg: Council of Europe Publishing, 2008).

[54] Committee of Ministers, 'Supervision of the Execution of Judgments of the ECtHR', *4th Annual Report* (Strasbourg: Council of Europe, 2011), at 31.

personal capacities of the Secretariat have not been increased, it is currently adopting a minimised and a prioritised supervision. The reforms have led to 'two (simplified and enhanced) practical supervision methods', which should be 'parallel and interdependent'.[55] The priority would be on three types of cases: the 'inter-state cases, pilot judgments and other cases raising significant and/or complex structural problems that may give rise to numerous repetitive cases, and judgments requiring urgent individual measures'.[56] In all cases, the approach is still of a non-coercive nature.[57] The 'simplified' procedure, which will be the most common, means that the supervision of the CoM will be purely formal, limiting itself to 'verifying whether or not action plans or action reports have been presented by member states'.[58] It is expected to speed-up the adoption of a final resolution and be less time-consuming for the Secretariat. Nevertheless, one may fear that, relying upon the *bona fides* of the State is not reassuring, as, without any political and collective pressure of the CoM, the implementation of some judgments might be less effective. If the States do not submit an action plan or an action report after six months, a reminder will be sent to the State concerned in the following three months. If the State still has not complied with its duties, the case may be analysed according to the enhanced procedure. If, in due time, the States do not fulfil their obligations (six months is a very short time period), which could occur, this simplified procedure will be a failure. The same assessment is to be applied to the execution of just satisfaction. At the request of some States, and despite the fact that the implementation of the just satisfaction has raised many problems in the past,[59] 'Registration would therefore become the standard procedure and

---

[55] Committee of Ministers, 'Supervision of the Execution of the Judgments and Decisions of the European Court of Human Rights: Implementation of the Interlaken Action Plan – Elements for a Roadmap', CM/Inf(2010)28 revised, 24 June 2010.
[56] *Ibid.*
[57] *Ibid.*, at 9: 'Thus, enhanced supervision by the CoM may be conducted by means other than debate, e.g. support by the Execution Department in drawing up and implementing action plans; more intensive bilateral consultations and/or enhanced technical cooperation programs with national authorities and regular reports to the CoM on the progress of execution.'
[58] Committee of Ministers, 'Supervision of the Execution of Judgments and Decisions of the European Court of Human Rights: Implementation of the Interlaken Action Plan – Modalities for a Twin-Track Supervision System', CM/Inf/DH(2010)37, 6 September 2010, at 12.
[59] Committee of Ministers, 'Monitoring of the Payment of Sums awarded by Way of Just Satisfaction: An Overview of the Committee of Ministers' Present Practice', CM/Inf/DH (2008)7 final, 15 January 2009.

supervision the exception' in these issues.[60] In practice, only in cases where the applicant complains within a short time will the Execution Department involve itself in the supervision process. Concerning the enhanced procedure, the Secretariat will have the duty to assist the States in the preparation and/or implementation of action plans, and provide them with expert assistance as regards the type of measures to be adopted. Such expertise is fundamental, as States often do not know how to abide by the judgment. Actually, the ignorance of the State about which measures to implement is relevant in many judgments, in particular those subject to the new standard procedure!

So, relying on the principle of effectiveness, the Court has come to realise that it should get more involved in recommending, or even ordering which measures the State has to take; as a consequence, this new policy also facilitates the responsibility of the CoM. But as the implementation process may be very technical, the Court is not always in the best position to address this task. However, the interference of the Court in some cases, in particular the pilot cases, is useful, in that it puts more pressure on the State to implement the judgment before the deadline prescribed by the Court (sometimes mentioning the measures and the deadline in the operative part of its judgment); although, if the Court goes too far, the risk is that competitive relations with the CoM may become even more complicated.

2.1.1 From competitive relations ...

Considering that the execution of judicial decisions is a component of the right to a fair process,[61] the European courts (the ECtHR as well as the European Court of Justice (ECJ)) have depoliticised the process of execution. This provides them with the conditions to interfere in that process, particularly when the execution takes time or seems difficult.[62] The basis for this evolution is the result of the 'implied powers' theory, the ECtHR using article 46 as the legal ground. By basing its reasoning on article 46, and undoubtedly on its paragraph 1 ('The High Contracting Parties undertake to abide by the final judgment of the Court in any case

---

[60] CM/Inf/DH(2010)37, Appendix II.
[61] ECtHR, *Hornsby* v. *Greece* (Appl. No. 18357/91), Judgment (Chamber), 19 March 1997, Report 1997-II, at 40. Cf., more recently, ECtHR, *Dubenko* v. *Ukraine* (Appl. No. 74221/01), Judgment (Second Section), 11 January 2005, not reported, at 44.
[62] See E. Lambert-Abdelgawad, 'L'Exécution des Décisions des Juridictions Européennes (Cour de Justice des Communautés Européennes et Cour Européenne des Droits de l'Homme)', *Annuaire Français de Droit International* 52 (2006) 676–724.

to which they are parties'), even if it does not explicitly mention it,[63] the Court recommends, or even orders specific measures to be adopted by the States, even if it reaffirms that the judgments are still, in principle, declaratory.[64] Moreover, the Court has the advantage of being the first actor which may decide on the implementation of the judgment, and so it may try to influence the CoM. This is clear for matters where the reopening of judicial procedures is required, or in the pilot cases. In its opinion on 1 December 2009, the CDDH considered 'Developing the emerging practice of interaction between the Committee of Ministers and the Court in relation to the pilot judgment procedure'.[65] Therefore, over the course of several years, the Court has assumed a more important role in the execution of its judgments and has become a major player. This is confirmed by the words couched for article 61 on the procedure for pilot judgments.[66]

The risk of competition between the ECtHR and the CoM may emerge when the two new mechanisms introduced by Protocol 14 in article 46 are implemented in order to speed up and improve the implementation of the judgments. The CoM used to have little power to sanction the reluctance of some States to abide by the judgments; in practice, interim resolutions have had no impact.[67] The infringement proceedings

---

[63] ECHR, article 46: 'Binding Force and Execution of Judgments': '1. The High Contracting Parties undertake to abide by the final judgment of the Court in any case to which they are parties. 2. The final judgment of the Court shall be transmitted to the Committee of Ministers, which shall supervise its execution.'

[64] See ECtHR, *Abbasov* v. *Azerbaijan* (Appl. No. 24271/05), Judgment (First Section), 17 January 2008, not reported, at 36: 'The Court reiterates that its judgments are essentially declaratory in nature and that, in general, it is primarily for the State concerned to choose, subject to supervision by the Committee of Ministers, the means to be used in its domestic legal order in order to discharge its obligation under Article 46 of the Convention.'

[65] Steering Committee for Human Rights, Report CDDH(2009)019 Report 69th Meeting, 24–7 November 2009, Addendum I, at C(5). This document includes a great number of proposals; it mentions the cooperation activities between national authorities and the CoM and the interaction between the CoM and the Court, but nothing with regard to the cooperation with the PACE.

[66] *Ibid.*, para. 9, holds that 'The CoM, the PACE, the Secretary General of the Council of Europe, and the Council of Europe's Human Rights Commissioner shall be informed of the adoption of a pilot judgment as well as of any other judgment in which the Court draws attention to the existence of a structural or systemic problem in a Contracting State.'

[67] See, for instance, Committee of Ministers, 'Execution of the Judgments of the European Court of Human Rights in 145 cases against the Russian Federation', Interim Resolution CM/ResDH(2009)43, 19 March 2009.

pursuant to article 46(4) ECHR allow the CoM to apply to the Court in order to have the refusal of a State to adhere to a judgment sanctioned. Neither the Assembly nor the applicants (nor their representatives, non-governmental organisations (NGOs), or lawyers) have been offered such a right, despite the fact that the Assembly was the first organ to launch the idea of incorporating the possibility of infringement proceedings in the ECHR.[68] The risk of abuse is not the main explanation; the idea was to create special links between the Court and the CoM and to give a political (and not a victim) approach to such an appeal. It was admitted that only the CoM (composed of ambassadors representative of the States) would be wise enough not to abuse such a power. The same reasoning has to be applied to the new competence of the CoM to ask the Court to interpret one of its former judgments pursuant to article 46(3) of the ECHR. The danger for the Court is that the way judgments are enacted could be criticised. The opinion shared at the time of the adoption of Protocol 14 was that neither the infringement nor the interpretation appeals would jeopardise the sharing of power between the CoM and the Court. 'The aim was not to give the Committee of Ministers authority over the work of the Court, but to inform the Court of the difficulties which could arise with certain of its judgments during the execution stage.'[69] Thus, from the beginning, there seems to have been a kind of 'deal' between the Court and the CoM that very little use of these new appeals will be made, whatever the States' practice might be, whether or not they abide by the judgments.

Nevertheless, owing to its composition, the CoM, certainly does not have the political willingness to go forward in this direction. Moreover, bringing a case to the Court on the ground of article 46(3) or (4) ECHR means that the CoM has failed in its function of supervising the implementation of the judgments; it will therefore probably be reluctant to display such a failure. Moreover, as the infringement proceedings are not coupled with daily fines, contrary to the practice applied before the ECJ, the impact of such an appeal will undoubtedly not be very high.

---

[68] See the references in E. Lambert-Abdelgawad, 'Le Protocole 14 et l'Exécution des Arrêts de la Cour Européenne des Droits de l'Homme', G. Cohen-Jonathan and J.F. Flauss (eds.), *La Réforme du Système de Contrôle Contentieux de la Convention Européenne des Droits de l'Homme* (Brussels: Bruylant, Nemesis, 2005) 79–113.

[69] Steering Committee for Human Rights, 'Activity Report on the Reinforcement of the Human Rights Protection Mechanism', CDDH-GDR(2001)010, 15 June 2001. This opinion was supported by the Venice Commission: 'Execution of Judgments of the European Court of Human Rights', Opinion No. 209/2002, 18 December 2002, at 61.

2.1.2 ... to some complicated relationship

Some cases illustrate that tensions may arise between the Court and the CoM regarding the implementation of the judgments. An illustrative example is *VGT v. Switzerland*. In this case, the applicant, an association, alleged that the continued prohibition on broadcasting a television commercial, after the Court had found a violation of the freedom of expression, constituted a breach of article 10. In this case the CoM had closed the implementation process by issuing a final resolution, whereas the reopening of the case at the national stage had not been granted yet. In fact, when an applicant is dissatisfied with the implementation of a judgment delivered by the ECtHR, he/she may come back before the Court itself, alleging a continuous violation. That was also the case for *Mehemi* and *Burdov*.[70] In these instances, the conflict was resolved by a new judgment of the Court. It declared the case inadmissible in the former, and established a violation in the latter case. In the latter case, the CoM will abide by the judgment and recommendations of the Court to have the judgment properly implemented.

If the Court's recommendations in a case concerning a general measure are not implemented, follow-up decisions may ensue, raising the same question. Those also evince a failure of the CoM to put pressure on States and have them abide by the first judgment of the Court. For example, *Rumpf v. Germany*[71] is a repetitive case following the *Sürmeli* judgment.[72] The *Greens and M.T. v. UK* case[73] is also a repetitive judgment after *Hirst (No. 2)*,[74] despite the interim resolution in this case.[75]

It is worth mentioning that the CoM closes its supervisory function when the applicant decides to bring his/her case before the ECtHR once more. This happened in the *Hertel v. Switzerland* and *Öcalan v. Turkey* cases.[76]

---

[70] ECtHR, *Mehemi v. France (No. 2)* (Appl. No. 53470/99), Judgment (Third Section), 10 April 2003, Reports 2003-IV; ECtHR, *Burdov v. Russia (No. 2)* (Appl. No. 33509/04), Judgment (First Section), 15 January 2009, Reports 2009.

[71] ECtHR, *Rumpf v. Germany* (Appl. No. 46344/06), Judgment (Fifth Section), 2 September 2010, Reports 2010.

[72] ECtHR, *Sürmeli v. Germany* (Appl. No. 75529/01), Judgment (Grand Chamber), 8 June 2006, Reports 2006-VII.

[73] ECtHR, *Greens and M.T. v. UK* (Appl. Nos. 60041 and 60054/08), Judgment (Fourth Section), 23 November 2010, Reports 2010.

[74] ECtHR, *Hirst v. UK (No. 2)* (Appl. No. 74025/01), Judgment (Grand Chamber), 6 October 2005, Reports 2005-IX.

[75] 'Execution of the Judgment of the ECtHR *Hirst v. UK (No. 2)*', Interim Resolution CM/ResDH(2009)160, 3 December 2009.

[76] ECtHR, *Öcalan v. Turkey* (Appl. No. 5980/07), Decision (Second Section), 6 July 2010, not reported.

Consequently, in many cases, the ECtHR's position will prevail, as was the situation in the *VGT* v. *Switzerland* judgment. The Swiss government had no other choice but to reopen the case, whereas the reopening had been refused by the Swiss Federal Tribunal following the first judgment of the Court. Another recent judgment, *Emre* v. *Switzerland (No. 2)*,[77] confirms the willingness of the majority of the Court[78] to play a greater role. But it would appear that if the Court goes too far, States will refer to the principle of subsidiarity alleging their margin of appreciation in implementing judgments. The risk is that States may refuse to implement some of the judgments of the ECtHR, which could jeopardise the whole system and the legitimacy of the judicial organ.

Another cause of further tension between the CoM and the Court could arise from a very recent proposal by some judges and the Registry of the Court, to send repetitive cases directly to the CoM instead of losing time dealing with them.[79] Until now, the idea has not been welcomed by the CoM.

2.2 The PACE's involvment in the implementation process and its impact

The PACE's involvement in the implementation process is to increase the pressure not on the Court, but mostly on the CoM; it focuses on the most urgent and serious cases.

2.2.1 A complementary role

The Assembly's involvement in the task of supervising the execution of judgments is the result of a gradual process, and currently takes a number of forms.[80] First, members of the Assembly do not hesitate to use written

---

[77] ECtHR, *Emre* v. *Switzerland (No. 2)* (Appl. No. 5056/10), Judgment (Second Section), 11 October 2011, not reported.

[78] See the Dissenting Opinion of Judge Malinverni.

[79] See L. Wildhaber, 'Rethinking the European Court of Human Rights', in J. Christoffersen and M.R. Madsen (eds.), *The European Court of Human Rights between Law and Politics* (Oxford University Press, 2011) 204–29, at 224: '... if class actions were handled collectively, and if repetitive matters were sent directly to the CM and/or the States, matters would definitely look more hopeful'.

[80] See A. Drzemczewski, 'Quelques Observations sur le Rôle de la Commission des Questions Juridiques et Droits de l'Homme de l'Assemblée Parlementaire dans l'Exécution des Arrêts de la Cour de Strasbourg', H. Hartig (ed.), *Trente Ans de Droit Européen des Droits de l'Homme: Études à la Mémoire de Wolfgang Strasser* (Brussels: Nemesis, Bruylant, 2007) 55–63.

questions to obtain explanations from the CoM concerning its failure to have certain judgments implemented correctly and within reasonable time.[81] The CoM is required to provide a written answer.[82] When oral questions are raised by members of the PACE to the Chair of the Ministers' Deputies at each session, the CoM is frequently called upon to provide an explanation concerning judgments which have not yet been executed. One of the PACE's four annual sessions now includes an agenda item on the implementation of the judgments. In addition to the drafting of a report, the discussion leads to the adoption of a recommendation and/or a resolution. With the adoption of Resolution 1226 (2000), the PACE decided to hold regular debates about the execution of judgments on the basis of a record of execution that it would keep. Its Committee on Legal Affairs and Human Rights decided to use two criteria when compiling this record: first, the time elapsed since the Court's decision (five years for the first record) and, second, the urgency attached to the implementation of certain decisions. The use of this procedure is based on the principle that only national delegations 'have the competence to call their governments to account within their own national parliamentary procedure',[83] in an objective manner, for action taken on a judgment. More generally, the Assembly 'again calls upon national delegations to monitor the execution of specific Court judgments concerning their governments through their respective parliaments and to take all necessary steps to ensure their speedy and effective execution'.[84]

The Assembly also envisages, in cases where States prove more reluctant, asking the minister of justice of the state concerned to give an

---

[81] For example, see Written Question No. 402 from Mr. Clerfayt (Doc. 9272) regarding Turkey's non-compliance with judgments concerning violations of article 5 of the Convention and the Committee's reply dated 16 January 2002, Parliamentary Assembly, 'Non-compliance of Turkey with European Court of Human Rights Judgments', Doc. 9327, 21 January 2002.

[82] For example, Parliamentary Assembly, 'Written Question No. 378', 10 September 1998, from certain members of the PACE asking the CoM to explain the length of time necessary for full execution of all the judgments pending for more than three years. See also, more recently, Parliamentary Assembly, CM/AS(2007)Quest487–488 final, 23 March 2007, 'Written Questions by Mr. Austin to the Chair of the CoM: a. No. 487: "Conditions of Detention for Mr Öcalan"; b. No. 488: "Execution of the Judgment of the ECtHR in the Öcalan case".'

[83] Parliamentary Assembly, 'Implementation of Decisions of the European Court of Human Rights', Resolution 1268 (2002), 22 January 2002, at 10.

[84] Ibid., at 11.

explanation to the Assembly in person. This measure was included in Resolution 1226 (2000) on 'Execution of judgments of the European Court of Human Rights'; in this Resolution, the Assembly also decided to 'adopt recommendations to the CoM, and through it to the relevant states, concerning the execution of certain judgments, if it [noticed] abnormal delays', to hold an 'urgent debate', if necessary, 'if the state in question [had] neglected to execute or deliberately refrained from executing the judgment', to open a monitoring procedure should a member state refuse to implement a decision of the Court, and even to 'envisage, if these measures [failed], making use of other possibilities, in particular those provided for in its own Rules of Procedure and/or of a recommendation to the CoM to make use of article 8 of the Statute [i.e. challenging the credentials of a national delegation]'. Finally, the Assembly has secured a promise from the CoM that a regular formal consultation will take place between the Committee's Rapporteur Group on Human Rights and the Assembly's Committee on Legal Affairs and Human Rights,[85] so that the different national delegations can question their governments without delay where the latter fail to fulfil their obligation to execute judgments. This measure was, however, a complete failure, as the CoM is jealous of its prerogatives and is opposed to such a sharing of responsibilities.[86]

Encouraged by official recognition of its role from the CoM itself,[87] the Assembly has decided to step up its supervision procedure by adopting a

---

[85] Committee of Ministers, see 'Reply from the CoM to Recommendation 1546 (2002) on the implementation of decisions of the ECtHR' PACE, First part of 2002 Session, Adopted texts, and Committee of Ministers, Notes on the Agenda, 782 Meeting, CM/Del/Dec (2002) 781/3.1, at 14.

[86] The year 2007 was marked especially by the adoption of the report by the Assembly, 'Council of Europe Commissioner for Human Rights – Stock-Taking and Perspectives'. The Assembly took note of the Commissioner's willingness to invest more into the control of the judgments, especially the pilot judgments. The Assembly focuses on the question of synergy between the organs at the European level. The Recommendation of the Assembly equally invites the CoM 'to make practical arrangements to fulfil the intention expressed in its Declaration of 19 May 2006 by organising, as quickly as possible, an initial annual tripartite meeting between representatives of the CoM, the Assembly and the Commissioner in order to promote stronger interaction with regard to the execution of Court judgments', see Parliamentary Assembly, 'Council of Europe Commissioner for Human Rights – stock-taking and perspectives' (J.C. Gardetto), Doc. 11376, 17 September 2007; Parliamentary Assembly, 'Resolution 1581 of 5 October 2007' and Parliamentary Assembly, 'Recommendation 1816 of 5 October 2007'. But it failed.

[87] Parliamentary Assembly, 'Implementation of Judgments of the European Court of Human Rights', Resolution 1516 (2006), 2 October 2006, at 4: 'In line with ... the

more proactive approach, giving priority to the examination of cases which concern major structural problems, and in which unacceptable delays of implementation have arisen. The PACE has further specified that it has 'reserve[d] the right to take appropriate action, notably by making use of Rule 8 of its Rules of Procedure, should the state concerned continuously fail to take all the measures required by a judgment of the Court, or should the national parliament fail to exert the necessary pressure on the government to implement judgments of the Court'.[88] The significance of the Assembly's involvement lies, above all, in the public nature of its denunciation; it seeks to heighten the Assembly's awareness of the international commitments of their own governments. In the author's view, this increasing activity of this organ can only be salutary at this stage, in particular as it complements the CoM's role.

Being inundated with cases, the Assembly was obliged to apply new and more selective criteria regarding the supervision of the implementation of the judgments by prioritising: 'judgments which raise important implementation issues as identified, in particular, by an interim resolution of the Committee of Ministers; and judgments concerning violations of a very serious nature'.[89]

Evidently the aim of the PACE is to increase the effectiveness of the implementation of judgments. Thus, priority will mostly be given to the pilot judgments and the judgments with serious violations, as is the case with the ECtHR and the CoM.

2.2.2 Putting more pressure on the CoM and indirectly on the Court

The PACE's involvement is crucial, as this organ has the political willingness to put pressure on the States to abide by their judgments. In its

---

Committee of Ministers Declaration of 19 May 2006 indicating that the Parliamentary Assembly will be associated with the drawing up of a recommendation on the efficient domestic capacity for rapid implementation of the Court's judgments, the Assembly feels duty-bound to further its involvement in the need to resolve the most important problems of compliance with the Court's judgments.' See also Steering Committee for Human Rights, 'CDDH Contribution to the Ministerial Conference Organised by the UK Chairmanship of the Committee of Ministers', CDDH(2012) R74 Addendum III, 15 February 2012, para. 14, encouraging 'closer involvement of the Parliamentary Assembly (...)'.

[88] See also Parliamentary Assembly, 'Implementation of Judgments of the European Court of Human Rights', Recommendation 1764 (2006), 2 October 2006.

[89] Declassified, Parliamentary Assembly, AS/Jur (2009) 36, Committee on Legal Affairs and Human Rights, 'Implementation of Judgments of the European Court of Human Rights Progress Report' 31 August 2009.

2009 report, the Assembly undertook 'to consider suspending the voting rights of a national delegation where its national parliament does not seriously exercise parliamentary control over the executive in cases of non-implementation of Strasbourg Court judgments'.[90] Punitive damages could also be a way of sanctioning serious repetitive violations.[91] Daily fines should also be reconsidered, in light of the deteriorating situation. In its report dated December 2010,[92] Mr. Pourgourides supported the view that 'the Assembly ought to consider – in the future – suspending the voting rights of national delegations when their parliaments do not seriously exercise parliamentary control over the executive in cases of non-implementation of judgments of the European Court of Human Rights'. Another measure is also indicated in this report, that is to say, the invitation made to 'the chairpersons of national parliamentary delegations – together, if need be, with the competent ministers – of states in which in situ visits were undertaken (or envisaged, in the case of Turkey) to present the results achieved in solving substantial problems highlighted in this resolution'.[93] The PACE recommended that the CoM 'increase pressure and take firmer measures in cases of dilatory and continuous non-compliance with the Court's judgments by state parties, and to work more closely on this subject with the Assembly', without expressly mentioning the infringement proceedings, as the CoM is the only organ which may seise the Court in such cases.

It is important to remember that NGOs, as well as the victim (and the victim's representative), play no part at the implementation stage. They are absent from the meetings of the CoM. This is a fundamental difference from the Inter-American system of human rights, where victims and their lawyers are very much involved in the monitoring process of the Court's judgments.[94] The execution of the judgment is therefore outside the control of the applicant (interstate applications are virtually

---

[90] *Ibid.*, at 23.
[91] Y. Grozev, 'How Human Rights Protection has Evolved: A Critical Analysis of Ten Years of Case Law', in ECtHR, *Ten Years of the 'New' European Court of Human Rights 1998–2008; Situation and Outlook* (Strasbourg: Council of Europe, 2009), at 39.
[92] Parliamentary Assembly, 'Implementation of Judgments of The European Court of Human Rights' (M.C. Pourgourides), Doc. 12455, 20 December 2010, Report, para. 213.
[93] *Ibid.*, at 10.4.
[94] See E. Lambert-Abdelgawad, 'L'Exécution des Décisions des Juridictions Internationales des Droits de l'Homme: vers une Harmonisation des Systèmes Régionaux', *Anuario Colombiano de Derecho Internacional*, 2010–3 Especial, 9–55 (www.anuariocdi.org/ anuario3a-capitulos-pdf/01_art.pdf).

THE COURT AS A PART OF THE COUNCIL OF EUROPE 287

non-existent). In addition, according to new Rule 9 of the rules adopted by the CoM for the implementation of article 46, NGOs, national institutions and applicants have been granted the right to provide documents to the CoM on the measures to be adopted. This may constitute a starting point for consideration by the Department for the Execution of Judgments.[95] NGOs and lawyers will certainly be encouraged by the PACE to ask the CoM to put more pressure on the State concerned, and to demand, for instance, the use of the infringement proceedings from the CoM. NGOs are well informed and it is fundamental that they share their expertise with the CoM.[96] According to the Rules adopted for the implementation of article 46, only NGOs have the competence to raise issues regarding general measures. Such documents may inform the CoM of the changes, or of the lack of changes, following the delivery of a particular judgment, such as the *Hirst* v. *UK* case settled in 2005 by the Grand Chamber;[97] NGOs have requested the use of the infringement proceedings in this case, as the UK opposed the reform on the right of prisoners to vote.[98] In another case, NGOs asked the CoM to adopt an interim resolution in order to put pressure on the State.[99] They also requested the enactment of precise recommendations on general measures which should be adopted, or to make comments on general measures the State had enacted or intended to adopt.[100] They have even

---

[95] Under Rules 9.1 and 9.2 adopted in 2006 by the CoM. National authorities are also able to appear before the CoM at the request of the Permanent Representative (Rules of the Committee of Ministers for the Supervision of the Execution of Judgments and of the Terms of Friendly Settlements, adopted on 10 May 2006).

[96] See the information sent by the NGO European Roma Rights Centre, DH-DD(2010)300, 7 June 2010. See also the documents sent by Human Rights Watch, DH-DD(2010)307, 9 June 2010.

[97] Communication by an NGO in the case *Hirst (No. 2)* v. *The United Kingdom* (Appl. No. 74025/01), Judgment (Grand Chamber), 6 October 2005, Reports 2005-IX; and Response of the Government, Information sent by the NGO UNLOCK, DH-DD (2010)3, 11 January 2010; see also Communications from different NGOs (AIRE, UNLOCK, PRI, PRT) in the case *Hirst (No. 2)* v. *The United Kingdom, ibid.*, DH-DD (2010)609, 1 December 2010.

[98] Communications from different NGOs (AIRE, UNLOCK, PRI, PRT) in *Hirst (No. 2)* v. *The United Kingdom, ibid.*, DH-DD(2010)609, 1 December 2010.

[99] Communications from Human Rights Watch in the case of ECtHR, *Sejdić and Finci* v. *Bosnia and Herzegovina* (Appl. Nos. 27996 and 34836/06), Judgment (Grand Chamber), 22 December 2009, Reports 2009, DH-DD(2010)307, 9 June 2010.

[100] Communication from NGOs in the cases of ECtHR, *DH and Others* v. *Czech Republic* (Appl. No. 57325/00), Judgment (Grand Chamber), 13 November 2007, Reports 2007-IV; ECtHR, *Sampanis and Others* v. *Greece* (Appl. No. 32526/05), Judgment (First Section), 5 June 2008, not reported; and ECtHR, *Oršuš and Others* v. *Croatia*

suggested that the CoM ask the Court for an advisory opinion on the compatibility of some national measures with the ECHR.[101]

2.3 A positive synergy between the Court, the PACE and the CoM

It would be too restrictive and biased to analyse the relationships between the Court, the PACE and the CoM only in terms of competition in the field of the implementation of judgments.

In his speech at the Izmir Conference, the Chairman of the PACE recalled that the CoM, which 'holds the principal responsibility for the supervision of the execution of the Court's judgments, has itself acknowledged the benefit of greater parliamentary involvement'. It is regrettable that the final Declaration adopted in Izmir on this matter only mentions the CoM, and even recalls 'the special role given to the Committee of Ministers in exercising its supervisory function under the Convention and underlines the requirement to carry out its supervision only on the basis of a legal analysis of the Court's judgments'.

There are many examples of good practices and progress emerging from the agreement of the three organs on some issues and the resulting pressure on States to comply with their obligations. In some instances these organs convinced States to adopt some specific measures, even without uniting their efforts, just through a positive cross-fertilisation of their work. It is necessary to illustrate this statement with a few examples. Concerning the payment of default interest after the expiry of the deadline to pay just satisfaction, even before the ECtHR imposed default interest on just satisfaction, the CoM required that the sum actually paid by States made full reparation for the harm sustained. That was the case in *Stran Greek Refineries and Stratis Andreadis*.[102]

(Appl. No. 15766/03), Judgment (Grand Chamber), 16 March 2010, Reports 2010; and observations of the Greek government regarding the case of *Sampanis* v. *Greece*, DH-DD (2010)586, 23 November 2010; Communications from Human Rights Watch in the case of *Sejdić and Finci* v. *Bosnia and Herzegovina*, DH-DD(2010)307, 9 June 2010. Communications from NGOs in the case of ECtHR, *Meltex Ltd. and Mesrop Movsesyan* v. *Armenia* (Appl. No. 32283/04), Judgment (Third Section), 17 June 2008, not reported, DH-DD(2010)375, 10 August 2010. Communication from an NGO in the case of ECtHR, *Bulves AD* v. *Bulgaria* (Appl. No. 3991/03), Judgment (Fifth Section), 22 January 2009, not reported, DH-DD(2010)377, 16 August 2010.

[101] Communication by an NGO in ECtHR, *Strain* v. *Romania* (Appl. No. 57001/00), Judgment (Third Section), 21 July 2005, Reports 2005-VII, DH-DD(2010)37F, 28 January 2010.

[102] The interest rate for compensation was in the region of 6 to 7 per cent of the principal established by the Court. See Committee of Ministers, Resolution DH (97) 184, 20 March

THE COURT AS A PART OF THE COUNCIL OF EUROPE   289

In this case, the three organs worked very effectively together to achieve reopening in the interest of the applicant. The practice was initiated by the CoM. Then some decisions of the PACE required the adoption of domestic measures to allow the reopening of national proceedings.[103]

These developments prompted a change in the Court's 'policy' in this field. The ECtHR now interprets the reopening of proceedings as a measure as close to *restitutio in integrum* as possible[104] and considers it to further 'the ideal form of reparation in international law'.[105] Consequently, it contends that the availability of such a procedure in national law 'demonstrat[ed] a Contracting State's commitment to the Convention and the case law to which it has given rise'.[106] The Court thus took a further step: instead of contenting itself with establishing the beneficial effects of the reopening of domestic proceedings after the violative act, it commended this measure prior to the event as offering the most appropriate remedy or an appropriate way of redressing the violation. Now the ECtHR proceeds as described, in particular in cases where the right to an independent and impartial tribunal has been violated.[107] The issue whether or not individuals must (instead of may) be released pending the new proceedings was discussed and eventually criticised by the PACE in the case of *Sadak, Zana, Dicle and Dogan* v. *Turkey*,[108] and also by the CoM in an interim resolution.[109] Relying on the presumption of

---

1997, concerning ECtHR, *Stran Greek Refineries and Stratis Andreadis* v. *Greece* (Appl. No. 13427/87), Judgment (Chamber), 9 December 1994, Series A, Vol. 301-B: 'stressing Greece's obligation to safeguard the value of the amounts awarded', the CoM ascertained that the sum paid, 'increased in order to provide compensation for the loss of value caused by the delay in payment, [corresponded] to the just satisfaction awarded by the Court'.

[103] See, for example, Parliamentary Assembly, 'Implementation of Decisions of the European Court of Human Rights', Recommendation 1684 (2004), 23 November 2004, and Parliamentary Assembly, 'Implementation of Decisions of the European Court of Human Rights', Resolution 1411 (2004), 23 November 2004, at 18.

[104] ECtHR, *Piersack* v. *Belgium (Article 50)* (Appl. No. 8692/79), 26 October 1984, Series A, Vol. 85, at 11.

[105] ECtHR, *Verein gegen Tierfabriken Schweiz (VgT)* v. *Switzerland* (Appl. No. 32772/02), Judgment (Fifth Section), 4 October 2007, Reports 2009, at 56.

[106] *Ibid.*, at 55.

[107] ECtHR, *Gençel* v. *Turkey* (Appl. No. 53431/99), Judgment (Third Section), 23 October 2003, not reported; ECtHR, *Ceylan* v. *Turkey (No. 2)* (Appl. No. 46454/99), Judgment (Second Section), 11 October 2005, not reported, at 38.

[108] Parliamentary Assembly, 'Implementation of Decisions of the European Court of Human Rights by Turkey' (M.E. Jurgens), Doc. 10192, at 7–9.

[109] Committee of Ministers, 'Interim Resolution', ResDH (2004) 31, 6 April 2004.

innocence and the Court's judgment, the CoM now considers that, in addition to the reopening of proceedings, the release of applicants is an integral part of the right to reparation 'in the absence of any compelling reasons justifying their continued detention pending the outcome of the new trial'.[110]

It is indisputable that these overall developments offer further incentives for States to allow reopening in their legal system. More explicitly, and more often than in the past, the Court also refers to interim resolutions enacted by the CoM in order to conclude that there is a systemic failure of the State to implement the ECHR on one or more issues.[111] It is certain that such references will increase in the years to come.

It may be concluded that the three organs interact on the implementation of judgments. Their actions complement one another most of the time. Yet, there is a risk for the ECtHR to get more involved in these technical and sensitive matters, in particular, at a time when States raise the subsidiarity principle, and thus challenge the imposition of specified measures in the implementation of judgments. Indeed, the Izmir Conference focused, first, on the 'new standard and enhanced procedures for supervision', whose aim is to speed-up the supervisory function by the CoM, and second, on the 'principle of subsidiarity' in this matter, and so on the 'choice of means' of States to implement the judgments. This approach reveals the pressure imposed by States on the European system of human rights. Currently, the reluctance of some States to implement some judgments *bona fide* seems to be the most problematic challenge. The CoM and the other European organs in charge of the supervisory function should be equipped to sanction such reluctance. The role of the Court, on the other hand, should be limited to an

---

[110] Ibid., 'Stressing, in this connection, the importance of the presumption of innocence as guaranteed by the Convention; deplores the fact that, notwithstanding the reopening of the impugned proceedings, the applicants continue to serve their original sentences ...; stresses the obligation incumbent on Turkey, under Article 46, paragraph 1, of the Convention, to comply with the Court's judgment in this case notably through measures to erase the consequences of the violation found for the applicants, including the release of the applicants in the absence of any compelling reasons.'

[111] ECtHR, *Vassilios Athanasiou and Others* v. *Greece* (Appl. No. 50973/08), Judgment (First Section), 21 December 2010, not reported, 45–53; ECtHR, *Gaglione and Others* v. *Italy* (Appl. Nos. 45867/07 and 474 others), Judgment (Second Section), 21 December 2010, not reported; ECtHR, *Konstantin Markin* v. *Russia* (Appl. No. 30078/06), Judgment (First Section), 7 October 2010, not reported; and ECtHR, *Wegera* v. *Poland* (Appl. No. 141/07), Judgment (Fourth Section), 19 January 2010, not reported, at 80.

objective examination of the violation of article 46,[112] so as not to get mixed up in political issues with States.

The ambition of the ECtHR to play a greater role could also be supported by an increased administrative, and perhaps financial, autonomy. On this issue, the ECtHR has also tried to make progress, but without the same success. This will be addressed in the next section.

3. The budgetary and administrative issues: the Court's dependence on the CoM

This section will discuss the pros and cons of a greater financial and administrative autonomy of the Court. On this question, a comparative approach with the practice of other regional and international tribunals will be adopted.

3.1 Deciding on the budget of the ECtHR: the involvement of the Secretary General

In conformity with article 50 of the ECHR, 'the expenditure on the Court shall be borne by the Council of Europe'. Accordingly, the Court does not have a separate budget; its budget is part of the general budget of the Council of Europe. As such, it is subject to the approval of the CoM as part of the overall Council of Europe budget. According to some authors, the Court is a body 'pris en pension' by the Council of Europe, as it is not really an organ of the Council of Europe.[113]

Article 20 of the Statute of the Council of Europe specifies that 'resolutions of the CoM, including adoption of the budget … require a two-thirds majority of the representatives casting a vote and a majority of the representatives entitled to sit on the Committee'. The PACE is involved in that process, but purely in an advisory capacity, having to provide two opinions (one on the Council of Europe's general budget, the

---

[112] See *Emre* v. *Switzerland (No. 2)*, where the Court concludes there was a violation of both articles 8 and 46.

[113] These are the words of H. Klebes, cited by J.F. Flauss, 'De l'indépendance de la Cour Européenne Des Droits de l'Homme', J.F. Flauss, (ed.), *La Mise en Œuvre du Protocole No.11: le Nouveau Règlement de la Cour EDH: Actes de la Journée d'Études du 23 octobre 1999 à la Mémoire de Louis Edmond Pettiti* (Brussels: Bruylant, 2000) 13–31 (hereinafter Flauss, 'De l'indépendance de la Cour'). For J.F. Flauss, 'institutionnellement, l'autonomie et partant l'indépendance budgétaire de la nouvelle Cour avoisine le degré zéro', at 29.

other on its own budget). Yet the PACE has complained that this advisory competence has been made 'without either having seen the draft budget submitted to the CoM by the Secretary General or being aware of the positions of the bodies involved in the budgetary process [Ministers' Deputies, Budget Committee]'.[114] The PACE has also required more budgetary powers, in light of what could be expected from a legislative assembly.[115] It needs to be stressed that the Secretary General is playing an important part in that process by submitting a draft of the budget to the CoM. According to interviews with the former President of the Court, Luzius Wildhaber, current disputes have not occurred between the CoM and the Court, nor between the Assembly and the Court, but between the Secretary General and the Court.[116] Luzius Wildhaber also confessed he was in favour of a separate budget for the Court.

With regard to this question, the ECtHR differs fundamentally from the other regional and international Courts. Indeed, article 72 of the American Convention on Human Rights holds that 'The Court shall draw up its own budget and submit it for approval to the General Assembly through the General Secretariat. The latter may not introduce any changes in it.' Article 26 of the Statute of the Court also repeats that the Court administers its own budget. This approach is also shared by the African system, even if it is not couched in such strict words. Article 26 of the Statute of the African Court of Justice and Human Rights states that: 'The Court shall prepare its draft annual budget and shall submit it to the Assembly through the Executive Council. 2. The budget of the Court shall be borne by the African Union. 3. The Court shall be accountable for the execution of its budget and shall submit reports thereon to the Executive Council in conformity with the Financial Rules and Regulations of the African Union.' Moreover, both the International Court of Justice (ICJ) and the ECJ submit a proposal for their own budget. Limiting ourselves to these examples, internationally, judicial independence seems to go hand-in-hand with budgetary independence. It would therefore be desirable for the ECtHR to co-decide on its own budget or,

---

[114] Recommendation 1155 (1991), Powers of the Assembly in Budgetary Matters, 28 June 1991.

[115] Parliamentary Assembly, 'Enlargement of the Council of Europe: the Budgetary and Administrative Powers of the Assembly' (M.A. Martinez), Doc. 7900, 8 September 1997: '1. The Assembly considers that its present budgetary and administrative powers are unsatisfactory and do not correspond to the normal prerogatives of a parliamentary assembly.'

[116] Interview with L. Wildhaber, 3 May 2011, Fribourg (on file with the author).

at least, to have the competence to propose it; the lack of financial autonomy is dangerous and could jeopardise the capacity of the Court to perform its functions in the future.

An autonomous budget would not necessarily mean a higher amount allocated to the Court. In 2010 the budget of the ECtHR (including the registry) was raised from €58 to €58.48 million; in 2011 the sum was €63.7 million.[117] At the same time, the ordinary budget for the Council of Europe in 2011 and in 2010 totalled €217 million, as it was subject to a zero growth policy. By contrast, in 2009 the budget of the Inter-American Court of Human Rights (IACtHR) and the Inter-American Commission of Human Rights (IACommHR) was US $5,526,600, whereas the overall budget of the Organization of American States (OAS) was US $90,125,000. The budget of the Commission and the Court amount to 4–5 per cent and 2 per cent of the overall budget of the OAS, respectively, whereas the budget of the ECtHR consumed slightly more than one-third of the total Council of Europe budget. These figures must be analysed in consideration of the number of cases submitted to these organs, as the number of cases before the ECtHR is infinitely higher than the number of applications the IACtHR has to deal with: with the annual budget of roughly €58 million for 2010, the Court decided 41,183 in total in that year. This means that the Court spent about €1,500 per decision. The IACtHR, by contrast, decided only 143 cases on a budget of US $3.7 million, which means the IACtHR has about US $25,000 per decision.

The budget of the ECtHR somehow increased during the last fifteen years, despite the fact that the budget of the Council of Europe was subject to the zero growth rule. The PACE required that the budget of the ECtHR be elevated, and that this budget be separated from the overall budget of the Council of Europe, without claiming an autonomous budget for the Court.[118] The PACE, opposing the redistribution of the budget of the

---

[117] ECtHR, *Annual Report 2010*, provisional edition (Strasbourg: Council of Europe, January 2011), at 17.

[118] Parliamentary Assembly, Recommendation 1812 (2007) and Parliamentary Assembly, 'Political Dimension of the Council of Europe Budget' (P. Wille), Doc. 11371, 12 September 2007: '6. The Assembly consequently asks the Committee of Ministers to place at the disposal of the Council of Europe the funds necessary to translate into action the tasks and priorities identified at the Warsaw Summit, which entails allocating financial and other resources not just to the European Court of Human Rights but also to all the other sectors whose activities ranked as a priority at the Summit.' '7.4. separate the budget of the European Court of Human Rights from the rest of the ordinary budget while keeping the Court within the Council of Europe's budgetary structure.'

Council of Europe in favour of the ECtHR, suggested 'the member states [to] face up to their responsibilities and finance all the needs of the European Court of Human Rights outside zero growth in real terms'.[119] In a Recommendation adopted in 2007, it also asked the CoM 'to 7.5. set minimum scales for member states' contributions so as to cover at least the administrative cost of a judge at the Court'. Indeed, it appears that some State contributions do not even cover the cost of their judge at the ECtHR.

Under the former chairmanship of Jean-Paul Costa, a sort of *modus vivendi* seemed to have been found between the Secretary General and the Court. Nevertheless, the situation is becoming more sensitive owing to the current financial crisis, and the budget allocated to the Court has even been reduced. In 2010, the Secretary General suggested that the budget of the Court be reduced by €251,600 and opposed the incorporation in the 2010 budget priorities of the third programme of reinforcement of the Court with the recruitment of an extra 225 staff. This view was fully endorsed by the CoM.[120] As one author wrote, 'judges depend on governments for the implementation of court decisions and for other forms of support, including budgetary support. The budget is obviously important given the severe backlog of cases.'[121]

3.2 Towards more autonomy of the ECtHR?

It is unsurprising that the issue of gaining more autonomy, mostly with regard to the budgetary questions, has been raised in the past.[122] In fact,

---

[119] Parliamentary Assembly, 'Budgets of the Council of Europe for the Financial Year 2008', Opinion No. 264 (2007), 24 May 2007.

[120] Committee of Ministers, Extract CM(2009)90, 'Meeting Report of the Budget Committee', May 2009 Session Court Enhancement Programme: '40. The Committee recognised that any significant reinforcement of the Court presented a serious challenge for the Organisation. If the €21.6M were to be financed by additional resources, made available through member states contributions, this would represent additional contributions of some 10 per cent for member states. The Committee considered that in the current economic climate it would not be possible in the foreseeable future to allocate additional resources to the Council of Europe by increasing Member States contributions in order to finance the programme of the Court. 41. The Committee also noted, that if the organisation had to finance some €21.6M on an annual basis for the Court programme within the Ordinary Budget this would only be possible by making dramatic reductions in other sectors of the Organisation...)'

[121] E. Voeten, 'Politics, Judicial Behavior, and Institutional Design', in Christoffersen and Madsen (eds.), *The European Court of Human Rights between Law and Politics*, 61–76, at 76.

[122] See ECtHR, *Ten Years of the 'New' European Court of Human Rights 1998-2008, Situation and Outlook*, Proceedings of the Seminar, 13 October 2008, 'Preface', President

more autonomy has been more highly prioritised than the issue of recruitment and the internal functioning of the Court. The Group of Wise Persons recommended '... in the interests of enhancing the Court's independence and effectiveness, ... granting it the greatest possible operational autonomy, as regards in particular the presentation and management of its budget and the appointment, deployment and promotion of its staff'.[123] The lack of administrative autonomy was also criticised by the former President, Jean-Paul Costa.[124] To a certain extent, such an autonomy *de facto* already exists, according to interviews with judges of the Court and members of the PACE. Indeed, the Secretary General leaves the Court to decide its policy of recruitment.

Despite the foregoing, currently the entire internal functioning of the Court seems to be subject to the CoM. Two aspects exemplify this lack of autonomy: first, the establishment and functioning of the Liaison Committee with the Court, second, the way the rules on the status of judges are enacted.

The Liaison Committee, a body of dialogue between the CoM and the Court,[125] was created in 2000 'to maintain a dialogue on the future of human rights protection in Europe and questions affecting the European Court of human rights'.[126] The Liaison Committee is chaired by an ambassador. In 2004, the Secretary General expressed the desire to be included in its work. The proposals concerning the modalities and procedures of the Liaison Committee mentioned that the draft agenda of the meetings of this Committee 'shall be agreed in advance with the Court', and that 'the Chair shall ensure that the judicial independence of the Court is respected in the proceedings of the Liaison Committee'.

Costa, at 15: 'How can one not raise the question of the Court's need for greater autonomy of management and funding, which would provide increased effectiveness?' See also 'Memorandum of the President of the ECtHR to the States with a view to preparing the Interlaken Conference', 3 July 2009: 'At the Conference, in addition to defining the relationship with States, it will be necessary to take steps to ensure that the Court is able to enjoy autonomy with regard to administrative and budgetary management. Steps must also be taken to meet the Court's resource needs.' This requirement will not be worded in exactly the same way one year later.

[123] 'Report of the Group of Wise Persons to the CoM,' CM(2006)203, 15 November 2006, at 124.

[124] 'Memorandum of the President of the ECtHR to the States with a View to Preparing the Interlaken Conference', 3 July 2009, at 4.

[125] There was an attempt to set up another Liaison Committee between the ECtHR and the PACE, but it did not work.

[126] Committee of Ministers, '706th meeting', 11 April 2010, Decisions, item 4.1.

If meetings are convened by the Chair, the Court only has the power to make proposals concerning the holding of meetings. Clearly the aim of the Liaison Committee was thus to allow the CoM to prepare and initiate the reforms of the future ECtHR.

Resolution (97)9 'on the status and conditions of service of judges of the European Court of Human Rights' governs the conditions of service of judges and ad hoc judges and exemplifies the dependence of the status of the ECtHR's judges on decisions of the CoM.[127] The ECtHR was not involved in the enactment of these rules.[128] Such rules were intended to be provisional and to be reviewed 'on the proposal of the Secretary General of the Council of Europe and in consultation with the President of the Court'. Nonetheless, it is surprising that the CoM has competence to enact these rules (following the text of the preamble to this resolution pursuant to article 16 of the Statute of the Council of Europe).[129] In addition, the Secretary General is given more powers than the President of the Court to review such rules.[130] This resolution has not been reviewed.

In 2004, discussions concerned the reform of the pension regime of judges. Under the prior regime, judges were to provide for their retirement or pension benefits at their own expense. On this issue, a majority of delegations clearly favoured the Budget Committee's recommendation over the judges' proposal, taking into account the budgetary constraints.[131] The main difference between the Secretary General's proposal

---

[127] It deals, in one appendix, with questions such as the annual salary, the place of residence, holiday and sick leave, the payment of expenses by the Council of Europe and social protection. Appendix II concerns the provisional regulations governing the conditions of service of ad hoc judges.

[128] Flauss, 'De l'indépendance de la Cour', at 17, note 6: 'La présence au sein du groupe de travail spécial du président et du greffe de l'ancienne Cour ne constitue qu'un pis-aller: ni l'un, ni l'autre n'avaient la moindre légitimité pour parler au nom de la nouvelle Cour. Leur âge les empêchait d'ailleurs, de jure ou de facto, d'être "renouvelés" dans leurs fonctions respectives.'

[129] According to article 16, 'the Committee of Ministers shall, subject to the provisions of Articles 24, 28, 30, 32, 33 and 35, relating to the powers of the Consultative Assembly, decide with binding effect all matters relating to the internal organisation and arrangements of the Council of Europe. For this purpose the Committee of Ministers shall adopt such financial and administrative arrangements as may be necessary.'

[130] Flauss, 'De l'indépendance de la Cour', at 17: 'Dans ces conditions, la résolution (97)9 a pu être comprise comme un coup de force ou à tout le moins, un coup de Jarnac asséné à la nouvelle Cour, avant même qu'elle ne soit constituée.'

[131] Committee of Ministers, 'Rapporteur Group on Administrative and Budgetary Questions', GR-AB(2004)CB9, 26 July 2004.

and the judges' proposal concerned the level of pension to be allocated to judges after six- and twelve-year- terms, respectively (25 per cent and 50 per cent according to the judges' proposal, 8 per cent and 16 per cent according to the Secretary General's proposal). The disagreement was also on the installation allowance (amounting to one month's remuneration for a judge who takes up residence in Strasbourg alone, and two months for judges whose spouse and children take up residence in Strasbourg, according to the judges' proposal).[132] Thus, in this case, the Court considered that the proposal failed 'completely the test of comparability with other international Courts ...'; it concluded that 'in sum, the proposed substantial reduction in salary, the low level of pension resulting and the non-retroactivity of the scheme combine to make the SG's proposal unacceptable to the Court'.[133]

Resolution 97(9) was replaced first in 2004, and finally in 2009.[134] The preamble to the rules adopted in 2009 refers only to the proposal of the Secretary General, and still mentions article 16 of the Statute of the Council of Europe. The central element of this text is article 10 on pensions, which holds that: 'Judges shall benefit from the pension Scheme for staff members which is in force at the Council of Europe at the time of their appointment, subject to any modifications rendered necessary by their particular status and conditions of service.' According to this general regime, the rate of contribution is 9.2 per cent of the basic salary. So the reference is made to the rules applied to staff members of the Council of Europe, despite the fact that judges benefit from a 'special status' (article 1), as their independence is to be preserved.

The current discussions regarding the enactment of a statute for the Court concern the increased autonomy of the Court and the way to facilitate the amendment of provisions relating to organisational matters. This idea has started to take shape since the Izmir and Interlaken

---

[132] See Committee of Ministers, 'Response to the Secretary General's Proposal for the Revision of Resolution (97)9 on the Status and Conditions of Service of Judges', Appendix E, 7 April 2004, in Committee of Ministers, CM(2004)69, 26 April 2004, Review of Resolution (97)9 on the Status and the Conditions of Service of the Judges of the ECtHR, Proposal of the Secretary General.

[133] *Ibid.*, Appendix E *in fine* (VII. Conclusions).

[134] Committee of Ministers, 'CM/Res(2004)50 on the Status and Conditions of Service of Judges of the ECtHR', 15 December 2004. Committee of Ministers, 'CM/Res(2009)5 on the Status and Conditions of Service of Judges of the ECtHR and of the Commissioner for Human Rights', 23 September 2009.

declarations.[135] The independence of the Court should be enhanced, not reduced.[136] At this stage, the content of the provisions that would be subject to the procedure is not clear. A committee of experts on a simplified procedure for amendment of certain provisions of the ECHR was set up; the Court is not represented, only the registry may send a representative(s) to meetings of this Committee.[137]

However, the issue is not so much about increasing the budget of the Court (the Court is aware of the financial crisis in Europe) as gaining more autonomy in the way the Court functions daily and uses its resources. The Interlaken Conference 'calls upon States Parties and the Council of Europe to ... grant to the Court, in the interest of its efficient functioning, the necessary level of administrative autonomy within the Council of Europe'. It also 'invites the Court to continue improving its internal structure and working methods and making maximum use of the procedural tools and the resources at its disposal'. The Izmir Declaration states that the conference invites the Court 'to present to the Committee of Ministers proposals, on a budget-neutral basis, for the creation of a training unit for lawyers and other professionals'! The conference even 'notes with satisfaction the arrangements made within the Registry of the Court that have allowed better management of budgetary and human resources'. Evidently the functioning of the Court is under strict scrutiny by the CoM and by the States.

Consequently, more and more pressure is put on the Court for a better use of its resources in its daily functioning.

4. Concluding remarks

During the last few years, the ECtHR has become increasingly involved in diverse issues. This is particularly true for the election of judges (indirectly through the panel of experts) and for the implementation of its judgments; the attempt to gain more autonomy at administrative and financial levels has been a failure so far. These attempts go hand-in-hand with the increasing activities of the Court and the willingness of some

---

[135] 'Interlaken Declaration', 19 February 2010, point G of the Action Plan. 'Izmir Declaration', 27 April 2011, point G of the Follow-up Plan.

[136] Speech of Former President Costa, Izmir, 26 April 2011: 'Toutefois, l'objectif doit être de renforcer l'indépendance, non de la réduire, ce qui serait le cas si certaines dispositions de notre Règlement étaient remontées au niveau d'un Statut.'

[137] Committee of Ministers, GT-SUIVI.Interlaken(2010)7, Appendix V, at 16.

judges, some politicians and members of the registry of the Court to reform the European system for the protection of human rights towards a Court which would deal with a limited number of cases and have a constitutional role.[138]

Such attempts are also linked to a certain confusion of powers between the three main organs of the Council of Europe, Indeed, this analysis has revealed that the overwhelming number of cases the ECtHR has to deal with has been used as a pretext for the governments in Europe and for the various actors of the Council of Europe to join forces. Although this mobilisation is understandable, as remedies have to be found to the current problems faced by the Court, the point is that it has blurred the distinction between the powers of the three organs (the CoM, the PACE and the Court) as stated in the Statute of the Council of Europe and the ECHR. The separation of powers between the legislative, executive and judicial bodies of the Council of Europe is put into question. The crisis, which is a crisis of the implementation of human rights in the national States, and not a crisis of the Court or of the European system, is used to legitimate the involvement of the other organs, and in particular of the CoM, to interfere in judicial matters. The independence of the Court is threatened by the CoM. The Brighton Declaration even indicates how the Court shall deliver judgments in repetitive and structural cases![139] It is not surprising that the previous proposal to enact a statute of the Court was addressed in only a few words in the Final Declaration of Brighton.[140] The most serious concern does not come from the lack of

---

[138] Steering Committee for Human Rights, 'CDDH Contribution to the Ministerial Conference organised by the UK Chairmanship of the Committee of Ministers', CDDH(2012) R74 Addendum III, 15 February 2012, para. 34.

[139] CoE, High Level Conference on the Future of the European Court of Human Rights, 'Brighton Declaration', 20 April 2012, para. 20 (c): 'Expresses continued concern about the large number of repetitive applications pending before the Court; welcomes the continued use by the Court of proactive measures, particularly pilot judgments, to dispose of repetitive violations in an efficient manner; and encourages the States Parties, the Committee of Ministers and the Court to work together to find ways to resolve the large numbers of applications arising from systemic issues identified by the Court, considering the various ideas that have been put forward, including their legal, practical and financial implications, and taking into account the principle of equal treatment of all States Parties; d) Building on the pilot judgment procedure, invites the Committee of Ministers to consider the advisability and modalities of a procedure by which the Court could register and determine a small number of representative applications from a group of applications that allege the same violation against the same respondent State Party, such determination being applicable to the whole group.'

[140] Ibid., para. 37 in the 'General and final provisions' part.

an autonomous budget of the Court, but mostly from the involvement of the executive organ representing the governments to impose its will upon the Court, even in its daily functioning and judicial policy. In his speech at Brighton, the President of the Court affirmed that the judges are, 'I have to say, uncomfortable with the idea that Governments can in some way dictate to the Court how its case-law should evolve or how it should carry out the judicial functions conferred on it', concluding that 'the need for the Convention and for a strong and independent Court is as pressing now as at any time in its history'.[141]

In the name of more efficiency of the European system of human rights, the current reforms represent a worrying infringement of the independence of the Court, which cannot be justified by the interference of the Court in the election process and in the implementation of its own judgments.

---

[141] CoE, High Level Conference, Brighton, 18–20 April 2012, Sir Nicolas Bratza, President of the European Court of Human Rights, Draft Speaking Notes.

8

Should the European Union ratify the European Convention on Human Rights? Some remarks on the relations between the European Court of Human Rights and the European Court of Justice

LEONARD F.M. BESSELINK[*]

1. Juxtaposed human rights orders and a twin peak system

This chapter focuses on the relationship between the European Court of Human Rights (ECtHR, the Court) and the European Union (EU) in light of the commitment of the EU to accede to the European Convention on Human Rights (ECHR).[1] It assesses what point there is or should be for the EU to accede.

As the process of accession is still underway at the time of writing, it is appropriate to look at what this process, and the complications it has run into so far, tell us about the importance of accession. In this context, it also highlights the role which both the ECtHR case law, and the ECtHR as an independent actor in the process of accession, have played until now.

In order to be able to assess what we are heading for, we first need to outline the existing relations between the EU and its European Court of Justice (ECJ) on the one hand and the ECHR and its ECtHR on the other, before the accession. In this regard we need to distinguish between the legal terms of the institutional relationship and the more factual institutional relationship as it takes shape in the contacts between the two courts. One might think that prior to the accession of the EU to the ECHR the relationship between the ECtHR and the ECJ has been one of

---

[*] This contribution has been written while the author was holder of the chair of European Constitutional Law at the University of Utrecht and Fellow of the Netherlands Institute for Advanced Studies (NIAS), Wassenaar, Netherlands, which have supported him with a generous grant. This text reflects the State of play per June 2012.

[1] Article 6(2) Treaty on European Union (TEU): 'The Union shall accede to the European Convention for the Protection of Human Rights and Fundamental Freedoms. Such accession shall not affect the Union's competences as defined in the Treaties.'

mere juxtaposition. This is formally true, but only trivially so. In fact, the relationship has been asymmetrical. This merits clarification.

Prior to accession, the ECtHR has had no official *legal* relationship with the EU, in the sense that there are mutually obligatory arrangements which create specific institutional relations with the ECJ on a mutually agreed legal basis such as a treaty or other bi- or multilateral treaty. Formally, the ECtHR has no official legal relation to the EU. It cannot, therefore, scrutinise its actions as it can scrutinise those of the states which are a party to the ECHR. But from the perspective of the EU, the relationship is not so in the same manner.

1.1 Asymmetric legal relations

In its case law, the ECJ unilaterally adopted a standard of fundamental rights protection based on two pillars: the rights of the constitutional traditions common to the member states and the rights of the human rights treaties to which the member states are party, in particular – but not exclusively – the ECHR. The rights found in these two pillars could neither be protected *qua* national constitutional rights nor *qua* treaty rights. The EU is not legally bound by national constitutions, nor is it legally bound by human rights treaties.[2] The power of the ECJ is limited to the interpretation of EU law. As it is neither bound by national law, nor to human rights treaties to which only member states are bound, it has no formal legal role in guaranteeing those rights. Nevertheless, in order to achieve such protection, these rights had to be transformed into EU law. This was done by declaring them part of the general principles of Community law, now Union law. Resorting to this somewhat roundabout approach was made necessary by the combination of the absence of a bill containing classic human rights in the European founding treaties, and the EC/EU not being a party the ECHR, together with the repeated warnings by German courts referring cases to the ECJ. The warnings were made in those national courts' explanation of the questions they posed in preliminary reference proceedings: if, in those instances, the ECJ were to refrain from taking a constructive approach to the protection of the rights in a manner equivalent to how they are protected under the German *Grundgesetz*, this would be reason for those German courts

---

[2] A recent exception is the Convention on the Rights of Persons with Disabilities (13 December 2006) 2515 UNTS 3, entered into force 3 May 2008, which the EU signed on 30 March 2007 and ratified on 23 December 2010.

no longer to grant direct effect to the disputed European law of which the compatibility with fundamental rights was in doubt.

Thus, via the convoluted route of the general principles of Union law, the ECHR rights became unilaterally incorporated into EU law, first in the ECJ case law only, and subsequently in the EU Treaty concluded in Maastricht in 1992 in a formula which we still find now in article 6(3) EU:

> Fundamental rights, as guaranteed by the European Convention for the Protection of Human Rights and Fundamental Freedoms and as they result from the constitutional traditions common to the Member States, shall constitute general principles of the Union's law.

1.2 From fundamental rights rejection to full scrutiny

It should be emphasised from the outset that the ECJ has gradually improved the standard of scrutiny it upholds when confronted with a claim that an act under EU law is contrary to fundamental rights guarantees. In its early case law, the Court simply refused to consider such a complaint. It could do so the more easily, since plaintiffs relied on fundamental rights as contained in national bills of rights, in particular, German plaintiffs by relying on the *Grundgesetz*.[3] As the Court is competent only to adjudicate on the basis of European law, not national law, the standard rejection was plausible. The turning point came in a series of German cases, of which the first is the case of a man called Erich Stauder, who wanted to remain anonymous and therefore did not want his name on the tickets for cheap butter for poor Germans to be handed in in shops – a European subsidised manner to reduce the quantity of over-produced butter stocked by the then EC to keep prices up at the time. The Court, incidentally, had the insensitivity not only of mentioning his name, making the man who sought anonymity famous among lawyers, but also of giving the precise details of his home address in Ulm.[4] This and the subsequent line of case law confirmed the ECJ's

---

[3] Case 1/58, 4 February 1959, *Friedrich Stork & Cie* v. *High Authority of the European Coal and Steel Community*; Joined Cases 36, 37, 38 and 40/59, 15 July 1960, *Präsident Ruhrkohlen- Verkaufsgesellschaft mbH, Geitling Ruhrkohlen- Verkaufsgesellschaft mbH, Mausegatt Ruhrkohlen- Verkaufsgesellschaft mbH and I. Nold KG* v. *High Authority of the European Coal and Steel Community*.

[4] Case 29/69, *Erich Stauder* v. *City of Ulm – Sozialamt* [1969] ECR 419.

power to protect such rights as general principles of Community law, but indeed, the scrutiny was lax. Mostly the Court found that a matter came within the scope of the right adduced, but that the measure which interfered with that right was taken in the interest of the Community and did not fully take away the core essence of the right, so was justified.[5] In the course of time, this approach was criticised as not 'taking rights seriously'.[6]

A quite definitive change in the intensity of scrutiny came in the *Connolly* judgment, an appeal against a judgment of the Court of First Instance on disciplinary measures against a Commission official who had written a book during a study leave on the many flaws of the making of the monetary union.[7] In the book, he used what is conceived of on the continent as Europhobic invective, but which presumably might just as well be qualified as colourful hyperbole in a long-standing tradition of English writing on anything 'European'.[8] He not only wrote, but also published the book without the prior consent of his superiors in the Commission,[9] under the title *The Rotten Heart of Europe*, with *Manneken Pis* (Petit Julien) weeing over the map of Europe on the cover. The fact that not everything in the book was kind, flattering or polite had – no doubt – added fuel to the conflict he had with his

---

[5] E.g., Case 11/70, *Internationale Handelsgesellschaft mbH* v. *Einfuhr- und Vorratsstelle für Getreide und Futtermittel* [1970] ECR 1125; Case 4/73, *J. Nold, Kohlen- und Baustoffgroßhandlung* v. *Commission of the European Communities* [1974] ECR 491; Case 44/79, *Liselotte Hauer* v. *Land Rheinland-Pfalz* [1979] ECR 03727.

[6] J. Coppell and A. O'Neill, 'The European Court of Justice: Taking Rights Seriously?', *Common Market Law Review* 29:4 (1992) 669–92; and the riposte by N.J.S. Lockhart and J.H.H. Weiler, '"Taking Rights Seriously" Seriously: The European Court and its Fundamental Rights Jurisprudence', *Common Market Law Review* 32:1 (1995) 51–94 (Part I), and 579–627 (Part II).

[7] Case C-273/99 P, *Bernard Connolly* v. *Commission of the European Communities* [2001] ECR I-1575.

[8] See M. Spiering, *Englishness: Foreigners and Images of National Identity in Postwar Literature. Studia Imagologica: Comparative Literature and European Diversity* (Amsterdam: Rodopi, 1992).

[9] Article 17 of the Staff Regulations, Regulation (EEC, Euratom, ECSC) No. 259/68 of the Council of 29 February 1968, OJ 56, 4.3.1968, pp. 1–7, as it then read: 'An official shall not, whether alone or together with others, publish or cause to be published without the permission of the appointing authority, any matter dealing with the work of the Communities. Permission shall be refused only where the proposed publication is liable to prejudice the interests of the Communities.' This provision has been amended by Council Regulation (EC, Euratom) No. 723/2004 of 22 March 2004, OJ L 124/1, replacing prior consent with prior notification.

Commission superiors, who imposed disciplinary sanctions, including his withdrawal from his post. The Court of First Instance in essence found the disciplinary measures justified, finding 'that the book at issue contains numerous aggressive, derogatory and frequently insulting statements, which are detrimental to the honour of the persons and institutions to which they refer' (para. 125 of its judgment). The Court of First Instance had rejected Connolly's reliance on article 10 ECHR. At the outset of doing so, it stated that the right contained in this provision is part of the general principles of Community law protected by the European courts, but instead of referring to and using the strict criterion of 'necessity in a democratic society' in the text of article 10, second paragraph, ECHR, translated the strict language of article 10 into the quite different standard developed in the ECJ case law. Compare the two texts:

ARTICLE 10(2) ECHR:	ECJ STANDARD FOR RESTRICTIONS AS USED IN *CONNOLLY* AT COURT OF FIRST INSTANCE:
The exercise of these freedoms, since it carries with it duties and responsibilities, may be subject to such formalities, conditions, restrictions or penalties as are prescribed by law and are *necessary in a democratic society, in the interests of* national security, territorial integrity or public safety, for the prevention of disorder or crime, for the protection of health or morals, for the protection of the reputation or rights of others, for preventing the disclosure of information received in confidence, or for maintaining the authority and impartiality of the judiciary.	[F]undamental rights do not constitute an unfettered prerogative but may be subject to restrictions, provided that the restrictions in fact correspond to objectives of general public interest pursued by the Community and do not constitute, with regard to the objectives pursued, a disproportionate and intolerable interference which infringes upon the very substance of the rights protected.

Against this standard, the Court of First Instance quickly concluded that its loose criteria for restricting freedom of expression were fulfilled. On appeal, the ECJ, quite to the contrary and for the very first time, construed the possibilities for restricting freedom of expression under article 10 ECHR strictly and totally in line with the quite strict case law of the ECtHR when it concerns prior restraints on expression. This, I would submit, constituted a revolution in the role of the ECJ as authentic fundamental rights umpire in the Union. Since then, overall the ECJ has lived up to the task of interpreting and applying the ECHR in line with the Strasbourg case law.

1.3   Factual relations between the two courts

The legal story on the state of affairs prior to the accession of the EU to the ECHR is not sufficient to sketch relations between the two courts.[10] There is also the more factual aspect of relations between them. This concerns the judicial dialogue which takes the form of regular meetings between the members of the two courts, which enable them to discuss matters of common interest in a round table meeting, usually on the basis of two or three presentations by members of each court. These exchanges usually take place during the late autumn or winter. The courts take it in turn to host the meetings. As one former judge of the ECtHR once remarked, the judges from Luxembourg each travel with their individual car and driver provided by the ECJ; the judges from Strasbourg go by bus.

It is hard to find out exactly when these periodic meetings began, but presumably they have taken place since the 1990s, and they may have their origin in the establishment of more direct contacts between the two courts after a little accident in 1989. This occurred in the judgment of the ECJ of 21 September 1989 in *Hoechst*, which is a very interesting case also from the substantive point of view.[11] In order to collect evidence of unlawful practices, the business premises of the company were searched by Commission officials under a warrant which ultimately had its basis in a piece of European legislation concerning such unlawful practices, and a fine was eventually imposed.[12] In a case against the imposition of the fine by the Commission, the company held that

---

[10] There is a *hausse* in literature and conferences on both the judicial and the non-judicial 'dialogue among judges'. Instead of many others, I refer to the 'Special Issue on Highest Courts and Transnational Interaction', *Utrecht Law Review* 8(2) (2012); especially the contributions by M. Claes and M. de Visser, 'Are You Networked Yet? On Dialogues in European Judicial Networks', at 100–14.

[11] Joined Cases 46/87 and 227/88, *Hoechst AG v. Commission of the European Communities* [1989] ECR 2859.

[12] Article 14 of EEC Council Regulation No. 17: First Regulation implementing articles 85 and 86 of the Treaty (as amended).

the search was an unlawful infringement of the right to the privacy of the relevant business premises, a fundamental right which forms an integral part of the general principles of Community law. In order to assess this claim, the Court had to establish whether such form of privacy is part of the constitutional traditions common to the member states, or is protected under article 8 of the ECHR (privacy and family life). The Court, however, held:

> that, although the existence of such a right must be recognized in the Community legal order as a principle common to the laws of the member states in regard to the private dwellings of natural persons, the same is not true in regard to undertakings, because there are not inconsiderable divergences between the legal systems of the member states in regard to the nature and degree of protection afforded to business premises against intervention by the public authorities ...
>
> No other inference is to be drawn from Article 8(1) of the European Convention on Human Rights....The protective scope of that article is concerned with the development of man's personal freedom and may not therefore be extended to business premises. Furthermore, *it should be noted that there is no case-law of the European Court of Human Rights on that subject.*[13]

Well, the last statement was not altogether true: there had been a judgment of the ECtHR, handed down on 30 March 1989, in which the Court had considered business premises on the second floor of an entrepreneur's private home to be protected by article 8 ECHR (a position confirmed by the ECtHR in 1992).[14] This judgment came after the reports of the hearing and further to the hearing (8 December 1988), and after the Opinion of the Advocate General, which was delivered at the sitting on 21 February 1989. We should be aware that in those days neither of the courts was connected to the World Wide Web and the judgments of the courts were made available digitally only years later. At any rate, this little accident has been understood to be a reason for establishing closer and more direct contacts between the two courts, of which the mutual visits have come to form part, on a regular basis since, at the latest, 1998.

The meetings did not yield members of the public much more than a press communique which mentions the visit. In 2007, the papers

---

[13] *Hoechst AG v. Commission of the European Communities*, paras. 17–18 (emphasis added).
[14] *Chappell v. UK* (Appl. No. 10461/83), Judgment (Chamber), 30 March 1989, Series A, Vol. 159; *Niemietz v. Germany* (Appl. No. 13710/88), Judgment (Chamber), 16 December 1992, Series A, Vol. 251-B.

presented by the courts for once were published on-line on the ECtHR website, but this has been the only time so far.[15] A novelty was the Joint Communication by the Presidents of the two courts, Skouris and Costa, of 17 January 2011, shortly before the negotiating group on the accession was to deal with the matter.[16] We return to that document below, when discussing the role of the courts in the accession negotiations.

2. The role of the *Bosphorus* doctrine

As regards the ECHR, the asymmetry between the ECJ and ECtHR mentioned above has a further aspect. Under the case law of the ECtHR, the starting point has been that of EU member state responsibility and EU immunity. For the ECtHR, the immunity of EU action under the ECHR as a consequence of its not being a contracting party, extends in some cases to EU member states according to the doctrine coined by the ECtHR in the *Bosphorus* judgment.[17] In it, the ECtHR developed the following approach.

Public authorities of member states of the EU are responsible, on account of their being a party to the ECHR, whenever they act outside the scope of EU law. When they act within the scope of EU law, there is an exception to their responsibility: when they have acted in a manner dictated by EU law and had no discretion under EU law not to apply it in a different manner, they are immune from ECHR responsibility. In this judgment, the ECtHR made this immunity – which implies that an application at the ECtHR in such a case is not admissible – dependent on the rebuttable assumption that the ECJ provides a protection of ECHR rights that is equivalent to that provided by the ECtHR. The ECtHR based this assumption on a twofold assessment of the standards applied by, and procedural protection available at, the ECJ.

---

[15] See the links to the papers on the following page under the heading 'Visit of Delegation From the Court of Justice of the European Communities' 09/11/2007: www.echr.coe.int/ ECHR/EN/Header/The+Court/The+President/Events/The_President_Events_2007.htm.

[16] See http://curia.europa.eu/jcms/jcms/P_64268/.

[17] *Bosphorus Hava Yollari Turizm ve Ticaret Anonim Şirketi* v. *Ireland* (Appl. No. 45036/98), Judgment (Grand Chamber), 30 June 2005, Reports 2005-VI, paras. 149–58. This doctrine was confirmed and applied in ECtHR, *Cooperatieve Producentenorganisatie Van De Nederlandse Kokkelvisserij U.A.* v. *The Netherlands* (Appl. No. 13645/05), Judgment (Third Section), 29 January 2009, Reports 2009, concerning the right to respond to Advocate Generals' opinions, which has been a point of controversy in the literature (and ECJ case law).

The first led the ECtHR to establish equivalence of the fundamental rights standard as contained in the general principles of Union law and the Charter. The Charter, as noted by the ECtHR, was 'not fully binding' at the time; the ECtHR *Bosphorus* judgment dates from June 2005, the Charter became binding only with the entry into force of the Lisbon Treaty in December 2009. So we may now say that since the entry into force of this Treaty, the Charter has become fully binding and the standard is therefore in principle raised further.

The second assessment concerned the judicial protection available in the EU to ensure observance of that standard. In this regard, the ECtHR judged that the system of judicial protection pre-Lisbon, notwithstanding the limitations on the *locus standi* of individuals at the ECJ, based as it is on the possibilities of legal protection through national courts, in combination with the preliminary reference procedures, as well as the possibility of state action and actions being brought by the institutions at the ECJ, warrants the conclusion 'that the protection of fundamental rights by EC law can be considered to be, and to have been at the relevant time, "equivalent" to that of the Convention system', and hence justifies a presumption of compliance with the ECHR. As we said, this presumption can be rebutted, which, according to the ECtHR, is the case if and when in the circumstances of a particular case the protection of ECHR rights is 'manifestly deficient'. Obviously, it is uniquely for the ECtHR to decide on attempts at rebuttal of the presumed equivalence of protection.

The *Bosphorus* judgment in the context of a conflict of treaty obligations (the EU Treaties versus the ECHR) addresses the dilemma on the one hand of effective protection of the rights of citizens under the ECHR, and the legitimate compliance with EU law of the state against which a complaint is directed on the other. However, it also effectively shields governments acting within the EU framework from scrutiny by the ECtHR. This effect of shielding is even stronger if it is not only the ECtHR that presumes EU compliance with the ECHR, but also if national courts refrain from scrutinising acts under EU law from compatibility with the ECHR on such a presumption.[18] As we remarked, it is for the ECtHR to decide on the equivalence of protection which the ECJ provides under EU

---

[18] This author is acquainted only with examples from the Netherlands case law in this respect, notably College van Beroep voor het bedrijfsleven (Industrial Appeals Court (a highest instance administrative court)) 23 April 2008, LJN BD0646, AB 2008, 233 (*Socopa*); President Rechtbank (District Court) Den Haag, 23 June 2009, LJN BJ0893.

law. In other words, the whole construct of the *Bosphorus* doctrine concerns the relations between the ECtHR and ECJ at the European level. Nevertheless, as we remarked there are national courts who have concluded from *Bosphorus* that member state action is also shielded from review against the ECHR by national courts – a not altogether illogical conclusion when looking only at the result of *Bosphorus* (i.e. immunity of the EU from scrutiny), but one which is totally illogical if we realise that the ECtHR never intended it as a task for *national* courts to assess whether the ECJ provides 'equivalent protection' as compared to the ECtHR. This type of national case law is a clear illustration of how the extension of comity between courts at European level into legal constructs has pernicious effects when viewed from the 'multilevel' perspective as regards its consequences of fundamental rights protection at national level.

As we presently explain, the accession may mean that some of the arguments which led the ECtHR to formulate the *Bosphorus* doctrine will no longer exist. So it is a major question whether this doctrine is tenable after accession.[19] During the accession negotiations, the question whether the doctrine should be retained or abandoned was consciously not raised. On the part of the EU, this was based on an early agreement between member states and the Commission not to request a codification of the *Bosphorus* doctrine in the accession agreement, despite some early calls to that effect.[20] This means that the negotiators left this important matter to the ECtHR to decide.

We briefly recapitulate some of the arguments for retaining and abandoning the *Bosphorus* approach.

2.1 Retaining the Bosphorus doctrine[21]

An argument in favour of retaining the doctrine is, first, that the rationale of the transfer of sovereignty from member states to the EU still exists

---

[19] On this matter, see L.F.M. Besselink, 'The European Union and The European Convention on Human Rights: From Sovereign Immunity in Bosphorus to Full Scrutiny under the Reform Treaty?', in I. Boerefijn and J.E. Goldschmidt (eds.), *Changing Perceptions of Sovereignty and Human Rights: Essays in Honour of Cees Flinterman* (Antwerp: Intersentia, 2008) 295–309.

[20] See Clemens Ladenburger, FIDE 2012 – Session on 'Protection of Fundamental Rights post-Lisbon', Institutional Report, section 5.1, p. 45, available at www.fide2012.eu/index.php?doc_id=88; the author is a member of the Legal Service of the EU Commission, and closely involved in the accession process, and wrote this institutional report on a personal title.

[21] For a number of politico-strategic reasons for retaining the *Bosphorus* approach concerning the relationship between the ECtHR and ECJ, see L. Scheeck, 'Diplomatic Intrusions, Dialogues, and Fragile Equilibria: The European Court as a Constitutional Actor of the

after accession. It is this transfer which can entail that a member state authority is compelled to act in a manner which causes an (alleged) violation of the ECHR. So it is this transfer, therefore, that causes the member state not to be held responsible for that violation, since this is exclusively caused by EU law compelling the member state authority to act the way it did. The member state was literally merely an 'agent' for the EU. The fact that the EU itself, which holds the powers transferred by the member states, has submitted to the ECHR after accession, adds an extra reason to refrain from scrutiny of the member states' actions. The so-called co-respondent mechanism – which we discuss below – ensures that retaining the *Bosphorus* doctrine does not lead to a void in cases where an applicant mistakenly directs his application to a member state, while it is the EU which should be the object of its application at the ECtHR.

A further reason which can justify retaining the *Bosphorus* doctrine is the accession of the EU to the ECHR. This reinforces the argument that protection offered within the EU is 'equivalent' to that required by the ECHR. After all, it imposes on the ECJ the duty in its case law to apply the ECHR directly, without the detour of the general principles under article 6(3) EU. Moreover, the EU fundamental rights protection 'post-Lisbon' has been strengthened: the EU Charter on Fundamental Rights has become legally binding; the ECJ will have jurisdiction with regard to what was previously called 'third pillar' law; and even the right of standing of individuals has been extended under article 263(4) TFEU.

In short, if, before Lisbon and accession to the ECHR, EU protection was equivalent to the protection offered under the ECHR, it must certainly even more easily meet the requirement of being equivalent after accession. This being the case, the ECtHR may have reason to maintain the immunity from scrutiny granted in *Bosphorus*.

2.2 Abandoning *the* Bosphorus *doctrine*

The most important argument in favour of abandoning the *Bosphorus* doctrine is that it seems to obviate major reasons for accession to the ECHR.[22] Exposure to ECtHR scrutiny is the very purpose of accession, and shielding from such scrutiny undermines that objective.

European Union', in J. Christoffersen and M.R. Madsen (eds.), *The European Court of Human Rights Between Law and Politics* (Oxford University Press, 2011) 164–80.

[22] See, e.g., T. Lock, 'EU Accession to the ECHR: Implications for the Judicial Review in Strasbourg', *European Law Review* 35:6 (2010) 777–98, at 797–8; T. Lock, 'The ECJ and

Moreover, it can be argued that from the start the *Bosphorus* doctrine was an inappropriate transplant of what was probably an appropriate construction for the *Bundesverfassungsgericht*, in the form of the '*solange*'-doctrine. It may be appropriate in the context of a domestic order to take a jurisdictional step back in favour of a European court. But it would seem inappropriate for a centralised special European court, whose very task it is to scrutinise compliance by domestic authorities and courts, to step back in favour of such domestic authorities. Whereas the former aims to avoid a double standard and divergences in establishing contradictory judgments, the latter allows for the possibility of divergent judgments concerning compliance with the ECHR, and creates a 'double standard'. On the latter point, after all, the ECtHR, as a Court with the exclusive and ultimate power to adjudicate compliance with the ECHR, should never be able to step back for, let us say, the German *Bundesverfassungsgericht*, because overall the protection provided is equivalent.

Accession would therefore seem to be the moment to set things right again, by abolishing the *Bosphorus* immunity. Whether the ECtHR will do so is, of course, uncertain.

3. The role of the European courts in accession negotiations

It may seem trite to make the observation that courts as institutions and their component members depend on each other, but certainly cannot be equated.[23] In this section, however, we shall see how the accession to the ECHR has changed from a matter for individual members of the ECJ representing the Court in a non-committal manner, as used to be the approach, to one in which the ECJ as an institution in its own right takes views in such a highly normative manner that the other actors in the negotiating process cannot ignore it without legal consequences.

In this context, there is of course already the procedure under Article 218(11) TEU, according to which a member state, the European Parliament, the Council or the Commission may obtain the opinion of the ECJ as to whether an international agreement envisaged by the EU is compatible with the Treaties. Where the opinion of the Court is adverse, the agreement

---

the ECtHR: The Future Relationship Between the Two European Courts', *Law and Practice of International Courts and Tribunals* 8:3 (2009) 375-98, at 395-6.

[23] On this, see L. Scheeck, 'The Relationship between the European Courts and Integration through Human Rights', *Zeitschrift für Ausländisches Öffentliches Recht und Völkerrecht* 65 (2005) 837-85.

envisaged may not enter into force unless it is amended or the Treaties are revised. A ruling under this provision makes the Court a powerful actor in the context of the conclusion of treaties. This is a role which, in the system of the EU Treaty, the Court plays *after* the treaty has been concluded by the political branches, but before it is ratified. The Commission had already announced that it would seek an opinion of the Court under Article 218 on the ECHR accession agreement. This makes the involvement by the Court in the negotiations all the more significant.

This involvement did not limit itself to the EU actors as addressees, but also those of the Council of Europe, by implicating the ECtHR through a Joint Communique of the Courts' presidents into the assertion of the ECJ's views on the desirability of mechanisms protecting its prerogatives. This centres around one particular issue that the ECJ began to consider crucial to its powers and its pivotal position within the EU legal order: the so-called 'prior involvement mechanism'. This is a procedural instrument by which a case brought to Strasbourg is suspended in order for the ECJ to give its judgment on the compatibility of an EU act with the ECHR rights involved, if the ECJ has not previously had the opportunity to adjudicate the matter.

There is a 'pre-history' to this. In the late 1970s, the Commission had opted for accession to the ECHR as a manner in which to solve the issue of fundamental rights protection within the European Communities. A memorandum was drawn up which provided the legal background, listed the legal and technical problems of accession, and the ways to solve them.[24] In this memorandum the issue was also raised of 'how to proceed in cases in which national courts have failed to fulfil their obligations to make a reference to the Court of Justice of the European Communities'. In this context, the first ideas for reference of the case from Strasbourg to Luxembourg were launched.[25] That in the late 1970s this was thought

---

[24] Bulletin of the European Communities, Supplement 2/79, Memorandum on the Accession of the European Communities to the Convention for the Protection of Human Rights and Fundamental Freedoms (adopted by the Commission on 4 April 1979), COM (79) 210 final, 2 May 1979. Cover title: Accession of the Communities to the European Convention on Human Rights. Commission Memorandum. Available digitally at http://aei.pitt.edu/6356.

[25] The quotation is at p. 20, left column. The next section of the Memorandum which addresses the question has all the symptoms of a text which was later inserted. In particular, considering the style of the rest of the document, a separate section number should have been provided. The relevant section reads as follows: 'Since it can hardly be envisaged that the Strasbourg organs would themselves refer questions to the Court of Justice, it would appear appropriate to introduce a procedure whereby the Community is

necessary in order to preserve the role of the ECJ is understandable; it was the period of consolidating the constitutionalisation of the then EC. Ever since, the idea of preserving that role through prior involvement, before Strasbourg would be allowed to judge, has remained. In the course of the accession negotiations, the ECJ took the following steps.

A first intervention in the direction of the negotiating actors was an intervention of the then Dutch ECJ judge, Timmermans, during a hearing of the competent European Parliament Committee in March 2010.[26] Judge Timmermans emphasised that he was a member of the Court, but that he spoke exclusively in a personal capacity: 'La Cour n'a pas de position officielle sur la question qui nous occupe aujourd'hui.'[27] That question concerned the position of the ECJ after the ECtHR would have become competent to adjudicate whether an act prescribed by EU law is compatible with the ECHR. The concern he expressed regarded particularly the cases in which the ECJ itself had not had the opportunity to adjudicate the relevant case. This is possible, because individuals cannot usually go directly to the ECJ with a complaint of violation of European constitutional rights – in the language of national constitutional law: the EU does not have a system of *recurso de amparo*, or *Verfassungsbeschwerde* – nor can an individual party force a national court by which the matter is to be decided to refer a case to Luxembourg, even if that would be appropriate, or even compulsory, under EU law. Judge Timmermans deemed it objectionable were the ECtHR to judge an act under EU law an infringement of the ECHR before the ECJ itself has been able to adjudicate the matter.[28] Hence, the proposal in such a case is to

---

obliged, in cases where the compatibility of a Community act with the ECHR is in question, to ask the Court of Justice for an opinion before it submits its own conclusions and to transmit this opinion together with its observations to the Strasbourg organs. This procedure should be employed both in the case of clear failure by national courts of last instance to comply with the third paragraph of Article 177 of the EEC Treaty and in the case of applications by non-member countries, which, for their part, where they are in doubt as to the conformity of a Community act with fundamental rights do not have the opportunity to make a reference to the Court of Justice.'

[26] See Annex to European Parliament 2009–2014, Committee Constitutional Affairs, AFCO PV (2010) 0317 1, Minutes of Meeting of 17 and 18 March 2010 Brussels; L'adhésion de l'Union Européenne à la Convention européenne des Droits de l'homme. Audition organisée par la Commission des affaires constitutionnelles, Bruxelles, 18 mars 2010, Christiaan Timmermans, Juge à la Cour de justice de l'UE, www.europarl.europa.eu/document/activities/cont/201003/20100324ATT71235/20100324ATT71235EN.pdf.

[27] Timmermans Statement, *ibid.*, at 1.

[28] It has been disputed whether this is actually correct; see *infra* note 46.

adjourn the matter in Strasbourg, which would give the ECJ the chance to judge on the validity of the relevant EU act.

This was the personal opinion of a judge of the Court of Justice. On 5 May 2010, there appeared on the website of the ECJ a 'Discussion Document' of the Court of Justice on the matter.[29] The document carries a date, but no signature or indication of its purpose. The title of the document, however, provides some indication. It is a 'Discussion Document', a 'document de réflexion de la Cour', a 'Reflexionspapier des Gerichtshofs'. Apparently, it contains the opinion of the Court and is destined for discussion and reflection on the modalities of accession to the ECHR. Nothing in the document suggests that it is intended for internal discussions within the Court. So we may conclude that it concerns the opinion of the Court which is given to others to reflect upon. The timing – a month before the Council established the definitive negotiating mandate for the accession negotiations (4 June 2010) – suggests that those others are the institutions negotiating the accession: the Council and Commission in particular (the Commission's Legal Service had not been in favour of the prior involvement mechanism, as we will have occasion to notice below).

In the document, the Court explains once again that 'the possibility must be avoided of the European Court of Human Rights being called on to decide on the conformity of an act of the Union with the Convention without the Court of Justice first having had an opportunity to give a definitive ruling on the point.'[30]

This is not a gratuitous preference of the Court. It explains that the principle of subsidiarity on which the ECHR is based makes it imperative that first within the internal order of the EU, the issue of whether an act infringes on the ECHR rights must be reviewed before an external review takes place.[31] This is, one can say, a matter of ECHR law. The Court, however, also uses an argument from internal EU law. This concerns the unique and sole power of the ECJ within the system of EU law:

> To maintain uniformity in the application of European Union law and to guarantee the necessary coherence of the Union's system of judicial protection, it is therefore for the Court of Justice alone, in an appropriate

---

[29] Discussion Document of the Court of Justice of the European Union on certain aspects of the accession of the European Union to the European Convention for the Protection of Human Rights and Fundamental Freedoms, 5 May 2010, http://curia.europa.eu/jcms/upload/docs/application/pdf/2010-05/convention_en_2010-05-21_12-10-16_272.pdf (last accessed 13 June 2012).
[30] Ibid., at 4, para. 9.   [31] Ibid., at 5, para. 11.

case, to declare an act of the Union invalid. That *prerogative* is an integral part of the competence of the Court of Justice, and hence of the 'powers' of the institutions of the Union, which, in accordance with Protocol No 8, must not be affected by accession.[32]

It is precisely to achieve this that the ECJ finds its prior involvement – before the ECtHR adjudicates an act under EU law – indispensable. In other words, absent 'prior involvement' by the ECJ, the accession would be incompatible with the special characteristics and nature of the EU legal order, and would consequently infringe the conditions set out in Protocol No. 8 of the Lisbon Treaty. The 'prior involvement mechanism' for the Court is a matter which affects the lawfulness of the accession. Note that this is not a private opinion of a member of the Court, it is the Court itself which pronounces on this point of law in its 'Discussion Document'. It also merits attention that Judge Timmermans had not explicitly spoken of 'prior ECJ involvement' as a strict legal requirement under Protocol No. 8.

The Discussion Document proved effective. From the little that has been made public on the negotiating mandate that the EU Council gave the Commission, it is clear that the ECJ desire of a 'prior involvement mechanism' was honoured.[33]

---

[32] *Ibid.*, at 4–5, para. 8.

[33] This can be found in a public Council document of 22 December 2010, which quotes from the otherwise strictly secret negotiating mandate; Council of the European Union, Brussels, 22 December 2010, DS 1930/10, Working Document from the Commission, [for the] FREMP meeting [in] Brussels, 10 January 2011, at 3: 'paragraph 11 of the negotiation directives of 4 June 2010 provides that the negotiations should ensure "*that the prior internal control by the Court of Justice of the European Union, in accordance with primary law, is applicable also in cases where the conformity with the* [ECHR] *of an act of an institution, body, office or agency of the Union is at stake in a case brought before the* [ECtHR] *but* [where] *the Court of Justice of the European Union has not had the opportunity to rule on the compatibility of that act with fundamental rights defined at the level of the Union. Any such procedural means, allowing the Court of Justice of the European Union to assess the compatibility of such act with fundamental rights, should be meant to safeguard the subsidiary nature of the procedure before the* [ECtHR] *and should not result in causing unreasonable delays in such procedure*"; in this connection the Council declaration annexed to the Council decision authorising the negotiation of the Accession Agreement of the European Union to the European Convention for the Protection of Human Rights and Fundamental Freedoms (Annex III) states that before the conclusion of the Accession Agreement "*the Council will unanimously adopt legally binding rules to the extent permitted by the Treaties, on the prior involvement of the Court of Justice of the European Union in assessing the compatibility of an act of an institution, body, office or agency of the Union with fundamental rights as defined at the level of the Union, as set out in paragraph 11 of the negotiation directives*"' (emphases in original).

SHOULD THE EUROPEAN UNION RATIFY THE ECHR? 317

As if this was not enough – evidently the Court found the matter of prime importance and feared omission – the matter was raised again shortly before the negotiating group was to deal with the 'prior involvement' mechanism at its 5th meeting, which took place on 25–8 January 2011.[34] The presidents of the ECtHR and ECJ issued a Joint Communication after the periodic meeting of members of the two courts.[35] The timing and substance of the Joint Communication was such that the matter was no longer one of the ECJ exercising its influence within the EU towards its own institutions, but a matter for all parties at the negotiating table.

The Joint Communication, after a brief remark on the desirability of 'parallel interpretation' of the EU Charter on Fundamental Rights and the ECHR, is entirely devoted to the 'prior involvement mechanism'. Unlike the Discussion Document, it does not address the lawfulness of dispensing with such a mechanism, but instead focuses on the desired procedural details to be observed in the introduction of the mechanism:

> In order that the principle of subsidiarity may be respected ... a procedure should be put in place [... which] would ensure that the CJEU may carry out an internal review before the ECHR carries out external review. The implementation of such a procedure, which does not require an amendment to the Convention, should take account of the characteristics of the judicial review which are specific to the two courts. In that regard, it is important that the types of cases which may be brought before the CJEU are clearly defined. Similarly, the examination of the consistency of the act at issue with the Convention should not resume before the interested parties have had the opportunity properly to assess the possible consequences of the position adopted by the CJEU and, where appropriate, to submit observations in that regard to the ECHR, within a time limit to be prescribed for that purpose in accordance with the provisions governing

---

[34] CDDH-UE(2011)03 Appendix II, 5th Working Meeting of the CDDH Informal Working Group on the Accession of the European Union to the European Convention on Human Rights (CDDH-UE) with the European Commission. Agenda, item 3: 'Elaboration of the accession instrument(s): a. Procedural means guaranteeing the prior involvement of the Court of Justice in cases in which it has not been able to pronounce on compatibility of an EU act with fundamental rights (item C.5 of the provisional list of issues).' The Agendas and Reports of the meetings are published on the website of the Council of Europe. See www.coe.int/t/dghl/standardsetting/hrpolicy/CDDH-UE/CDDH-UE_documents_en.asp.

[35] Only available in the working languages of the ECtHR, see http://curia.europa.eu/jcms/jcms/P_64268/.

procedure before the ECHR. In order to prevent proceedings before the ECHR being postponed unreasonably, the CJEU might be led to give a ruling under an accelerated procedure.[36]

Finally, I draw attention to the fact that the ECJ formed part of the Council working group establishing the negotiating mandate, as an observer (FREMP). This was not really intended as a 'silent' observer, as is apparent from the invitation of the Swedish Council Presidency already extended to the Court in December 2009.[37] It is unclear whether the Court was supposed to be a 'silent witness' when its membership of the Council Committee in charge of supervising the negotiations and outcome thereof was extended beyond the period of preparing the negotiating mandate.[38] Nor is there any information on the role of the Court representative in that committee.

The ECJ was not the only court that participated in the negotiations; so did the ECtHR. Its participation was not limited to the Joint Communication of the two presidents. The ECtHR also was a member of the negotiating group in the person of its Registrar and Deputy Registrar.

---

[36] Section 2, last paragraph of the Communication.

[37] See Council Document, Brussels, 5 January 2010, 17807/09, JAI 948, INST 255; this contains a memo of the presidency to COREPER, which was an 'I' item, that is to say, a document which is not an object for deliberations in COREPER, from which it appears that the member states were consulted on the admission of a representative of the Court to 'the discussions regarding a draft recommendation for the opening of the negotiations with a view to the accession of the European Union to the European Convention on Human Rights, as from their preparatory phase. [...] Given the technicalities of the accession of the European Union to that Convention, and in particular considering its procedural and jurisdictional aspects and the effect that such accession could produce in relations between the Court of Justice of the European Union and the ECHR, the delegations agreed that an involvement of the Court of Justice in these discussions would be of paramount importance [...] throughout the duration of the discussions on a draft recommendation for the opening of negotiations for the accession of the European Union to the European Convention on Human Rights.'

[38] The committee is the Working Party on Fundamental Rights, Citizens Rights and Free Movement of Persons, alias FREMP. Its task was defined in article 3 of the partially declassified negotiation mandate (declassification decision of September 2010) Council Document 10817/10 EXT 2. The invitation to the ECJ to participate in FREMP is in Council Document of 17 September 2010, 13714/10, at 2, and was this time more restricted 'to the extent that the issues for discussion on the FREMP agenda require such an expertise and the Court of Justice of the European Union agrees on such a participation'. Enquiries at the ECJ show that a representative indeed acted as observer, but no further details have been communicated on his activities.

4. The expected outcome of accession negotiations

At the time this chapter is written (May 2012), the accession negotiations have not yet reached a definitive result. As a consequence of intra-EU disagreement between member state governments over the Draft Accession Agreement, multilateral negotiations have been suspended since July 2011.[39]

It had looked so promising. The negotiations had started in July 2010, and much progress was made in the negotiating group, composed of a select group of equal numbers of EU and non-EU Council of Europe members on an expert basis, together with the EU Commission negotiators. The agenda flowed naturally from the inventory of all the mainly quite technical issues, as they had been assembled since the Commission proposed accession in 1979. They were contained in a set of equally technical documents, proposing solutions to the various points. They were deftly dealt with. In June 2011 agreement was reached, and in July the negotiated text of the Draft Accession Agreement with a Draft Explanatory Report to the Agreement and two other draft legal instruments were published in a definitive form.[40]

A solemn session in October had been planned to adopt the results formally, if possible plan the Agreement's signature, and to celebrate. All this fell through. The UK and France had too many objections. The UK had a long list of what can be considered pretty cosmetic and editorial issues, France on the scope of ECtHR jurisdiction, in particular as regards cases concerning the European Foreign and Security Policy (on which the ECJ has quite limited jurisdiction). On some issues there were more member states venting second thoughts. These concerned the exercise of voting rights in the Council of Europe's Committee of Ministers, when supervising the compliance of states with ECtHR judgments,

---

[39] See Steering Committee for Human Rights (CDDH), Report to the Committee of Ministers on the elaboration of legal instruments for the accession of the European Union to the European Convention on Human Rights. Strasbourg, 14 October 2011 CDDH(2011)009; Council of the European Union, Brussels, 6 December 2011, Council Document 18117/11, Fremp 112/Jai 918/Cohom 284/Cosce 22.

[40] CDDH-UE(2011)16, Final Version, 8th Working Meeting of the CDDH Informal Working Group on the Accession of the European Union to the European Convention on Human Rights (CDDH-UE) with the European Commission; Draft Legal Instruments on the Accession of the European Union to the European Convention on Human Rights, Strasbourg, 20–4 June 2011.

the unaffected member states' competences as a result of the accession, and the extent of application of the co-respondent mechanism.[41]

At least in part, the objections concerned issues which in a sense are quite technical, but in part they concerned matters of high diplomacy. The voting rights issue is particularly sensitive, as it is viewed as at least a potential precedent for similar issues in other international organisations, which could work to the detriment of the member states. The issue basically concerns EU states forming a majority in the Committee of Ministers which, under normal voting rules, could always block an unfavourable view of the non-EU member states as to the compliance of the EU, or an EU member state, with an ECtHR judgment. Depriving EU member state governments of the right to cast their individual vote turned out to be equally problematic.

Another issue touching on 'sovereignty' sensitivities is the Foreign and Security Policy. The overall negative attitude of the UK – more or less tacitly supported by some other ECtHR-sceptic countries – can be explained by the prevailing anti-European, and especially the more than traditionally anti-ECtHR political climate in the UK Parliament.

At the moment, unofficial reports from Brussels circles have it that a set of compromise texts which were designed and negotiated after the *déconfiture* in the autumn of 2011 have been agreed in the course of April 2012 in the relevant FREMP and in general terms was adopted in the JHA Council Meeting in the same month, calling for early resumption of negotiations in the framework of the Council of Europe.[42]

4.1 Prior ECJ involvement

Although unconfirmed rumours suggest that something in the text of the Draft Agreement on the 'prior involvement mechanism' may still have been amended, it is certain that such a mechanism will be included.[43] An

---

[41] See, e.g., the document published on Statewatch, www.statewatch.org/news/2011/nov/eu-council-echr-accession-1638-11.pdf: Council of the European Union, Brussels, 8 November 2011, Document 16385/11 LIMITE, FREMP 100, JAI 795, COHOM 257, COSCE 20.

[42] Council of the European Union, 'Press Release, 3162nd Council meeting (Justice and Home Affairs)' (27 April 2012) 16, www.consilium.europa.eu/ueDocs/cms_Data/docs/pressData/en/jha/129870.pdf. What form these negotiations were to take was still unclear in June 2012, when this chapter was finalised, as it was said to be unlikely that it would take place again in the working group of experts. Uncertainty as to the forum may explain the delay in resuming the negotiations.

[43] The text of the Draft Agreement of July 2011 reads in art. 3: '6. In proceedings to which the European Union is co-respondent, if the Court of Justice of the European Union has not yet assessed the compatibility with the Convention rights at issue of the provision of

area of uncertainty is the scope of the cases which can be referred from Strasbourg to Luxembourg. Initially, one seemed to be thinking of cases which raise issues of the 'validity' of EU acts (cf. the statement by Timmermans and the Discussion Document). In this option, the mechanism could not be invoked for issues of 'interpretation' of EU law; if issues concerning the 'interpretation of EU law' are included, this would concern a considerably larger category of cases than cases which concern the 'validity' of EU acts.[44] The outcome of this matter will have to be awaited. Suffice to remark that the text of the Draft Accession Agreement of July 2011 is not very explicit as to whether it limits the matter to a judgment on the 'validity' of EU acts only.

Another important point is that nothing so far is known about the internal EU rules under which the mechanism is to function. It has been suggested that 'accelerated proceedings' will be used, for which existing procedural rules under the 'urgent preliminary ruling' proceedings may serve as inspiration. Unclear is what the standing of the appellant in Strasbourg is under this procedure in Luxembourg, nor is it clear on what basis what kind of rulings can be handed down by the ECJ, and what the consequences are for *res judicata* in the case brought to Strasbourg by plaintiffs, to mention just a few important outstanding issues which

---

European Union law as under paragraph 2 of this Article, then sufficient time shall be afforded for the Court of Justice of the European Union to make such an assessment and thereafter for the parties to make observations to the Court. The European Union shall ensure that such assessment is made quickly so that the proceedings before the Court are not unduly delayed. The provisions of this paragraph shall not affect the powers of the Court.'

[44] The French delegation in the Council Working Group has proposed such a wide-ranging formulation in November 2011, for art. 3(6) of the Accession Agreement to read as follows:

> In proceedings to which the European Union is co-respondent, if the Court of Justice of the European Union has not yet assessed the compatibility with **or interpretation with regard to** the Convention rights at issue of the provision of European Union law as under paragraph 2 of this Article, then sufficient time shall be afforded for the Court of Justice of the European Union to make such an assessment and thereafter for the parties to make observations to the Court. The European Union shall ensure that such assessment is made quickly so that the proceedings before the Court are not unduly delayed. The provisions of this paragraph shall not affect the powers of the Court **in matters relating to the interpretation of the Convention** (bold text in original).

This proposal can be found in Council document DS 1675/11, at 7, para. 19, available at www.statewatch.org/news/2011/nov/eu-council-echr-accession-fop-ds-1675-11.pdf.

must be dealt with within the EU. Initially, the Commission found it unnecessary to introduce the prior involvement procedure, while the Legal Service of the Commission held that an amendment of the Treaty on the Functioning of the European Union was necessary,[45] but it seems that that position has been abandoned by the Commission.

4.2 The merits of the prior involvement mechanism: institutional prerogative or access to justice through the back door

It is, nevertheless, possible to give a preliminary assessment of the proposal for having such a mechanism at all. In this regard, it is striking that the ECJ has formulated the necessity for its introduction in terms of keeping its judicial 'prerogative' within the EU untouched.[46] This reveals an unexpected sensitivity which echoes quasi-'sovereigntist' sentiments among the states which did not want an ECtHR at the time of the negotiation of the ECHR.[47] It was found that such a Court would be a court of fourth instance of appeal, which would upset the national system of judicial protection. It would rule on what as a net result would be the validity of national law, a power which was the monopoly of national legislatures, or if it had to be courts, constitutional courts. This has clear analogies in the arguments propounded by and on behalf of the ECJ. In reality, of course, the ECJ in these respects is no different from national courts, and the response to such fears is identical. The ECtHR does not rule on the validity of internal law of states party to the ECHR. It can only adjudicate concrete allegations of infringements of ECHR rights and do little more than order compensation in cases where an infringement is established.

Nor is the argument correct that it is unique to the EU that a case might arise that has not been adjudicated by a competent domestic court. As I have already indicated, such a case can arise as a result of failure of

---

[45] See Council Document Brussels, 2 June 2010, 10568/10, at 3–4 (footnote 1), and at 6 (footnote 1), which refers to document Doc. 9693/10 of Council containing the Legal Service's views, which document was partially released for publication in February 2012, not containing anything on the substance of that opinion, however.

[46] See the ECJ's Discussion Document, para. 8, *supra* note 29.

[47] For the various positions of the governments at the origins of the ECHR, see E. Bates, 'The Birth of the European Convention of Human Rights and the European Court of Human Rights', in Christoffersen and Madsen (eds.), *The European Court of Human Rights Between Law and Politics*, 17–42, at 25–7 and *passim*; for the British position, A.W. Brian Simpson, *Human Rights and the End of Empire: Britain and the Genesis of the European Convention* (Oxford University Press, 2001) 330, 612–16, 654–6, 678–80.

a national court to refer EU law questions for preliminary rulings to the ECJ, which individual parties in a case cannot force national courts to do, while individuals do not have standing at the ECJ for alleged infringements of EU fundamental rights alone – there is no EU equivalent of a *recurso de amparo*, or *Verfassungsbeschwerde*. When we look at national systems of judicial protection, often the situation is no different. In truth, there are many cases in which the national court competent to protect constitutional rights and to adjudicate the constitutional validity of acts of public authorities, especially legislatures, is not brought to such a court, precisely because a recourse like *amparo* or *Verfassungsbeschwerde* does not exist in all states. So it can, and indeed, does happen, that the ECtHR rules in cases which might not have been dealt with nationally: in fact, it is established case law that the national judicial remedies should be exhausted only on the assumption that there is an effective domestic remedy available in respect of the alleged violation; the only remedies which the Convention requires to be exhausted are those that relate to the breaches alleged and are at the same time available and sufficient.[48] The point is that in a range of cases (in particular, the preliminary proceedings) there is no such procedure available in EU law. It would seem that now the ECJ is trying to repair the gap in judicial protection through the back door: a form of *Verfassungsbeschwerde* via the route of Strasbourg.

Was the introduction of the prior involvement mechanism inevitable, given the make-up of judicial protection in the EU? Ultimately it is the architect who determines the constitutional design. There is very little inevitable in the choice of the design. The Court could, for instance, have resolved the matter by pleading for the creation of a *ius standi* in a special appeal concerning an infringement of EU fundamental rights. This was pleaded for regularly in the literature, in particular the German literature, at the time of the Constitutional Convention.[49]

---

[48] Recently, e.g., *Scoppola v. Italy* (Appl. No. 10249/03), Judgment (Grand Chamber), 17 September 2009, not reported, paras. 68–70.

[49] E.g., N. Reich, 'Zur Notwendigkeit einer Europäischen Grundrechtsbeschwerde', *Zeitschrift für Rechtspolitik* (2000) 6 375–8; H.-W. Rengeling, 'Brauchen wir die Verfassungsbeschwerde auf Gemeinschaftsebene?', *Festschrift für Ulrich Everling* (Baden-Baden: Nomos, 1995) 1187 ff.; Th. Giegerich, 'Die Verfassungsbeschwerde an der Schittstelle von Deutschem, Internationalem und Supranationalem Recht', C. Grabenwarter and S. Hammer (eds.), *Allgemeinheit der Grundrechte und Vielfalt der Gesellschaft* (Stuttgart: Richard Boorberg Verlag, 1994) 101 ff.; for a critical discussion of this and other proposals to strengthen individual judicial protection, B. Hansel, 'Effektiver Rechtsschutz in Grundrechtsfragen durch Vorlagepflicht oberster Bundesgerichte oder europäische Verfassungsbeschwerde', Walter Hallstein-Institut, WHI Paper 6/03, 2003.

However, this was not the route the ECJ propounded: not EU law, but ECHR law needed to cater for a special recourse to Luxembourg in relevant cases. There may be political arguments for this position, prominently the fact that EU Treaty amendments of an architectural nature are more and more complicated to achieve. It is hard to see, however, why it should be more feasible to have this matter resolved by putting it through a procedure which not only requires the ratification of the 27 EU member states, but also that of the twenty non-EU state parties to the ECHR.

Not only is the prior involvement proceedings not something inevitable, there is a body of scholarly views, and views within the institutions, which thinks it unnecessary anyway, which, as we mentioned, also initially included those of the Legal Service of the Commission. The prior involvement procedure is premised on a situation which is unlawful. Both under EU law, ECtHR case law and also the case law of the national constitutional courts like the *Bundesverfassungsgericht*, a failure to refer a case for a preliminary ruling to the ECJ is an unlawful infringement of article 267 TFEU, article 6 ECHR[50] and article 101 *Grundgesetz*, respectively. This means that at any rate access to these respective courts is given as a consequence, which seems to obviate the necessity of introducing a special prior ECJ involvement mechanism.[51]

The prior involvement mechanism may be considered a more controversial instrument than the co-respondent mechanism, which we shall describe presently, since its inspiration seems to be not primarily the interest of the applicant, but it is motivated by defending what the Court itself terms the institutional prerogative of the ECJ. However, a second thought is possible. If the applicant has standing at the ECJ under this procedure, he has acquired access to the Luxembourg court which otherwise he would not have had. In fact, the prior involvement procedure has opened access to justice through the back door.

---

[50] See, e.g., *Schweighofer and Others v. Austria* (Appl. Nos. 35673, 35674, 36082 and 37579/97), Judgment (Third Section), 24 August 1999, not reported; *John v. Germany* (Appl. No. 15073/03), Judgment (Fifth Section), 13 February 2007, not reported; and for a refinement, *Ullens De Schooten and Rezabek v. Belgium* (Appl. Nos. 3989 and 38353/07), Judgment (Second Section), 20 September 2011, not reported.

[51] For the Commission's initial views, see *supra* note 40; in the academic literature, for instance, N. Reich, 'Wer hat Angst vor Straßburg?', *Europäische Zeitschrift für Wirtschaftsrecht* 10 (2011) 379.

4.3 The miraculous multiplication of respondents

One other aspect which deserves mention in this context is the equally complicated mechanism of co-respondents, to which the prior involvement procedure is linked. It amounts to the following. On a decision of the ECtHR, and at its own request, the EU becomes a co-respondent in proceedings instituted against an EU member state, or vice versa: a member state can become co-respondent in a case brought against the EU. The EU, or a member state, can become a co-respondent only following its own request.

The co-respondent mechanism is triggered if it appears that an alleged violation of the ECHR calls into question the compatibility of 'a provision of EU law' (if the EU is respondent and a member state co-respondent, this should be 'a provision of primary EU law') with the Convention, 'notably where that violation could have been avoided only by disregarding an obligation under European law'. Whether the latter is the case is a matter which, given the insertion of the word 'notably', is not a matter which needs to be established with full certainty by the ECtHR; the Court thus does not need to be drawn into an interpretation of EU law in order to decide whether a party can rightly become a co-respondent.[52]

---

[52] The relevant text of art. 3 of the Draft Accession Agreement of July 2011 reads as follows:

> 2. Where an application is directed against one or more member States of the European Union, the European Union may become a co-respondent to the proceedings in respect of an alleged violation notified by the Court if it appears that such allegation calls into question the compatibility with the Convention rights at issue of a provision of European Union law, notably where that violation could have been avoided only by disregarding an obligation under European Union law.
>
> 3. Where an application is directed against the European Union, the European Union member States may become co-respondents to the proceedings in respect of an alleged violation notified by the Court if it appears that such allegation calls into question the compatibility with the Convention rights at issue of a provision of the Treaty on European Union, the Treaty on the Functioning of the European Union or any other provision having the same legal value pursuant to those instruments, notably where that violation could have been avoided only by disregarding an obligation under those instruments.
>
> 4. Where an application is directed against and notified to both the European Union and one or more of its member States, the status of any respondent may be changed to that of a co-respondent if the conditions in paragraph 2 or paragraph 3 of this Article are met.
>
> 5. A High Contracting Party shall become a co-respondent only at its own request and by decision of the Court. The Court shall seek the views of all parties to the proceedings. When determining a request of this nature

Different from the existing 'third party intervention' under article 36 ECHR, a co-respondent is a party to the case. This means that a judgment becomes binding on it. In principle this is positive for the applicant *if* the ECtHR finds in his favour; this is no doubt the greatest advantage of the co-respondent procedure for applicants. But we should not exaggerate this clear advantage any further than it goes. This is an advantage *only* if the ECtHR finds in favour of the applicant. The chances of finding in favour of an applicant may diminish with the number of opponents. The co-respondent mechanism implies, after all, that an applicant is faced with more parties at the other end of the table in Strasbourg than he had reason to expect. In most cases this will, moreover, be at a stage at which the application is not considered manifestly ill-founded (although, of course, the co-respondent mechanism can also be triggered in admissibility proceedings).[53] Another weakness is that a party becomes co-respondent only at its own request. So it is definitely a weakness that a party which qualifies to be both co-respondent and share in responsibility for the infringement of an ECHR right can withdraw from the bindingness of an adverse judgment by choosing not to become co-respondent. So the aim of binding responsible parties is not always guaranteed by the co-respondent mechanism, and actually undermines the objective which it is supposed to serve.[54]

A further reason not to exaggerate the advantages of the mechanism is that a co-respondent may not actually have caused the alleged violation, and is not going to be a party against which a judgment is to be executed.[55] In this case it makes no difference whether the co-respondent

> the Court shall assess whether, in the light of the reasons given by the High Contracting Party concerned, it is plausible that the conditions in paragraph 2 or paragraph 3 of this Article are met.

[53] The Draft Accession Agreement, in art. 3(1), proposes to amend art. 36(4) ECHR, of which the last sentence is to read: 'The admissibility of an application shall be assessed without regard to the participation of a co-respondent in the proceedings.' This merely means that the wrong choice of respondent will not affect the judgment on admissibility; it does not mean that the co-respondent mechanism cannot be triggered at the admissibility stage of proceedings.

[54] See N. O'Meara, 'A More Secure Europe of Rights? The European Court of Human Rights, the Court of Justice of the European Union and EU Accession to the ECHR', *German Law Journal* 12 (2011) 1813–32, at 1821.

[55] See the Explanatory Report to the Draft Accession Agreement, para. 37: '[T]he mechanism would also be applied if the EU or its member State was not the party that acted or omitted to act in respect of the applicant, but was instead the party that provided the legal basis for that act or omission.'

was a party to the proceedings or merely an intervening third party, as it can be already under the present article 36 ECHR.

4.4 An example

The various complications can perhaps best be illustrated by a concrete example. Take the case of *Šneersone and Kampanella* v. *Italy*,[56] and see what could have happened under the co-respondent mechanism. The case concerned a Latvian mother, Šneersone, who brought her son, Kampanella, from Italy to Latvia without the father's permission ('child abduction'). There is a piece of EU legislation which ensures that in such cases a national court ruling (in this case in Italy) is to be executed without further ado by the Latvian courts and authorities.[57] This case concerned an Italian court order to send the child back to Italy to its father, who had had minimal participation in his upbringing, never had the child in his care, and had not had contact with the child for several years, with no attempt to establish such contact. In the ECtHR judgment as it was handed down, it established that the Italian court's order in this case constituted an interference with family life between mother and son (article 8(1) ECHR), for which it had to determine whether it could be justified as 'necessary in a democratic society' (see article 8(2) ECHR). It concluded that the interference with the applicants' right to respect for their family life was not 'necessary in a democratic society' within the meaning of article 8(2) of the Convention; there had been a violation of article 8 of the Convention on account of the Italian courts' order for the child's return to Italy.

If the text of the draft Accession Agreement enters into force, this creates the possibility for the EU to intervene against Ms. Šneersone. Arguably, the case concerned the application of a Regulation which calls into question the Regulation's compatibility with an ECHR right; the alleged infringement of article 8 ECHR could only have been avoided by disregarding the obligation under the Regulation to apply the Italian court order in Latvia without making this dependent on an assessment of an infringement of an ECHR right by the Latvian authorities and courts.

---

[56] *Šneersone and Kampanella* v. *Italy* (Appl. No. 14737/09), Judgment (Second Section), 12 July 2011, not reported.
[57] Council Regulation (EC) No. 2201/2003 of 27 November 2003 concerning jurisdiction and the recognition and enforcement of judgments in matrimonial matters and matters of parental responsibility (hereinafter 'the Regulation').

If this reading of the conditions under which the co-respondent mechanism is triggered is correct, Ms. Šneersone will be confronted with the EU as her opponent, and possibly any of the other EU member states, who, after all, may be presumed to have a stake in compliance with the Regulation.

Probably the EU – whom so ever represents it[58] – and other member states would explain that the whole point of the Regulation is one of mutual trust on which the mechanism of mutual recognition of national court judgments on matters of matrimony and parental responsibility is based. Introducing a further requirement in the country of execution of a foreign judgment to review compatibility with the ECHR would undermine that system.

Note that it would not have been possible for the Republic of Latvia to intervene as respondent on the side of Ms. Šneersone, because Latvia is then not 'respondent'. It remains possible, nevertheless, that the ECtHR would allow Latvia to take part as third-party intervener (article 36 ECHR in its present form).

Note also that again in this case the conditions for co-respondent status for the EU and any other member state wishing to oppose Ms. Šneersone have been fulfilled, but neither of these co-respondents necessarily have a share in the liability, since they themselves have not acted in this case; they have only provided a legal basis for the act which Šneersone complained of, or not even that. This shows that Ms. Šneersone will not need to execute the judgment against these co-respondents. Co-respondents may have made it harder for Ms. Šneersone to plead her case, but there is nothing in return for her even in the case where the ECtHR rules in her favour.

An interesting further question is whether the 'prior involvement mechanism' can be triggered in a scenario of co-respondents in a case like *Šneersone*. The Draft Accession Agreement links this mechanism to the co-respondent mechanism: only when the EU is co-respondent and the ECJ has not been able to pronounce on the compatibility of the

---

[58] During the FIDE conference of 31 May–2 June 2012 in Tallinn, a discussant from one of the institutions found it not self-evident that the EU would be represented in all cases only by the Commission, but could also have an agent representing the Council, although this would not be in line with the current state of the law and practice. The matter needs to be clarified in the internal EU rules, which at the time of writing are being drafted. Council Document 10744/12 of 1 June 2012 on 'Draft internal rules to be adopted in the context of the EU's accession to the European Convention on Human Rights (ECHR) – Representation of the Union before the European Court of Human Rights (ECtHR)' is not accessible to the public.

EU law provision with the ECHR, may the case be suspended to give the ECJ the chance to adjudicate this matter. This may occur, since neither the Italian nor the Latvian national courts involved in *Šneersone* found it necessary to refer a question to the ECJ as to how to interpret and apply the Regulation at stake. So ultimately, the effect of the co-respondent mechanism may be that the matter can be settled in a different court from that where the case was brought – or, at least, this is what one would expect the prior involvement mechanism to deliver if the judgment is in favour of the applicant. Whether it will, depends of course, on the status of judgment at the ECJ under this procedure, which is still unclear. If the outcome is unfavourable for the applicant, the case will be resumed in Strasbourg, which will independently assess the case. If the *Bosphorus* doctrine is maintained, however, in cases in which the relevant member state authority had no discretion in applying EU law, Strasbourg may refrain from proceeding to an independent assessment of conformity with the ECHR. Arguably, this is the case in the example we are dealing with. The ECJ will probably (it will again depend on the nature and effect of its judgment under the prior involvement procedure) then have settled the matter by rejecting the claim of Ms. Šneersone. That it would actually judge unfavourably for Ms. Šneersone is, of course, uncertain. But the ECJ judgment in *Aguire Zarraga* does not augur well. In this judgment, the ECJ held that, in the execution of a court order in cases of child abduction, it is not for the courts in the country where the order is to be executed to review the compatibility of the order with fundamental rights.[59] However, this case was not entirely identical to *Šneersone*.

4.5 Was there an alternative? Binding the EU to ECtHR rulings

Alternatives to the co-respondent mechanism can always be thought of, but it is uncertain whether and to what extent these could secure the applicant his benefits in a significantly less complicated manner, and would avoid him being confronted with a potential multitude of opponents. Thus, one might think, for instance, of adopting a provision in article 36 ECHR stating that in proceedings involving EU law in which the EU and member states are not both respondents, the ECtHR should adjudicate the case without regard to the question whether responsibility

---

[59] Case C-491/10, PPU *Joseba Andoni Aguirre Zarraga v. Simone Pelz* [2010] ECR nyr.

for a violation devolves on a member state, or the Union, or both. It could be left to the ECtHR to allow the relevant other contracting party (EU or member state, according to which is the case) to act with some flexibility in such cases as third-party intervener, while it is left to an internal EU instrument to divide responsibility and mutual indemnification in cases where the ECtHR held there was a violation and awarded damages. This would leave the matter as an internal EU matter, which it is, anyway, without the applicant being burdened with the complexities of the division of powers and responsibilities under EU law. It would not necessarily mean he is faced with fewer opponents when it comes to it, except that in Strasbourg, some of them would then act not as co-respondent, but as third-party interveners.

To come to a normative assessment of the co-respondent mechanism, one needs to balance the disadvantage of the number of opponents in the proceedings against the advantage of binding the co-respondent to the outcome of the proceedings. In light of the availability of alternative courses to achieve a result which guarantees successful appellants in Strasbourg the execution of its judgments, the assessment might be negative, should one still have the opportunity to do away with what is now in the Draft Accession Agreement. Given the state of negotiations, the option for alternatives is illusory. So one might as well make the best of it, and hope for a practice and internal EU implementation rules which are, indeed, less burdensome for applicants, and bring something positive.[60]

5. What's the point of accession?

All of the above suggests that the record for accession is quite mixed when looked at from the perspective of the relations between the ECtHR and the ECJ. Since the *Connolly* judgment, the ECJ has brought its standard of fundamental rights protection up to the level of the ECtHR. It has beyond doubt extended the scope of protection to primary level since its judgments in *Schmidberger* and *Kadi I*. It was precisely this

---

[60] In this regard, the disagreement about voting rights in the Council of Europe Committee of Ministers when it is supervising the compliance with ECtHR judgments may be reason for cautiousness: if the EU member states retain the right to vote, they will easily outvote non-EU members of the Committee, which might not be to the advantage of successful applicants. Also in this respect, we have to await the definitive outcomes of the compromises on amending the Draft Accession Agreement.

increased level of scrutiny which could allow for the exception of ECtHR scrutiny in the latter's *Bosphorus* judgment, which acknowledged the overall presumption of equivalent protection. This would have seemed to make the issue of which is the prime court in Europe redundant. At least part of the literature on 'comity' between the courts seemed to be premised on a form of jealousy. But the two courts seemed to have moved far beyond this, not just due to the friendly relations established by their mutual visits and exchanges, but even more importantly, by concentrating on the substance of their core tasks: providing protection of the rights of litigants.

Accession to the ECHR, however, seems to have triggered a very different dynamic. The accession negotiations sometimes seemed to have lost sight of the objective of improving the judicial protection of fundamental rights, and instead acquired the appearance of the diplomacy of high politics, far removed from anything which might have to do with the rights of ordinary citizens. The ECJ has found it necessary to protect its autonomy, perceived uniqueness, and the fear of upsetting its prerogatives inherent in the system of judicial protection of the EU; and doing so in a manner which can, in fact, merit the qualification of 'jealously' protecting its position. In this, the ECJ has echoed the quasi-sovereigntist objections of some states against the introduction of an ECtHR with competence to adjudicate complaints from individuals at the time of the negotiation of the ECHR – and, as we noted above, also some of the EU member states themselves are acting within a political climate in which the ECtHR has become the object of strong semi-sovereigntist criticism. In that climate, arguments concerning 'subsidiarity' of the fundamental rights protection at the domestic level of the parties to the Convention lose their innocence. Warnings to respect this subsidiarity imply that otherwise the internal constitutional order is upset: in member states the division of powers between courts and legislatures and the particular role of the national constitutional courts, in the EU the prerogatives of the ECJ within a balance of powers between the EU and member states.

These counter-dynamics have inspired much of the introduction of the co-respondent mechanism and, more clearly, the 'prior ECJ involvement' mechanism. Each of these, and the two combined, are uniquely complex mechanisms of which the actual functioning in practice must be awaited. Hopefully, the internal EU rules implementing these mechanisms will more clearly serve the interests of ordinary citizens seeking protection of their fundamental rights than has been the case so far.

If this is the state of affairs, the question must arise: what is the point of accession? Is it really improving the rights of individuals, and does it still also serve any further constitutional interest? The answer to these questions is clearly a matter of normative and political assessment, and allows for different answers.

It may seem paradoxical after all that was written above, but this author would strongly defend accession to the ECHR on the following grounds. First, accession does indeed increase the opportunities for protection of individual rights. Acts of the institutions are now screened off from ECtHR supervision; accession no doubt creates further access to justice than is available now. This is intended to be regular scrutiny by the ECtHR after exhaustion of domestic remedies, including remedies under EU law at the ECJ, to the extent that they are available. Moreover, we noted above that the 'prior involvement' procedure may open access to justice at the ECJ through the back door. This may diminish the access to justice deficit which has been noticed in the literature on the ECJ, and the right of standing of individuals in the Luxembourg court.

Second, there is a constitutional aspect to the accession; accession of the Union to the ECHR, to use the words of the ECJ in Opinion 2/94, is of 'constitutional importance' (*d'envergure constitutionnelle*). So far, the two courts have enjoyed an asymmetric form of fundamental rights protection, as we explained above. This will be redressed by opening scrutiny by the ECtHR. Of course, this redress will only be truly effective if the ECtHR abandons the so-called *Bosphorus* doctrine. Whether this will, indeed, occur is something which only the future will tell. Formally redressing the somewhat lopsided formal legal relations between the two courts is of importance because of what the ECtHR can bring to the EU.

In this regard, it is often said that the accession will not change much, since overall the EU lives up to the standards set by the ECHR. This makes one think of what the governments of the first generation told their parliaments on ratification to the ECHR (and they may have genuinely believed it): it is a document of the values we not only believe in, but which we believe we are already living up to. The history and case law of the ECtHR tell a different story. So it may be after the accession of the EU to the ECHR.

An area in which the ECtHR may gradually be deploying a scrutiny which is more intense than is the case within the EU comprises data protection, privacy and ICT-related issues like 'digital identities'. Another area is that of 'transnational' integration in the EU context. With this expression I refer to the areas of the law which are based on more or less 'automatic' forms of mutual recognition in the fields of criminal law and procedure (think of the European Arrest Warrant), as well as civil law and procedure (we mentioned the child abduction cases), and asylum law (think of the so-called 'Dublin Regulation' concerning the country which is responsible for the processing of asylum applications).[61] Mutual recognition in all of these fields is based on the assumption of mutual trust in each other's systems of judicial protection of fundamental rights. However, the ECtHR has consistently held that this cannot go so far as obviating responsibility under the ECHR for the states automatically giving effect to administrative and judicial decisions of other member states.[62] Far from 'undermining' the system of mutual recognition, the ECtHR has a useful role to play in reminding the EU and member state authorities, when they act within the scope of EU law, that mutual recognition may be good for European integration, but that it should not undermine core values on which it is founded: respect for the minimal rights contained in the ECHR. Respect of these is a precondition of EU membership, and should be a precondition to which the EU itself must also live up. Making the EU do this is the particular contribution which the ECtHR has to make within a mature mutual relationship with the EU and its Court of Justice.

---

[61] For relevant issues concerning the Schengen Information System, see E. Brouwer, *Digital Borders and Real Rights: Effective Remedies for Third-country Nationals in the Schengen Information System* (Leiden: Nijhoff, 2008).

[62] See, recently, in the field of the Dublin Regulation, *M.S.S. v. Belgium and Greece* (Appl. No. 30696/09), Judgment (Grand Chamber), 21 January 2011, Reports 2011, which has now been followed by the ECJ in Case C-411/10, *N.S. v. Secretary of State for the Home Department and Others* [2011] nyr. See also the case of *Šneersone and Kampanella*, in the field of mutual recognition of civil judgments in the field of matrimony and parenthood, which can be contrasted with, Case C-491/10, *supra* note 59.

9

The European Court of Human Rights and the United Nations

CHRISTIAN TOMUSCHAT

1. The European Court of Human Rights and international organisations

The European Court of Human Rights (ECtHR, or the Court) was not established with a mandate to control the activities of any international organisation. Neither the Council of Europe nor the organisations of the process of European integration were originally placed under its jurisdiction, let alone the United Nations (UN). According to the original version of article 59 of the European Convention on Human Rights (ECHR), only members of the Council of Europe – namely, states – were entitled to become parties to that instrument and thereby potentially subject to the jurisdiction of the ECtHR. Under the prevailing circumstances, this was an appropriate determination. At the time when the ECHR was signed, the process of European integration had not yet been translated into law. The signing of the Treaty establishing the European Coal and Steel Community (ECSC) took place on 18 April 1951, and it is at that moment only that the necessity of ensuring legal and judicial protection also against international institutions became clearly visible. Fortunately, the authors of the ECSC Treaty realised in good time that individual citizens should not be deprived of remedies, which they enjoyed in their home states as a matter of fact, when being transported into a new international environment. A French working document, which served as the basis for the drafting process, provided for a cumbersome procedure entrusted to an ad hoc arbitral body, a mechanism that would have operated like a deterrent. By contrast, acknowledging the needs of the persons subject to the powers of the 'High Authority', the executive body of the ECSC, the German delegation requested from the very outset an effective system of judicial protection. Their views prevailed.[1] Accordingly, articles 33, 35 and 41 of the

---

[1] See H. Mosler, 'Die Entstehung des Modells supranationaler und gewaltenteilender Staatenverbindungen in den Verhandlungen über den Schuman-Plan', E. von Caemmerer

ECSC Treaty shaped the mechanism which, in principle, has remained the determinative model of judicial protection for all later integration treaties.

At the same time, this European model provides a blueprint for judicial protection against acts of other international organisations that directly affect individuals. According to a traditional pattern, international organisations are endowed with immunity before national courts exactly like states before the courts of another state. This legal configuration does not do justice any longer to situations where an international organisation becomes an actor who operates like an administrative agency in the territory of any of its member states. Judicial protection belongs today to the key building blocks of a system of governance under the rule of law. It will be the main aim of the following pages to scrutinise in that light the procedures available to victims of wrongdoing by the UN, and to inquire, where lacunae have been identified, whether and to what extent the two European courts, the Court of Justice of the European Union and, in particular, the ECtHR may step in to fill that vacuum.

2. Judicial protection against the UN

In 1950, the UN was already an operative entity. Originally, it was not expected that the world's highest authority on matters of peace and war might be prompted, in the exercise of its powers, directly to interfere with individual rights of private persons outside armed hostilities. Such a prospect seemed to lack any real bases.[2] Indeed, the Charter does not specifically provide for determinations of the Security Council to be made *vis-à-vis* individuals. The system presupposes that under Chapter VII orders may be issued to states which then are required to implement those orders by enacting decisions under national law on the basis of the relevant national instruments.

2.1 Staff disputes

The general assumption that the UN would act exclusively with regard to states was so deeply entrenched in the minds of the drafters

---

et al. (eds.), *Probleme des europäischen Rechts: Festschrift für Walter Hallstein* (Frankfurt/Main: Vittorio Klostermann, 1966) 355–86, at 368–71.

[2] See also, M. Bothe, 'Security Council's Targeted Sanctions against Presumed Terrorists', *Journal of International Criminal Justice* 6 (2008) 541–55, at 541 (hereinafter Bothe, 'Security Council's Targeted Sanctions').

that they even forgot to establish a judicial review procedure with regard to personnel disputes, i.e. instances where members of the staff complain about non-compliance with the stipulations of their contracts or the applicable staff rules and regulations. Very soon, it emerged that a judicial mechanism of dispute settlement was indispensable for the organisation to function properly. Accordingly, the UN Administrative Tribunal (UNAT) was set up by a resolution of the General Assembly.[3] Only recently, this institution was subjected to radical reforms (with effect as from 1 July 2009). The single-instance body was replaced by a Dispute Tribunal on first instance and an Appeals Tribunal on appeal.[4] Thus, claimants are granted ample opportunities to assert rights which, in their view, have been unlawfully denied to them.

Whereas the UN has its main headquarters in New York, i.e. outside the territorial scope of application of the ECHR, it also maintains European offices in Geneva and in Vienna. Additionally, many of the specialised agencies have their headquarters in Western Europe. The International Criminal Tribunal for the former Yugoslavia (ICTY), an entity established by the Security Council,[5] has its seat in The Hague. Inevitably, therefore, the question arises as to whether the relevant territorial states do not have an obligation, both under their constitutions and the ECHR, to guarantee adequate legal protection against any infringement of the private rights of the staff of those organisations, irrespective of the quality of the employer and the immunity it might enjoy.[6] With regard to the UN itself, the appropriateness of the UNAT and of the recently established successor institutions[7] has never been questioned. Likewise, the conformity of the procedures under the ICTY's jurisdiction has been tacitly acknowledged by the ECtHR by denying any attributability of the ICTY's acts

---

[3] UN General Assembly (GA), Establishment of a United Nations Administrative Tribunal, Resolution 351A (IV), 24 November 1949.

[4] See UN GA, Administration of Justice at the United Nations, Resolutions 61/261, 4 April 2007; 62/228, 22 December 2007; 63/253, 24 December 2008.

[5] UN Security Council (SC) Resolution 827(1993), Establishment of an International Tribunal for the Prosecution of Persons Responsible for Serious Violations of International Humanitarian Law committed in the Territory of the Former Yugoslavia, 25 May 1993.

[6] The UN enjoys immunity from legal action under Art. 105(1) UN Charter and the implementing Convention on the Privileges and Immunities of the UN, 1 UNTS 15, 13 February 1946, entered into force 17 September 1946.

[7] UN Dispute Tribunal on first instance and UN Appeals Tribunal on second instance.

to the Netherlands.[8] However, criticisms levelled against the composition and the proceedings of the Administrative Tribunal of the International Labour Organisation (ILOAT), endowed with competence to adjudicate labour disputes within a number of the UN specialised agencies led, at least in one case, to a proceeding before the Italian courts. The Food and Agriculture Organization of the UN (FAO), located in Rome, is one of the organisations that have entrusted the ILOAT with jurisdiction in respect of staff disputes. In *FAO v. Colagrossi*, the Corte di cassazione rejected those objections, ruling that the immunity granted to the FAO under the Convention on the Privileges and Immunities of the Specialized Agencies[9] could not be overturned or circumvented by way of allegations that major deficiencies marred the mechanism of judicial protection provided by the ILOAT.[10] Some applications concerning other international organisations reached the ECtHR but were all dismissed, since the system of legal protection met, according to the Strasbourg judges, all the requirements of a fair trial as required by article 6 ECHR.[11]

2.2 Disputes arising from peacekeeping activities

It should not have come as a surprise to observers that outside New York and Geneva, too, the UN could incur international responsibility by infringing basic rules of conduct. Peacekeeping activities, apart from their beneficial effects for the assisted groups of people, have also quite understandably caused injuries in situations where chaotic circumstances in the areas of operation obtained. Thus, the UN was confronted with numerous reparation claims arising from the operation in the Congo

---

[8] ECtHR, *Galić and Blagojević v. The Netherlands* (Appl. Nos. 22617 and 49032/07), Decision (Third Section), 9 June 2009, not reported, para. 46.
[9] Convention on the Privileges and Immunities of the Specialized Agencies, 33 UNTS 261, 21 November 1947, entered into force 2 December 1948.
[10] *FAO v. Colagrossi*, Judgment, 18 May 1992, *Rivista di diritto internazionale* 75 (1992) 407, at 411. See also ECtHR, *Boivin v. 34 State Members of the Council of Europe* (Appl. No. 73250/01), Decision (Fifth Section), 9 September 2008, Reports 2008.
[11] See with regard to the European Space Agency, located in Darmstadt (Germany), ECtHR, *White and Kennedy v. Germany* (Appl. No. 26083/94), Judgment (Grand Chamber), 18 February 1999, Reports 1999-I, 393, paras. 40, 69; ECtHR, *Beer and Regan v. Germany* (Appl. No. 28934/95), Judgment (Grand Chamber), 18 February 1999, not reported, paras. 30, 59. Another decision, relating to NATO, which dismissed an application as inadmissible; ECtHR, *AL v. Italy* (Appl. No. 41387/98), Decision (Second Section), 11 May 2000, not reported.

(ONUC) from July 1960 to June 1964. With the growth of peacekeeping activities, the characteristics of such claims have increased both in quantity as well as in complexity.

2.3 Disputes arising from targeted sanctions

Another field of grievances has been opened up by the practice of targeted sanctions initiated by the Security Council in its quest for effective measures that hit responsible political leaders but not the entire population of a country that has come within the scope of application of Chapter VII of the Charter.[12] These sanctions are of two types. On the one hand, travel bans may be imposed on members of the political elite of a country that has committed grave breaches of the principle of non-use of force or has engaged in massive violations of human rights. On the other hand, the Security Council has developed a strategy of freezing of assets, in particular of persons known or supposed to be involved in terrorism or sponsoring terrorism. Generally, a special committee of the Security Council ('Sanctions Committee') produces 'blacklists' containing the names of the persons subject to the relevant measures of constraint. In implementing these types of sanctions, the UN is compelled to rely on the cooperation of its member states.

3. UN action susceptible of causing harm

In the following, it will be attempted to focus in greater detail on the possible points of intersection between the ECHR and the UN. Some hints were already given in the preceding sections as to circumstances where an individual might seek the protection of the ECtHR against actions undertaken or initiated by the UN.

3.1 Human rights protection against the UN: general considerations

Since judicial protection is one of the key elements of the rule of law, a concept embraced by the UN in many of its principled statements,[13] one

---

[12] See I. Cameron, 'Protecting Legal Rights. On the (in)Security of Targeted Sanctions', in P. Wallensteen and C. Staibano (eds.), *International Sanctions. Between Words and Wars in the Global System* (London and New York: Routledge, 2005) 181–206 (hereinafter Cameron, 'Protecting Legal Rights').

[13] See, in particular, UN GA Resolution 60/1, World Summit Outcome, 16 September 2005, para. 134. See also the UN's special website: www.un.org/en/ruleoflaw/index.shtml.

might assume that in response to the expanding field of activity of the UN institutions, in particular the Security Council, the world organisation would have correspondingly developed appropriate mechanisms for the protection of potential victims of such activities. However, this has not happened. The observer must note a complete standstill. Thus, the question arises as to recourse to any subsidiary mechanisms capable of providing legal remedies. Among all the institutions entrusted with granting such remedies for the protection of human rights, the ECtHR is certainly the most effective one. However, the fact remains that the ECtHR is only a regional judicial body with a limited mandate both *ratione materiae* and *ratione personae*.

The ECHR cannot directly control the activities of the UN.[14] It is a regional instrument that does not aim to govern the world at large. Its parties are exclusively state members of the Council of Europe; and the opening which Protocol No. 14 to the ECHR[15] has introduced for the European Union, hitherto not implemented,[16] remains confined to the European Union and does not cover any other international organisations. Furthermore, it would be preposterous to seek to generally subject the world organisation to the requirements of the ECHR. Accordingly, the ECHR will never become an instrument that may be directly invoked against the UN in matters of universal scope. Seen from a structural viewpoint, it is clear from the very outset that the ECHR and its executive arm, the ECtHR, can only come into play when a state party to the ECHR acts for the implementation of some UN measure, which will then open up the possibility of implicitly reviewing the lawfulness of that measure in light of the human rights guarantees of the ECHR. Obviously, such remedies, which operate 'through the back door', will generally lack the requisite effectiveness that would be inherent in remedies permitting directly to challenge acts of the Security Council or the General Assembly.

Additionally, it should be specified that communications submitted to the Human Rights Committee, the body entrusted with supervising

---

[14] See ECtHR, *Stephens* v. *Cyprus, Turkey and the UN* (Appl. No. 45267/06), Decision (First Section), 11 December 2008, not reported; ECtHR, *Blagojević* v. *The Netherlands* (Appl. No. 49032/07), Decision (Third Section), 9 June 2009, not reported, para. 36.
[15] CETS 194, 13 May 2004, entered into force 1 June 2010, art. 17, included in the ECHR as art. 59(2).
[16] It may indeed appear doubtful whether the introduction of a complaint procedure against judgments of the ECJ would be a wise decision, given the workload of the ECtHR. Proceedings might be extended *ad infinitum*.

compliance with the International Covenant on Civil and Political Rights (ICCPR), are confined to allegations of breaches of the ICCPR by states. The blueprint of the ICCPR and of the (First) Optional Protocol supplementing it is the same as that of the ECHR. Only states may become parties, and communications can only be directed against states parties. While, in Europe, the vacuum left by the ECHR regarding governmental acts of supranational institutions has always been filled by the specific remedies made available within the framework of the European integration treaties, this has not happened at UN level. As already pointed out, the new window of activity of the Security Council consisting of targeting individuals, is of recent date, and this aspect of its activity does not belong to its ordinary functions, but still has features of exceptionality. Therefore, to establish a specific judicial body to review such targeting measures may originally have appeared as a marginal concern which does not satisfy any appreciable public interest. Another reason for this obvious lack of enthusiasm is the reluctance of the Security Council (in particular, its permanent members), to be subjected to a judicial control mechanism. Understandably, the members of the Security Council are predominantly of the view that their acts and decisions are generally based on the exercise of broad discretionary powers that should not be submitted to control of a judicial type.[17] Obviously, different philosophies clash at this point. On the one hand, the general political context at world level can never be rejected as irrelevant, and it may justify measures which reach beyond common usages. On the other hand, the fundamental rights and freedoms of individuals should never be lightly sacrificed on the altar of the common interest. In the absence of comprehensive institutional answers, compromise solutions at a balanced midpoint must be found.[18]

One of the paths to be embarked upon in order to facilitate judicial control could be to enquire whether the contributory acts of national

---

[17] See B. Fassbender, 'Targeted Sanctions Imposed by the UN Security Council and Due Process Rights. A Study Commissioned by the UN Office of Legal Affairs and Follow-up Action by the United Nations', *International Organizations Law Review* 3 (2006) 437–85, at 438; Cameron, 'Protecting Legal Rights', at 199.

[18] See G. Nolte, 'Human Rights Protection against International Institutions in Kosovo: The Proposals of the Venice Commission of the Council of Europe and their Implementation', in P.M. Dupuy *et al.* (eds.), *Common Values in International Law. Essays in Honour of Christian Tomuschat* (Kehl: N.P. Engel, 2006) 245–58; C. Stahn, *The Law and Practice of International Territorial Administration* (Cambridge University Press, 2008) 602–16.

delegates in the organs of the UN are bound by the requirements established by their national constitutions as well as by the human rights instruments applicable in their home states. Since the General Assembly is generally prevented from adopting acts producing a binding effect, it is mainly the Security Council which might be scrutinised along that line. If, for example, a proposed embargo decision risks injuring the weakest part of the targeted country – women, children and people suffering from severe diseases – then can at least any one of the permanent members be held to account, given the fact that they could have blocked the controversial resolution by simply saying: no? A similar question came up before the German Constitutional Court a few years ago with regard to the approval of a Directive of the European Community on coordination of the television activities of the member states of the Community.[19] The *Land* of Bavaria argued that the Federal Government should have taken into account the interests of the German *Länder* in giving its approval to the Community instrument, since, according to the internal distribution of powers, the *Länder* hold authority over the broadcasting and television sector. For the Constitutional Court, there was no doubt that acting in Brussels was also subject to the provisions of the Basic Law and could thus be challenged if a *Land* opined that the Federation had infringed the dividing line separating federal from *Länder* powers, or had failed to behave according to the standards of 'federal loyalty' (*Bundestreue*).[20]

It is not easy to say whether the same logic should apply to the Security Council of the UN. The Security Council is an organ of the international community, or, in other words, of mankind at large. If one assumed that every delegate in the General Assembly and in the Security Council, when acting in that capacity, was subject to its national constitution, and additionally to any international treaty binding on his or her country, the decision-making process at the UN would find itself greatly hampered. One may argue that to accept such an extensive arsenal of checks contradicts not only article 27 of the Vienna Convention on the Law of Treaties (VCLT), according to

---

[19] Council Directive 89/552/EEC, 3 October 1989 on the coordination of certain provisions laid down by Law, Regulation or Administrative Action in Member States concerning the pursuit of television broadcasting activities, *Official Journal* L298/23, 17 October 1989.

[20] Judgment, 22 March 1995, *Entscheidungen des Bundesverfassungsgerichts* (BVerfGE) 92, 203, at 228. See also the decision of the Court of 7 September 2011, 2 BvR 987/10, www.bundesverfassungsgericht.de/entscheidungen/rs20110907_2bvr098710.html, para. 114, where it rejected constitutional complaints against the participation of Germany in the establishment of the European Financial Stability Facility (EFSF).

which no state may invoke the provisions of its domestic law as justification for its failure to perform a treaty, but also article 103 of the Charter, the provision claiming precedence of the Charter over any other treaty commitments. In fact, in *Behrami and Saramati*, the ECtHR held (para. 149):

> Since operations established by UNSC Resolutions under Chapter VII of the UN Charter are fundamental to the mission of the UN to secure international peace and security and since they rely for their effectiveness on support from member states, the Convention cannot be interpreted in a manner which would subject the acts and omissions of Contracting Parties which are covered by UNSC Resolutions and occur prior to or in the course of such missions, to the scrutiny of the Court. To do so would be to interfere with the fulfilment of the UN's key mission in this field including, as argued by certain parties, with the effective conduct of its operations. It would also be tantamount to imposing conditions on the implementation of a UNSC Resolution which were not provided for in the text of the Resolution itself. This reasoning equally applies to voluntary acts of the respondent States such as the vote of a permanent member of the UNSC in favour of the relevant Chapter VII Resolution and the contribution of troops to the security mission: such acts may not have amounted to obligations flowing from membership of the UN but they remained crucial to the effective fulfilment by the UNSC of its Chapter VII mandate and, consequently, by the UN of its imperative peace and security aim.[21]

In other words, the ECtHR shows great respect for the Security Council.[22] Without explicitly mentioning article 103 of the Charter, the quoted passage is visibly influenced by that provision.[23] It is not easy to reject the reasoning of the Strasbourg judges.[24] The UN Charter stands above the great mass of other multilateral treaties. Without characterising it as a

---

[21] ECtHR, *Behrami and Behrami v. France* and *Saramati v. France, Germany and Norway* (Appl. Nos. 71412 and 78166/01), Judgment (Grand Chamber), 2 May 2007, not reported (*Behrami and Saramati*).

[22] T. Tridimas and J.A. Gutierrez-Fons, 'EU Law, International Law, and Economic Sanctions against Terrorism: The Judiciary in Distress?', *Fordham International Law Journal* 32 (2008–9) 660–730, at 686 (hereinafter Tridimas and Gutierrez-Fons, 'EU Law, International Law, and Economic Sanctions against Terrorism'), call it a 'deferential judgment'.

[23] In a series of subsequent decisions, the ECtHR has maintained its line of reasoning: *Kasumaj v. Greece* (Appl. No. 6974/05), Decision (First Section), 5 July 2007, not reported; *Gajic v. Germany* (Appl. No. 31446/02), Decision (Fifth Section), 28 August 2007, not reported; *Berić and Others v. Bosnia and Herzegovina* (Appl. No. 36357/04), Decision (Fourth Section), 16 October 2007, not reported, paras. 27–8.

[24] For a different view, see Cameron, 'Protecting Legal Rights', at 187.

'world constitution',[25] one must acknowledge that the Charter contains the great structural principles of today's world order, concretised by General Assembly Resolution 2625 (XXV),[26] in particular, as rightly emphasised by the ECtHR, the 'imperative peace and security aim'.[27] This core element of the contemporary international legal order should not be lightly ignored.

3.2 Peacekeeping operations and the ECHR

The main areas of intersection between the UN and the ECtHR are constituted by military activities of the world organisation to the extent that troops provided by states that are bound by the ECHR are involved. Under such circumstances, a person having sustained injury through a UN operation may envisage complaining about an infringement of his/her rights and eventually bringing the ensuing dispute to the ECtHR. To date, only a few cases have found their way to Strasbourg, but it must be expected that in the future the number of such cases will grow not only in quantity, but also in complexity.

3.2.1 UN peacekeeping – general principles

It is well known that the original concept of UN military power, reflected in article 43 of the Charter, has remained abortive. Member states were to put at the disposal of the UN troop contingents designed to assist the UN in its task of ensuring international peace and security. This concept failed, in particular, because of the mistrust of the great powers *vis-à-vis* one another. It was feared that a UN force might be employed abusively in the power struggle between the 'West', on the one hand, and the socialist states, on the other.

At the present juncture, reality is dominated by the structural elements that have arisen as some kind of *Ersatz* for combat forces under article 43. On the one hand, at the height of the Cold War, the concept of 'peacekeeping' was invented, a device originally having a truly innocuous

---

[25] The most prominent protagonist of this approach is B. Fassbender, *UN Security Council Reform and the Right of Veto* (The Hague: Kluwer Law International, 1998), at 89.

[26] UN GA, Declaration on Principles of International Law concerning Friendly Relations and Co-operation among States in accordance with the Charter of the United Nations, GA Resolution 2625, 24 October 1970.

[27] ECtHR, *Behrami and Saramati*.

character.[28] Peacekeeping troops were sent, when somewhere after armed hostilities a truce had been reached, to pacify the situation in border areas that were still impacted by the preceding conflict. UNEF I, ONUC, UNIFIL and UNDOF[29] were among the first examples of such military forces under the command of the UN that initially were always deployed with the consent of the relevant territorial state(s). Peacekeepers had no combat or enforcement mandate. Just by their presence, they were expected to separate the warring parties and to consolidate an unstable armistice until a definitive solution could be found in political and legal terms – and not only on the basis of the facts as they had arisen as a result of armed conflict.

In later decades, in particular due to the wars on the soil of the former Yugoslavia, peacekeeping operations attained a higher degree of variety. Experience taught many bitter lessons. Peacekeepers who stood idly by when human beings were murdered, tortured, and driven from their homes, because they had no mandate to intervene, as happened many times in Bosnia-Herzegovina within the framework of UNPROFOR, were likely to discredit the instrument of peacekeeping as a whole. Accordingly, the concept of 'robust' peacekeeping emerged, peacekeeping that was not strictly confined to observing and trying to settle disputes by peaceful methods, but comprising also resort to the use of military methods according to the needs of a victimised population. Today, the concept of peacekeeping has attained an enormous variety of configurations.[30] Generally, however, the basic rule remains that peacekeepers have no mandate to proceed against an aggressor.

3.2.2 Peacekeepers as UN organs

Peacekeeping operations are UN operations. States put certain contingents of their military force at the disposal of the UN, and those troops operate exclusively under the command of the UN. Supreme political authority to authorise a peacekeeping operation is vested in the Security

---

[28] For a comprehensive account, see M. Bothe, 'Peace-Keeping', in B. Simma (ed.), *The Charter of the United Nations: A Commentary*, 2nd edn, vol. I (Oxford University Press, 2002) 648–700; M. Bothe, 'Peacekeeping Forces', in R. Wolfrum (ed.), *The Max Planck Encyclopedia of Public International Law* (Oxford University Press, 2008).

[29] For summary accounts, see Bothe, 'Peace-Keeping', at 665–7.

[30] For an overview of the earlier practice until 1995, see also S.R. Ratner, *The New UN Peacekeeping* (New York: St. Martin's Press, 1995); R.C.R. Siekmann, *National Contingents in United Nations Peace-Keeping Forces* (Dordrecht: Martinus Nijhoff, 1991).

Council.³¹ The Security Council delegates responsibility for the conduct of an operation to the Secretary-General who, on his part, as a rule entrusts an Under-Secretary-General with organising and managing the operation in logistical detail.³² Additionally, for each mission, a Special Representative of the Secretary-General is appointed who, as Head of Mission, holds political authority over the operation, sometimes having to take decisions under difficult circumstances when the superior authorities in New York are unable to provide good advice due to their distance from the daily occurrences.³³ Eventually, on the ground, a military commander exercises operational command in military terms. Where the territory to be covered is extensive, several regional sub-commanders may be needed. As for the different national contingents, they remain subject to their national commanders to some limited extent. In effect, the command of the UN is not of a sweeping nature. As far as issues of discipline are concerned, in particular, the national commanders retain full authority.³⁴ For that reason, peacekeepers serve in a double capacity, both as UN organs and, to a limited extent, as elements of their national armed forces.

3.2.3 Responsibility for injuries caused by peacekeeping activities

The consequences of this configuration in respect of responsibility leave no doubts. All the actions of peacekeeping troops are attributable to the UN, provided they act within the scope of the assignment imparted to them by the Security Council.³⁵ Apart from a judgment of the British House of Lords

---

[31] Theoretically, on the basis of the Uniting for Peace Resolution of the General Assembly (Resolution 377 (V) A, 3 November 1950), also the General Assembly might establish an operation. However, the original enthusiasm of the Western group of states for the resolution has faded away long since. After UNEF I, no other operation was brought to life by the General Assembly, see C. Tomuschat, 'Uniting for Peace', http://untreaty.un.org/cod/avl/ha/ufp/ufp.html; D. Zaum, 'The Security Council, the General Assembly, and War: The Uniting for Peace Resolution', in V. Lowe et al., *The United Nations Security Council and War* (Oxford University Press, 2008) 154–74.

[32] As of April 2012, Frenchman Hervé Ladsous is the head of the Department of Peace-keeping Operations.

[33] Unfortunately, the lack of resolve of the Japanese Special Representative, Yasushi Akashi, contributed to some extent to the genocide committed in Srebrenica.

[34] See Model Agreement Between the United Nations and Member States Contributing Personnel and Equipment to United Nations Peace-Keeping Operations, UN doc. A/46/185, 23 May 1991, paras. 8, 25.

[35] Letter of the UN Legal Counsel of 3 February 2004, *UN Juridical Yearbook* 2004, 352–6, at 354, paras. 6, 7; M. Hirsch, *The Responsibility of International Organizations Toward*

in the opposite sense, where the alternative between assigning liability to the UN or to the UK that had placed British troops at the disposal of a peacekeeping operation, was not sufficiently probed into,[36] this has always been recognised in practice. However, there seems to exist a slight divergence between the position of the UN, represented by the Secretary-General, which qualifies peacekeeping forces as a 'subsidiary organ' of the UN[37] – in other words, a full UN organ – and the International Law Commission (ILC), also a UN body, but made up of independent experts, which subsumes peacekeeping contingents provided by member states to the UN under article 7 of its articles on the 'Responsibility of international organizations' (DARIO) approved by the ILC on first reading on 11 June 2011[38] on the basis of the work done by Giorgio Gaja, its special rapporteur for the topic.[39] Pursuant to article 7 DARIO, organs or agents placed at the disposal of an international organisation 'shall be considered' under international law as an act of the organisation, provided the organisation exercises 'effective control' over the relevant conduct. However, as far as the actual conclusions to be drawn, the two constructions do not evince or imply any significant differences. The practice of the UN, which consists of unrestrictedly assuming liability *vis-à-vis* an injured third party,[40] at the same time corresponds fully to draft article 8 DARIO, according to which the international organisation concerned is prevented from rejecting attribution, even if the organ or agent concerned has exceeded its authority or has contravened its instructions. On the other hand, nothing stands in the way of internally recovering the amounts paid to injured third parties if the peacekeepers concerned have acted with gross negligence or in wilful disregard of the law to be complied with by them.[41]

Third Parties: Some Basic Principles (Dordrecht: Martinus Nijhoff, 1995) 66–71 (hereinafter Hirsch, *The Responsibility of International Organizations*); ECtHR, *Stephens v. Cyprus, Turkey and the UN* (Appl. No. 45267/06), Decision (First Section), 11 December 2008, not reported.

[36] *Attorney-General v. Nissan* [1969] 1 All ER 639. The House of Lords instead examined primarily the question of whether the UK or the country of deployment, Cyprus, had to bear the financial responsibility for the damage caused.

[37] See Letter of UN Legal Counsel of 3 February 2004.

[38] ILC 2011 Report, UN Doc. A/66/10, 52. For the response of the GA, see Resolution 66/98, Report of the International Law Commission on the work of its sixty-third session, 9 December 2011, para. 4.

[39] Commentary on Art. 7, *ibid.*, at 85, para. 1.

[40] Letter of UN Legal Counsel of 3 February 2004, at 354, para. 7.

[41] *Ibid.*, para. 9, referring to the Model Memorandum of Understanding between the UN and contributing states, Annex to the note of the Secretary-General on Reform of the

In such instances there will generally be no possibility of resorting to the remedy of application to the ECtHR, since the UN is not under its jurisdiction. It would also appear that the original model of peacekeeping, even after its development into 'complex' forms, has not given rise in actual practice to disputes that would have led to attempts to seise the Strasbourg system.[42] The fact remains, however, that any third party claims are settled by the UN itself, which does not correspond to the modern logic of human rights where, to a considerable extent, individuals may take disputes with public authorities to a judicial body. However, it would be extremely difficult to devise a juridical construction to the effect that, notwithstanding the UN's authorship, the troop-contributing countries must bear liability. Their integration into the relevant UN force is a fact that cannot be disputed. Where the UN acts as a subject of international law, it has to shoulder liability, even when, for injured third parties, the regime of responsibility lacks the ultimate finish of perfection. In the language of civil law, this is a case of vicarious liability, where the principal must make good any damage caused by its agents.[43] This inference can also be seen as the result of a functional theory according to which the determinative question is on whose behalf the relevant agent had acted.[44]

3.3 Military operations mandated by the Security Council by authorisation or 'delegation'

3.3.1 Factual background

Another model of UN operations was essentially initiated in 1990–1 at the time of the invasion of Kuwait by Iraqi forces. Its characteristic is the restricted role of the Security Council, which limits itself to authorising

---

process for determining reimbursement to Member States for contingent-owned equipment, UN doc. A/51/967, 27 August 1997, art. 9: 'The United Nations will be responsible for dealing with any claims by third parties where the loss of or damage to their property, or death or personal injury, was caused by the personnel or equipment provided by the Government in the performance of services or any other activity or operation under this Memorandum. However, if the loss, damage, death or injury arose from gross negligence or wilful misconduct of the personnel provided by the Government, the Government will be liable for such claims.'

[42] See, however, the case of *Behrami and Saramati*.
[43] Similar considerations by D. Sarooshi, *International Organizations and Their Exercise of Sovereign Powers* (Oxford University Press, 2005) 40 *et seq*.
[44] See Superior Court of Appeal, Vienna, Judgment, 26 February 1979, 77 ILR 470, at 472.

an operation carried out by a group of states ready to shoulder the corresponding burden.[45] For the first time in the history of the UN,[46] it proved feasible to activate the system for the protection and preservation of international peace and security with the aim of stopping an aggressor. It would certainly have been possible to establish a UN force under the authority of a UN commander. However, none of the powers ready to assist Kuwait was prepared to accept that traditional formula. Instead, by Resolution 678 (1990),[47] the Security Council '[a]uthorize[d] Member States co-operating with the government of Kuwait ... to use all necessary means to uphold and implement resolution 660 (1990) and all subsequent relevant resolutions and to restore international peace and security in the area'.[48] First and foremost, this authorisation was relied upon by the United States which, through massive deployment of its superior military might, succeeded in bringing about the withdrawal of Iraqi troops from Kuwait and defeating the Iraqi army.

The model of authorisation was subsequently used many times, in particular with regard to Kosovo, where Security Council Resolution 1244 (1999)[49] determined that for a transitional period, two 'presences' would be deployed there – an international civil presence (UNMIK) under the authority of the Secretary-General (para. 10) as well as an international security presence. As far as this latter presence was concerned, Annex 2 of Resolution 1244 (1999) provided (para. 4):

> The international security presence with substantial North Atlantic Treaty Organization participation must be deployed under unified command

---

[45] For an extensive study of this type of operations, see N. Blokker, 'Is the Authorization Authorized? Powers and Practice of the UN Security Council to Authorize the Use of Force by "Coalitions of the Able and Willing"', *European Journal of International Law* 11 (2000) 541–68 (hereinafter Blokker, 'Is the Authorization Authorized?'); E. de Wet, *The Chapter VII Powers of the United Nations Security Council* (Oxford and Portland: Hart Publishing, 2004) 260–310 (hereinafter de Wet, *The Chapter VII*); and recently, A. Peters, 'Die Anwendbarkeit der EMRK In Zeiten komplexer Hoheitsgewalt und das Prinzip der Grundrechtstoleranz', *Archiv des Völkerrechts* 48:1 (2010) 22–41 (hereinafter Peters, 'Die Anwendbarkeit der EMRK'); J.-P. Schütze, *Die Zurechenbarkeit von Völkerrechtsverstößen im Rahmen mandatierter Friedensmissionen der Vereinten Nationen* (Berlin: Duncker & Humboldt, 2011) 43–8, 148–69 (hereinafter Schütze, *Die Zurechenbarkeit*).

[46] I do not take into account the Korea operation, which was not placed under the authority of the UN, see *infra*, text accompanying n. 82.

[47] UN SC, Resolution 678 (1990) concerning Iraq and Kuwait, 29 November 1990.

[48] *Ibid.*, operative para. 2. The resolution was preceded by the much weaker Resolution 665 (1990), 25 August 1990.

[49] UN SC, Resolution 1244 (1999) concerning Kosovo, 10 June 1999.

and control and authorized to establish a safe environment for all people in Kosovo and to facilitate the safe return to their homes of all displaced persons and refugees.

In a similar fashion, the recent operation against Libya was linked to the UN only by virtue of a mandate given to an undefined group of states ready to take action. Under paragraph 4 of Resolution 1973 (2011),[50] the Security Council:

> *Authorize[d]* Member States that have notified the Secretary-General, acting nationally or through regional organizations or arrangements, and acting in cooperation with the Secretary-General, to take all necessary measures, notwithstanding paragraph 9 of resolution 1970 (2011), to protect civilians and civilian populated areas under threat of attack in the Libyan Arab Jamahiriya, including Benghazi...

It is easily understandable why this model of indirect command has become a success story. For the UN, which has its headquarters in New York, mostly far away from the theatre of hostilities, to organise and manage a huge operation which encompasses thousands of armed soldiers constitutes a challenge which it can handle only with a tremendous effort that goes to the outer limits of its capabilities.[51] For the armed forces of the main troop-contributing countries, the effort required is far less significant, inasmuch as it corresponds to what a military force is required to accomplish.

3.3.2 Responsibility

The question who can be made accountable if such an operation, which has been 'authorised' by the UN but not directly steered by it, produces injuries for which the victims seek reparation.

3.3.2.1 General rules of responsibility Recourse may be had to the articles prepared by the ILC that set out the rules governing the responsibility of international organisations (DARIO),[52] since those articles essentially reflect customary international law.[53] It stands to reason that

---

[50] UN SC, Resolution 1973 (2011), concerning Libya, 17 March 2011.
[51] Currently, the operation MONUSCO in the Democratic Republic of the Congo comprises more than 20,000 persons, military and civilian personnel.
[52] *Supra* note 35.
[53] See doubts raised by C. Ryngaert, 'The European Court of Human Rights Approach to the Responsibility of Member States in Connection with Acts of International Organizations', *International and Comparative Law Quarterly* 60 (2011) 997–1016, at 998–9 (hereinafter Ryngaert, 'ECtHR Approach to Responsibility').

in the case of mandated operations, article 6 on attribution[54] cannot apply. Where the UN confines itself to issuing an authorisation to a group of states or an international organisation, the troop contingents involved in the operation concerned do not become organs of the UN. Accordingly, it would seem that article 7 DARIO must be relied upon, where 'effective control' is chosen as the decisive criterion.[55]

The test of effectiveness has been derived from articles 6 and 8 of the ILC Articles on Responsibility of States for internationally wrongful acts (ARS).[56] However, given the structural differences between states and international organisations, different language can be found in the ARS, on the one hand, and in the 'Gaja draft', on the other. Article 6 ARS, which from the point of view of substance is closest to article 7 of the 'Gaja draft', expresses the idea of intimate connection as a requirement of attribution by the words: 'if the organ is acting in the exercise of elements of the governmental authority of the State at whose disposal it is placed'. Rapporteur Gaja and, following his lead, the ILC, did not find that formula adequate, since in their view international organisations do not exercise 'governmental' authority[57] – which, however, seems rather, to be a semantic problem.[58] On the other hand, article 8 ARS clearly endorses the test of effectiveness by stating:

> The conduct of a person or group of persons shall be considered an act of a State under international law if the person or group of persons is in fact acting on the instructions of, or under the direction or control of, that State in carrying out the conduct.

---

[54] Art. 6 'Conduct of organs or agents of an international organization

1. The conduct of an organ or agent of an international organization in the performance of functions of that organ or agent shall be considered an act of that organization under international law, whatever position the organ or agent holds in respect of the organization.
2. The rules of the organization apply in the determination of the functions of its organs and agents.'

[55] 'Conduct of organs of a State or organs or agents of an international organization placed at the disposal of another international organization The conduct of an organ of a State or an organ or agent of an international organization that is placed at the disposal of another international organization shall be considered under international law as an act of the latter organization if the organization exercises effective control over that conduct.'

[56] Taken note of by UN GA, Resolution 56/83, 12 December 2001, Responsibility of States for Internationally Wrongful Acts.

[57] See ILC 2011 Report, Commentary on art. 7, 86, para. 4.

[58] It is true that an international organisation does not exercise 'sovereign' powers.

THE EUROPEAN COURT OF HUMAN RIGHTS AND THE UN   351

3.3.2.2 Identifying the author: issues of attribution (imputability)   If an application is brought to the ECtHR, two initial questions arise. On the one hand, in terms of attribution, it must be clarified who was the author of the act complained of, an issue to be assessed in light of the rules of general international law.[59] Within a purely domestic context, this question normally has no actual relevance. All the acts and measures taken by one of the three branches of government are attributable to the state behind them. No specific inquiry is needed if a measure is taken by a national authority on the basis of a law enacted by the respective national legislature. However, when states and international organisations cooperate, the issue of attribution takes a pivotal role. Acts performed by national authorities in pursuing a UN mandate can be attributed either to the state concerned or to the UN, according to the circumstances. The same or similar questions may arise in assessing whether acts or omissions come within the scope of applicability of the ECHR *ratione personae*, since the relevant criteria overlap to a wide extent.

A functional approach, according to which it must first be asked on whose behalf an organ or agent has acted, found full recognition by the ECtHR in the case of *Drozd and Janousek*, where the question arose whether France's and Spain's readiness to lend justices to Andorra for the administration of justice in that country entailed the responsibility of those two countries. The Court denied any such responsibility, holding that French and Spanish judges sitting as members of Andorran courts did not do so in their capacity as French or Spanish judges, since those courts exercised their functions in an autonomous manner, their judgments not being subject to supervision by the authorities of France or Spain.[60] That was a situation not confronting the ECtHR with any real difficulties, since France and Spain were not substantively involved in the proceedings.

By contrast, the case of *Behrami and Saramati*[61] has hitherto raised the most complex issues regarding the authorship of the measures which the applicants had submitted to the review of the ECtHR. All the

---

[59] Quite erroneously, it is many times contended that 'attribution' is *exclusively* a concept of international responsibility. Logically, the precondition of any inquiry into international relations is to know who acted. Thereafter, the specific operation of attribution commences. Both intellectual operations may overlap to a significant degree.
[60] ECtHR, *Drozd and Janousek* v. *France and Spain* (Appl. No.12747/87), Judgment (Plenary), 26 June 1992, Series A, Vol. 240, para. 96. At that time, Andorra was not yet a state party to the ECHR.
[61] *Behrami and Saramati*.

commentators of the decision of the ECtHR in *Behrami and Saramati* have observed that the test adopted in that decision – namely, 'ultimate authority and control' (para. 133) – seems to be irreconcilable with the straightforward test of effectiveness, as it has been chosen by the two drafts in the field of international responsibility. In cautious words, the UN distanced itself from the assessment of the legal position by the ECtHR.[62] Likewise, in the legal literature the Court's formula has found few supporters,[63] among them, in particular, Antonio Cassese[64] who, as rapporteur in the *Tadic* appeal judgment of the ICTY, had opted for a somewhat looser test, namely, 'overall control'.[65] In fact, there may be substantive grounds fully justifying the approach preferred by the ECtHR.[66]

In *Behrami*, where the application was directed against France, the basic facts were simple. Of two children of the applicant Behrami, one

---

[62] UN SG, Report of the Secretary-General on the UN Interim Administration in Kosovo, UN Doc. S/2008/354, 12 June 2008, para. 16: 'It is understood that the international responsibility of the United Nations will be limited to the extent of its effective operational control.'

[63] See, for instance, the critical voices of A. Breitegger, 'Sacrificing the Effectiveness of the European Convention on Human Rights on the Altar of the Effective Functioning of Peace Support Operations: A Critique of *Behrami & Saramati* and *Al Jedda*', *International Community Law Review* 11 (2009) 155–83, at 167 (hereinafter Breitegger, 'Sacrificing the Effectiveness'); L. Doswald-Beck, *Human Rights in Times of Conflict and Terrorism* (Oxford University Press, 2011) 22–5; C. Janik, 'Die EMRK und Internationale Organisationen', *Zeitschrift für Ausländisches Öffentliches Recht und Völkerrecht* 70 (2010) 126–79, at 143 (hereinafter Janik, 'Die EMRK'); M. Milanović and T. Papić, 'As Bad As It Gets: The European Court's *Behrami* and *Saramati* Decision and General International Law', *The International and Comparative Law Quarterly* 58:2 (2009) 267–96, at 267 *et seq.* (hereinafter Milanović and Papić, 'As Bad As it Gets'); Peters, 'Die Anwendbarkeit der EMRK', at 34, 42, Ryngaert, 'ECtHR Approach to Responsibility', 1008; Schütze, 'Die Zurechenbarkeit' at 164.

[64] A. Cassese, 'The *Nicaragua* and *Tadic* Tests Revisited in Light of the ICJ Judgement on Genocide in Bosnia', *European Journal of International Law* 18 (2007) 649–68, at 667; also P. Lagrange, 'Responsabilité des Etats pour actes accomplis en application du Chapitre VII de la Charte des Nations Unies', *Revue Générale de Droit International Public* 112 (2008) 85–110, at 108; A. Sari, 'Jurisdiction and International Responsibility in Peace Support Operations: The *Behrami* and *Saramati* Cases', *Human Rights Law Review* 8 (2008) 151–70, at 162 (hereinafter Sari, 'Jurisdiction').

[65] Case IT-94-1-A, *The Prosecutor v. Dusko Tadic*, 15 July 1999, ILM 38 (1999) 1518, at 1540 *et seq.*, paras. 116–45.

[66] The ECtHR has continued its jurisprudence in *Kasumaj v. Greece* (Appl. No. 6974/05), Decision (First Section), 5 July 2007, not reported; *Gajic v. Germany* (Appl. No. 31446/02), Decision (Fifth Section), 28 August 2007, not reported; *Beric v. Bosnia and Herzegovina* (Appl. No. 36357/04), Decision (Fourth Section), 16 October 2007, not reported. See also decision in *Galić and Blagojević*.

had died and the other remained gravely injured, as a consequence, as the applicant argued, of a grossly negligent omission of the responsible French contingent, which had not de-mined the area concerned as provided for. Here, according to the internal delimitation of responsibilities, UNMIK was found to be in charge of de-mining activities, not the French troops which were deployed in the area. Since UNMIK was a subsidiary organ of the UN, the failure to act had to be attributed directly to the UN.[67] Thus, the question of whether the parent organisation had 'effective control' was essentially moot and was not looked into.[68] Curiously enough, the Court did not reflect on whether, alongside the UN, France could possibly also be made accountable for its inertia in taking the requisite measures of precaution.

The situation regarding KFOR was infinitely more complex. As already noted, the mandate given to KFOR departed from the usual model of peacekeeping, in that the UN had refrained from assuming full responsibility for the military presence required in Kosovo, but had 'authorized' member states and 'relevant international organizations' to establish that presence 'with substantial North Atlantic Treaty Organization participation'. The chain of command ran from the Security Council and the Secretary-General to NATO, which established the requisite 'unified command' for KFOR. There could be no doubt that the political direction of the operation in Kosovo remained in the hands of the UN. KFOR was meant to ensure public safety and order until UNMIK could take responsibility for that task. It was enjoined to support UNMIK and cooperate with it; thus, it was part of a concerted action by the UN.

On the other hand, it is certainly doubtful whether the UN kept 'effective control' according to the scheme of responsibility developed by the International Court of Justice (ICJ) in *Nicaragua* v. *United States* with regard to international responsibility of states.[69] The ECtHR does not engage in a lengthy discussion on what the appropriate yardstick is. It confines itself to the straightforward statement that the Security Council retained 'ultimate authority and control'.[70] The subsequent considerations on whether such 'authority and control' did in fact exist add little,

---

[67] *Behrami and Saramati*, para. 142.   [68] *Ibid.*, paras. 142–3.
[69] *Military and Paramilitary Activities in and against Nicaragua (Nicaragua* v. *United States of America)*, Merits, ICJ Reports (1986) 14, at 61–5, paras. 105–15. This line was continued in *Application of the Convention on the Prevention and Punishment of the Crime of Genocide (Bosnia and Herzegovina* v. *Serbia and Montenegro)*, ICJ Reports (2007) 43, at 207, para. 397.
[70] *Behrami and Saramati*, para. 133.

almost nothing, to the correctness of the choice of the relevant parameter. In particular, the distinction between 'authorisation' and 'delegation' on which the Court relies is of no great help in understanding the rationale of the Court. Security Council 1244 simply speaks of an authorisation (para. 7: '*Authorizes*'), without having recourse to the term 'delegation': in fact, nothing is resolved by semantic games.[71] The true – and only – question is to what extent the Security Council may be considered authorised to entrust third parties with discharging its specific tasks, whatever the name that may be given to such a mandate, and to which degree it ensures its control of an operation.

That the ECtHR remained fairly reticent in explaining its reliance on the formula 'ultimate authority and control' may be due to its earlier jurisprudence where similar, though not identical, situations had to be addressed. In *Loizidou*, where it had to adjudicate the claim of a Greek Cypriot who was barred from accessing her house in the northern part of Cyprus, the crucial question was whether that property was placed under the jurisdiction of Turkey. Turkey, which maintains strong contingents of military forces in that part of the island since its invasion in 1974, where under its aegis the Turkish Republic of Northern Cyprus (TRNC) was proclaimed, denied that it could be made accountable for the actions of the local authorities. But the ECtHR held that, although the concept of jurisdiction was primarily territorial, extra-territorial activities of a contracting party could also be comprised in the scope of application *ratione territorii* of the ECHR. With very few words, it stated:

> Bearing in mind the object and purpose of the Convention, the responsibility of a Contracting Party may also arise when as a consequence of military action – whether lawful or unlawful – it exercises effective control of an area outside its national territory. The obligation to secure, in such an area, the rights and freedoms set out in the Convention derives from the fact of such control whether it be exercised directly, through its armed forces, or through a subordinate local administration.[72]

---

[71] Rightly, therefore, de Wet, *The Chapter VII*, 258–60, treats the two terms as synonyms. On the other hand, D. Sarooshi, *The United Nations and the Development of Collective Security: The Delegation by the UN Security Council of its Chapter VII Powers* (Oxford: Clarendon Press, 1999) 4–15, 142–55, 163–6, draws a sharp distinction between authorisation and delegation. Ultimately, the issue of responsibility depends essentially on the degree of control retained by the Security Council.

[72] ECtHR, *Loizidou v. Turkey (Preliminary Objections)* (Appl. No. 15318/89), 23 March 1995, Series A, Vol. 310, para. 62.

Although the words 'effective control' are presented as the key notion in this passage, the subsequent elaboration does not correspond to the general premise. Control exercised through a 'subordinate local administration' can hardly be effective control in the sense that the superior authority determines conduct at the grass roots level in a comprehensive fashion at any point in time. When coming to the merits of the case, the ECtHR had another opportunity to particularise its concept of control. It specified that under the prevailing circumstances in northern Cyprus, taking into account the great number of Turkish troops deployed there, it was not necessary to find out whether Turkey actually exercised 'detailed control over the policies and actions of the authorities of the "TRNC"'. It was obvious that her army exercised 'effective overall control over that part of the island. Such control ... entails her responsibility for the policies and actions of the "TRNC"... Those affected by such policies or actions therefore come within the "jurisdiction" of Turkey for the purposes of article 1 of the Convention'.[73] In other words, the Court applied a softened concept of 'effective control', viewing the system of governance in northern Cyprus as a well-functioning integrated whole where, in the last analysis, every governmental act could be attributed to Turkey which, as the determinative factual power, held sway over the 'TRNC'. In the later judgment on the inter-state application brought by Cyprus against Turkey, the same reasoning was upheld. The Court re-affirmed that in the 'TRNC', Turkey exercised 'effective overall control' and was therefore responsible for any official act in that entity.[74]

It seems hardly promising to engage in a semantic study of the differences between the various formulations employed by the ECtHR and the ICJ. One thing is certain, however. Two tendencies are opposed to one another. According to a strict yardstick, that of 'effective control', the authority of the superior command entity must be total and without any major gaps, taking into account, however, that in human relationships absolute perfection can never be obtained. On the other hand, there are those who plead for a somewhat more flexible approach that emphasises the organisational unity of an operative system of governance or

---

[73] ECtHR, *Loizidou* v. *Turkey* (*Merits*) (Appl. No. 15318/89), Judgment (Grand Chamber), 18 December 1996, Reports 1996-VI, para. 56.

[74] ECtHR, *Cyprus* v. *Turkey* (Appl. No. 25781/94), Judgment (Grand Chamber), 10 May 2001, Reports 2011-IV, para. 77. Doswald-Beck, 'Human Rights in Times of Conflict and Terrorism', at 17, speaks of 'a fairly wide interpretation to the term "effective control"'.

military command. Indeed, as Antonio Cassese has suggested, issues of responsibility should be assessed in their specific context.[75]

The criterion of 'effective control', taken as determinative by the ICJ both in *Nicaragua v. United States*[76] and in *Bosnia-Herzegovina v. Serbia*,[77] is well suited for certain configurations. In the international community of equal sovereign states, which are supposed to respect one another, it can hardly ever be presumed that one state incites insurgents in another state to carry out armed activities, hoping to topple the government of that state. Such activities are strictly forbidden by general rules of international law. The Friendly Relations Declaration of the General Assembly provides in its elaboration on the principle of non-use of force that '[e]very State has the duty to refrain from organizing or encouraging the organization of irregular forces or armed bands, including mercenaries, for incursion into the territory of another State'.[78] Not to comply with this rule constitutes a grave infringement of basic commitments under international law. Therefore, the relevant criteria of attribution must be strict and clear-cut. To derive international responsibility of a state from any kind of linkage it has with opposition or insurgent movements in another state would lead to absurd results in the world of today where all the former barriers to communication have been swept away. Article 8 ARS, to which the ICJ explicitly refers in its judgment in *Bosnia-Herzegovina v. Serbia and Montenegro*,[79] hence deserves full approval for such situations.

The same considerations apply when a state is charged with interfering by armed force in the territory of a neighbouring state and participating in genocidal acts, which was the complaint brought by Bosnia-Herzegovina against Serbia. Charges of armed interference and genocide are of the utmost gravity. It should never be lightly presumed that a state engages in such conduct in open breach of the fundamental

---

[75] 'The *Nicaragua* and *Tadić* Tests Revisited', 661.
[76] See *Military and Paramilitary Activities in and against Nicaragua (Nicaragua v. United States of America)*.
[77] *Application of the Convention on the Prevention and Punishment of the Crime of Genocide (Bosnia and Herzegovina v. Serbia and Montenegro)* ICJ Reports (2007) 43, paras. 396–407.
[78] UN GA Resolution 2625 (XXV), Declaration on Principles of International Law Concerning Friendly Relations and Co-operation among States in Accordance with the Charter of the United Nations (Sixth Committee) (A/8082), 24 October 1970.
[79] *Application of the Convention on the Prevention and Punishment of the Crime of Genocide (Bosnia and Herzegovina v. Serbia and Montenegro)*, para. 398.

principles of the international legal order.[80] Only where such flagrant breaches take place under the decisive influence of the wrongdoer should its responsibility be entailed.

Where, on the other hand, a common enterprise is openly brought into being, in particular in the form of an operation under Chapter VII of the Charter, the general presumption goes in the opposite direction. States that join a UN operation or a UN-mandated operation may thereby manifest their will to contribute to attaining a common goal. They do not have their own agenda, but subordinate themselves voluntarily under the command of the UN, no matter how long the chain of command. Therefore, one may see this type of situation as vicarious liability. The UN, the principal, should thus bear all the consequences of the conduct of its agents. In a system of voluntary cooperation, the principal may generally assume that its orders and wishes are executed bona fide by the entire machinery created for the performance of the common project. There is no need to establish specific control mechanisms that ensure that even the slightest movement is steered from above. Generally, even without such strict supervision, the ship will sail in the right direction.

In other words, it is imperative to distinguish between the different factual configurations when analysing attribution.[81] The general connotation of a societal organisation cannot be neglected. Therefore, it does not seem appropriate to rely on the criterion of 'effective control' in the case of true UN operations under Chapter VII of the Charter, however organised. The debate on article 7 of the 'Gaja draft' is not yet finished. The parallelism between responsibility of states and the responsibility of international organisations may sometimes be a fallacy. In general, states rely on their own organs and agents when performing their duties. In the case of international organisations, the situation is entirely different. Their administrative apparatus is generally fairly small, and they are widely dependent on assistance by their members, securing peace in the international arena constituting the main example of that intimate inter-relationship. Here, it can generally be presumed that everything being performed lies in the interest of the organisation. Accordingly, in

---

[80] It is another question altogether whether the ICJ did everything in its power to elucidate the relationship between the Bosnian Serbs and the Serbian Army.
[81] When identifying 'effective control' as the determinative criterion, Hirsch, 'The Responsibility of International Organizations Toward Third Parties', at 77, did not yet have to consider the alternatives that emerged after the publication of his book (1995).

such cooperative organisational structures, attribution to the organisation should be the general maxim to follow. From the viewpoint of human rights protection, this is not an ideal stance to take, inasmuch as legal remedies against the UN, in particular, are either non-existent or defective. States are much better controlled in respect of their actions, in particular, all the states members of the ECHR. However, it would not be correct to attribute responsibility specifically on that ground to troop-contributing countries where, indeed, the military or other contingents concerned acted exclusively in the performance of the mandate given to them by the UN without any interference by their national governments.

A caveat must be added to this conclusion. It will always be necessary to examine the relevant facts very closely. Under specific circumstances the UN may, from the very outset, manifest that it declines to assume any responsibility for an operation that enjoys its political support. When, in the absence of the Soviet Union from the Security Council in June 1950, the Council recommended to the members of the world organisation to 'furnish such assistance to the Republic of Korea as may be necessary to repel the armed attack and to restore international peace and security in the area',[82] it specified at the same time that the operation was to be conducted under the command of the United States; the only link between the operation and the UN was the authorisation to use the UN flag and the request to provide the Security Council with reports 'as appropriate' on the course of action taken under the unified command.[83] These stipulations made it clear that the operation of defence against the North Korean attack was not a UN operation, although it enjoyed the political backing of the world organisation.

Second, overall control by the UN must be real and not only fictitious. Examination of the institutional structure of the operation must show that, indeed, the UN is the decisive control centre and that the operation is truly placed under its direction.[84] This was the situation in Kosovo, where KFOR had to act as an instrument for the attainment of the general strategy determined by the Security Council, which was ensured through its obligation to submit regular reports to the Security Council and through the required close cooperation with UNMIK.[85] None of that

---

[82] UN SC, Resolution 83 (1950) concerning Korea, 27 June 1950, UN Doc. S/1511.
[83] UN SC, Resolution 84 (1950) concerning Korea, 7 July 1950, UN Doc. S/1588.
[84] Persuasively shown by de Wet, *The Chapter VII*, 308.
[85] UN SC, Resolution 1244 (1999) concerning Kosovo, 10 June 1999, UN Doc. S/RES/1244, paras. 9(f) and 20. The criticism by L.-A. Sicilianos, 'L'(Ir)responsabilité des Forces

existed in the case of Iraq, where the invasion came first and where only afterwards some very limited recognition was granted to the Coalition Provisional Authority established by the United States and the United Kingdom (UK).[86] The same picture could be observed with regard to Libya. Willy-nilly, the Security Council granted to a coalition of willing states the right to resort to armed force in order to protect the civilian population.[87] This authorisation, however, was not backed up by any institutional elements that would have secured the direction of the UN. The only obligation incumbent upon such a coalition was to 'inform' the Secretary-General immediately. No parallel UN mechanism was established.[88] As far as the EULEX Rule of Law mission of the EU is concerned, it was formally brought under the roof of Security Council Resolution 1244 (1999), but follows its own strategy; there are no institutional links of subordination between EULEX and the Security Council, just a somewhat loose relationship of mutual accommodation.[89]

3.3.2.3 The troop-contributing countries' own responsibility

The proposed ground rule of attribution should not detract from the responsibility of a troop contingent placed at the disposal of the UN, which may exist alongside the responsibility of the UN.[90] In the ordinary course of

Multinationales', in L. Boisson de Chazournes and M.G. Kohen (eds.), *Liber Amicorum Vera Gowlland-Debbas* (Leiden and Boston: Brill, 2010) 95–125, at 102–6, 116 does not take account of the real situation in that case, basing itself on a purely dogmatic distinction between peacekeeping operations and operations authorised by the Security Council.

[86] UN SC, Resolution 1511 (2003) concerning Iraq, 16 October 2003, UN Doc. S/RES/1511, para. 1.

[87] UN SC, Resolution 1973 (2011) concerning Libya, 17 March 2011, UN Doc. S/RES/1973, para. 4.

[88] The contention that as a consequence of *Behrami and Saramati* the actions of the coalition in Iraq must be attributed to the UN reveals bad judgment, see Milanović and Papić, 'As Bad As it Gets', 292.

[89] See, e.g., the Report of the European Union High Representative for Foreign Affairs and Security Policy to the Secretary-General on the activities of the European Union Rule of Law Mission in Kosovo, Annex I to the Report of the Secretary-General on the United Nations Interim Mission in Kosovo, UN Doc. S/2011/281, 3 May 2011.

[90] Suggested already by Hirsch, 'The Responsibility of International Organizations', 65. This is now a common view; see, in particular, G. Gaja, First Report on Responsibility of International Organizations, UN Doc. A/CN.4/532, 26 March 2003, at 20, para. 38. See also, P. Bodeau-Livinec *et al.*, 'Case Note', *American Journal of International Law* 102 (2008) 323–31, at 328; Breitegger, 'Sacrificing the Effectiveness', 160; A. Clapham, 'The Subject of Subjects and the Attribution of Attribution', in Boisson de Chazournes and Kohen (eds.), *Liber Amicorum Vera Gowlland-Debbas*, 45–58, at 56; T. Dannenbaum,

executing a Security Council mandate, the members of a national troop contingent may act solely on behalf of the UN. Thus, the Norwegian Commander of KFOR (COMKFOR), who ordered the detention of Saramati, exercised exclusively powers entrusted to him by KFOR. His role as commander had nothing to do with the governmental authority of Norway. On the other hand, if a troop contingent is faced with issues of life and death, like de-mining, and if, in that case, it is clearly visible that failure to de-mine could easily lead to loss of human lives, the letter and spirit of the ECHR require that appropriate steps be taken with a view to eliminating the glaring risk factor. Accordingly, it would have been advisable for the ECtHR to distinguish between the two cases of *Behrami* and *Saramati*. In the case of 'Dutchbat', the Dutch unit charged with protecting the inhabitants of Srebrenica in 1995, the Gerechtshof (Court of Appeal) in The Hague rightly came to the conclusion that because of the tight involvement of the Dutch government in the negotiations held with the UN Secretary-General on the conduct to be observed in the case of the expected attack by Bosnian Serb forces, the Netherlands had to assume responsibility, possibly alongside the UN, an issue that was not, however, under the jurisdiction of the Court.[91]

3.3.2.4 The constitutional requirement of Security Council control

The Security Council is embedded in a constitutional framework of tight checks and balances. In particular, the veto right of the permanent members prevents any easy abuses. This bulwark against rash and inconsiderate decisions must not suffer any inroads by a practice of authorisations pursuant to which the Security Council remains only *de jure* the

---

'Translating the Standard of Effective Control into a System of Effective Accountability: How Liability Should Be Apportioned for Violations of Human Rights by Member State Troop Contingents Serving as United Nations Peacekeepers', *Harvard International Law Journal* 51 (2010) 113–92, at 169; S. Dorigo, 'Imputazione e Responsabilità Internazionale per l'Attività delle Forze di Peacekeeping delle Nazioni Unite', *Rivista di Diritto Internazionale* 85 (2002) 903–45, at 936–40; F. Messineo, 'The House of Lords in *Al-Jedda* and Public International Law', *Netherlands International Law Review* 56 (2009) 35–62, at 40 (hereinafter Messineo, 'The House of Lords in *Al-Jedda*'); Milanović and Papić, 'As Bad As it Gets', *supra* note 63, 289; Peters, 'Die Anwendbarkeit der EMRK', 34; Sari, 'Jurisdiction', 167; Schütze, 'Die Zurechenbarkeit', 199.

[91] *Mustafic v. Netherlands*, Judgment, case 200-020.173/01, 5 July 2011, http://zoeken.rechtspraak.nl/detailpage.aspx?ljn=BR0132&u_ljn=BR0132; English translation: http://srebrenica-genocide.blogspot.com/2011/08/srebrenica-appeals-court-ruling.html; for a comment, see A. Nollkaemper, 'Dual Attribution: Liability of the Netherlands for Conduct of Dutchbat in Srebrenica', *Journal of International Criminal Justice* 9 (2011) 1143–57.

THE EUROPEAN COURT OF HUMAN RIGHTS AND THE UN   361

ultimate centre of attribution, but in fact cedes its authority to 'coalitions of the willing', which then act according to their own political preferences. In principle, authorisations are by now an acknowledged feature of the system under Chapter VII of the Charter. The international community recognises that the general mandate conferred on the Security Council could not be satisfactorily discharged if the Council invariably had to act under its sole and exclusive responsibility.[92] But it must be clear that it retains the 'ultimate' responsibility and that, by authorising or delegating enforcement powers, it will not be freed from its obligation to remain at the helm of such operations.[93]

3.3.3 Jurisdiction under article 1 ECHR

The second question which stands at the commencement of any proceedings before the ECtHR relates to article 1 ECHR. The scope of application *ratione personae* of the ECHR extends to 'everyone within [the] jurisdiction' of one of the contracting parties. An applicant must be able to submit that he/she is placed under the protection of the ECHR by virtue of the commitments undertaken by the respondent state. Both questions are intimately related to one another. As was already pointed out, the UN is not bound by the ECHR. Generally, jurisdiction *ratione personae* on the passive side has already been discussed under the heading of attribution or authorship. Accordingly, in the following, the main accent will be on the dimension *ratione personae* on the active side, the entitlement to assert rights under the ECHR. Since the states parties to the ECHR are bound *vis-à-vis* 'everyone', they are obligated not only vis-à-vis their own nationals and the nationals of other states parties, but also in respect of persons holding other nationalities, or no nationality at all.

Jurisdiction *ratione personae* in this sense is intimately tied up with jurisdiction *ratione territorii*. The most instructive example regarding the territorial component of jurisdiction is provided by the *Bankovic* case.[94] Bankovic and others were victims of one of the air raids carried out by NATO aircraft during the war against Yugoslavia when the Western

---

[92] See, e.g., Blokker, 'Is the Authorization Authorized?', 552, 554.
[93] This was explicitly recognised in *Behrami and Saramati*, para. 132. For an overview of the different strategies employed to ensure the control of the Security Council, see Blokker, 'Is the Authorization Authorized?', 561–7.
[94] ECtHR, *Bankovic and Others v. (all involved NATO states)* (Appl. No. 52207/99), Judgment (Grand Chamber), 12 December 2001, Reports 2001-XII.

alliance intervened on behalf of the Kosovar Albanians. Through applications to the ECtHR, the next of kin of the deceased requested compensation for their deaths. The ECtHR rejected the applications. It did not inquire into the complex issue of who should shoulder the responsibility for the air operations, which had taken place under the command of NATO. Instead, it concluded that in any event the persons affected on the ground in Belgrade were not placed under the jurisdiction of any of the respondent states. Acts of warfare did not bring the victims of such acts under the jurisdiction of the military power having caused the injuries complained of.[95]

3.3.3.1 **The concept of jurisdiction** As reflected in *Bankovic*, the ECtHR has taken as its starting point the concept of jurisdiction as it is generally understood in international law. Stating that jurisdiction is primarily territorial, it has nevertheless acknowledged that there exist other forms of jurisdiction which have an extra-territorial dimension, in particular, personal jurisdiction or jurisdiction which stems from the fact of establishing elements of governmental authority in a foreign country.[96] Thus, governmental agents are not exempt from any commitments under the ECHR as soon as they leave their national territory. This means that any troop contingent operating abroad travels with the constraints imposed upon its home state, irrespective of its place of deployment. However, since responsibility for operations under the aegis of the UN must be shouldered by the UN, such additional responsibility of the national state will arise only exceptionally, in particular if the unit concerned has taken discretionary decisions not predetermined by the mission to be accomplished. Originally, in the *Bankovic* judgment (§ 80), the ECtHR had suggested that the it was 'a constitutional instrument of *European* public order'. It added that the ECHR was a multilateral treaty

---

[95] The later judgment in ECtHR, *Mansur Pad and Others* v. *Turkey* (Appl. No. 60167/00), Decision (Third Section), 28 June 2007, not reported, paras. 55, 56, is not consistent with the *Bankovic* judgment. To date, however, the authority of the Grand Chamber judgment prevails.

[96] For a comprehensive account of the ECtHR's case law on 'jurisdiction' under art. 1, see ECtHR, *Al-Skeini and Others* v. *United Kingdom* (Appl. No. 55721/07), Judgment (Grand Chamber), 7 July 2011, not reported, paras. 130–42. For a similar line of reasoning with regard to the ICCPR, see ICJ, *Legal Consequences of the Construction of a Wall in the Occupied Palestinian Territory*, Advisory Opinion, ICJ Reports (2004) 136, at 179–89, paras. 109–11; *Armed Activities on the Territory of the Congo (Democratic Republic of the Congo* v. *Uganda)*, Judgment, ICJ Reports (2005) 168, at 243, para. 216.

operating in an essentially regional context and notably in the legal space (*espace juridique*) of the Contracting States. Since the Federal Republic of Yugoslavia, as a non-state party, did not fall within this legal space, the ECHR could not be invoked to assess the bombings in Belgrade. The Convention was not designed to be applied throughout the world.

3.3.3.2 Extra-territorial activities   This cautious attitude could not be maintained. The ECtHR was faced, in subsequent years, with facts where a denial of the applicability of the ECHR would have appeared as a recourse to a double standard harmful for the ideal of human rights. The extra-territorial effect of the ECHR was first reaffirmed in *Ilascu*,[97] although in that case the alleged violations – deprivation of personal freedom in violation of article 5 ECHR – took place on the soil of an area formally under the jurisdiction of Moldova, a state party to the ECHR, but where the Moldovan government, because of the proclamation of a secessionist state (the Moldovan Republic of Transdniestria, MRT) had little real power. The jurisprudence was taken a step further in *Issa*, where the ECtHR considered whether Turkish jurisdiction could possibly have been entailed by inroads into the northern part of Iraq by Turkish troops when combating Kurdish rebel groups.[98] This decision of the Second Section of the Court received its final approval in the case of Kurdish leader Öcalan. Öcalan, the political leader of the insurgent Kurds, had been retrieved in Kenya. On the basis of communications between the intelligence services of Turkey and Kenya, Öcalan was arrested in Nairobi, brought on board a Turkish aircraft and flown to Turkey. Without the least hesitation, the Grand Chamber of the Court examined whether Öcalan's arrest in Nairobi could have violated his rights under article 5 ECHR,[99] relying on a short passage in the preceding judgment of the First Section, where it had been noted that the applicant had been handed over by the Kenyan authorities to Turkish officials which forced him to return to Turkey, thus already establishing Turkey's jurisdiction over him on Kenyan soil.[100]

---

[97] ECtHR, *Ilascu and Others* v. *Moldova and Russia* (Appl. No. 48787/99), Judgment (Grand Chamber), 8 July 2004, Reports 2004-VII, para. 314.
[98] ECtHR, *Issa and Others* v. *Turkey* (Appl. No. 31821/96), Judgment (Second Section), 16 November 2004, paras. 68, 69.
[99] ECtHR, *Öcalan* v. *Turkey* (Appl. No. 46221/99), Judgment (Grand Chamber), 12 May 2005, Reports 2005-IV, paras. 103–5.
[100] ECtHR, *Öcalan* v. *Turkey* (Appl. No. 46221/99), Judgment (First Section), 12 March 2003, not reported, para. 93.

If any doubts might have remained after the decision in *Öcalan*, they were definitely removed by the more recent judgments in *Al-Skeini*[101] and *Al-Jedda*.[102] In the former case, the ECtHR had to examine a number of deaths which had occurred in Iraq at the hands of the British occupation forces. Four of the victims had been shot dead in the streets of Basra, or in their homes, whereas one of the victims had been beaten up in a police station in such a brutal manner that he died from the wounds inflicted upon him. The latter case had as its subject matter the detention by British military units in Iraq of a British citizen of Iraqi origin, Mr. Al-Jedda. From October 2004 to 30 December 2007, he had been held in a British-run prison in Basra without being treated in accordance with the guarantees of article 5 ECHR.

In *Al-Skeini*, the British courts admitted that the death in a UK military prison had occurred under UK jurisdiction, while they held that the shooting incidents did not come under UK jurisdiction.[103] Rightly, the ECtHR saw this assessment of the case as erroneous, since the shooting incidents did not happen during armed hostilities at the time when the coalition invaded Iraq, but later, after the UK had already established its authority as an occupying power, thereby assuming responsibility for the area and its inhabitants.[104] Neither in *Al-Skeini* nor in *Al-Jedda* did the Court devote lengthy considerations to the question of whether the cases of detention could possibly be attributed to the UN instead of the UK. Although the Security Council, after the invasion, had twice granted an authorisation to the occupation forces to administer the country, the Court rightly felt that the applicants' confinement to a UK military prison definitely brought them under UK jurisdiction.

At first glance, it might appear as if the ECtHR had run into a contradiction with its holdings in *Behrami and Saramati*. Closer

---

[101] *Al-Skeini and Others* v. *United Kingdom*.
[102] ECtHR, *Al-Jedda* v. *United Kingdom* (Appl. No. 27021/08), Judgment (Grand Chamber), 7 July 2011, not reported. See comments by C. Chinkin, 'International Humanitarian Law, Human Rights and the UK Courts', in Boisson de Chazournes and Kohen (ed.) *Liber Amicorum Vera Gowlland-Debbas*, 243–64, at 252–64; C. Tomuschat, 'Human Rights in a Multi-Level System of Governance and the Internment of Suspected Terrorists', *Melbourne Journal of International Law* 9 (2008) 391–404 (predicting that the judgment would not stand scrutiny by the ECtHR); and Messineo, 'The House of Lords in *Al-Jedda*'.
[103] House of Lords, Judgment, 13 June 2007, [2007] UKHL 26; critical comments by R. Wilde, *American Journal of International Law* 102 (2008) 628–34, at 632–4.
[104] *Al-Skeini and Others* v. *United Kingdom*, paras. 143–50.

examination of the facts, however, shows that this is not the case. Already at their origins, the two operations were fundamentally different. The assumption of power in Kosovo by UNMIK and KFOR had been determined by the Security Council through Resolution 1244 of 10 June 1999, while the invasion of Iraq in March 2003 was an undertaking by a coalition of the willing under the leadership of the United States, primarily supported by the United Kingdom. Also, the first resolution of the Security Council after the invasion simply took note of the fact that the United States and the UK had established a Coalition Provisional Authority, specifying, in this connection, that the two nations had to assume the obligations of an occupying power under international law.[105] It was only through Resolution 1511 of 16 October 2003 that some legal recognition was given to the Coalition Provisional Authority to ensure security and stability in Iraq until the establishment of a new government.[106] Lastly, in a third resolution of 8 June 2004,[107] emphasis was placed on the fact that the multinational force was present in Iraq 'at the request of the incoming Interim Government'. Obviously, the coalition forces in Iraq had a character that differed fundamentally from KFOR in Kosovo. The Coalition Provisional Authority owed its birth to the unlawful invasion of Iraq by the US-led coalition of the willing, and the UN confined itself to extending some legal umbrella that was suited to bring the situation in Iraq back into the framework of international law. No powers of control and direction were demanded or obtained by the Security Council; nor did it request that it be regularly informed by the submission of reports. In order to establish its own contacts with

---

[105] UN SC, Resolution 1483 (2003) concerning Iraq, 22 May 2003, UN Doc. S/RES/1483, Preamble, para. 13.

[106] UN SC, Resolution 1511 (2003) concerning Iraq, 16 October 2003, UN Doc. S/RES/1511, para. 1: '1. *Reaffirms* the sovereignty and territorial integrity of Iraq, and *underscores*, in that context, the temporary nature of the exercise by the Coalition Provisional Authority (Authority) of the specific responsibilities, authorities, and 1483 (2003), which will cease when an internationally recognized, representative government established by the people of Iraq is sworn in and assumes the responsibilities of the Authority ...'; para. 13: '...*authorizes* a multinational force under unified command to take all necessary measures to contribute to the maintenance of security and stability in Iraq, including for the purpose of ensuring necessary conditions for the implementation of the timetable and programme as well as to contribute to the security of the United Nations Assistance Mission for Iraq, the Governing Council of Iraq and other institutions of the Iraqi interim administration, and key humanitarian and economic infrastructure.'

[107] UN SC, Resolution 1546 (2004) concerning Iraq, 8 June 2004, UN Doc. S/RES/1546, para. 9.

the country, the Security Council established a mission of its own – which again had no authority over the coalition forces.[108] Under these circumstances, any factual elements were lacking that could have justified attribution of the acts of the coalition forces to the UN. The fate of the victims in *Al-Skeini* and in *Al-Jedda* may not even have come to the knowledge of the Secretary-General of the UN.

Al-Skeini and *Al-Jedda* are the final elements in a chain of judgments that make clear, once and for all, that the extra-territorial activities of the states parties to the ECHR remain bound by their contractual commitments wherever they act, inside or outside their territories, provided only that they may be deemed to have jurisdiction over a person. This applies also to instances where, on the high seas, a state takes control of a vessel by its military forces.[109] Outside the national borders, such assignment of jurisdiction will take place only exceptionally. However, in particular when a person is kept in detention, the responsible authorities of the detention centre will always have jurisdiction over that person.

For the ECtHR, it will certainly not be easy to live up to its responsibilities under article 1 ECHR when it has to pronounce on occurrences outside Europe, where the taking of evidence is hampered by considerable difficulties. However, on account of the requirement of exhaustion of national remedies, the underlying facts will often have been clarified to a sufficient degree. In particular, when a case comes under the jurisdiction of a state party to the ECHR, the requirement of exhaustion of local remedies leads inexorably to proceedings at home, within the borders of the relevant state. Thus, in *Al-Skeini* and in *Al-Jedda*, where the measures complained of took place in Iraq, On each occasion the dispute was considered in last instance by the House of Lords. Given the scrupulous attention of the UK courts in general, the Strasbourg judges could rely on the facts as they were recounted in the national judgments.

---

[108] UN SC, Resolution 1500 (2003) concerning Iraq and establishing the United Nations Assistance Mission for Iraq (UNAMI), 14 August 2003, UN Doc. S/RES/1500, which mandate was determined by SC Resolution 1546 (2004), para. 7.

[109] See ECtHR, *Medvedyev and Others* v. *France* (Appl. No. 3394/03), Judgment (Grand Chamber), 29 March 2010, Reports 2010, paras. 66–7. The Court held: '... as this was a case of France having exercised full and exclusive control over the *Winner* and its crew, at least *de facto*, from the time of its interception, in a continuous and uninterrupted manner until they were tried in France, the applicants were effectively within France's jurisdiction for the purposes of Article 1 of the Convention'. Already in *Bankovic and Others* v. *(all involved NATO states)*, para. 73, the Court had stated that states also exercised jurisdiction on board aircraft and vessels registered by them or flying their flag.

4. Enforcement of international directions or orders by national authorities

Cases where state authorities act directly vis-à-vis an individual without being integrated into a cooperative system at the executive level, do not offer the same degree of complexity at the initial stage. No question arises as to who is the author of the relevant order or measure. Every state has to assume full responsibility of all the acts of its three branches of government performed on the national territory.[110] Accordingly, anyone who feels adversely affected is free to file for the domestic remedies available in such cases. However, if the national agency concerned did nothing other than execute a regulation or order issued by an international institution, it may appear doubtful whether, in abiding by the general principle of the rule of law, the judicial body seised with the matter also has the authority to review those orders from another legal world as to their validity.

4.1 The European Union

In the European Union, a truly intelligent device was framed at the very inception of the integration process. Obviously, the general intention was to see Community law applied and enforced in no other way than domestic law as a matter of everyday routine. However, special provision was made for instances where the application of that law could prove fraught with uncertainties. The procedure of preliminary rulings (now article 267 TFEU) combines both respect for national sovereignty and Community/Union control over the development of the entire legal order of the Union, comprising both the primary level of the treaties and the secondary law of the instruments enacted on the basis of those treaties. National judges are authorised to request the ECJ to provide an authentic interpretation of rules of Union law whose interpretation they consider controversial, and the highest tribunals are required to make such a request where the interpretation poses objective problems. On the other hand, where the validity of an act of secondary law is in issue, the national judges are denied any discretion: if they regard an act of secondary law as incompatible with superior norms, they are denied the right to strike down or leave aside that act according to their

---

[110] ECtHR, *Al-Saadoon and Mufdhi* v. *UK* (Appl. No. 61498/08), Judgment (Fourth Section), 2 March 2010, Reports 2010, paras. 126–8.

judgment, but must beforehand seek a preliminary ruling of the ECJ. Thus, national judges have the authority – and are even obligated – to examine the validity of a regulatory act of the Union, but they cannot set aside such an act in an autonomous fashion.[111] If no preliminary ruling is sought, persons alleging a violation of their rights under the ECHR may eventually, after having exhausted the available domestic remedies, take their grievances to the ECtHR by an application against the state concerned, emphasising the existing links to the domestic legal order of that state.[112]

4.2 The UN

As far as the law of the UN is concerned, no such procedure exists. Here, again, the lack of foresight by the drafters is amply explained by their assumption that the General Assembly and the Security Council would entertain legal relationships only at the high level of inter-state relationships. It has already been observed that this idyllic picture has proven not to be in conformity with realities, inasmuch as the Security Council has begun a practice according to which specific individual human beings, identified by their names and addresses, are targeted in a quasi-direct fashion, although the execution on the ground of such measures is left to domestic authorities. This came as a surprise to most commentators, who took note of the new development, especially through the *Kadi* case that had to be adjudicated by the ECJ – and yet has a strong virtual link with the ECtHR.

In recent years, the Security Council has intensified its practice of 'targeted' sanctions out of the realisation that comprehensive ('dumb') sanctions against a country mostly hit the 'wrong' people, while the power wielders, those to be blamed for endangering international peace and security, could easily avoid any negative consequences for themselves.[113] The sanctions imposed on Iraq after the aggression against

---

[111] Case 314/85, *Foto Frost v. Hauptzollamt Lübeck-Ost* [1987] ECR 4199, paras. 15–20; Case C-119/05, *Ministero dell'Industria, del Commercio e dell'Artigianato v. Lucchini SpA* [2007] ECR I-6199, para. 53; Case C-188 and 189/10, *Melki and Abdeli* [2010] ECR I-5667, para. 54.

[112] For an extensive study of the openings generated by the jurisprudence of the ECtHR, see Janik, 'Die EMRK'.

[113] Consideration clearly exposed by Tridimas and Gutierrez-Fons, 'EU Law, International Law, and Economic Sanctions against Terrorism', 672. A general overview of targeted sanctions is given by A. Ciampi, 'Security Council Targeted Sanctions and Human

Kuwait were characterised by numerous critics as conducive to the death of thousands of children.[114] When, instead, only those responsible for the denounced wrongs are interfered with, innocent victims will generally be spared, although it may happen that persons are included in the circle of addressees who were not involved in any kind of wrongdoing. On the other hand, sanctions against criminal insurgent movements were deemed to deprive such movements of any legitimacy and to cut off their connections with foreign countries.

4.2.1 Travel bans

Two instruments have been developed by the Security Council that correspond to the philosophy of targeting exclusively the responsible perpetrators. On the one hand, travel bans have been issued.[115] Such bans were issued, for example, against members of the white racist regime in Southern Rhodesia (Zimbabwe),[116] members of the UNITA rebel movement in Angola,[117] members of the Iraqi Government on the eve of the invasion by the US–UK coalition,[118] and members of the

---

Rights' in B. Fassbender (ed.), *Securing Human Rights? Achievements and Challenges of the UN Security Council* (Oxford University Press, 2011) 98–140 (hereinafter Ciampi, 'Security Council Targeted Sanctions'), and E. de Wet, 'Human Rights Considerations and the Enforcement of Targeted Sanctions in Europe: The Emergence of Core Standards of Judicial Protection', in *ibid.*, 141–71 (hereinafter de Wet, 'Human Rights Considerations').

[114] See, e.g., A. Reinisch, 'Developing Human Rights and Humanitarian Law Accountability of the Security Council for the Imposition of Economic Sanctions', *American Journal of International Law* 95 (2001) 851–72, at 852 (with further references); C. Tomuschat, *Human Rights Between Idealism and Realism*, 2nd edn (Oxford University Press, 2008) 101; de Wet, *The Chapter VII*, 227–33.

[115] For a comprehensive study, including a few case studies, see E. Cosgrove, 'Examining Targeted Sanctions. Are Travel Bans Effective?', in P. Wallensteen and C. Staibano (eds.), *International Sanctions: Between Words and Wars in the Global System* (London and New York: Routledge, 2005) 207–28. Rich empirical data is provided by R.W. Conroy, 'The UN Experience with Travel Sanctions: Selected Cases and Conclusions', in D. Cortright and G.A. Lopez (eds.), *Smart Sanctions: Targeting Economic Statecraft* (Lanham: Rowman & Littlefield, 2002) 145–69.

[116] UN SC, Resolution 253 (1968) concerning Southern Rhodesia (Zimbabwe), 29 May 1968, para. 5(b).

[117] UN SC, Resolution 1127 (1997) concerning Angola, 28 August 1997, UN Doc. S/RES/1127, para. 4. This ban seems to have been particularly porous, see Cosgrove, 'Examining Targeted Sanctions', 152–6.

[118] UN SC, Resolution 1137 (1997) concerning Iraq, 12 November 1997, UN Doc. S/RES/1137, para. 4.

Taliban in Afghanistan,[119] to exert pressure on account of the massive violations of human rights in the Sudan,[120] to counteract similar efforts by Iran,[121] with a view to stifling North Korea's attempts to produce nuclear weapons,[122] sanctioning persons fomenting civil strife in Côte d'Ivoire,[123] or recently against the leadership of Libya that fought a merciless war against its own people.[124] According to a standard formulation in these resolutions, member states are required to prevent 'entry into or transit through their territories'.[125] Technically, the procedure, which also applies in respect of freezing orders, follows a consistent pattern.[126] On the basis of information received mainly from intelligence services, a Sanctions Committee of the Security Council, on which all members of the Security Council are represented, identifies the persons subject to the ban or to be hit by a freezing order. Their names are included in a Consolidated List that is communicated to all states.[127] Governments then have to enforce the determinations which, since adoption under Chapter VII of the Charter, are binding on all members of the world organisation.

It can easily be imagined that someone covered by a ban finds himself/herself on the soil of a state party to the ECHR, being stopped there or

---

[119] UN SC, Resolutions 1333 (2000) concerning Afghanistan, 19 December 2000, UN Doc. S/RES/1333, para 14; 1390 (2002) concerning Afghanistan, 28 January 2002, UN Doc. S/RES/1390, para. 2(b).

[120] UN SC, Resolution 1591 (2005) concerning the Sudan, 29 March 2005, UN Doc. S/RES/1591, para. 3(f).

[121] UN SC, Resolutions 1737 (2006) concerning Iran, 25 December 2005, UN Doc. S/RES/1737, para. 10; 1747 (2007), 24 March 2007, UN Doc. S/RES/1747, para. 2; 1803 (2008), UN Doc. S/RES/1803, para. 5.

[122] UN SC, Resolution 1718 (2006) concerning the Democratic People's Republic of Korea, 14 October 2006, UN Doc. S/RES/1718, para. 8(e).

[123] UN SC Resolution 1572 (2004) concerning Côte d'Ivoire, 15 November 2004, UN Doc. S/RES/1572, para. 9.

[124] UN SC, Resolutions 1970 (2011) concerning Libya, 26 February 2011, UN Doc. S/RES/1970, paras. 15, 16; 1973 (2011), 17 March 2011, UN Doc. S/RES/1973, para. 22. The earlier embargo against Libya, imposed by UN SC Resolution 748 (1992), 31 March 1992, UN Doc. S/RES/748, prohibited any kind of air traffic with the country (para. 4).

[125] For a full list, see the official website of the UN Security Council Sanctions Committees, www.un.org/sc/committees/.

[126] See, e.g., the Guidelines of the 1267 Sanctions Committee, 30 November 2011, www.un.org/sc/committees/1267/pdf/1267_guidelines.pdf. By virtue of UN SC Resolutions 1988 (2011) and 1989 (2011), 17 June 2011, UN Doc. S/RES/1988 and UN Doc. S/RES/1989, the mandate of the 1267 Sanctions Committee was confined to Al-Qaida.

[127] For the latest list, see www.un.org/sc/committees/1267/AQList.htm (updated 13 April 2012).

being arrested for the purpose of his/her expulsion to the relevant home country. Hitherto there seems to be only one case which has come before the competent courts. In *Abdelrazik* v. *The Minister of Foreign Affairs*, a Federal Court of Canada found that Mr. Abdelrazik's right under the Canadian Charter of Rights and Freedoms to enter Canada, his country of citizenship which had been denied to him because he was listed and purchasing an airline ticket on his behalf, was precluded by a ban on transferring assets to a listed entity, had been breached. The judge held that the remedy to which Mr. Abdelrazik was entitled required the Canadian government to take immediate action so that he be returned to Canada.[128] It has also been observed by UK judges that through the effect of a freezing order, a person may be cut off from any opportunity to travel, making him or her effectively a 'prisoner of the state'.[129] The insignificant number of court cases may simply be due to the fact that in matters of immigration all states are endowed with extensive discretionary powers, since decisions on who is admitted to the national territory pertain to the core of national sovereignty. Generally, as opposed to nationals, aliens enjoy no right of admission.

Travel bans, although based on orders issued by the Security Council, are truly domestic measures of the acting state concerned, and can hence be challenged before the competent courts like any other measures adversely affecting individual rights. By contrast, as to the merits, the defence would be restricted. Not only are governments fairly free to take decisions as they see fit on political grounds, additionally, since the Security Council also enjoys broad discretion as to the assessment whether a given situation falls within the scope of Chapter VII of the

---

[128] *Abdelrazik* v. *The Minister of Foreign Affairs*, Decision, June 2009, 2009 FC 580, referred to in the Eleventh Report of the Analytical Support and Sanctions Implementation Monitoring Team established pursuant to Security Council resolution 1526 (2004) and extended by Resolution 1904 (2009) concerning Al-Qaida and the Taliban and associated individuals and entities, UN Doc. S/2011/245, 13 April 2011, para. 62; see also comment by A. Tzanakopoulos, 'United Nations in Domestic Courts: From Interpretation to Defiance in *Abdelrazik* v. *Canada*', *Journal of International Criminal Justice* 8 (2010) 249–67.

[129] Sedley LJ, UK Court of Appeal, *A and others* v. *HM Treasury* [2008] EWCA Civ 1187; [2009] 3 WLR 25, para. 125. In *Her Majesty's Treasury (Respondent)* v. *Mohammed Jabar Ahmed and Others (FC) (Appellants) Her Majesty's Treasury (Respondent)* v. *Mohammed al-Ghabra (FC) (Appellant) R (on the application of Hani El Sayed Sabaei Youssef) (Respondent)* v. *Her Majesty's Treasury (Appellant)*, Judgment, 27 January 2010, [2010] UKSC 2, this view was shared at the level of the Supreme Court by Lord Hope, joined by Lord Walker and Lady Hale, para. 60: 'the effect ... can be devastating'.

Charter, no complainant could persuasively argue that the Security Council has misused its discretion. Yet, the question is whether he or she may contend that the inclusion in the list established by the Security Council is due to a mistake, and lastly, a determination is required as to the fairness of a procedure that does not provide for any hearing before decisions are taken. In the last instance, such cases, as long as the implementation of travel bans is entrusted to national rule-setting,[130] could arrive at the Court after the available national remedies have been exhausted.[131] The problem raised by the fairness of the proceedings will be discussed in the following section in relation to the judgments delivered by the ECJ on the lawfulness of freezing orders.

4.2.2 Freezing orders

4.2.2.1 Freezing orders implemented by European Union regulations The second type of sanctions, namely, the freezing of assets, has not (yet) come before the ECtHR,[132] but has been handled by the ECJ in a number of key decisions, due to the fact that the freezing orders issued by the Security Council had to be implemented inside the European Union by Community (now Union) regulations that, like the resolutions of the Security Council, specifically identified their addressees and could therefore be challenged before the European CFI.[133] Under the current system, the relevant powers were/are held by the European Community/Union. Whereas originally, when members of a specific ruling elite were targeted, it was relatively easy to determine who belonged to that group, the borderlines became difficult to trace as soon as the fight against terrorism through the freezing of assets was elevated to the international agenda.[134] An elaborate system, directed primarily against the Taliban operating in Afghanistan, was introduced by

---

[130] Obviously, individual decisions denying someone entry into the territory or preventing him/her from leaving a country will always be taken by national authorities, because the EU lacks immigration services of its own.

[131] According to A. Frank, 'UNO-Sanktionen gegen terrorismus und Europäische Menschenrechtskonvention (EMRK)', in S. Breitenmoser et al., *Human Rights, Democracy and the Rule of Law: Liber amicorum Luzius Wildhaber* (Zürich and Baden-Baden: Dike & Nomos, 2007) 237–60, at 242 (hereinafter Frank, 'UNO-Sanktionen gegen Terrorismus'), unlimited travel bans are hardly compatible with the ECHR.

[132] Applications may be pending, but the ECtHR has not yet made any determination on the issue.

[133] Pursuant to art. 230(4) EC, the admissibility of an action for annulment depended on the applicant being individually affected ('individual concern').

[134] See Cameron, 'Protecting Legal Rights', at 190.

Security Council Resolution 1267 of 15 October 1999[135] and was progressively intensified to cover additionally terrorist activities carried out by Al-Qaida.[136] Any territorial linkage was hence abandoned.[137]

After the initial stage, the system was modified to take care of requirements of the rule of law and also of the humanitarian needs of those designated as authors of terrorist acts or sponsors of terrorism. First of all, steps were taken to ensure the basic vital needs of the targeted persons, lifting the ban on that part of the frozen funds necessary for daily survival.[138] Additionally, the procedure was ameliorated. States seeking listing of a suspect person were required to submit detailed information. Permanent review of the Consolidated List was made obligatory. Resolution 1904 (2009) has provided that targeted individuals themselves are entitled to address the newly established institution of the Ombudsperson with requests for delisting.[139] A careful perusal of the guidelines of the Sanctions Committee under Resolution 1267,[140] which were recently again amended by Resolution 1989 (2011)[141] in order to take care of legitimate complaints, reveals that a tremendous effort has

---

[135] See para. 4(b): 'Decides further that ... all States shall (b) Freeze funds and other financial resources, including funds derived or generated from property owned or controlled directly or indirectly by the Taliban, or by any undertaking owned or controlled by the Taliban, as designated by the Committee established by paragraph 6 below, and ensure that neither they nor any other funds or financial resources so designated are made available, by their nationals or by any persons within their territory, to or for the benefit of the Taliban or any undertaking owned or controlled, directly or indirectly, by the Taliban, except as may be authorized by the Committee on a case-by-case basis on the grounds of humanitarian need.'

[136] UN SC, Resolution 1333 (2000) concerning Afghanistan, 19 December 2000, UN Doc. S/RES/1333, para 8(c); UN SC, Resolution 1390 (2002) concerning Afghanistan, 28 January 2002, UN Doc. S/RES/1390, para. 2(a).

[137] See J.A. Almquist, 'A Human Rights Critique of European Judicial Review: Counter-Terrorism Sanctions', *The International and Comparative Law Quarterly* 57 (2008) 303–31, at 306 (hereinafter Almquist, 'A Human Rights Critique').

[138] UN SC, Resolution 1452 (2002) concerning terrorism, 20 December 2012, UN Doc. S/RES/1452, para. 1(b).

[139] UN SC, Resolution 1904 concerning terrorism, 17 December 2009, UN Doc. S/RES/1904, paras. 20, 21.

[140] Security Council Committee Established Pursuant to Resolution 1267 (1999) Concerning Al-Qaida and the Taliban and Associated Individuals and Entities, Guidelines of the Committee for the conduct of its work, 30 November 2011, www.un.org/sc/committees/1267/pdf/1267_guidelines.pdf (hereinafter 'Guidelines').

[141] In particular, more information is now made accessible. Individuals seeking delisting are encouraged to submit a petition to the Ombudsperson, UN SC Resolution 1989 concerning threats to international peace and security caused by terrorist acts, para. 26. The Security Council admonishes its Sanctions Committee to ensure 'fair and clear'

been made to organise the system in such a fashion that it meets the requirements of equity and fairness to the greatest extent. Perhaps the most serious weakness of the system is that any delisting eventually requires the full consent of all 15 members of the Security Council.[142] However, Resolution 1989 (2011) gives considerable weight to recommendations of the Ombudsperson to delist a person or entity and also to similar recommendations of a state on whose request a person was listed (paras. 21, 27). Such recommendations can be rejected by the Sanctions Committee only by consensus, and a tight time-calendar eliminates any room for manipulation by postponement. If no consensus on delisting emerges, the Security Council itself, where the veto remains unaffected, will have to make the final determination. This means that, although once a name has been placed on the Consolidated List it will remain difficult to get it removed, the recent reform has profoundly modified the essential features of the delisting procedure.[143] In any event, procedural safeguards have been created that prevent the responsible Sanctions Committee from becoming a simple rubber-stamping machine obediently fulfilling the wishes of certain great powers.

To date, the ECJ has not been persuaded by these manifold changes designed to give more room to human rights.[144] The first judgments on the issue were delivered by the CFI (now General Court), which had been resorted to by several applicants who challenged the Community regulations transposing the relevant resolution of the Security Council into Community law.[145] The applicants contended that the regulations were invalid, since they infringed basic principles of the Community's legal order, in particular, as far as procedural fairness was concerned. The CFI

---

procedures, *ibid.*, para. 42. This is a response to a call by the World Summit Outcome, UN GA Resolution 60/1, 16 September 2005, UN Doc. A/RES/60/1, paras. 108, 109.

[142] 'Guidelines', Section 4(a).

[143] Thus, the criticism voiced by G. Abi-Saab, 'The Security Council *Legibus Solutus*? On the Legislative Forays of the Council', in Boisson de Chazournes and Kohen (eds.), *Liber Amicorum Vera Gowlland-Debbas*, 23–44, at 40 ('sheer arbitrariness'); J.A. Frowein, 'The UN Anti-Terrorism Administration and the Rule of Law', in P.M. Dupuy *et al.* (eds.), *Common Values in International Law, Essays in Honour of Christian Tomuschat* (Kehl: N.P. Engel, 2006) 785–95, at 790–3; and D.L. Tehindrazanarivelo, 'Targeted Sanctions and Obligations of States on Listing and De-listing Procedures', in Boisson de Chazournes and Kohen (eds.), *Liber Amicorum Vera Gowlland-Debbas* 127–71, has lost much of its weight.

[144] However, the relevant judgments have not been able to take into account the latest procedural improvements of June/November 2011.

[145] Case T-315/01, *Kadi v. Council and Commission* [2005] ECR II-3649; T-Case 306/01, *Yusuf and Al Barakaat v. Council and Commission* [2005] ECR II-3353.

noted that to review the lawfulness of the regulations amounted to an indirect review of the Security Council's resolutions, since the Community institutions had done nothing other than, word for word, translate those resolutions into Community law. To undertake such kind of control would lead to a violation of article 103 of the UN Charter, which provides that the Charter takes precedence over any other treaty, and had therefore to be excluded; however, the UN was embedded in the framework of the international legal order where rules of *jus cogens* were the central pillars, to be respected also by the Security Council. After examining the objections of the applicants one by one, the Court of First Instance (CFI) came to the conclusion that none of the legal principles invoked by them partook of the nature of *jus cogens*.

The decision triggered a considerable number of comments.[146] The positive aspect was that the CFI proceeded from a concept of unity of international law, graduated hierarchically, where European Community law found its place a step lower than the UN system, which on its part was subordinated to the rules of *jus cogens*.[147] The negative aspect was the scarcity of *jus cogens* rules, so that in cases of errors or mistakes of lesser gravity, no remedy would be available.[148]

The judgment of the CFI was appealed. In his Opinion submitted to the Court of Justice of the European Union (CJEU), Advocate-General Poiares Maduro made a fervent plea in favour of the integrity of the legal

---

[146] See, *inter alia*, Almquist, 'A Human Rights Critique', 319–26; H.P. Aust and N. Naske, 'Rechtsschutz gegen den UN-Sicherheitsrat durch Europäische Gerichte?', *Austrian Journal of Public and International Law* 61 (2006) 587–623; V. Bore Eveno, 'Le contrôle juridictionnel des résolutions du Conseil de Sécurité: Vers un constitutionnalisme international?', *Revue Générale de Droit International Public* 110 (2006) 827–60; J. Klabbers, 'Kadi Justice at the Security Council?', *International Organizations Law Review* 4 (2007) 293–304 (hereinafter Klabbers, 'Kadi Justice'); M. Payandeh, 'Rechtskontrolle des UN-Sicherheitsrates durch staatliche und überstaatliche Gerichte', *Zeitschrift für Ausländisches Öffentliches Recht und Völkerrecht* 66 (2006) 41–71; G. Thallinger, 'Sense and Sensibility of the Human Rights Obligations of the United Nations Security Council', *Zeitschrift für Ausländisches Öffentliches Recht und Völkerrecht* 67 (2007) 1015–40, at 1032–4 (hereinafter Thallinger, 'Sense and Sensibility'); Tridimas and Gutierrez-Fons, 'EU Law, International Law, and Economic Sanctions against Terrorism', 679–702.

[147] This was underlined by C. Tomuschat, 'Case Law Comment', *Common Market Law Review* 43 (2006) 537–51.

[148] However, in *Ayadi*, Case T-253/02, Judgment (Second Chamber), 12 July 2006, wishing to compensate for the less than satisfying outcome for the applicant in *Kadi*, the CFI stated that national governments were placed under a legal obligation to provide diplomatic assistance to their nationals in support of requests for delisting (paras. 145–9).

order under the treaties for European integration.[149] Even decisions of the Security Council of the UN must conform to the tenets of that system; accordingly, there was no obstacle to reviewing Community instruments that were a genuine textual reflection of Security Council resolutions. The applicable yardstick was the European legal order as a whole, not only the core substance of *jus cogens*. In actual terms, the Advocate-General considered that the denial of information, as well as the denial of judicial remedies, were incurable defects of the challenged regulations. The Advocate-General brushed aside the argument of a violation of article 103 UN Charter as being a matter of international responsibility that could afterwards be settled in some way.[150]

The ECJ itself followed its Advocate-General to the greatest conceivable extent.[151] It emphasised the autonomy of the Community legal order and observed that the obligations imposed by an international agreement cannot have the effect of prejudicing the constitutional principles of the EC Treaty, which include the principle that all Community acts must respect fundamental rights, that respect constituting a condition of their lawfulness which it is for the Court to review in the framework of the complete system of legal remedies established by the Treaty.[152]

Thus, for the ECJ, as for its Advocate-General, article 103 of the UN Charter – which it did not even mention – was irrelevant. Proceeding from that premise, on matters of substance it also shared the view of its Advocate-General that the lack of information,[153] as well as the non-availability of judicial remedies,[154] could not be reconciled with the fundamental principles of the Community legal order. Therefore, the contested regulation was annulled.[155]

---

[149] Case C-402 and C-415/05P, *Yassin Abdullah Kadi and Al Barakaat International Foundation v. Council of the European Union and Commission of the European Communities* [2008] ECR I-6351, Opinion of Advocate-General Poiares Maduro (16 January 2008).

[150] *Ibid.*, para. 39.

[151] *Ibid.*, Comments by P.J. Cardwell, D. French and N. White, *International and Comparative Law Quarterly* 58 (2009) 233–40 (hereinafter Cardwell *et al.*, 'Comments').

[152] Opinion of Advocate-General Poiares Madura, para. 285.

[153] *Ibid.*, para. 325.   [154] *Ibid.*, paras. 334–7.

[155] But only in respect of *Kadi and Al Barakaat*, *supra* note 149. At the same time, the Court ordered the effects of Regulation (EC) No. 881/2002 to be maintained, as far as the two applicants were concerned, for a period that should not exceed three months, running from the date of delivery of the judgment. See criticism by A. Bradford and E.A. Posner, 'Universal Exceptionalism in International Law', *Harvard International Law Journal* 52 (2011) 1–54, at 16; G. de Búrca, 'The European Court of Justice and the International Legal Order after *Kadi*', *Harvard International Law Journal* 51 (2010) 1–49, at 4;

The Community responded by enacting a new regulation[156] with effect from 3 December 2008, reinserting the names of the successful applicants in the Consolidated List after having communicated the narrative summaries of reasons provided by the UN Al-Qaida and Taliban Sanctions Committee (1267 Committee) to Mr. Kadi and to the Al Barakaat International Foundation, and given them the opportunity to comment on these grounds in order to make their point of view known, which both did. Eventually, the Commission came to the conclusion that the listing of Mr. Kadi and the Al Barakaat International Foundation was justified for reasons of their association with the Al-Qaida network.[157]

Mr. Kadi again brought an action against this continued interference with his rights. By judgment of 30 September 2010, the General Court of the EU confirmed the earlier findings in the case, therefore annulling Regulation (EC) No. 1190/2008.[158] It reiterated that under Community law a person affected by measures of governmental authority must be provided with a full review of the underlying facts and the supporting evidence. The system of the Sanctions Committee was inadequate in that regard because it did not permit challenge of the relevant evidence, and under no circumstances could the requirement of effective judicial protection be forgone. One of the main grounds for the verdict was the fact that the freezing had been in effect for no less than ten years, with no end in sight, therefore causing a violation of the principle of proportionality.[159] The judgment has been appealed and is currently pending before the Grand Chamber of the ECJ.

This is not the place to discuss the pros and cons of executive mechanisms on the one hand and judicial procedures on the other. The observer gets the impression that in the judgments of the European judicature the principle of judicial protection is given an importance which it does not possess at universal level – and not even under European regional law. It must be noted that article 13 ECHR – or

---

C. Tomuschat, 'The *Kadi* Case: What Relationship is there between the Universal Legal Order under the Auspices of the United Nations and the EU Legal Order?', *Yearbook of European Law* 28 (2009) 654–63, at 662.

[156] Commission Regulation (EC) No. 1190/2008 of 28 November 2008, amending for the 101st time Council Regulation (EC) No. 881/2002 imposing certain specific restrictive measures directed against certain persons and entities associated with Usama bin Laden, the Al-Qaida network and the Taliban, OJ 2008 L 322/25.
[157] *Ibid.*, Preamble.
[158] Case T-85/09, *Yassin Abdullah Kadi v. European Commission* [2010] ECR nyr.
[159] *Ibid.*, paras. 149, 150.

article 2(3) ICCPR – does not demand that states make available to their citizens recourse to judicial bodies in a comprehensive fashion;[160] explicitly, article 6(1) ECHR – and article 14(1) ICCPR – confine that requirement to specific configurations, the main one of which is criminal proceedings and disputes about 'civil rights'. However, most of the disputes that have arisen concern 'civil rights' as understood by the ECtHR, in particular where assets have been frozen. Should such a case be brought to the ECtHR from a non-member of the European Union, the Strasbourg judges would be confronted with the same difficulty of whether to affirm the primacy of the European standard, embodied in the ECHR, or to acknowledge the superior authority of the Security Council. The UN mechanism would be on a par with judicial proceedings the day when the veto, capable of blocking any request for delisting, was to be abolished.

In the international arena, the answers given to the *Kadi* problematique vary enormously. In Switzerland, the Supreme Federal Court has determined that the supremacy clause of article 103 of the UN Charter must be complied with, excluding any review of the correctness of freezing orders of the Security Council.[161] In the UK, by contrast, the Supreme Court held that all the improvements of the procedures of the 1267 Sanctions Committee were not enough to ensure an adequate defence of a person struck by a freezing order.[162] However, the debate in the Supreme Court centred mainly on whether section 1(1) of the United

---

[160] With regard to Art. 13 ECHR, see ECtHR, *M.S.S. v. Belgium and Greece* (Appl. No. 30696/09), Judgment (Grand Chamber), 21 January 2011, not reported, paras. 288, 289.

[161] Swiss Federal Court, *Nada v. SECO*, Judgment, 14 November 2007, French text (translation from German), *Revue suisse de droit international et de droit européen* (2008) 467–72, at 468–70, para. 5. However, the Swiss Federal Court sees the powers of the Security Council limited by the rules of *jus cogens* (471, para. 7), following in that respect the European CFI in *Kadi*. Comments by R. Kolb, 'Le Contrôle de Résolutions Contraignantes du Conseil de Sécurité des Nations Unies par des Juridictions Internationales ou Nationales Sous l'Angle du Respect du Jus Cogens', in *ibid.*, 401–11. In *NADA v. Switzerland* (Appl. No. 10593/08), Judgment (Grand Chamber), 12 September 2012, the ECtHR eventually found against Switzerland for not having made use of a less burdensome measure, but did not touch upon the issue of the hierarchy between obligations under the UN Charter and obligations under the ECHR (para. 197).

[162] *Her Majesty's Treasury (Respondent) v. Mohammed Jabar Ahmed and others (FC) (Appellants) Her Majesty's Treasury (Respondent) v. Mohammed al-Ghabra (FC) (Appellant) R (on the application of Hani El Sayed Sabaei Youssef) (Respondent) v. Her Majesty's Treasury (Appellant)*, Judgment, 27 January 2010, [2010] UKSC 2. Criticising the procedure under the 1267 Sanctions Committee were, in particular, Lord Hope (para. 80), Lord Phillips (para. 146) and Lord Mance (para. 239).

Nations Act 1946[163] provided an appropriate legal basis for the executive orders by virtue of which the freezing orders had been made.

The legal position is, of course, entirely different where the Security Council confines itself to generally enjoining states to combat terrorism, as it did through its Resolution 1373 (2001).[164] Under such circumstances, states bear unrestricted responsibility for all the actions taken by them ('autonomous listing'). They must see to it that they implement the wishes of the Security Council by taking measures in full consonance with their respective domestic orders, including their commitments under the ECHR. In such instances, the European Community/ Union is also called upon to respect fully the constitutional principles as they are laid down in the basic treaties, as well as in the applicable customary law.[165] Where the act complained of is an act of the European Community/Union that directly interferes with individual rights, the responsibility of the member states cannot be engaged. Hitherto, a strict separation between Community/Union acts and national measures has been maintained; the former have never been attributed to the member states collectively.[166]

4.2.2.2 Freezing orders implemented through national legislation

The last class of cases to be examined comprises those where national authorities act for the implementation of directions issued by the Security

---

[163] 'If, under Article forty-one of the Charter of the United Nations ... the Security Council of the United Nations call upon His Majesty's Government in the United Kingdom to apply any measures to give effect to any decision of that Council, His Majesty may by Order in Council make such provision as appears to Him necessary or expedient for enabling those measures to be effectively applied, including (without prejudice to the generality of the preceding words) provision for the apprehension, trial and punishment of persons offending against the Order.'

[164] UN SC Resolution 1373 (2001) concerning terrorism, 28 September 2001, UN Doc. S/RES/1373, para. 1.

[165] See CFI, Case T-228/02, *Organisation des Modjahedines du peuple d'Iran* v. *Council of the European Union* [2006] ECR II-4665, paras. 99–103; Case T-47/03, *Jose Maria Sison* v. *Council of the European Union* [2009] ECR II-1483, paras. 137–55; Case T-256/07, *People's Mojahedin Organization of Iran* v. *Council of the European Union* [2008] ECR II-3019, paras. 130, 131; see also Opinion of Advocate-General Sharpston of 14 July 2011 in Case C-27/09 P, *French Republic* v. *People's Mojahedine Organization of Iran* [2011] ECR nyr.

[166] See ECtHR, *Kokkelvisserij* v. *Netherlands* (Appl. No. 13645/05), Decision (Third Section), 20 January 2009, Reports 2009. See also Institut de droit international, Resolution on The Legal Consequences for Member States of the Non-fulfilment by International Organizations of their Obligations toward Third Parties, adopted at its 66th session in Lisbon, 1966, article 6, www.idi-iil.org/idiE/resolutionsE/1995_lis_02_en.pdf.

Council that were made domestically applicable by national acts of legislation. In such instances, remedies may be filed with the responsible national courts. The judicature of the European Union will not get involved, except for situations (which to date have not materialised) where a national court might find it advisable to request a preliminary ruling of the ECJ. Because, within the European Community/Union legislative, competence for freezing assets lies with the Brussels authorities, almost all relevant disputes were adjudicated by the judicature of the European Union.

Reference has been made to the Swiss case of *Nada* v. *SECO*, again a dispute about freezing bank accounts, where the Swiss Federal Tribunal held that it was debarred from reviewing the lawfulness of lists of names determined by the Security Council, since article 103 UN Charter provided for the primacy of the Charter over any other treaties.[167]

In the *Bosphorus* case, an aircraft, leased to the Turkish corporation Bosphorus by JAT, the Yugoslav Airlines, was impounded at Dublin Airport by Irish authorities. By Resolution 820 (1993), the Security Council had issued an order to all states to impound all aircraft owned by Yugoslav citizens or entities. Transposition of the resolution into the Community legal order was effected by EEC Regulation 990/93, which served as the legal basis of the impoundment on 28 May and 8 June 1993. Protracted legal battles followed. At a first stage, the ECJ was requested to give a preliminary ruling on the interpretation of Regulation 990/93, the text of which was not clear as to whether an aircraft leased to a corporation of a third state was also covered by the embargo. This was confirmed by the ECJ on the advice of its Advocate-General.[168] Curiously enough, neither one spent a single word on whether the ECJ was empowered to verify the lawfulness of the relevant Security Council resolution. At a further stage of the proceedings, the case came before the ECtHR. The Court reiterated a proposition which it had affirmed in many previous judgments, according to which a state is responsible for all acts and omissions of its organs, regardless of whether the act or omission in question was a consequence of domestic law or of the

---

[167] *Nada* v. *SECO*. It has been reported that an application was filed against the judgment with the ECtHR, see Ciampi, 'Security Council Targeted Sanctions', 129; and de Wet, 'Human Rights Considerations', at 145.

[168] Case C-84/95, *Bosphorus Hava Yollari Turızm ve Ticaret AS* v. *Minister of Transport, Energy and Communications and others* [1996] ECR I-3953; Opinion of Advocate-General Jacobs, *ibid.*, 3956–77, at 3967 (interesting question which need not be addressed).

necessity to comply with international legal obligations.[169] On the other hand, it took account of the fact that the European Community had evolved an autonomous system for the protection of human rights, manifesting its trust in the effectiveness of that system:

> State action taken in compliance with such legal obligations is justified as long as the relevant organisation is considered to protect fundamental rights, as regards both the substantive guarantees offered and the mechanisms controlling their observance, in a manner which can be considered at least equivalent to that for which the Convention provides ... By "equivalent" the Court means "comparable"; any requirement that the organisation's protection be "identical" could run counter to the interest of international cooperation pursued .... However, any such finding of equivalence could not be final and would be susceptible to review in the light of any relevant change in fundamental rights protection.
>
> If such equivalent protection is considered to be provided by the organisation, the presumption will be that a state has not departed from the requirements of the Convention when it does no more than implement legal obligations flowing from its membership of the organisation. However, any such presumption can be rebutted if, in the circumstances of a particular case, it is considered that the protection of Convention rights was manifestly deficient.[170]

These holdings clearly refer to the European Community, affirming its grown-up status as a defender of human rights. Consequently, the complaint of Bosphorus was rejected in implicit application of the principle of subsidiarity, which has received strong emphasis in the recent jurisprudence of the ECtHR: since the European Community (EC) (now European Union (EU)) handled human rights issues responsibly, there was no need for an additional stage of international review. However, on its part, too, the ECtHR failed to address the

---

[169] ECtHR, *Matthews* v. *UK* (Appl. No. 24833/94), Judgment (Grand Chamber), 18 February 1999, Reports 1999-I, para. 32; recently reconfirmed: *Al-Saadoon and Mufdhi* v. *UK*, paras. 126–8.

[170] ECtHR, *Bosphorus Hava Yollari Turızm ve Ticaret AS* v. *Ireland* (Appl. No. 45036/98), Judgment (Grand Chamber), 30 June 2005, Reports 2005-VI, paras. 155, 156. Confirmation of this jurisprudence in ECtHR, *Biret* v. *France* (Appl. No. 13762/04), Decision (Fifth Section), 9 December 2008, not reported, para. 2. On the other hand, in ECtHR, *M.S.S.* v. *Belgium and Greece* (Appl. No. 30696/09), Judgment (Grand Chamber), 21 January 2011, Reports 2011, paras. 338–40, the Court noted that, when acting under the Dublin Convention, Belgium had a considerable degree of discretion. Therefore, its impugned measure – the expulsion of the applicant – did not strictly fall within Belgium's international legal obligations. Accordingly, the presumption of equivalent protection did not apply in the case.

issue of whether the binding nature of Security Council resolutions may be challenged.[171] One may assume that the Court had no doubts as to the soundness of the political decision to impose an embargo on the former Yugoslavia because of its involvement in the hostilities subsequent to its collapse and the proclamations of independence of its former component republics. Accordingly, the dispute centred exclusively on the lawfulness of the relevant EEC regulation, in particular on whether the principle of proportionality had been respected.[172]

Not by accident, many observers have evaluated the *Bosphorus* judgment as a parallel to the judgment of the German Federal Constitutional Court in *Solange II*, where the Karlsruhe judges stated that they would refrain from reviewing acts of secondary law of the European (Economic) Community/Union as long as, in general, the level of protection of human rights at European level was equivalent to the level as ensured in Germany.[173] One may, indeed, view the reservation shown by the ECtHR as a gesture of inter-institutional subsidiarity. In any event, the caveat announced by the ECtHR has not come into operation. The same could be observed in Germany. For more than a quarter of a century, the Constitutional Court has abstained from considering the merits of complaints that fundamental rights under the Basic Law had been infringed by European Community/Union acts.[174]

---

[171] Likewise, no attention is given to this issue in their lucid commentaries by B. Conforti, 'Le principe d'equivalence et le contrôle sur les actes communautaires dans la jurisprudence de la cour européenne des droits de l'homme', in S. Breitenmoser *et al*. (eds.), *Human Rights, Democracy and the Rule of Law: Liber Amicorum Luzius Wildhaber* (Zürich and Baden-Baden: Dike & Nomos, 2007) 173–82, and G. Gaja, 'The Review by the European Court of Human Rights of Member States' Acts Implementing European Union Law: "Solange" Yet Again?', in M. Shaw *et al*. (eds.), *Common Values in International Law: Essays in Honour of Christian Tomuschat* (Kehl: N.P. Engel, 2006) 517–26.

[172] However, when a person accused before the ICTY filed a complaint against the Netherlands, the ECtHR noted that the ICTY offered all the guarantees required by the standard of a fair and equitable trial, see decisions in *Galić* and *Blagojević*, para. 46.

[173] Judgment, 22 October 1986, Entscheidungen des Bundesverfassungsgerichts 73, 339; English translation, *Decisions of the Federal Constitutional Court*, Vol. 1, Part II (Baden-Baden: Nomos, 1992) 613.

[174] In the *Banana Market* case, BVerfGE 102, 147, 7 June 2000, the Federal Constitutional Court held that a request for a preliminary ruling on the validity of EEC Regulation No. 404/93, 13 February 1993 on the common organisation of the market in bananas failed to show that the level of protection of human rights had 'generally' fallen below the required level of equivalence. In the *Honeywell* case, BVerfGE 126, 286, 6 July 2010, the Federal Constitutional Court specified that its mandate to intervene was triggered only

Notwithstanding the generosity the ECtHR has shown in *Bosphorus*, the question remains whether that judgment must be understood as a reminder that the requirements of the rule of law constitute an indispensable cornerstone of the architecture of the ECHR, entailing the need to submit any action of national authorities, irrespective of their legal background, to strict scrutiny. Did the Court wish to suggest that its holdings are generally applicable, even when the action complained of was performed in compliance with an international obligation flowing from the Security Council, or did it implicitly suggest that decisions under Chapter VII of the UN Charter enjoy a special status? For the time being, no definitive answer can be given to this question. In any event, in *Gasparini* v. *Italy and Belgium*, a case where objections were raised against NATO's system of settling staff disputes, a section of the ECtHR reiterated its *monitum* to contracting parties to the ECHR:

> ... les Etats membres ont l'obligation, au moment où ils transfèrent une partie de leurs pouvoirs souverains à une organisation internationale à laquelle ils adhèrent, de veiller à ce que les droits garantis par la Convention reçoivent au sein de cette organisation une 'protection équivalente' à celle assurée par le mécanisme de la Convention. En effet, la responsabilité d'un Etat partie à la Convention pourrait être mise en jeu au regard de celle-ci s'il s'avérait ultérieurement que la protection des droits fondamentaux offerte par l'organisation internationale concernée était entachée d'une 'insuffisance manifeste'.[175]

Clearly, this passage goes beyond what was stated in *Bosphorus*, by requiring that states must take care of adequate protection of human rights at the point in time when, through the conclusion of a treaty, they transfer powers to an international organisation. Apparently, where a structural gap can be perceived, a state may incur responsibility even if it had no decisive influence on the actual running of the organisation concerned.

---

by acts *ultra vires* which led to a 'structurally significant shifting of powers to the detriment of member states' (English translation, www.bverfg.de/entscheidungen/rs20100706_2bvr266106en.html). But that case did not centre on human rights guarantees.

[175] ECtHR, *Gasparini* v. *Italy and Belgium* (Appl. No. 10750/03), Judgment (Second Section), 12 May 2009, not reported; comment by E. Rebasti, 'Corte Europea dei diritti dell'uomo e responsabilità degli stati per trasferimento di poteri ad una organizzazione internazionale', *Rivista di Diritto Internazionale* 93 (2010) 65–88; Ryngaert, 'ECtHR Approach to Responsibility', 1005; see also Janik, 'Die EMRK', 165.

After the ECJ as well as the UK Supreme Court have voiced their dissatisfaction with the procedures of the different UN Sanctions Committees, the ECtHR will also be under strong pressure to align itself with that critical position if a case is submitted to it, probably from a member state of the Council of Europe that does not belong to the EU. It would then have to inquire whether the listing and delisting of persons meets the requirements of the ECHR. Some weighty reasons speak against an outcome in consonance with the jurisprudence of the ECJ. First of all, considerable improvements of the procedure of the UN Sanctions Committees have been introduced in recent years, doubtless in response to the critical voices, primarily from Europe. None of the judgments referred to above has been able to assess the impact of the latest reforms brought about, especially by Security Council Resolution 1989 (2011) of 17 June 2011.

On a technical level, one can argue that the Charter of the UN came into force in 1945, long before the ECHR was drafted. In fact, no state has the potential to demand a review of the Charter at the time of its admission.[176] The Charter must be equated with a *rocher de bronce*. It develops essentially through practice, since to obtain the necessary consent for a formal amendment is so demanding that not even the most undisputed changes have been operated, like, for instance, the deletion of the special provisions on 'enemy states' (articles 53, 107).[177] Only two major changes were introduced by formal amendments, namely, the increase of the number of members of the Security Council from 11 to 15, and the increase of the members of the Economic and Social Council from 18 to 54.

These 'technical' arguments to some extent reflect the exceptional features of the UN Charter. As already noted, the Charter is not just any one of thousands of multilateral treaties, but has acquired aspects of a constitution of the world. No single state is able to bring about an amendment of the Charter; on the other hand, states remain subject to the powers conferred on the General Assembly and the Security Council. Although accession to the UN is a voluntary act, *de facto* the pressure to join the nations of the world is almost irresistible. Even states that would prefer to remain outsiders are brought under the discipline of the Charter

---

[176] This is also acknowledged by Frank, 'UNO-Sanktionen gegen Terrorismus', 254.
[177] At the World Summit in 2005, consensus was reached in concluding that those provisions of the UN Charter were obsolete and should be deleted, UN GA Resolution 60/1, 16 September 2005, para. 177.

by article 2(6). Therefore, to postulate that at the time of their joining the UN states parties to the ECHR must make sure that they can fully live up to their commitments under the ECHR, is no more than a pious wish that hurts against a wall of immutable political realities.

In *Behrami and Saramati*, the ECtHR has unequivocally indicated that it acknowledges the special tasks entrusted to the Security Council as the guardian of international peace and security under Chapter VII of the Charter.[178] If the Security Council were bound to respect all of the constitutional and international obligations of the members of the organisation, its action would be seriously hampered. This does not mean that human rights could be thrown overboard, and neither should the level of protection be lowered to the bare minimum of *jus cogens*, as suggested by the CFI in *Kadi I*. A reasonable standard of protection must be maintained, whose precise benchmarks can only be determined on a case-by-case basis, in light of the prevailing circumstances. In any event, article 103 UN Charter cannot be the decisive argument against any restriction of the powers of the Security Council by virtue of human rights rules.[179]

On one hand, the international community has acknowledged the paramount authority of the Security Council through its membership in the world organisation. On the other hand, article 103 UN Charter is no blank cheque for the Security Council to engage in arbitrary conduct. Article 24(2) UN Charter provides that the Security Council 'shall act in accordance with the Purposes and Principles of the United Nations'. This means that the rights and interests of persons affected by measures under Chapter VII may not be disregarded. Core human rights must never be interfered with. Even alleged interests of preserving peace and international security would never justify a strategy of ethnic cleansing, for example, rightly, in *Al-Jedda* the ECtHR has embraced a presumption with the help of which any serious difficulties may be overcome:

> The Court considers that, in interpreting its resolutions [scil. the resolutions of the Security Council], there must be a presumption that the

---

[178] *Behrami and Saramati*, paras. 148, 149.
[179] See the weighty arguments advanced by Cardwell *et al.*, 'Comments', 240; M. Lugato, 'Sono le sanzioni del Consiglio di Sicurezza incompatibili con il rispetto delle garanzie procedurali?', *Rivista di Diritto Internazionale* 93 (2010) 309–42, at 324; Thallinger, 'Sense and Sensibility', 1028. Suggestions as to the requisite balancing process have been advanced by S. Zappalà, 'Reviewing Security Council Measures in the Light of International Human Rights Principles', in *Securing Human Rights? Achievements and Challenges of the UN Security Council* (Oxford University Press, 2011) 172–94.

Security Council does not intend to impose any obligation on Member States to breach fundamental principles of human rights. In the event of any ambiguity in the terms of a Security Council Resolution, the Court must therefore choose the interpretation which is most in harmony with the requirements of the Convention and which avoids any conflict of obligations. In the light of the United Nations' important role in promoting and encouraging respect for human rights, it is to be expected that clear and explicit language would be used were the Security Council to intend States to take particular measures which would conflict with their obligations under international human rights law.[180]

An assessment should not be blinded by slogans not connected to realities. The requirement of judicial protection does not belong to the arsenal of *jus cogens* norms, as recently clarified by the ICJ in *Germany v. Italy*.[181] Obviously, the individual will best be served by protective mechanisms that operate fast and effectively. As already pointed out, the listing and delisting procedures of the Security Council have been greatly improved in the recent past. In any event, remedial action by the ECtHR is conceivable only after exhaustion of all available domestic remedies, which may take many years. In contradistinction to the CJEU, the ECtHR, in particular in the recent past, has emphasised, its subsidiary role *vis-à-vis* national authorities, whose margin of appreciation it respects to a large extent. One of the reasons relied on by it in this respect is the better democratic legitimacy of national authorities,[182] where, indeed, the ECJ is on safer ground than the ECtHR, which may be characterised as the outcome of a truly inter-governmental only system. Compliance with orders issued by the UN Security Council as the central institution of the international community is one of those choices by a state party to which the ECtHR will certainly show deference if it can be proven that the system of listing and delisting, as it has taken shape within the UN framework, operates in an appropriate manner, taking the rights of the individual into due account.

It is true that reflection on the adequate standards of protection has benefited enormously from the judgment of the ECJ in *Kadi* and from

---

[180] *Al-Jedda v. UK*, para. 102.
[181] *Jurisdictional Immunities of the State (Germany v. Italy: Greece Intervening)*, nyr, 3 February 2012, paras. 93–5.
[182] ECtHR, *Hatton v. United Kingdom* (Appl. No. 36022/97), Judgment (Grand Chamber), 8 July 2003, Reports 2003-VIII, para. 97; ECtHR, *Van der Heijden v. Netherlands* (Appl. No. 42857/05), Judgment (Grand Chamber), 3 April 2012, not reported, para. 55.

the judgment of the UK Supreme Court of 27 January 2010. However, a serious debate is necessary on the pros and cons of effective legal protection. Access to judges is the traditional and well-proven method. However, to establish adequate mechanisms at world level is an immensely challenging undertaking. One cannot take it for granted that in situations where complex configurations of wrongdoing must be assessed, judges are the best-qualified persons as far as preventative measures are concerned.[183]

5. Concluding observations

To the extent that the UN is changing its conduct – and thereby also its substance – by taking measures that directly affect individual rights, legal remedies should be introduced or improved. The ideal solution would be to bring into being a centralised system that provides adequate legal protection while, at the same time, preventing abusive review practices by individual states. Such a system, which would operate less as a threat to the authority of the Security Council and more as a device to strengthen its legitimacy,[184] is not in sight at the present juncture. By force, hence, regional courts, among them in particular the ECJ and the ECtHR, are compelled to fill the gap left by the lack of adequate mechanisms of dispute settlement at universal level. However, care must be taken not to exaggerate the advantages of judicial remedies. In complex configurations with manifold intertwined political and legal aspects, procedures conducted by expert bodies may sometimes be the better solution, as long as the vital needs of the persons concerned are duly taken into account. The actions of the Security Council cannot be reviewed in the same fashion as decisions of national administrative authorities if, and to the extent that, they are embedded in a wider political context. Not only does the Security Council enjoy a large measure of discretion explicitly granted to it by the entire community of nations, it also has a background of knowledge and expertise that national judges, or even international judges, will never be able to attain. Moreover, individuals struggling against the UN without the assistance of their state of nationality, can never be in a comfortable procedural

---

[183] Bothe, 'Security Council's Targeted Sanctions', 550–5 advocates a 'soft system of remedies' modelled on the World Bank Inspection Panel. Likewise, Klabbers, 'Kadi Justice', pronounces himself for a flexible system of 'Kadi justice'.
[184] See Frank, 'UNO-Sanktionen gegen Terrorismus', 258 et seq.

situation. However, in no circumstances whatsoever may certain borderlines be crossed under the rule of law. Forfeiture of rights or confiscation of assets, administrative detention, true punishments and targeted killings could never be justified under the authority of the Security Council. *Jus cogens* rules may not be pushed aside where the personal fate of individuals is at stake. To avoid such occurrences, fair and open proceedings are the best tools of prevention. Through open exchange of arguments, unjustifiable measures can be identified and thereby be avoided.

10

Conclusions

ANDREAS FØLLESDAL, BIRGIT PETERS AND GEIR ULFSTEIN

1. The ECtHR at 50: constituting Europe?

In 2008, Keller and Stone Sweet concluded their study on the reception of the European Convention by its member states: 'National officials are, gradually but inexorably, being socialized into a Europe of rights, a unique transnational legal space now seeking to develop its own logic of political and juridical legitimacy.'[1] Five years onwards, this book finds that the member states, the organs of the Council of Europe – including the Court itself – the EU and, possibly, the UN, are still seeking to calibrate and develop the ECtHR's legitimacy within the European sphere of fundamental rights.

In the months preceding the 2012 Brighton Conference, discussions on the Court's legitimacy had reached a new height. The UK suggested curtailing the Court drastically. It should examine only those cases where the national court had erred in its interpretation of the Convention rights, or raised other serious questions of interpretation of the Convention.[2] The Brighton Declaration used much softer terms, affirming the member states' primary responsibility for protecting human rights, but acknowledging the essential role of the Court controlling states' protection. The Brighton brouhaha showed that the ECtHR's legitimate function in the greater European sphere of rights is far from settled.

When looking at the Court's relations with the EU and the UN, exchanges on the Court's legitimate role have just begun. A Draft Accession Agreement with the EU has been prepared, but awaits further negotiations. And the Court increasingly deals with cases that concern member state action mandated or authorised by the UN or other

---

[1] H. Keller and A. Stone Sweet, *A Europe of Rights: The Impact of the ECHR on National Legal Systems* (Oxford University Press, 2008) 710.

[2] Draft Brighton Declaration, 28 February 2012, para 23(c)(i) and (ii) available at: www.guardian.co.uk/law/interactive/2012/feb/28/echr-reform-uk-draft (last accessed 5 July 2012).

international organisations. Discussions about the Court's proper role and function in such cases await further clarification.

The assessments in this book concerning the Court's relations with the member states revolve around roles and functions which are already to a large extent constitutional – disagreements about the definition of 'constitutional' notwithstanding (Cameron). In analogy with the functions of domestic constitutional courts, consider several shared characteristics frequently referred to in debates on the constitutional role of the ECtHR:

- Constitutional courts deal with cases of high political or societal importance that often raise deeply contested issues of the fundamental rights and values of a society.[3]
- There is usually a certain system of case selection; constitutional courts may exercise wide discretion in determining which cases to decide.[4]
- Constitutional courts often perform some sort of extraordinary judicial review; some are not embedded into the regular appeal structure within a judicial review system.[5]
- Their general competence spans individual complaints against administrative and judicial decisions and often includes the judicial review of a piece of general legislation and the annulment of legislative acts as unconstitutional.[6]

In light of these features, it is difficult to deny the ECtHR's constitutional role in its relations with the member states. This is not to say that the ECtHR is formally embedded in the general judicial review structure at the member state levels. Nonetheless, it decides on the compatibility of

---

[3] M. O'Boyle in E. Myjer *et al.* (eds.), *The Conscience of Europe: 50 Years of the European Court of Human Rights* (London: Council of Europe, Third Millennium Publishing Limited, 2010), at 201, speaks of cases of 'constitutional import'.

[4] J. Gerards, 'Judicial Deliberations in the European Court of Human Rights', in N. Huls *et al.* (eds.), *The Legitimacy of Highest Courts' Rulings: Judicial Deliberations and Beyond* (The Hague: T.M.C. Asser Press, 2009) 407–36, 417.

[5] *Ibid.*, 410 *et seq.* The judicial review of legislation, however, is a much-contested part of constitutional adjudication which not all countries subscribe to. Compare A.W. Heringa and P. Kiiver, *Constitutions Compared: An Introduction to Comparative Constitutional Law* (2nd edn, Ius Commune Europaeum) (Antwerp, Oxford, Maastricht: Intersentia, Metro, 2009) 23.

[6] This has been highlighted, for example, by M. O'Boyle, 'On Reforming the Operation of the European Court of Human Rights', *European Human Rights Law Review* 1 (2008) 3–4; J.A. Frowein, 'The Transformation of Constitutional Law through the European Convention on Human Rights', *Israel Law Review* 41 (2008) 489–99, 493.

legislative as well as administrative and judicial acts with the Convention. Pilot judgment cases, in particular, may entail a declaration of incompatibility of particular legal provisions with the Convention (Leach).

Many of the Court's judgments are of crucial importance for fundamental rights conceptions in the wider Europe, among them the recent *A, B and C* v. *Ireland*, *Lautsi* v. *Italy*, and *Stübing* v. *Germany* decisions. Sometimes the Court has been at the forefront of standard-setting, such as on the role of human rights in environmental protection issues. The Court's evolutive or dynamic interpretation is also constantly developing the rights enshrined in the Convention. For instance, the ECtHR now protects the rights of transsexuals and guarantees a certain standard of environmental protection or social security. The Court has often relied on the rights and values enshrined in international conventions to further advance the rights of the ECHR. Hence, the ECtHR defines a common moral reading of the Convention along the lines of autonomous international values (Letsas). The Court's findings on non-pecuniary remedies, in particular in pilot judgments, illustrate the significance of its findings beyond the individual case (Leach).

The reformed admissibility criteria permit a selection of cases by the Court. The Brighton Conference adopted a modification of article 35, incorporating the so-called *de minimis* rule which allows review by the ECtHR only in cases concerning a 'significant disadvantage'.[7] In addition, the Court has already developed its own priority policy and adopted a pilot judgment procedure, both of which allow a selective and prioritised treatment of cases. It is also interesting to note that the 2011 output of the court generated a success rate for applicants of no more than 2 per cent. The success rate before the German Constitutional Court, which receives about 6,000 applications each year, is about the same.[8] We will return to further aspects of the ECtHR's constitutional nature, such as the Court's adherence to the principle of subsidiarity and to division of powers in the Council of Europe, under the respective headings below.

Yet, in the multilevel setting in which the Court is placed, it appears more constitutional in one relationship and less constitutional in another. Even after the EU's accession to the ECHR, the ECtHR will remain one of two constitutional courts in the EU. The

---

[7] Council of Europe, *High Level Conference on the Future of the European Court of Human Rights Brighton Declaration* (Strasbourg, 2012), para. 15(c).
[8] 2.4%, see BVerfG, 'Verfahren', at www.bundesverfassungsgericht.de/organisation/gb2011/A-I-1.html (last accessed 21 June 2011).

Draft Accession Agreement allows and requires a prior review by the CJEU, before the case can continue before the ECtHR. Prior to the adoption of the Draft Accession Agreement, the ECtHR acknowledged the primary review of member states' implementation of EU legislation by the CJEU in the *Bosphorus* jurisprudence. This jurisprudence may possibly continue to apply even after the EU's accession to the ECHR (Besselink). But the ECtHR will have the competence to determine with binding effect whether the EU acts in accordance with the ECHR.

The ECtHR is a regional organ, which, *qua* treaty, cannot assume functions of constitutional review in relation to the UN (Tomuschat). The ECtHR's earlier decisions limited the extra-territorial application of the ECHR in military operations. Now, the Court is more open to the extra-territorial application, but the concepts of ultimate authority and control represent a great level of deference to the UN. Judicial control of UN-mandated operations by ECHR member states remain a challenge, and requires arrangements which can accommodate both global and regional needs for effective protection of peace as well as human rights.

2. The ECtHR's legitimacy

2.1 Scepticism and rejection

The legitimacy of the ECtHR is increasingly questioned by member states, young and old. The latter, in particular, criticise the Court for what they see as a retreat in the use of the margin of appreciation doctrine (Letsas) and overuse of the doctrine of dynamic interpretation.[9] The former, some of which are responsible for the bulk of the caseload before the ECtHR, are equally critical towards the Court – but on other grounds. The Court has been subject to political and press criticism in Russia, and Russian courts have argued that they are not bound by the ECtHR's decisions (Andenas and Bjorge). On some occasions, Russian courts have invoked sovereignty considerations to reject Strasbourg's interpretations and findings (*ibid*.). The antecedents to the Brighton Conference illustrated those sensitivities. In fact, the discussions at Brighton resulted in agreement that both

---

[9] B. Hale, '"Argentoratum Locutum": Is Strasbourg or the Supreme Court Supreme?', *Human Rights Law Review* 12 (2012) 65–78, at 67 *et seq.*

the margin of appreciation doctrine and the principle of subsidiarity be included in the preamble to the ECHR.

2.2 Causes of the legitimacy crisis

The causes of the Court's legitimacy crisis are manifold. The most obvious is the high number of individual applications, which threatens to paralyse the Court's institutional capacities. It has constantly grown since Strasbourg's inauguration as a full-time court in the late 1990s and stagnated only with the coming into force of Protocol 14 on 1 June 2010. In December 2011, the backlog of cases had reached 151,600. That year, six states, namely, Russia (26.6%), Turkey (10.5%), Italy (9.1%), Romania (8.1%), Ukraine (6.8%) and Serbia (4.5%) accounted for over two-thirds of the case law of the Court.[10]

Another issue contributing to the Court's legitimacy deficit with the member states is the variety of violations reaching Strasbourg. As one court for a Europe of more than 820 million potential applicants, the Court is competent to decide on violations of the ECHR, no matter the stage of development of the justice structures in the individual member states. It needs to handle serious, gross, and systematic human rights violations as well as cases of a less egregious nature, possibly involving conflicting human rights, on a daily basis. States with a functioning judiciary and a stable commitment to the rule of law are left suspicious of the ECtHR's human rights expertise to decide on their behalf. Some argue that national supreme constitutional courts are better placed to deal with the human rights issues at the national level (Letsas). As the recent emphasis on the subsidiarity principle shows, it is felt that the Court falls short of living up to this latter expectation. Hence, the ECtHR needs to engage in a daily balancing act of providing a firm answer to serious and systematic human rights violations, as well as a more deferential approach to those states which undertake a comprehensive examination of human rights complaints.

2.3 Explanations

The chapters in this book have provided various explanations of this legitimacy crisis. One is a lack of authorship and influence of the

---

[10] On the latest figures of the Court, see Registry of the European Court of Human Rights, *Annual Report 2011* (Strasbourg, 2012), available at www.echr.coe.int.

changing institutional functions of the Court from the viewpoint of the member states (Cameron). The Court's shift towards a *de facto* constitutional function in this relationship can be understood as *reaction* to constraints threatening the Court's workability and functionality (*ibid.*). It may be argued that the Court was forced into this role by some few states with systemic problems, which hardly comply with the Court's recommendations. Moreover, the Court's *de facto* constitutional functions have been decided in multiple fora and by various actors, even though the member states are and remain the main addressee of the Court's decisions, bearing the main obligation to implement and give effect to the rights enshrined in the Convention in relation to their citizens.[11] Reform suggestions come from inside the Court, from the member states, and from the other organs of the Council of Europe (Lambert-Abdelgawad). They do not concentrate on shaping a specific ideal of what the Court should become or be *for* (Cameron). Rather, they address all fields of the court's activity, perhaps with the primary aim of increasing the Court's efficiency in dealing with the backlog.

3. Developments and further solutions

The analyses in this book have addressed the present and future relations and functions of the Court towards the member states, the EU, and the UN, along the lines of an open set of qualitative principles, reaching from legal conceptions such as proportionality balancing and subsidiarity, to broader conceptions of effectiveness and comity.

3.1 The implied powers and ultra vires concepts

The implied powers doctrine allows an international institution to expand its powers based on the institution's objectives, beyond the expressly provided competence in the founding treaty. Lambert-Abdelgawad assessed the Court's expansion of authority into areas formerly occupied by the other organs of the Council of Europe. She concluded, perhaps not surprisingly, that the Court's expansion of institutional authority beyond its original *jus dicere* role on questions concerning the election of judges, or in the area of remedies, did not violate this principle.

---

[11] See art. 1 ECHR.

Nonetheless, the Court's expansion of institutional authority in its relations with the CoM and the PACE may put significant pressure on this relationship (Lambert-Abdelgawad). The *ultra vires* doctrine refers to cases where an institution has acted beyond its competence. This may provide a basis for challenging such decisions. One could, for example, argue that the Court's constitution of an advisory committee on the appointment of judges amounted to an act *ultra vires*, since the election of the Court's judges was a power initially assigned to the PACE, according to article 22 of the ECHR. Yet, the committee assumes mainly an advisory role (*ibid.*). It might exercise some influence on the election, but could it be held to *interfere* with the actual election of judges by the PACE?

As these examples exhibit, the implied powers and the *ultra vires* doctrine allow institutional powers to develop over time. There is great leeway in the assumption of new institutional authority. At the same time, discussions around the ECtHR's legitimate exercise of authority continue. Neither of the two doctrines fully captures the conflicts of authority which are currently debated in the ECtHR.[12] Further insights may be gained from analyses which take account of considerations of efficiency, effectiveness, proportionality, subsidiarity, and comity.[13]

3.2 The efficiency and effectiveness of the Convention system

3.2.1 Efficiency

There is a need to differentiate between predications about the system's efficiency, on the one hand, and its effectiveness on the other (Cameron). The former concept is understood here in terms of its ability to quantitatively deal with the caseload before it. Following the ECHR's notion of effectiveness in articles 1, 13 and 34, the latter concept refers to qualitative criteria such as the ability to provide individual claimants with a swift, prompt, just, and reasoned decision, which will eventually be implemented at the member state level.[14]

---

[12] On the authority of the international judiciary, compare A. von Bogdandy and I. Venzke, 'International Judicial Institutions as Lawmakers', *German Law Journal* 12:5 (2011) 979–1004; A. von Bogdandy and I. Venzke, 'On the Democratic Legitimation of International Judicial Lawmaking', *German Law Journal* 12 (2011) 1341–70.

[13] For a definition of those concepts, see A. Føllesdal, B. Peters and G. Ulfstein, Introduction, in this book.

[14] Compare arts. 1 and 13 ECHR. E. Voeten, 'Does a Professional Judiciary Induce More Compliance?' (at www.jus.uio.no/english/research/projects/multirights/docs/voeten-legal-justifications.pdf), at 1 and 29, also finds the professionalism of judges can contribute to

The past reforms of the Convention system have primarily sought to increase the Court's efficiency. They were not without results: as we illustrated earlier, the pilot judgment procedure, the Court's priority policy, as well as the adoption (and adjustment) of the *de minimis* rule in article 35(3)(b) of the Convention, have already had an impact on the Court's adjudicatory output. The same is true for the reform proposals to improve the Court's speed in dealing with incoming applications, in particular, the introduction of the single-judge formation to deal with admissibility decisions. The year 2011 saw the Court delivering more decisions than in the years before. From 2010 to 2011, the number of decisions rendered by the Court has risen by 30 per cent.[15]

3.2.2 Effectiveness

Some ways to increase the efficiency of the Strasbourg court may hinder its overall effectiveness (Cameron). Some filtering mechanisms may illustrate this loss. The states which produce the majority of cases provide the Court with a high number of inadmissible, *as well as* admissible cases. Streamlining Strasbourg's admissibility criteria in order to filter the inadmissible cases can impede the system's overall ability to render just decisions if the Court also employs these tools to deal with the admissible cases. One way to deal with this problem could be to abandon the ideal that Strasbourg should be a court of individual justice – an idea still favoured by many – and accept that the system has already developed into a *de facto* system of constitutional justice (*ibid.*).[16]

This difference of view concerns what the ECtHR should be *for* (*ibid.*). There are also many other factors which influence the ECtHR's ability to provide prompt, fair, just and reasoned decisions. One aspect which has received particular attention in this book is the qualifications and professional background of the judges elected and sworn in at

---

the effectiveness of a decision. But see K.L.R. Helfer, K.J. Alter and M.F. Guerzovich, 'Islands of Effective International Adjudication: Constructing an Intellectual Property Rule of Law in the Andean Community', *American Journal of International Law* (2009) 1–47, at 2, note 6, who refer to the 'degree to which international rules or tribunal rulings produce "observable, desired changes in behaviour"', the definition of effectiveness commonly referred to in international relations theory.

[15] The total number of judgments rendered by the Court in 2011 was 1,157. See *Annual Report 2011*, at 14.

[16] This applies to the Court's relation with the member states. See section 1 above. The idea is not new. Compare L. Wildhaber, 'A Constitutional Future for the European Court of Human Rights?', *Human Rights Law Journal* 23:5/7 (2002) 161–5.

Strasbourg (Cameron, Letsas, Lambert-Abdelgawad). The qualifications of judges nominated must live up to the demands of article 21(1) of the Convention so that only judges of 'high moral character' who 'possess the qualifications required for appointment to high judicial office or be jurisconsults of recognised competence' are elected to Strasbourg. The nomination and election processes in the PACE and the CoM must be transparent, to increase acceptance among the greatest possible number of member states.

The current process could be further improved. Currently, the PACE is electing the judges, but a consultative committee of the Court comments upon the qualifications and suitability of the candidates who stand for election. The CoM also maintains an *ad hoc* group which comments upon candidates. Finally, the CoM has adopted guidelines on the nomination by member states of judges to the Court (Lambert-Abdelgawad). Hence, in addition to the member states nominating the candidates, all organs of the Council of Europe have stakes in the election process. There may be advantages to a more formalised procedure concentrated in the hands of one organ, possibly the PACE (*ibid.*).

Many other measures and aspects can be mentioned with regard to improving the Court's ability to render swift, prompt, just, and well-reasoned decisions which will also be implemented at the member state level. The criterion of a reasoned decision applies at the substantive law level to the Court's approach to interpreting the Convention, above all, to the margin of appreciation and dynamic interpretation doctrines. Letsas and Arai-Takahashi have both advanced views as to how this approach could be understood to resonate at the member state level: the Court should apply autonomous interpretations of the rights enshrined in the ECHR. These should derive from international (moral) standards and not from majoritarian definitions deduced from the national levels.

The Court's overall approach to interpretation of the ECHR seems to resonate at the member state level. The consistent interpretation of the ECHR and the case law of the ECtHR is so uniform in many of the European member states that it exemplifies the universality and the successful domestication of the Convention at the national level (Andenas and Bjorge). In addition, national courts do not look to the ECtHR alone when applying and interpreting the Convention: they frequently invoke the practice of other member states (*ibid.*).

The Court's judgments may be implemented more readily at the member state level if the Court continues to develop its approach to non-pecuniary remedies. They can, for instance, include requirements concerning the release of prisoners, the resumption or reopening of domestic proceedings, as well as further recommendations (Leach). This more concrete approach can also assist the CoM in its supervision of the implementation of judgments. It should accept the more active role of the Court in this field, as it is unlikely that the CoM will further increase its capacities on implementation of the Convention (Lambert-Abdelgawad). Nonetheless, this approach may have unwanted and devastating consequences in individual cases if it is met by outright rejection at the member state level, such as in the *Hirst* decision against the UK (Leach).

Another useful procedure to improve implementation of the Court's judgments was introduced with the new article 46 of the ECHR. It offers the possibility to obtain a second ruling where issues arise from the interpretation of the Court's judgments. Though the Court has not yet been addressed under this new procedure (Lambert-Abdelgawad), this may prove an interesting way to reduce tensions between the Court and the member states, in particular on sensitive issues involving national interests. It provides another opportunity to bring justice to the claimant, who is usually the one who is suffering the most from the non-implementation stalemate. Another procedure aimed at more effective implementation of the Court's judgments is the preliminary reference mechanism, introduced by the Brighton Conference. This procedure awaits formal inclusion in the Convention.

Finally, some may question whether the co-respondent mechanism and the primary involvement procedure introduced in the Draft Accession Agreement of the EU will provide justice to the individual complainant (Besselink). Before the ECtHR, he or she will get another powerful respondent, eager to defend the EU legislation. The hope is that the ECtHR will also be ready to ensure effective protection of Convention rights in relation to a strong regional organisation. As regards ECHR member states' participation in UN operations, the Court has found the Convention to apply where individuals were under direct rule of such states, such as detention situations, notwithstanding the fact that the prisons were placed outside Europe's borders (Tomuschat).

3.3 Proportionality

Proportionality allows striking a balance between individual rights and the community interest. Accordingly, balancing plays a prominent role in cases before member states' highest or constitutional courts and the ECtHR (Andenas and Bjorge). Proportionality balancing is an example of the reception of the ECHR in national member states' courts and a growing Europeanisation of fundamental rights conceptions within the Council of Europe. Cases from the UK and Germany, in particular, epitomise how proportionality considerations may facilitate and further guide the reconciliation of national constitutional rights interpretations with Strasbourg's jurisprudence (*ibid.*). Thus, proportionality considerations can indicate ways to harmonise Strasbourg's human rights conceptions with Karlsruhe's, London's, and Oslo's.[17] Even formally dualist countries like Germany, Italy or Russia chose proportionality balancing over pure formalist arguments such as the *lex posterior* or *lex superior* principle, for the sake of integration of the international obligations into national constitutional systems (*ibid.*).

3.4 Subsidiarity

The contributions in this book illustrate that subsidiarity is relevant for several aspects of the Convention. It shapes admissibility considerations, as well as the application and interpretation of the substantive law, and impacts considerations on remedies. It applies to the implementation of the ECHR at member state level, in the Court's relations with the EU and, possibly, in its relations with the UN. Normatively, the principle urges deference to the lower level, where a hierarchically higher and lower level interact. In the multi-layered, multi-faceted relationships of the ECtHR with the member states, the Council of Europe organs, the EU and the UN, subsidiarity considerations may need to be accompanied by proportionality considerations, which can moderate between the various interests at the various levels involved.[18]

The exhaustion of local remedies provision in article 35(1) ECHR, as well as the present version of article 35(3)(b) ECHR, can be considered to incorporate subsidiarity considerations at the admissibility stage. As the Court's jurisprudence evinces, the margin of appreciation doctrine may be held to moderate between national protection and the ECHR on the other hand (Arai-Takahashi). Thus, in *A and Others* v. *UK*, the Court

---

[17] B. Peters, 'Germany's Dialogue with Strasbourg: Extrapolating the Bundesverfassungsgericht's Relationship with the European Court of Human Rights in the Preventive Detention Decision', *German Law Journal* 13 (2012) 757–72, 772.

[18] Compare M. Kumm, 'The Legitimacy of International Law: A Constitutionalist Framework of Analysis', *European Journal of International Law* 15 (2004) 907–31, 921.

affirmed the doctrine had 'always been meant as a tool to define relations between domestic authorities and the Court' (*ibid.*).

The Court's standard predominant approach to remedies has also corresponded to subsidiarity considerations and, as Leach demonstrated, maybe overly so. Earlier, it merely contained a declaration that the Convention had been violated and an appeal to the member states to award compensation. This rendered much deference to the national levels. For example, only in exceptional cases were member states asked to alter their legislation (Leach). But the Court's expanding jurisprudence on non-pecuniary remedies may not necessarily constitute a breach of the subsidiarity principle, since the main responsibility for implementation of the Court's judgments still rests with the member states. Accordingly, it has until now met surprisingly little opposition from member states (*ibid.*). By contrast, the Court's recommendations on the reopening of domestic proceedings, which serve as *restitutio in integrum* in cases concerning, for example, unfair domestic proceedings, or criminal cases, give more weight to subsidiarity considerations, since national courts must decide the case anew. This approach should possibly be made obligatory, to increase its overall effectiveness (*ibid.*). It can also be questioned whether this approach is appropriate and effective in complaints against states with systemic human rights problems and weak judicial systems.[19]

Finally, subsidiarity considerations can also be held to moderate the relations between the ECtHR and the CJEU. After accession of the EU to the ECHR, the Draft Accession Agreement will allow for the CJEU's primary right of review of violations of the ECHR in the EU before passing the case on to the ECtHR. Today, the ECtHR's *Bosphorus* doctrine lends deference to the EU standard of human rights protection in member states' implementation of EU legislation (Besselink, Tomuschat). It is debatable whether there is a need to uphold the *Bosphorus* doctrine after the accession of the EU (Besselink). A continued application of the doctrine could be seen to entail an unequal treatment of the parties to the ECHR, as it would shield the member states of the EU from the ECtHR's substantive jurisprudence.[20]

---

[19] H. Keller, A. Fischer and D. Kühne, 'Debating the Future of the European Court of Human Rights after the Interlaken Conference: Two Innovative Proposals', *European Journal of International Law* 21:4 (2010) 1032.

[20] T. Lock, 'The ECJ and the ECtHR: The Future Relationship between the Two European Courts', *The Law and Practice of International Courts and Tribunals* 8:3 (2009) 375–98, 395.

3.5 Comity: the dialogue des juges

Andenas and Bjorge's and Besselink's assessments highlighted comity as a further element shaping the Court's inter-institutional relations to the national constitutional and highest courts at the member state level and to other European courts, like the CJEU. Comity here is an overall description of various practices which facilitate cooperation, exchange and interaction among Europe's constitutional and supreme courts and their judges. Strasbourg has institutionalised the exchange with the highest national and constitutional court judges in the *dialogue des juges,* an annual meeting which debates salient issues arising in the Convention context. Since about 2006, the ECtHR has published the proceedings of these joint annual seminars with constitutional court judges and the plenary of the Court.[21] Meetings have debated central elements of ECtHR doctrine, such as the role of consensus in the ECHR system, the evolutive interpretation doctrine, and the subsidiarity principle,[22] and thus contributed to a common understanding of the ECHR's concepts and interpretations by the ECtHR, further shaping the European sphere of fundamental rights.

The Court's relations with other courts concern not only the national levels. Besselink illustrated the importance of Strasbourg's judicial dialogue with Luxemburg, initiated after the ECJ's decision in the *Hoechst* case. This case concerned the searching of premises of Hoechst Ltd., an incorporation, and thus needed to answer whether legal persons could benefit from the protection of article 8 ECHR. Whereas the ECJ assumed that this question had not yet been tackled by the ECtHR, the Court had, in fact, affirmed a few months earlier in the *Niemitz* judgment that article 8 could indeed lend protection to legal persons (Besselink). It is hoped that the two courts will continue those dialogues even after the accession of the EU to the ECHR.

4. The future: constituting Europe?

Previous assessments have described the Court as a janus-headed animal pursuing individual justice on the one hand, and constitutional justice on the other.[23] It is disputable whether those two attributes really describe

---

[21] See ECtHR, 'Dialogue between judges', at www.echr.coe.int/ECHR/FR/Header/Reports+and+Statistics/Seminar+documents/Dialogue+between+Judges/.

[22] See the seminars for 2008, 2010 and 2011.

[23] J. Christoffersen and M.R. Madsen (eds.), *The European Court of Human Rights between Law and Politics* (Oxford University Press, 2011), chapter 1.

an antagonism. Be that as it may, this book finds that the Court's current role in relation to the member states in many respects is constitutional. The Court selects and prioritises cases and denies admissibility in more than 90 per cent of the cases before it. The various reform suggestions that introduce new admissibility criteria, procedures, and implementation suggestions further shape the Court's constitutional role. It will likely continue to develop in this direction. Some of the recent changes adopted at Brighton, in particular on the modified admissibility criterion of article 34(3)(a) ECHR, affirm this point.

Even though the ECtHR's constitutional role is not so clear in relation to the EU and to the UN, some 'constitutionalist' tendencies also influence these relations. The *Bosphorus* and the *Al-Skeini* jurisprudence exemplify how the Convention may continue to apply, no matter whether the member state act was mandated by the EU or authorised by the UN.

Future discussions on the further development of the Court's jurisprudence should thus revolve around how its constitutional role is to be understood, and along which lines it needs to be further developed. This book suggests that a combination of the principles of effectiveness, proportionality, and subsidiarity should guide some of the further debates to come.

Those findings notwithstanding, the political and role model function of the Court should not be underestimated. The Court has already been the motor of fundamental changes in the European human rights architecture. We must hope it will not suffocate, be it from its own success, or from other challenges.

BIBLIOGRAPHY

Abi-Saab, G. 'The Security Council Legibus Solutus? On the Legislative Forays of the Council', in L. Boisson de Chazournes and M.G. Kohen (eds.), *International Law and the Quest for its Implementation: Liber Amicorum Vera Gowlland-Debbas* (Leiden and Boston: Brill, 2010) 23–44

Ackerman, B. 'Constitutional Politics/Constitutional Law', *Yale Law Journal* 99 (1989) 453–547

Ahmed, T. 'The European Union and Human Rights: An International Law Perspective', *European Journal of International Law* 17:4 (2006) 771–801

Alexy, R. *A Theory of Constitutional Rights* (Oxford University Press, 2002)
  'Balancing, Constitutional Review, and Representation', *International Journal of Constitutional Law* 3 (2005) 572–581
  'The Construction of Constitutional Rights', *Law and Ethics of Human Rights* 4 (2010) 20–32

Alkema, E.A. 'The European Convention as a Constitution and its Court as a Constitutional Court', in P. Mahoney et al. (eds.), *Protecting Human Rights: The European Perspective: Studies in Memory of Rolv Ryssdal* (Cologne: Karl Heymanns Verlag, 2000) 41–63

Almquist. J.A. 'A Human Rights Critique of European Judicial Review: Counter-Terrorism Sanctions', *The International and Comparative Law Quarterly* 57 (2008) 303–31

Alvarez, J.A. *International Organizations as Law-Makers* (Oxford University Press, 2005)

Andenas, M. 'The Federal Russian Law on Foreign Treaties', in R. Mullersohn (ed.), *Constitutional Reform and International Law in Central and Eastern Europe* (The Hague: Kluwer Law International, 1998), at 259–65
  '"There is A World Elsewhere" – Lord Bingham and Comparative Law', in M. Andenas et al. (eds.), *Tom Bingham and the Transformation of the Law: A Liber Amicorum* (Oxford University Press, 2009) 831–66

Andenas, M. and Bjorge, E. 'Juge national et interprétation évolutive de la Convention européenne des droits de l'homme', *Revue du droit public* 4 (2011) 997–1014
  Menneskerettene og oss (Oslo: Universitetsforlaget, 2012)

'Norske domstoler og utviklingen av menneskerettene', *Jussens Venner* 46:5 (2011) 251–86
Andenas, M. and Kravik, A.M. 'Norske verdier og EMK', *Lov og Rett* 49:10 (2010) 579–99
Arai-Takahashi, Y. 'Administrative Discretion in German Law: Doctrinal Discourse Revisited', *European Public Law* 6:1 (2000) 69–80
'Disharmony in the Process of Harmonisation? – The Analytical Account of the Margin of Appreciation Doctrine as an Interpretive Device of the ECHR', in C. Andersen and M. Andenas (eds.), *Theory and Practice of Harmonisation* (Cheltenham: Edward Elgar Publishers, 2012) 95–114
The Margin of Appreciation Doctrine and the Principle of Proportionality in the Jurisprudence of the ECHR (Antwerp: Intersentia, 2002)
Arden, M. 'Peaceful or Problematic? The Relationship between National Supreme Courts and Supranational Courts in Europe', in P. Eeckhout *et al.* (eds.), *Yearbook of European Law 2010* (Oxford University Press, 2010) 3–20
Aust, H.P. and Naske, N. 'Rechtsschutz gegen den UN-Sicherheitsrat durch Europäische Gerichte?', *Austrian Journal of Public and International Law* 61 (2006) 587–623
Badinter, R. *Les épines et les roses* (Paris: Fayard, 2011)
Barber, N. 'The Commission on the Human Rights Act and the European Court of Human Rights', *UK Constitutional Law Group* (27 September 2011)
Barkhuysen, T. and van Emmerik, M. 'Legitimacy of European Court of Human Rights Judgments: Procedural Aspects', in N. Huls, M. Adams and J. Bornhoff (eds.), *The Legitimacy of Highest Courts' Rulings* (The Hague: T.M.C. Asser Press, 2009) 437–49
Bates, E. 'The Birth of the European Convention of Human Rights and the European Court of Human Rights', in Christoffersen and Madsen (eds.), *The European Court of Human Rights Between Law and Politics* (Oxford University Press, 2012) 17–42, at 25–7
The Evolution of the European Convention on Human Rights: From its Inception to the Creation of a Permanent Court of Human Rights (Oxford University Press, 2010) 436–72
Bell, J. *et al. Principles of French Law*, 2nd edn. (Oxford University Press, 2008)
'A Fragment on Government', F.C. Montague (ed.) (Oxford: Clarendon Press, 1891)
Bentham, J. *Rationale of Judicial Evidence*, Vol. II, Bk. III (London: Hunt and Clarke, 1827)
Benvenisti, E. 'Margin of Appreciation, Consensus, and Universal Standards', *New York University Journal of International Law and Politics* 31 (1998–9) 843–54
Bergmann, J.M. 'Diener dreier Herren?: Der Instanzrichter zwischen BVerfG, EuGH und EGMR', *Europarecht* 41:1 (2006) 101–17

Bermann, G.A. 'Taking Subsidiarity Seriously: Federalism in the European Community and the United States', *Columbia Law Review* 94 (1994) 332–456

Bernhardt, R. 'Human Rights and Judicial Review: The European Court of Human Rights', in D.M. Beatty (ed.), *Human Rights and Judicial Review: A Comparative Perspective* (Dordrecht: Martinus Nijhoff, 1994) 297–319

Besselink, L.F.M. 'Entrapped by the Maximum Standard: On Fundamental Rights, Pluralism and Subsidiarity in the European Union', *Common Market Law Review* 35 (1998) 629–80

  'The European Union and The European Convention on Human Rights: From Sovereign Immunity in Bosphorus to Full Scrutiny under the Reform Treaty?', in I. Boerefijn and J.E. Goldschmidt (eds.), *Changing Perceptions of Sovereignty and Human Rights: Essays in Honour of Cees Flinterman* (Antwerp: Intersentia, 2008) 295–309

Besson, S. 'European Human Rights, Supranational Judicial Review and Democracy – Thinking Outside the Judicial Box', in P. Popelier, C. Van den Heyning and P. Van Nuffel (eds.), *Human Rights Protection in the European Legal Order: Interaction, between European Courts and National Courts* (Cambridge: Intersentia, 2011) 97–143

Bindman, C. 'Deputy PM Nick Clegg Defends UK Human Rights Laws' *BBC News UK Politics* (26 August 2011)

Bindman, G. 'Britain should be proud of the Human Rights Act – and protect it', *The Guardian* (29 August 2011)

Bingham, T. *Lives of the Law: Selected Essays and Speeches 2000–2010* (Oxford University Press, 2011)

  Widening Horizons: The Influence of Comparative Law and International Law on Domestic Law (Cambridge University Press, 2010)

Bix, B. *Law, Language, and Legal Determinacy* (Oxford: Clarendon Press, 1993)

  'Questions in Legal Interpretation', in A. Marmor (ed.), *Law and Interpretation: Essays in Legal Philosophy* (Oxford: Clarendon Press, 1995) 137–54

Bjorge, E. 'Exceptionalism and Internationalism in the Supreme Court: *Horncastle* and *Cadder*', *Public Law* 3 (2011) 475–82

  'National Supreme Courts and the Development of ECHR Rights', *International Journal of Constitutional Law* 9:1 (2011) 5–31

  'Torture and "Ticking Bomb" Scenarios', *Law Quarterly Review* 127 (2011) 196–9

Blackburn, D. 'Human Rights Wrangle', *The Spectator* (2 September 2011)

Blackburn, R. and Polakiewicz, J. *Fundamental Rights in Europe: The European Convention on Human Rights and its Member States, 1950–2000* (Oxford University Press, 2001)

Blackstone, W. *Commentaries on the Law of England*, Bk. III, 12th edn (London: Cadell, 1794)

Bleckmann, A. 'Der Beurteilungsspielraum im Europa – und im Völkerrecht', *Europäische Grundrechte Zeitschrift* (1979) 485–95

Die Bindung der Europäischen Gemeinschaft an die Europäische Menschenrechtskonvention (Cologne: C. Heymann, 1986)

Blokker, N. 'Is the Authorization Authorized? Powers and Practice of the UN Security Council to Authorize the Use of Force by "Coalitions of the Able and Willing"', *European Journal of International Law* 11 (2000) 541–68

Bodeau-Livinec, P. et al., 'Case Note', *American Journal of International Law* 102 (2008) 323–31

Bore Eveno, V. 'Le contrôle juridictionnel des résolutions du Conseil de Sécurité: Vers un constitutionnalisme international?', *Revue Générale de Droit International Public* 110 (2006) 827–60

Bossuyt, M. *'It is by Ever Widening its Jurisdiction that the Court of Strasbourg is Going too far'*, Paper presented at the 'Expert Seminar: The Future of the European Court of Human Rights', Institute for Human Rights, Katholieke Universiteit Leuven, 2 September 2011 (on file with the author)

Bothe, M. 'Peace-Keeping', in B. Simma (ed.), *The Charter of the United Nations. A Commentary*, 2nd edn, Vol. I (Oxford University Press, 2002) 648–700

'Peacekeeping Forces', in R. Wolfrum (ed.), *The Max Planck Encyclopedia of Public International Law* (Oxford University Press, 2008)

'Security Council's Targeted Sanctions against Presumed Terrorists', *Journal of International Criminal Justice* 6 (2008) 541–55

Boulouis, J. 'De la compétence de la Communauté européenne pour adhérer à la Convention de sauvegarde des droits de l'homme et des libertés fondamentales: Avis 2/94 de la Cour de justice des Communautés', *Libertés* 315–22

Bradford, A. and Posner, E.A. 'Universal Exceptionalism in International Law', *Harvard International Law Journal* 52 (2011) 1–54

Bratza, N. 'The Relationship between the UK Courts and Strasbourg', *European Human Rights Law Review* 5 (2011) 505–12

Brauch, J.A. 'The Margin of Appreciation and the Jurisprudence of the European Court of Human Rights: Threat to the Rule of Law', *Columbia Journal of European Law* 11:1 (2004/2005) 113–50

Breitegger, A. 'Sacrificing the Effectiveness of the European Convention on Human Rights on the Altar of the Effective Functioning of Peace Support Operations: A Critique of *Behrami and Saramati* and *Al Jedda*', *International Community Law Review* 11 (2009) 155–83

Human Rights: Universality and Diversity (The Hague: Kluwer, 2001)

'The Margin of Appreciation Doctrine in the Case-Law of the European Court of Human Rights', *Zeitschrift für ausländisches öffentliches Recht und Völkerrecht* 56:1–2 (1996) 240–314

Breyer, S. 'Introduction of President Luzius Wildhaber', *American University International Law Review* 22:4 (2007) 517–20

Brian Simpson, A. *Human Rights and the End of Empire: Britain and the Genesis of the European Convention* (Oxford University Press, 2001)

Brouwer, A. *Digital Borders and Real Rights: Effective Remedies for Third-country Nationals in the Schengen Information System* (Leiden: Nijhoff, 2008)

Brown, L.N. et al. *French Administrative Law*, 5th edn (Oxford: Clarendon Press, 1998)

Bruinsma, F.J. and Parmentier, S. 'Interview with L. Wildhaber, President of the ECHR', *Netherlands Quarterly Review of Human Rights* 21:2 (2003) 185–201

Buyse, A. 'The Court's New Priority Policy', 17 November 2010, http://echrblog.blogspot.com/2010/11/courts-new-priority-policy.html

Caflisch, L. 'Les conventions américaine et européenne des droits de l'homme et le droit international général', *Révue générale du droit international* 108:5 (2004) 9–22

Çalı, B. *'The Legitimacy of the European Court of Human Rights: The View from the Ground'* (Department of Political Science, University College London, 2011)

Callewaert, J. 'Quel avenir pour la marge d'appréciation?', in Mahoney et al. (eds.), *Protecting Human Rights: The European Perspective: Studies in Memory of Rolv Ryssdal*, 147–66

Cameron, I. 'Competing Rights?', in S. de Vries, S. Weatherill and U. Bernitz (eds.), *The Protection of Fundamental Rights in the EU after Lisbon* (Oxford: Hart Publishing, 2013)

'Protecting Legal Rights: On the (in)security of Targeted Sanctions', in P. Wallensteen and C. Staibano (eds.), *International Sanctions: Between Words and Wars in the Global System* (London and New York: Routledge, 2005) 181–206

'Protocol 11 to the ECHR: the European Court of Human Rights as a Constitutional Court?', *Yearbook of European Law* 15 (1995) 219–62

Canivet, G. *Cours suprêmes nationales et convention européenne des droits de l'homme: nouveau rôle ou bouleversement de l'ordre juridique interne?* (Paris: Cour de Cassation, 2005)

Cardwell, P.J., French, D. and White, N. 'Comments', *International and Comparative Law Quarterly* 58 (2009) 233–40

Carozza, P.G. 'Subsidiarity as a Structural Principle of International Human Rights Law', *American Journal of International Law* 97 (2003) 38–79

Cassel, D. 'The Expanding Scope and Impact of Reparations Awarded by the Inter-American Court of Human Rights', in K. De Feyter et al. (eds.), *Out of the Ashes: Reparation for Victims of Gross and Systematic Human Rights Violations* (Antwerp: Intersentia, 2005)

Cassese, A. 'The *Nicaragua* and *Tadic* Tests Revisited in Light of the ICJ Judgment on Genocide in Bosnia', *European Journal of International Law* 18 (2007) 649–68

Chinkin, C. 'International Humanitarian Law, Human Rights and the UK Courts', in Boisson de Chazournes and Kohen (eds.), *International Law and the Quest for its Implementation: Liber Amicorum Vera Gowlland-Debbas*, 243–64

Christoffersen, J. 'Individual and Constitutional Justice', in Christoffersen and Madsen (eds.), *The European Court of Human Rights between Law and Politics*, 181–203

'Primaritetsprinsippet – nye tanker om EMRKs stilling i dansk ret', in Christoffersen and Madsen (eds.), *Menneskerettighedsdomstolen – 50 års samspil med dansk ret og politik* (Copenhagen: Thomson 2009)

and Madsen, M.R. *The European Court of Human Rights between Law and Politics* (Oxford University Press, 2011)

Ciampi, A. 'Security Council Targeted Sanctions and Human Rights', in B. Fassbender (ed.), *Securing Human Rights? Achievements and Challenges of the UN Security Council* (Oxford University Press, 2011)

Claes, M. and de Visser, M. 'Are You Networked Yet? On Dialogues in European Judicial Networks', *Utrecht Law Review* 8:2 (2012) 100–14

Clapham, A. 'The Subject of Subjects and the Attribution of Attribution', in Boisson de Chazournes and Kohen (eds.), *International Law and the Quest for its Implementation: Liber Amicorum Vera Gowlland-Debbas*, 45–58

Clarke, K. Speech by Rt. Hon. Kenneth Clarke QC MP, Secretary of State for Justice, Lord Chancellor, 26 April 2011, High Level Conference on the Future of the European Court of Human Rights, Izmir, 26–7 April 2011. Available at: www.coe.int/t/dghl/standardsetting/conferenceizmir/Speeches/Speech%20UK.pdf

Cohen-Eliya, M. and Porat, I. 'Proportionality and the Culture of Justification', *American Journal of Comparative Law* 59:2 (2010) 463–90

'The Hidden Foreign Law Debate in Heller: The Proportionality Approach in American Constitutional Law', *San Diego Law Review* 46:2 (2009) 367–413

Conforti, B. 'Le principe d'équivalence et le contrôle sur les actes communautaires dans la jurisprudence de la Cour européenne des droits de l'homme', in S. Breitenmoser et al. (eds.), *Human Rights, Democracy and the Rule of Law: Liber Amicorum Luzius Wildhaber* (Zürich and Baden-Baden: Dike & Nomos, 2007) 173–82

Conroy, R.W. 'The UN Experience with Travel Sanctions: Selected Cases and Conclusions', in D. Cortright and G.A. Lopez (eds.), *Smart Sanctions: Targeting Economic Statecraft* (Lanham: Rowman & Littlefield, 2002) 145–69

Coomber, A. 'Judicial Independence: Law and Practice of Appointments to the European Court of Human Rights', *European Human Rights Law Review* 5 (2003) 486–500

Coppell, J. and O'Neill, A. 'The European Court of Justice: Taking Rights Seriously?', *Common Market Law Review* 29:4 (1992) 669–92

Cosgrove, E. 'Examining Targeted Sanctions. Are Travel Bans Effective?', in Wallensteen and Staibano (eds.), *International Sanctions: Between Words and Wars in the Global System*, 207–28

Costa, J.-P. 'Interview exclusive de Jean-Paul Costa, président de la Cour européenne des droits de l'homme', *Droits de l'homme – jurisprudence de la cour européenne des droits de l'homme*, 5 (2007) 77–80

Craig, P. 'Perspectives on Process: Common Law, Statutory and Political', *Public Law* (2010) 275–96

  'The European Union Act 2011: Locks, Limits and Legality', in P. Craig and G. de Búrca (eds.), *The Evolution of EU Law* (Oxford University Press, 2012)

Crawford, J. 'International Law as an Open System', in J. Crawford (ed.), *International Law as an Open System* (London: Cameron May Press, 2002) 17–38

Crema, L. 'Disappearance and New Sightings of Restrictive Interpretation(s)', *European Journal of International Law* 21 (2010) 681–700

Daillier, P. *et al. Droit international public* (Paris: Librairie générale de droit et de jurisprudence, 2009)

Dannenbaum, T. 'Translating the Standard of Effective Control into a System of Effective Accountability: How Liability Should Be Apportioned for Violations of Human Rights by Member State Troop Contingents Serving as United Nations Peacekeepers', *Harvard International Law Journal* 51 (2010) 113–92

de Búrca, G. 'The European Court of Justice and the International Legal Order after Kadi', *Harvard International Law Journal* 51 (2010) 1–49

  'The Influence of European Legal Concepts on UK Law: Proportionality and *Wednesbury* Unreasonableness', *European Public Law* 3 (1993) 561–87

  and Weiler, J.H.H., 'Introduction', in G. de Búrca and J.H.H. Weiler (eds.), *The Worlds of European Constitutionalism* (Cambridge University Press, 2012) 1–7

de Lange, R. 'Judicial Deliberations and Human Rights Adjudication', in N. Huls, M. Adams and J. Bornhoff (eds.), *The Legitimacy of Highest Courts' Ruling* (The Hague: T.M.C. Asser Press, 2009)

de Schutter, O. 'L'interprétation de la Convention européenne des droits de l'homme: un essai en démolition', *Revue de Droit International de Sciences Diplomatiques, Politiques, et Sociales* 70 (1992) 83–127

de Wet, E. 'Human Rights Considerations and the Enforcement of Targeted Sanctions in Europe: The Emergence of Core Standards of Judicial Protection', in Fassbender (ed.), *Securing Human Rights? Achievements and Challenges of the UN Security Council* 141–71

  The Chapter VII Powers of the United Nations Security Council (Oxford and Portland: Hart Publishing, 2004)

Devlin, P. *The Judge* (Oxford University Press, 1981)

Dorigo, S. 'Imputazione e responsabilità internazionale per l'attività delle forze di Peacekeeping delle Nazioni Unite', *Rivista di Diritto Internazionale* 85 (2002) 903–45

Doswald-Beck, L. *Human Rights in Times of Conflict and Terrorism* (Oxford University Press, 2011) 22–5

Dowling, J. and Pfeffer, J. 'Organizational Legitimacy: Social Values and Organizational Behavior', *The Pacific Sociological Review* 18:1 (1975) 122-36

Doyle, M. 'Kant, Liberal Legacies and Foreign Affairs', *Philosophy and Public Affairs* 12 (1983) 205-23

Drzemezewski, A. 'Election des juges à la Cour Européenne de Strasbourg: un aperçu', *L'Europe des libertés* 33 (2010) 6-10

'Quelques observations sur le rôle de la Commission des questions juridiques et droits de l'homme de l'Assemblée parlementaire dans l'exécution des arrêts de la Cour de Strasbourg', H. Hartig (ed.), *Trente ans de droit européen des droits de l'homme: études à la mémoire de Wolfgang Strasser* (Brussels: Nemesis, Bruylant, 2007), 55-63

'The European Human Rights Convention: A New Court of Human Rights in Strasbourg as of 1 November 1998', *Washington and Lee Law Review* 55:3 (1998) 697-736

'The Internal Organisation of the European Court of Human Rights: The Composition of Chambers and the Grand Chamber', *European Human Rights Law Review* 3 (2000) 233-48

Dunt, I. 'Clarke: "No question" of human rights withdrawal' (www.politics.co.uk/news/legal-and-constitutional/clarke-no-question-of-human-rights-withdrawal-$21387359.htm)

Dupuy, P.M. 'Evolutionary Interpretation of Treaties: Between Memory and Prophecy', in E. Cannizzaro (ed.), *The Law of Treaties Beyond the Vienna Convention* (Oxford University Press, 2011) 123-37

Dutheillet de Lamothe, O. 'Olivier Dutheillet de Lamothe Member, Conseil constitutionnel France', *International Journal of Constitutional Law* 3:4 (2005) 550-6

Dworkin, R. *A Matter of Principle* (Cambridge, MA: Harvard University Press, 1985)

'Do Values Conflict? A Hedgehog's Approach', *Arizona Law Review* 43 (2001) 251-9

'Even Bigots and Holocaust Deniers Must Have Their Say', *The Guardian*, 14 February 2006

'Hart's Postscript and the Character of Political Philosophy', *Oxford Journal of Legal Studies* 24:1 (2004) 1-37

Justice in Robes (Cambridge, MA: Harvard University Press, 2006)

Law's Empire (Oxford: Hart Publishing, 1986)

'Rights as Trumps', in J. Waldron (ed.), *Theories of Rights* (Oxford University Press, 1984) 153-67

Taking Rights Seriously (London: Duckworth, 1977)

Dzehtsiarou, K. 'Does Consensus Matter? Legitimacy of European Consensus in the Case Law of the European Court of Human Rights', *Public Law* (July 2011) 534-53 and Greene, A. 'Legitimacy and the Future of the European Court of Human Rights: Critical Perspectives from Academia and Practitioners', *German Law Journal* 12:10 (2011) 1707–15

Eaton, M. 'The New Judicial Filtering Mechanism: Introductory Comments', in Directorate General of Human Rights (ed.), *Future Developments of the European Court of Human Rights in the Light of the Wise Persons' Report: Colloquy organized by the San Marino chairmanship of the Committee of Ministers of the Council of Europe*, San Marino, 22–3 March 2007 (France: Council of Europe, 2007)

Eckhoff. T. *Rettskildelære* (Oslo: Universitetsforlaget, 2001)

Ejima, A. 'Yoroppa Jinken-Saibansho-niokeru "Hyoka-no-yochi" Riron-no Aratana Hatten' ('New Development of the "Margin of Appreciation" Doctrine in the European Court of Human Rights'), *Meiji University Graduate School (Law) Review* 29 (1992) 55–73

Endicott, T.A.O. 'Law and Language', in J. Coleman and S. Shapiro (eds.), *The Oxford Handbook of Jurisprudence and Philosophy of Law* (Oxford University Press, 2002) 935–68

Endo, K. 'Subsidiarity and its Enemies: To What Extent is Sovereignty Contested in the Mixed Commonwealth of Europe?', *EUI Working Papers*, RSC No. 2001/24 at 36, available at www.eui.eu/RSCAS/WP-Texts/01_24.pdf

'The Principle of Subsidiarity: From Johannes Althusius to Jacques Delors', *Hokkaido Law Review* 44:6 (1994) 553–652

English, R. 'Human Rights – Strasbourg or Luxembourg?', *UK Human Rights Blog* (9 September 2011)

Everling, U. 'Europäische Union, Europäische Menschenrechtskonvention und Verfassungsstaat: Schlusswort auf dem Symposion am 11. Juni 2005 in Bonn', *Europarecht* 40:4 (2005) 411–18

Fairgrieve, D. and Muir Watt, H. *Common Law et tradition civiliste: convergence ou concurrence?* (Paris: Presses Universitaires de France, 2006)

Fassbender, B. *Securing Human Rights? Achievements and Challenges of the UN Security Council* (Oxford University Press, 2011)

'Targeted Sanctions Imposed by the UN Security Council and Due Process Rights: A Study Commissioned by the UN Office of Legal Affairs and Follow-up Action by the United Nations', *International Organizations Law Review* 3 (2006) 437–85

UN Security Council Reform and the Right of Veto (The Hague: Kluwer Law International, 1998)

Finnis, J. 'Natural Law: The Classical Tradition', in Coleman and Shapiro (eds.), *The Oxford Handbook of Jurisprudence and Philosophy of Law*, 1–60

Fitzmaurice, M. 'Dynamic (Evolutive) Interpretation of Treaties I', *Hague Yearbook of International Law* 21 (2008) 101–57

Flauss, J.-F. 'De l'indépendance de la Cour Européenne des droits de l'homme', J.-F. Flauss (ed.), *La mise en œuvre du Protocole n°11: le nouveau règlement*

de la CourEDH: actes de la journée d'études du 23 octobre 1999 à la mémoire de Louis Edmond Pettiti (Brussels: Bruylant 2000) 13–31
and Cohen-Jonathan, G. 'La Cour EDH et le Droit international', Annuaire Français de Droit International 50 (2004) 778–802
Føllesdal, A. 'Legitimacy Deficits beyond the State: Diagnoses and Cures', in A. Hurrelmann, S. Schneider and J. Steffek (eds.), Legitimacy in an Age of Global Politics (Basingstoke: Palgrave, 2007) 211–28
'Subsidiarity', Journal of Political Philosophy 6 (1998) 190–218
'The Legitimacy of International Human Rights Review: The Case of the European Court of Human Rights', Journal of Social Philosophy 40:4 (2009) 595–607
Franck, T. 'Legitimacy in the International System', American Journal of International Law 82:4 (1988) 705–59
The Power of Legitimacy among Nations (New York: Oxford University Press, 1990)
Frank, A. 'UNO-Sanktionen gegen Terrorismus und Europäische Menschenrechtskonvention (EMRK)', in S. Breitenmoser et al. (eds.), Human Rights, Democracy and the Rule of Law: Liber Amicorum Luzius Wildhaber (Zürich and Baden-Baden: Dike & Nomos, 2007) 237–60
French, D. 'Treaty Interpretation and the Incorporation of Extraneous Legal Rules', The International and Comparative Law Quarterly 55:2 (2006) 281–314
Die Kontrolldichte bei der gerichtlichen Überprüfung von Handlungen der Verwaltung (Berlin: Springer, 1993)
"The Transformation of Constitutional law through the European Convention on Human Rights", Israel Law Review 41 (2008) 489–99
'The UN Anti-Terrorism Administration and the Rule of Law', in P.M. Dupuy et al. (eds.), Common Values in International Law: Essays in Honour of Christian Tomuschat (Kehl: N.P. Engel, 2006) 785–95
Furtado, C.F. 'Guess Who's Coming to Dinner? Protection for National Minorities in Eastern and Central Europe under the Council of Europe', Columbia Human Rights Law Review 34 (2003) 333–412
Gaja, G. 'The Review by the European Court of Human Rights of Member States' Acts Implementing European Union Law: "Solange" Yet Again?', in M. Shaw et al. (eds.), Common Values in International Law: Essays in Honour of Christian Tomuschat (Kehl: N.P. Engel, 2006) 517–26
Gardiner, R. Treaty Interpretation (Oxford University Press, 2008)
Gerards, J. 'Judicial Deliberations in the European Court of Human Rights', in Huls et al. (eds.), The Legitimacy of Highest Courts' Rulings: Judicial Deliberations and Beyond, 407–36
'The Pilot Judgment Procedure before the European Court of Human Rights as an Instrument for Dialogue', in M. Claes and P. Popelier (eds.), Constitutional Conversations (Antwerp, Oxford, Portland: Intersentia, forthcoming, available at http://papers.ssrn.com/sol3/papers.cfm?abstract_id=1924806

Giegerich, T. 'Die Verfassungsbeschwerde an der Schittstelle von deutschem, internationalem und supranationalem Recht', C. Grabenwarter and S. Hammer (eds.), *Allgemeinheit der Grundrechte und Vielfalt der Gesellschaft* (Stuttgart: Richard Boorberg Verlag, 1994) 101ff

'Wirkung und Rang der EMRK in den Rechtsordnungen der Mitgliedstaaten', R. Grote, (ed.), *EMRK/GG: Konkordanzkommentar zum europäischen und deutschen Grundrechtsschutz* (Tübingen: Mohr Siebeck, 2006) 61–98

Grant, R. and Keohane, R. 'Accountability and Abuses of Power in World Politics', *American Political Science Review* 99:1 (2005) 29–43

Greenberg, M. 'The Standard Picture and its Discontents' (available at http://papers.ssrn.com/sol3/papers.cfm?abstract_id=1103569)

Greenberg, S. 'New Horizons for Human Rights: The European Convention, Court and Commission', *Columbia Law Review* 63:8 (1963) 1384–412

Greer, S. '"Balancing" and the European Court of Human Rights: A Contribution to the Habermas–Alexy Debate', *Cambridge Law Journal* 63 (2004) 412–34

'Constitutionalising Adjudication under the European Convention on Human Rights', *Oxford Journal of Legal Studies* 23 (2003) 405–33

The European Convention on Human Rights: Achievements, Problems and Prospects (Cambridge University Press, 2006)

The Margin of Appreciation: Interpretation and Discretion under the European Convention on Human Rights, Human Rights Files No. 17 (Strasbourg: Council of Europe, 2000)

'What's Wrong with the European Convention on Human Rights?', *Human Rights Quarterly* 30 (2008) 680–702

Groussot, X. 'European Rights' and Dialogues in the Context of Constitutional', *Scandinavian Studies in Law* 55 (2010) 45–75

Groves, J. 'Human Rights Act is GOOD for us, insists Clegg in direct challenge to Cameron', *Mail Online* (27 August 2011)

Grozev, Y. 'How Human Rights Protection has Evolved: A Critical Analysis of Ten Years of Case Law', in ECtHR (ed.), *Ten Years of the 'New' European Court of Human Rights 1998–2008, Situation and Outlook* (Strasbourg: Council of Europe, 2009) 34–9

Guyomar, M. 'Conclusions sur Conseil d'État, Assemblée, 14 December 2007, M. Planchenault (1re espèce), et Garde des sceaux, ministre de la Justice c/ M. Boussouar (2e espèce)', *Revue Française de Droit Administratif* (2008)

'Le dialogue des jurisprudences entre le Conseil d'État et la Cour de Strasbourg: appropriation, anticipation, émancipation', in *Mélanges en l'honneur de Jean-Paul Costa* (Paris: Dalloz, 2011) 311–20

et al., Contentienx Administratif (Paris: Dalloz, 2010)

Habermas, J. *Between Facts and Norms* (Cambridge, MA: MIT Press, 1996)

'Intolerance and Discrimination', *International Journal of Constitutional Law* 1 (2003) 2–12

'Toward a Cosmopolitan Europe', *Journal of Democracy* 14 (2003) 86–100

Hale, B. '"Argentoratum Locutum": Is Strasbourg or the Supreme Court Supreme?', *Human Rights Law Review* 12 (2012) 65–78

'Beanstalk or Living Instrument?' in ECtHR (ed.), *Dialogue between Judges* (Strasbourg: Council of Europe, 2011)

'European Court of Human Rights: The Limits to the Evolutive Interpretation of the Convention' at www.echr.coe.int/ECHR/EN/Header/The+Court/Events+at+the+court/Opening+of+the+judicial+year/ (15 April 2011)

Hale, Sir M. *The History of the Common Law of England*, 6th edn (London: H. Butterworth, 1820)

Halpérin, J.L. *Les mondialisations du droit* (Paris: Dalloz, 2009)

L'impossible code civil (Paris: Presses Universitaires de France, 1992)

Hampson, F. 'The Future of the European Court of Human Rights', in G. Gilbert, F. Hampson and C. Sandoval (eds.), *Strategic Visions for Human Rights: Essays in Honour of Professor Kevin Boyle* (London and New York: Routledge, 2011) 141–66

Hansel, B. 'Effektiver Rechtsschutz in Grundrechtsfragen durch Vorlagepflicht oberster Bundesgerichte oder europäische Verfassungsbeschwerde', Walter Hallstein-Institut, WHI Paper 6/03 (2003)

Haratsch, A. 'Die Solange-Rechtsprechung des Europäischen Gerichtshofs für Menschenrechte: das Kooperationsverhältnis zwischen EGMR und EuGH', *Zeitschrift für Ausländisches Öffentliches Recht und Völkerrecht* 66:4 (2006) 927–47

Harmsen, R. 'The European Court of Human Rights as a "Constitutional Court"', in J. Morison, K. McEvoy and G. Anthony (eds.), *Judges, Transition and Human Rights* (Oxford University Press, 2007) 33–53

Harris, D.J. *et al. Law of the ECHR*, 2nd edn (Oxford University Press, 2009)

Hart, H.L.A. 'Positivism and the Separation of Law and Morals', *Harvard Law Review* 71 (1957) 593–629

The Concept of Law, 2nd edn (Oxford University Press, 1994)

Heckscher, S. 'Finns det någon europeisk rätt?' C. Wong (ed.), *Festskrift till Per Ole Träskman* (Stockholm: Norstedts, 2011)

Hedigan, J. 'The Election of Judges to the European Court of Human Rights', in M.G. Kohen (ed.), *Promoting Justice, Human Rights and Conflict Resolution through International Law: Liber Amicorum Lucius Caflish* (Leiden and Boston: Brill, 2007) 235–53

Helfer, L.R. Alter, K.J. and Guerzovich, M.F. 'Islands of Effective International Adjudication: Constructing an Intellectual Property Rule of Law in the Andean Community', *American Journal of International Law* (2009) 1–47

Helgesen, J.E. 'What are the Limits to the Evolutive Interpretation of the Convention?', in ECtHR (ed.), *Dialogue between Judges* (Strasbourg: Council of Europe, 2011) 19–28

Hennette-Vauchez, S. 'Constitutional v. International? When Unified Reformatory Rational Mismatch the Plural Paths of Legitimacy of ECHR Law', in Christoffersen and Madsen (eds.), *The European Court of Human Rights Between Law and Politics*, 144–63

Heringa, A.W. and Kiiver, P. *Constitutions Compared: An Introduction to Comparative Constitutional Law*, 2nd edn (Ius Commune Europaeum, Antwerp, Oxford, Maastricht: Intersentia, Metro, 2009)

Herne Hill, Lord Lester of. 'The European Court of Human Rights after 50 Years', *European Human Rights Law Review* 4 (2009) 461–78

 'Universal versus Subsidiarity: A Reply', *European Human Rights Law Review* (1998) 73–81

Herring, J. 'Who Decides on Human Rights?', *Law Quarterly Review* 125 (2009) 1–5

Hershovitz, S. 'Integrity and Stare Decisis', in S. Hershovitz (ed.), *Exploring Law's Empire* (Oxford University Press, 2006) 103–18

Heun, W. *The Constitution of Germany: A Contextual Analysis* (Oxford: Hart Publishing, 2011)

Heuschling, L. 'Comparative Law in French Human Rights Cases', in E. Örücü (ed.), *Judicial Comparativism in Human Rights Cases* (United Kingdom National Committee of Comparative Law, 2003) 23–47

Hilf, M. 'Europäische Union und Europäische Menschenrechtskonvention', Max Planck Institute for Comparative Public Law and International Law (ed.), *Recht zwischen Umbruch und Bewahrung: Festschrift für Rudolf Bernhardt* (Berlin and Heidelberg: Springer, 1995) 1193–1210

Himma, K.E. 'Inclusive Legal Positivism', in Coleman and Shapiro (eds.), *The Oxford Handbook of Jurisprudence and Philosophy of Law*, 125–65

Hirsch, M. *The Responsibility of International Organizations Toward Third Parties: Some Basic Principles* (Dordrecht: Martinus Nijhoff, 1995) 66–71

Hirschl, R. *Towards Juristocracy: The Origins and Consequences of the New Constitutionalism* (Cambridge, MA: Harvard University Press, 2004)

Hoffmann, L. 'Human Rights and the House of Lords', *Modern Law Review* 62 (1999) 159–66

 'The Universality of Human Rights', *Judicial Studies Boards Annual Lecture* (2009)

Hofmann, M. 'Zum zweiten "Lissabon-Urteil" des Tschechischen Verfassungsgerichts', *Europäische Grundrechtzeitschrift* 37: 5–6 (2010) 153–6

Hölderlin, F. 'Patmos', in E.L. Santner (ed.), *Hyperion and Selected Poems* (New York: Continuum, 1990)

Human Rights Association. 'Cameron Warned over Human Rights', *The Guardian*, 21 August 2011

Hurd, I. 'Legitimacy and Authority in International Politics', *International Organization* 53:2 (1999) 379–408

Isensee, J. 'Subsidiarität, das Prinzip und seine Prämissen', P. Blickle, T.O. Hüglin and D. Wyduckel (eds.), *Subsidiarität als rechtliches und politisches Ordnungsprinzip in Kirche, Staat und Gesellschaft*, Beiheft 20 (Berlin: Duncker und Humboldt, 2001) 129–77

Jaag, T. 'Beitritt der EG zur EMRK?: zum Gutachten 2/94 des Europäischen Gerichtshofs', *Aktuelle Juristische Praxis* 5:8 (1996) 980–4

Janik, C. 'Die EMRK und internationale Organisationen – Ausdehnung und Restriktion der equivalent protection Formel in der neuen Rechtsprechung des EGMR', *Zeitschrift für Ausländisches Öffentliches Recht und Völkerrecht* 70 (2010) 127–79

Jennings, C. *Oppenheim's International Law*, Vol. I (London: Longman, 1992)

Kaboğlu, I.O. and Koutnatzis, S.I.G. 'The Reception Process in Greece and Turkey', in Keller and Stone Sweet (eds.), *A Europe of Rights: The Impact of the ECHR on National Legal Systems*, 452–531

Kastanas, E. *Unité et diversité: notions autonomes et marge d'appréciation des États dans la jurisprudence de la Cour européenne des droits de l'homme* (Brussels: Bruylant, 1996)

Kavanagh, A. 'Defending Deference in Public Law and Constitutional Theory', *Law Quarterly Review* 126 (2010) 222–50

Keller, H. and Stone Sweet, A. *A Europe of Rights: The Impact of the ECHR on National Legel Systems* (Oxford University Press, 2008)

Keller, H., Fischer, A. and Kühne, D. 'Draft Statute for the European Court of Human Rights – A Contribution to Reforming the European System', *Human Rights Law Journal* 30 (2011) 1–12

'Debating the Future of the European Court of Human Rights after the Interlaken Conference: Two Innovative Proposals', *European Journal of International Law* 21:4 (2010) 1025–48

Keller, H., Forowicz, M. and Engi, L. *Friendly Settlements before the European Court of Human Rights: Theory and Practice* (Oxford University Press, 2010)

Keller, P. 'Re-thinking Ethnic and Cultural Rights in Europe', *Oxford Journal of Legal Studies* 18 (1998) 29–59

Klabbers, J. '*Kadi* Justice at the Security Council?', *International Organizations Law Review* 4 (2007) 293–304

Klabbers, J., Ulfstein G. and Peters, A. *The Constitutionalization of International Law* (Online edn Oxford Scholarship Online, Oxford University Press, 2009)

Kolb, R. 'Le contrôle de Résolutions contraignantes du Conseil de sécurité des Nations Unies par des jurisdictions internationales ou nationales sous l'angle du respect du jus cogens', *Revue Suisse de Droit International et Européen* (2008) 401–41

Koroteev, K. 'Judgment of the Russian Constitutional Court on Supervisory Review in Civil Proceedings: Denial of Justice, Denial of Europe', *Human Rights Law Review* 7 (2007) 619–32

Kress, K. 'Legal Indeterminacy', *California Law Review* 77 (1989) 283–337
Krzyżanowska-Mierzewska, M., 'The Reception Process in Poland and Slovakia', in Keller and Stone Sweet (eds.), *A Europe of Rights: The Impact of the ECHR on National Legal Systems*
Kumm, M. 'Constitutional Rights as Principles: On the Structure and Domain of Constitutional Justice' – A Review Essay on "A Theory of Constitutional Rights"', *International Journal of Constitutional Law* 2:3 (2004) 574–96
 'The Legitimacy of International Law: A Constitutionalist Framework of Analysis', *European Journal of International Law* 15:5 (2004) 907–31
Lagrange, P. 'Responsabilité des Etats pour actes accomplis en application du Chapitre VII de la Charte des Nations Unies', *Revue Générale de Droit International Public* 112 (2008) 85–110
Lambert, P. 'Marge nationale d'appréciation et contrôle de proportionnalité', F. Sudre (ed.), *L'interprétation de la Convention européenne des droits de l'homme* (Brussels: Bruylant, 1998) 63–89
Lambert-Abdelgawad, E. 'L'exécution des décisions des juridictions internationales des droits de l'homme: vers une harmonisation des systèmes régionaux', *Anuario Colombiano de Derecho Internacional* 2010–3 Especial, 9–55
 'L'exécution des décisions des juridictions européennes (Cour de Justice des Communautés Européennes et Cour Européenne des Droits de l'Homme)', *Annuaire Français de Droit International* 52 (2006) 676–724
 'Le Protocole 14 et l'exécution des arrêts de la Cour européenne des droits de l'homme', in G. Cohen-Jonathan and J.F. Flauss (eds.), *La réforme du système de contrôle contentieux de la Convention européenne des droits de l'homme* (Brussels: Bruylant, Nemesis, 2005) 79–113
 Preventing and Sanctioning Hindrances to the Right of Individual Petition before the ECtHR (Antwerp: Intersentia, 2011)
 'The Execution of the Judgments of the ECtHR: Towards a Non-coercive and Participatory Model of Accountability', *Zeitschrift für ausländisches öffentliches Recht und Völkerrecht* 69:3 (2009) 471–506
 The Execution of Judgments of the European Court of Human Rights, 2nd edn (Strasbourg: Council of Europe Publishing, 2008)
Lasser, M.D.S. *Judicial Deliberations: A Comparative Analysis of Judicial Transparency and Legitimacy* (Oxford University Press 2004)
Leach, P. 'Access to the ECtHR – From a Legal Entitlement to a Lottery?', *Human Rights Law Journal* 27 (2006) 11–25
 'Quelles sont les réparations adéquates dans les affaires de 'disparitions'? Leçons issues des affaires sur la Tchétchénie', E. Lambert-Abdelgawad and K. Martin-Chenut (eds.), *Réparer les violations graves et massives des droits de l'homme: La Cour InterAméricaine, pionnière et modèle?*, Collection de L'UMR De Droit Comparé de Paris, Vol. XX (Paris: Société de Législation Comparée, 2010)

  Responding to Systemic Human Rights Violations: An Analysis of Pilot Judgments of the European Court of Human Rights and their Impact at National Level (Antwerp, Oxford, Portland: Intersentia, 2010)

  Taking a Case to the European Court of Human Rights, 3rd edn (Oxford University Press, 2011) 466–8

  'The Chechen Conflict: Analysing the Oversight of the European Court of Human Rights', *European Human Rights Law Review* (2008) 732–61

Lester, A. 'Beyond *Wednesbury*: Substantive Principles of Administrative Law', *Public Law* (1987) 368

  'The European Court of Human Rights after 50 Years', in Christoffersen and Madsen (eds.), *The European Court of Human Rights Between Law and Politics*, 98–115

Letsas, G. *A Theory of Interpretation of the European Convention on Human Rights* (Oxford University Press, 2007)

  'Judge Rozakis's Separate Opinions and the Strasbourg Dilemma', in D. Spielmann, M. Tsirli and P. Voyatzis (eds.), *The European Convention on Human Rights: A Living Instrument, Essays in Honour of Christos L. Rozakis* (Brussels: Bruylant, 2011)

  'No Human Right to Adopt?', *UCL Human Rights Review* 1:1 (2008) 134–53

  'Strasbourg's Interpretive Ethic: Lessons for the International Lawyer', *European Journal of International Law* 21:3 (2010) 509–41

  'The Truth in Autonomous Concepts: How to Interpret the ECHR', *European Journal of International Law* 15:2 (2004) 279–305

  'Two Concepts of the Margin of Appreciation', *Oxford Journal of Legal Studies* 26:4 (2006) 705–32

Limbach, J. et al. *Judicial Independence: Law and Practice of Appointments to the European Court of Human Rights* (London: Interights, 2003)

Lock, T. 'Accession of the EU to the ECHR: Who Would Be Responsible in Strasbourg?' in D. Ashiagbor, N. Countouris and I. Lianos (eds.), *The European Union after the Treaty of Lisbon* (Cambridge University Press, 2012)

  'EU Accession to the ECHR: Implications for the Judicial Review in Strasbourg', *European Law Review* 35:6 (2010) 777–98

  'The ECJ and the ECtHR: The Future Relationship between the Two European Courts', *The Law and Practice of International Courts and Tribunals* 8:3 (2009) 375–98

Lockhart, N.J.S. and Weiler, J.H.H. '"Taking Rights Seriously" Seriously: The European Court and its Fundamental Rights Jurisprudence', *Common Market Law Review* 32:1 (1995) 51–94 (Part I) and 579–627 (Part II)

Lorange Backer, I. 'Begrunnelse for avsiling av en sivil ankesak', *Lov og Rett* 48:8 (2009) 49–51

Lucy, W. 'Adjudication', in Coleman and Shapiro (eds.), *The Oxford Handbook of Jurisprudence and Philosophy of Law*, 206–67

Lugato, M. 'Sono le sanzioni del Consiglio di Sicurezza incompatibili con il rispetto delle garanzie procedurali?', *Rivista di Deritto Internazionale* 93 (2010) 309–42

Macdonald, R.St.J. 'The Margin of Appreciation', in R.St.J. Macdonald, F. Matscher and H. Petzold (eds.), *The European System for the Protection of Human Rights* (Dordrecht/London: Martinus Nijhoff, 1994) 83–124

Machinska, H. 'Pilot Lowyer Project Developed by the Council of Europe to Make Direct Access to the ECtHR Easier and More Effective for Individuals', in Lambert-Abdelgawad, *Preventing and Sanctioning Hindrances*

Macklem, P. 'Militant Democracy, Legal Pluralism, and the Paradox of Self-Determination', *International Journal of Constitutional Law* 4 (2006) 488–516

Mahoney, P. 'Judicial Activism and Judicial Self-Restraint in the European Court of Human Rights: Two Sides of the Same Coin', *Human Rights Law Journal* 11 (1990) 57–80

'Marvellous Richness of Diversity or Invidious Cultural Relativism?', *Human Rights Law Journal* 19:1 (1998) 1–6

'New Challenges for the European Court of Human Rights Resulting from the Expanding Case Load and Membership', *Penn State International Law Review* 21:1 (2002) 101–14

'Universality versus Subsidiarity in the Strasbourg Case Law on Free Speech: Explaining Some Recent Judgments', *European Human Rights Law Review* 4 (1997) 364–79

Marchenko, M.N. 'Yuridicheskaya priroda i charakter resheny Evropeyskogo Suda po pralam cheloveka', *Gusodarstvo i Pravo*, 2 (2006)

Matscher, E. 'Methods of Interpretation of the Convention', in Macdonald *et al.* (eds.), *The European System for the Protection of Human Rights*

Maurer, A. 'The Federal Constitutional Court's Emergency Power to Intervene: Provisional Measures Pursuant to Article 32 of the Federal Constitutional Court Act', *German Law Journal* 2 (2001)

McGoldrick, D. 'Multiculturalism and its Discontents', *Human Rights Law Review* 5 (2005) 27–56

McNair, A. *The Law of Treaties* (Oxford University Press, 1968)

Merkel, G. 'Incompatible Contrasts? Preventive Detention in Germany and the European Convention on Human Rights', *German Law Journal* 11 (2010) 1046–66

Meron, T. 'Martens Clause, Principles of Humanity, and Dictates of Public Conscience', *American Journal of International Law* 94 (2000) 78–89

Messineo, F. 'The House of Lords in *Al-Jedda* and Public International Law', *Netherlands International Law Review* 56 (2009) 35–62

Metcalf, E. 'Time for the UK Supreme Court to Think Again on Hearsay', *The Guardian*, 15 December 2011

Milanović, M. and Papić, T. 'As Bad As It Gets: The European Court's Behrami and Saramati Decision and General International Law', *The International and Comparative Law Quarterly* 58:2 (2009) 267–96

Minichmayr, G. *Der Beitritt der Europäischen Gemeinschaft zur Konvention zum Schutze der Menschenrechte und Grundfreiheiten* (Euro-Jus, Schriftenreihe der Abteilung für Europäische Integration, Krems: Donau Universität, 1999)

Möller, K. 'Balancing and the Structure of Constitutional Rights', *International Journal of Constitutional Law* 5:3 (2007) 453–68

Møse, E. 'Norway', in Blackburn and Polakiewicz (eds.), *Fundamental Rights in Europe: The European Convention on Human Rights and its Member States, 1950–2000*, 636–7

Mosler, H. 'Die Entstehung des Modells supranationaler und gewaltenteilender Staatenverbindungen in den Verhandlungen über den Schuman-Plan', E. von Caemmerer *et al.* (eds.), *Probleme des europäischen Rechts: Festschrift für Walter Hallstein* (Frankfurt/Main: Vittorio Klostermann, 1966) 355–86

Mowbray, A. 'A Study of the Principle of Fair Balance in the Jurisprudence of the European Court of Human Rights', *Human Rights Law Review* 10 (2010) 289–317

'The Consideration of Gender in the Process of Appointing Judges to the European Court of Human Rights', *Human Rights Law Review* 8:3 (2008) 549–59

'The Interlaken Declaration: The Beginning of a New Era for the European Court of Human Rights?', *Human Rights Law Review* 10:3 (2010) 519–28

Myjer, E. *et al.* (eds.), *The Conscience of Europe: 50 Years of the European Court of Human Rights* (London: Council of Europe, Third Millennium Publishing Limited, 2010)

Ní Aoláin, F. 'The Emergence of Diversity: Differences in Human Rights Jurisprudence', *Fordham International Law Journal* 19 (1995–6) 101–42

Nishikata, T. 'Oushu-Jinken-Joyaku derogation-joko-to "Hyoka-no-Yochi": Jinken-Saibansho-no Tosei-wo Chushin-ni' ('The Derogation Clause of the ECHR – Judicial Control by the European Court of Human Rights'), *Kobe Hogaku-Zasshi (Kobe Law Journal)* 50:2 (2000) 149–86

Nollkaemper, A. 'Dual Attribution: Liability of the Netherlands for Conduct of Dutchbat in Srebrenica', *Journal of International Criminal Justice* 9 (2011) 1143–57

Nolte, G. 'General Principles of German and European Administrative Law – A Comparison in Historical Perspective', *Modern Law Review* 57 (1994) 191–212

'Human Rights Protection against International Institutions in Kosovo: The Proposals of the Venice Commission of the Council of Europe and their Implementation', in Dupuy *et al.* (eds.), *Common Values in International Law: Essays in Honour of Christian Tomuschat*, 245–58

Norges offentlige Utredninger, *Makt og demokrati, Sluttrapport fra Makt-og demokratiutredningen* (Oslo: Statens forvaltningstjeneste Informasjonsforvaltning, 2003)

Nowlin, C. 'The Protection of Morals under the European Convention for the Protection of Human Rights and Fundamental Freedoms', *Human Rights Quarterly* 24 (2002) 264–86

Nußberger, A. 'The Reception Process in Russia and Ukraine', in Keller and Stone Sweet (eds.), *A Europe of Rights: The Impact of the ECHR on National Legal Systems*, 604–77

O'Boyle, M. 'On Reforming the Operation of the European Court of Human Rights', *European Human Rights Law Review* 1 (2008) 3–4

'The Future', in Myjer et al. (eds.), *The Conscience of Europe: 50 Years of the European Court of Human Rights*

O'Donnell, T. 'The Margin of Appreciation Doctrine: Standards in the Jurisprudence of the European Court of Human Rights', *Human Rights Quarterly* 4 (1982) 474–96

O'Meara, N. 'A More Secure Europe of Rights? The European Court of Human Rights, the Court of Justice of the European Union and EU Accession to the ECHR', *German Law Journal* 12 (2011) 1813–32

Oeter, S. 'Die Kontrolldichte hinsichtlich unbestimmter Begriffe und des Ermessens', in Frowein (ed.), *Die Kontrolldichte bei der gerichtlichen Überprüfung von Handlungen der Verwaltung* (Berlin: Springer, 1993) 266–91

Pache, E. and Rösch, F. 'Europäischer Grundrechtsschutz nach Lissabon: die Rolle der EMRK und der Grundrechtecharta in der EU', *Europäische Zeitschrift für Wirtschaftsrecht* 19:17 (2008) 519–22

Pannick, D., 'Principles of Interpretation of Convention Rights under the Human Rights Act and the Discretionary Area of Judgment', *Public Law* (1998) 545–51

Paul, J.R. 'Comity in International Law', *Harvard International Law Journal* 32:1 (1991) 1–80

Pavlakos, G. 'Constitutional Rights, Balancing and the Structure of Autonomy', *Canadian Journal of Law and Jurisprudence* 24:1 (2011) 129–54

Payandeh, M. 'Constitutional Review of EU Law After *Honeywell*: Contextualizing the Relationship Between the German Constitutional Court and the EU Court of Justice', *Common Market Law Review* 48 (2011) 9–38

'Rechtskontrolle des UN-Sicherheitsrates durch staatliche und überstaatliche Gerichte', *Zeitschrift für ausländisches öffentliches Recht und Völkerrecht* 66 (2006) 41–71

Pérez, J.R.-Z. 'The Dynamic Effect of the Case-law of the European Court of Human Rights and the Role of the Constitutional Courts', in ECtHR (ed.), *Dialogue between Judges* (Strasbourg: Council of Europe, 2007) 36–52

Peters, A. 'Die Anwendbarkeit der EMRK in Zeiten komplexer Hoheitsgewalt und das Prinzip der Grundrechtstoleranz', *Archiv des Völkerrechts* 48:1 (2010) 22–41

'Rechtsordnungen und Konstitutionalisierung: Zur Neubestimmung der Verhältnisse', *Zeitschrift für Öffentliches Recht* 65 (2010) 3–63

Peters, B. 'Germany's Dialogue with Strasbourg: Extrapolating the Bundesverfassungsgericht's Relationship with the European Court of Human Rights in the Preventive Detention Decision', *German Law Journal* 13 (2012) 757–72

Petzold, H. 'The Convention and the Principle of Subsidiarity', in Macdonald *et al.* (eds.), *The European System for the Protection of Human Rights*, 41–62

Philippi, N. 'Divergenzen im Grundrechtsschutz zwischen EuGH und EGMR', *Zeitschrift für europarechtliche Studien* 3:1 (2000) 97–126

Pinna, A. 'Filtering Applications, the Number of Judgments Delivered and Judicial Decisions by Supreme Courts: Some Thoughts based on the French Example', in Huls, Adams and Bornhoff (eds.), *The Legitimacy of Highest Courts' Ruling*

Polakiewicz, J. 'The European Union's Charter of Fundamental Rights and the European Convention on Human Rights: Competition or Coherence in Fundamental Rights Protection in Europe', *Revue européenne de droit public* 14:1 (2002) 853–78

Pollicino, O. *et al.* 'Report on Italy', in O. Pollicino (ed.), *The National Judicial Treatment of the ECHR and EU Laws: A Comparative Perspective* (Groningen: Europa Law Publishing, 2010) 269–95

Popelier, P., Heyning, C.V.D. and Nuffel, P.V. *Human Rights Protection in the European Legal Order: The Interaction between the European and the National Courts* (Law and Cosmopolitan Values) (Cambridge, Portland: Intersentia, 2011)

Proelss, A. 'Der Grundsatz der völkerrechtsfreundlichen Auslegung im Lichte der Rechtsprechung des BVerfG', H. Rensen and S. Brink (eds.), *Linien der Rechtsprechung des Bundesverfassungsgerichts – erörtert von den wissenschaftlichen Mitarbeitern* (Berlin: De Gruyter Recht, 2009) 553–84

Puente Egido, I. 'Adhesión de la Unión Europea al Convenio Europeo para la Protección de los Derechos Humanos?', *Soberanía del estado y derecho internacional* 2 (2005) 1119–44

Quinn, G. 'The European Union and the Council of Europe on the Issue of Human Rights: Twins Separated at Birth?', *McGill Law Journal* 46:4 (2001) 849–74

Raab, D.J. *Strasbourg in the Dock: Prisoner Voting, Human Rights and the Case for Democracy* (London: Civitas, 2011)

Ratner, S.R. *The New UN Peacekeeping* (New York: St. Martin's Press, 1995)

Rawls, J. *Political Liberalism* (New York: Columbia University Press, 1993)

Raz, J. *Ethics in the Public Domain* (Oxford: Clarendon Press, 1995)

The Authority of Law (Oxford: Clarendon Press, 1979)

The Morality of Freedom (Oxford University Press, 1986)

'The Problem of Authority: Revisiting the Service Conception', *Minnesota Law Review* 90 (2006) 1003–44

Rebasti, E. 'Corte Europea dei diritti dell'uomo e responsabilità degli Stati per trasferimento di poteri ad una organizzazione internazionale', *Rivista di Diritto internazionale* 93 (2010) 65–88

Rehnquist, W. 'The Notion of a Living Constitution', *Texas Law Review* 54 (1976) 693–706

Reich, N. 'Wer hat Angst vor Straßburg?', *Europäische Zeitschrift für Wirtschaftsrecht* 22:10 (2011) 379–84

'Zur Notwendigkeit einer Europäischen Grundrechtsbeschwerde', *Zeitschrift für Rechtspolitik* (2000) 6 375–8

Reinisch, A. 'Developing Human Rights and Humanitarian Law Accountability of the Security Council for the Imposition of Economic Sanctions', *American Journal of International Law* 95 (2001) 851–72

Rengeling, H.W. 'Brauchen wir die Verfassungsbeschwerde auf Gemeinschaftsebene?', O. Duel, M. Lutter, and J. Schwarze (eds.), *Festschrift für Ulrich Everling* (Baden-Baden: Nomos, 1995) 1187f.

Rivers, J. 'Proportionality and Variable Intensity of Review', *Cambridge Law Journal* 65:1 (2006) 174–207

Rozenberg, J. 'Draft Brighton Declaration is a breath of fresh air', *The Guardian*, 9 April 2012

Ruffert, M. 'Die künftige Rolle des EuGH im europäischen Grundrechtsschutzsystem: Bemerkungen zum EuGH-Urteil v. 20.5.2003', *Europäische Grundrechte-Zeitschrift* 31:16/18 (2004) 466–71

Ryngaert, C. 'The European Court of Human Rights Approach to the Responsibility of Member States in Connection with Acts of International Organizations', *International and Comparative Law Quarterly* 60 (2011) 997–1016

Ryssdal, R. 'Opinion: The Coming of Age of the European Convention on Human Rights', *European Human Rights Law Review* 1:1 (1996) 18–29

Sadurski, W. 'Law's Legitimacy and "Democracy-Plus"', *Oxford Journal of Legal Studies* 26:2 (2006) 377–409

'Partnering with Strasbourg: Constitutionalisation of the European Court of Human Rights, the Accession of Central and East European States to the Council of Europe, and the Idea of Pilot Judgments', *Human Rights Law Review* 9 (2009) 397–453

Sager, L. 'The Incorrigible Constitution', *New York University Law Review* 65 (1990) 893–961

Sales, P. 'The General and the Particular: Parliament and the Courts under the Scheme of the European Convention on Human Rights', in Andenas *et al.* (eds.), *Tom Bingham and the Transformation of the Law: A Liber Amicorum*, 163–82

et al. 'Rights-Consistent Interpretation and the Human Rights Act 1998', *Law Quarterly Review* 127 (2011) 217–38

Salvioli, F. 'Un Analisis desde el principio pro persona sobre el valor juridica de las Decisiones de la Comision Interamericana de Derechos Humanos', *En Defensa de la Constitución: Libro Homenaje a Germán Bidart Campos* (Buenos Aires: Ediar, 2003)

Sandoval, C. and Duttwiler, M. 'Redressing Non-pecuniary Damages of Torture Survivors: The Practice of the Inter-American Court of Human Rights', in G. Gilbert, F. Hampson and C. Sandoval (eds.), *The Delivery of Human Rights: Essays in Honour of Professor Sir Nigel Rodley* (London and New York: Routledge, 2011) 114–36

Sands, P. 'Lord Bingham of Cornhill Obituary', *The Guardian*, 11 September 2010

Sari, A. 'Jurisdiction and International Responsibility in Peace Support Operations: The Behrami and Saramati Cases', *Human Rights Law Review* 8 (2008) 151–70

Sarooshi, D. *International Organizations and Their Exercise of Sovereign Powers* (Oxford University Press, 2005)

  The United Nations and the Development of Collective Security: The Delegation by the UN Security Council of its Chapter VII Powers (Oxford: Clarendon Press, 1999)

Scalia, A. 'Common Law Courts in a Civil Law System: The Role of United States Federal Courts in Interpreting the Constitution and Laws', in A. Gutmann (ed.), *A Matter of Interpretation: Federal Courts and the Law* (Princeton University Press, 1998) 3–48

Schapiro, R.A. *Polyphonic Federalism: Toward the Protection of Fundamental Rights* (University of Chicago Press, 2009)

Scharpf, F. 'Problem-Solving Effectiveness and Democratic Accountability in the EU', *MPIfG Working Paper* 03/1 (2003)

Scheeck, L. 'Diplomatic Intrusions, Dialogues, and Fragile Equilibria: The European Court as a Constitutional Actor of the European Union', in Christoffersen and Madsen (eds.), *The European Court of Human Rights Between Law and Politics*, 164–80

  'The Relationship between the European Courts and Integration through Human Rights', *Zeitschrift für ausländisches öffentliches Recht und Völkerrecht* 65 (2005) 837–85

Schlütter, B. (now B. Peters) 'Aspects of Human Rights Interpretation by the UN Treaty Bodies', in G. Ulfstein and H. Keller (eds.), *UN Treaty Bodies: Law and Legitimacy* (Cambridge: University Press, 2012) 261–319

  'Crucifixes in Italian Classrooms: Lautsi v Italy', *European Human Rights Law Review* 6 (2011) 86–92

Schütze, J.P. *Die Zurechenbarkeit von Völkerrechtsverstößen im Rahmen mandatierter Friedensmissionen der Vereinten Nationen* (Berlin: Duncker & Humboldt, 2011)

'Subsidiarity after Lisbon: Reinforcing the Safeguards of Federalism?', *Cambridge Law Journal* 68 (2009) 525–36

Shany, Y. 'Assessing the Effectiveness of International Courts: Can the Unquantifiable be Quantified?', *Hebrew University International Law Research Paper* No. 03/10

Regulating Jurisdictional Relations betwen National and International Courts (International Courts and Tribunals) (Oxford University Press, 2007)

'Toward a General Margin of Appreciation Doctrine in International Law?', *European Journal of International Law* 16:5 (2005) 907–40

Sharpe, R. 'The Impact of a Bill of Rights on the Role of the Judiciary: A Canadian Perspective', in P. Alston (ed.), *Promoting Human Rights through Bills of Rights: Comparative Perspectives* (Oxford University Press, 1999) 431–53

Shelton, D. *Remedies in International Human Rights Law*, 2nd edn (Oxford University Press, 2005)

Sherwin, E., 'Rule-Oriented Realism', *Michigan Law Review* 103 (2005) 1578–94

Sicilianos, L.A. 'L'(ir)responsabilité des forces multinationales', in Boisson de Chazournes and Kohen (eds.), *Liber Amicorum Vera Gowlland-Debbas* (Leiden and Boston: Brill, 2010)

Siekmann, R.C.R. *National Contingents in United Nations Peace-Keeping Forces* (Dordrecht: Martinus Nijhoff, 1991)

Simma, B. 'Harmonizing Investment Protection and International Human Rights: First Steps towards a Methodology', in C. Binder (ed.), *International Investment Law for the 21st Century* (Oxford University Press, 2009) 685–94

Simmons, B. *Mobilizing for Human Rights: International Law in Domestic Politics* (Cambridge University Press, 2009)

Singh, M.P. *German Administrative Law: In Common Law Perspective*, 2nd edn (Berlin: Springer, 2001).

Singh, R. 'Is There a Role for the "Margin of Appreciation" in National Law after the Human Rights Act?', *European Human Rights Law Review* (1999) 15–22

Sitaropoulos, N. 'Implementation of the European Court of Human Rights' Judgments concerning National Minorities or why Declaratory Adjudication does not Help', *European Society of International Law Conference Paper Series*, No. 4/2011

Skoghøy, J.E.A. 'Norske domstolers lovkontroll i forhold til inkorporerte menneskerettskonvensjoner', *Lov og Rett* 41:06 (2002) 337–54

Smith, C. 'The Interaction between the European Convention and the Protection of Human Rights and Fundamental Freedoms within the Norwegian Legal System', in Mahoney *et al.* (eds.), *Protecting Human Rights: The European Perspective*, 1306–7

Spielmann, D. 'Allowing the Right Margin; the European Court of Human Rights and the National Margin of Appreciation Doctrine: Waiver or Subsidiarity of European Review?', *CELS Working Paper Series*, February 2012

Spiering, M. *Englishness: Foreigners and Images of National Identity in Postwar Literature. Studia Imagologica: Comparative Literature and European Diversity* (Amsterdam: Rodopi, 1992)

Stahn, C. *The Law and Practice of International Territorial Administration* (Cambridge University Press, 2008)

Stavropoulos, N. 'Why Principles?' (available at http://papers.ssrn.com/sol3/papers.cfm?abstract_id=1023758)

Stirn, B. *Les Libertés en Question*, 7th edn (Paris: Lextenso Editions, 2010)

  Les sources constitutionnelles du droit administratif: Introduction au droit public, 6th edn (Paris: Lextenso Editions, 2008)

  et al. *Droits et libertés en France et au Royaume-Uni* (Paris: Odile Jacob, 2006)

Stone Sweet, A. 'A Cosmopolitan Legal Order: Constitutional Pluralism and Rights Adjudication in Europe', *Journal of Global Constitutionalism* 1:1 (2012) 53–90

  'Assessing the Impact of the ECHR on National Legal Systems', in A. Stone Sweet (ed.), *A Europe of Rights: The Impact of the ECHR on National Legal Systems* (Oxford University Press, 2008) 677–712

  Governing with Judges: Constitutional Politics in Europe (Oxford University Press, 2000)

  'Proportionality Balancing and Global Constitutionalism', *Columbia Journal of Transnational Law* 47 (2008) 73

  'Sur la constitutionalisation de la Convention Européenne des Droits de l'Homme: Cinquante ans après son installation, la Cour Européenne des Droits de l'Homme conçue comme une Cour constitutionelle', *Revue Trimestrielle des Droits de l'Homme* 80 (2009) 923–44

  and Mathews, J. 'Proportionality, Judicial Review, and Global Constitutionalism', in G. Bongiovanni, G. Sartor and C. Valentini (eds.), *Reasonableness and Law* (Law and Philosophy Library) (Dordrecht, Heidelberg: Springer Netherlands, 2009) 171–214

  'Introduction: The Reception of the ECHR in National Legal Order', in Stone Sweet (ed.) *A Europe of Rights: The Impact of the ECHR on National Legal Systems*, 11–36

Sudre, F. 'Du "dialogue des juges" à l'euro-compatibilité', *Le dialogue des juges: Mélanges en l'honneur du président Bruno Genevois* (Paris: Dalloz, 2009) 1015–31

Sweeney, A. 'Margins of Appreciation: Cultural Relativity and the European Court of Human Rights in the Post-Cold War Era', *International and Comparative Law Quarterly* 54 (2005) 459–74

Tehindrazanarivelo, D.L. 'Targeted Sanctions and Obligations of States on Listing and De-listing Procedures', in Boisson de Chazournes and Kohen (eds.), *Liber Amicorum Vera Gowlland-Debbas* 127–71

Terris, D. et al. *The International Judge: An Introduction to the Men and Women Who decide the World's Cases* (International Courts and Tribunal Series, Oxford University Press, 2007)

Thallinger, G. 'Sense and Sensibility of the Human Rights Obligations of the United Nations Security Council', *Zeitschrift für ausländisches öffentliches Recht und Völkerrecht* 67 (2007) 1015–40

Tomuschat, C. 'Case Law Comment', *Common Market Law Review* 43 (2006) 537–51

'Die staatsrechtliche Entscheidung für die internationale Offenheit', J. Isensee and P. Kirchhoff (eds.), *Handbuch des Staatsrechts der Bundesrepublik Deutschland*, Vol. VII (Heidelberg: C. F. Müller, 1992) 483–524

Human Rights Between Idealism and Realism, 2nd edn (Oxford University Press, 2008)

'Human Rights in a Multi-Level System of Governance and the Internment of Suspected Terrorists', *Melbourne Journal of International Law* 9 (2008) 391–404

'The Effects of the Judgments of the European Court of Human Rights According to the German Constitutional Court', *German Law Journal* 11 (2006) 513–26

'The *Kadi* Case: What Relationship is there between the Universal Legal Order under the Auspices of the United Nations and the EU Legal Order?', *Yearbook of European Law* 28 (2009) 654–63

Torres Pérez, A. *Conflicts of Rights in the European Union: A Theory of Supranational Adjudication* (Oxford University Press, 2009)

Tridimas, T. and Gutierrez-Fons, J.A. 'EU Law, International Law, and Economic Sanctions against Terrorism: The Judiciary in Distress?', *Fordham International Law Journal* 32 (2008–9) 660–730

Tsakyrakis, S. 'Proportionality: An Assault on Human Rights?', *International Journal of Constitutional Law* 7:3 (2009) 468–93

'Proportionality: An Assault on Human Rights?: A Rejoinder to Madhav Khosla', *International Journal of Constitutional Law* 8:2 (2010) 307–10

Tulkens, F. 'The European Convention on Human Rights between International Law and Constitutional Law', in ECtHR (ed.), *Dialogue between Judges* (Strassbourg: Council of Europe, 2007) 8–15

and Donnay L. 'L'usage de la marge d'appréciation par la Cour européenne des droits de l'homme. Paravent juridique superflu ou mécanisme indispensable par nature?', *Revue de science criminelle et de droit pénal comparé* 1 (2006) 3–23

Tzanakopoulos, A. 'United Nations in Domestic Courts: From Interpretation to Defiance in *Abdelrazik v. Canada*', *Journal of International Criminal Justice* 8 (2010) 249–67

Tzevelekos, V.P. 'The Use of Article 31(3)(c) of the VCLT in the Case Law of the ECtHR: An Effective Anti-Fragmentation Tool for the Reinforcement of Human Rights Teleology? Between Evolution and Systemic Integration', *Michigan Journal of International Law* 31 (2010) 621–90

Ulfstein, G. 'International Constitutionalization: A Research Agenda', Guest Editorial, *ESIL Newsletter* (2010)

'The International Judiciary', in J. Klabbers, G. Ulfstein and A. Peters (eds.), *The Constitutionalization of International Law* (Oxford University Press, 2009) 126-52

van Drooghenbroeck, S. *La proportionnalité dans le droit de la Convention européenne des droits de l'homme – Prendre l'idée simple au sérieux* (Brussels: Bruylant, 2001)

Vitruk, N.V. 'O nekotorykh osobennostyakh ispol'zovaniya resheniy Evropeyskogo Suda po pravam cheloveka v. pratike Konstitutsionnogo Suda Rossiyskoy Fedreratsii i inykh sudov', *Sravnitel'noe konsituttsionnoe obozrenie*, 1 (2006)

Voeten, E. 'Politics, Judicial Behavior, and Institutional Design', in Christoffersen and Madsen (eds.), *The European Court of Human Rights between Law and Politics*, 61-76

'The Impartiality of International Judges: Evidence from the European Court of Human Rights', *American Political Science Review* 102:4 (2008) 417-33

von Bernstorff, J. *Kerngehalte im Grund- und Menschenrechtsschutz* (Berlin: Duncker und Humboldt, 2012)

von Bogdandy, A. 'On the Democratic Legitimation of International Judicial Lawmaking', *German Law Journal* 12 (2011) 1341-70

'Pluralism, Direct Effect, and the Ultimate Say: On the Relationship between International and Domestic Constitutional Law', *International Journal of Constitutional Law* 6 (2008) 397-413

'Prinzipien der Rechtsfortbildung im europäischen Rechtsraum: Überlegungen zum Lissabon-Urteil des BVerfGE', *Neue Juristische Wochenzeitung* 63:1 (2010) 1-5

and Venzke, I. 'International Judicial Institutions as Lawmakers', *German Law Journal* 12:5 (2011) 979-1004

von Staden, A. 'The Democratic Legitimacy of Judicial Review Beyond the State: Normative Subsidiarity and Judicial Standards of Review', *Jean-Monnet Working Paper* 10/11 (2011)

Voßkuhle, A. 'Europa als Gegenstand wissenschaftlicher Reflexion – eine thematische Annäherung in 12 Thesen', C. Franzius *et al.* (eds.), *Strukturfragen der Europäischen Union* (Baden-Baden: Nomos 2011) 37-45

'Multilevel Cooperation of the European Constitutional Courts: Der Europäische Verfassungsgerichtsverbund', *European Constitutional Law Review* 6 (2010) 175-98

Voyiakis, A. 'International Law and the Objectivity of Value', *Leiden Journal of International Law* 22:1 (2009) 51-78

Wagner, A. 'Bill of Rights Commission publishes advice (and squabbles) on European Court of Human Rights reform', *UK Human Rights Blog* (9 September 2011)

Waldock, H. 'The Effectiveness of the System set up by the European Convention on Human Rights', *Human Rights Law Journal* 1 (1980) 1-12

Waldron, J. 'Judges as Moral Reasoners', *International Journal of Constitutional Law* 7 (2009) 2–24
  'The Core of the Case against Judicial Review', *Yale Law Journal* 115 (2006) 1346–1406
Weiler, J.H.H. *Un' Europa Cristiana: Un saggio esplorativo* (Saggi: BUR, 2003)
  'Editorial', *European Journal of International Law* 21:1 (2010) 1–6
Wheatley, S. 'Minorities under the ECHR and the Construction of a "Democratic Society"', *Public Law* (2007) 770–92
White, R. and Ovey, R. *The European Convention on Human Rights*, 5th edn (Oxford University Press, 2010)
Wieacker, F. 'Geschichtliche Wurzeln des Prinzips der verhältnismäßigen Anwendung', M. Lutter, W. Simpel and H. Wiedemann (eds.), *Festschrift für Robert Fischer* (Berlin, New York: Walter de Gruyter, 1997) 867–81
Wildhaber, L. 'A Constitutional Future for the European Court of Human Rights?', *Human Rights Law Journal* 23:5/7 (2002) [N.P. Engel] 161–5
  'Europäischer Grundrechtsschutz aus der Sicht des Europäischen Gerichtshofs für Menschenrechte', *Europäische Grundrechtezeitschrift* (2005) 689–92
  'Rethinking the European Court of Human Rights', in Christoffersen and Madsen (eds.), *The European Court of Human Rights between Law and Politics*, 204–29
  'The European Court of Human Rights in Action', *Ritsumeikan Law Review* 83 (2004) 83–92
Winkler, S. *Der Beitritt der Europäischen Gemeinschaften zur Europäischen Menschenrechtskonvention* (Baden-Baden: Nomos, 2000)
Worster, W.T. 'Competition and Comity in the Fragmentation of International Law', *Brooklyn Journal of International Law* 34:1 (2008) 119–49
Young, K.A. *The Law and Process of the U.N. Human Rights Committee* (The Procedural Aspects of International Law Monograph Series) (Ardsley, New York: Transnational Publishers, 2002)
Yourow, H.C. *The Margin of Appreciation Doctrine in the Dynamics of European Human Rights Jurisprudence* (The Hague: Martinus Nijhoff Publishers, 1996)
Zappalà, S. 'Reviewing Security Council Measures in the Light of International Human Rights Principles', in Fassbender (ed.), *Securing Human Rights? Achievements and Challenges of the UN Security Council*, 172–94
Zaum, D., 'The Security Council, the General Assembly, and War: The Uniting for Peace Resolution', in V. Lowe *et al.* (eds.), *The United Nations Security Council and War* (Oxford University Press, 2008) 154–74
Zimnenko, B.L. *Mezhdunarodnoe pravo in pravovaya sistema Rossiyskoy Federatsii* (Moscow: Statut, 2006)

INDEX

accession of EU to ECHR, 8–9, 23, 301–33, 398
   Bosphorus doctrine and, 310–12, 332
   co-respondent mechanism and, 325–31, 398
   current suspension of negotiations, 319–20
   'Discussion Document' on (ECJ), 315–16, 321
   European Commission and, 313, 315, 322
   new issues raised by, xi, 4
   point or purpose of, 330–3
   prior involvement mechanism and, 313–17, 320, 328, 331–2, 398
   procedural issues and, 58
   relationship between ECJ and ECtHR prior to, 301–8
   role of European courts in negotiations, 312–18
administration and budget of ECtHR, 291–8
administrative discretion, origins in concept of margin of appreciation in, 64–5
Administrative Tribunal of the International Labour Organisation (ILOAT), 337
admissibility criteria, 36–8, 51–3, 55–9, 391
advisory opinion of ECtHR on election of judges, 268–71
advisory opinions, 48–50
Albania
   legal representation in, 48
   remedies in unfair domestic legal proceedings, 152

Alexy, Robert, 75, 82
Andenas, Mads, vii, 22, 181, 392, 397–8, 401
Andorra
   legal representation in, 48
   responsibility for administration of justice in, 351
Arai-Takahashi, Yutaka, vii, 21, 62, 397, 399
Armenia, legal representation in, 48
Article 46 judgments, 161, 166–71
asymmetrical relationship between ECJ and ECtHR, 302–3
Austria
   court fees in, 46
   legal representation in, 48
authority-based legitimacy, 126–35
autonomous concepts doctrine, 113, 122, 124, 189–90
Azerbaijan, legal representation in, 48

Bandinter, Robert, 236
Barkhuysen, T., 55
Belgium
   judges, nomination of, 267
   legal representation in, 48
   national implementation of ECHR rights in, 204–6, 260
Bernhardt, Rudolf, 1
Bernstorff, Jochen von, 234
Besselink, Leonard, vii, 23, 301, 392, 398, 400–1
Bingham, Lord, 203–4
Bjorge, Eirik, vii, 22, 181, 392, 397–9, 401
blacklists, UN, 338
Bogdandy, Armin von, 183

INDEX

Bosnia and Herzegovina
  pilot judgment procedures involving, 163–4
  remedies in unfair domestic legal proceedings, 152
  UN peacekeepers and military operations in, 344, 356
Bosphorus doctrine, 310–12, 332, 380–3, 400
Bratza, Sir Nicholas, 213
Brauch, J. A., 81
Breyer, S., 42
Brighton Declaration (2012), 3, 6, 8, 43–54, 178, 299
budget and administration of ECtHR, 291–8
Bulgaria, pilot judgment procedures involving, 162

Cameron, Iain, vii, 20–1, 25, 390, 394–7
Canada, on travel bans, 371
Carozza, Paolo G., 91
Cassese, Antonio, 352, 356
CDDH (Steering Committee for Human Rights), 44–7, 50–1, 279
Centre for Advanced Study, Norway, xi
Chechnya, 171, 174
Christoffersen, Jonas, 2, 4
CJEU. *See* Court of Justice of the European Union (CJEU) and ECtHR
Clarke, Kenneth, 166
coordination-based legitimacy, 133–5
co-respondent mechanism, 325–31, 398
Cohen-Eliya, Moshe, 94, 104
CoM. *See* Committee of Ministers
comity, principle of, 15–16, 401
commitment-based legitimacy, 126, 136–41
committee form, decision of cases in, 53
Committee of Ministers (CoM)
  advisory opinion of ECtHR on election of judges and, 268–71
  budget of ECtHR and, 291–4
  expert panel to advise on election of judges, 272–5
  implementation of Court judgments by, 275–91, 398
  judges, involvement in election of, 264, 266, 268–75, 296–8
  Liaison Committee, 295
  relationship with ECtHR and PACE, 264, 288, 299–300, 395, 397
  remedies used by ECtHR and, 152, 161, 176, 179
  Resolution (97)9 on status and conditions of service of ECtHR judges, 296–8
  unfair domestic legal proceedings, re-opening of, 152
  voting rights, 319–20
common law, development of rights in, 203–4
competing rights and freedoms, balancing, 77–8
consistency issues
  case law, 53–4, 60
  margin of appreciation doctrine, 79–80
  principles, Court obligation of consistency of, 140
constitutional issues, 11, 106, 332, 390–1, 394, 402
Costa, Jean-Paul, 186, 272, 294–5
Council of Europe institutions and ECtHR, 8, 22–3, 263–300. *See also* Committee of Ministers; Parliamentary Assembly of Council of Europe
  autonomy of ECtHR, 294–8
  budget and administration, 291–8
  implementation of Court judgments, 275–91, 398
  judges, election of, 264–75
  judicial role of Court, expansion of, 263–4
  relationship between PACE, CoM, and ECtHR, 264, 288, 299–300, 394–5
court fees, proposal to introduce, 46–7
Court of First Instance of the European Union (CFI; now General Court), on freezing orders, 374–6

INDEX

Court of Justice of the European
  Union (CJEU) and ECtHR.
  See also European Court of Justice
  CFI (now General Court) on freezing
    orders, 374–6
  EU and ECtHR, relationship
    between, 8–9, 23
  general interpretative guidelines for
    national courts, CJEU's efforts
    to create, 49
  prior review by CJEU, 392
  proportionality, use of principle
    of, 19
  relationship between, xi, 4
  subsidiarity principle and, 400
CPT (European Committee for the
  Prevention of Torture and
  Inhuman or Degrading Treatment
  or Punishment), 207
Crawford, James, 181, 190
Croatia, legal representation in, 48
cultural values, recognition/rejection of,
  97–103
Czech Republic
  legal representation in, 48
  national implementation of
    ECHR rights in, 184–5, 192,
    202–3, 260

damages, pecuniary and non-
  pecuniary, 147–8
de minimis rule, 391, 396
democratic control and independence
  of Court, balancing, 14
detainees, release of, 157–60
Directorate General for Human Rights,
  265
Dublin Regulation, 333
Dworkin, Ronald, 76, 82–3, 86, 124,
  140
dynamic interpretation doctrine, 2, 21,
  106–41, 397
  after reform of Protocol 11 (1998),
    115–22
  autonomous concepts doctrine and,
    113, 122, 124
  before reform of Protocol 11 (1998),
    109–15

common or shared standards as
  factor, 108
constitutions and, 106
emergent consensus or common
  value, reliance on, 116–22
human rights law and, 107–8
legitimacy of moral reading of
  ECHR, 125–6.
  See also legitimacy of ECtHR
margin of appreciation versus, 89,
  113–15, 121, 125, 188
moral reading of ECHR, 122–5, 397
national implementation of ECHR
  rights and, 185–6, 188, 190–2,
  259
present-day standards as factor, 108
respondent state's standards,
  decisive importance not
  assigned to, 109

ECHR. *See* European Convention for
  the Protection of Human Rights
  and Fundamental Freedoms
ECJ. *See* European Court of Justice
ECSC (European Coal and Steel
  Community) protections
  regarding international
  organisations, 334
ECtHR. *See* European Court of Human
  Rights
effective control doctrine, 350–7
effectiveness, principle of, 10–12,
  17–19, 263, 278, 396–8
efficiency of ECtHR system, 395–6
Eisenhower, Dwight, 42
enforced disappearance cases, 171
erga omnes, 3, 53
Estonia, legal representation in, 48
EULEX, 359
European Coal and Steel Community
  (ECSC) protections regarding
  international organisations, 334
European Commission, on accession of
  EU to ECHR, 313, 315, 322
European Committee for the
  Prevention of Torture and
  Inhuman or Degrading Treatment
  or Punishment (CPT), 207

European consensus
  dynamic interpretation doctrine and, 109–15
  margin of appreciation doctrine and, 87–9, 99–100
European Convention for the Protection of Human Rights and Fundamental Freedoms (ECHR). *See also* accession of EU to ECHR; dynamic interpretation doctrine; national implementation of ECHR rights
  effectiveness, principle of, 17–19
  effectuation of, ECtHR's focus on, 2
  extra-territorial jurisdiction under Article 1 ECHR, 361–6, 392, 398
  immunity of EU action under (*Bosphorus* doctrine), 310–12, 332
  moral reading of, 122–5
  procedural statute, creation of, 44–6
European Court of Human Rights (ECtHR), xi
  accession of EU to ECHR and, 8–9, 23, 301–33, 398. *See also* accession of EU to ECHR
  advisory opinions on election of judges, 268–71
  autonomy of, 294–8
  budget and administration, 291–8
  changing circumstances and institutional setting, in 1–6
  CJEU and, xi, 4. *See also* Court of Justice of the European Union (CJEU) and ECtHR
  common legal principles guiding analysis of, xii, 10–12
  Council of Europe institutions and, 8, 22–3, 263–300. *See also* Council of Europe institutions and ECtHR
  democratic control and independence of Court, balancing, 14
  dynamic interpretation doctrine, 2, 21, 106–41, 397. *See also* dynamic interpretation doctrine
  ECJ, relationship to, 301–8, 317
  efficiency of, 395–6
  EU and, 8–9, 23, 301–33. *See also* European Union and ECtHR
  expert panel to advise on election of judges, 272–5
  extra-territiorial jurisdiction, 361–6, 392, 398
  implementation of judgments, role in, 276, 291
  importance of decisions for fundamental rights conceptions, 391
  international organisations and, 9–10, 334–5
  judges, Court involvement in election of, 268–75
  judicial cooperation and interaction, principles governing, 15–17
  judicial role, expansion of, 263–4
  jus dicere role of, 263
  legitimacy issues, 12–15, 389–94. *See also* legitimacy of ECtHR
  margin of appreciation doctrine, 21, 62–105. *See also* margin of appreciation doctrine
  member states and, 6–8, 20–1
  national courts and, 22, 181–262, 397–8. *See also* national implementation of ECHR rights
  procedural issues, 20–1, 25–61. *See also* procedural issues
  remedies, 22, 142–80, 397. *See also* remedies
  success rates of applicants, 391
  UN and, 4, 24, 334–88, 392. *See also* United Nations and ECtHR
European Court of Justice (ECJ)
  accession negotiations, role in, 312–18
  autonomy and uniqueness, efforts to protect, 331
  co-respondent mechanism and, 329, 331

European Court of Justice (ECJ) (cont.)
  'Discussion Document' on accession negotiations, 315–16, 321
  exhaustion of domestic remedies, 332
  freezing orders, on 372–87
  Joint Communication with ECtHR on accession, 317
  national enforcement of international directions or orders, on 367–8
  prior involvement mechanism, 313–17, 320, 328, 331–2, 398
  relationship between ECtHR and ECJ prior to EU accession to ECHR, 301–8
  standard of scrutiny for claims regarding fundamental rights, 303
European Union and ECtHR, 8–9, 23, 301–33. *See also* accession of EU to ECHR
  Bosphorus doctrine, 310–12, 332
  co-respondent mechanism, 325–31, 398
  ECJ and ECtHR, 301–8
  Foreign and Security Policy of EU, 319–20
  national enforcement of international directions or orders, 367–8
evolutive interpretation. *See* dynamic interpretation
exhaustion of domestic remedies, 53, 332
expert panel to advise on election of judges, 272–5
expertise-based legitimacy, 129–33
extra-territorial jurisdiction of ECtHR, 361–6, 392, 398

FAO (Food and Agriculture Organisation), 337
fees, proposal to introduce, 46–7
filtering, 33–5, 50–1, 57
Føllesdal, Andreas, viii, 1, 389
Food and Agriculture Organisation (FAO), 337

Foreign and Security Policy, EU, 319–20
France
  accession of EU to ECHR, objections to, 319
  administrative discretion in, 65
  Andorra, responsibility for administration of justice in, 351
  appeals accepted by Cours de Cassation, 56
  legal representation in, 48
  national implementation of ECHR rights in, 194–7, 217, 219, 236, 260
Franck, Thomas, 14
freezing orders, 372–87
FREMP (Working Party on Fundamental Rights, Citizens Rights and Free Movement of Persons), 318, 320

Gaja, Giorgio, 346
General Court (formerly Court of First Instance of the European Union or CFI), on freezing orders, 374–6
Georgia, legal representation in, 48
Germany
  administrative discretion in, 65
  federal responsibility for interests of *Länder* in, 341
  national implementation of ECHR rights in, 183, 218–37, 239, 260–1
  pilot judgment procedures involving, 163
Giegerich, Thomas, 219
good faith, obligation of ECtHR to reason in, 140
Grant, Ruth W., 276
Greece, pilot judgment procedures involving, 163
Greer, Stephen, 74, 84–5
Group of Wise Persons Report (2007), 30–2, 57, 295
Guyomar, Mattias, 195, 217

Habermas, Jürgen, 104–5
Hale, Lady, 193, 203–4

INDEX 435

Hart, H. L. A., 72–3
Hölderlin, Friedrich, 233
HRC (Human Rights Committee), UN, 339
Huber, Max, 192
Human Rights Committee (HRC), UN, 339
Hungary, legal representation in, 48

IACtHR. *See* Inter-American Court of Human Rights
ICCPR. *See* International Covenant on Civil and Political Rights
ICESCR (International Covenant on Social, Economic and Cultural Rights), no withdrawal from ratification of, 107
ICJ (International Court of Justice), responsibility doctrine of, 353, 355–6
ICTY (International Criminal Tribunal for the former Yugoslavia), 336, 352
ILC (International Law Commission), 346, 349–50
ILOAT (Administrative Tribunal of the International Labour Organisation), 337
immunity of EU action under ECHR (*Bosphorus* doctrine), 310–12, 332
implementation of ECHR rights
  Court judgments, CoM implementation of, 275–91, 398
  national implementation. *See* national implementation of ECHR rights
implied powers doctrine, 10–12, 15, 263, 278, 394–5
inadmissibility criteria, 36–8, 51–3, 55–9, 391
inconsistency. *See* consistency issues
independence of the Court and democratic control, balancing, 14
individual rights and public interests, balancing, 74–7

institutional/structural dimension of subsidiarity and margin of appreciation, 92–3
Inter-American Court of Human Rights (IACtHR)
  budget of, 293
  remedies of, 22, 172–7
interim measures, requests for, 52
Interlaken Declaration (2010), 6, 35, 43–54, 178
International Court of Justice (ICJ), responsibility doctrine of, 353, 355–6
International Covenant on Civil and Political Rights (ICCPR)
  ECHR and, 339
  no withdrawal from ratification of, 107
International Covenant on Social, Economic and Cultural Rights (ICESCR), no withdrawal from ratification of, 107
International Criminal Tribunal for the former Yugoslavia (ICTY), 336, 352
international directions or orders, national enforcement of. *See* national enforcement of international directions or orders
International Law Commission (ILC), 346, 349–50
international organisations. *See also specific institutions*
  ECSC and, 334
  ECtHR and, 9–10, 334–5
  legitimacy of, 11
interpretation of ECHR. *See* dynamic interpretation doctrine, margin of appreciation doctrine
Iraq, international military operations in, 347, 359, 364–6
Italy
  legal representation in, 48
  national implementation of ECHR rights in, 237–9, 260
  repetitive cases, 41
Izmir Declaration (2011), 6, 43–54

Joint Communication of ECJ and ECtHR on accession, 317
judges
  advisory opinion of ECtHR on election of, 268–71
  CoM involvement in election of, 264, 266, 268–75, 296–8
  Court involvement in election of, 268–75
  election to ECtHR by PACE, 264–75
  expert panel to advise on election of, 272–5
  member states, nomination by, 266–7, 302–3
  national implementation of ECHR rights and, 259
  procedural issues and, 33–5, 38
  Resolution (97)9 on status and conditions of service of, 296–8
judicial cooperation and interaction, principles governing, 15–17
judicial deference and judicial restraint, 65
judicial dialogue between ECtHR and ECJ, 306–8
jus cogens, 137
jus dicere role of ECtHR, 263

Keller, Helen, 182, 206, 259, 389
Keohane, Robert O., 276
Khodorkovsky, Mihail, 158, 184, 261
Korean War, 358
Koskenniemi, Martii, 91
Kosovo, international military operations in, 348, 351–3, 358, 360, 365
Kumm, Mathias, 17
Kuwait, international military operations in, 347

Lambert-Abdelgawad, Elisabeth, viii, 22–3, 394–5, 397–8
Latvia, legal representation in, 48
Leach, Philip, viii, 22, 142, 391, 398
legal representation before ECtHR, 47–8
legitimacy, national. *See* national sovereignty
legitimacy of ECtHR, 12–15, 389–94
  authority-based legitimacy, 126–35
  causes of and explanations for crisis regarding, 393–4
  coordination-based legitimacy, 133–5
  commitment-based legitimacy, 126, 136–41
  continuing scepticism about and rejection of, 389–90, 392–3
  expertise-based legitimacy, 129–33
  good faith application of consistent principles, as 140
  moral reading of ECHR, justification for, 125–6
  procedural issues and, 54–61
legitimacy of international institutions generally, 11
Letsas, George, viii, 21, 74, 93, 106, 123–4, 391, 393, 397
Liaison Committee between CoM and ECtHR, 295
Libya, international military operations in, 349, 359
Liechtenstein, legal representation in, 48
Lisbon Treaty, 9–10, 309, 311, 316
Lithuania, Article 46 judgments against, 170
living instrument, ECHR as. *See* dynamic interpretation doctrine
London, Treaty of (1949), 1
Luxembourg, legal representation in, 48

Maastricht Treaty, 303
Macdonald, Ronald. St. J., 63
Macedonia, former Yugoslav Republic of, legal representation in, 48
Madsen, Mikael Rask, 2, 4
Mahoney, Paul, 1
majoritarian preferences, 96–7, 101, 123, 397
Manneken Pis (Petit Julien), 304
Marchenko, Mihail N., 240
margin of appreciation doctrine, 21, 62–105
  administrative discretion, origins in concept of, 64–5

Brighton Conference on, 7
circumstances in which doctrine may
  be evoked, 69–78
competing rights and freedoms,
  balancing, 77–8
criticisms of, 78–82
cultural values, recognition/rejection
  of, 97–103
defined, 62
derogating measures, in context
  of, 65
development of, in ECtHR
  jurisprudence, 65–8
dynamic interpretation versus, 89,
  113–15, 121, 125, 188
European consensus, lack of, 87–9,
  99–100
fact-finding and ascertaining facts,
  69–70
general principle, as 82–4
human rights norms, evaluating,
  71–4
inconsistency of, 79–80
individual rights and public interests,
  balancing, 74–7
national implementation of ECHR
  rights and, 186–8, 247–50, 260
national law, appraisal of, 70–1
national sovereignty concerns and,
  13, 63, 94–5
nature of, 82–7
policy standard, as 86–7
procedural issues and, 51
progressive jurisprudence,
  willingness of ECtHR to
  develop, 2
proportionality, principle of, 188
rule of law, corrosive effect on, 80
secondary order principle, as 84–5
subjective and relativist standards,
  introduction of, 81
subsidiarity and, 90–3, 399
substantive dimensions of, 94–103
tyranny of the majority and, 96–7,
  101, 123, 397
Martinico, Giuseppe, 238
Member States and ECtHR, 6–8, 20–1.
  See also margin of appreciation
  doctrine; national implementation
  of ECHR rights
Bosphorus doctrine, 310–12, 332
co-respondent mechanism, 325–31,
  398
CoM voting rights, 319–20
judges nominated by, 266–7, 302–3
military operations of UN,
  responsibility for, 359–60
sovereignty concerns, 13.
  See also national sovereignty
'translation' problem, 48–50, 53–4
UN actions, responsibility for,
  340–1
military operations of UN, 347–66
attribution or imputation of
  responsibility, 351–9
constitutional requirement of
  Security Council control, 360
ECtHR jurisdiction *ratione personae*
  under Article 1 ECHR, 361–6
effective control doctrine, 350–7
member states, responsibilities of,
  359–60
responsibility for, 349–61
Milton, John, 204
minority protections from tyranny of
  majority, 96–7, 101, 123, 397
Moldavian Republic of Transdniestria,
  158
Moldova
  Article 46 judgments against, 168
  pilot judgment procedures involving,
    163
Monaco, legal representation in, 48
Montesquieu, Charles-Louis 263
moral reading of ECHR, 122–5, 397
Mowbray, Alastair, 78–82

national enforcement of international
  directions or orders, 367–87
EU, in 367–8
extra-territorial jurisdiction of
  ECtHR over, 361–6, 392, 398
failure of UN to properly provide
  for, 368–9
freezing orders, 372–87
travel bans, 369–72

national implementation of ECHR rights, 22, 181–262, 397–8.
See also specific countries
autonomous concepts doctrine and, 189–90
CJEU, efforts to create general interpretative guidelines by, 49
dynamic interpretation and, 185–6, 188, 190–2, 259
issues, principles, and doctrines involved in, 182–90
judges, importance of, 259
margin of appreciation and, 186–8, 247–50, 260
matters not explicitly resolved by ECtHR, 250–5
multilateral relationship between national courts, 259–62
proportionality, principle of, 188, 228, 260, 398–9
tort remedies for violations, 255–9
unfair domestic legal proceedings, remedies in, 152–7
national sovereignty
accession of EU to ECHR and, 320, 331
margin of appreciation and, 13, 63, 94–5
Member State concerns regarding, 13
pilot judgment procedure and, 166
procedural issues and, 53
NATO (North Atlantic Treaty Organisation), 10, 353
Netherlands
judges, nomination of, 267
UN military operations, responsibility for, 360
Neuberger of Abbotsbury, Lord, 261
non-disclosure of investigative files, 174
non-judicial rapporteurs, 33–5
Normal Justification Thesis, 127
North Atlantic Treaty Organisation (NATO), 10, 353
Norway
Kosovo, responsibility for UN military operations in, 360
national implementation of ECHR rights in, 183, 197–202, 206, 260
Nußberger, Angelika, 239

O'Boyle, Michael, 57
Öcalan, 363
open textured norms, 72

PACE. *See* Parliamentary Assembly of Council of Europe
pacta sunt servanda, 136
Papier, Hans-Jürgen, 236
Parliamentary Assembly of Council of Europe (PACE)
budget of ECtHR, role in, 291, 293
implementation of ECtHR judgments, role in, 264, 276, 278–89
judges, election of, 264–75
relationship with ECtHR and CoM, 264, 288, 299–300, 394–5
peacekeeping activities of UN, 343–7
general principles of, 343–4
judicial protections for disputes arising from, 337
organs of UN, peacekeepers as, 344–5
responsibility for injuries caused by, 345–7
Permanent International Court of Justice (PICJ)
property, restitution of, 149
unfair domestic legal proceedings, on 154
Peters, Birgit, viii, 1, 389
pilot judgment procedure, 161–6, 391, 396
Poiares Maduro, Luis Miguel, 185, 375
Poland
filtering under Protocol 14, 33–4
legal representation in, 48
pilot judgment procedures involving, 162
repetitive cases, 41
Polliciono, Oreste, 238
Porat, Iddo, 94, 104
Portugal, legal representation in, 48
Pourgourides, M. Christos, 286
principles, Court obligation of consistency of, 140
prior involvement mechanism, 313–17, 320, 328, 331–2, 398

INDEX 439

priority policy, 42–3, 57, 391.
procedural issues, 20–1, 25–61
　See also Protocol 14
　additional chambers, plan to add, 35
　admissibility criteria, 36–8, 51–3, 55–9, 391
　advisory opinions, 48–50
　committee form, decision of cases in, 53
　context of, 25
　de minimis rule, 391, 396
　fees, proposal to introduce, 46–7
　filtering, 33–5, 50–1, 57
　Group of Wise Persons Report (2007) on, 30–2, 57
　inconsistency of case law, 53–4, 60
　Interlaken, Izmir and Brighton Declarations, 43–54
　legal representation, 47–8
　legitimacy problems and, 54–61
　nature of court and, 58–9
　priority policy, 42–3, 57, 391, 396
　repetitive cases, 25, 38–42
　Satellite Offices, proposal to establish, 30
　significant disadvantage, new admissibility ground of, 36–8
　statute, creation of, 44–6
　subsidiarity principle, application of, 51–3, 60
　substantive issues and, 26
　Woolf Report (2005) proposals, 27, 57
property, restitution of, 149–52
proportionality, principle of, 10–12, 19–20, 188, 228, 260, 398–9
Protocol 14
　additional chambers, plan to add, 35
　entry into force (2010), 27
　filtering, 33–5
　priority policy and, 43
　purpose of, 27
　repetitive cases, 38–42
　significant disadvantage, new admissibility ground of, 36–8
　structural sense of subsidiarity and, 92
public interests and individual rights, balancing, 74–7

ratification of ECHR. *See* accession of EU to ECHR
Raz, Joseph, 127–9
release of detainees, 157–60
remedies, 22, 142–80, 397
　Article 46 judgments, 161, 166–71
　damages, pecuniary and non-pecuniary, 147–8
　exhaustion of domestic remedies, 53, 332
　IACtHR, of 22, 172–7
　increasingly prescriptive and expansive approach of Court to, 142–3, 145–9, 178–80
　legal basis for, 143–8
　non-disclosure of investigative files, for 174
　pilot judgment procedure, 161–6, 391, 396
　property, restitution of, 149–52
　purpose of, 142
　release of detainees, 157–60
　repetitive cases due to lack of effective local remedies, 39
　restitutio in integrum, 143, 145, 179
　serious, systematic human rights violations, for 171–7
　subsidiarity. principle of, 152–7, 177–8, 400
　systemic and structural violations of ECHR, for 161–71
　tort remedies for violations of ECHR rights, national implementation of, 255–9
　unfair domestic legal proceedings, in 152–7
repetitive cases, 25, 38–42
res judicata, 15
Resolution (97)9 on status and conditions of service of ECtHR judges, 296–8
restitutio in integrum, 143, 145, 179
Romania
　filtering under Protocol 14, 33–4
　legal representation in, 48
　pilot judgment procedures involving, 162, 164
　repetitive cases, 41

440   INDEX

Rozakis, Christos, 121
rule of law, 10–12, 80, 359
Russia
    approval of Protocol 14 and, 27, 44
    court fees in, 46
    filtering under Protocol 14, 33–4
    legal representation in, 48
    national implementation of ECHR rights in, 183, 202–3, 239–42, 260–1
    pilot judgment procedures involving, 163
    repetitive cases, 39–40, 47, 56
    serious, systematic human rights violations, remedies for, 171, 173–4
Ryssdal, Rolv, 188

Sadurski, W., 97
Sands, Philippe, 203
Satellite Offices, 30
Scotland, national implementation of ECHR rights in, 182–3, 243–6
Shelton, D., 171, 175
'Should states ratify human rights conventions?' research project, xi
significant disadvantage, new admissibility ground of, 36–8
Simpson, A. W. Brian, 260
single judge procedure, 33–5
Slovakia, legal representation in, 48
Slovenia
    Article 46 judgments against, 169
    legal representation in, 48
sovereignty. *See* national sovereignty
Spain
    Andorra, responsibility for administration of justice in, 351
    legal representation in, 48
Spielmann, Dean, 76
states parties. *See* member states and ECtHR
statute, procedural, creation of, 44–6
Steering Committee for Human Rights (CDDH), 44–7, 50–1, 279
Stone Sweet, Alec, 181, 206, 259, 389

structural/institutional dimension of subsidiarity and margin of appreciation, 92–3
structured balancing, 74
subsidiarity, principle of, 7, 10–12, 16–17, 51–3, 60, 90–3, 152–7, 177–8, 315, 331, 399
Sweden
    filtering under Protocol 14, 34
    legal representation in, 48
Switzerland
    court fees in, 46
    Interlaken Conference organised by, 44
    legal representation in, 48

targeted sanctions of UN, 337
Timmermans, Christian, 314, 316, 321
Tomuschat, Christian, ix, 24, 181, 190, 334, 392, 400
tort remedies for violations of ECHR rights, 255–9
'translation' problem, 48–50, 53–4
travel bans, 369–72
Turkey
    Article 46 judgments against, 168–9
    extra-territorial jurisdiction of ECHR over actions of, 363
    filtering under Protocol 14, 33–4
    repetitive cases, 39–40, 47, 56
    serious, systematic human rights violations, remedies for, 171, 174
    TRNC (Turkish Republic of Northern Cyprus), responsibility for troop actions in, 354–5
tyranny of the majority, 96–7, 101, 123, 397

Ukraine
    filtering under Protocol 14, 33–4
    legal representation in, 48
    pilot judgment procedures involving, 163
    repetitive cases, 39–40, 47, 56
Ulfstein, Geir, ix, 1, 389
ultra vires doctrine, 394–5

unfair domestic legal proceedings, remedies in, 152–7
United Kingdom
  accession of EU to ECHR, objections to, 319–20
  Article 46 judgments against, 169
  common law, development of rights in, 203–4
  extra-territorial jurisdiction of ECHR over actions of, 364–6
  municipal margin of appreciation, rejection of, 187
  national implementation of ECHR rights by, 187
    changes in, 182–3
    dynamic interpretation, 193–4, 203, 206–19, 243–6, 260
    margin of appreciation, 187, 247–50, 260
    multilateral relationship between national courts, 260–2
    proportionality, 260
    tort remedies, 255–9
  pilot judgment procedures involving, 163, 165–6
  remedies used by ECtHR, criticism of, 166, 177
  travel bans, on 371
  UN peacekeepers as organs of UN, on 346
United Nations and ECtHR, 4, 24, 334–88, 392. *See also* military operations of UN; national enforcement of international directions or orders; peacekeeping activities of UN
  blacklists, 338
  extra-territorial jurisdiction of ECtHR and, 361–6, 392, 398
  freezing orders, 372–87
  harm, UN actions capable of causing, 338–66

human rights protections, 338–43
international organisations and ECtHR generally, 9–10, 334–5
judicial protections against UN, 335
no withdrawal from ratification of covenants, 107
staff disputes, resolution of, 335–7
targeted sanctions, 337
travel bans, 369–72
United States Supreme Court
  fees, 46
  judicial deference and judicial restraint, 65
  racial equality judgments, implementation of, 41

van Emmerik, Michiel, 55
Venice Commission, 46–7
Vienna Convention on the Law of Treaties, 18, 86, 242
Vitruk, N. V., 240
Voßkuhle, Andreas, 219, 233, 236, 259, 261

Waismann, Friedrich, 72
Waldock, Humphrey, 63
Weiler, Joseph H. H., 187
Wildhaber, Luzius, 58, 61, 186, 272
Wise Persons Report (2007), 30–2, 57, 295
Wittgenstein, Ludwig, 84
Woolf Report (2005), 27, 57
Working Party on Fundamental Rights, Citizens Rights and Free Movement of Persons (FREMP), 318, 320

Zimnenko, B. L., 240
Zorkin, Valery, 183, 240–1